T0373092

Walter Benjamin

SELECTED WRITINGS

Michael W. Jennings
General Editor

Marcus Bullock, Howard Eiland, Gary Smith
Editorial Board

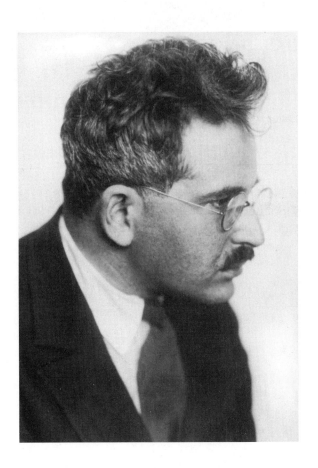

Walter Benjamin

SELECTED WRITINGS
VOLUME 2, PART 2
1931–1934

Translated by Rodney Livingstone
and Others

Edited by Michael W. Jennings,
Howard Eiland, and Gary Smith

THE BELKNAP PRESS OF HARVARD UNIVERSITY PRESS
Cambridge, Massachusetts, and London, England

This work is a translation of selections from Walter Benjamin, *Gesammelte Schriften, Unter Mitwirkung von Theodor W. Adorno und Gershom Sholem, herausgegeben von Rolf Tiedemann und Hermann Schweppenhäuser,* copyright © 1972, 1974, 1977, 1982, 1985, 1989 by Suhrkamp Verlag. Some of the pieces in this volume were previously published in English, as follows: "Unpacking My Library" and "Franz Kafka" apppeared in Walter Benjamin, *Illuminations,* edited by Hannah Arendt, English translation copyright © 1968 by Harcourt Brace Jovanovich, Inc. "Karl Kraus," "The Destructive Character," "Berlin Chronicle," "Hashish in Marseilles," "On the Mimetic Faculty," and "The Author as Producer" appeared in Walter Benjamin, *Reflections,* English translation copyright © 1978 by Harcourt Brace Jovanovich, Inc. Published by arrangement with Harcourt Brace Jovanovich, Inc. "A Family Drama in the Epic Theater" appeared in Walter Benjamin, *Understanding Brecht* (London: NLB/Verso, 1973). "Little History of Photography" appeared in Walter Benjamin, *"One-Way Street" and Other Writings* (London: NLB/Verso, 1979, 1985). "Doctrine of the Similar" appeared in *New German Critique* 17 (Spring 1979). "Left-Wing Melancholy" appeared in *Screen* 15, no. 2 (Summer 1974). "The Rigorous Study of Art" appeared in *October* 47 (Winter 1988), translation © 1988 by October Magazine Ltd. and the Massachusetts Institute of Technology.

Publication of this book has been aided by a grant from Inter Nationes, Bonn.

Frontispiece: Walter Benjamin, Berlin, 1929. Photo by Charlotte Joël. Courtesy of the Theodor W. Adorno Archiv, Frankfurt am Main.

Library of Congress Cataloging in Publication Data

Benjamin, Walter, 1892–1940.
[Selections. English. 1999]
Selected writings / Walter Benjamin; edited by Michael W. Jennings, Howard Eiland, and Gary Smith
    p. cm.
"This work is a translation of selections from Walter Benjamin, Gesammelte Schriften . . . copyright 1972 . . . by Suhrkamp Verlag"—T.p. verso.
Includes index.
Contents: v. 1. 1913–1926.—v. 2. 1927–1934.—v. 3. 1935–1938.—v. 4. 1938–1940.
ISBN 0-674-94585-9 (v. 1: alk. paper)   ISBN 0-674-94586-7 (v. 2: alk. paper)
ISBN 0-674-00896-0 (v. 3: alk. paper)   ISBN 0-674-01076-0 (v. 4: alk. paper)
ISBN 0-674-01355-7 (v. 1: pbk.)   ISBN 0-674-01588-6 (v. 2, pt. 1: pbk.)
ISBN 0-674-01746-3 (v. 2, pt. 2: pbk.)
I. Jennings, Michael William. II. Title.
PT2603.E455A26 1996
833'.91209—dc20 96-23027

Designed by Gwen Nefsky Frankfeldt

Contents

IBIZAN SEQUENCE, 1932

THOUGHT FIGURES, 1933

THE AUTHOR AS PRODUCER, 1934

The Destructive Character, 1931

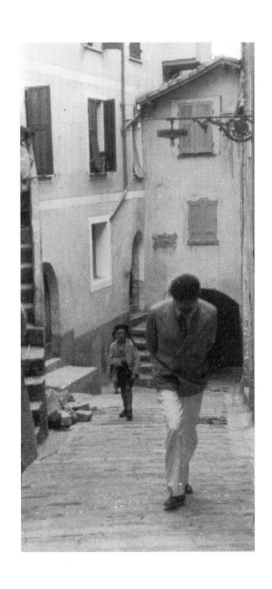

Walter Benjamin in Saint-Paul de Vence, France, May 1931. Photo by Gert Wissing. Collection of the Werkbundarchiv Museum der Dinge, Berlin.

In Parallel with My Actual Diary

In parallel with my actual diary, my intention here is to put down some notes on gambling. I would like to begin with a thesis that tackles the matter from the outside but is nonetheless important. It is the assertion that the most primitive link (precondition) of a game that is successful over a longer period is the player's clear understanding about his own economic existence. Nothing is more common than for people to make gambling into a drug, which will enable them to escape the consciousness of their economic situation. These people must lose; it may be that, for them, losing is a stronger drug than winning. Since wealthy people find it easier than poor people to contemplate their economic situation dispassionately, it follows that, independently of all technical considerations about the actual game, their chances of winning are greater.

Certain cells have the peculiar ability to take on bodily forms as the need arises, so that fingers or nose, flippers or tail, can be formed from the same cells. In the same way, great passions have the ability to stand in vicariously for quite different forms of life. We can perhaps go even further than Anatole France in his profound understanding of these things and demonstrate that gambling may be a substitute not only for religion but also for love, and even for marriage, for a man's profession, and even for a creative life.[1] Most miraculous of all, however, is that gambling can take possession not only of the future—in the form of feverish expectation—but also of the past. Indeed, isn't its ability to alter the visage of the past the greatest expression of its power over the gambler's heart? I sometimes believe that most gamblers are the stepchildren of love, whether of parental or sexual love, and that here at the gaming tables they are looking to fate to provide them with an adoption that ennobles them more than the origins that repudiated them.

A short register of superstitions / psychological and ontological study of gambling / gambling at the seaside.

Why do anxious people have an irresistible tendency toward games of chance? Perhaps because their policy is to bury their heads in the sand, or because they are able to endure the prospect of the future only if it is grotesquely disguised.

Fragment written 1929–1931; unpublished in Benjamin's lifetime. *Gesammelte Schriften,* VI, 190–191. Translated by Rodney Livingstone.

Notes

1. Anatole France (1844–1924), French writer and ironic, skeptical, urbane critic, was widely regarded in his day as the ideal man of letters. He was elected to the French Academy in 1896 and won the Nobel Prize for Literature in 1921.

Criticism as the Fundamental Discipline of Literary History

Criticism as the fundamental discipline of literary history. In Franz Mehring, literature appears solely as documentary material.[1] The disadvantage of his popularizing treatment is that he chose to treat only works that lend themselves to this approach. In consequence, he ignores Romanticism almost entirely.

Magical criticism as a manifestation of the highest stage of criticism. Opposite it on the same plane is the scholarly (literary-historical) treatise.

Max Dessoir, *Gesammelte Abhandlungen* (properly: *Beiträge zur allgemeinen Kunstwissenschaft;* Stuttgart: Ferdinand Enke, 1929).—Contains an essay on criticism.

The fundamental distinction between literary history and criticism must be rejected.

The theory of the life of works should be explored with reference to the most important works of Wiesengrund[2]—on *Wozzeck*, "New Tempi," and so on. This theory is closely linked both to the fact that works cannot be judged, and to the strategically judging stance of criticism.

Two modes, if we may put it thus, of transcendental criticism: one directed at authors, the other at the public.

On the theory of the survival of works—see Wiesengrund's theory of shrinkage [*Schrumpfung*]. This shrinkage can be seen in a twofold context. (1) In connection with my theory of packaging [*Verpackung*]. The theory of the ruins created by time should be complemented by the process of deconstruction [*Abmontieren*], which is the task of the critic. (2) In connection with my work on [Goethe's] *Wahlverwandtschaften* [Elective Affinities], shrinkage should be defined as the entrance of truth-content into material content. This formula represents the "hallowed sobriety" of that continued life.[3]

The whole critique of materialist literary criticism turns on the argument that it lacks a "magical," nonjudging side—that it always (or almost always) gets to the bottom of the mystery.

On the theory of shrinkage, see Wiesengrund, "New Tempi."

The third section, the theory of the survival of works, is dominated by the idea that this survival unmasks the terrain of "art" as semblance [*Schein*].

Fragment written in 1930 or 1931; unpublished in Benjamin's lifetime. *Gesammelte Schriften*, VI, 173–174. Translated by Rodney Livingstone.

Notes

1. Franz Mehring (1846–1919) was a radical journalist, a historian of the German Social Democratic party, and a biographer of Karl Marx.
2. That is, the work of Theodor Wiesengrund Adorno. Adorno's essay on Alban Berg's opera *Wozzeck* was published in *Musikalische Schriften* 5 (1982): 472–479. His theory of "shrinkage" is found in his essay "Neue Tempi" (New Tempi), *Musikalische Schriften* 4 (1984): 66–73.
3. "Hallowed sobriety" alludes to the swans in Friedrich Hölderlin's poem "Hälfte des Lebens" (Halves of Life), who dip their heads into the "hallowed-sober water."

Critique of the New Objectivity

Critique of the New Objectivity.[1] Expressionism signaled the energetic politicization of the intelligentsia. It could be shown how the movement is both the expression of that politicization and also the attempt to give it an idealist turn, despite its desire to have an impact in practice. This idealist stance was revised, and the New Objectivity was the result. But there was also a corresponding revision of the revolutionary practice whose modest beginnings Expressionism had inaugurated (examples!). Needless to say, this revision could not take place openly. The practical impulses atrophied, in line with the "stabilization" of the day, and simultaneously the absolute political significance of left-wing writing was proclaimed. Moreover, it was believed that this significance could not be better demonstrated than by ascribing an immediate effect to this entire body of writing. The first consequence was that every theoretical consideration was thrown overboard. Theory and reflection both seem and actually are detrimental to any immediate effect. It is high time to acknowledge that the fashionable appeal to "facts" is a two-edged sword. On the one hand, it is undoubtedly hostile to fictions removed from reality—to *belles lettres,* in short. On the other hand, it attacks theory. Experience proves this. Never has a generation of young writers been less interested in the theoretical legitimation of its activities than the generation that exists today. Everything which goes beyond an *argumentatio ad hominem* lies beyond their horizon. And how are they to arrive at a theoretical analysis of their position when this position is so confused and precludes any penetrating insight into itself? Such an insight would be insight into the class situation of the writers themselves. It is circumvented from the outset by the claim these writers make about the immediate political impact of their writings. It is this claim that will be scrutinized here.

The claim to immediate political impact will not just turn out to be a bluff; it will also be exposed as the attempt to liquidate an almost hopeless situation by a series of completely hopeless maneuvers. In short, it resembles nothing so much as Baron Münchhausen's claim that he pulled himself out of a swamp by his own hair.[2] This left-radical wing of writing and reportage may posture as much as it likes—it will never succeed in eliminating the fact that the proletarianization of the intellectual hardly ever turns him into a proletarian. Why? Because from childhood on, the middle class gave him a means of production in the form of an education—a privilege that establishes his solidarity with it and, perhaps even more strongly, its solidarity with him. This solidarity may become blurred superficially, or even be undermined, but it almost always remains powerful enough to exclude the intellectual from the constant state of alert, the sense of living your life at the front, which is characteristic of anyone who has been politicized by the proletarian class. Hence, it also remains powerful enough to deny him the energies flowing from struggles that have been personally experienced in the course of political practice. These energies, which only direct participation in struggle can confer, are called theory and knowledge. It is from Lenin's writings that we can see most clearly the huge distance separating the literary yield of political practice from the crude factual, journalistic stuff which is forced on us today under the guise of political writing, and that we can learn to understand the preeminently theoretical nature of this literature.

Fragment written in 1930 or 1931; unpublished in Benjamin's lifetime. *Gesammelte Schriften*, VI, 179–180. Translated by Rodney Livingstone.

Notes

1. *Neue Sachlichkeit* (New Objectivity) was the term originally applied by the museum curator G. F. Hartlaub to an emergent figuration in postwar German painting. It gradually came to designate the Weimar "period style" in art, architecture, design, literature, and film: cool, objective, analytical.
2. Karl Friedrich Hieronymus, Baron von Münchhausen (1720–1797), was a German storyteller. Some of his tales passed into popular consciousness, becoming sayings and anecdotes.

We Ought to Reexamine the Link between Teaching and Research

We ought to reexamine the link between teaching and research on which traditional academic activity is based. Such a link is not always the most appropriate form for the learning that the academy still wishes to impart today. It is suitable for matters that stand at the center of modern life, and for fields that have just become the object of research and are only now about to become living constituents of contemporary culture. In contrast, subjects that have long been investigated and appropriated by scholars need to be emancipated from the forms in which such scholarly acquisition took place, if they are still to have any value and any defined character today. In other words, it is precisely here that teaching and research should again part company and that both should seek to establish rigorous new forms. The whole pernicious spectrum of critical methods must disappear to make way for more enterprising researchers, on the one hand, and above all for a less banal, more considered learning, on the other. In these areas, in short, we should not look to research to lead a revival in teaching; instead, it is more important to strive with a certain intransigence for an—albeit very indirect—improvement in research to emerge from the teaching. These are insights that in the case of literary history force themselves quite urgently on the attention of anyone who has studied the *Outline of German Literary History* and the *Philosophy of Literary Science*.[1] The first displays the sterility of the complacent total approach; the second, the failure of research to turn teaching at the present time and in its present state into a fruitful activity. And if the alternative approach adumbrated above will be able to deliver the goods, this will only be because in principle teaching is capable of adapting to new strata of students in such a way that a rearrangement of the subject matter would give rise to entirely new forms of knowledge.

Examine the sense in which "Outlines," "Guides," and so on are touchstones for the state of a discipline. Show that they are the most demanding of all, and how clearly even their phrasing betrays every half-measure.

Fragment written in 1930 or 1931; unpublished in Benjamin's lifetime. *Gesammelte Schriften,* VI, 172–173. Translated by Rodney Livingstone.

Notes

1. H. A. Korff and W. Linden, *Aufriss der deutschen Literaturgeschichte nach neueren Gesichtspunkten* (Leipzig, 1930); E. Ermatinger, *Philosophie der Literaturwissenschaft* (Berlin, 1930).

Hofmannsthal and Aleco Dossena

Establish a connection between Hofmannsthal and Aleco Dossena.[1] Dossena, too, made forgeries without knowing it. He did his thing, and then others turned up and said, "What a unique Giotto!" or "What an incomparable Greco-Roman torso!" And having ascribed authorship in this fashion, they would then proceed to expose the artist. Hofmannsthal produced forgeries without knowing it, but of course he was inspired by the works that blossomed anew within him. Nowhere are we confronted more urgently by the question of what really drives the forger; but there can be no doubt that the great masterpieces of the past filled him with that very drive. This is why "translation" is such an inadequate term to describe his treatment of *Oedipus, Electra, Venice Preserved, Everyman, Life Is a Dream,* and so much else.[2] He used these works much as he used Goethe's *Novelle* or the fairy tale of the woman without a shadow, which is anything but a translation. At the same time, it gives us an insight into what is happening here, and what all these works have in common. In every instance, they amount to an almost unbearable condensation of the most personal features of those works. No novella is as Goethean as *Die Frau ohne Schatten* [The Woman without a Shadow]; no play of Calderón's is as Calderonic as *Der Turm* [The Tower]. And if there is any way of expressing the peculiarly cool element in these works, their remoteness from life, it is this: they present us with all the materials of their originary images [*Urbilder*], and they do so in their most condensed and most highly sublimated forms; but they have not been truly assimilated. We may perhaps put it best by saying that they are nourishing, but not really edible. To call them edible would mean they were digestible, and very little of what Hofmannsthal wrote is digestible.—

His genius could be summed up in a single phrase as a genius for quoting; and this comes very close to defining what we meant by forging. The great forger who has little or nothing to do with forgery as a purely commercial activity cites the originary image. And this is Hofmannsthal's situation: he quotes not single lines, purple passages, or the like, but the entire great work, the originary image in its entirety. He elevates it to the status of a quotation, but also of a manifestation. For in fact the forger cites the work in that other sense: he conjures it up. For Hofmannsthal, the art of conjuring was inseparable from the idea of culture [Bildung], whose lost authority he hoped to reestablish on the foundation of the magic of the past. The enterprise of founding culture on magic powerfully expresses what is great about Hofmannsthal, but also what is chimerical. This culture was without doubt legitimate, but it was no longer viable. For as long as possible, all essential events could be preserved as reflections of tradition. He had an infallible instinct for the topical relevance of even the remotest cultural goods. But when the current reality failed to discover its own reflection in the "eternal possessions of culture," Hofmannsthal found himself deprived of his own authentic faculty of expression. His ideal of authority and culture acquired chimerical overtones, and his synthesis of Protestant humanism and Hapsburg imperialism gradually collapsed. The culture he conjured up in the political Palatinate of postwar Germany was a Helen of Troy whose beauty was essentially impotent.

Fragment written in 1930 or 1931; unpublished in Benjamin's lifetime. *Gesammelte Schriften*, VI, 145–146. Translated by Rodney Livingstone.

Notes

1. Aleco Dossena (1878–1937) was an Italian sculptor. In 1928 a number of supposed classical Greek sculptures, as well as works said to be from the Trecento and Quattrocento, were shown to be forgeries made by Dossena.
2. Hugo von Hofmannsthal made adaptations, often very free, of Sophocles' *Oedipus Rex* and *Electra*; the latter was one of the key works in Hofmannsthal's long collaboration with Richard Strauss. He also adapted Thomas Otway's *Venice Preserved*. The medieval parable of *Everyman* was produced for the Salzburg Festival in 1911. Hofmannsthal's late play *Der Turm* (The Tower; 1927) was inspired by Calderón's *La vida es sueño* (Life Is a Dream).

Left-Wing Melancholy

Today Kästner's poems are already available in three imposing volumes.[1] Anyone wishing to study the character of these verses, however, is advised to stick to the form in which they originally appeared. In books they are too crowded and somewhat stifling, but they dart through the daily papers like fish in water. If this water is not always the cleanest and has quite a lot of refuse floating in it, all the better for the author, whose poetic minnows can fatten themselves thereon.

The popularity of these poems is linked to the rise of a stratum which took unconcealed possession of its commercial positions of power and prided itself like none other on the nakedness, the unmasked character, of its economic physiognomy. This is not to say that this stratum, whose only aim was success and which recognized nothing else, had now conquered the strongest positions. Its ideal was too asthmatic for that. It was the ideal of childless agents, parvenus of insignificant origin, who, unlike financial magnates, did not provide for their families over decades but provided only for themselves, and that hardly beyond the end of the season. Who cannot see them—their dreamy baby eyes behind horn-rimmed spectacles, their broad, pale cheeks, their halting voices, their fatalism in gesture and mode of thought? From the beginning, it is to this stratum and to this stratum alone that the poet has something to say; it is this stratum that he flatters, insofar as from dawn to dusk he holds up a mirror less *to* them than *against* them. The gaps between his stanzas are the folds of fat in their necks, his rhymes their thick lips, his caesuras dimples in their flesh, his punchlines the pupils in their eyes. Subject matter and effect remain restricted to this stratum, and Kästner is as incapable of striking the dispossessed with his rebellious accents as he is of touching the industrialists with his irony. This is because, despite appearances, this lyricism protects above all the status interests of the middle stratum—agents, journalists, heads of departments. The hatred it proclaims meanwhile toward the petty bourgeoisie has itself an all-too-intimate petty-bourgeois flavor. On the other hand, it noticeably abandons any striking power against the big bourgeoisie, and betrays its yearning for patronage at last in the heartfelt sigh: "If only there were a dozen wise men with a great deal of money." No wonder Kästner, in settling accounts with the bankers in "A Hymn," is as obliquely familial as he is obliquely economic when he presents the nocturnal thoughts of a proletarian woman under the title "A Mother Takes Stock." Ultimately, home and income remain the strings with which a better-off class leads the mewling poet.

This poet is dissatisfied—indeed, heavy-hearted. But this heaviness of heart derives from routine. For to be in a routine means to have sacrificed one's idiosyncrasies, to have forfeited the gift of being disgusted. And that makes one heavy-hearted. It is this circumstance which gives this case a certain similarity with Heine's. The notes with which Kästner indents his poems, to give these lacquered children's balls the appearance of rugby balls, are routine. And nothing is more routine than the irony which, like baking powder, helps to raise the kneaded dough of private opinion. It is only unfortunate that his impertinence is as much out of all proportion to the ideological forces at his disposal as it is to the political ones. Not least does the grotesque underestimation of the opponent that underlies these provocations betray how much the position of this left-radical intelligentsia is a lost one. It has little to do with the labor movement. Rather, as a phenomenon of bourgeois dissolution, it is a counterpart to the mimicry of feudalism that the *Kaiserreich* admired in the reserve lieutenant. Left-radical publicists of the stamp of Kästner, Mehring, and Tucholsky are the decayed bourgeoisie's mimicry of the proletariat.[2] Their function is to give rise, politically speaking, not to parties but to cliques; literarily speaking, not to schools but to fashions; economically speaking, not to producers but to agents. And indeed, for the past fifteen years this left-wing intelligentsia has been continually the agent of all intellectual booms, from Activism, via Expressionism, to the New Objectivity.[3] Its political significance, however, was exhausted by the transposition of revolutionary reflexes (insofar as they arose in the bourgeoisie) into objects of distraction, of amusement, which can be supplied for consumption.

Thus was Activism able to impose the face of a quasi-classless sound common sense on the revolutionary dialectic. It was in some sense the sale week on this intelligentsia's department store. Expressionism exhibited the revolutionary gesture, the raised arm, the clenched fist in papier-mâché. After this advertising campaign, the New Objectivity, from which Kästner's poems spring, was added to the catalogue. What, then, does the "intellectual elite" discover as it begins to take stock of its feelings? Those feelings themselves? They have long since been remaindered. What is left is the empty spaces where, in dusty heart-shaped velvet trays, the feelings—nature and love, enthusiasm and humanity—once rested. Now the hollow forms are absentmindedly caressed. A know-all irony thinks it has much more in these supposed stereotypes than in the things themselves; it makes a great display of its poverty and turns the yawning emptiness into a celebration. For this is what is new about this objectivity—it takes as much pride in the traces of former spiritual goods as the bourgeois do in their material goods. Never have such comfortable arrangements been made in such an uncomfortable situation.

In short, this left-wing radicalism is precisely the attitude to which there is no longer, in general, any corresponding political action. It is not to the left of this or that tendency, but simply to the left of what is in general possible. For from the beginning all it has in mind is to enjoy itself in a negativistic quiet. The metamorphosis of political struggle from a compulsory decision into an object of pleasure, from a means of production into an article of consumption—that is this literature's latest hit. Kästner, who is a considerable talent, has all its means at his fingertips. By far the most important of these is an attitude expressed even in the titles of many of his poems. Among them are "Elegy with Egg," "Chemically Purified Christmas Carol," "Suicide in the Public Pool," "Fate of a Stylized Negro," and so on. Why these dislocations? Because criticism and knowledge are ready to intervene; but they would be spoilsports and should on no condition be allowed to speak. So the poet must gag them, and their desperate convulsions now have the same effect as the tricks of a contortionist—that is, they amuse a wide public, insecure in its taste. In Morgenstern, nonsense was only the obverse of a flight into theosophy.[4] But Kästner's nihilism conceals nothing, as little as a mouth that cannot close for yawning.

Poets early became acquainted with a curious variety of despair: tortured stupidity. For the truly political poetry of the past decades has for the most part hurried on ahead of things as a harbinger. It was in 1912 and 1913 that Georg Heym's poems anticipated the then inconceivable constitution of the masses that came into the open in August 1914, in repellent descriptions of never-glimpsed collectivities: of suicides, of prisoners, of the sick, of sailors, of the insane.[5] In his lines, the earth armed itself for its submergence in the red deluge. And long before the Ararat of the goldmark was the only peak sticking up above the flood—every inch of it besieged by Feeding Trough, Belly Liner, and Sweet Tooth—Alfred Lichtenstein, who fell in the first days of the war, had brought into view the sad and flabby figures for which Kästner has found the stereotypes.[6] Now, what distinguishes the bourgeois in this early, still pre-expressionist version from the later, post-expressionist one is his eccentricity. It was no accident that

Lichtenstein dedicated one of his poems to a clown. The clowning of despair was still deep in the bones of his bourgeois. They had not yet shifted eccentricity outside themselves as an object of urban amusement. They were not yet so totally satiated, nor had they so totally become agents, that they did not feel their obscure solidarity with a commodity whose sales crisis is already on the horizon. Then came peace—the collapse of the market for the human commodity, a collapse with which we have become familiar as unemployment. And the suicide for which Lichtenstein's poems are propaganda is like dumping—the disposal of a commodity at ruinous prices. Kästner's verses have forgotten all this. Their beat very precisely follows the notes according to which poor rich folk play the blues; they correspond to the mournfulness of the satiated man who can no longer devote all his money to his stomach. Tortured stupidity: this is the latest of two millennia of metamorphoses of melancholy.

Kästner's poems are for people in the higher income bracket, those mournful, melancholy dummies who trample anything and anyone in their path. With the rigidity of their armor, the slowness of their advance, the blindness of their action, they are the rendezvous that tank and bedbug have made in people. These poems teem with them like a city café after the stock exchange closes. Is it surprising that their function is to reconcile this type of person to himself, and to establish that identity of professional and private life which these men understand by the name "humanity" but which is in truth the genuinely bestial, since authentic humanity—under present conditions—can arise only from a tension between these two poles? In this tension, consciousness and deed are formed. To create it is the task of all political lyricism, and today this task is most strictly fulfilled by Bertolt Brecht's poems. In Kästner, it has to give way to complacency and fatalism. This is the fatalism of those who are most remote from the process of production and whose obscure courting of the state of the market is comparable to the attitude of a man who yields himself up entirely to the inscrutable accidents of his digestion. The rumbling in these lines certainly has more to do with flatulence than with subversion. Constipation and melancholy have always gone together. But since the juices began to dry up in the body social, stuffiness meets us at every turn. Kästner's poems do not improve the atmosphere.

Published in *Die Gesellschaft*, 1931. *Gesammelte Schriften*, III, 279–283. Translated by Ben Brewster.

Notes

1. Erich Kästner (1899–1974), best-known for the children's book *Emil und die Detektive* (Emil and the Detectives; 1928), was a well-regarded poet, novelist,

and journalist during the Weimar Republic. His mostly ironic light verse in the detached mode of the New Objectivity appealed to middle-class readers in the late 1920s.

2. Franz Mehring (1846–1919) was a radical journalist, an important historian of the German Social Democratic party, and author of a widely influential biography of Karl Marx (1918). Kurt Tucholsky (1890–1935) was a journalist, poet, and satirical essayist. He is best-known for his biting cabaret lyrics and his work for the leading left-liberal journal in Germany, *Die Weltbühne.*

3. Activism *(Aktivismus)* was a movement dating back to the World War I years. It called for the elite—that is, artists and intellectuals—to engage actively in a new kind of spiritual politics. *Neue Sachlichkeit* (New Objectivity) was the term originally applied by the museum curator G. F. Hartlaub to an emergent figuration in German postwar painting. It gradually came to designate the Weimar "period style" in art, architecture, design, literature, and film: cool, objective, analytical.

4. Christian Morgenstern (1871–1914) was a German poet and humorist best-known for his nonsense verse. His collection *Galgenlieder* (Gallows Songs) appeared in 1905.

5. Georg Heym (1887–1912) was one of the leading poets of early German Expressionism. Examples of his visionary and apocalyptic verse appeared in the volumes *Der ewige Tag* (Eternal Day; 1911) and *Umbra Vitae* (1912). He drowned while skating on the frozen Havel, in Berlin.

6. Alfred Lichtenstein (1889–1914) was an early Expressionist poet. His work, characterized by grotesque images, was published posthumously in 1919. He was killed in action on the western front.

Theological Criticism

Willy Haas, *Gestalten der Zeit* [Figures of the Age] (Berlin: Gustav Kiepenheuer Verlag, 1930), 247 pages.

In a man's life the truly productive experiences are like seeds, unprepossessing and encapsulated. The most fruitful things are enclosed within the hard shell of immediacy. Nothing separates genuine productivity so clearly from the deficient kind, and above all from the false kind, as the question: What befell that particular man early on in life, between the ages of fifteen and twenty-five? Did he experience things that silenced him, that made him taciturn, conscious, and reflective, that furnished him with experience for which he could vouch and that he would never betray, never blurt out? Among these "figures of the age" are two to whom the author of this book is indebted for such incommunicable experiences—experiences that oblige him to testify in public. These are figures with whom he has kept faith, and who now act as patron saints, presiding over his book on its path through the contemporary world: Franz Kafka and Hugo von Hofmannsthal. Both, the reader will find, were encountered at the very heart of danger. Kafka, in Prague, in the camp of the degenerate Jewish intelligentsia, where in the name of Judaism he renounced Judaism, turning his back on it with a threatening, enigmatic gesture. Hofmannsthal, at the heart of the collapsing Hapsburg monarchy, where, in a kind of posthistorical maturity, he entirely transformed the energy on which it had thrived into formal structures.

It would be anything but surprising if the author were to regard as arbitrary the emphases we have given to his text. It would indeed be far-fetched to dwell on what Hofmannsthal and Kafka might have in common. But the question of what the two might mean to an author like Haas is a very different matter. He has discussed them in two quite separate essays. But to have discussed them in this way—in such masterful fashion, so uninfluenced by his own sentences and yet in such complete harmony with them—this is something that a writer achieves only when tackling the subjects closest to his heart. It is by no means crucial to his writing that he was personally acquainted with both Kafka and Hofmannsthal. For all that, it is no run-of-the-mill spectacle to see how in a mere six pages he conjures up the spirit of Kafka with an account of the laconic, precisely noted words that passed in a brief encounter with the writer. And we touch only the surface of things if we observe that Hofmannsthal's works provide a concentrate of the world of Catholicism, while Kafka's synthesize the Jewish world. What Haas wrote in 1929 under the impact of the news of Hofmannsthal's death—it was almost the only piece in the entire German press that did anything like justice to the event—inserted him into the space of the old Catholic monarchy, as a sort of descendant of the mother country that had lost all her sons, as a poetic genius of the state who had come too late. The country no longer had a future. And so—this is what we find in his second essay on Hofmannsthal—the time that was yet to come was, as it were, all rolled up into the past, like a scroll, and became a sort of underworld of the future, one haunted by only the oldest of things. In that realm of the "unborn children" with which *Die Frau ohne Schatten* [The Woman without a Shadow] opens, Haas has discerned the nebulous core of Hofmannsthal's world of images. Max Mell, the poet's friend, has recently done the same thing.[1] In no other writer have the worlds of image and semblance become more intimately, dangerously, intertwined. Indeed, this hidden ambiguity in Hofmannsthal's image-world is what gives it its spiritual gloss—that ideal significance, that surplus, which gives it its distinguishing character. Or, as Haas expresses it, "Never has spirit so magically become poetic experience."

The surprising feature of all this is that the deeper the reader immerses himself in the world of this essayist, the more he realizes that the world of semblance [*Schein*] constantly demands its due in a hundred different ways, whatever is depicted—whether it be the semblance of the hermaphrodite, as in André Gide, the semblance of eternal recurrence, as in Anatole France, or the semblance of a mediated reality, as in Hermann Bahr.[2] In truth, however, what we discover in these studies is that theology has pitched its tent near semblance itself, one of its favorite objects. The book abounds in discussions of the Talmud and Kierkegaard, of Thomas Aquinas and Pascal, of Ignatius Loyola and Léon Bloy.[3] But what commands the author's complete attention is not the study of theologians proper, so much as the works of those who grant asylum to theological contents [*Gehalte*] at their moment of maximum jeopardy, in their most threadbare disguise. One of these disguises is semblance itself. Popular fiction, colportage, is another. This explains why, alongside the exemplary analyses of Hofmannsthal, we find the perhaps even more significant discussions of Kafka. They point the way to future exegeses of this writer through an interpretation that energetically presses forward to theological questions at every point. In so doing, the author occasionally comes close to a theory of colportage. What he discovers in Kafka is a theology on the run which lies at the base of a number of essays that explore the topic of colportage. This is how we should classify his "theology in the detective novel," his superb characterization of Luden-dorff,[4] and his analysis of the Jewish joke.

We thought it right to regard Hofmannsthal and Kafka as the presiding geniuses in this book, particularly since the most perfect essays in it are devoted to them. What the author sets out to do in this collection is so difficult and dangerous that even the most resolute might keep an eye out for assistance. For what has Haas undertaken here? He has attempted to beat a path to the work of art by destroying the theory of the "sphere" of art. The theological approach gains its full significance through an attack on art which is all the more destructive for being covert. The ground motif of this book is that the theological illumination of works provides an authentic model with which to interpret their political aspects as much as their fashionable ones, their economic features as much as their metaphysical ones. As can be seen, this is a basic stance that opposes historical materialism with a radicalism that turns it into its very antithesis. "Where everyone else can make progress only through a series of compromises," Haas writes, "the Church can still advance its thought in profoundly true syntheses." But there are cases when this Catholic splicing of thesis and antithesis can take a rather convoluted form. Haas walks this tightrope with dizzying assurance. Nevertheless, the sight might trigger anxiety in spectators, were there not present here a more reliable and higher-grade safety element: the art of knowing how to fall. "To be able to stake one's entire life on an expedition—an expedition that can't be precisely calculated in advance—against some minor detail of this world: this and nothing else is what is meant by 'thinking'." Is it only by chance that this profound definition which we encounter on the last page of the book is that of a man in free fall? The author will have learned the hard way, risking his neck. But when he once again touches terra firma after his breathtaking fall, he stands firmly on his own two feet.

There have never been a great many writers who could combine authorial substance with the stance of the virtuoso—or rather, the schooled man of letters—as successfully as here. It is easy to believe that such people were more frequently to be found on the right of the political spectrum than on the left. However this may be, Haas is the editor of a left-leaning weekly magazine that always intervenes actively in the literary controversies of the day.[5] But as a scholar, he is really much more of a disciple of Adam Müller, Burke, or de Maistre than of Voltaire, Gutzkow, or Lassalle.[6] Fundamentally, his lineage stretches back much further into the past. We should have to go back as far as the literature and chronicles of the seventeenth century in order to discover anything comparable to the framework of universal history characteristic of these essays, both as the expression of an overall metaphysical stance and as a form of virtuoso writing that mediates effectively, even though it does not always create a satisfactory synthesis. In his obituary for Hofmannsthal, Haas himself has given a definitive account of this method, which is his own. It creates a perspective, like the backdrop for a stage set. It strives for a plasticity comprised of thick layers of meaning superimposed on one another. "This never results in a corporeal plasticity, but it does produce a perspectival one." The phenomenal form of his figures corresponds to this. They are figures of the age—there can be no doubt about that. But their life is that of epic pasts that have not been carried to decision, and whose contestation reveals to the author the true image of his age.

Published in *Die neue Rundschau*, February 1931. *Gesammelte Schriften*, III, 275–278. Translated by Rodney Livingstone.

Notes

1. Max Mell (1882–1971) was an Austrian poet whose work reflects his ties to popular and conservative traditions, as well as to the Catholic Church.
2. Hermann Bahr (1863–1934), Austrian playwright and critic, was an important conduit for French modernist ideas; he championed (successively) Naturalism, Romanticism, and Symbolism.
3. Léon Bloy (1846–1917), French novelist, critic, and polemicist, was a devout Roman Catholic convert who advocated spiritual revival through suffering and poverty.
4. Erich Ludendorff (1865–1937) was a German general who served as chief of staff to Field Marshal Hindenburg in World War I; he bore primary responsibility for German military strategy. During the Weimar Republic he was an important supporter of the Nazis. His writings idealize the Aryan race and attack the pope, Jews, Jesuits, and Freemasons.
5. Willy Haas (1891–1973) was a well-known writer and critic. He was editor of *Die literarische Welt* and *Die Welt im Wort*.
6. Adam Müller (1779–1829) was a German political pamphleteer of strongly conservative and authoritarian views. Edmund Burke (1729–1797), British political writer and statesman, entered Parliament in 1765; his most famous work, *Reflections on the Revolution in France* (1790), expresses his opposition to the Revolution. Joseph de Maistre (1753–1821), French diplomat and writer, was

one of the leading intellectual opponents of the French Revolution. Karl Gutzkow (1811–1878) was a journalist associated with the liberal and radical Young Germany movement in the 1830s. He was jailed in 1836 for having brought the Christian religion into disrepute with his novel *Wally die Zweiflerin* (Wally the Doubter). Ferdinand Lassalle (1825–1864) was one of the founding fathers of German Social Democracy.

Karl Kraus

Dedicated to Gustav Glück

1. Cosmic Man [*Allmensch*]

How noisy everything grows.
—Kraus, *Words in Verse II*

In old engravings, there is a messenger who rushes toward us crying aloud, his hair on end, brandishing a sheet of paper in his hands—a sheet full of war and pestilence, of cries of murder and pain, of danger from fire and flood—spreading everywhere the Latest News. "News" in this sense, in the sense that the word has in Shakespeare, is disseminated by *Die Fackel* [The Torch].[1] Full of betrayal, earthquakes, poison, and fire from the *mundus intelligibilis*. The hatred with which it pursues the tribe of journalists that swarms into infinity is not only a moral hatred but a vital one, such as is hurled by an ancestor upon a race of degenerate and dwarfish rascals that has sprung from his seed. The very term "public opinion" outrages Kraus. Opinions are a private matter. The public has an interest only in judgments. Either it is a judging public, or it is none. But it is precisely the purpose of the public opinion generated by the press to make the public incapable of judging, to insinuate into it the attitude of someone irresponsible, uninformed. Indeed, what is even the most precise information in the daily newspapers in comparison to the hair-raising meticulousness observed by *Die Fackel* in the presentation of legal, linguistic, and political facts? *Die Fackel* need not trouble itself about public opinion, for the blood-steeped novelties of this "newspaper" demand a passing of judgment. And on nothing more impetuously, urgently, than on the press itself.

A hatred such as that which Kraus has heaped on journalists can never be founded simply on what they do—however obnoxious this may be; this hatred must have its reason in their very being, whether it be antithetical or akin to his own. In fact, it is both. His most recent portrait, in its very first sentence, characterizes the journalist as "a person who has little interest either in himself and his own existence, or in the mere existence of things, but who feels things only in their relationships, above all where these meet in events—and only in this moment become united, substantial, and alive." What we have in this sentence is nothing other than the negative of an image of Kraus. Indeed, who could have shown a more burning interest in himself and his own existence than the writer who is never finished with this subject? Who, a more attentive concern for the mere existence of things, their origin? Whom does that coincidence of the event with the date, the witness, or the camera cast into deeper despair than him? In the end, he brought together all his energies in the struggle against the empty phrase, which is the linguistic expression of the despotism with which, in journalism, topicality sets up its dominion over things.

This side of his struggle against the press is illuminated most vividly by the life's work of his comrade-in-arms, Adolf Loos. Loos found his providential adversaries in the arts-and-crafts mongers and architects who, in the ambit of the "Vienna Workshops," were striving to give birth to a new art industry. He sent out his rallying cry in numerous essays—particularly, in its enduring formulation, in the article "Ornamentation and Crime," which appeared in 1908 in the *Frankfurter Zeitung*. The lightning flash ignited by this essay described a curiously zigzag course. "On reading the words with which Goethe censures the way the philistine, and thus many an art connoisseur, run their fingers over engravings and reliefs, the revelation came to him that what may be touched cannot be a work of art, and that a work of art must be out of reach." It was therefore Loos's first concern to separate the work of art from the article of use, as it was that of Kraus to keep apart information and the work of art. The hack journalist is, in his heart, at one with the ornamentalist. Kraus did not tire of denouncing Heine as an ornamentalist, as one who blurred the boundary between journalism and literature, as the creator of the feuilleton in poetry and prose; indeed, he later placed even Nietzsche beside Heine as the betrayer of the aphorism to the impression. "It is my opinion," he says of the former, "that to the mixture of elements . . . in the decomposing European style of the last half century, he added psychology, and that the new level of language he created is the level of essayism, as Heine's was that of feuilletonism." Both forms appear as symptoms of the chronic sickness of which all attitudes and standpoints merely mark the temperature curve: inauthenticity. It is from the unmasking of the inauthentic that this battle against the press arose. "Who was it that brought into the world this great excuse: 'I can do what I am not'?"

The empty phrase. It, however, is an abortion of technology. "The newspaper industry, like a factory, demands separate areas for working and selling. At certain times of day—twice, three times in the bigger newspapers—a particular quantity of work has to have been procured and prepared for the machine. And not from just any material: everything that has happened in the meantime, anywhere, in any region of life—politics, economics, art, and so on—must by now have been reached and journalistically processed." Or, as Kraus so splendidly sums it up: "It ought to throw light on the way in which technology, while unable to coin new platitudes, leaves the spirit of mankind in the state of being unable to do without the old ones. In this duality of a changed life dragging on in unchanged forms, the world's ills grow and prosper." In these words, Kraus deftly tied the knot binding technology to the empty phrase. True, its untying would have to follow a different pattern, journalism being clearly seen as the expression of the changed function of language in the world of high capitalism. The empty phrase of the kind so relentlessly pursued by Kraus is the label that makes a thought marketable, the way flowery language, as ornament, gives a thought value for the connoisseur. But for this very reason the liberation of language has become identical with that of the empty phrase—its transformation from reproduction to productive instrument. *Die Fackel* itself contains models of this, even if not the theory: its formulas are the kind that tie up, never the kind that untie. The intertwining of biblical magniloquence with stiff-necked fixation on the indecencies of Viennese life—this is its way of approaching phenomena. It is not content to call on the world as witness to the misdemeanors of a cashier; it must summon the dead from their graves.—Rightly so. For the shabby, obtrusive abundance of these scandals in Viennese coffeehouses, the press, and society is only a minor manifestation of a foreknowledge that then, more swiftly than anyone could perceive, suddenly arrived at its true and original subject: two months after the outbreak of war, Kraus called this subject by its name in his speech "In These Great Times," with which all the demons that inhabited this possessed man passed into the herd of swine who were his contemporaries.

> In these great times, which I knew when they were small, which will again be small if they still have time, and which, because in the field of organic growth such transformations are not possible, we prefer to address as fat times and truly also as hard times; in these times, when precisely what is happening could not be imagined, and when what must *happen* can no longer be *imagined,* and if it could it would not happen; in these grave times that have laughed themselves to death at the possibility of growing serious and, overtaken by their own tragedy, long for distraction and then, catching themselves in the act, seek words; in these loud times, booming with the fearful symphony of deeds that engender reports, and of reports that bear the blame for deeds; in these unspeakable times, you can expect no word of my own from me. None except this, which just preserves silence from misinterpretation. Too deeply am I awed

by the unalterability of language, the subordination of language to misfortune. In the empires bereft of imagination, where man is dying of spiritual starvation though feeling no spiritual hunger, where pens are dipped in blood and swords in ink, that which is not thought must be done, but that which is only thought is inexpressible. Expect from me no word of my own. Nor should I be capable of saying anything new; for in the room where someone writes, the noise is great, and whether it comes from animals, from children, or merely from mortars shall not be decided now. He who addresses deeds violates both word and deed and is twice despicable. This profession is not extinct. Those who now have nothing to say because it is the turn of deeds to speak, talk on. Let him who has something to say step forward and be silent!

Everything Kraus wrote is like that: a silence turned inside out, a silence that catches the storm of events in its black folds and billows, its livid lining turned outward. Notwithstanding their abundance, each of the instances of this silence seems to have broken upon it with the suddenness of a gust of wind. Immediately, a precise apparatus of control is brought into play: through a meshing of oral and written forms, the polemical possibilities of every situation are totally exhausted. With what precautions this is surrounded can be seen from the barbed wire of editorial pronouncements that encircles each edition of *Die Fackel,* as from the razor-sharp definitions and provisos in the programs and lectures accompanying his readings from his own work. The trinity of silence, knowledge, and alertness constitutes the figure of Kraus the polemicist. His silence is a dam before which the reflecting basin of his knowledge is constantly deepened. His alertness permits no one to ask it questions, forever unwilling to conform to principles offered to it. Its first principle is, rather, to dismantle the situation, to discover the true question the situation poses, and to present this in place of any other to his opponents. If in Johann Peter Hebel we find, developed to the utmost, the constructive, creative side of tact, in Kraus we see its most destructive and critical face. But for both, tact is moral alertness—Stössl calls it "conviction refined into dialectics"—and the expression of an unknown convention more important than the acknowledged one.[2] Kraus lived in a world in which the most shameful act was still the faux pas; he distinguishes between degrees of the monstrous, and does so precisely because his criterion is never that of bourgeois respectability, which, once above the threshold of trivial misdemeanor, becomes so quickly short of breath that it can form no conception of villainy on a world-historical scale.

Kraus knew this criterion from the first; moreover, there is no other criterion for true tact. It is a theological criterion. For tact is not—as narrow minds imagine it—the gift of allotting to each, on consideration of all relationships, what is socially befitting. On the contrary, tact is the capacity to treat social relationships, though not departing from them, as natural, even paradisal, relationships, and so not only to approach the king as if he had been born with the crown on his brow, but the lackey like an Adam in livery. Hebel possessed this *noblesse* in his priestly bearing; Kraus, in armor. His concept of creation contains the theological inheritance of speculations that last possessed contemporary validity for the whole of Europe in the seventeenth century. At the theological core of this concept, however, a transformation has taken place that has caused it, quite without constraint, to coincide with the cosmopolitan credo of Austrian worldliness, which made creation into a church in which nothing remained to recall the rite except an occasional whiff of incense in the mists. Stifter gave this creed its most authentic stamp, and his echo is heard wherever Kraus concerns himself with animals, plants, children. Stifter writes:

> The stirring of the air, the rippling of water, the growing of corn, the tossing of the sea, the verdure of the earth, the shining of the sky, the twinkling of the stars, I hold great. The thunderstorm approaching in splendor, the lightning flash that cleaves houses, the storm driving the surf, the mountains spewing fire, the earthquake laying waste to countries, I do not hold greater than the former phenomena; indeed, I believe them smaller, because they are only effects of far higher laws . . . When man was in his infancy, his spiritual eye not yet touched by science, he was seized by what was close at hand and obtrusive, and was moved to fear and admiration; but when his mind was opened, when his gaze began to be directed at the connections between things, particular phenomena sank from sight and the law rose even higher, miracles ceased, and wonder increased . . . Just as in nature the general laws act silently and inces-santly, and conspicuous events are only single manifestations of these laws, so the moral law acts silently, animating the soul through the infinite intercourse of human beings, and the miracles of the moment when deeds are performed are merely small signs of this general power.[3]

Tacitly, in these famous sentences, the holy has given place to the modest yet questionable concept of law. But this nature of Stifter's and his moral universe are transparent enough to escape any confusion with Kant, and to be still recognizable in their core as creation. This insolently secularized thunder and lightning, storms, surf, and earthquakes—cosmic man has won them back for creation by making them its world-historical answer to the criminal existence of men. Only the span between Creation and the Last Judgment here finds no redemptive fulfillment, let alone a historical over-coming. For as the landscape of Austria fills unbroken the captivating expanse of Stifter's prose, so for him, Kraus, the terrible years of his life are not history but nature, a river condemned to meander through a landscape of hell. It is a landscape in which every day fifty thousand trees are felled for sixty newspapers. Kraus imparted this information under the title "The End." For the fact that mankind is losing the fight against the creaturely is to him just as certain as the fact that technology, once deployed against creation, will not stop short of its master, either. His defeatism is of a supranational—that is, planetary—kind, and history for him is merely the wilderness dividing his race from creation, whose last act is world confla- gration. As a deserter to the camp of animal creation—so he measures out this wilderness. "And only the animal that is conquered by humanity is the hero of life": never was Adalbert Stifter's patriarchal credo given so gloomy and heraldic a formulation.

It is in the name of the creature that Kraus again and again inclines toward the animal and toward "the heart of all hearts, that of the dog," for him creation's true mirror of virtue, in which fidelity, purity, gratitude smile from times lost and remote. How lamentable that people usurp its place! These are his followers. More numerously and eagerly than about their master, they throng with unlovely sniffings about the mortally wounded opponent. Indeed, it is no accident that the dog is the emblematic beast of this author: the dog, the epitome of the follower, who is nothing except devoted creature. And the more personal and unfounded this devotion, the better. Kraus is right to put it to the hardest test. But if anything makes plain what is infinitely questionable in these creatures, it is that they are recruited solely from those whom Kraus himself first called intellectually to life, whom he conceived and convinced in one and the same act. His testimony can deter- mine only those for whom it can never become generative.

It is entirely logical that the impoverished, reduced human being of our day, the contemporary, can seek sanctuary in the temple of living things only in that most withered form: the form of a private individual. How much renunciation and how much irony lie in the curious struggle for the "nerves"—the last root fibers of the Viennese to which Kraus could still find Mother Earth clinging. "Kraus," writes Robert Scheu, "discovered a great subject that had never before set in motion the pen of a journalist: the rights of the nerves. He found that they were just as worthy an object of impas- sioned defense as were property, house and home, political party, and constitution. He became the advocate of the nerves and took up the fight against petty, everyday imitations; but the subject grew under his hands, became the problem of private life. To defend this against police, press, morality, and concepts, and ultimately against neighbors in every form, constantly finding new enemies, became his profession." Here, if anywhere, is manifest the strange interplay between reactionary theory and revolution- ary practice that we find everywhere in Kraus. Indeed, to secure private life against morality and concepts in a society that perpetrates the political radioscopy of sexuality and family, of economic and physical existence, in a society that is in the process of building houses with glass walls, and terraces extending far into the living rooms that are no longer living rooms— such a watchword would be the most reactionary of all, were not the private life that Kraus made it his business to defend precisely that which, unlike the bourgeois form, is in strict accordance with this social upheaval; in other words, the private life that is dismantling itself, openly shaping itself, that of the poor, from whose ranks came Peter Altenberg, the agitator, and Adolf Loos. In this fight—and only in this fight—his followers also have their uses, since it is they who most sublimely ignore the anonymity with which the satirist has tried to surround his private existence, and nothing holds them in check except Kraus's decision to step in person before his threshold and pay homage to the ruins in which he is a "private individual."

As decisively as he makes his own existence a public issue when the fight demands it, he has always just as ruthlessly opposed the distinction between personal and objective criticism—a distinction which has been used to discredit polemics, and which is a chief instrument of corruption in our literary and political affairs. That Kraus attacks people less for what they are than for what they do, more for what they say than for what they write, and least of all for their books, is the precondition of his polemical authority, which is able to lift the intellectual universe of an author—all the more surely the more worthless it is, with confidence in a truly prestabilized, reconciling harmony—whole and intact from a single fragment of sentence, a single word, a single intonation. But the coincidence of personal and objective elements, not only in his opponents but above all in himself, is best demonstrated by the fact that he never puts forward an opinion. For opinion is false subjectivity that can be separated from the person and incorporated in the circulation of commodities. Kraus has never offered an argument that did not engage his whole person. Thus, he embodies the secret of authority: never to disappoint. Authority has no other end than this: it dies or it disappoints. It is not in the least undermined by what others must avoid: its own despotism, injustice, inconsistency. On the contrary, it would be disappointing to observe how it arrived at its pronouncements—by fairness, for example, or even self-consistency. "For a man," Kraus once said, "being right is not an erotic matter, and he gladly prefers others' being right to his being wrong." To prove his manhood in this way is denied to Kraus; his existence demands that at most the self-righteousness of others is opposed to his wrongness, and how right he then is to cling to this. "Many will be right one day. But it will be a rightness resulting from my wrongness today." This is the language of true authority. Insight into its operations can reveal only one thing: that it is binding, mercilessly binding, toward itself in the same degree as toward others; that it does not tire of trembling before itself, though never before others; that it never does enough to satisfy itself, to fulfill its responsibility toward itself; and that this sense of responsibility never allows him to accept arguments derived from his private constitution or even from the limits of human capacity, but always only from the matter at hand, however unjust it may be from a private point of view.

The characteristic of such unlimited authority has for all time been the union of legislative and executive power. But it was never a more intimate union than in the theory of language. This is therefore the most decisive expression of Kraus's authority. Incognito like Haroun al Rashid, he passes by night among the sentence constructions of the journals, and, from behind the petrified façades of phrases, he peers into the interior, discovering in the orgies of "black magic" the violation, the martyrdom, of words:

> Is the press a messenger? No: it is the event. Is it speech? No: life. The press not only claims that the true events are its news of events, but it also brings about a sinister identification that constantly creates the illusion that deeds are reported before they are carried out, and frequently also the possibility of a situation (which in any case exists) that when war correspondents are not allowed to witness events, soldiers become reporters. I therefore welcome the charge that all my life I have overestimated the press. It is not a servant—How could a servant demand and receive so much? It is the event. Once again the instrument has run away with us. We have placed the person who is supposed to report outbreaks of fire, and who ought doubtless to play the most subordinate role in the State, in power over the world, over fire and over the house, over fact and over our fantasy.

Authority and word against corruption and magic—thus are the catchwords distributed in this struggle. It is not idle to offer a prognosis. No one, Kraus least of all, can leave the utopia of an "objective" newspaper, the chimera of an "impartial transmission of news," to its own devices. The newspaper is an instrument of power. It can derive its value only from the character of the power it serves; not only in what it represents, but also in what it does, it is the expression of this power. When, however, high capitalism defiles not only the ends but also the means of journalism, then a new blossoming of paradisal, cosmic humanity can no more be expected of a power that defeats it than a second blooming of the language of Goethe or Claudius.[4] From the one now prevailing, it will distinguish itself first of all by putting out of circulation ideals that debase the former. This is enough to give a measure of how little Kraus would have to win or lose in such a struggle, of how unerringly *Die Fackel* would illuminate it. To the ever-repeated sensations with which the daily press serves its public, he opposes the eternally fresh "news" of the history of creation: the eternally renewed, uninterrupted lament.

2. Demon

Have I slept? I am just falling asleep.
—Kraus, *Words in Verse IV*

It is deeply rooted in Kraus's nature, and the stigma of every debate concerning him, that all apologetic arguments miss their mark. The great work of Leopold Liegler springs from an apologetic posture. To certify Kraus as an "ethical personality" is his first objective. This cannot be done. The dark background from which Kraus's image detaches itself is not formed by his contemporaries, but is the primeval world [*Vorwelt*], or the world of the demon. The light of the day of Creation falls on him—thus he emerges from this darkness. But not in all parts; others remain that are more deeply immersed in it than one suspects. An eye that cannot adjust to this darkness will never perceive the outline of this figure. On it will be wasted all the gestures that Kraus tirelessly makes in his unconquerable need to be perceived. For, as in the fairy tale, the demon in Kraus has made vanity the expression of his being. The demon's solitude, too, is felt by him who gesticulates wildly on the hidden hill: "Thank God nobody knows my name is Rumpelstiltskin." Just as this dancing demon is never still, in Kraus eccentric reflection is in continuous uproar. "The patient of his gifts," Berthold Viertel called him. In fact, his capacities are maladies; and over and above the real ones, his vanity makes him a hypochondriac.

If he does not see his reflection in himself, he sees it in the adversary at his feet. His polemics have been, from the first, the most intimate intermingling of a technique of unmasking that works with the most advanced means, and a self-expressive art that works with the most archaic. But in this zone, too, ambiguity, the demon, is manifest: self-expression and unmasking merge in it as self-unmasking. Kraus has said, "Anti-Semitism is the mentality that offers up and means seriously a tenth of the jibes that the stock-exchange wit holds ready for his own blood"; he thereby indicates the nature of the relationship of his own opponents to himself. There is no reproach to him, no vilification of his person, that could not find its most legitimate formulation in his own writings, in those passages where self-reflection is raised to self-admiration. He will pay any price to get himself talked about, and is always justified by the success of these speculations. If style is the power to move freely in the length and breadth of linguistic thinking without falling into banality, it is attained chiefly by the cardiac strength of great thoughts, which drives the blood of language through the capillaries of syntax into the remotest limbs. While such thoughts are quite unmistakable in Kraus, the powerful heart of his style is nevertheless the image he bears of himself in his own breast and exposes in the most merciless manner. Yes, he is vain. As such he has been portrayed by Karin Michaelis, who describes how he crosses a room with swift, restless bounds to reach the lecture podium. And if he then offers a sacrifice to his vanity, he would not be the demon that he is were it not finally himself, his life and his suffering, that he exposes with all its wounds, all its nakedness. In this way his style comes into being, and with it the typical reader of *Die Fackel*, for whom in a subordinate clause, in a particle, indeed in a comma, fibers and nerves quiver; from the obscurest and driest fact, a piece of his mutilated flesh hangs. Idiosyncrasy as the highest critical organ—this is the hidden logic of that self-reflection and the hellish state known only to a writer for whom every act of gratification becomes at the same time a station of his martyrdom, a state experienced, apart from Kraus, by no one as deeply as by Kierkegaard.

"I am," Kraus has said, "perhaps the first instance of a writer who simultaneously writes and experiences his writing theatrically." Thus he shows his vanity its most legitimate place: in mime. His mimetic genius, imitating while it glosses, pulling faces in the midst of polemics, is festively unleashed in the readings of dramas whose authors, with good reason, occupy a peculiarly intermediate position: Shakespeare and Nestroy, dramatists and actors; Offenbach, composer and conductor. It is as if the demon in the man sought the tumultuous atmosphere of these dramas, shot through with all the lightning flashes of improvisation, because it alone offered him the thousand opportunities to break out, teasing, tormenting, threatening. In them his own voice tries out the abundance of personae inhabiting the performer ("per-sona": that through which sound passes), and about his fingertips dart the gestures of the figures populating his voice. But in his polemics, too, mimesis plays a decisive role. He imitates his subjects in order to insert the crowbar of his hate into the finest joints of their posture. This quibbler, probing between syllables, digs out the larvae that nest there in clumps. The larvae of venality and garrulity, ignominy and bonhomie, childishness and covetousness, gluttony and dishonesty. Indeed, the exposure of inauthenticity—more difficult than that of the merely bad—is here performed behavioristically. The quotations in *Die Fackel* are more than documentary proof: they are the props with which the quoter unmasks himself mimetically. Admittedly, what emerges in just this connection is how closely the cruelty of the satirist is linked to the ambiguous modesty of the interpreter, which in his public readings is heightened beyond comprehension. "To creep"—this is the term used, not without cause, for the lowest kind of flattery; and Kraus creeps into those he impersonates, in order to annihilate them. Has courtesy here become the mimicry of hate, hate the mimicry of courtesy? However that may be, both have attained perfection, absolute pitch. "Torment," of which there is so much talk in Kraus in such opaque allusions, here has its seat. His protests against letters, printed matter, documents are nothing but the defensive reaction of a man who is himself implicated. But what implicates him so deeply is more than deeds and misdeeds; it is the language of his fellow men. His passion for imitating them is at the same time the expression of and the struggle against this implication, and also the cause and the result of that ever-watchful guilty conscience in which alone the demon is in his element.

The economy of his errors and weaknesses—more a fantastic edifice than the totality of his gifts—is so delicately and precisely organized that all outward confirmation only disrupts it. Well it may, if this man is to be certified as the "pattern of a harmoniously and perfectly formed human type," if he is to appear—in a term as absurd stylistically as semantically—as a philanthropist, so that anyone listening to his "hardness" with "the ears of the soul" would find the reason for it in compassion. No! This incorruptible, piercing, resolute assurance does not spring from the noble poetic or humane disposition that his followers are so fond of attributing to him. How utterly banal, and at the same time how fundamentally wrong, is their derivation of his hatred from love, when it is obvious how much more elemental are the forces here at work: a humanity that is only an alternation of malice and sophistry, sophistry and malice, a nature that is the highest school of aversion to mankind and a pity that is alive only when interlaced with vengeance. "Oh, had I only been left the choice / to carve the dog or the butcher, / I should have chosen." Nothing is more perverse than to try to fashion him after the image of what he loves. Rightly, Kraus the "timeless world-disturber" has been confronted with the "eternal world-improver," on whom benign glances not infrequently fall.

"When the age laid hands upon itself, he was the hands," Brecht said. Few insights can stand beside this, and certainly not the comment of his friend Adolf Loos. "Kraus," he declares, "stands on the threshold of a new age." Alas, by no means.—For he stands on the threshold of the Last Judgment. Just as, in the most opulent examples of Baroque altar painting, saints hard-pressed against the frame extend defensive hands toward the breathtakingly foreshortened extremities of the angels, the blessed, and the damned floating before them, so the whole of world history presses in on Kraus in the extremities of a single item of local news, a single phrase, a single advertisement. This is the inheritance that has come down to him from the sermons of Abraham a Sancta Clara. Thence the overwhelming immediacy, the ready wit, of the wholly uncontemplative moment; and the inversion that allows his will only theoretical, his knowledge only practical, expression. Kraus is no historic type. He does not stand on the threshold of a new age. If he ever turns his back on creation, if he breaks off in lamentation, it is only to file a complaint at the Last Judgment.

Nothing is understood about this man until it has been perceived that, of necessity and without exception, everything—language and fact—falls, for him, within the sphere of justice. All his fire-eating, sword-swallowing philology in the newspapers pursues justice just as much as language. It is to misunderstand his theory of language to see it as other than a contribution to the linguistic rules of court, the word of someone else in his mouth as other than a *corpus delicti,* and his own as other than a judging word. Kraus knows no system. Each thought has its own cell. But each cell can in an instant, and apparently almost without cause, become a chamber, a legal chamber over which language presides. It has been said of Kraus that he has to "suppress the Jewishness in himself," even that he "travels the road from Jewishness to freedom"; nothing better refutes this than the fact that, for him, too, justice and language remain founded in each other. To worship the image of divine justice in language—even in the German language—this is the genuinely Jewish *salto mortale* by which he tries to break the spell of the demon. For this is the last official act of this zealot: to place the legal system itself under accusation. And not in a petty-bourgeois revolt against the enslavement of the "free individual" by "dead formulas." Still less in the posture of those radicals who storm the legal code without ever for a moment having taken thought of justice. Kraus accuses the law in its substance, not in its effect. His charge: high treason of the law against justice. More exactly, betrayal of the word by the concept, which derives its existence from the word: the premeditated murder of imagination, which dies of the absence of a single letter and for which, in his "Elegy on the Death of a Sound," he has sung the most moving lament. For over jurisdiction, right-saying, stands orthography, right-spelling, and woe to the former if the latter should be wanting. Here, too, therefore, he confronts the press; indeed, in this charmed circle he holds his fondest rendezvous with the *lemures*. He has seen through law as have few others. If he nevertheless invokes it, he does so precisely because his own demon is drawn so powerfully by the abyss it represents. By the abyss that, not without reason, he finds most gaping where mind and sexuality meet—in the trial for sexual offenses—and has sounded in these famous words: "A trial for sexual offenses is the deliberate development from an individual immorality to a general immorality, against which dark background the proven guilt of the accused stands out luminously."

Mind and sexuality move in this sphere with a solidarity whose law is ambiguity. The obsession of demonic sexuality is the ego that, surrounded by sweet feminine mirages "such as the bitter earth does not harbor," enjoys itself. And no different is the loveless and self-gratifying trope of the obsessed mind: the joke. Neither reaches its object: the ego does not attain women any more than the joke attains words. Decomposition has taken the place of procreation; stridency, that of secrecy. Now, however, they shimmer in the most winsome nuances: in repartee, lust comes into its own; and in onanism, the joke. Kraus portrayed himself as hopelessly subjugated to the demon; in the pandemonium of the age, he reserved for himself the most melancholy place in the icy wilderness lit by reflected flames. There he stands on the Last Day of Humankind[5]—the "grumbler" who has described the preceding days. "I have taken the tragedy, which disintegrates into scenes of disintegrating humanity, on myself, so that it might be heard by the spirit who takes pity on the victims, even though he may have renounced for all time his connection with a human ear. May he receive the keynote of this age, the echo of my bloodstained madness, through which I share the guilt for these noises. May he accept it as redemption!"

"I share the guilt . . ." Because this has the ring of the manifestos—even if they are finally self-accusations—of an intelligentsia seeking to call to mind the memory of an epoch that seemed to be turning away from it, there is something to be said about this guilt feeling in which private and historical consciousness so vividly meet. This guilt will always lead to Expressionism, from which his mature work was nourished by roots that cracked open their soil. The slogans are well known—with what scorn did not Kraus himself register them: *geballt, gestuft, gesteilt* [clenched, stepped, steeped]; stage sets, sentences, paintings were composed.—Unmistakable—and the Expressionists themselves proclaim it—is the influence of early medieval miniatures on the world of their imagination. But anyone who examines their figures—for example, in the Vienna Genesis[6]—is struck by something very mysterious, not only in their wide-open eyes, not only in the unfathomable folds of their garments, but also in their whole expression. As if falling sickness had overtaken them thus, in their running which is always headlong, they lean toward one another. "Inclination" may be seen, before all else, as the deep human affect tremulously pervading the world of these miniatures, as it does the manifestos of that generation of poets. But only one, as it were inwardly curved, aspect of this relation is revealed by the front of these figures. The same phenomenon appears quite different to someone who looks at their backs. These backs are piled—in the saints of the adorations, in the servants of the Gethsemane scene, in the witnesses of the entrance into Jerusalem—into terraces of human necks and human shoulders that, really clenched in steep steps, lead less toward heaven than downward to and even under the earth. It is impossible to find, for their pathos, an expression that ignores the fact that they could be climbed like heaped rocks or rough-hewn steps. Whatever powers may have fought out their spiritual battles on these shoulders, one of them, from our experience of the condition of the defeated masses immediately after the end of the war, we are able to call by its name. What finally remained of Expressionism, in which an originally human impulse was converted almost without residue into a fashion, was the experience and the name of that nameless power toward which the backs of people bent: guilt. "That obedient masses are led into danger not by an unknown will but by an unknown guilt makes them pitiable," Kraus wrote as early as 1912. As a "grumbler" he participates in their lot in order to denounce them, and denounces them in order to participate. To meet them through sacrifice, he one day threw himself into the arms of the Catholic Church.

In those biting minuets that Kraus whistled to the *chassé-croisé* of Justitia and Venus, the leitmotif—that the philistine knows nothing of love—is articulated with a sharpness and persistence that have a counterpart only in the corresponding attitude of *décadence,* in the proclamation of art for art's sake. For it was precisely art for art's sake, which for the decadent movement applies to love as well, that linked expertise as closely as possible to craftsmanship, to technique, and allowed poetry to shine at its brightest only against the foil of hack writing, as it made love stand out against perversion. "Penury can turn every man into a journalist, but not every woman into a prostitute." In this formulation Kraus betrayed the false bottom of his polemic against journalism. It is much less the philanthropist, the enlightened friend of man and nature, who unleashed this implacable struggle than the literary expert, artiste, indeed the dandy, whose ancestor is Baudelaire. Only Baudelaire hated, as Kraus did, the satiety of healthy common sense, and the compromise that intellectuals made with it in order to find shelter in journalism. Journalism is betrayal of the literary life, of mind, of the demon. Idle chatter is its true substance, and every feuilleton poses anew the insoluble question of the relationship between the forces of stupidity and malice, whose expression is gossip. It is, fundamentally, on the complete agreement of two forms of existence—life under the aegis of mere mind, and life under the aegis of mere sexuality—that the solidarity of the man of letters with the whore is founded, a solidarity to which Baudelaire's existence is once again the most inviolable testimony. So Kraus can call by their name the laws of his own craft, intertwined with those of sexuality, as he did in *Die Chinesische Mauer* [The Great Wall of China]. Man "has wrestled a thousand times with the other, who perhaps does not live but whose victory over him is certain. Not because he has superior qualities but because he is the other, the latecomer, who brings woman the joy of variety and who will triumph as the last in the sequence. But they wipe it from her brow like a bad dream, and want to be the first." Now, if language—this we read between the lines—is a woman, how far the author is removed, by an unerring instinct, from those who hasten to be the first with her; how multifariously he forms his thought, thus inciting her with intuition rather than slaking her with knowledge; how he lets hatred, contempt, malice ensnare one another; how he slows his step and seeks the detour of followership, in order finally to end her joy in variety with the last thrust that Jack holds in readiness for Lulu![7]

The life of letters is existence under the aegis of mere mind, as prostitution is existence under the aegis of mere sexuality. The demon, however, who leads the whore to the street exiles the man of letters to the courtroom. This is therefore, for Kraus, the forum that it has always been for the great journalist—for a Carrel, a Paul-Louis Courier, a Lassalle. Evasion of the genuine and demonic function of mere mind, to be a disturber of the peace; abstention from attacking the whore from behind—Kraus sees this double omission as defining the journalist.—Robert Scheu rightly perceived that for Kraus prostitution was a natural form, not a social deformation, of female sexuality. Yet it is only the interlacing of sexual with commercial intercourse that constitutes the character of prostitution. It is a natural phenomenon as much in terms of its natural economic aspect (since it is a manifestation of commodity exchange) as in terms of its natural sexuality. "Contempt for prostitution? / Harlots worse than thieves? / Learn this: not only is love paid, / but payment, too, wins love!" This ambiguity—this double nature as twofold naturalness—makes prostitution demonic. But Kraus "enlists with the power of nature." That the sociological realm never becomes transparent to him—no more in his attack on the press than in his defense of prostitution—is connected with this attachment to nature. That for him the fit state of man appears not as the destiny and fulfillment of nature liberated through revolutionary change, but as an element of nature per se, of an archaic nature without history, in its pristine, primeval state, throws uncertain, disquieting reflections even on his ideas of freedom and humanity. They are not removed from the realm of guilt that Kraus has traversed from pole to pole: from mind to sexuality.

But in the face of this reality, to which Kraus exposed himself more harrowingly than any other, the "pure mind" that his followers worship in the master's activity is revealed as a worthless chimera. For this reason, none of the motives for his development is more important than the constant curbing and checking of mind. *Nachts* [By Night] is the title he gives to the logbook of this control. For night is the mechanism by which mere mind is converted into mere sexuality, mere sexuality into mere mind, and where these two abstractions hostile to life find rest in recognizing each other. "I work day and night. So I have a lot of free time. In order to ask a picture in the room how it likes work; in order to ask the clock whether it is tired and the night how it has slept." These questions are sacrificial gifts that he throws to the demon while working. His night, however, is not a maternal night, or a moonlit, romantic night: it is the hour between sleeping and waking, the night watch, the centerpiece of his threefold solitude: that of the coffeehouse, where he is alone with his enemy; of the nocturnal room, where he is alone with his demon; of the lecture hall, where he is alone with his work.

3. Monster [*Unmensch*]

Already the snow falls.
—Kraus, *Words in Verse III*

Satire is the only legitimate form of regional art. This, however, was not what people meant by calling Kraus a Viennese satirist. Rather, they were attempting to shunt him for as long as possible onto this siding, where his work could be assimilated into the great store of literary consumer goods. The presentation of Kraus as a satirist can thus yield the deepest insight both into what he is and into his most melancholy caricatures. For this reason, he was at pains from the first to distinguish the genuine satirist from the scribblers who make a trade of mockery and who, in their invectives, have little more in mind than giving the public something to laugh about. In contrast, the great type of the satirist never had firmer ground under his feet than amid a generation about to mount tanks and put on gas masks, a mankind that has run out of tears but not of laughter. In him civilization prepares to survive, if it must, and communicates with him in the true mystery of satire, which consists in the devouring of the adversary. The satirist is the figure in whom the cannibal was received into civilization. His recollection of his origin is not without filial piety, so that the proposal to eat people has become an essential constituent of his inspiration, from Jonathan Swift's pertinent project concerning the use of the children of the less wealthy classes, to Léon Bloy's suggestion that landlords of insolvent lodgers be conceded a right to the sale of the lodgers' flesh. In such directives, great satirists have taken the measure of the humanity of their fellow men. "Humanity, culture, and freedom are precious things that cannot be bought dearly enough with blood, understanding, and human dignity"—thus Kraus concludes the dispute between the cannibal and human rights. One should compare his formulation with Marx's treatment of the "Jewish question," in order to judge how totally this playful reaction of 1909—the reaction against the classical ideal of humanity—was likely to become a confession of materialist humanism at the first opportunity. Admittedly, one would need to understand *Die Fackel* from the first number on, literally word for word, to predict that this aesthetically oriented journalism, without sacrificing or gaining a single motif, was destined to become the political prose of 1930. For this it had to thank its partner, the press, which disposed of humanity in the way to which Kraus alludes in these words: "Human rights are the fragile toy that grownups like to trample on and so will not give up." Thus, drawing a boundary between the private and public spheres, which in 1789 was supposed to inaugurate freedom, became a mockery. Through the newspaper, says Kierkegaard, "the distinction between public and private affairs is abolished in private-public prattle . . ."

To open a dialectical debate between the public and private zones that commingle demonically in prattle, to lead concrete humanity to victory— this is operetta's purpose, which Kraus discovered and which in Offenbach he raised to its most expressive level.[8] Just as prattle seals the enslavement of language through stupidity, so operetta transfigures stupidity through music. To fail to recognize the beauty of feminine stupidity was for Kraus always the blackest philistinism. Before its radiance the chimeras of progress evaporate. And in Offenbach's operettas the bourgeois trinity of the true, the beautiful, and the good is brought together, freshly rehearsed and with musical accompaniment, in its star turn on the trapeze of idiocy. Nonsense is true, stupidity beautiful, weakness good. This is Offenbach's secret: how in the deep nonsense of public discipline—whether it be that of the upper ten thousand, a dance floor, or a military state—the deep sense of private licentiousness opens a dreamy eye. And what, in the form of language, might have been judicial strictness, renunciation, discrimination, becomes cunning and evasion, obstruction and postponement, in the form of music.—Music as the preserver of the moral order? Music as the police of a world of pleasure? Yes, this is the splendor that falls on the old Paris ballrooms, on the Grande Chaumière, on the Clôserie des Lilas in Kraus's rendering of *La vie parisienne*. "And the inimitable duplicity of this music, which simultaneously puts a plus and a minus sign before everything it says, betraying idyll to parody, mockery to lyricism; the abundance of musical devices ready to perform all duties, uniting pain and pleasure—this gift is here developed to its purest pitch." Anarchy as the only international constitution that is moral and worthy of man becomes the true music of these operettas. The voice of Kraus speaks, rather than sings, this inner music. It whistles bitingly about the peaks of dizzying stupidity, reverberates shatteringly from the abyss of the absurd; and in Frescata's lines it hums, like the wind in the chimney, a requiem to the generation of our grandfathers.—Offenbach's work is touched by the pangs of death. It contracts, rids itself of everything superfluous, passes through the dangerous span of this existence and re-emerges saved, more real than before. For wherever this fickle voice is heard, the lightning flashes of advertisements and the thunder of the Métro cleave the Paris of omnibuses and gas jets. And the work gives him all this in return. For at moments it is transformed into a curtain, and with the wild gestures of a fairground showman with which he accompanies the whole performance, Kraus tears aside this curtain and suddenly reveals the interior of his cabinet of horrors. There they stand: Schober, Bekessy, Kerr, and the other skits, no longer enemies but curiosities, heirlooms from the world of Offenbach or Nestroy[9]—no, older, rarer still, *lares* of the troglodytes, household gods of stupidity from prehistoric times. Kraus, when he reads in public, does not speak the words of Offenbach or Nestroy: they speak from him. And now and then a breathtaking, half-blank, half-glittering whoremonger's glance falls on the crowd before him, inviting them to the unholy marriage with the masks in which they do not recognize themselves, and for the last time invokes the evil privilege of ambiguity.

It is only now that the satirist's true face, or rather true mask, is revealed. It is the mask of Timon the misanthrope. "Shakespeare had foreknowledge of everything"—yes. But above all of Kraus. Shakespeare portrays inhuman figures—Timon the most inhuman of them—and says: Nature would produce such a creature if she wished to create something befitting the world as your kind have fashioned it, something worthy of it. Such a creature is Timon; such is Kraus. Neither has, or wants, anything in common with men. "An animal feud is on, and so we renounce humanity"; from a remote

village in the Swiss mountains Kraus throws down this challenge to mankind, and Timon wants only the sea to weep at his grave. Like Timon's
verse, Kraus's poetry stands opposite the colon of the *dramatis persona,* of
the role. A Fool, a Caliban, a Timon—no more thoughtful, no more dignified or better—but, nevertheless, his own Shakespeare. All the figures
thronging about him should be seen as originating in Shakespeare. Always
he is the model, whether Kraus is speaking with Otto Weininger about man
or with Peter Altenberg about women, with Frank Wedekind about the stage
or with Adolf Loos about food, with Else Lasker-Schüler about the Jews or
with Theodor Haecker about the Christians. The power of the demon ends
at this realm. His semihuman or subhuman traits are conquered by a truly
inhuman being, a monster. Kraus hinted at this when he said, "In me a
capacity for psychology is united with the greater capacity to ignore the
psychological." It is the inhuman quality of the actor that he claims for
himself in these words: the cannibal quality. For in each of his roles the
actor assimilates bodily a human being, and in Shakespeare's baroque ti-
rades—when the cannibal is unmasked as the better man, the hero as an
actor, when Timon plays the rich man, Hamlet the madman—it is as if the
actor's lips were dripping blood. So Kraus, following Shakespeare's example,
wrote himself parts that let him taste blood. The endurance of his convictions is persistence in a role, in its stereotypes, its cues. His experiences are,
in their entirety, nothing but this: cues. This is why he insists on them,
demanding them from existence like an actor who never forgives a partner
for denying him his cue.

Kraus's public readings of Offenbach, his recital of couplets from Nestroy,
are bereft of all musical means. The word never gives way to the instrument;
but by extending its boundaries further and further, it finally depotentiates
itself, dissolving into a merely creaturely voice. A humming that is to the
word what his smile is to the joke is the holy of holies of this performer's
art. In this smile, this humming—in which, as in a crater lake amid the most
monstrous crags and cinders, the world is peacefully and contentedly mirrored—irrupts the deep complicity with his listeners and models that Kraus
has never allowed to enter his words. His service to the word permits no
compromise. But as soon as the word turns its back, he is ready for anything.
Then the tormenting, inexhaustible charm of these recitals makes itself felt:
the charm of seeing the distinction between like and unlike minds annulled
and the homogeneous mass of false friends created—the charm that sets the
tone of these performances. Kraus confronts a world of enemies, seeks to
coerce them to love, yet coerces them to nothing but hypocrisy. His defense-
lessness before the latter has a precise connection to the subversive dilettan-
tism that is particularly prominent in his Offenbach renderings. Here Kraus
confines music to limits narrower than were ever dreamed of in the manifestos of the George school.[10] This cannot, of course, obscure the antithesis

between the linguistic gestures of the two men. Rather, an exact correlation exists between the factors which give Kraus access to both poles of linguistic expression—the enfeebled pole of humming and the armed pole of pathos—and those which forbid his sanctification of the word to take on the forms of the Georgean cult of language. To the cosmic rising and falling that for George "deifies the body and embodies the divine," language is simply a Jacob's ladder with ten thousand word-rungs. Kraus's language, by contrast, has done away with all hieratic moments. It is the medium neither of prophecy nor of domination. It is the theater of a sanctification of the name—with this Jewish certainty, it sets itself against the theurgy of the "word-body." Very late, with a decisiveness that must have matured in years of silence, Kraus entered the lists against the great partner whose work had arisen at the same time as his own, beneath the threshold of the century. George's first published book and the first volume of *Die Fackel* are dated 1899. And only retrospectively, in "After Thirty Years" (1929), did Kraus issue the challenge. There, as the zealot, he confronts George, the object of worship,

> who dwells in the temple from which
> he never had to drive the traders and the lenders,
> nor yet the pharisees and scribes,
> who therefore—camped about the place—describe it.
> The *profanum vulgus* praises this renouncer,
> who never told it what it ought to hate.
> And he who found the goal before the way
> did not come from the origin [*Ursprung*].

"You came from the origin—the origin is the goal" is received by the "Dying Man" as God's comfort and promise. To this Kraus alludes here, as does Berthold Viertel when, in the same way as Kraus, he calls the world a "wrong, deviating, circuitous way back to paradise." "And so," he continues in this most important passage of his essay on Kraus, "I attempt to interpret the development of this odd talent: intellectuality as a deviation . . . leading back to immediacy; publicity—a false trail back to language; satire—a detour to the poem." This "origin"—the seal of authenticity on the phenomenon—is the subject of a discovery that has a curious element of recognition. The theater of this philosophical recognition scene in Kraus's work is poetry, and its language is rhyme: "A word that never tells an untruth at its origin" and that, just as blessedness has its origin at the end of time, has its at the end of the line. Rhyme—two putti bearing the demon to its grave. It died at its origin because it came into the world as a hybrid of mind and sexuality. Its sword and shield—concept and guilt—have fallen from its hands to become emblems beneath the feet of the angel that killed it. This is a poetic, martial angel with a foil in his hand, as only Baudelaire knew him: "practicing alone fantastic swordsmanship,"

> Flairant dans tous les coins les hasards de la rime,
> Trébuchant sur les mots comme sur les pavés,
> Heurtant parfois des vers depuis longtemps révés.

> [Scenting rhyme's hazards in every corner,
> Stumbling on words as on uneven pavements,
> Jostling now and then long-dreamed-of lines.]

Also, to be sure, a licentious angel, "here chasing a metaphor that has just turned the corner, there coupling words like a procurer, perverting phrases, infatuated with similarities, blissfully abusing chiastic embraces, always on the lookout for adventure, impatient and hesitant to consummate in joy and torment." So, finally, the hedonistic impulse of the work finds its purest expression in this melancholy and fantastic relationship to existence in which Kraus, in the Viennese tradition of Raimund and Girardi, arrives at a conception of happiness that is as resigned as it is sensual.[11] This must be borne in mind if one is to understand the urgency with which he decried the dancing pose affected by Nietzsche—not to mention the wrath with which the monster [*Unmensch*] was bound to greet the Superman [*Übermensch*].

The child recognizes by rhyme that it has reached the ridge of language, from which it can hear the rushing of all springs at their origin. Up there, creaturely existence is at home; after so much dumbness in the animal and so much lying in the whore, it has found its tongue in the child. "A good brain must be capable of imagining each fiber of childhood with all its manifestations so intensely that the temperature is raised"—in statements such as this, Kraus aims further than it appears. He himself, at any rate, satisfied this requirement to the extent that he never envisaged the child as the object of education; rather, in an image from his own youth, he saw the child as the antagonist of education who is educated by this antagonism, not by the educator. "It was not the cane that should be abolished, but the teacher who uses it badly." Kraus wants to be nothing except the teacher who uses it better. The limit of his philanthropy, his pity, is marked by the cane, which he first felt in the same class at school to which he owes his best poems.

"I am only one of the epigones"—Kraus is an epigone of school anthologies. "The German Boy's Table Grace," "Siegfried's Sword," "The Grave in the Busento," "Kaiser Karl Inspects a School"—these were his models, poetically re-created by the attentive pupil who learned them. So "The Steeds of Gravelotte" became the poem "To Eternal Peace," and even the most incandescent of his hate poems were ignited by Hölty's "Forest Fire," whose glow pervaded the anthologies of our schooldays. And if on the last

day not only the graves but the school anthologies open, to the tune of
"How the Trumpets Blow, Hussars Away," the true Pegasus of the little folk
will burst from them and, with a shriveled mummy, a puppet of cloth or
yellowish ivory, hanging dead and withered from the shoulders of his horse,
this unparalleled fashioner of verses will go careening off; but the two-edged
saber in his hand, as polished as his rhymes and as incisive as on the First
Day, will belabor the green woods, and blooms of style will bestrew the
ground.

Language has never been more perfectly distinguished from mind, never
more intimately bound to eros, than by Kraus in the observation, "The more
closely you look at a word, the more distantly it looks back." This is a
Platonic love of language. The only closeness from which the word cannot
escape, however, is rhyme. So the primal erotic relationship between near-
ness and distance is, in his language, given voice as rhyme and name. As
rhyme, language rises up from the creaturely world; as name, it draws all
creatures up to it. In "The Forsaken" the most ardent interpenetration of
language and eros, as Kraus experienced them, expresses itself with an
innocent grandeur that recalls the perfect Greek epigrams and vase pictures.
"The Forsaken" are forsaken by each other. But—this is their great solace—
also with each other. On the threshold between dying and rebirth, they
pause. With head turned back, joy "in unheard-of fashion" takes her eternal
leave; turned from her, the soul "in unwonted fashion" silently sets foot in
an alien world. Thus forsaken with each other are joy and soul, but also
language and eros, also rhyme and name.—To "The Forsaken" the fifth
volume of *Words in Verse* is dedicated. Only the dedication now reaches
them, and this is nothing other than an avowal of Platonic love, which does
not satisfy its desire in what it loves, but possesses and holds it in the name.
This self-obsessed man knows no other self-renunciation than giving thanks.
His love is not possession, but gratitude. Thanking and dedicating—for to
thank is to put feelings under a name. How the beloved grows distant and
lustrous, how her minuteness and her glow withdraw into name: this is the
only experience of love known to *Words in Verse*. And, therefore, "To live
without women, how easy. / To have lived without women, how hard."

From within the linguistic compass of the name, and only from within it,
can we discern Kraus's basic polemical procedure: citation. To quote a word
is to call it by its name. So Kraus's achievement exhausts itself at its highest
level by making even the newspaper quotable. He transports it to his own
sphere, and the empty phrase is suddenly forced to recognize that even in
the deepest dregs of the journals it is not safe from the voice that swoops
on the wings of the word to drag it from its darkness. How wonderful if
this voice approaches not to punish but to save, as it does on the Shake-
spearean wings of the lines in which, before the town of Arras, someone
sends word home of how in the early morning, on the last blasted tree beside

the fortifications, a lark began to sing. A single line, and not even one of his, is enough to enable Kraus to descend, as savior, into this inferno, and insert a single italicization: "It was a nightingale and not a lark which sat there on the pome*granate* tree and sang."[12] In the quotation that both saves and punishes, language proves the matrix of justice. It summons the word by its name, wrenches it destructively from its context, but precisely thereby calls it back to its origin. It appears, now with rhyme and reason, sonorously, congruously, in the structure of a new text. As rhyme, it gathers the similar into its aura; as name, it stands alone and expressionless. In citation the two realms—of origin and destruction—justify themselves before language. And conversely, only where they interpenetrate—in citation—is language consummated. In it is mirrored the angelic tongue in which all words, startled from the idyllic context of meaning, have become mottoes in the book of Creation.

From its two poles—classical humanism and materialist humanism—the whole world of this man's culture is embraced by citation. Schiller, admittedly unnamed, stands beside Shakespeare: "There is also a moral nobility. Mean natures pay / With that which they do; noble, with that which they are"—this classical distich characterizes, in the convergence of manorial *noblesse* and cosmopolitan rectitude, the utopian vanishing point where Weimar humanism was at home, and which was finally fixed by Stifter. It is decisive for Kraus that he locates origin at exactly this vanishing point. It is his program to reverse the development of bourgeois-capitalist affairs to a condition that was never theirs. But he is nonetheless the last bourgeois to claim his justification from Being, and Expressionism was portentous for him because in it this attitude had for the first time to prove its worth in the face of a revolutionary situation. It was precisely the attempt to do justice to this situation not by actions but by Being that led Expressionism to its clenched, precipitous voice. So it became the last historical refuge of personality. The guilt that bowed it and the purity it proclaimed—both are part of the phantom of the unpolitical or "natural" man who emerges at the end of that regression and was unmasked by Marx. He writes:

> Man as member of bourgeois society, unpolitical man, necessarily appears as natural man . . . Political revolution dissolves bourgeois life into its component parts without revolutionizing or criticizing these components themselves. It stands to bourgeois society, to the world of needs, work, private interests, private right, in the same relation as it does to the foundation of its existence . . . and therefore to its natural basis . . . The real man is acknowledged only in the form of the egoistical individual; the true man, only in the form of the abstract *citoyen* . . . Only when the really individual man takes back into himself the abstract citizen and, as an individual man, has become in his empirical life, in his individual work, in his individual circumstances a species-being . . . and therefore no longer separates social power from himself in the form of political power, only then is human emancipation complete.[13]

The materialist humanism which Marx here opposes to its classical counterpart manifests itself for Kraus in the child, and the developing human being raises his face against the idols of ideal man—the romantic child of nature as much as the dutiful citizen. For the sake of such development, Kraus revised the school anthology, investigated German education, and found it tossing helplessly on the waves of journalistic caprice. Hence his "Lyrik der Deutschen" [Lyric of the Germans]:

He who *can* is their man and not he who *must*;
they strayed from being to seeming.
Their lyrical case was not Claudius
but Heine.

The fact, however, that the developing man actually takes form not within the natural sphere but in the sphere of mankind, in the struggle for liberation, and that he is recognized by the posture which the fight with exploitation and poverty stamps upon him, that there is no idealistic but only a materialistic deliverance from myth, and that at the origin of creation stands not purity but purification—all this did not leave its trace on Kraus's materialist humanism until very late. Only when despairing did he discover in citation the power not to preserve but to purify, to tear from context, to destroy; the only power in which hope still resides that something might survive this age—because it was wrenched from it.

Here we find confirmation that all the martial energies of this man are innate civic virtues; only in the melee did they take on their combative aspect. But already no one recognizes them any more; no one can grasp the necessity that compelled this great bourgeois character to become a comedian, this guardian of Goethean linguistic values a polemicist, or why this irreproachably honorable man went berserk. This, however, was bound to happen, since he thought fit to change the world by beginning with his own class, in his own home, in Vienna. And when, admitting to himself the futility of his enterprise, he abruptly broke it off, he placed the matter back in the hands of nature—this time destructive not creative nature:

Let time stand still! Sun, be consummate!
Make great the end! Announce eternity!
Rise up with menace, let your light boom thunder,
that our strident death be silenced.

You golden bell, melt in your own heat,
Make yourself a gun against the cosmic foe!
Shoot firebrands in his face! Had I but Joshua's power,
I tell you, Gideon would be again![14]

On this unfettered nature Kraus's later political credo is founded, though in antithesis to Stifter's patriarchal code; it is a confession that is in every respect astonishing, but incomprehensible only in the fact that it has not been preserved in *Die Fackel*'s largest type, and that this most powerful of postwar bourgeois prose must be sought in the now-vanished issue of November 1920:

> What I mean is—and now for once I shall speak plainly to this dehumanized brood of owners of property and blood, and to all their followers, because they do not understand German and from my "contradictions" are incapable of deducing my true intention . . .—what I mean is, Communism as a reality is only the obverse of their own life-violating ideology, admittedly by the grace of a purer ideal origin, a deranged remedy with a purer ideal purpose: the devil take its practice, but God preserve it as a constant threat over the heads of those who have property and would like to compel all others to preserve it, driving them, with the consolation that worldly goods are not the highest, to the fronts of hunger and patriotic honor. God preserve it, so that this rabble who are beside themselves with brazenness do not grow more brazen still, and so that the society of those exclusively entitled to enjoyment, who believe they are loving subordinate humanity enough if they give it syphilis, may at least go to bed with a nightmare! So that at least they may lose their appetite for preaching morality to their victims, take less delight in ridiculing them!

A human, natural, noble language—particularly in the light of a noteworthy declaration by Loos: "If human work consists only of destruction, it is truly human, natural, noble work." For far too long, the accent was placed on creativity. People are only creative to the extent that they avoid tasks and supervision. Work as a supervised task—its model being political and technical work—is attended by dirt and detritus, intrudes destructively into matter, is abrasive to what is already achieved and critical toward its conditions, and is in all this opposite to the work of the dilettante luxuriating in creation. His work is innocent and pure, consuming and purifying masterliness. And therefore the monster stands among us as the messenger of a more real humanism. He is the conqueror of the empty phrase. He feels solidarity not with the slender pine but with the plane that devours it, not with the precious ore but with the blast furnace that purifies it. The average European has not succeeded in uniting his life with technology, because he has clung to the fetish of creative existence. One must have followed Loos in his struggle with the dragon "ornament," heard the stellar Esperanto of Scheerbart's creations, or seen Klee's *New Angel* (who preferred to free men by taking from them, rather than make them happy by giving to them) to understand a humanity that proves itself by destruction.[15]

Justice, therefore, is destructive in opposing the constructive ambiguities of law, and Kraus destructively did justice to his own work: "All my errors stay behind to lead." This is a sober language that bases its dominance on permanence. The writings of Kraus have already begun to last, so that he might furnish them with an epigraph from Lichtenberg, who dedicated one of his most profound works to "Your Majesty Forgetfulness." So his modesty now appears—bolder than his former self-assertion, which dissolved in demonic self-reflection. Neither purity nor sacrifice mastered the demon; but where origin and destruction come together, his reign is over. Like a creature sprung from the child and the cannibal, his conqueror stands before him: not a new man—a monster, a new angel. Perhaps one of those who, according to the Talmud, are at each moment created anew in countless throngs, and who, once they have raised their voices before God, cease and pass into nothingness. Lamenting, chastising, or rejoicing? No matter—on this evanescent voice the ephemeral work of Kraus is modeled. Angelus— that is the messenger in the old engravings.

Published in the *Frankfurter Zeitung und Handelsblatt,* March 1931. *Gesammelte Schriften,* II, 334–367. Translated by Edmund Jephcott.

Notes

1. Karl Kraus (1874–1936) edited and wrote for *Die Fackel* from 1899 to 1936.
2. Otto Stössl, *Lebensform und Dichtungsform* [Life Form and Poetic Form] (Munich, 1914). Johann Peter Hebel (1760–1826) was a journalist and author who developed a number of innovative short prose forms during his work as editor and chief writer at the *Badischer Landkalendar,* an annual publication not unlike the American *Old Farmer's Almanach.* See Benjamin's essays on Hebel in Volume 1 of this edition.
3. This quotation by Adalbert Stifter (1805–1868) comes from the introduction to his *Bunte Steine* (1853), a volume of short stories. Stifter's prose is characterized by an unusually graceful style and a reverence for natural processes. See Benjamin's essay "Stifter" in Volume 1 of this edition.
4. Matthias Claudius (1740–1815), German poet, was perhaps the most notable poetic voice between Klopstock and Goethe. He served as editor of the important journal *Der Wandsbecker Bote.*
5. *Die letzten Tage der Menschheit* (The Last Days of Humankind) is the title of Kraus's mammoth apocalyptic drama, which sought to expose the bureaucratic mediocrity and political criminality that he believed had brought Europe to the Great War. The play was published in its final form in 1923. Due to its length (it has 220 scenes and approximately 500 characters), it was first performed in Vienna only in 1964—and even then in a shortened version.
6. "Vienna Genesis" refers to an illuminated manuscript—a copy of the book of Genesis—in the collection of the Austrian National Library. Its dating (early Byzantine, perhaps 500–600 A.D.) and place of origin (Constantinople or Syria) are disputed. The linkage of Expressionism and late Antiquity had been a concern of Benjamin's from the time he read Alois Riegl's *Die spätrömische Kunst-Industrie* (The Late Roman Art Industry) during the years of the First World War; the linkage plays an important role in Benjamin's *Ursprung des deutschen Trauerspiels* (Origin of the German Trauerspiel).

7. Benjamin refers here to the "Lulu" cycle, two dramas by the German playwright Frank Wedekind (1864–1918). In *Erdgeist* (Earth Spirit; 1895) and *Die Büchse der Pandora* (Pandora's Box; 1904), the conflict of a desiccated, hypocritical bourgeois morality with a personal and above all sexual freedom is played out in the fate of the amoral femme fatale Lulu. Alban Berg based his opera *Lulu* on Wedekind's plays.

8. Kraus translated and edited the operetta *La vie parisienne* (music by Offenbach and libretto by Henri Meilhac and Ludovic Halévy). See "Karl Kraus Reads Offenbach," in this volume.

9. Johann Schober (1874–1932), a police official, was twice prime minister of Austria (1921–1922 and 1929–1930). He was best-known for his attempts to negotiate a union between Austria and Germany. Alfred Kerr (pseudonym of Alfred Klemperer; 1867–1948) was Berlin's most prominent and influential theater critic. Johann Nestroy (1801–1862), Austrian dramatist and character actor, used satire, irony, and parody as weapons against the newly rising bourgeoisie. His best-known work is *Einen Jux will er sich machen* (He Intends to Have a Fling; 1842), adapted by Thornton Wilder as *The Matchmaker* and later turned into the musical play and film *Hello, Dolly!*

10. "George school" refers to the circle of conservative intellectuals around the poet Stefan George (1868–1933), whose high-modernist verse appeared in such volumes as *Das Jahr der Seele* (The Year of the Soul; 1897) and *Der siebente Ring* (The Seventh Ring; 1907). George's attempt to "purify" German language and culture exerted a powerful influence on younger poets.

11. Ferdinand Raimund, Austrian comic dramatist, was—along with Johann Nestroy—among the preeminent playwrights of Vienna in the mid-nineteenth century.

12. Kraus cites this line in *Die Fackel* and attributes it to an anonymous Belgian soldier. *Granat* means "pomegranate"; *Granate,* "grenade" or "shell."

13. This is the conclusion of Karl Marx's 1844 review of Bruno Bauer's "On the Jewish Question."

14. Karl Kraus, *Worte in Versen II* (Words in Verse II).

15. The reference is to Paul Klee's ink wash drawing *Angelus Novus* (1920), which Benjamin owned for a time. See the discusssion under "1921" in the Chronology to Volume 1 of this edition.

Literary History and the Study of Literature

Scholars attempt again and again to present the history of individual disciplines in terms of one self-contained development. They like to speak of "autonomous disciplines." And even though this formulation initially refers only to the conceptual system of individual disciplines, the idea of autonomy easily spills over into the historical domain. It then leads to the attempt to portray the history of scholarship as an independent, separate process set apart from overall political and intellectual developments. There is no need to debate the rights and wrongs of this procedure here; independently of any judgment on this issue, one must, in a survey of the current situation in a particular discipline, consider any findings not just as a link in the autonomous historical development of the subject, but also as an element of the prevailing cultural situation at that point in time. If, as is maintained in what follows, literary history is in the depths of a crisis, this crisis must be seen as part of a much broader one. Literary history is not only a discipline in its own right; in its development, it is also a moment of history in general.

It certainly is the latter. But is it really the former? Is literary history a historical discipline? The following will clarify the sense in which this must be denied. It is fair to say in advance that despite what the term might lead us to expect, "literary history" did not make its initial appearance in the context of historical studies. In the eighteenth century it was a branch of aesthetic education, a kind of applied taxonomy of taste, and it stood halfway between a textbook of aesthetics and a bookseller's catalogue.

The first pragmatic historian of literature was Gervinus, the first volume of whose *Geschichte der poetischen Nationalliteratur der Deutschen* [History of the Poetic National Literature of the Germans] appeared in 1835.[1] He saw himself as a member of the historical school. In his eyes, great works are "historical events, poets are geniuses of activity, and judgments about them have far-reaching public effects . . . This analogy to world history is as much a part of Gervinus' own individual attitude as his method of filling the gap due to the absence of art-historical analysis by 'comparing' great works with 'related' ones."[2] The true relationship between literature and history—let alone the relationship between history and literary history—is something that this brilliant but methodologically naive work could not focus on. And if we survey the attempts made prior to the middle of the century, we see how the position of literary history, and the extent to which it was a part of history or something *outside* it but related to it, remained unclarified. With men like Michael Bernays, Richard Heinzel, and Richard Maria Werner, this epistemological perplexity was followed by a reaction.[3] With varying degrees of intention the link with history was abandoned in favor of a leaning toward the exact natural sciences. Whereas previously even bibliographic compilations tended to give an idea of the overall historical development, scholars now doggedly fell back on individual studies and on "collecting and cherishing." To be sure, this period of positivist doctrine brought forth a plethora of histories of literature for use by the layman, as a complement to scholarly research in the strict sense. But the panorama of universal history that they unfolded was nothing but a kind of narrative comforter for both writer and reader. Wilhelm Scherer's history of literature, with its factual underpinning and its great rhythmic periodization (three phases over each of three centuries), can be seen as a synthesis of the two great basic trends of scholarship at the time.[4] Commentators have been right to emphasize the cultural-political and organizational intentions which underlie this work, together with the Makart-like vision on which it is based[5]—that of a colossal triumphal procession of ideal German figures. Scherer's bold conception makes the dominant figures "arise sometimes from the political sphere and sometimes from the realm of literature, religion, or philosophy, without creating the impression of a higher necessity, or even of external consistency. He cancels out their effects with those of individual works, fetishized ideas, or literary giants, and the entire project ends up a colorful jumble that is the very antithesis of historical order."[6]

What we see emerging here is the false universalism of the methods of cultural history. It is a development that culminates logically in the concept of the "cultural sciences" [*Kulturwissenschaften*] as formulated by Rickert and Windelband.[7] Indeed, the victory of these cultural sciences was so complete that with Karl Lamprecht's *Deutsche Geschichte* [German History] it even went on to become the epistemological foundation of pragmatic history. With the proclamation of "values," history was distorted once and for all in the service of modernism, while research was demoted to the status of an auxiliary in a cult in which the "eternal values" were celebrated in accordance with a syncretist rite. It is always worth reflecting how short the path is from here to the wildest aberrations of the most recent forms of literary history, and what charms the castrated methodologies have succeeded in extracting from the repulsive neologisms that lurk behind the golden gates of the "values." "Just as all poetry ultimately aspires to a world of 'verbalizable' [wortbaren] values, so too in formal terms it signifies an ultimate intensification and interiorization of the immediate expressive powers of speech."[8] After this assertion the reader will have become anesthetized, for good or ill, to the shock of recognition with which the poet himself experiences this "ultimate intensification and interiorization" as "the pleasures of verbalizing" [Wortungs-Lust].[9] This is the same world in which the "verbal artwork" is at home. Rarely has a word that has been so much abused displayed so much nobility as the word "poetry." And with all that, this science throws its weight around while simultaneously betraying itself through the "breadth" of its object and through its "synthesizing" comportment. The profligate drive toward totalities is its misfortune. Just listen: "Spiritual values come to the fore with overwhelming power and purity . . . as 'ideas' which make the poet's soul soar aloft and impel him to create symbolic forms. Unsystematically, yet with complete clarity, the poet makes us feel at every moment which values or which value-strata he privileges; and also perhaps, what priority he gives to values in general."[10]

In this quagmire, the hydra of scholastic aesthetics is at home with its seven heads: creativity, empathy, freedom from time, imitation, sympathetic understanding, illusion, and aesthetic enjoyment. Whoever wishes to explore the world of its acolytes could not do better than to take a look at its latest, representative handbook—Philosophie der Literaturwissenschaft, edited by Emil Ermatinger—in which the German literary historians of the present attempt to give an account of their work and from which these quotations have been taken. This does not mean that all the contributors to this volume take responsibility for one another in a spirit of solidarity. Undoubtedly, writers like Gumbel, Cysarz, Muschg, and Nadler stand out from the chaotic background in which they appear.[11] It is all the more revealing, then, that even men who have notable scholarly achievements to their credit have brought few of the attitudes that ennobled the study of German literature in its early days into the community of their colleagues. For anyone who is at home in literature, the entire enterprise creates the uncanny impression that the beautiful, well-built house of poetry has been invaded by a company of mercenaries who clump around with their heavy boots in the ostensible desire to admire its treasures and wonders. At the sight of them, everything immediately becomes clear: these people do not give a damn for the order and inventory of the house. They have moved in because it is strategically situated and because it is a convenient vantage point from which to bombard a railway or bridgehead whose defense is important in the civil war. And this is how literary history has established itself in the house of literature: the "beautiful," the "worthwhile experience," the "ideal," and so on are all apertures from which it is easy to bombard the enemy.

It cannot be said that the troops caught up in this crossfire are adequately trained. They operate under the command of the materialist literary historians, among whom old Franz Mehring still stands head and shoulders above the rest.[12] What this man means can be seen anew from every attempt at materialist literary history since his death. Most clearly in Alfred Kleinberg's *Deutsche Dichtung in ihren sozialen, zeit- und geistesgeschichtlichen Bedingungen* [German Literature in Its Social, Historical, and Intellectual Context]—a work that slavishly colors all the stereotypes of a Leixner or a Koenig and then frames them with a few ornaments of free thought.[13] The whole thing is a real blessing for the ordinary man. For his part, Mehring is a materialist far more because of the scope of his general historical and economic knowledge than through his methodology. His ideology derives from Marx; his intellectual discipline, from Kant. The result is that the work of this man—who held unswervingly to the belief that "the noblest possessions of the nation" had to be preserved at all cost—is conservative in the best sense of the word, rather than revolutionary.

But the Fountain of Youth of history is fed by Lethe. Nothing is so rejuvenating as oblivion. With the crisis in education, the use of literary history for the creation of "representative examples" is growing, as can be seen most obviously in the many popular handbooks on the subject. It is always the same blurred text that makes its appearance in one format or another. Such achievements have long since ceased to have anything in common with scholarship; their function is limited to giving certain social strata the illusion that they are participating in the cultural and literary heritage. Only a discipline that abandons its museum characteristics can replace illusion with reality. That would call not just for the courage to omit much, but also for the ability to bring the entire business of literary history into an age in which the number of writers—and this means more than the poets and literati—is growing daily and has a much more urgent technical interest in the problems of writing than in those of edification. More recent scholars can take this into account, and have already begun to do so in part, with analyses of anonymous writing—calendar stories and colportage—as well as of the sociology of the reading public, writers' associations, and the history of the publishing industry. But this is perhaps a matter less of renewing teaching through research than of renewing research through teaching. For the crisis in education stands in precise correlation to the fact that literary history has now completely lost sight of its most important challenge—namely, its pedagogical task, the task with which it began its life as the "science of belles lettres."

So much for the social context. Just as modernism has flattened out the tension between knowledge and practice with its museum-like concept of culture, the same fate has afflicted the historical sphere: the distinction has fallen away between past and present—that is to say, between criticism and literary history. The literary history of modernism is not concerned with legitimating itself prematurely by a creative interaction with the past. It imagines that it can do this better with acts of patronage toward contemporary writing. It is astonishing to see how academic scholarship goes along with this trend. In former times, German literary scholars refused to regard the literature of their age as a suitable subject for research. This was not, as is believed today, a matter of prudence, but sprang from the ascetic attitudes of researchers who served their age directly by attempting to do justice to the past. The style and attitude of the Brothers Grimm testify to the fact that the regimen required for such work is no less demanding than that needed for great artistic creativity. This attitude has been replaced by the ambition of scholars to demonstrate that they are as well informed as the midday edition of any metropolitan newspaper.

Present-day German studies are eclectic—that is to say, unphilological through and through. This is to measure them not by the positivistic yardstick of the Scherer school but by that of the Brothers Grimm, who never sought to grasp material content except through words and who would have shuddered to hear contemporary talk of a literary analysis that was "transparent" or "pointed beyond itself." Needless to say, no later generation has been able to approach their talent for interweaving critical and historical analysis. True, there is some remarkable literary history emerging in a few isolated cases (Hellingrath, Kommerell) from the work of the George circle—history that does succeed in combining the literary with the academic.[14] But if this is so, it is because in their own way these writers breathe something of the same antiphilological spirit. The panoply of Alexandrian learning that is familiar from the works of the George circle—"genius" and "virtus," "kairos" and "daemon," Fortuna and Psyche—is really designed to exorcize the historical. And the ideal of this trend would really be to divide up the whole of German literature into sacred groves containing temples to poets of timeless worth. Last, the abandonment of the philological approach leads (not least in the George circle) to that fallacious question that is increasingly a source of confusion in the field of literary history— namely, whether, and to what extent, reason is ever capable of comprehending the work of art. We are now very far from grasping the fact that the existence of a work of art in time and the understanding of it are but two sides of the same thing. The task of opening literary history to reason has been consigned to the monographic treatment of works and forms.

"For the present," writes Walter Muschg, "we may say that in its essential works literary history is almost exclusively focused on monographs. Faith in the possibility of a comprehensive description has been almost entirely lost by the present generation. Instead it struggles with individuals and problems that it mostly found missing in the age of universal histories." It struggles with individuals and problems—this may well be accurate. The truth, however, is that it should struggle above all with the works. Their entire life and their effects [*Wirkung*] should have the right to stand along-side the history of their composition. In other words, their fate, their reception by their contemporaries, their translations, their fame. For with this the work is transformed inwardly into a microcosm, or indeed a micro-eon. What is at stake is not to portray literary works in the context of their age, but to represent the age that perceives them—our age—in the age during which they arose. It is this that makes literature into an organon of history; and to achieve this, and not to reduce literature to the material of history, is the task of the literary historian.

Published in *Die literarische Welt,* April 1931. *Gesammelte Schriften,* III, 283–290. Translated by Rodney Livingstone.

Notes

1. Georg Gottfried Gervinus (1805–1871), historian, literary historian, and politician, held professorships at Heidelberg and Göttingen and was a delegate to the German National Assembly in Frankfurt in 1848. His literary history broke new ground in its effort to embed the discussion of literature within a larger historical narrative.
2. Walter Muschg, "Das Dichterporträt in der Literaturgeschichte" [The Portrait of the Poet in Literary History], in Emil Ermatinger, ed., *Philosophie der Literatur-wissenschaft* [Philosophy of Literary Scholarship] (Berlin: Junker und Dünn-haupt, 1930), p. 288.
3. Michael Bernays (1834–1897), German literary historian, was best-known for his work on Goethe and Shakespeare. Richard Heinzel (1835–1905), literary historian, attempted to bring the exactitude of the natural sciences to the study of language and literature. Richard Maria Werner (1854–1913), literary historian, was best-known for his work on the dramatist Hebbel.
4. Wilhelm Scherer (1841–1886), one of the nineteenth century's leading linguists and literary historians, sought to replace descriptive literary history with a comparative approach which emphasized the "genetic" development of a national literature.
5. Hans Makart (1840–1884) was an Austrian painter who made his reputation with vast historical and allegorical canvases that made his name a byword for empty monumentality.
6. Muschg, "Das Dichterporträt," p. 290.
7. The philosopher Heinrich Rickert (1863–1936) founded, together with Wilhelm Windelband, one of the principal schools of Neo-Kantian philosophy in Ger-

many. His work in epistemology emphasized the role of transcendental subjectivity in the acquisition of knowledge. Both Benjamin and Heidegger studied with Rickert. Wilhelm Windelband (1848–1915), also a philosopher, taught in Zürich, Freiburg, and Strasbourg before joining Rickert in Heidelberg. He is best-known for the way in which he differentiated the methods of the humanities from those of the natural sciences.

8. Robert Petsch, "Die Analyse des Dichtwerks" [Analysis of the Poetic Work], in Ermatinger, ed., *Philosophie,* p. 263.

9. Ibid., p. 255.

10. Ibid., p. 259.

11. Emil Julius Gumbel (1891–1966), literary scholar, was forced to resign his position at Heidelberg because of his pronounced republican and pacifist ideas. He emigrated first to France and then to the United States, where he ended his career at the New School for Social Research in New York. Herbert Cysarz (1896–1985), literary historian, concentrated much of his work on Baroque literature. Benjamin cites Cysarz extensively in his *Ursprung des deutschen Trauerspiels* (Origin of the German Trauerspiel). Walter Muschg (1898–1965) was a Swiss poet, dramatist, and literary historian. Josef Nadler (1884–1963) was a German literary historian.

12. Franz Mehring (1846–1919), radical journalist, was a historian of the German Social Democratic Party and the biographer of Karl Marx.

13. Otto Leixner von Grünberg (1847–1907), literary historian, editor, and author, was coeditor of the journal *Die Gegenwart,* which published several of Benjamin's articles.

14. Friedrich Norbert Theodor von Hellingrath (1888–1916), literary historian, caused a sensation in Germany with his historical-critical edition of the works of Friedrich Hölderlin. Benjamin's own early work on Hölderlin is indebted to Hellingrath. In the years before World War I, Hellingrath became associated with the circle around Stefan George; he died in the Battle of Verdun. Max Kommerell (1902–1944), literary critic, author, and translator, belonged intermittently to the George circle. He was a widely influential critical voice in the Weimar Republic. See also Benjamin's "Against a Masterpiece," in this volume.

German Letters

I

The series of German letters that is inaugurated here is not to be thought of as an anthology. However much the attentive reader may learn from it about the value and honor of the German language, and however clearly some of these letters enable him to glimpse a human being where previously he had perceived only an achievement, this is not the intention of the present writer—any more than he wishes to advance the general education of the reader.[1] The intention of this series is, rather, to reveal the lineaments of a "secret Germany" that people nowadays would much prefer to shroud in heavy mist. For a secret Germany really exists. It is merely that its secretness is not simply the expression of its inwardness and depth, but—albeit in a different sense—the product of raucous and brutal forces that have prevented it from playing an effective role in public life and have condemned it to a secret one. And these forces are the same ones that drove Georg Forster from his native land, that led Hölderlin to try to earn his living as a tutor in France, and that made Johann Seume play into the hands of the recruiting officers from Hesse, who then sent him to fight in America. Must we define these forces more precisely? Forster and Seume call them by name, and, in his greatest poems, Hölderlin confronts them as never before with the figure of the German genius. For none of these men—and this holds good for the others who will appear later in this sequence—has ever in his creative work sought an alibi that might enable him to evade the call of civic duty in an emergency. It is because these letters make this so clear that they have remained so unknown. This is as true of Forster as of Seume. And although Hölderlin's letters were read, they were misunderstood most in what they said to the Germans about Germany. One consolation in all this is that these letters have remained quite untouched. They were overlooked by public speakers and those who commemorate anniversaries. And if the latter occasionally managed to pervert the works of these men, as if they had no message to convey to us, or rather no witness to bear, a glance at their letters is sufficient to show where that Germany stands today—a Germany that unfortunately remains a secret one.

Georg Forster (1754–1794) died at the age of forty. He was, to vary a famous saying, at every moment of his life a man who dies at the age of forty. The age of manhood was the age of his maturity, and everything about him that became mature was manly. Forster was as familiar with the *misère* of the German intellectuals of his day as any Hölderlin or Seume. But he had a particular affinity with the latter because, like Seume's, his own misfortune did not derive from being a private tutor. Instead, the theater of his misfortune was Europe as a whole, which he came to know in the course of extensive traveling. This is why he was almost the only German who was destined to understand the European response to the prevailing conditions, which is how he interpreted the French Revolution. In 1795 he went to Paris as a delegate from the city of Mainz; and after the Germans reconquered the town and made his return there impossible by outlawing him, he remained in Paris until his death.

Hölderlin (1770–1843) can have entertained no doubts about the insignificance of the play that Böhlendorff sent him and for which he thanks him in the following letter. Yet it is not just tact that moved him to respond with such a magnanimous letter, but his consciousness of the superhuman difficulties that his friend faced in his life—difficulties that were so unfavorable to any poetic production and that were so similar to Hölderlin's own. The writing and the terrible fate of Schubart, who was imprisoned in a house of correction for eleven years by the duke of Württemberg, and who was never informed of the reason for this punishment, had a powerful influence on Hölderlin in his youth.[2] He hardly ever spoke out against despotism. But anyone who takes the measure of the profundity of his philosophical thoughts about everything German will be able also to gauge the depth of the silence about conditions in Germany that had been imposed on him.

Johann Gottfried Seume (1763–1810) was no great writer. Yet it is not this that distinguishes him from many others who occupy a position in the history of German literature, but his unfailingly irreproachable attitude at times of crisis and the imperturbability with which—after he had been press-ganged by Hessian recruiters and shipped off to America as a soldier—

he consistently stood for the dependable citizen long after he had shed his officer's uniform and had become a proofreader for the publisher Göschen. What the eighteenth century understood by the phrase *honnête homme* can be seen as clearly in Seume as in Tellheim.[3] The only difference is that for Seume the honor of an officer is not so far removed from that of the kind of highwayman his contemporaries revered in *Rinaldo Rinaldini*.[4] When at one point he has fallen into the deepest poverty and is on the verge of despair, he considers going back into the army, and the one thought which consoles him is that in no profession is the man of honor so sorely needed as in that of the soldier.

Written either in early April 1931 or after 1933; unpublished in Benjamin's lifetime. *Gesammelte Schriften*, IV, 945–947. Translated by Rodney Livingstone.

Notes

1. Benjamin's involvement with the publication of a series of German letters spans the years 1931–1936. In 1931 and 1932, the *Frankfurter Zeitung* published twenty-seven letters from the years 1783–1883; Benjamin had chosen and edited the letters, but his name was not mentioned in association with them. In the months leading up to and during the publication of the letters, he composed both a provisional introduction—the text at hand—and a text probably intended as a radio broadcast (see "On the Trail of Old Letters," in this volume). The twenty-seven letters, together with a foreword to the collection and a brief introduction to each selection, were published in book form in Switzerland in 1936 under the title *Deutsche Menschen*. The three letters Benjamin would have included here, by Forster, Hölderlin, and Seume, are not identical with the ones included in the later collection. The letters are: Georg Forster to his wife, July 26, 1793; Friedrich Hölderlin to Casimir Böhlendorff, December 4, 1801; and Johann Gottfried Seume to Karl Böttiger, November 1805.
2. Christian Friedrich Daniel Schubart was a poet and publicist, known for his outspoken religious, patriotic, and democratic views. The duke of Württemberg imprisoned him in the fortress of Hohenasperg from 1777 to 1787. Friedrich Schiller visited him there in 1781. After his release he was appointed Master of Music to the Württemberg court.
3. Tellheim is one of the two chief characters in Lessing's *Minna von Barnhelm*. He is a model of rectitude and dignity.
4. *Rinaldo Rinaldini* was a three-volume novel written in 1798 by Goethe's brother-in-law, Christian August Vulpius. It was widely read in its day.

May–June 1931

Juan-les-Pins, May 4, 12:45 in the morning. I'm going to save my remaining sheets of paper for a diary. On the assumption that what lies ahead of me is not worth making much of a fuss about, I will concentrate on the past. A number of factors have prompted this project. The most important, however, is that I feel tired. Tired above all of the struggle, the struggle for money, of which I now have enough in reserve to enable me to stay here. But tired also of aspects of my personal life with which strictly speaking— apart from my economic situation—I have no reason to be dissatisfied. But the very sense of tranquillity that has taken possession of me inwardly to a degree that has always been rare with me leads me to probe more deeply into the life I am now leading. And then this fatigue. It not only dredges up memories from the past; what is crucial is that of the events in my past which surface in my memory from time to time, it is the factors that make them moments of my life, make them mine, that have become clear, whereas previously I never gave them a thought. Last, this fatigue combines in a strange way with the causes of my dissatisfaction with my life. This dissatisfaction involves a growing aversion to, as well as a lack of confidence in, the methods I see chosen by people of my kind and my situation to assert control over the hopeless situation of cultural politics in Germany. What torments me is the lack of clarity and precision with which the few people close to me divide into factions. What disturbs my inner peace, which is also a peaceable attitude, is the disproportion between the bitterness with which they debate their differences of opinion in my presence—though they have long since ceased to do so among themselves—and the frequently minimal differences in substance. It is actually the consistent characters among the writers who are the worst of all; but in the interests of professional solidarity, they are hardly ever exposed. I have often wondered whether my particular irenic nature is not linked to the contemplative spirit engendered by the use of drugs. The universal reservations toward one's own way of life, which are forced upon every writer—without exception, I believe—by the contemplation of the situation in Western Europe, are related in a bitter way to the attitude toward other human beings that is induced in the drugtaker by the poison he takes. And to take the full measure of the ideas and impulses that preside over the writing of this diary, I need only hint at my growing willingness to take my own life. This willingness is not the product of a panic attack; but profound though its connection is with my exhaustion from my struggles on the economic front, it would not have been conceivable without my feeling of having lived a life whose dearest wishes had been granted, wishes that admittedly I have only now come to recognize as the original text on a page subsequently covered with the handwritten marks of my destiny.

The morning of the same day. Further thoughts about wishes. People would have fewer doubts about the assertion that everyone has his dearest wishes granted, if they would only realize that these wishes are almost always unconscious—in other words, are different from the wishes they know of and which (they may rightly complain) they have not been granted. Fairy tales make this very clear with the motif of the three wishes. We have no right to be astonished at the folly and shortsightedness of the use people make of those magic wishes. For we are those people. Except that our dearest wishes are never present in our minds, as they are to the lucky fairy-tale characters who have them granted; we become aware of them only as events in the past, and often we find that they have unfortunately come true and that we have been duped. The true characteristic of these wishes, however, was that no price was too high for what one desired; and in retrospect these wishes can best be recognized by the fact that this limitless willingness was actually exploited and by the actual cost of their fulfillment. Of the three greatest wishes of my life, the one I recognized soonest was the wish for distant and, above all, long journeys. This was also the wish I became aware of most quickly before it was granted, if only by the violence of my reaction. At first it may simply have been the irresistible impulse to flee Germany, a desire that gripped people during the war years with the same force as the wish for an automobile during the inflation and the period of reconstruction. Then came the moment when I had enough money to enable me, in an emergency, to spend some time abroad; I arranged to spend time in Capri with some friends. I have a very clear memory of the shock I received when I saw the headline in an evening paper in the hand of a woman selling newspapers on the corner of Friedrichsstrasse and Unter den Linden: "Ban on Foreign Travel." A regulation had been issued restricting foreign travel to those people who were able to deposit a sum that was perhaps tenfold what I had available. The regulation was due to come into force in two or three days' time. It was evident to me that, in the circumstances, I could not wait for the departure date that I had agreed on with my friends and that happened to fall just before the deadline. Only when I came to unpack my suitcase in Capri or Naples did I discover what a mad rush I'd been in: I had just packed whatever came immediately to hand. Many essentials were missing, while a hundred superfluous things had been brought along. Yet the real turning point of that trip was not my swift resolve to leave Berlin (my friends managed, with difficulty, to leave a few days later) but, five or six weeks later, when my financial resources were exhausted, my decision to put up with anything as long as I did not have to leave the island. I even considered in all seriousness the possibility of living in one of its large caves, and the images I still have of this are so vivid that today I no longer know whether they were mere fantasies or were based on one of the adventure stories that abound on the island. There have been similar reports of someone actually doing this during the war. In this way my wish was granted with my stay on the island, and later because of it. For I am convinced that to have lived for a long time on Capri gives you a claim on distant journeys, so strong is the belief of anyone who has long lived there that he has all the threads in his hand and that in the fullness of time everything he needs will come to him.

Juan-les-Pins, May 5, in the morning. Before continuing with my three wishes, I want to write down my thoughts about Hemingway. Entirely successful, entirely meaningful ventures can sometimes best be perceived when placed next to complete failures, things that are completely banal. Compare Hemingway with a bad writer. A bad writer is a writer who always says more than he thinks. A good writer—and here we must be careful if we wish to arrive at any real insight—is a writer who does not say more than he thinks. This definition will probably be read as a request for "clear and simple writing"; people will imagine that a good writer is one who says exactly what he thinks. But it is this obvious inference that must be avoided at all costs. The foundation of every insight into questions of style is the realization that there is no such thing as "saying what you think." The fact is that speech is not so much the expression as the making real of thought, a process that subjects thought to the profoundest modifications—much as running toward a goal is not just the expression of a wish to reach it, but a making real, a process that likewise subjects the wish to profound modification. Yet the way these modifications turn out—whether they ennoble the wish, refine it, or allow it to become too vague and general—depends on the writer's training regimen. The more he disciplines his body, and the more he limits his body to running and avoids superfluous, uncoordinated, or slack movements, the more his gait will itself become a criterion of the goal of his wish, will refine it, or drop it if it is not worth the trouble. The magic of Hemingway is his ability to make these phenomena, which normally only the practiced eye can discern in a rigorously and intelligently trained body, visible in his style. It would be a mistake to overemphasize individual technical achievements, such as his skill in knowing what to omit, or his talent for dialogue. His prose presents us with the great drama of an education in right thinking through correct writing. He does not say more than he thinks, and hence the whole power of his writing redounds to the benefit of what he really thinks.

As I returned, dead tired, from the Casino de la Lotée in Nice to Juan-les-Pins by bus on the night of May 5, an illuminating etymological insight occurred to me. The French say *allure* [walk, gait, bearing]; we say *Haltung*. Both words come from the idea of walking. But in order to say the same thing (and just how little it is the "same" can be seen from this observation), the French emphasize the process of walking—*allure*—while the Germans talk of its interruption—*Haltung* [posture, stance, attitude].

On the way here, I spent the night with Egon in Basel.[1] We shared a room; and although it was after two or even three A.M. when we went to bed and our train was due to leave at seven in the morning, we stayed awake talking about this and that. It so happened that I expressed for the first time an idea that had struck me several times during the previous few weeks. Egon made a comment about the Bauhaus style that coincided with the negative opinions I used to hold. His criticism was based on his aesthetic reservations about the formal idiom of Bauhaus furniture, and this gave me my cue to indicate how—even though my views had not become fully clarified—it had given me a remarkable insight into the famous manorial style of the very rich. And in fact, the intentions of the Bauhaus people and their like can be seen far less well from the theories they proclaim than from the hidden laws that determined the architectural style of the immediately preceding generations. If you enter one of the bourgeois rooms of the 1880s, the main impression you receive, for all the "coziness" it may well radiate, is one that says, "You have no business here." You have no business there because there is not an inch on which the owner has not left a trace of his own. What this means is made clear enough by a fine phrase of Brecht's. "Erase the traces" is the refrain of the first poem in his *Lesebuch für Städtebewohner* [Reader for Citydwellers]. Here, in the bourgeois room the opposite behavior has become an ethos in the strictest sense—that is to say, a habit. Indeed, leaving traces is not just a habit, but the primal phenomenon of all the habits that are involved in inhabiting a place. What is possible among the pieces of furniture of the Bauhaus is no more than a bare lodging [*ein Hausen*] when compared with life in a bourgeois dwelling, whose interior compels the inhabitant to adopt a maximum number of habits; and indeed these habits are better calculated to celebrate the interior in which he lives than to do justice to himself. This will be readily understood by anyone who still remembers the absurd fuss people made in those days when anything was broken. Even their way of showing their anger—and this emotion, which is gradually starting to atrophy, was one they could turn on and off to spectacular effect—was, above all, the reaction of someone denied his habits. The modern style of building, whatever else may be said of it, has now created rooms in which it is hard to leave such traces (this is why glass and metal have become so important) and which make it almost impossible to acquire habits in the first place. This is why the rooms are empty and often adjustable at will.

May 6, evening. Lay around yesterday with Gert and Egon. We spoke about experiences of love, and in the course of this conversation I understood something for the first time in my life: every time I've experienced a great love, I've undergone a change so fundamental that I've amazed myself and have been forced to realize that the man who said such unexpected things and behaved in such unpredictable ways was myself. This is based on the fact that a genuine love makes me resemble the woman I love. I was delighted to hear Gert confirm this so emphatically, even though she did so by asserting that this was the true mark of feminine love in general. This transformation into the realm of the similar—which is so indispensable that in the view of the Church it has to be guaranteed by the sacrament of marriage, for nothing makes people resemble each other more than living together in marriage—was something I experienced most powerfully in my relationship with Asja, with the result that I discovered many things in myself for the first time. On the whole, however, the three great loves of my life have influenced me not just chronologically, in terms of periodization, but also in terms of experience. I have come to know three different women in the course of my life, and three different men in myself.[2] To write the story of my life would mean describing the rise and fall of these three men and the compromise among them—one could also say, the triumvirate—that represents my life.

Sanary, May 13, 1931. I wonder whether the enjoyment of the world of images isn't fed by a sullen defiance of knowledge. I gaze out over the landscape. Before me lies the sea, which in the bay is as smooth as a mirror; forests extend up to the hilltop, an immobile, silent mass; to one side, ruined castle walls stand there as they have for centuries; the sky is cloudless—a heavenly blue, as the phrase goes. This is what the dreamer who immerses himself in this landscape wants to see. The fact that the sea rises and falls in thousands upon thousands of waves every moment; that the forests tremble anew every second, from their roots to the very last leaf; that in the stones of the castle ruins, there is a constant crumbling and crashing; that in the sky, gases surge invisibly to and fro in conflict with each other before they condense into clouds; that science pursues all this movement into the innermost heart of matter, sees in atoms nothing but electron storms—all this he must forget and wishes to deny so as to surrender to the images that will give him peace, rest, eternity. Every gnat that hums in his ears, every gust of wind that makes him shiver, everything near that strikes him gives the lie to his dreams, but every distance rebuilds them again. They spring to life at every mountain ridge in the dusk, or every lighted window. And the dream appears at its most perfect when he succeeds in removing the sting from movement itself, in translating the trembling of the leaves above him into the top of a tree, the flitting and darting of the birds above his head into a flock of migrating birds. To command Nature herself to stand still in the name of faded images—this is the black magic of sentimentality. But to utter a call that will freeze it anew is the gift of poets.

In the evening, a brief conversation with Speyer sitting next to a fire in the hearth.[3] As I watched the flame licking around the logs just as we were talking about a novel, the two topics of conversation merged in my mind. I suddenly imagined that the way the logs were piled represented the true model of composition in the novel. The plot must be just as loosely arranged, and should be designed for consumability in just the same way. In other words, it must be completely opposed to architectonic—and, even more, monumental—construction. Of course, the Germans in their novels have never been able to free themselves from the idea of architecture. Even Gottfried Keller lacked the touch to pile up the logs of his story artistically like Balzac or Dostoevsky. The actual adversary of this novelistic technique—which produces books that can warm the reader as much as an open fire—is the great constructor Flaubert, whose works have the same impact on the reader as a splendid Delft stove in which there is no fire.

Juan-les-Pins, May 17, 1931. Attempted to set down some of what was said about Eva Hermann[4] in conversation partly with Wilhelm and partly with Maria Speyer.

May 21. Went with Speyer by car to Saint-Paul de Vence. One ought to spend ten days in this extraordinary place sometime. Unfortunately, however remote and self-contained a place may be, nowadays a chink in its armor will soon be discovered. I had no sooner said to Speyer—we were alone together briefly, since Wissing's and Speyer's wives had gone on ahead— "Quel bonheur que ça ne soit pas encore découvert par les cinéastes" [How lucky that the place has not yet been discovered by film enthusiasts], than Willy Fritsch and Lilian Harvey suddenly appeared in the marketplace with a large party.[5] Anyway, the place can't really be described as undiscovered;

otherwise, how would it have acquired a celebrated tea room run by two young girls, friends, lesbians, with candles lighting up the interior and old-fashioned copper kettles, ladles, and similar implements to give it cachet. Still, it is all very charming and tasteful. In addition, the tea salon is combined with the sale of postcards and an antique shop. And just outside the town, in front of the gates, there are two inns. Of these we saw the Colombe d'Or, a beautifully maintained hostelry, with gardens laid out in terraces going down to the valley floor, and tables standing ready for guests under blossoming orange trees surrounded by flower beds. Without seeing anything, the Berlin film company thundered around the market square, which satisfies all the requirements for show simply by the unsurpassable economy of a tiny arcade and a single Empire fountain, and whose very modesty succeeds in bringing out the very best in the tiny dimensions of the town. Of course, it unobtrusively takes its revenge, since, as I suddenly discovered, it has found room in the confined space for no fewer than two sundials. Neither of these has an inscription.—Some of this reminds me of San Gimignano, but the authority of the fortifications is greater here. It allows no space for the development of any splendor, or even leisureliness. Even the marketplace is tiny. And amid the network of crisscrossing streets, there is not a single spot that invites the visitor to linger—apart, that is, from one place in front of the church and the spaces around the fortifications. The strict, uninterrupted contrast between house and street completely dominates the architecture; all mediations are avoided, and even the presumably indispensable presence of shops has actually been rendered invisible. So unified is the row of house façades that you can scarcely tell whether they are inhabited, let alone whether they conceal stores or workshops. At most you catch a glimpse of a room with a man and a woman sorting orange blossoms, or laying them out to dry. The ten days I wished for in Saint-Paul would certainly be necessary to get to know the place. In such a town, there is hardly anything that does not lie concealed and would not be worth the trouble of discovering: the narrow shafts between the houses that frame the green depths of the landscape beyond like a chimney; the sundials affixed at right angles to two gabled walls on the market square; the view through the monumental arches of the gateways; the fringed profile of the ruins of the town ramparts. In a courtyard that made us pause in surprise as we passed by, and above which it was impossible to see the sky—we were standing at an angle, and the houses here were very tall—someone had put up a poster with the one word "Cinema" on it. The painter may have painted the word with a stencil, or perhaps had just designed it himself, since only this clumsy, rustic lettering would have matched the dull browns and grays of this shady neighborhood so perfectly. Even if it had been the courtyard of a Lyons monastery, the monks would scarcely have been able to fix a more inexorably styled pious motto over the portal. We stood around for a long time on the ancient ramparts and gazed down into the countryside lying beneath an overcast sky. In the even light, all the lines that human labor had incised in the landscape emerged more starkly. Hedges and furrows idiosyncratically drew their lines and angles. But one would have had to know all the plants by name in order to be able to decode their geometry. Indeed, faced with this supremely cultivated landscape, the untutored townsman stands baffled, like a Westerner confronted by a page of Chinese script. To think that such ignorance is the only common foundation of the majority of descriptions! In most cases, the further apart these Provençal farms are, the more admirably they are built, and the more you realize how snugly they fit into the landscape and how natural their forms are, compared to the inexorably geometric lines of the groves, beds, and fields. The town has the *grandezza* that work on the land confers on the villages: before nightfall hardly anyone is to be seen on the streets.

June 3, 1931. In front of the Potinière in Le Lavandou. A very cold wind is blowing. I am there with Brecht, Hesse-Burri, Elisabeth Hauptmann, the Brentanos, and Marie Grossmann.[6] Of course, I could record all sorts of things from my conversations with Brecht. The most diverse topics were touched on: the international society of materialist friends of the Hegelian dialectic; the idea of a detective play; the trial of Friedrich Schiller; and last of all Proust, in an hour-long conversation yesterday at which Marie Grossmann was present. But I prefer to describe a different scene, one in which my own behavior is quite inscrutable. I had gone for a walk on my own to Saint Clair. It was the first for a long time—the first walk, not just the first one on my own, for a long time. On the way, I was struck by the dog roses. I picked one; it did not disappoint me, since it had a wonderful fragrance. I removed the thorns from the end of the stalk and carried it in my hand. On the way back I passed a bush full of peonies. They reminded me vividly of the bunch of flowers Jula Cohn once gave me years ago for my birthday; that, too, had consisted entirely of peonies. With some difficulty I broke off a small twig and put it, together with the dog rose, between the pages of Jouhandeau's *Journal du Coiffeur,* which I was carrying. On the way, as I was passing the Villa Mar Belo, where Brecht and the others were staying, I thought I would stop in. I did so, even though I said to myself that they would still be at table. And in the somewhat labile state this first walk on my own for such a long time had induced in me, I probably did so at least partly because I had grown tired of following a pretty girl in a red beach-jacket and blue trousers who had been walking along the highroad in front of me in the twilight. The worst thing was that she suddenly stopped to talk to a man she had met, so that I would have been forced to walk on past her. So I went down the side path to the villa and entered the hall. They had seen me coming, and at the door to the dining room Brecht came out to meet me. Despite my protestations, he refused to go back to the table and took me into the next room. We stayed there and talked for about two hours, partly on our own, and partly with the others, mainly just with Frau Grossmann, until I felt it was time to go. As I picked up my book the flowers peeked out of it, and when someone joked about them my embarrassment grew, since even before I had entered the house I had been wondering why I was arriving bearing flowers and whether I shouldn't throw them away. But I hadn't done so, God knows why. There was undoubtedly an element of defiance in it. Needless to say, I realized there would be no opportunity to give my rose to Elisabeth Hauptmann, so I decided I would at least hoist it like a flag. But this idea was a complete failure. In the face of Brecht's ironic jokes, I no less ironically presented him with the peony, keeping a firm grip on the dog rose. Of course, Brecht refused to accept it. I ended up putting the peony unobtrusively into a large vase full of blue flowers next to me. The dog rose, however, I threw in among the blue flowers from above. There it stuck, looking as if it were growing out of the blue flowers—a veritable botanical curiosity. And there it remained quite clearly. So the bunch of flowers had hoisted my flag after all, and had to take the place of her for whom it was intended.

The previous evening, a conversation with Brecht, Brentano, and Hesse in the Café du Centre. The conversation turned to Trotsky; Brecht maintained there were good reasons for thinking that Trotsky was the greatest living European writer. We exchanged episodes from his books. Brecht contributed the following anecdote. It concerned a particular account of Lenin's first days in Leningrad, as reported in Trotsky's book. Trotsky tells how completely isolated Lenin was in the Communist party immediately after his arrival, and how finally there was to be a particularly important vote, at which Lenin declared that he would leave if he were outvoted. Brecht was talking to Brik about this, and asked him with some anxiety what he thought of such monstrous proceedings, and what he thought of Lenin's undisciplined reaction. And now Brik's reply—Brecht repeated it full of admiration: "That was like the tree trunk saying to the foliage, 'I'm leaving.'"[7]

June 6. Brecht regards Kafka as a prophetic writer. He says that he knows him as well as his own pocket. But what he means by this is not so easy to find out. So much is clear: he believes that Kafka has just one theme, and that the richness of Kafka as a writer is simply the rich variety of this one theme. According to Brecht, this theme, in its most general sense, is astonishment. The astonishment of a man who feels that huge shifts are in the offing in every aspect of life, without being able to find a niche for himself in the new order of things. For this new order—if I have understood Brecht correctly—is governed by the dialectical laws that dictate the life of the masses to themselves and to the individual. But the individual as such must react with astonishment tinged with panic-stricken horror to the almost incomprehensible deformations of life that are revealed by the emergence of these laws.—Kafka, it seems to me, is dominated by this to the point that he is quite incapable of portraying any event without distortion. In other words, everything he describes makes statements about something other than itself. The permanent, visionary presence of distorted things is met with the writer's own gaze, full of inconsolable earnestness and despair. As a result of this stance, Brecht is inclined to regard Kafka as the only authentic Bolshevist writer. Kafka's fixation on his one and only theme can give the reader an impression of obsessiveness. But in reality this impression is only a sign that Kafka has broken with the tradition of pure narrative prose. It may be that his prose proves nothing; but it is so constructed that it can be inserted into passages of argument at any time. This is reminiscent of the form of the Haggadah. That is what Jews call the stories and anecdotes in the Talmud that serve to elucidate and confirm the teachings— the Halachah.[8] Admittedly, the teachings as such are never enunciated by Kafka. The only possibility is to read them from the astonishing behavior of people—behavior that is either born of fear or that causes it in others.

One can gain some insight into Kafka by observing that he attributes the most interesting forms of behavior to animals. The reader follows these animal tales for a fair distance without even noticing that they do not deal with human beings at all. Then, when the animal is identified for the first time—as a mouse or a mole—you are suddenly jolted and realize how far you have drifted away from the continent of human beings. As far away from it as a future society will be. Incidentally, it is worth paying attention to the kinds of animals Kafka chooses to embody his ideas. They always dwell in the interior of the earth, or, like the beetle in "Die Verwandlung" [The Metamorphosis], they are creatures that hide away on the ground, in cracks and crannies. This scurrying away seems to the author the only appropriate behavior for the isolated members of his generation and their context, with their ignorance of the law.

Brecht contrasts Kafka—and the figure of K.—with Schweik: the man who is astonished by everything with the one who is astonished by nothing. Schweik puts to the test the monstrous nature of the existence into which he has been placed by making it seem as if nothing is impossible for him. In his experience, conditions are so completely bereft of laws that he has long since abandoned the expectation that laws might be found. Kafka, on the other hand, comes up against the law at every turn; indeed, one could even say that he bloodies his brow smashing up against the law (see the Mole, and see also p. 213);[9] but it is no longer the law governing the real world of things in which he lives, or any world of things whatsoever. It is the law of a new order in which all the things in which it expresses itself are misshapen, a law that deforms all things and all the people it touches.

June 7. In conversation with Brentano the other day, Brecht let fall a remark that seems to me to be worth preserving. Brentano was in the midst of one of his blustering speeches about the revolutionizing of the intellectual workers, the situation of the intelligentsia, and so forth, when Brecht interrupted rather fiercely. What was wrong with the position of the intellectuals, and what prospects could the revolution hold out to them? "The intelligentsia," he said, "is not overworked. And even if there are doctors and lawyers who are slaving away, what does that matter? It's a kind of work that suits them; it cannot be compared with the work of the proletariat by any stretch of the imagination. And so what if they ask themselves what they should do when they're sixty and haven't saved anything? That's really going too far!" he said angrily. "For God's sake, let them croak! It's far too late then, anyway. It would be better if they died right away." A day or so later, we touched on the same subject when I spoke about the lack of pretentiousness of the Surrealists—a trait that made it easier to form a grouping in France and that was precluded in Germany by the far-reaching demands made by German writers. To be sure, it is only right for a collective to moderate its demands; for the individual, it is mainly a mistake.

June 8. A truly unusual afternoon with Brecht. A discussion about "propositions"—the kind of propositions that one hears from Brecht almost every day—took a strange turn, thanks to an objection from me. I disagreed with his search for "ideas" [*Vorstellungen*] and instead called for a study of modes of behavior. I focused on my favorite topic, dwelling [*das Wohnen*]. Brecht entered into the discussion enthusiastically and produced an extraordinary account of his manner of dwelling—which I then followed up with a different one, without identifying it as my own. I kept a record of what was said and so can repeat it accurately. The two accounts were seen to be dialectical and were represented as polar opposites. Brecht's starting point was a "sympathetic" [*mitahmend*] dwelling.[10] This is a mode of dwelling that "shapes" its environment, arranges it in a suitable, adaptable, and compliant way—a world in which the dweller is at home in his own way. Brecht contrasted this with a different approach: the habit of always behaving like a guest. Such a person refuses to take responsibility for what he makes use of; he feels invited by the chair on which he sits, and when he gets up he feels himself to be disinvited. At this point, I set out to explain a different dialectic of living. I managed to convince Brecht that my account was not just a paraphrase of his own views. I made a distinction between a way of dwelling that gives the inhabitant a maximum of habits, and a way of dwelling that gives him a minimum. Both extremes are pathological. The probable difference between this approach and the one outlined by Brecht is that the attitudes he described tend to diverge, whereas those I defined tend to converge. The mode of dwelling that reinforces habits is the one imagined by the landladies of rented accommodations. For them, a human being becomes a function of the activities that the furnishings require of him. The person inhabiting a dwelling has a completely different relationship to the world of things from the relationship involved in "sympathetic" dwelling. The objects are taken seriously (whether or not they are "property" in the legal sense), whereas for "sympathetic" dwelling they have roughly the same meaning as a stage set. We might even say that one mode takes place in a stage set; the other, in an interior. What is less easily defined is the element of habit in "sympathetic" dwelling, whereas for living as a guest, it is completely captured by Nietzsche's statement, "I love ephemeral habits."[11] Last, the fourth mode of dwelling—the dwelling that gives you the fewest habits—is just simple lodging [Hausen]. This idea, too, appears best-developed in the mentality of landladies. At its center are the idea of the bad lodger and the concept of wear and tear. For simple lodging is destructive dwelling—a mode of dwelling that undoubtedly prevents the development of any habits, because it constantly clears away its basis: the objects.

June 10. A few days ago, a conversation with Speyer's wife, who reported this astounding statement by Eva Hermann from the period of her greatest depression: "The fact that I'm unhappy doesn't mean that I have to run around with a face full of wrinkles." This made a number of things clear to me. Above all, that my recently acquired peripheral contact with the world of these creatures—Gert, Eva Hermann, and so on—is only a belated and feeble echo of one of the fundamental experiences of my life: that of semblance [Schein]. I expressed this view yesterday in the course of a conversation with Speyer, who has also begun to reflect about these people, and who made the astonishing comment that they had no conception of honor—or, rather, that their code of honor was actually to say everything they thought. This is very true, and basically it is merely a proof of the obligation they feel to semblance. For this "saying everything" means destroying what has been said. Or, better: once these people have destroyed what has been said, it is turned into a subject of conversation. Only when it has become semblance-like are they able to digest it. Speyer and I also spoke about the fact that the stance of this circle is very much the complement of that attitude of pseudo-maturity, pseudo-knowledge, characteristic of people who have the answer to everything. The microcosm of a false childhood in which these people shield themselves from life is the other side of the coin from the would-be gigantic scale on which others (I'm thinking of Lawrence above all) experience life. Speyer's friend Max Mohr must be a person of this type.[12] For him, everything that followed Mycenae is decadence, and today tourism seems to him to represent the greatest guarantee of health.

June 12. Yesterday, with Speyer's wife up in Mar Belo. It was the first real contact between Brecht and Speyer, and I was very pleased that it went off so well. I had not actually been anxious about it, given Brecht's behavior during the past few days. But it was a stroke of luck that Brecht started talking about his childhood and hence about things to which Speyer feels especially sympathetic. Above all, he talked about the school of strategy from which he had graduated: the battles between different school classes at the bleaching grounds on the River Lech, and the battles with tin soldiers in the garden. The incidental stories he told about his school life reminded me very powerfully of Kraus's attitude toward school. "We learned," Brecht said, "everything we needed later on. In our eyes, the teacher was simply the human being as such: vigilant, bad-tempered, unjust. And the faking, cheating, and inventing excuses—all this had to be learned. We had to do our English homework during math class and our German homework during English class—all this had to be learned." But as already mentioned, he talked mainly about the battles with tin soldiers. "There were set-piece encounters with four or five thousand such soldiers. The battles had to follow strict rules: at every move the infantry was allowed to advance a distance equivalent to its own height, while the cavalry could move twice its own height. Of course, only soldiers were usable when you were on the attack. Other tin soldiers would have deprived the conflict of every illusion." Brecht told us about a march that had acquired historical fame: one of his friends had succeeded in moving a 300-strong body of troops over a meadow without any cover in such a way that 180 were still alive at the end of it. While these troops were advancing, they came under fire from cannons that pelted them with tiny missiles (crackers). The secret was to hit them broadside; otherwise they did not fall over. If we reflect that just moving the soldiers around manually on that march must have taken hours, this really was a great achievement. In these battles, villages were marked by strips of cardboard, rivers were crossed on pontoons, and tree roots represented mountains. Moreover, Brecht claimed that in those days he had learned by heart a whole series of the battles of world history—that he had studied *De Bello Gallico* and all the battles of Frederick the Great.[13] He believed that he could probably reconstruct the Battle of Waterloo even now.

This morning he made his appearance at nine, and, as luck would have it, he continued where he had left off with stories from his youth. Today, though, he talked about the later years. He was "very cheerful," as he said himself, because the political news from Berlin had shaken his conviction that Germany would have to wait for years for a revolutionary situation to arise. Everything could turn around very suddenly, he thought. And he based this prognosis on some very interesting theses about the masses, which I will simply set down here. The intelligence of the capitalists grows in proportion to their isolation; that of the masses, in proportion to their solidarity. The proletariat's sense of reality is incorruptible. You can give workers as many assurances as you wish, but if they come to the conclusion that the person giving these assurances cannot fulfill them, even if he wanted to, then they will simply proceed as if nothing had happened—very much in contrast to intellectuals. Moreover, capitalism had now reached the point where even its well-intentioned promises would find no credence with the masses.—The masses wished to be treated as individuals: this was the main dialectical proposition to bear in mind when dealing with them. For all these assertions Brecht appealed to the period at the outbreak of the revolution in Munich, when he had effectively been in charge of a military ward for patients with venereal disease, even though formally he was only a junior doctor.[14] Of all the wards, this was the only one in which patients were not allowed to leave the barracks—a regulation that could not be enforced anywhere else. Brecht was very funny in his description of the various methods he used to keep the patients where they were. He first tried to persuade the masses to organize, and to get the cleverest and strongest of their leaders on his side. He then tried to join with the masses in a united front of illegality: he procured blankets for them through deception, coal through a break-in, and so on. What helped him most was that he was better at giving injections than the other doctors. "I could do it skillfully—but I could also do it unskillfully." And he acted out a splendid solo scene for me, showing how, when he had to inject a patient who had pulled a fast one, he would gradually work himself into a state while preparing the injection, so that the patient began to worry about how deeply upset the doctor was and to realize how very unpleasant this procedure might be, just from the way the doctor washed out the syringe. Brecht sometimes took measures that affected the collective as a whole; one evening, for example, he confiscated all the blankets in one dormitory.—He also gave very curious reasons in favor of such collective measures, in our discussion about the German situation. If he were on the Berlin executive committee, he would devise a five-day plan according to which at least 200,000 Berliners would be eliminated within that period. Simply because this would ensure that "people get involved." "If this were done, I would know that at least 50,000 proletarians would have been made to participate actively."

June 17, 1931. The following emerged from several conversations with Brecht about the Epic Theater. Speyer was present at some of these conversations, and Carola Neher at others.[15] Brecht seems to regard Georg Kaiser (alongside Strindberg) as the greatest technician among modern dramatists, and thinks that *Der gerettete Alkibiades* [Alcibiades Saved], in particular, is one of the greatest achievements and models of the Epic Theater.[16] He describes Kaiser as the last idealist dramatist, but claims that in his works dramatic technique has reached a level that makes it unusable for idealist purposes. He is the last dramatist before the great change. Other examples of Epic Theater from Calderón and Shakespeare.[17] I referred him particularly to *El mayor monstruo, los celos* [The Greatest Monster, Jealousy], and *La gran Cenobia* [The Great Zenobia], and Brecht asked me if I would at some point prepare a description of these plays for publication. And then Shakespeare. He kept returning to his favorite passage—that great speech by a mother to her son, the speech that is supposed to induce Coriolanus to withdraw from Rome and that achieves its purpose even though it could hardly have been more wretched and incoherent. "It's a miracle," Brecht says of Shakespeare, "where he could have got this speech from; he must have spent enough time looking for it." And yet it is this speech that leads the mother to her goal. How this comes about is explained by Coriolanus in the sentence which sums up the situation: "I have sat too long," he says, and nothing more.[18] Further examples from Shakespeare. I talk about Gloucester's leap from the cliff that isn't a cliff;[19] it was this episode that first gave me an inkling of other possibilities for the stage than were contained in Freytag's *Die Technik des Dramas* [Dramatic Technique]. It might not be the worst idea to explicate the laws of Epic Theater by comparing them with that book. I also gleaned a very important idea from a remark made in the course of a conversation between Brecht and Neher on the journey from Le Lavandou to Marseilles. Brecht was saying that he would like little descriptions from people about human "behavior" taken from direct experience. It appears that Neher had been making similar experiments of this sort for some time. Brecht was keen to encourage her in this. She should simply write down what she had been able to discover. "And above all, no punch lines. That would ruin them." In my view, this would tell us a lot not only about the Epic Theater but also about Brecht. He seems to hate and abhor nothing so much as activities and modes of behavior that bring their own reward.—Very curious is what Brecht has to say about *Romeo and Juliet* in the context of a defense of the Epic Theater. The conversation was triggered by a comment that Speyer had made about the play years ago—about how very significant and also how bold it was of Shakespeare to have introduced Romeo as the most passionate lover of Rosaline in order to show how much he is in love with Juliet.[20] Brecht instantly added an astonishing variation to this theme by saying that Romeo was not just the most passionate but also the most fortunate lover—namely, a totally exhausted one, quite bereft of his manly powers. And if Brecht is to be believed, this really seemed to be the "epic" theme of the play—namely, that it was primarily for physiological reasons that the couple were unable to come together. For just as "it is well known" that the sexual act does not work if the partners have only sexual intentions, so too the love of Romeo and Juliet failed because they were trying too hard, were too eager.

June 21. On the last day of our journey from Marseilles to Paris, we paused for a break in the open air. The Brentanos stayed on the road, while I went higher, climbing up an embankment. I then lay down under a tree. There was a bit of a breeze; the tree was a willow or a poplar—in any case, a tree with very pliant, swaying boughs. As I looked up into the foliage and followed its movements, it suddenly occurred to me how many images and metaphors are nesting in a single tree. The branches and the treetop sway up and down reflectively, and bend away in rejection; the boughs, depending on the way the wind is blowing, lean toward you or fly upward; the mass of leaves resists the demands of the wind, recoils from them, or comes to meet them; the trunk has the solid ground on which it stands; and one leaf casts a shadow on another.

Postscript to Brecht's studies on dwelling and ideas in general: dwelling in a hotel—the idea that life is a novel.

Written May–June 1931; unpublished in Benjamin's lifetime. *Gesammelte Schriften,* VI, 422–441. Translated by Rodney Livingstone.

Notes

1. Egon Wissing, a physician, was Benjamin's cousin. They were neighbors on Prinzregentenstrasse in Berlin. In 1932, when Benjamin again contemplated taking his own life, he wrote a farewell letter to Wissing and made him the executor of his will. Egon's wife, Gert, died in 1933.
2. According to Gershom Scholem, the three women were presumably Dora Benjamin (Walter's wife), Jula Cohn, and, Asja Lacis. For more information on Benjamin's relations with them, see the Chronologies to volumes 1 and 2 of this edition.
3. Wilhelm Speyer (1887–1952) was a novelist and dramatist whom Benjamin accompanied on a motoring tour of Italy in 1929 and with whom he collaborated on a novel and several plays.
4. Eva Hermann (1901–1978) was a graphic artist friendly with Klaus and Erika Mann.
5. Willy Fritsch (1901–1973) and Lilian Harvey (1907–1968) were prominent German film actors who had recently appeared together in two popular films, *Die Drei von der Tankstelle* (1930) and *Der Kongreß tanzt* (1931).
6. Emil Hesse-Burri was a writer and producer who collaborated with Brecht on his *Saint Joan of the Stockyards.* Elisabeth Hauptmann (1897–1973) was a major

collaborator of Brecht's—on *The Threepenny Opera, Mahagonny,* and other works. Bernhard von Brentano (1901–1964) was a left-wing journalist and novelist.

7. Osip Maximovich Brik (1888–1945) was a friend and associate of the poet Vladimir Mayakovsky. Originally a Formalist writer, he later helped to found the Levy front iskusstva (Left Front of Art), known as LEF—a Marxist literary group.

8. The term *Lehre* figured prominently in Benjamin's discussions with Gershom Scholem during the World War I years. It signifies something between "religious doctrine" and "teachings."

9. K. is the protagonist of Kafka's novel *Das Schloß* (The Castle). Schweik is the protagonist of the satirical novel *The Good Soldier Schweik* (3 vols., 1920–1933), by the Czech writer Jaroslav Hašek (1883–1923). See also "The Burrow," in Franz Kafka, *The Collected Short Stories* (Harmondsworth: Penguin, 1983), p. 328; and "The Great Wall of China," ibid., p. 244. "The Mole" is Benjamin's name for the narrator of "The Burrow." His page reference is to Franz Kafka, *Beim Bau der Chinesischen Mauer* (Berlin: Kiepenheuer, 1931).

10. Brecht's word *mitahmend* is a coinage combining elements of *nachahmend* ("imitative") and *Mitgefühl* ("sympathy").

11. Nietzsche, *Die fröhliche Wissenschaft* (The Gay Science), aphorism 295.

12. Max Mohr (1891–1944) was a physician and the author of novels and plays. He emigrated to China in 1934.

13. Julius Caesar's *De Bello Gallico* (On the Gallic War) is his account of the Romans' conquest of Gaul in 58–50 B.C.

14. Brecht had in fact been a medical orderly. The reference is to the socialist revolution of 1918–1919 in Munich.

15. Carola Neher (1905–1942) was an actress who performed in many of Brecht's plays, including the original version of *The Threepenny Opera.* She emigrated to the USSR in 1933, was arrested in 1939, and was murdered in one of the camps three years later.

16. Georg Kaiser (1878–1945) was one of the leading dramatists of the German Expressionist theater. His most important works include *Die Bürger von Calais* (The Burghers of Calais; 1914), *Von Morgens bis Mitternachts* (From Morn to Midnight; 1916), and the *Gas* trilogy, consisting of *Die Koralle* (The Coral; 1917), *Gas I* (1918), and *Gas II* (1920).

17. Pedro Calderón de la Barca (1600–1681) was one of the premier dramatists and poets of Spain's Golden Age. His best-known secular dramas include *El médico de su honra* (The Surgeon of His Honor; 1635), *La vida es sueño* (Life Is a Dream; 1635), *El alcalde de Zalamea* (The Mayor of Zalamea; ca. 1640), and *La hija del aire* (The Daughter of the Air; 1653).

18. See *Coriolanus,* Act 5, scene 3, line 131.

19. See *King Lear,* Act 4, scene 6.

20. See *Romeo and Juliet,* Act 1, scene 2.

Unpacking My Library

A Talk about Collecting

I am unpacking my library. Yes, I am. The books are not yet on the shelves, not yet touched by the mild boredom of order. I cannot march up and down their ranks to pass them in review before a friendly audience. You need not fear any of that. Instead, I must ask you to join me in the disorder of crates that have been wrenched open, the air saturated with wood dust, the floor covered with torn paper, to join me among piles of volumes that are seeing daylight again after two years of darkness, so that you may be ready to share with me a bit of the mood—certainly not an elegiac mood but, rather, one of anticipation—which these books arouse in a genuine collector. For such a man is speaking to you, and on closer scrutiny he proves to be speaking only about himself. Would it not be presumptuous of me if, in order to appear convincingly objective and matter-of-fact, I enumerated for you the main sections or prize pieces of a library—if I presented you with their history, or even their usefulness to a writer? I, for one, have in mind something less obscure, something more palpable than that; what I am really concerned with is giving you some insight into the relationship between a collector and his possessions, into collecting rather than a collection. If I do this by elaborating on the various ways of acquiring books, this is something entirely arbitrary. This or any other procedure is merely a dam against the spring tide of memories which surges toward any collector as he contemplates his possessions. Every passion borders on the chaotic, but the collector's passion borders on the chaos of memories. More than that: the chance, the fate, which suffuse the past before my eyes are conspicuously present in the accustomed confusion of these books. For what else is this collection but a disorder to which habit has accommodated itself to such an extent that it can appear as order? You have all heard of people whom the loss of their books has turned into invalids, or of those who in order to acquire books became criminals. These are the very areas in which any order is nothing more than a hovering above the abyss. "The only exact knowledge there is," said Anatole France, "is the knowledge of the date of publication and the format of books."[1] And indeed, if there is a counterpart to the confusion of a library, it is the order of its catalogue.

Thus, the life of a collector manifests a dialectical tension between the poles of disorder and order.

Naturally, his existence is tied to many other things as well: to a very mysterious relationship to ownership (something about which we shall have more to say later); also, to a relationship to objects which does not emphasize their functional, utilitarian value—that is, their usefulness—but studies and loves them as the scene, the stage, of their fate. The most profound enchantment for the collector is the locking of individual items within a magic circle in which they are frozen as the final thrill, the thrill of acquisition, passes over them. Everything remembered and thought, everything conscious, becomes the pedestal, the frame, the base, the lock of his property. The period, the region, the craftsmanship, the former ownership—for a true collector, the whole background of an item adds up to a magic encyclopedia whose quintessence is the fate of his object. In this circumscribed area, then, it may be surmised how the great physiognomists—and collectors are the physiognomists of the world of things—turn into interpreters of fate. One has only to watch a collector handle the objects in his glass case. As he holds them in his hands, he seems to be seeing through them into their distant past, as though inspired. So much for the magical side of the collector—his old-age image, I might call it.—*Habent sua fata libelli.* These words may have been intended as a general statement about books.[2] So books like *The Divine Comedy,* Spinoza's *Ethics,* and *The Origin of Species* have their fates. A collector, however, interprets this Latin saying differently. For him, not only books but also *copies of books* have their fates. And in this sense, the most important fate of a copy is its encounter with him, with his own collection. I am not exaggerating when I say that to a true collector the acquisition of an old book is its rebirth. This is the childlike element which, in a collector, mingles with the element of old age. For children can accomplish the renewal of existence in a hundred unfailing ways. Among children, collecting is only one process of renewal; other processes are the painting of objects, the cutting out of figures, the application of decals—the whole range of childlike modes of acquisition, from touching things to giving them names. To renew the old world—this is the collector's deepest desire when he is driven to acquire new things, and this is why a collector of older books is closer to the wellsprings of collecting than the acquirer of luxury editions. How do books cross the threshold of a collection and become the property of a collector? The history of their acquisition is the subject of the following remarks.

Of all the ways of acquiring books, writing them oneself is regarded as the most praiseworthy method. At this point, many of you will remember with pleasure the large library which Jean Paul's poor little schoolmaster Wutz gradually acquired by writing, himself, all the works whose titles interested him in book-fair catalogues; after all, he could not afford to buy them.[3] Writers are really people who write books not because they are poor, but because they are dissatisfied with the books which they could buy but do not like. You, ladies and gentlemen, may regard this as a whimsical definition of a writer. But everything said from the angle of a real collector is whimsical.—Of the customary modes of acquisition, the one most appropriate to a collector would be the borrowing of a book and the subsequent failure to return it. The book borrower of real stature whom we envisage here proves himself an inveterate collector of books not so much by the fervor with which he guards his borrowed treasures and by the deaf ear which he turns to all reminders from the everyday world of legality as by his failure to read these books. If my experience may serve as evidence, a man is more likely now and then to return a borrowed book than to read it. And the nonreading of books, you will object, should be characteristic of collectors? This is news to me, you may say. It is not news at all. Experts will bear me out when I say that it is the oldest thing in the world. Suffice it to quote the answer which Anatole France gave to a philistine who admired his library and then finished with the standard question, "And you have read all these books, Monsieur France?" "Not one-tenth of them. I don't suppose you eat off of your Sèvres china every day?"

Incidentally, I have put the right to such an attitude to the test. For years, for at least the first third of its existence, my library consisted of no more than two or three shelves which increased only by inches each year. This was its militant age, when no book was allowed to enter it without the certification that I had not read it. Thus, I might never have acquired a library extensive enough to be worthy of the name if there had not been the inflation. Suddenly the emphasis shifted; books acquired real value, or, at any rate, were difficult to obtain. At least, this is how it seemed in Switzerland. At the eleventh hour I sent my first major book orders from there and in this way was able to secure such irreplaceable items as *Der blaue Reiter* and Bachofen's *Sage von Tanaquil,* which could still be obtained from the publishers at that time.—[4] Well (so you may say), after exploring all these byways we should finally reach the wide highway of book acquisition— namely, the purchasing of books. This is indeed a wide highway, but not a comfortable one. The purchasing done by a book collector has very little in common with that done in a bookshop by a student getting a textbook, a man of the world buying a present for his lady, or a businessman intending to while away his next train journey. I have made my most memorable purchases on trips, as a transient. Property and possession belong to the tactical sphere. Collectors are people with a tactical instinct; their experience teaches them that when they capture a strange city, the smallest antique shop can be a fortress, the most remote stationery store a key position. How many cities have revealed themselves to me in the marches I undertook in pursuit of books!

Many of the most important purchases, though, are not made on the premises of a dealer. Catalogues play a far greater part. And even though the purchaser may be thoroughly acquainted with the book ordered from a catalogue, the individual copy always remains a surprise and the order always a bit of a gamble. There are grievous disappointments, but also happy finds. I remember, for instance, that I once ordered a book with colored illustrations for my old collection of children's books only because it contained fairy tales by Albert Ludwig Grimm and was published at Grimma, Thuringia. Grimma was also the place of publication of a book of fables edited by the same Albert Ludwig Grimm. With its sixteen illustrations, my copy of this book of fables was the only extant example of the early work of the great German book illustrator Lyser, who lived in Hamburg around the middle of the last century. Well, my reaction to the consonance of the names had been correct. In this case, too, I discovered the work of Lyser—namely, *Linas Märchenbuch,* a book which has remained unknown to his bibliographers and which deserves a more detailed reference than this first one I am introducing here.[5]

The acquisition of books is by no means a matter of money or expert knowledge alone. Not even both factors together suffice for the establishment of a real library, which is always somewhat impenetrable and at the same time uniquely itself. Anyone who buys from catalogues must have flair in addition to the qualities I have mentioned. Dates, place names, formats, previous owners, bindings, and the like: all these details must tell him something—not as dry, isolated facts, but as a harmonious whole. From the quality and intensity of this harmony, he must be able to recognize whether a book is for him or not.—An auction requires yet another set of qualities in a collector. To the reader of a catalogue, the book itself must speak—or possibly its previous ownership, if the provenance of the copy has been established. A man who wishes to participate at an auction must pay equal attention to the book and to his competitors, in addition to keeping a cool enough head to avoid being carried away in the competition. It frequently happens that someone gets stuck with a high purchase price because he kept raising his bid—more to assert himself than to acquire the book. On the other hand, one of the finest memories of a collector is the moment when he rescued a book to which he might never have given a thought, much less a wishful look, because he found it lonely and abandoned in the marketplace and bought it to give it its freedom—the way the prince bought a beautiful slave girl in the *Thousand and One Nights*. To a book collector, you see, the true freedom of all books is somewhere on his shelves.

To this day, Balzac's *Peau de chagrin* stands out from long rows of French volumes in my library as a memento of my most exciting experience at an auction. This happened in 1915 at the Rümann auction held by Emil Hirsch, one of the greatest of book experts and most distinguished of dealers. The edition in question appeared in 1838 in Paris, place de la Bourse. When I pick up my copy, I see not only its number in the Rümann Collection, but even the label of the shop in which the first owner bought the book more than ninety years ago, for one-eightieth of today's price. "Papeterie I. Flanneau," it says. A fine age, in which it was still possible to buy such a de luxe edition at a stationery dealer's! The steel engravings of this book were designed by the foremost French graphic artist and executed by the foremost engravers. But I was going to tell you how I acquired this book. I had gone to Emil Hirsch's for an advance inspection and had handled forty or fifty volumes; that particular volume had inspired in me the ardent desire to hold on to it forever. The day of the auction came. As chance would have it, in the sequence of the auction this copy of *La peau de chagrin* was preceded by a complete set of its illustrations printed separately on India paper. The bidders sat at a long table; diagonally across from me sat the man who was the focus of all eyes at the first bid, the famous Munich collector Baron von Simolin. He was greatly interested in this set, but he had rival bidders; in short, there was a spirited contest which resulted in the highest bid of the entire auction—far in excess of three thousand marks. No one seemed to have expected such a high figure, and all those present were quite excited. Emil Hirsch remained unconcerned, and whether he wanted to save time or was guided by some other consideration, he proceeded to the next item, with no one really paying attention. He called out the price, and with my heart pounding and with the full realization that I was unable to compete with any of those big collectors I bid a somewhat higher amount. Without arousing the bidders' attention, the auctioneer went through the usual routine—"Do I hear more?" and three bangs of his gavel, with an eternity seeming to separate each from the next—and proceeded to add the auctioneer's charge. For a student like me, the sum was still considerable. What happened the following morning at the pawnshop is no longer part of this story. I prefer to speak about another incident, which I would like to call the negative of an auction. It occurred last year at a Berlin auction. The books offered were a motley collection in both quality and subject matter, and only a number of rare works on occultism and natural philosophy were worthy of note. I bid for a number of them, but each time I noticed a gentleman in the front row who seemed only to have waited for my bid to counter with his own, evidently prepared to top any offer. After this had been repeated several times, I gave up all hope of acquiring the book which I was most interested in that day. It was the rare *Fragmente aus dem Nachlass eines jungen Physikers* [Posthumous Fragments by a Young Physicist], which Johann Wilhelm Ritter had published in two volumes at Heidelberg in 1810. This work has never been reprinted, but I have always considered its preface, in which the author-editor tells the story of his life in the guise of an obituary for a supposedly deceased unnamed friend—with whom he is really identical—as the most important example of personal prose in German Romanticism. Just as the item came up, I had an illumination. It was simple enough: since my bid was bound to give the item to the other man, I must not bid at all. I controlled myself and remained silent. What I had hoped for came about: no interest, no bid, and the book was put aside. I deemed it wise to let several days go by; and when I appeared on the premises after a week, I found the book in the secondhand department, and profited from the lack of interest when I acquired it.

Once you have approached the mountains of crates in order to mine the books from them and bring them to the light of day—or, rather, of night—what memories crowd in upon you! Nothing highlights the fascination of unpacking more clearly than the difficulty of stopping this activity. I had started at noon, and it was midnight before I had worked my way to the last crates. Now I put my hands on two volumes, bound in faded boards, which—strictly speaking—do not belong in a bookcase at all: two albums with paste-in pictures which my mother had glued in as a child and which I inherited. They are the seeds of a collection of children's books which is growing steadily even today, though no longer in my garden.—There is no living library that does not harbor a number of booklike creations from fringe areas. They need not be paste-in albums or family albums, autograph books or portfolios containing pamphlets or religious tracts. Some people become attached to leaflets and prospectuses; others, to handwriting facsimiles or typewritten copies of unobtainable books. And certainly periodicals can form the prismatic fringes of a library. But to get back to those albums: Actually, inheritance is the soundest way of acquiring a collection. For a collector's attitude toward his possessions stems from an owner's feeling of responsibility toward his property. Thus it is, in the highest sense, the attitude of an heir, and the most distinguished trait of a collection will always be its heritability. You should know that, in saying this, I fully realize that my discussion of the mental climate of collecting will confirm many of you in your conviction that this passion is behind the times, in your distrust of the collector type. Nothing is further from my mind than to shake either your conviction or your distrust. But one thing should be noted: the phenomenon of collecting loses its meaning when it loses its subject. Even though public collections may be less objectionable socially and more useful academically than private collections, the objects get their due only in the latter. I do know that night is coming for the type that I am discussing here and have been representing before you a bit *ex officio*. But, as Hegel put it, only when it is dark does the owl of Minerva begin its flight.[6] Only in extinction is the collector comprehended.

Now I am on the last half-emptied crate, and it is way past midnight. Other thoughts fill me than the ones I am talking about—not thoughts but images, memories. Memories of the cities in which I found so many things: Riga, Naples, Munich, Danzig, Moscow, Florence, Basel, Paris; memories of Rosenthal's sumptuous rooms in Munich, of the Danzig Stockturm, where the late Hans Rhaue was domiciled, of Süssengut's musty book cellar in North Berlin; memories of the rooms where these books had been housed, of my student's den in Munich, of my room in Bern, of the solitude of Iseltwald on the Lake of Brienz, and finally of my boyhood room, the former location of only four or five of the several thousand volumes that are piled up around me. O bliss of the collector, bliss of the man of leisure! No one has had less expected of him and no one has had a greater sense of well-being than the man who has been able to carry on his disreputable existence in the guise of Spitzweg's "Bookworm."[7] For inside him there are spirits, or at least little genii, which have seen to it that for a collector—and I mean a real collector, a collector as he ought to be—ownership is the most intimate relationship that one can have to things. Not that they come alive in him; it is he who lives in them. So I have erected before you one of his dwellings, with books as the building stones; and now he is going to disappear inside, as is only fitting.

Published in *Die literarische Welt*, July 1931. *Gesammelte Schriften*, IV, 388–396. Translated by Harry Zohn.

Notes

1. Anatole France (pseudonym of Jacques-Anatole-François Thibault; 1844–1924), writer and ironic, skeptical, urbane critic, was widely regarded in his day as the ideal French man of letters. He was elected to the French Academy in 1896 and was awarded the Nobel Prize for Literature in 1921.
2. *Habent sua fata libelli:* "Books have their own fates," or "Every book has its fate."
3. The poor little schoolmaster Wutz, a perpetually happy figure, appears in Jean Paul's *Leben des vergnügten Schulmeisterlein Maria Wutz in Auenthal* (Life of the Contented Little Schoolmaster Maria Wutz in Auenthal; 1793).
4. *Der blaue Reiter* was edited by Wassily Kandinsky and Franz Marc and published in 1912. A compendium of reproductions of works of art and theoretical texts, it served as the manifesto of the group of artists known as Der blaue Reiter. *Die Sage von Tanaquil* [The Legend of Tanaquil] is a rare book by Johann Jakob

Bachofen (1815–1887), Swiss professor of law, historian, and anthropologist best-known for his study of matriarchal societies.

5. Johann Peter Lyser (1804–1870) was an author, graphic artist, and music critic. Benjamin admired his illustrations for children's books; see "Notes for a Study of the Beauty of Colored Illustrations in Children's Books" and "Old Forgotten Children's Books" in the first volume of this edition.

6. Hegel, introduction to *Grundlinien der Philosophie des Rechts* (Elements of the Philosophy of Right).

7. Carl Spitzweg (1808–1885), German painter, established himself with humorous and often satirical scenes from bourgeois life. "The Bookworm" depicts a collector on a ladder, examining his vast collection.

Franz Kafka: *Beim Bau der Chinesischen Mauer*

Let me begin by recounting a little story that has been taken from the collection with the title given above[1] and that will show you two things: the greatness of this writer and the difficulty of articulating it. Kafka purports to be retelling a Chinese legend:

> The emperor, so the story goes, has sent you a message—you, the individual, his paltry subject, the insignificant shadow cowering in the remotest distance before the imperial sun. The emperor, from his deathbed, has sent a message to you alone. He commanded the messenger to kneel down by his bedside and whispered the message to him. So important to the emperor was this message that he ordered the messenger to repeat it back in his ear. He confirmed the accuracy of the statement with a nod of his head. And in the presence of all those assembled to witness his death—all the obstructing walls having been broken down, the grandees of his empire had gathered round in a circle on the vast and lofty staircases—he dispatched the messenger. The messenger sets out without delay. A powerful, indefatigable man, he forces a path for himself through the crowd, thrusting out now one arm, now the other. If he encounters resistance he points to his chest, on which the symbol of the sun is emblazoned. He makes rapid progress, more so than anyone else would have done. But the throng is so vast, their dwellings have no end. If only he could reach the open fields, how he would fly! And soon you would hear the glorious sound of his fists hammering at your door. But instead, how vainly he labors—he is still struggling to make his way through the chambers of the innermost palace. Never will he get to the end of them. And even if he succeeded in this, nothing would be gained—he would still have to fight his way down the stairs. And even if he succeeded in this, nothing would be gained—he would still have the

courtyards to cross. And after the courtyards, came the second, outer palace; then more staircases and courtyards; then beyond them another palace; and so on for thousands of years. And even if he managed at long last to force a path through the outermost gateway—but never, never can this happen—he would find the imperial capital lying before him, the center of the world, crammed to bursting with its dregs. No one can fight his way through that, let alone with a message from a dead man.—But you sit at your window and dream it to yourself when evening comes.

I will not interpret this story for you. You need no guidance from me to realize that the person addressed here is, primarily, Kafka himself. But who, then, was Kafka? He has done everything in his power to bar the way to an answer. It is impossible to overlook the fact that he stands at the center of his novels, but what happens to him there is designed to reduce to insignificance the person who experiences it, to render him invisible by concealing him at the heart of banality. And the cipher "K.," which designates the protagonist of his novel *Das Schloß* [The Castle], tells us no more than the initials on a handkerchief or the lining of a hat, and is certainly not enough to enable us to recognize the person who has disappeared. The most we can do is weave a legend around this man Kafka. It is as if he had spent his entire life wondering what he looked like, without ever discovering that there are such things as mirrors.

But to return to the initial story: I would like at least to suggest how *not* to interpret Kafka, since unfortunately this is almost the only way to establish a link with what has been said about him up to now. Admittedly, to provide a religious interpretation of Kafka's books, as has been done, is plausible enough. And such ideas may very possibly be aroused or even confirmed by the sort of close acquaintance with the writer enjoyed by Max Brod, to whom we are indebted for the publication of Kafka's works. Nevertheless, this approach amounts to a particular way of evading—or, one might almost say, of dismissing—Kafka's world. Doubtless, it is impossible to refute the assertion that in his novel *Das Schloß* Kafka wished to depict the higher powers, the realm of grace, whereas in *Der Prozeß* [The Trial] his aim was to portray the lower world of the law courts, and in his last great work, *Amerika,* he described earthly existence—all of these topics to be understood in a theological sense. The only problem is that such methods are far less productive than the admittedly much more challenging task of interpreting a writer from the center of his image world. To give but one example: the case against Joseph K. is played out in an everyday world, in backyards or waiting rooms, but always in different and unexpected places which the accused does not so much enter as find himself in by mistake. One day, for instance, he finds himself in an uppermost gallery. The banks of seats are packed full of people who have crowded in to follow the proceedings. They have come expecting a lengthy session, but conditions up there are almost unbearable. The ceiling (ceilings are almost always low in Kafka) presses down on them. So they have even brought cushions with them to lean their heads on.—But this is an image that precisely copies the grotesque faces familiar to us from the capitals surmounting the pillars in so many medieval churches. Of course, this is not to imply that Kafka intended to imitate them. But if we think of his works as a reflecting surface, a long-forgotten capital of this sort might easily appear to be the actual unconscious object of such descriptions. In that case, the interpreter would have to look for its reflection at precisely the same distance from the mirror as the reflected model, only in the opposite direction. In other words, it would have to be sought in the future.

Kafka's work is prophetic. The precisely registered oddities that abound in the life it deals with must be regarded by the reader as no more than the little signs, portents, and symptoms of the displacements that the writer feels approaching in every aspect of life without being able to adjust to the new situation. His only reaction to the almost incomprehensible distortions of existence that betray the emergence of these new laws is a sense of astonishment, mixed with elements of panic-stricken horror. Kafka is so possessed by this that he is incapable of imagining any single event that would not be distorted by the mere act of describing it—though by "description" here we really mean "investigation." In other words, everything he describes makes statements about something other than itself. Kafka's fixation on the sole topic of his work—namely, the distortion of existence—may appear to the reader like obsessiveness. But this impression, as well as the inconsolable earnestness, the despair, in the writer's gaze, is merely a sign that Kafka has abandoned the idea of a purely poetic prose. His prose may prove nothing; but it is so constructed that it can be inserted into passages of argument at any time. We may remind ourselves here of the form of the Haggadah, the name Jews have given to the rabbinical stories and anecdotes that serve to explicate and confirm the teachings—the Halachah. Like the haggadic parts of the Talmud, these books, too, are stories; they are a Haggadah that constantly pauses, luxuriating in the most detailed descriptions, in the simultaneous hope and fear that it might encounter the halachic order, the doctrine itself, en route.

Indeed, procrastination is the true meaning of that noteworthy and often striking fullness of detail which according to Max Brod lay at the heart of Kafka's search for perfection and the true way. Brod observes: "Of all the aspects of life to be taken seriously, we may say what a girl in *Das Schloß* says of the enigmatic letters from the authorities—namely, that 'the reflections to which they give rise are interminable.'" But what Kafka enjoys about these interminable reflections is the very fear that they might come to an end. Hence, his love of detail has a quite different meaning from that of an episode in a novel. Novels are sufficient unto themselves. Kafka's books are never that; they are stories pregnant with a moral to which they never give birth. This is why Kafka learned—if we must discuss matters in these terms—not from the great novelists but from much more modest writers, from mere storytellers. The moralist Johann Peter Hebel and the enigmatic Swiss Robert Walser were among his favorite writers.[2]—We have drawn attention to the dubious religious interpretations of Kafka's work, according to which the Castle is to be seen as the seat of grace. Yet it is the fact that his books are incomplete which shows the true working of grace in his writings. The fact that the Law never finds expression as such—this and nothing else is the gracious dispensation of the fragment.

Whoever doubts this truth may be persuaded by Max Brod's account of what Kafka told him in conversation about the planned conclusion to the novel. After a long, restless life in the village, a life without rights, K. lies exhausted on his deathbed, exhausted by his struggles. Then, at last, at long last, the messenger arrives from the Castle, bringing the decisive piece of news: K. has indeed no legal right to live in the village, but because of various subsidiary factors he is to be allowed to stay and work there. At this point, however, K.'s life ebbs away.—You can see that this story inhabits the same mental world as the tale with which I began. We also learn from Max Brod that Kafka had a particular village in mind—Zürau, in the Erzgebirge—as a model for the village at the foot of the Castle hill. For my own part, I am reminded of the village referred to in a legend from the Talmud. It is a legend related by a rabbi in reply to the question why Jews prepare a festive meal on Friday evenings. He tells the story of a princess who is pining away in exile, far from her fellow countrymen, among a people whose language she does not understand. One day this princess receives a letter bearing the news that her fiancé has not forgotten her and has set out on the journey to see her. The fiancé, says the rabbi, is the Messiah, the princess is the soul, and the village to which she has been exiled is the body. And because she has no other way of communicating her joy to the people around her who do not know her language, the soul prepares a festive meal for the body.

It needs only a minute shift of emphasis in this story from the Talmud for us to find ourselves in Kafka's world. Modern man dwells in his body as K. does in the village: as a stranger, an outcast who is ignorant of the laws that connect this body to higher and vaster orders. Much light is shed on this aspect of his works by the fact that Kafka frequently places animals at the center of his tales. The reader follows these animal tales for a fair distance without even noticing that they do not deal with human beings at all. Then, when the animal is identified for the first time—as a mouse or a mole—you are suddenly jolted and realize how far you have drifted away from the continent of human beings. Incidentally, it is worth paying attention to the kinds of animals Kafka chooses to embody his ideas. They always dwell in the interior of the earth, or, like the beetle in "Die Verwandlung" [The Metamorphosis], they are creatures that hide away on the ground, in cracks and crannies. This scurrying away seems to the author the only appropriate behavior for the isolated members of his generation and their context, with their ignorance of the law. Yet this absence of law is the result of a process of development. Kafka never tires of describing his fictional realm as dust-laden, rotten, and outmoded. The dingy rooms in which the Trial is enacted are just like the regulations that hold sway in the Penal Colony, or the sexual habits of the women who lend K. moral support. But the depravity of this realm is palpable, and not just in the unbounded promiscuity of the women characters. The same uninhibited brazenness can be seen in the activities of the higher authorities, who have rightly been seen to play as cruel a game of cat and mouse with their victims as the one played by the lower organs of power. "Both worlds are a murky, dust-covered, poky, airless labyrinth of chancelleries, offices, waiting rooms, with an endless hierarchy of junior, senior, very senior, and quite unapproachable officials and subofficials, lawyers, clerks, and messenger boys who look outwardly like a parody of a ludicrous and senseless bureaucracy."[3] As we see, even the people in power are as lawless as those at the bottom of the pile, and creatures from every level of society mix indiscriminately; the only bond that unites them is a unique feeling of anxiety. This anxiety is not a reaction, but something organic. And we can readily specify what it is constantly and infallibly alert to. But before its object is defined, the remarkable dual nature of this organic fear should give us pause. For it is—and this takes us back to the mirror image with which we began—at one and the same time and in equal measure both fear of the primeval, the immemorial, and also fear of what is close by, the immediate future with all its urgency. In a word, it is fear of an unknown guilt and of the atonement, which brings only one blessing: it makes the guilt explicit.

For the clearest deformation that is characteristic of Kafka's world has its roots in the fact that what is great, new, and liberating here manifests itself as atonement, in cases where the past has not seen through itself, confessed, and been finished with. This is why Willy Haas was fully justified in decoding the unadmitted guilt that the trial of Joseph K. conjures up: it is guilt over forgetting. Kafka's writing is simply full of configurations of forgetting—of silent pleas to recall things to mind. And this holds good whether we think of "Die Sorge des Hausvaters" [The Cares of a Family Man]—of that strange talking spool called Odradek, whom no one can classify; or of the dung beetle, the hero of "Die Verwandlung," whom we know all too well to have been a human being; or of the "Kreuzung"

[Crossbreed], the animal that is half-kitten, half-lamb, and for which the butcher's knife might well come as salvation.

> If to my garden I go
> To water flowers among the trees,
> A little hunchback's standing there
> And he begins to sneeze.

These lines come from a mysterious folk song.[4] The little hunchback, too, is something that has been forgotten, something we once used to know; he was then at peace with himself, but now he blocks our way to the future. It is highly revealing that Kafka was able to recognize (though unable to create) the figure of a supremely religious man, a man who is in the right. And where did he find him? In none other than Sancho Panza, who has freed himself from a promiscuous relationship with his demon by directing the demon toward another object than himself, so that he might pursue a peaceful life in which he has no need to forget anything. As Kafka's brief but magnificent interpretation expresses it: "Sancho Panza succeeded in the course of the years, by feeding him with a great quantity of romances of chivalry and adventure during the evening and night hours, in diverting from himself his demon, whom he later called Don Quixote. This demon knew no restraint in carrying out the maddest exploits—which, however, for lack of a preordained object (one that should have been Sancho Panza himself), did no one any harm. A free man, Sancho Panza philosophically followed Don Quixote on his crusades, perhaps from a certain feeling of responsibility, and derived great and useful entertainment from them to the end of his days."

If the author's large-scale novels are the well-tended fields that he has bequeathed to us, the new volume of stories from which this interpretation has been taken is the sower's bag that is filled with seeds—ones which have the strength of the natural seeds that sprout from graves even after millennia, and that we know will still bear fruit.

Radio talk broadcast July 1931. *Gesammelte Schriften*, II, 676–683. Translated by Rodney Livingstone.

Notes

1. *Beim Bau der Chinesischen Mauer* (The Great Wall of China) is a posthumous collection of Kafka's short fiction edited by his friend Max Brod and published in 1931.
2. Johann Peter Hebel (1760–1826), German journalist and author, was much esteemed for his use of dialect in his writings. As editor and chief writer for the *Badischer Landkalendar,* an annual publication not unlike the American *Old*

Farmer's Almanac, he produced an enormous volume of poetry and prose. Robert Walser (1878–1956), Swiss poet, novelist, and short-story writer, was revered by Benjamin for his mastery of the brief impressionistic sketch. See Benjamin's essay "Robert Walser" (1929), in this volume.

3. Willy Haas, *Gestalten der Zeit* (Berlin: Kiepenheuer, 1930), p. 176. See also Benjamin's review of Haas (titled "Theological Criticism") in this volume.

4. The source is Achim von Arnim and Clemens Brentano, *Des Knaben Wunderhorn* (Munich: Winkler, 1966), pp. 824–825.

Diary from August 7, 1931, to the Day of My Death

This diary does not promise to become very long. Today I received a negative response from Anton Kippenberg,[1] and this gives my plan the relevance that only futility can guarantee. I need to discover "a method that is just as convenient but somewhat less definitive," I said to I. today.[2] My hope of making any such discovery is fast disappearing. But if anything can strengthen still further the determination, indeed the peace of mind, with which I think of my intention, it must be the shrewd, dignified use to which I put my last days or weeks. Those just past leave a lot to be desired in this respect. Incapable of action, I just lay on the sofa and read. Frequently, I fell into so deep a reverie that I forgot to turn the page. I was mainly preoccupied with my plan, with wondering whether or not it was unavoidable, whether it should best be implemented here in the studio or back at the hotel, and so on.

I read *Das Friedensfest* [The Peace Festival] and *Einsame Menschen* [Lonely People].[3] People really were uncivilized in that Friedrichshagen milieu. But the fact is that the members of Bruno Wille and Wilhelm Bölsche's "New Community" do indeed seem to have behaved childishly.[4] The modern reader cannot but ask himself whether he belongs to a new race of Spartans—so disciplined is he in comparison, and above all, so much better able to detach himself and to look beyond his own immediate interests. That Johannes Vockerat whom Hauptmann depicts with such evident sympathy is certainly a nasty piece of work: bad manners and lack of discretion seem to be the prerequisites of heroism in these plays.[5] At the same time, these figures enable us to see how the characters in a play can be invalidated, if the author listens to them too attentively. Anyone who turns to them after forty years and tries to enter into their spirit finds it impossible to gain entry, because from every window a word or a turn of phrase stares out at him; these characters are merely tenements full of worn-out reactions and sentiments. They enable us to formulate one of the laws governing the truly great characters of drama: they contain vacant cavities, uninteresting cells that ensure that they have a real life, chambers of silence or empty staterooms of pathos in which a guest can find accommodation or make himself at home after decades or even centuries.— A remarkable feature of a different kind in these Hauptmann plays is sickness. Here, as in Ibsen, the various illnesses seem to be a cover for the sickness of the turn of the century, the *mal du siècle*. In those half-failed Bohemians like Braun and Dr. Scholz, the yearning for freedom is at its most powerful; but on the other hand, it often seems as if it is the intense preoccupation with art, with social questions, and the like that is making people ill. In other words, illness here is like a social emblem, much like madness among the ancients. Sick people have a special insight into the state of society; their private casting off of inhibitions is converted into an inspired sensitivity to the atmosphere their "contemporaries" breathe. But the form taken by this conversion is "nerves." It might be important to establish whether this word had not become a fashionable concept in the Jugendstil [Art Nouveau] period. At any rate the nerves are inspired threads; they resemble those fiberlike lines that trailed around furniture and house façades, redolent of unsatisfied rejuvenations and curves full of yearning. As for the figures of the Bohemian and the emancipated woman, Naturalism liked to dwell on them in the shape of a Daphne pursued by reality and changing into a bundle of nerves, laid bare, plantlike, trembling in the fresh air of the now [*Jetztzeit*].

Yesterday evening, a meeting with Albert Salomon and Fritz Holborn.[6] The conversation turned on questions of methodology in history. Someone quoted an excellent remark by Johan Huizinga: run-of-the-mill history answers more questions than a wise man will ask. My attempt to explain a theory of history in which the concept of development is entirely supplanted by the concept of origins. Understood in this way, history cannot be sought in the riverbed of a process of development. Instead, as I have remarked elsewhere, the image of a riverbed is replaced by that of a whirlpool. In such a whirlpool earlier and later events—the prehistory and posthistory of an event, or, better, of a status, swirl around it. The actual objects of such a view of history are not specific events but specific unchanging *statuses* of a conceptual or sensual kind—for example, the Russian agrarian system, the city of Barcelona, population shifts in the Mark of Brandenburg, barrel vaulting, and so on. If this approach is determined by its firm rejection of the possibility of an evolutionary or universalist dimension in history, it is determined *internally* by a productive polarity. The twin poles of such a view are the historical and the political—or, to point up the distinction even more sharply, the historical and the event. These two factors occupy two completely different planes. We can never say, for example, that we experience history; nor can we maintain that a historical account brings the events so close to us that it has the same impact as a historical event (such an account would be worthless), or that we have experienced events that are destined to become history (since such a view is journalistic).

Before the closing of the gates, I shall confer on myself a title thought up by Lichtenberg: *professor philosophiae extraordinariae.*

August 12. In conversation with Gustav Glück,[7] I discovered the true reason for Kraus's reaction to my series of essays.[8] Kraus's attitude toward his followers undoubtedly played a role, but the real key to his behavior is surely to be found in "The Diebold Case" in the latest issue of *Die Fackel.* If my essays had only contained Diebold's name somewhere, however inconspicuously, and had alluded, however indirectly, to his denigration of Kraus, he would have overwhelmed the work with compliments. But as it was, he sought the name Diebold in vain throughout its length and breadth, and he was not willing to modify his negative attitude toward the *Frankfurter Zeitung* on my account—all the less as I failed to supply him with any ammunition.

The older you get as a writer, the more you're struck from time to time by a word that you've never written. Such a word can evoke an entire period. And it's not just the older you get the more you're struck, but you're also struck more frequently. For this openness to the glossy stamp of words comes only in later years, the more frequently you encounter worn-out words, indeed words that have become worn out by your own use.

August 16, at the home of Willy Haas.[9] On the little glass veranda built onto the house—present were his wife, Tritsch, Artur Rosen, and Peter Huchel—a conversation took place, some of which seems worth preserving.[10] I told them about the meeting that had been held on the thirteenth in the Schubert Rooms to protest the censorship. This led to the related topic of Marxism and art, which enabled me to discuss the dialectic of this relationship. I advanced two theses that have always—or rather, since the rise of capitalism—been in conflict with each other:

1. Art is for the people.
2. Art is for the connoisseurs.

It is obvious that on the surface everything speaks for the second thesis. Above all, it has always been the case that an artistic practice very quickly degenerates if it addresses itself more to the undifferentiated needs of consumers than to the critical collaboration of experts. In recent times, this is most strikingly borne out by the novel. The novel seems from the outset to be more evidently aimed at consumption, unproductive enjoyment, than other forms of art. Elsewhere, I have explored the analogy between the novel and food in greater depth.[11] The time when this type of food possessed any nutritional value has long since passed, and the "popularity" of art, something that today is represented by popular novels, has long since ceased to have anything productive or nourishing about it—unlike the novel at the time of the incipient emancipation of the bourgeoisie. Nowadays it is rather the expression of the complete integration of this kind of writing into the world of commodity circulation. Its sole purpose is to pander to the need for comfort. As long as a century ago, the Romantics made the most daring efforts to introduce expertise into the reading of the novel; but the only result was to deprive the novel of any popularity. Thus, at the very point at which bourgeois writing achieves its greatest productivity, the antinomy is at its starkest. On the other hand, however, in the long run every class and every social stratum will open the door to the forms of their life and language only to the person who is active on their behalf, and who reproduces in modified form for their benefit the themes that they make available to him. This means that every form of art that systematically sets out to dispense with popularity will rightly find itself consigned to the luxury segment of the market, and thus subject to the dictates of fashion. Of course, every flourishing literature has always undergone a whole series of transitions between the popular and the esoteric. The decisive factor, however, was that these intermediate products possessed a continuity—not just externally, in terms of commercial success or size of edition, but an internal continuity—between the specific provinces of writing in itself. In our day this continuity has been broken, meaning that precisely the most important tasks—namely, work on the new art forms on the basis of the entire arsenal of proletarian life and language—have become insoluble and, we might even say, incapable of formulation. This is the situation that has led to the so-called crisis of art and to calls for art's abolition, or even to the demand that it be replaced by journalism. Incomprehensible though such a demand is under the class hegemony of the bourgeoisie, the fact that it could be made is significant, as is its value as a prognosis of things to come. The complete takeover of literature by the newspaper—which by publishing fiction in serial form has even appropriated the novel, decisively modifying it in the process—is in fact a dialectical process. On the one hand, it spells the demise of literature in contemporary social conditions, but, on the other, it prepares the way for its reinstatement when conditions change. And since the contemporary situation and the changed circumstances are basically already having an impact on each other, the symptoms of future developments can already be discerned. Admittedly, the first result of the predominance of the newspaper is to expose the fact that literary production has been integrated into the production of commodities—to reveal this fact in every sphere where it had not previously been evident. But the second result stands in a dialectical relationship to the first. For as writing gains in breadth what art loses in depth, the separation between the author and the public—a separation that journalism maintains in a corrupt way—starts to be overcome in an admirable way. The reader is ready at any moment to become a writer—that is to say, a describer and prescriber. From every form of material knowledge, a path leads to the writing about it: in short, work itself finds a voice. And its representation in words becomes a part of the ability that is needed for its exercise. Literary competence is based not on consumption, but on working practices; in other words, it becomes a popular activity. The popular nature of writing is based not on consumption, but on production; it is part of an expertise. In a word, it is the literarization of living conditions, which becomes master of what are otherwise the insoluble antinomies that dominate all artistic activity in our age. And the stage on which we see enacted the profoundest debasement of the printed word—that is, the newspaper—will be the site of its regeneration in a new society. Moreover, this is not the most contemptible ruse of reason. It is poverty that compresses the creativity of our best talents today, with an enormous atmospheric pressure. In this way, talent finds a refuge in the belly of the cultural section of the newspaper—as if in the belly of a wooden horse, from which one day this creativity will emerge and set alight the Troy of the modern press.

Diary entries from late 1931; unpublished in Benjamin's lifetime. *Gesammelte Schriften*, VI, 441–446. Translated by Rodney Livingstone.

Notes

1. Anton Kippenberg was the head of the Insel publishing company. Benjamin had hoped that Insel would publish a book by him, commemorating Goethe's centenary.
2. "I." probably refers to Inge Buchholz, a close friend of Benjamin's in the early 1930s. Nothing else is known about her.
3. These are plays by Gerhart Hauptmann. *Das Friedensfest* (The Peace Festival; 1890) is an analysis of the troubled relations within a neurotic family. *Einsame Menschen* (Lonely People; 1891) describes the tragic end of an unhappy intellectual torn between his wife and a young woman with whom he can share his thoughts. Friedrichshagen lies on the outskirts of Berlin. For a slightly different version of this section, see "Thought Figures" (1933), in this volume.
4. Bruno Wille (1860–1928), German author, editor, and impresario, founded one of Berlin's most important theaters, the Freie Volksbühne Berlin, in 1901. He also

established, with Wilhelm Bölsche (1861–1939), an alternative school called the Freie Hochschule. Bölsche, poet and novelist, was a founder of Berlin Naturalism in the 1890s. The "New Community" was bound together by belief in Darwinism, positivism, and determinism; its members envisioned a harmonious, nonreligious, and scientifically based world.

5. Gerhart Hauptmann (1862–1946), German playwright, poet, and novelist, established himself as the leading voice in German Naturalism in the 1890s. In 1912 he received the Nobel Prize for Literature.

6. Albert Salomon (1891–1966), sociologist and political scientist, was editor of *Die Gesellschaft*. He left Germany in 1933 for Switzerland and then the United States, where he became a professor at the New School for Social Research in New York.

7. Gustav Glück (1902–1973), perhaps Benjamin's closest friend during the 1930s, was a director of the foreign section of the Reichskreditgesellschaft (Imperial Credit Bank) in Berlin until 1938. He was able to arrange the transfer to Paris of the fees Benjamin received from his occasional contributions to German newspapers until 1935. In 1938 Glück emigrated to Argentina; after World War II, he was a board member of the Dresdner Bank.

8. Benjamin's essay on Karl Kraus, included in this volume, appeared in four installments in the *Frankfurter Zeitung* in March 1931, with a dedication to Gustav Glück. Despite its positive view, it provoked an ironic response from Kraus which Benjamin attempts to explain here. Bernhard Diebold was a Nazi critic who had condemned the works of Kraus, Brecht, and Kurt Tucholsky as morally rootless, while he praised the "healthy" ideas of "artists" like Josef Goebbels. Kraus attacked Diebold on a number of occasions in *Die Fackel*. Following Kraus's response to his essay, Benjamin, who had been preoccupied with Kraus since around 1916, vowed to write nothing further about him. He was also deeply shocked by Kraus's endorsement of Engelbert Dollfuss's Austro-Fascism in 1932 as "the lesser evil."

9. Willy Haas (1891–1973) was a well-known writer and critic. He was editor of *Die literarische Welt* and *Die Welt im Wort*.

10. Artur Rosen was managing editor of *Die literarische Welt*. Peter Huchel (1903–1981), poet and editor, was the editor-in-chief of the important East German journal *Sinn und Form* from 1949 to 1962. He left the German Democratic Republic in 1971.

11. See the section "Reading Novels" in the piece entitled "Little Tricks of the Trade" (1933), in this volume.

Little History of Photography

The fog that surrounds the beginnings of photography is not quite as thick as that which shrouds the early days of printing; more obviously than in the case of the printing press, perhaps, the time was ripe for the invention, and was sensed by more than one—by men who strove independently for the same objective: to capture the images in the camera obscura, which had been known at least since Leonardo's time. When, after about five years of effort, both Niepce and Daguerre simultaneously succeeded in doing this, the state, aided by the patenting difficulties encountered by the inventors, assumed control of the enterprise and made it public, with compensation to the pioneers.[1] This paved the way for a rapid ongoing development which long precluded any backward glance. Thus it is that the historical or, if you like, philosophical questions suggested by the rise and fall of photography have gone unheeded for decades. And if they are beginning to enter into consciousness today, there is a definite reason for it. The latest writings on the subject point up the fact that the flowering of photography—the work of Hill and Cameron, Hugo and Nadar—came in its first decade.[2] But this was the decade which preceded its industrialization. Not that hucksters and charlatans did not appropriate the new techniques for gain, even in that early period; indeed, they did so en masse. But that was closer to the arts of the fairground, where photography is at home to this day, than to industry. Industry made its first real inroads with the visiting-card picture, whose first manufacturer, significantly, became a millionaire. It would not be surprising if the photographic methods which today, for the first time, are harking back to the preindustrial heyday of photography had an underground connection with the crisis of capitalist industry. But that does not make it any easier to use the charm of old photographs, available in fine recent publications,[3] for real insights into their nature. Attempts at theoretical mastery of the subject have so far been entirely rudimentary. And no matter how extensively it may have been debated in the last century, basically the discussion never got away from the ludicrous stereotype which a chauvinistic rag, the *Leipziger Stadtanzeiger,* felt it had to offer in timely opposition to this black art from France. "To try to capture fleeting mirror images," it said, "is not just an impossible undertaking, as has been established after thorough German investigation; the very wish to do such a thing is blasphemous. Man is made in the image of God, and God's image cannot be captured by any machine of human devising. The utmost the artist may venture, borne on the wings of divine inspiration, is to reproduce man's God-given features without the help of any machine, in the moment of highest dedication, at the higher bidding of his genius." Here we have the philistine notion of "art" in all its overweening obtuseness, a stranger to all technical considerations, which feels that its end is nigh with the alarming appearance of the new technology. Nevertheless, it was this fetishistic and fundamentally antitechnological concept of art with which the theoreticians of photography sought to grapple for almost a hundred years, naturally without the smallest success. For they undertook nothing less than to legitimize the photographer before the very tribunal he was in the process of overturning. Far different is the tone of the address which the physicist Arago, speaking on behalf of Daguerre's invention, gave in the Chamber of Deputies on July 3, 1839.[4] The beautiful thing about this speech is the connections it makes with all aspects of human activity. The panorama it sketches is broad enough not only to make the dubious project of authenticating photography in terms of painting—which it does anyway—seem beside the point; more important, it offers an insight into the real scope of the invention. "When inventors of a new instrument," says Arago, "apply it to the observation of nature, what they expect of it always turns out to be a trifle compared with the succession of subsequent discoveries of which the instrument was the origin." In a great arc Arago's speech spans the field of new technologies, from astrophysics to philology: alongside the prospects for photographing the stars and planets we find the idea of establishing a photographic record of the Egyptian hieroglyphs.

Daguerre's photographs were iodized silver plates exposed in the camera obscura, which had to be turned this way and that until, in the proper light, a pale gray image could be discerned. They were one of a kind; in 1839 a plate cost an average of 25 gold francs. They were not infrequently kept in a case, like jewelry. In the hands of many a painter, though, they became a technical adjunct. Just as seventy years later Utrillo painted his fascinating views of Paris not from life but from picture postcards,[5] so the highly regarded English portrait painter David Octavius Hill based his fresco of

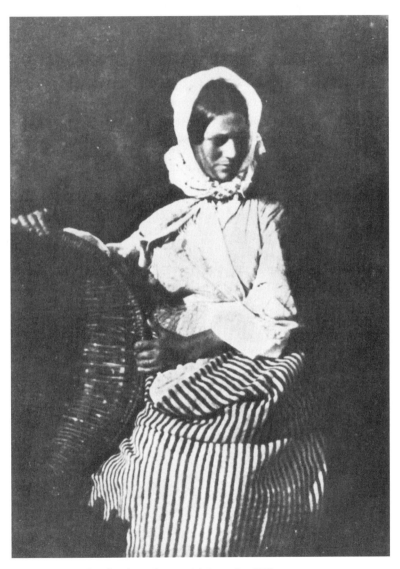

Newhaven Fishwife. Photo by David Octavius Hill.

the first general synod of the Church of Scotland in 1843 on a long series of portrait photographs. But these pictures he took himself. And it is they, unpretentious makeshifts meant for internal use, that gave his name a place in history, while as a painter he is forgotten. Admittedly a number of his studies lead even deeper into the new technology than this series of portraits—anonymous images, not posed subjects. Such figures had long been the subjects of painting. Where the painting remained in the possession of a particular family, now and then someone would ask about the person portrayed. But after two or three generations this interest fades; the pictures, if they last, do so only as testimony to the art of the painter. With photography, however, we encounter something new and strange: in Hill's Newhaven fishwife, her eyes cast down in such indolent, seductive modesty, there remains something that goes beyond testimony to the photographer's art, something that cannot be silenced, that fills you with an unruly desire to know what her name was, the woman who was alive there, who even now is still real and will never consent to be wholly absorbed in "art."

> And I ask: How did the beauty of that hair,
> those eyes, beguile our forebears?
> How did that mouth kiss, to which desire
> curls up senseless as smoke without fire?[6]

Or you turn up the picture of Dauthendey the photographer, the father of the poet, from the time of his engagement to that woman whom he found one day, shortly after the birth of her sixth child, lying in the bedroom of his Moscow house with her veins slashed. Here she can be seen with him. He seems to be holding her, but her gaze passes him by, absorbed in an ominous distance. Immerse yourself in such a picture long enough and you will realize to what extent opposites touch, here too: the most precise technology can give its products a magical value, such as a painted picture can never again have for us. No matter how artful the photographer, no matter how carefully posed his subject, the beholder feels an irresistible urge to search such a picture for the tiny spark of contingency, of the here and now, with which reality has (so to speak) seared the subject, to find the inconspicuous spot where in the immediacy of that long-forgotten moment the future nests so eloquently that we, looking back, may rediscover it. For it is another nature which speaks to the camera rather than to the eye: "other" above all in the sense that a space informed by human consciousness gives way to a space informed by the unconscious. Whereas it is a commonplace that, for example, we have some idea what is involved in the act of walking (if only in general terms), we have no idea at all what happens during the fraction of a second when a person actually takes a step. Photography, with its devices of slow motion and enlargement, reveals the secret. It is through photography that we first discover the existence of this

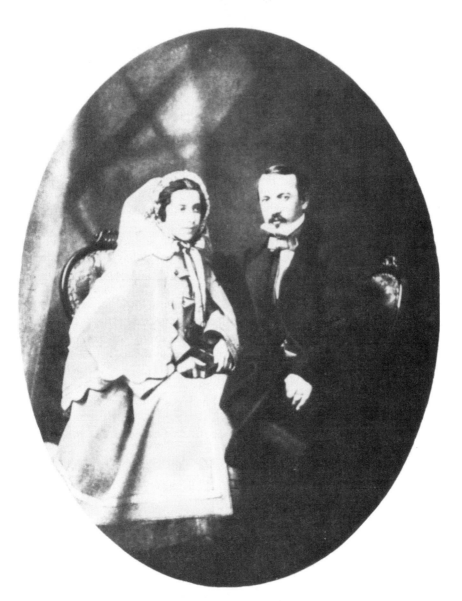

Karl Dauthendey (Father of the Poet), with His Fiancée.
Photo by Karl Dauthendey.

optical unconscious, just as we discover the instinctual unconscious through psychoanalysis. Details of structure, cellular tissue, with which technology and medicine are normally concerned—all this is, in its origins, more native to the camera than the atmospheric landscape or the soulful portrait. Yet at the same time, photography reveals in this material physiognomic aspects, image worlds, which dwell in the smallest things—meaningful yet covert enough to find a hiding place in waking dreams, but which, enlarged and capable of formulation, make the difference between technology and magic visible as a thoroughly historical variable. Thus, Blossfeldt with his astonishing plant photographs[7] reveals the forms of ancient columns in horse willow, a bishop's crosier in the ostrich fern, totem poles in tenfold enlargements of chestnut and maple shoots, and gothic tracery in the fuller's thistle. Hill's subjects, too, were probably not far from the truth when they described "the phenomenon of photography" as still being "a great and mysterious experience"—even if, for them, this was no more than the consciousness of "standing before a device which in the briefest time could capture the visible environment in a picture that seemed as real and alive as nature itself." It has been said of Hill's camera that it kept a discreet distance. But his subjects, for their part, are no less reserved; they maintain a certain shyness before the camera, and the watchword of a later photographer from the heyday of the art, "Don't look at the camera," could be derived from their attitude. But that did not mean the "They're looking at you" of animals, people, and babies, which so distastefully implicates the buyer and to which there is no better counter than the way old Dauthendey talks about daguerreotypes: "We didn't trust ourselves at first," he reported, "to look long at the first pictures he developed. We were abashed by the distinctness of these human images, and believed that the little tiny faces in the picture could see *us,* so powerfully was everyone affected by the unaccustomed clarity and the unaccustomed fidelity to nature of the first daguerreotypes."

The first people to be reproduced entered the visual space of photography with their innocence intact—or rather, without inscription. Newspapers were still a luxury item which people seldom bought, preferring to consult them in the coffeehouse; photography had not yet become a journalistic tool, and ordinary people had yet to see their names in print. The human countenance had a silence about it in which the gaze rested. In short, the portraiture of this period owes its effect to the absence of contact between contemporary relevance and photography. Many of Hill's portraits were made in the Edinburgh Greyfriars cemetery—and nothing is more characteristic of this early period, except perhaps the way his subjects were at home there. And indeed the cemetery itself, in one of Hill's pictures, looks like an interior, a separate closed-off space where the gravestones propped against gable walls rise up from the grass, hollowed out like chimneypieces,

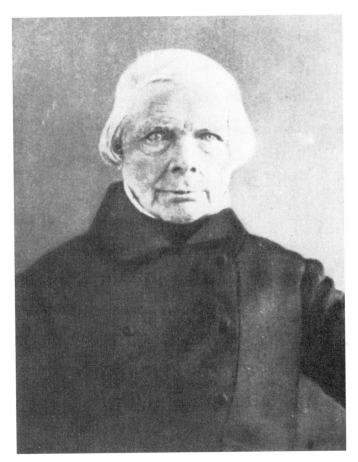

The Philosopher Schelling, ca. 1850. Photographer (German) unknown.

with inscriptions inside instead of flames. But this setting could never have been so effective if it had not been chosen on technical grounds. The low light-sensitivity of the early plates made prolonged exposure outdoors a necessity. This in turn made it desirable to take the subject to some out-of-the-way spot where there was no obstacle to quiet concentration. "The synthetic character of the expression which was dictated by the length of time the subject had to remain still," says Orlik of early photography, "is the main reason these photographs, apart from their simplicity, resemble well-drawn or well-painted pictures and produce a more vivid and lasting impression on the beholder than more recent photographs."[8] The procedure itself caused the subject to focus his life in the moment rather than hurrying on past it; during the considerable period of the exposure, the subject (as it were) grew into the picture, in the sharpest contrast with appearances in a snapshot—which is appropriate to that changed environment where, as Kracauer has aptly noted, the split second of the exposure determines "whether a sportsman becomes so famous that photographers start taking his picture for the illustrated papers." Everything about these early pictures was built to last. Not only the incomparable groups in which people came together—and whose disappearance was surely one of the most precise symptoms of what was happening in society in the second half of the century—but the very creases in people's clothes have an air of permanence. Just consider Schelling's coat. It will surely pass into immortality along with him: the shape it has borrowed from its wearer is not unworthy of the creases in his face. In short, everything suggests that Bernard von Brentano was right in his view that "a photographer of 1850 was on a par with his instrument"—for the first time, and for a long while the last.[9]

To appreciate the full impact made by the daguerreotype in the age of its discovery, one should also bear in mind that *plein air* painting was then opening up entirely new perspectives for the most advanced painters. Conscious that in this very area photography had to take the baton from painting, even Arago, in his historical review of the early attempts of Giovanni Battista Della Porta, explicitly commented: "As regards the effect produced by the imperfect transparency of our atmosphere (which has been loosely termed 'atmospheric degradation'), not even experienced painters expect the camera obscura"—i.e., the copying of images appearing in it— "to help them to render it accurately."[10] At the moment when Daguerre succeeded in fixing the images of the camera obscura, painters parted company on this point with technicians. The real victim of photography, however, was not landscape painting but the portrait miniature. Things developed so rapidly that by 1840 most of the innumerable miniaturists had already become professional photographers, at first only as a sideline, but before long exclusively. Here the experience of their original livelihood stood them in good stead, and it is not their artistic background so much as their training as craftsmen that we have to thank for the high level of their photographic achievement. This transitional generation disappeared very gradually; indeed, there seems to have been a kind of biblical blessing on those first photographers: the Nadars, Stelzners, Piersons, Bayards all lived well into their eighties and nineties.[11] In the end, though, businessmen invaded professional photography from every side; and when, later on, the retouched negative, which was the bad painter's revenge on photography, became ubiquitous, a sharp decline in taste set in. This was the time photograph albums came into vogue. They were most at home in the chilliest spots, on occasional tables or little stands in the drawing room—leather-bound tomes with repellent metal hasps and those gilt-edged pages as thick as your finger, where foolishly draped or corseted figures were displayed: Uncle Alex and Aunt Riekchen, little Trudi when she was still a baby, Papa in his first term at university . . . and finally, to make our shame complete, we ourselves—as a parlor Tyrolean, yodeling, waving our hat before a painted snowscape, or as a smartly turned-out sailor, standing rakishly with our weight on one leg, as is proper, leaning against a polished door jamb. The accessories used in these portraits, the pedestals and balustrades and little oval tables, are still reminiscent of the period when, because of the long exposure time, subjects had to be given supports so that they wouldn't move. And if at first head clamps and knee braces were felt to be sufficient, "further impedimenta were soon added, such as were to be seen in famous paintings and therefore had to be 'artistic.' First it was pillars, or curtains." The most capable started resisting this nonsense as early as the 1860s. As an English trade journal of the time put it, "in painting the pillar has some plausibility, but the way it is used in photography is absurd, since it usually stands on a carpet. But anyone can see that pillars of marble or stone are not erected on a foundation of carpeting." This was the period of those studios—with their draperies and palm trees, their tapestries and easels—which occupied so ambiguous a place between execution and representation, between torture chamber and throne room, and to which an early portrait of Kafka bears pathetic witness. There the boy stands, perhaps six years old, dressed up in a humiliatingly tight child's suit overloaded with trimming, in a sort of greenhouse landscape. The background is thick with palm fronds. And as if to make these upholstered tropics even stuffier and more oppressive, the subject holds in his left hand an inordinately large broad-brimmed hat, such as Spaniards wear. He would surely be lost in this setting were it not for his immensely sad eyes, which dominate this landscape predestined for them.

This picture, in its infinite sadness, forms a pendant to the early photographs in which people did not yet look out at the world in so excluded and godforsaken a manner as this boy. There was an aura about them, a medium that lent fullness and security to their gaze even as it penetrated

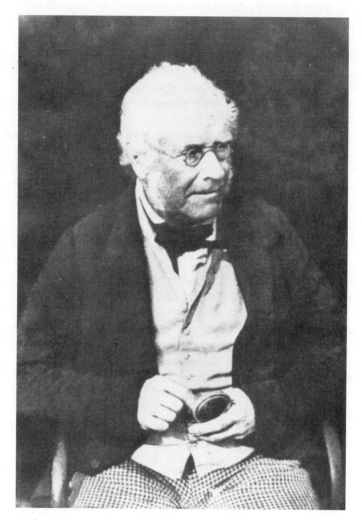

Robert Bryson. Photo by David Octavius Hill.

that medium. And once again the technical equivalent is obvious: it consists in the absolute continuum from brightest light to darkest shadow. Here, too, we see in operation the law that new advances are prefigured in older techniques, for the earlier art of portrait painting, before its disappearance, had produced the strange flower of the mezzotint. The mezzotint process was of course a technique of reproduction, which was only later combined with the new photographic reproduction. The way light struggles out of darkness in the work of a Hill is reminiscent of mezzotint: Orlik talks about the "comprehensive illumination" brought about by the long exposure times, which "gives these early photographs their greatness."[12] And among the invention's contemporaries, Delaroche had already noted the "unprecedented and exquisite" general impression, "in which nothing disturbs the tranquillity of the composition."[13] So much for the technical determinedness of the auratic appearance. Many group photos in particular still preserve an air of animated conviviality for a brief time on the plate, before being ruined by the print. It was this breathy halo that was sometimes captured with delicacy and depth by the now old-fashioned oval frame. That is why it would be a misreading of these incunabula of photography to make too much of their "artistic perfection" or their "taste." These pictures were made in rooms where every client was confronted, in the person of the photographer, with a technician of the latest school; whereas the photographer was confronted, in the person of every client, with a member of a rising class equipped with an aura that had seeped into the very folds of the man's frock coat or floppy cravat. For this aura was by no means the mere product of a primitive camera. Rather, in this early period subject and technique were as exactly congruent as they become incongruent in the period of decline that immediately followed. For soon advances in optics made instruments available that wholly overcame darkness and recorded appearances as faithfully as any mirror. After 1880, though, photographers made it their business to simulate the aura which had been banished from the picture with the suppression of darkness through faster lenses, exactly as it was being banished from reality by the deepening degeneration of the imperialist bourgeoisie. They saw it as their task to simulate this aura using all the arts of retouching, and especially the so-called gum print. Thus, especially in Jugendstil [Art Nouveau], a penumbral tone, interrupted by artificial highlights, came into vogue. Notwithstanding this fashionable twilight, however, a pose was more and more clearly in evidence, whose rigidity betrayed the impotence of that generation in the face of technical progress.

And yet, what is again and again decisive for photography is the photographer's attitude to his techniques. Camille Recht has found an apt metaphor: "The violinist," he says, "must first produce the note, must seek it out, find it in an instant; the pianist strikes the key and the note rings out. The painter and the photographer both have an instrument at their disposal.

Drawing and coloring, for the painter, correspond to the violinist's production of sound; the photographer, like the pianist, has the advantage of a mechanical device that is subject to restrictive laws, while the violinist is under no such restraint. No Paderewski will ever reap the fame, ever cast the almost fabulous spell, that Paganini did."[14] There is, however—to continue the metaphor—a Busoni of photography, and that is Atget.[15] Both were virtuosos, but at the same time precursors. The combination of unparalleled absorption in their work and extreme precision is common to both. There was even a facial resemblance. Atget was an actor who, disgusted with the profession, wiped off the mask and then set about removing the makeup from reality too. He lived in Paris poor and unknown, selling his pictures for a trifle to photographic enthusiasts scarcely less eccentric than himself; he died recently, leaving behind an oeuvre of more than 4,000 pictures. Berenice Abbott from New York has gathered these together, and a selection has just appeared in an exceptionally beautiful volume published by Camille Recht.[16] The contemporary journals "knew nothing of the man, who for the most part hawked his photographs around the studios and sold them for next to nothing, often for the price of one of those picture postcards which, around 1900, showed such pretty town views, bathed in midnight blue, complete with touched-up moon. He reached the Pole of utmost mastery; but with the bitter modesty of a great craftsman who always lives in the shadows, he neglected to plant his flag there. Therefore many are able to flatter themselves that they have discovered the Pole, even though Atget was there before them." Indeed, Atget's Paris photos are the forerunners of Surrealist photography—an advance party of the only really broad column Surrealism managed to set in motion. He was the first to disinfect the stifling atmosphere generated by conventional portrait photography in the age of decline. He cleanses this atmosphere—indeed, he dispels it altogether: he initiates the emancipation of object from aura, which is the most signal achievement of the latest school of photography. When avant-garde periodicals like *Bifur* or *Variété* publish pictures that are captioned "Westminster," "Lille," "Antwerp," or "Breslau" but that show only details, here a piece of balustrade, there a treetop whose bare branches crisscross a gas lamp, or a gable wall, or a lamppost with a life buoy bearing the name of the town—this is nothing but a literary refinement of motifs that Atget discovered. He looked for what was unremarked, forgotten, cast adrift. And thus such pictures, too, work against the exotic, romantically sonorous names of the cities; they suck the aura out of reality like water from a sinking ship.—What is aura, actually? A strange weave of space and time: the unique appearance or semblance of distance, no matter how close it may be. While at rest on a summer's noon, to trace a range of mountains on the horizon, or a branch that throws its shadow on the observer, until the moment or the hour become part of their appearance—this is what it means to breathe

the aura of those mountains, that branch. Now, to bring things *closer* to us, or rather to the masses, is just as passionate an inclination in our day as the overcoming of whatever is unique in every situation by means of its reproduction. Every day the need to possess the object in close-up in the form of a picture, or rather a copy, becomes more imperative. And the difference between the copy, which illustrated papers and newsreels keep in readiness, and the original picture is unmistakable. Uniqueness and duration are as intimately intertwined in the latter as are transience and reproducibility in the former. The peeling away of the object's shell, the destruction of the aura, is the signature of a perception whose sense for the sameness of things has grown to the point where even the singular, the unique, is divested of its uniqueness—by means of its reproduction. Atget almost always passed by the "great sights and so-called landmarks." What he did not pass by was a long row of boot lasts; or the Paris courtyards, where from night to morning the handcarts stand in serried ranks; or the tables after people have finished eating and left, the dishes not yet cleared away—as they exist by the hundreds of thousands at the same hour; or the brothel at No. 5, Rue ——, whose street number appears, gigantic, at four different places on the building's façade. Remarkably, however, almost all these pictures are empty. Empty is the Porte d'Arceuil by the fortifications, empty are the triumphal steps, empty are the courtyards, empty, as it should be, is the Place du Tertre. They are not lonely, merely without mood; the city in these pictures looks cleared out, like a lodging that has not yet found a new tenant. It is in these achievements that Surrealist photography sets the scene for a salutary estrangement between man and his surroundings. It gives free play to the politically educated eye, under whose gaze all intimacies are sacrificed to the illumination of detail.

It is obvious that this new way of seeing stands to gain least in an area where there has been the greatest self-indulgence: commercial, conventional portrait photography. On the other hand, to do without people is for photography the most impossible of renunciations. And anyone who did not know it was taught by the best Russian films that milieu and landscape, too, reveal themselves most readily to those photographers who succeed in capturing their anonymous physiognomy, as it were presenting them at face value. Whether this is possible, however, depends very much on the subject. The generation that was not obsessed with going down to posterity in photographs, rather shyly drawing back into their private space in the face of such proceedings—the way Schopenhauer withdrew into the depths of his chair in the Frankfurt picture, taken about 1850—for this very reason allowed that space, the space in which they lived, to get onto the plate with them. That generation did not pass on its virtues. So the Russian feature film was the first opportunity in decades to put before the camera people who had no use for their photographs. And immediately the human face appeared on film with new and immeasurable significance. But it was no longer a portrait. What was it? It is the outstanding service of a German photographer to have answered this question. August Sander[17] has compiled a series of faces that is in no way inferior to the tremendous physiognomic gallery mounted by an Eisenstein or a Pudovkin, and he has done it from a scientific viewpoint.[18] "His complete work comprises seven groups which correspond to the existing social order, and is to be published in some forty-five folios containing twelve photographs each." So far we have a sample volume containing sixty reproductions, which offer inexhaustible material for study. "Sander starts off with the peasant, the earthbound man, takes the observer through every social stratum and every walk of life up to the highest representatives of civilization, and then goes back down all the way to the idiot." The photographer did not approach this enormous undertaking as a scholar, or with the advice of ethnographers and sociologists, but, as the publisher says, "from direct observation." It was assuredly a very impartial, indeed bold sort of observation, but delicate too, very much in the spirit of Goethe's remark: "There is a delicate empiricism which so intimately involves itself with the object that it becomes true theory." So it was quite in order for an observer like Döblin to have hit on precisely the scientific aspects of this work, commenting: "Just as there is comparative anatomy, which helps us to understand the nature and history of organs, so this photographer is doing comparative photography, adopting a scientific standpoint superior to that of the photographer of detail."[19] It would be a pity if economic considerations should prevent the continuing publication of this extraordinary body of work. Apart from this basic encouragement, there is a more specific incentive one might offer the publisher. Work like Sander's could overnight assume unlooked-for topicality. Sudden shifts of power such as are now overdue in our society can make the ability to read facial types a matter of vital importance. Whether one is of the Left or the Right, one will have to get used to being looked at in terms of one's provenance. And one will have to look at others the same way. Sander's work is more than a picture book. It is a training manual.

"In our age there is no work of art that is looked at so closely as a photograph of oneself, one's closest relatives and friends, one's sweetheart," wrote Lichtwark back in 1907, thereby moving the inquiry out of the realm of aesthetic distinctions into that of social functions.[20] Only from this vantage point can it be carried further. It is indeed significant that the debate has raged most fiercely around the aesthetics of photography-as-art, whereas the far less questionable social fact of art-as-photography was given scarcely a glance. And yet the impact of the photographic reproduction of artworks is of very much greater importance for the function of art than the greater or lesser artistry of a photography that regards all experience as fair game for the camera. The amateur who returns home with great piles of artistic shots is in fact no more appealing a figure than the hunter who comes back

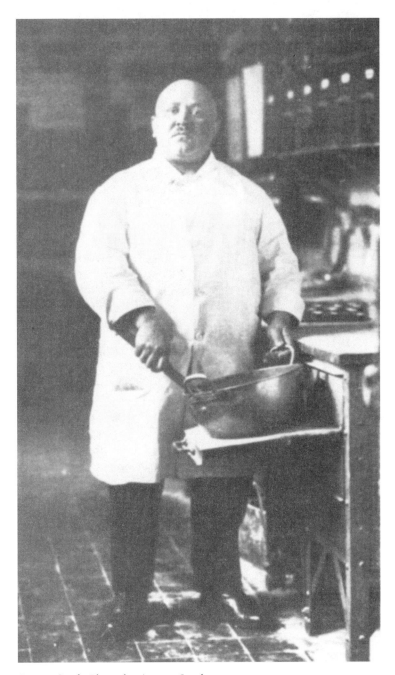

Pastry Cook. Photo by August Sander.

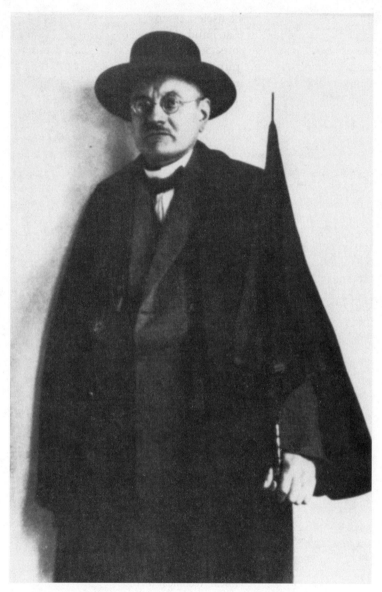

Parliamentary Representative (a Democrat). Photo by August Sander.

with quantities of game that is useless to anyone but the merchant. And the day does indeed seem to be at hand when there will be more illustrated magazines than game merchants. So much for the snapshot. But the emphasis changes completely if we turn from photography-as-art to art-as-photography. Everyone will have noticed how much easier it is to get hold of a painting, more particularly a sculpture, and especially architecture, in a photograph than in reality. It is all too tempting to blame this squarely on the decline of artistic appreciation, on a failure of contemporary sensibility. But one is brought up short by the way the understanding of great works was transformed at about the same time the techniques of reproduction were being developed. Such works can no longer be regarded as the products of individuals; they have become a collective creation, a corpus so vast it can be assimilated only through miniaturization. In the final analysis, mechanical reproduction is a technique of diminution that helps people to achieve control over works of art—a control without whose aid they could no longer be used.

If one thing typifies present-day relations between art and photography, it is the unresolved tension between the two introduced by the photography of works of art. Many of those who, as photographers, determine the current face of this technology started out as painters. They turned their back on painting after attempts to bring its expressive resources into a living and unequivocal relationship with modern life. The keener their feel for the temper of the times, the more problematic their starting point became for them. For once again, as eighty years before, photography has taken the baton from painting. As Moholy-Nagy has said:

> The creative potential of the new is for the most part slowly revealed through old forms, old instruments and areas of design which in their essence have already been superseded by the new, but which under pressure from the new as it takes shape are driven to a euphoric efflorescence. Thus, for example, futurist (structural) painting brought forth the clearly defined problematic of the simultaneity of motion, the representation of the instant, which was later to destroy it—and this at a time when film was already known but far from being understood . . . Similarly, some of the painters (neoclassicists and verists) today using representational-objective methods can be regarded—with caution—as forerunners of a new representational optical form which will soon be making use only of mechanical, technical methods.[21]

And Tristan Tzara, 1922: "When everything that called itself art was stricken with palsy, the photographer switched on his thousand-candle-power lamp and gradually the light-sensitive paper absorbed the darkness of a few everyday objects. He had discovered what could be done by a pure and sensitive flash of light—a light that was more important than all the constellations arranged for the eye's pleasure."[22] The photographers who

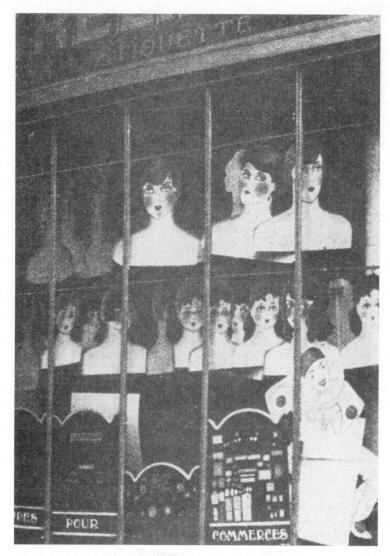

Display Window. Photo by Germaine Krull.

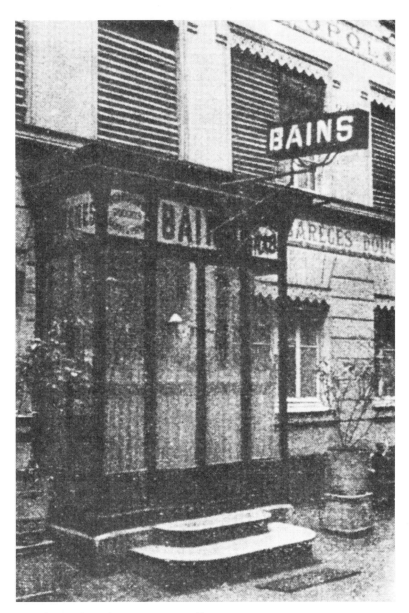

Storefront. Photo by Germaine Krull.

went over from figurative art to photography not on opportunistic grounds, not by chance, not out of sheer laziness, today constitute the avant-garde among their colleagues, because they are to some extent protected by their background against the greatest danger facing photography today: the touch of the commercial artist. "Photography-as-art," says Sascha Stone, "is a very dangerous field."[23]

When photography takes itself out of context, severing the connections illustrated by Sander, Blossfeldt, or Germaine Krull, when it frees itself from physiognomic, political, and scientific interest, it becomes *creative*.[24] The lens now looks for interesting juxtapositions; photography turns into a sort of arty journalism. "The spirit that overcomes mechanics translates exact findings into parables of life." The more far-reaching the crisis of the present social order, and the more rigidly its individual components are locked together in their death struggle, the more the creative—in its deepest essence a variant (contradiction its father, imitation its mother)—becomes a fetish, whose lineaments live only in the fitful illumination of changing fashion. The creative in photography is its capitulation to fashion. *The world is beautiful*—that is its watchword.[25] In it is unmasked the posture of a photography that can endow any soup can with cosmic significance but cannot grasp a single one of the human connections in which it exists, even when this photography's most dream-laden subjects are a forerunner more of its salability than of any knowledge it might produce. But because the true face of this kind of photographic creativity is the advertisement or association, its logical counterpart is the act of unmasking or construction. As Brecht says: "The situation is complicated by the fact that less than ever does the mere reflection of reality reveal anything about reality. A photograph of the Krupp works or the AEG tells us next to nothing about these institutions.[26] Actual reality has slipped into the functional. The reification of human relations—the factory, say—means that they are no longer explicit. So something must in fact be *built up*, something artificial, posed." We must credit the Surrealists with having trained the pioneers of such photographic construction. A further stage in this contest between creative and constructive photography is typified by Russian film. It is not too much to say that the great achievements of Russian directors were possible only in a country where photography sets out not to charm or persuade, but to experiment and instruct. In this sense, and in this only, there is still some meaning in the grandiloquent salute offered to photography in 1855 by that uncouth painter of ideas Antoine Wiertz.[27]

> For some years now the glory of our age has been a machine which daily amazes the mind and startles the eye. Before another century is out, this machine will be the brush, the palette, the colors, the craft, the experience, the patience, the

dexterity, the sureness of touch, the atmosphere, the luster, the exemplar, the perfection, the very essence of painting . . . Let no one suppose that daguerreotype photography will be the death of art . . . When the daguerreotype, that infant prodigy, has grown to its full stature, when all its art and strength have been revealed, then will Genius seize it by the scruff of the neck and shout: "Come with me—you are mine now! We shall work together!"

How sober—indeed, pessimistic—by contrast are the words in which Baudelaire announced the new technology to his readers, two years later, in his *Salon of 1857*. Like the preceding quotation, they can be read today only with a subtle shift of emphasis. But as a counterpart to the above, they still make sense as a violent reaction to the encroachments of artistic photography. "In these sorry days, a new industry has arisen that has done not a little to strengthen the asinine belief . . . that art is and can be nothing other than the accurate reflection of nature . . . A vengeful god has hearkened to the voice of this multitude. Daguerre is his messiah." And: "If photography is permitted to supplement some of art's functions, they will forthwith be usurped and corrupted by it, thanks to photography's natural alliance with the mob. It must therefore revert to its proper duty, which is to serve as the handmaiden of science and the arts."

One thing, however, both Wiertz and Baudelaire failed to grasp: the lessons inherent in the authenticity of the photograph. These cannot be forever circumvented by a commentary whose clichés merely establish verbal associations in the viewer. The camera is getting smaller and smaller, ever readier to capture fleeting and secret images whose shock effect paralyzes the associative mechanisms in the beholder. This is where inscription must come into play, which includes the photography of the literarization of the conditions of life, and without which all photographic construction must remain arrested in the approximate. It is no accident that Atget's photographs have been likened to those of a crime scene. But isn't every square inch of our cities a crime scene? Every passer-by a culprit? Isn't it the task of the photographer—descendant of the augurs and haruspices—to reveal guilt and to point out the guilty in his pictures? "The illiteracy of the future," someone has said, "will be ignorance not of reading or writing, but of photography." But shouldn't a photographer who cannot read his own pictures be no less accounted an illiterate? Won't inscription become the most important part of the photograph? Such are the questions in which the interval of ninety years that separate us from the age of the daguerreotype discharges its historical tension. It is in the illumination of these sparks that the first photographs emerge, beautiful and unapproachable, from the darkness of our grandfathers' day.

Published in *Die literarische Welt*, September–October 1931. *Gesammelte Schriften*, II, 368–385. Translated by Edmund Jephcott and Kingsley Shorter.

Notes

1. Joseph-Nicéphore Niepce (1765–1833), French inventor, succeeded in making the first permanent photographic image. In 1826–1827, he used a camera to produce a view from his studio that was captured on a pewter plate. His death cut off his collaboration with Louis Jacques Mandé Daguerre (1787–1851), French painter and physicist, who went on to refine Niepce's work. Daguerre reduced the exposure time from Niepce's eight hours to twenty minutes and invented a process that was widely applicable.

2. David Octavius Hill (1802–1870), Scottish painter and photographer, collaborated with the chemist Robert Adamson on a series of remarkable portraits. Julia Margaret Cameron (1815–1879), English photographer, was, unlike many of the most important early photographers, an amateur. She is considered one of the greatest portrait photographers of the nineteenth century. Victor Hugo (1802–1885), poet, novelist, and dramatist, was the most important of the French Romantic writers. Hugo and indeed his entire family were enthusiastic amateur photographers and produced a sizable body of work. Nadar (pseudonym of Gaspard-Félix Tournachon; 1820–1910), French writer, caricaturist, and photographer, emerged from a large group of Parisian studio portraitists as one of the great portraitists of the century. Among his many innovations are his natural posing of his subjects, a patent on the use of photographs in mapmaking and surveying, the first aerial photograph (from a balloon), and the first photographic interview: twenty-one images of the scientist Eugène Chevreul, accompanied by text.

3. Helmut Bossert and Heinrich Guttmann, *Aus der Frühzeit der Photographie, 1840–1870: Ein Bildbuch nach 200 Originalen* (Frankfurt: Societäts Verlag, 1930). Heinrich Schwarz, *David Octavius Hill: Der Meister der Photographie* (Leipzig: Insel, 1931), with 80 plates. [Benjamin's note]

4. Dominique François Jean Arago (1786–1853), French physicist, was active in the study of light. He devised an experiment that proved the wave theory of light and contributed to the discovery of the laws of light polarization.

5. Maurice Utrillo (1883–1955), French painter, was known for his Montmartre street scenes.

6. Stefan George, *Der Teppich des Lebens und die Lieder von Traum und Tod* (The Carpet of Life and the Songs of Dream and Death), "Standbilder, das Sechste," verses 13–16.

7. Karl Blossfeldt, *Urformen der Kunst: Photographische Pflanzenbilder*, edited and with an introduction by Karl Nierendorf (Berlin: Ernst Wasmuth, 1928), with 120 plates. [Benjamin's note. Blossfeldt, a professor of drawing and painting in Berlin, created a sensation in the 1920s with the publication of his magnified photos of plant parts; see "News about Flowers" (1928), in this volume.—*Trans.*]

8. Emil Orlik, *Kleine Aufsätze* (Berlin: Propyläen Verlag, 1924), pp. 38ff. Orlik (1870–1932) was a German graphic artist and painter whose work was influenced by Jugendstil (Art Nouveau).

9. Bernard von Brentano (1901–1964), leftist novelist and journalist, wrote for the *Frankfurter Zeitung* and the *Berliner Tageblatt.* He is perhaps best-known for the historical novel *Theodor Chindler,* which depicts the transition from the empire to the Weimar Republic.

10. Giovanni Battista (Giambattista) Della Porta (1535–1615) was an Italian physicist and dramatist whose works contain descriptions of the camera obscura, as well as of a special lens he developed for it.

11. Carl Ferdinand Stelzner (ca. 1805–1895) was a German painter and photographer who, like many miniaturist painters, turned to daguerreotypy; together with Hermann Biow, he shot some of the earliest news photographs. Pierre-Louis Pierson (1822–1913) was a prominent French studio portraitist; his firm, Mayer and Pierson, catered to high society and the court. In 1862 Pierson and his partners, the brothers Léopold Ernest Mayer and Louis Frédéric Mayer, were named official photographers to Napoleon III. Hippolyte Bayard (1801–1887), French photographer, was active as an inventor in the earliest days of photography. He is widely regarded as one of photography's first significant artists, and held the first known photographic exhibition, displaying thirty of his own works.

12. Orlik, *Kleine Aufsätze,* p. 38.

13. Paul Delaroche, cited in Schwarz, *David Octavius Hill,* p. 39. Delaroche (1757–1859) was a French academic painter who specialized in historical subjects.

14. Eugène Atget, *Lichtbilder,* with an introduction by Camille Recht (Paris and Leipzig, 1930), p. 10. [Benjamin's note]

15. Eugène Atget (1857–1927), French photographer, spent his career in obscurity making pictures of Paris and its environs. He is widely recognized as one of the leading photographers of the twentieth century.

16. Berenice Abbott (1898–1991), American photographer, preserved Atget's work and oversaw its earliest publication. She undertook, very much in the spirit of Atget, a photographic documentation of New York City in the 1930s and 1940s.

17. August Sander, *Das Antlitz der Zeit: Sechzig Aufnahmen deutscher Menschen des 20. Jahrhunderts,* with an introduction by Alfred Döblin (Munich, 1929). [Benjamin's note. Sander (1876–1964), a German photographer, sought to compile a photographic portrait of the German people; *Das Antlitz der Zeit* (The Face of Our Time) was the first precipitate of this sociologically oriented project, which included portraits of peasants, workers, artisans, capitalists, and artists, among many others.—*Trans.*]

18. Sergei Mikhailovich Eisenstein (1898–1948), Soviet film director and theorist, produced a large body of work. His best-known films include *Battleship Potemkin* (1925), *Alexander Nevsky* (1938), and *Ivan the Terrible* (released in two parts, 1944 and 1958). Vsevolod Illarionovich Pudovkin (1893–1953) was a Soviet film director and theorist whose work often focused on heroic figures caught in violent historical change. His films include *Mat* (Mother; 1926), based on Gorky's novel; *Konets Sankt-Peterburga* (The End of St. Petersburg; 1927);

Potomok Chingis-Khan (Heir to Genghis Khan, or Storm over Asia; 1928); and the sound films *Dezertir* (Deserter; 1933), *Suvorov* (General Suvorov; 1941), and *Admiral Nakhimov* (1946–1947).

19. Alfred Döblin, introduction to Sander, *Antlitz der Zeit,* p. vi.
20. Alfred Lichtwark, introduction to Fritz Matthies-Masuren, *Künstlerische Photographie: Entwicklung und Einfluss in Deutschland* [Artistic Photography: Development and Influence in Germany] (Berlin: Marrquardt, 1907), p. 16.
21. László Moholy-Nagy, *Malerei Fotographie Film* (Munich: Langen, 1925). Moholy-Nagy (1895–1946), Hungarian painter, photographer, and art teacher, emerged as a dominant figure at the Bauhaus, where he was responsible for the famous Preliminary Course. As a photographer, he moved freely between the abstract photogram and representational photography. He is arguably the most influential photographer of the 1920s in Europe.
22. Tristan Tzara, "La photographie à l'envers" (Photography from the Verso), translated by Benjamin as "Die Photographie von der Kehrseite," in *G: Zeitschrift für elementare Gestaltung,* July 1924, p. 30. Tzara (1896–1963), Romanian-born French poet and essayist, was one of the founders of Dada in Zurich. He carried Dada ideas to Paris after World War I.
23. Sascha Stone (pseudonym of Alexander Sergei Steinsapir; 1895–1940), German-Jewish photographer, worked as a professional photographer in Berlin, primarily for the illustrated magazines published by Ullstein Verlag. Stone was active at the borders of the group around the journal *G,* which included Moholy-Nagy, Mies van der Rohe, Hans Richter, El Lissitsky, and Benjamin. He created the photomontage for the book jacket of Benjamin's *One-Way Street* (see Volume 1 of this edition).
24. Germaine Krull (1897–1985), German photographer, emigrated to Paris in 1924, where she became known for her work in portraiture, as well as in architectural, industrial, and fashion photography.
25. *Die Welt ist schön* (The World Is Beautiful) is the title of a photo volume by Albert Renger-Patzsch; it became the most influential of all of the photo essays published in the Weimar Republic. Benjamin was involved in a long-standing polemic against Renger-Patzsch's work. See especially "The Author as Producer" (1934), in this volume.
26. The Krupp works at Essen was the original plant in the Krupp steel, armaments, and shipbuilding empire, which had been founded in 1811 by Friedrich Krupp. The AEG is the Allgemeine Elektricitäts Gesellschaft, or General Electric Company, founded in Berlin in 1833 by the industrialist Emil Rathenau; it was largely responsible for building the electrical infrastructure of modern Germany.
27. Antoine Wiertz (1806–1865), Belgian painter, was known for his large, frequently grotesque paintings. Wiertz plays an important role in Benjamin's *Passagen-Werk* (Arcades Project).

P aul Valéry

On His Sixtieth Birthday

O langage chargé de sel, et paroles véritablement marines![1]

Valéry once wanted to become a naval officer. Elements of this youthful
dream can still be discerned in what he did become. First, there is his poetry
with its sustained formal abundance, which language garners from thought
as the sea does from a calm. Second, there is the thought itself, imbued with
the spirit of mathematics—a thought that leans over its objects as if they
were maritime charts and that, without indulging itself in contemplation of
the "depths," is content if it can hold a safe course. The sea and mathematics: they come together in a captivating union in one of the most beautiful
passages he has written, the one in which Socrates tells Phaedra of the
discovery he has made on the shore. His find is puzzling. Is it ivory, or
marble, or an animal bone? At any rate, the object washed up by the tide
could almost be a head with the features of Apollo. And Socrates wonders
whether it is the work of an artist or of the waves. He weighs it in his hand.
How long would the ocean take to create this shape rather than millions of
others, and how long the artist? Socrates may well assert "that an artist is
worth a thousand centuries or a hundred thousand, or many more . . . This
is an unusual measuring rod for works of art."[2] If the admirers of the author
of this outstanding work, *Eupalinos, ou l'Architecte* [Eupalinos, or the
Architect], had decided to honor his sixtieth birthday by making a surprise
presentation of an Ex Libris, it might have taken the form of a giant
compass, with one arm firmly anchored in the seabed and the other stretched
out wide toward the horizon. It would be a metaphor for the broad span
encompassed by this man. Tension is the dominating impression of his

physical appearance; tension is in the expression of his face, whose deep-set eyes hint at a reverie that is remote from earthly images and that enables him to set the course of his interior life by them as well as by those of the stars. Solitude is the night out of which such images shine, and Valéry has had long experience with solitude. Having published his first poems and his first two essays at the age of twenty-five, he began a twenty-year hiatus in his public activities from which he emerged with glory in 1917 with the poem "La jeune Parque." Eight years later, a series of outstanding works and ingenious maneuverings in society brought him membership in the Académie Française. Not without malice, he was assigned the seat previously occupied by Anatole France. Valéry parried the thrust with an exceedingly elegant address—the obligatory eulogy of his predecessor—in which France's name did not occur once. Aside from that, the speech contains a survey of literature that is sufficiently out of the ordinary to provide a clue to its author. He talks there of the "Valley of Jehoshaphat"[3] which is crowded with the mass of writers past and present: "Everything new is lost in something else new. Every illusion of being original disappears. The soul is cast down and turns its thoughts, with pain, albeit mixed with irony and a profound compassion, to those millions of feathered creatures, those innumerable agents of the mind, each of whom appears to himself to be the man of the moment, a free creator, the first mover, the possessor of an irrefragable certainty, a unique, distinctive source; and he who has spent his days in toil and who has used up his best moments in preserving his distinctiveness finds himself annihilated by the multitudes and swallowed up in the ever-growing swarms of those like himself."[4] In Valéry, this entirely vain exercise of the will to distinguish oneself is replaced by another goal: the will to endure, the endurance of the written word. The endurance of the written word, however, is quite different from the immortality of the writer, and has often taken place without it. Endurance, not originality, is the mark of the classical in writing, and Valéry is indefatigable in his search for what makes it possible. "A classical writer," he remarks, "is a writer who conceals or absorbs the associations of his ideas."[5] In those passages where the author's inspiration soars to the heights and where he feels himself to be above the demands of construction, sees no joints, and (because he cannot see them) does not feel them—it is at these points that the mildew of old age sets in. In order to recognize the joints, the limits of thought, one needs self-criticism. Valéry sets out to explore the writer's and especially the poet's intelligence like an inquisitor, and calls for a break with the widely held view that it is self-evident that writers are intelligent, as well as with the even more widely held idea that intelligence is irrelevant to the poet. He himself possesses intelligence of a kind that is anything but self-evident. Nothing can be more disconcerting than its embodiment: Monsieur Teste. Again and again, from his earliest writings to his later ones, Valéry has recourse to this strange figure around whom a whole series of little writings has grown up—"La soirée avec Monsieur Teste," a letter to Teste's wife, a preface, and of course a logbook. Monsieur Teste ("Mr. Head") is a personification of the intellect that reminds us very strongly of the God conceived by the negative theology of Nicholas of Cusa.[6] Everything we learn about Teste ends up in negation. What is so very seductive about him is not theorems, but the tricks of a way of behaving that impinges as little as possible on nonbeing and follows the maxim, "Every sense of excitement, every feeling, is the sign of a failure of construction and adaptation."[7] However human Monsieur Teste feels himself to be, he has taken to heart Valéry's aperçu that the most important ideas are those that contradict our feelings. He represents, therefore, the negation of the "human." "Behold, the twilight of the approximate breaks in, and before the door stands the reign of the dehumanized that will emerge from precision, rigor, and purity in human affairs."[8] No expansive, pathos-filled gestures, nothing "human," comes into the ambit of this Valéryesque eccentric, for whom thought is the only substance from which perfection may arise. One of its attributes is continuity. Thus, art and science are a continuum through which Leonardo's method (Valéry's first work was his "Introduction à la méthode de Léonard de Vinci," and Leonardo may be seen as a forerunner of Monsieur Teste) opens up paths that must not be misunderstood as boundaries. It is this method that, when applied to poetry, led Valéry to the celebrated concept of *poésie pure,* an idea that was certainly not made to be dragged through the literary magazines of France for months on end by a belletristically minded abbé in order to force Valéry to admit that it was identical with the concept of prayer.[9] Time and again, and with a remarkable degree of success, Valéry himself has recorded the different stages in the history of poetic theory—from Poe down to Baudelaire and Mallarmé—in which the constructive and musical elements of lyric poetry sought to demarcate their particular domains, defining them against each other, until they culminated in reflections whose core is formed by his lyrical masterpieces "Le cimetière marin," "La jeune Parque," and "Le Serpent"—poems in which we find the perfect interplay of voice and intelligence. The ideas in his poems rise like islands out of the sea of the voice. This is what separates this "reflective poetry" [*Gedankenlyrik*] from everything that we Germans understand by the term: at no point does the idea it contains come into contact with "life" or "reality." The idea has no connection with anything but the voice: this is the essence of *poésie pure.* "Lyric poetry is that mode of literature which is predicated on the voice in action—the voice as it speaks spontaneously, or as it is awakened by the things we see or the things we feel in their presence."[10] Or again, "The strict requirements of prosody are the artistic device which confers on natural speech the qualities of a resistant material that is alien to our soul and remains deaf to our desires."[11] And this is the peculiar feature of pure intelligence. But this *intelligence pure* that in Valéry has taken up its winter quarters on the inhospitable mountain peaks of esoteric poetry is, after all, identical with the intelligence under whose aegis the European bourgeoisie embarked on its voyages of conquest in the Age of Discovery. The Cartesian doubts about knowledge have been extended in Valéry in an almost reckless but also profound manner, to the point where they become doubts about the questions themselves: "The realms of chance, the powers of the gods or Fate, are nothing but the symptoms of our own mental deficiencies. If we had an answer to everything—a precise answer, that is—these powers would not exist . . . We feel this ourselves, and this is why we end up turning against our own questions. But that should be just the beginning. We ought to be able to formulate a question for ourselves that precedes all others and tests them in turn to see what they are worth."[12] The strict return of such ideas to their context in the heroic period of the European bourgeoisie allows us to master the surprise at encountering once more the idea of progress at such an advanced stage of the old European humanism. It is, furthermore, the valid and genuine idea of a progress transferable at the level of "methodology"—a term that corresponds to Valéry's concept of "construction" as neatly as it conflicts with the *idée fixe* of inspiration. As one of his contemporaries has claimed, "The work of art is not a creation, but a construction in which analysis, calculation, and planning play the principal roles." The ultimate merit of the systematic process of leading the investigator to excel himself has proved its worth in Valéry. For who is Monsieur Teste except the individual who is ready to cross the threshold where he will vanish into history—but who, like a disappearing shade, answers the call one last time, only to become submerged once again where he enters into an order of things whose approach Valéry describes in these terms: "In the age of Napoleon, electricity had roughly the same significance as Christianity in the age of Tiberius. Gradually it became apparent that this general infusion of energy was of greater consequence and better able to change the future than any 'political' event from Ampère to the present day."[13] The gaze Valéry turns on this approaching world is no longer that of the officer, but simply that of the experienced sailor who feels the approach of the storm and has too clear-eyed a vision of the changed world-historical situation ("with the increase in precision and exactitude, a corresponding increase in effect") not to realize that today, "faced with these changes, the profoundest thoughts of a Machiavelli or a Richelieu have about the same value and efficacy as a stock market tip."[14] Thus he stands there, "upright, on the pinnacle of thought, keeping as sharp a lookout as he can for the limits of things or of his own vision."[15]

Published in *Die literarische Welt*, October 1931. *Gesammelte Schriften*, II, 386–390. Translated by Rodney Livingstone.

Notes

1. "O language filled with salt, and words that are truly of the sea!" From Paul Valéry, *Eupalinos, ou l'Architecte,* in Valéry, *Oeuvres,* ed. Jean Hytier (Paris: Pléiade, 1971), vol. 2, p. 117.
2. Ibid., p. 119.
3. The Valley of Jehoshaphat was the site of Jehovah's apocalyptic judgment upon the nations (Joel 4:14).
4. "Remerciement à l'Académie française," in Valéry, *Oeuvres,* vol. 1, p. 731.
5. Ibid., p. 793.
6. Nicholas of Cusa (1401–1464) propounded a theology that stressed the limitations of human knowledge of God, which must be content with conjecture or approximation to the truth. The absolute truth escapes man; his proper attitude is "learned ignorance."
7. *Mauvaises pensées et autres,* in Valéry, *Oeuvres,* vol. 2, p. 866.
8. *Rhumbs,* in Valéry, *Oeuvres,* vol. 2, p. 621.
9. The reference is to the abbé Henri Bremond, who presented a report to the Académie Française on October 24, 1925, entitled "Poésie pure: D'où s'élève une querelle entre poètes, critiques et esthéticiens."
10. "La Poésie," in Valéry, *Oeuvres,* vol. 2, p. 549.
11. "Au sujet d'Adonis," in Valéry, *Oeuvres,* vol. 1, p. 480.
12. "Rhumbs: Arrière-pensées," in Valéry, *Oeuvres,* vol. 2, p. 647.
13. *"Regards sur le monde actuel" et autres essais,* in Valéry, *Oeuvres,* vol. 2, pp. 919–920. Jean-Jacques Ampère (1800–1864), French historian and philologist, studied the origins of western European languages and mythology.
14. Ibid., p. 925.
15. "Extraits du log-book de *Monsieur Teste,*" in Valéry, *Oeuvres,* vol. 2, p. 39.

The Lisbon Earthquake

Have you ever had to wait at the drug store, watching a prescription being made up? The pharmacist measures out on a scale all the substances and powders that are needed for the finished medicine, using a finely calibrated set of weights, gram by gram or ounce by ounce. I feel like a chemist when I talk to you over the radio. My weights are the minutes, and I have to measure them out very accurately: so much of this and so much of that, if the final mixture is going to come out right. "How come?" you will ask. "If you want to tell us about the Lisbon earthquake, begin by telling us how it started. And then you can go on to tell us what happened next." But if I followed this advice, I don't think the description would be much fun. One house after another collapses; one family after another loses their lives. The panic created by the spreading fire, the flood of water, the darkness, the plundering, the groans of the injured, and the cries of people searching for their loved ones—to hear of all this and nothing else would please no one. And besides, those are the very things that recur in more or less the same form in every natural disaster.

But the earthquake that destroyed Lisbon on November 1, 1755, was not a disaster like a thousand others. In many respects it was remarkable, even unique. And this is what I would like to tell you about. In the first place, it was one of the largest and most destructive earthquakes of all time. Yet it is not for this reason alone that it excited and preoccupied the entire world like few other events in that century. The destruction of Lisbon in 1755 was roughly equivalent to the destruction of London or Chicago today. In the middle of the eighteenth century, Portugal was at the height of its power as a colonial empire. Lisbon was one of the most prosperous trading cities in the world. Year in, year out, its port at the mouth of the Tagus was filled with ships, and its streets were lined with the great trading houses of English, French, and German—especially Hamburg—merchants. The city had 30,000 houses and well over 250,000 inhabitants, of whom roughly a fourth perished in the earthquake. The king's court was famous for its strictness and its pomp. The many accounts of the city that appeared in the period preceding the earthquake contain the most curious descriptions of the stiffness and solemnity that could be seen on summer evenings in the main square of the city, the Rucio, when the courtiers and their families congregated in their carriages and chatted together for a while without descending from their vehicles. Moreover, people had such an exalted conception of the king of Portugal that one of the many pamphlets which spread precise descriptions of the catastrophe throughout Europe was quite unable to come to terms with the fact that such a great king had been affected by it. This extraordinary reporter notes: "Just as the magnitude of a disaster can be fully appreciated only once it has been overcome, so too you can grasp the awful import of this dreadful catastrophe only when you reflect that a great king, together with his wife, spent the entire day in a carriage, in the most wretched state, abandoned by all." The pamphlets in which such accounts can be studied took the place of newspapers at that time. Whoever was able to do so obtained eyewitness descriptions in as much detail as possible, and then printed and sold them. In what follows, I shall read to you from such a report—one which records the experiences of an Englishman who was then residing in Lisbon.

There is a further, special reason that helps to explain why this event affected people's minds so powerfully—why countless pamphlets passed from hand to hand, and indeed why new descriptions continued to make their appearance almost a century later. The reason is that this earthquake was the most powerful on record. Its impact was felt throughout Europe and as far away as Africa. It has been calculated that, together with its most distant tremors, it affected two and a quarter million square kilometers—a huge area. Its most powerful shocks extended from the Moroccan coast to the shores of Andalusia and France. The cities of Cádiz, Jerez, and Algeciras were almost completely destroyed. An eyewitness in Seville claimed that the cathedral spires shook like reeds in the wind. But the most powerful tremors were transported by the sea. From Finland to the Dutch East Indies, mighty tidal waves were felt; and it was calculated that they moved with amazing speed—in a quarter of an hour!—from the Portuguese coast to the mouth of the Elbe. And these were just the events actually experienced at the time of the disaster. Even more significant is the way in which people's imaginations brooded on the strange phenomena of nature that had been observed in the weeks preceding the earthquake and that subsequently—and probably not always without justification—were regarded as portents of the catastrophe to come. In Locarno, in the south of Switzerland, for example, some two weeks before the disaster, steam was seen coming out of the earth; within a couple of hours it had transformed itself into a red mist, which, toward evening, fell as purple rain. From then on, people claimed to have observed terrible hurricanes, with cloudbursts and floods in western Europe. Eight days before the earthquake, the ground near Cádiz was found to be covered with a vast quantity of worms.

No one was more fascinated by these remarkable events than the great German philosopher Kant, whose name may be familiar to some of you. At the time of the earthquake he was a young man of twenty-four, who had never left his hometown of Königsberg—and who would never do so in the future. But he eagerly collected all the reports of the earthquake that he could find, and the slim book he wrote about it probably represents the beginnings of scientific geography in Germany. And certainly the beginnings of seismology. I would gladly tell you something of the route taken by this science from that description of the earthquake of 1755 down to the present day. But I must take care lest the Englishman whose first-hand account I still wish to read to you gets lost in the crowd. He is waiting impatiently, because after 150 years in which no one has taken any notice of him, he would welcome the opportunity to speak once again and hence will permit me to say only a few words about our present knowledge of earthquakes. A word to the wise: it is not what you imagine. I would wager that if I were to interrupt my talk briefly and ask you how you would go about explaining earthquakes, your first thoughts would be of volcanos. And the fact is that volcanic eruptions often are associated with earthquakes, or at least announced by them. And this is why people have imagined for two thousand years—from the ancient Greeks down to Kant, and indeed even longer, roughly until 1870—that earthquakes came from the fiery gases and steam arising from the interior of the earth and suchlike. But when people began to take measurements and to make calculations whose subtlety and precision you and I can scarcely conceive of—in short, when they started to look at the problem scientifically—the truth turned out to lie in quite a different direction, at least insofar as major earthquakes like the one in Lisbon were concerned. They arise not from the innermost core of the earth, which to this day is thought of as being liquid, or at least mudlike, a sort of seething sludge, but from events in the earth's crust. The earth's crust is a layer about 3,000 kilometers thick. It is in a state of permanent turmoil; the masses of matter it contains are constantly shifting and striving to achieve equilibrium. We know some of the factors that disturb this equilibrium, and are striving unceasingly to discover others. So much is clear: that the most important changes are caused by the constant cooling of the earth. This gives rise to huge tensions in the rock formations and ends up fracturing them, seeking a new equilibrium through a reconfiguration that we experience as an earthquake. Other changes arise from the erosion of the mountains, making them lighter, and accretions in the seabed, which thus becomes denser. Storms that rage around the globe, especially in autumn, have an impact on the earth's surface. And last, scientists are in the process of establishing what effect the gravitational pull of extraterrestrial bodies might have on the surface of the globe. "But," you might say, "in that case, the earth can never come to rest. There must be a continuous series of earth tremors!" You're quite right about that. The extremely sensitive instruments that we have nowadays—in Germany alone, there are thirteen earthquake-monitoring stations in various towns—these sensitive instruments are never entirely still. In other words, the earth experiences tremors all the time, but for the most part not so violently that we notice.

All the worse if suddenly, out of the blue, we feel a tremor. This "out of the blue" should be taken quite literally. "For," says our Englishman, who has at long last managed to have his say,

the sun now shone in its full glory. The sky was completely blue and clear, and there was not the least sign of any natural event. Then, between nine and ten in the morning, I was sitting at my desk when my table moved, and since I could not discern any reason, I felt some surprise. I was wondering what could possibly have been the cause when the house suddenly shook from top to bottom. From beneath the ground arose a sound of thunder, as if a storm were raging at a great distance. I put my pen down quickly and leaped to my feet. The danger was great, but I was still hopeful that the matter would pass without much ill effect; but the very next moment put an end to any doubts on that score. There was a shattering noise, as if all the buildings in town were collapsing at the same time. My house, too, was profoundly affected: the upper stories instantly collapsed, and the rooms I was staying in swayed so much that all the utensils came crashing down. I truly thought my last moment had arrived, for the walls were bursting apart and great stones were falling out of the joints—all the beams seemed to be supported by thin air. At this very moment the sky went dark, and it became possible to recognize any object. Everything was in Stygian gloom, either from the immeasurable amounts of dust caused by the collapsing buildings, or because of the volumes of sulphurous fumes that arose from the bowels of the earth. At last the night became light once more, and the force of the tremors abated. I regained some of my composure and began to look about me. I realized that my life had been spared up to then thanks to a trivial circumstance. Had I been fully clothed, I would surely have fled into the street, where I would have been buried beneath the buildings crashing all around. I threw on my coat and shoes and rushed out into the street in the direction of St. Paul's cemetery, convinced that the high ground on which it was situated would afford me some measure of safety. No one was able to recognize the street in which he lived; many were unable to describe what had happened to them. Everything was scattered, and no one knew what had happened to his family or possessions. From the heights of the cemetery, I now became witness to a terrifying spectacle: out on the ocean, as far as the eye could see, there was a throng of ships being tossed about by the waves and crashing into each other as if they were the playthings of a mighty storm. Suddenly the huge quay by the shore sank into the sea and vanished, together with all the people who had imagined that standing on it ensured their safety. At the same time, the boats and vehicles in which so many were trying to escape all suddenly became victims of the sea.

As we know from other reports, it was about an hour after the second and most destructive tremor that the vast wave—twenty meters high—which the Englishman could see from a distance came crashing down over the city. As the tide withdrew, the bed of the Tagus was suddenly left completely dry: the ebb was so powerful that it drained all the water from the river. The Englishman's account concludes as follows: "When evening settled on the desolate city, the landscape seemed to turn into a sea of fire; the brightness was such that you could have read a letter by it. At a hundred different points at least, the flames rose to the sky, and they blazed for six days. What the earthquake had spared, they now consumed. As if petrified by fear, thousands gazed at the flames, while women and children prayed to the saints and angels for help. The ground continued to tremble more or less violently, often for a quarter of an hour on end."

So much for that day of misfortune, November 1, 1755. The catastrophe it brought in its wake is one of the very few that can render men as impotent now as they were 170 years ago. But here, too, technology will find ways to combat it, even if in a roundabout way: by prediction. For the moment, however, the senses of some animals are still superior to our most sensitive instruments. Dogs, especially, are said to display unmistakable signs of agitation days before the eruption of an earthquake, so that people keep them as helpers in the lookout posts in earthquake-prone regions. This brings me to the end of my twenty minutes, and I hope they have not passed too slowly for you.

Children's narrative broadcast by Berliner Rundfunk, October 1931. *Gesammelte Schriften*, VII, 220–226. Translated by Rodney Livingstone.

The Destructive Character

It could happen to someone looking back over his life that he realized that almost all the deeper obligations he had endured in its course originated in people who everyone agreed had the traits of a "destructive character." He would stumble on this fact one day, perhaps by chance, and the heavier the shock dealt to him, the better his chances of representing the destructive character.

The destructive character knows only one watchword: make room. And only one activity: clearing away. His need for fresh air and open space is stronger than any hatred.

The destructive character is young and cheerful. For destroying rejuvenates, because it clears away the traces of our own age; it cheers, because everything cleared away means to the destroyer a complete reduction, indeed a rooting out, of his own condition. Really, only the insight into how radically the world is simplified when tested for its worthiness for destruction leads to such an Apollonian image of the destroyer. This is the great bond embracing and unifying all that exists. It is a sight that affords the destructive character a spectacle of deepest harmony.

The destructive character is always blithely at work. It is Nature that dictates his tempo, indirectly at least, for he must forestall her. Otherwise she will take over the destruction herself.

The destructive character sees no image hovering before him. He has few needs, and the least of them is to know what will replace what has been destroyed. First of all, for a moment at least, empty space—the place where the thing stood or the victim lived. Someone is sure to be found who needs this space without occupying it.

The destructive character does his work; the only work he avoids is creative. Just as the creator seeks solitude, the destroyer must be constantly surrounded by people, witnesses to his efficacy.

The destructive character is a signal. Just as a trigonometric sign is exposed on all sides to the wind, so he is exposed to idle talk. To protect him from it is pointless.

The destructive character has no interest in being understood. Attempts in this direction he regards as superficial. Being misunderstood cannot harm him. On the contrary, he provokes it, just as oracles, those destructive institutions of the state, provoked it. The most petty bourgeois of all phenomena, gossip, comes about only because people do not wish to be misunderstood. The destructive character tolerates misunderstanding; he does not promote gossip.

The destructive character is the enemy of the étui-man. The étui-man looks for comfort, and the case is its quintessence. The inside of the case is the velvet-lined trace that he has imprinted on the world. The destructive character obliterates even the traces of destruction.

The destructive character stands in the front line of traditionalists. Some people pass things down to posterity, by making them untouchable and thus conserving them; others pass on situations, by making them practicable and thus liquidating them. The latter are called the destructive.

The destructive character has the consciousness of historical man, whose deepest emotion is an insuperable mistrust of the course of things and a readiness at all times to recognize that everything can go wrong. Therefore, the destructive character is reliability itself.

The destructive character sees nothing permanent. But for this very reason he sees ways everywhere. Where others encounter walls or mountains, there, too, he sees a way. But because he sees a way everywhere, he has to clear things from it everywhere. Not always by brute force; sometimes by the most refined. Because he sees ways everywhere, he always stands at a crossroads. No moment can know what the next will bring. What exists he reduces to rubble—not for the sake of the rubble, but for that of the way leading through it.

The destructive character lives from the feeling not that life is worth living, but that suicide is not worth the trouble.

Published in the *Frankfurter Zeitung*, November 1931. *Gesammelte Schriften*, IV, 396–398. Translated by Edmund Jephcott.

Reflections on Radio

The crucial failing of this institution has been to perpetuate the fundamental separation between practitioners and the public, a separation that is at odds with its technological basis. A child can see that it is in the spirit of radio to put as many people as possible in front of a microphone on every possible occasion; the public has to be turned into the witnesses of interviews and conversations in which now this person and now that one has the opportunity to make himself heard. Whereas in Russia they are in the process of drawing out the logical implications of the different apparatuses, with us the mindless notion of the "offering," under whose aegis the practitioner presents himself to the public, still has the field to itself. What this absurdity has led to after long years of practice is that the public has become quite helpless, quite inexpert in its critical reactions, and has seen itself more or less reduced to sabotage (switching off). There has never been another genuine cultural institution that has failed to authenticate itself by taking advantage of its own forms or technology—using them to create in the public a new expertise. This was as true of the Greek theater as of the Meistersingers, as true of the French stage as of orators from the pulpit. But it was left to the present age, with its unrestrained development of a consumer mentality in the operagoer, the novel reader, the tourist, and other similar types to convert them into dull, inarticulate masses—and create a "public" (in the narrower sense of the word) that has neither yardsticks for its judgments nor a language for its feelings. This barbarism has reached its zenith in the attitude of the masses toward radio programs, and now seems on the point of reversing itself. Only one thing is needed for this: listeners must direct their reflections at their own real reactions, in order to sharpen and justify them. This task would of course be insoluble if their behavior really were—as radio managers and especially presenters like to imagine—more or less impossible to calculate, or simply dependent upon the content of the programs. But the most superficial reflection proves the opposite. No reader has ever closed a just-opened book with the finality with which the listener switches off the radio after hearing perhaps a minute and a half of a talk. The problem is not the remoteness of the subject matter; in many cases, this might be a reason to keep listening for a while before making up one's mind. It is the voice, the diction, and the language—in a word, the formal and technical side of the broadcast—that so frequently make the most desirable programs unbearable for the listener. Conversely, for the same reason but very rarely, programs that might seem totally irrelevant can hold the listener spellbound. (There are speakers who can hold your attention while reading weather forecasts.) Accordingly, it is the technical and formal aspects of radio that will enable the listener to train himself and to outgrow this barbarism. The matter is really quite obvious. We need only reflect that the radio listener, unlike every other kind of audience, welcomes the human voice into his house like a visitor. Moreover, he will usually judge that voice just as quickly and sharply as he would a visitor. Yet no one tells it what is expected of it, what the listener will be grateful for or will find unforgivable, and so on. This can be explained only with reference to the indolence of the masses and the narrowmindedness of broadcasters. Not that it would be an easy task to describe the way the voice relates to the language used—for this is what is involved. But if radio paid heed only to the arsenal of impossibilities that seems to grow by the day—if, for example, it merely provided from a set of negative assumptions a typology of comic errors made by speakers—it would not only improve the standard of its programs but would win listeners over to its side by appealing to them as experts. And this is the most important point of all.

Fragment written no later than November 1931; unpublished in Benjamin's lifetime. *Gesammelte Schriften*, II, 1506–1507. Translated by Rodney Livingstone.

Mickey Mouse

From a conversation with Gustav Glück and Kurt Weill.[1]—Property relations in Mickey Mouse cartoons: here we see for the first time that it is possible to have one's own arm, even one's own body, stolen.

The route taken by Mickey Mouse is more like that of a file in an office than it is like that of a marathon runner.

In these films, mankind makes preparations to survive civilization.

Mickey Mouse proves that a creature can still survive even when it has thrown off all resemblance to a human being. He disrupts the entire hierarchy of creatures that is supposed to culminate in mankind.

These films disavow experience more radically than ever before. In such a world, it is not worthwhile to have experiences.

Similarity to fairy tales. Not since fairy tales have the most important and most vital events been evoked more unsymbolically and more unatmospherically. There is an immeasurable gulf between them and Maeterlinck or Mary Wigman.[2] All Mickey Mouse films are founded on the motif of leaving home in order to learn what fear is.[3]

So the explanation for the huge popularity of these films is not mechanization, their form; nor is it a misunderstanding. It is simply the fact that the public recognizes its own life in them.

Fragment written in 1931; unpublished in Benjamin's lifetime. *Gesammelte Schriften*, VI, 144–145. Translated by Rodney Livingstone.

Notes

1. Gustav Glück (1902–1973), perhaps Benjamin's closest friend during the 1930s, was director of the foreign section of the Reichskreditgesellschaft (Imperial Credit Bank) in Berlin until 1938. He was able to arrange the transfer to Paris of the fees Benjamin received from his occasional contributions to German newspapers until 1935. In 1938 Glück emigrated to Argentina; after World War II, he was a board member of the Dresdner Bank.

2. Maurice Maeterlinck (1862–1949), Belgian writer and dramatist, was one of the leading figures of the Symbolist movement at the end of the nineteenth century. He was awarded the Nobel Prize in 1911. Mary Wigman (1886–1973) was one of the greatest German dancers of the twentieth century. A pupil of Emile Jaques-Dalcroze, she developed her own school in Dresden and Leipzig, creating expressionist solo and group dances that were mainly performed without music except for percussion accompaniment. The idea was that the shape of the dance would emerge from the dancer's own rhythmic movement.

3. This refers to a fairy tale by the Brothers Grimm—"The Boy Who Left Home in Order To Learn the Meaning of Fear"—which also served as a principal theme in Wagner's version of the Siegfried legend.

In Almost Every Example We Have of Materialist Literary History

In almost every example we have of materialist literary history, what we find is a thick-skinned tracing out of the lines in the works themselves, whose social content—if not social tendency—lies partly on the surface. In contrast, the sociologist's detective-like expectation, which this method above all others might be expected to satisfy, is almost always disappointed.

Literary history burdened by value judgment. The scientific value of my theory of the fame of great works.

The enjoyability of all works of art: not simply because they can be explained but because—thanks to these explanations—they become the repositories not only of abstract or specific truth-contents, but of truth-contents that are shot through with material contents.

For the true critic, the actual *judgment* is the ultimate step—something that comes with a struggle after everything else, never the basis of his activities. In the ideal case, he forgets to pass judgment.

On the point that criticism is internal to the work: in the case of great works, art is merely a transitional stage. They were something else (in the course of their gestation) and become something else again (in the state of criticism).

Fragment written in 1931; unpublished in Benjamin's lifetime. *Gesammelte Schriften*, VI, 172. Translated by Rodney Livingstone.

The Task of the Critic

Reading is only one of a hundred ways of gaining access to a book. Always ultimately essential (within limits) as a means of verification, but often no more than this. What does it mean to have a sense of the aura surrounding a book? Perhaps it means the ability to forget. To forget a word or conversation about a book, or a glance through its pages, means perhaps consigning it to the judgment of our unconscious. The unconscious—which has the power to turn impressions and images, however fleeting, into extracts we often recognize in our dreams. This explains why the true critic often has waking dreams about a book even before he comes to know it. Moreover, this is what he has in common with a good publisher. It was no accident that these connections occurred to us in the course of a conversation with a Berlin publisher.

Regarding the terrible misconception that the quality indispensable to the true critic is "his own opinion": it is quite meaningless to learn the opinion of someone about something when you do not even know who he is. The more important the critic, the more he will avoid baldly asserting his own opinion. And the more his insights will absorb his opinions. Instead of giving his own opinion, a great critic enables others to form *their* opinion on the basis of his critical analysis. Moreover, this definition of the figure of the critic should not be a private matter but, as far as possible, an objective, strategic one. What we should know about a critic is what he stands for. He should tell us this.

Investigate why the concept of taste is obsolete. It emerged in the early stages of capitalism. Now we are in the late stages. Lexicon of literary history.

The section "Critical Technique" will include a number of major topics: theory of the critical quotation. Praise and censure. Theory of polemics.

The section "The Task of the Critic" will include a critique of the great figures of today, a critique of the sects. Physiognomic criticism. Strategic criticism.

Dialectical criticism: judgment and the events within the work itself.

Max Dessoir, *Kunstphilosophische Studien* (properly: *Beiträge zur allgemeinen Kunstwissenschaft,* Stuttgart, 1929).

Fragment written ca. 1931; unpublished in Benjamin's lifetime. *Gesammelte Schriften,* VI, 171–172. Translated by Rodney Livingstone.

Ibizan Sequence, 1932

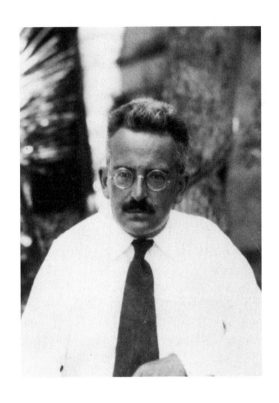

Walter Benjamin on Ibiza, ca. 1932. Photographer unknown. Courtesy of the Theodor W. Adorno Archiv, Frankfurt am Main.

Experience

The character type that learns by experience is the exact opposite of the gambler as a type.

Experiences are lived similarities.

There is no greater error than the attempt to construe experience—in the sense of life experience—according to the model on which the exact natural sciences are based. What is decisive here is not the causal connections established over the course of time, but the similarities that have been lived.

Most people have no wish to learn by experience. Moreover, their convictions prevent them from doing so.

That experience and observation are identical has to be shown. See the concept of "romantic observation" in my dissertation.[1]—Observation is based on self-immersion.

Fragment written in 1931 or 1932; unpublished in Benjamin's lifetime. *Gesammelte Schriften,* VI, 88–89. Translated by Rodney Livingstone.

Notes

1. See Volume 1 of the present edition, pp. 147–148.

On Ships, Mine Shafts, and Crucifixes in Bottles

On ships, mine shafts, and crucifixes in bottles, as well as panopticons.

"While reading Goethe's rebuke to philistines and many other art lovers who like to touch copper engravings and reliefs, the idea came to him that anything that can be touched cannot be a work of art, and anything that is a work of art should be placed out of reach." Franz Glück on Adolf Loos, in *Adolf Loos: Das Werk des Architekten* [Adolf Loos: The Architect's Works], edited by Heinrich Kulka (Vienna, 1931), p. 9.

Does this mean that these objects in bottles are works of art *because* they have been placed out of reach?

Fragment written no later than 1932; unpublished in Benjamin's lifetime. *Gesammelte Schriften*, VI, 127. Translated by Rodney Livingstone.

On the Trail of Old Letters

What I would like to tell you about today, Ladies and Gentlemen, has its focus in a number of documents—some old letters, in fact—and in the circumstances that led me to them.[1] I would like to confine myself here to a few brief words of introduction. I will not discuss the various bibliographic and library techniques that enable the researcher to find his way around the mass of letters that German history has bequeathed to us. About all this, let us say merely that in the case of many of the most valuable of these letters, the real work comes after they have been discovered; for they confront us with the challenge of making them comprehensible in their proper context and from every angle. No, what I would like to tell you about are the motives that guide me in my search. I won't say "the motives that guided me from the outset," since, as with so many enterprises (and not the least interesting among them), what triggered my search initially was no more than an idea, a whim, which contained little more than the dim outlines of what I perceive with greater clarity today. And if I am clearer about my own intentions now, I owe this in no small measure to the editors of the *Frankfurter Zeitung,* who were happy to place their trust in a casual suggestion and to make room for this small selection—the beginnings of a series for which I have already obtained many useful ideas.

Many of you will perhaps recall the stratification that Gundolf once proposed for analyzing the mountain of a great artist's life; we do not wish to adopt his scheme, but it is useful to describe it.[2] Any conversations that have survived form the foothills of the peak, which begin an almost imperceptible rise. This would be followed by the broad layer of the correspondence that has been handed down and is closer to the final shape, while the summit contains the genuinely creative achievement. Now if we can stick with this metaphor for a moment, the situation with the age of German Classicism, which was my starting point and to which we should confine ourselves, is that this mountain is covered by a glacier. For it cannot be denied that the canon of German Classicism has long been fixed and is no longer open to debate, and its rigid immobility threatens to be matched by its present lack of influence. Anyone who has become aware of this will also realize that the huge mass of correspondence we possess from that period represents (to continue the metaphor) something like the snow line. Not that there has been a dearth of attempts to extend the debilitating concept of Classicism to various collections of letters, to label them canonical and condemn them to impotence. I need only name the correspondence between Goethe and Schiller, Feuerbach's letters to his mother, and Wilhelm von Humboldt's letters to Karoline, his future wife—volumes that can even be acquired in gilt-edged editions. But this does not change the fact that the overwhelming mass of these great collections of letters has been ignored by schools, the press, and the speechifying industries and has for that reason been prevented from falling into the all-consuming and insatiable maw of culture. In other words, a knowledge of these letters has hitherto been the preserve of scholars—indeed, of specialists. But this means that, even among them, hardly anyone has turned his attention to the letters for their own intrinsic interest. In most cases they have remained evidence, treasure trove, source material, or whatever else you may care to call it. Hence, Gervinus is right to assert in the introduction to his extremely important study of Goethe's correspondence: "Literary historians have obviously extracted the chief benefits that these collections of letters can confer . . . They make possible a literary-historical pragmatism that was previously inconceivable and that in earlier times was neither known nor needed. For . . . desire and the pleasure of peeking through a writer's windows can result only from the author's desire to conceal the writer behind the man, or vice versa. But this effort is particularly characteristic of the modern age and its authors, even though it is as foolish and futile as the attempt to keep political matters a secret."[3] With these words Gervinus introduces his considered project of allowing an image of Goethe, and more especially the old Goethe, to emerge from his correspondence. This is one of the very few exhaustive and penetrating attempts to analyze a corpus of letters, an attempt that is as different from the scholarly industry that followed as it is from the misuse of important collections of letters to underpin a cult of the writer as hero.

But I do not commend this exemplary piece of research to you without reservation. It must not be overlooked that Gervinus published his study five years after Goethe's death, and that he lacked the necessary historical distance for a proper appraisal of the letters. Yet it is this very historical distance which dictates the laws governing our own examination, chief among them that of content: the fact that with the passage of time those distinctions between man and author, the private and the objective, the person and the thing, gradually lose their validity. To the point where it becomes clear that to do justice to a single significant letter, to illuminate it in all of its factual references, its allusions and details, means going to the very heart of the person's humanity. If this humanity does not amount to a striking character, a hero or genius, but instead to something that facilitates communication with his lesser contemporaries, this will merely make it the more noble, creditable, and rich in substance. We do not shy away from saying straight out: the more deeply the historian enters into the past, the more the psychology characteristic of someone like Emil Ludwig in his slick and cheap biographies becomes devalued, and the more the facts, the data, and the names come into their own—an achievement that need be no mere philological accretion, but a true human gain.[4]

What follows are some modest attempts to live up to these intentions.

[The typescript here contains a gap, which was presumably to be filled by a number of letters and the relevant commentaries.]

So much for today. It would give me great pleasure if the few letters that I now lay before you were to whet your appetite for a further series which the *Frankfurter Zeitung* proposes to publish shortly. And it would please me even more if I have managed to convince you that these publications are not intended to gratify either philological ambition or a dubious need for culture, but are meant instead to transmit a living tradition.

Undelivered talk written in late 1931 or early 1932. *Gesammelte Schriften*, IV, 942–944. Translated by Rodney Livingstone.

Notes

1. From April 1931 to May 1932, Benjamin published a series of twenty-seven letters from the period 1783–1883 in the *Frankfurter Zeitung*. The present talk, which may have been intended for radio broadcast, serves as a kind of introduction to the series, which did not bear Benjamin's name.
2. Friedrich Gundolf (pseudonym of Friedrich Gundelfinger; 1880–1931), a disciple of Stefan George, was a prominent literary critic and, after 1920, a professor at Heidelberg. Benjamin was engaged in a long polemic against Gundolf in the Teens and Twenties. See "Comments on Gundolf's *Goethe*" and "Goethe's Elective Affinities," in Volume 1 of this edition.
3. Georg Gottfried Gervinus, *Ueber den Göthischen Briefwechsel* [On Goethe's Correspondence] (Leipzig, 1836), pp. 2–3. Gervinus (1805–1871), a historian,

literary historian, and politician, held professorships at Heidelberg and Göttingen and was a delegate to the German National Assembly in Frankfurt in 1848. His literary history broke new ground in its effort to embed the discussion of literature within a larger historical narrative.

4. Emil Ludwig (1881–1948), German biographer, gained an international reputation for his popular biographies. His biography of Goethe (1925) established him as a writer in the "new school" of biography, which emphasized the personality of the subject.

A Family Drama in the Epic Theater

On the occasion of the world premiere of Brecht's play *Die Mutter* [The Mother].

Brecht has said of Communism that it is "the middle term." "Communism is not radical. It is capitalism that is radical." How radical it is can be seen in its attitude toward the family—as in every other matter. It insists upon the family at any price, even where intensification of family life can only aggravate the suffering already caused by conditions utterly unworthy of human beings. Communism is not radical. Therefore, it has no intention of simply abolishing family relations. It merely tests them to determine their capacity for change. It asks itself: Can the family be dismantled so that its components may be socially refunctioned? These components are not so much the family members themselves as their relationships with one another. Of these, it is clear that none is more important than the relationship between mother and child. Furthermore, the mother, among all family members, is the most unequivocally determined as to her social function: she produces the next generation. The question raised by Brecht's play is: Can this social function become a revolutionary one, and how? In a capitalist economic system, the more directly a person is engaged in production relations, the more he or she is subject to exploitation. Under today's conditions, the family is an organization for the exploitation of the woman as mother. Pelagea Vlassova, "widow of a worker and mother of a worker," is therefore someone who is doubly exploited: first, as a member of the working class, and, second, as a woman and mother. The doubly exploited childbearer represents the exploited in their most extreme oppression. If mothers are revolutionized, there is nothing left to revolutionize. Brecht's subject is a sociological experiment concerning the revolutionizing of a mother. This explains a number of simplifications which are not agitational but constructive. "Widow of a worker, mother of a worker"—here lies the first simplification. Pelagea Vlassova is the mother of only one worker, and for this reason she somewhat contradicts the original meaning of the word "proletarian woman" (*proles,* in Latin, means descendants). This mother has only one son. The one is enough. For it turns out that with this one lever she can operate the mechanism which channels her maternal energies toward the entire working class. Her first duty is to cook. Producer of a man, she becomes the reproducer of his working strength. But there is no longer enough to eat for such reproduction. The son looks with contempt at the food she puts in front of him. How easily this look can wound the mother. She cannot help herself because she does not yet know that "the decision about the meat lacking in the kitchen is not made in the kitchen." This, or something like it, is surely written in the leaflets she goes out to distribute. Not in order to help Communism, but in order to help her son, whose turn it is to distribute them. This is how her work for the party begins. And in this way she transforms the antagonism which threatened to develop between herself and her son into an antagonism against their mutual enemy. This attitude of a mother is the sole suitable form of help—followed here into its true, original housing, the folds of a mother's skirt—that can at the same time acquire a social validity (as the solidarity of the oppressed) which it possessed before only in an animal sense. The road which the mother travels is that from this first kind of help to the ultimate form, the solidarity of the working class. Her speech to the mothers who queue up to hand in their copper kitchenware is not a pacifist one; it is a revolutionary exhortation to the childbearers who, by betraying the cause of the weak, also betray the cause of their own young, their children. And so we see that the mother's way to the party starts first with helping, and comes to theory only afterward. This is the second constructive simplification. The purpose of these simplifications is to underline the simplicity of the lessons they teach. It is in the nature of Epic Theater to replace the undialectical opposition between the form and content of consciousness (which meant that a character can refer to his own actions only by reflections) by the dialectical one between theory and praxis (which meant that any action making a breakthrough opens up a clearer view of theory). Epic Theater, therefore, is the theater of the hero who is beaten. A hero who is not beaten never makes a thinker. "Spare the rod and spoil the hero," to modify one of our forefathers' pedagogical maxims. There is something special about the "lessons" with which the mother occupies herself, as if with commentary on her own behavior, during her times of defeat or of waiting (for Epic Theater, there is no difference between the two): she sings them. She sings, "What Are the Objections to Communism?" She sings, "Learn, Woman of Sixty!" She sings, "In Praise of the Third Cause." And she sings these songs as a mother. For they are lullabies. Lullabies for Communism, which is small and weak but irresistibly growing. This Communism she has taken unto herself as a mother. It becomes clear, too, that she is loved by Communism as only a mother is loved: she is loved not for the sake of her beauty or her fame or her excellence, but as the inexhaustible source of help. She represents help at its source, where it is still pure-flowing, where it is still practical and not false, from where it can still be channeled without reservation to that which, without reservation, needs help—namely, Communism. The mother is praxis incarnate. We see this when she makes tea, and we see it when she wraps up the piroshkis; when she is visiting her son in prison, we see that every single thing she does with her hands serves Communism; and when she is hit by stones and the policemen strike her with their rifle butts, we see that whenever a hand is raised against her it is in vain. The mother is praxis incarnate. This means that we shall find in her not enthusiasm but reliability. Yet she would not be reliable if she had not, at first, raised objections against Communism. But—and this is the decisive fact—her objections were not those of an interested party but those of common sense. "It's necessary, therefore it isn't dangerous"—she'll never accept statements like that. And she has just as little use for utopias. "Does Mr. Sukhlinov own his factory or doesn't he? Well, then!" You can explain to her, however, that his ownership of the factory is a limited one. And so, step by step, she travels along the path of ordinary common sense.—"If you've a disagreement with Mr. Sukhlinov, what has that got to do with the police?" This step-by-step advance of ordinary common sense, the opposite of radicalism, leads the mother to the head of the May Day demonstration, where she is beaten down. So much for the mother. It is time to turn the tables and ask: If the mother leads, what is happening to the son? It is the son, after all, who reads books and prepares himself for leadership. There are four characters—mother and son, theory and praxis—and they regroup themselves; they play a game of change and change about. Once the critical moment arrives when ordinary common sense becomes the leader, theory is only good enough to do the housework. The son must cut bread while the mother, who is illiterate, works the printing press; the necessity of life no longer catalogues people according to their sex. In the workers' room, space is made for a blackboard between the kitchen range and the bed. When the State is turned upside down for the sake of a kopeck, much will change within the family, too; and at that moment the place of the bride, who personifies the ideals of the future, will be taken by the mother, who, with all her forty years' experience, will confirm Marx and Lenin. The dialectic has no need of a far distance shrouded in mist. It is at home within the four walls of praxis, and it stands on the threshold of the moment to speak the closing words of the play: "And 'Never' becomes, 'Before the day is out!'"

Published in *Die literarische Welt*, February 1932. *Gesammelte Schriften*, II, 511–514. Translated by Anna Bostock.

The Railway Disaster at the Firth of Tay

When people first attempted to smelt iron and build steam engines at the beginning of the nineteenth century, that was a very different matter from what happens today when scientists and engineers go about developing a new airplane or even a space rocket or some other new machine. Today we know what technology is. Such scientists and engineers have the attention of the whole world; newspapers inform us of their achievements, and great industrial concerns provide them with money for their research. But as for the men who made those inventions at the turn of the past century and who transformed the face of the earth—the inventors of the mechanical loom or gaslighting, iron smelting or the steam engine—basically the average person had no idea what they were doing, and even they could form no conception of the implications of their own work. It is difficult to call any one of these major discoveries more important than the others. For people in our day, they can scarcely be thought of independently of their applications. Even so, we may say that the most striking alterations to the globe in the course of the previous century were all in some way or other connected with the railway. I am going to tell you today about a railway disaster. Not so much to recount a horrifying story, but rather to put the event in the context of the history of technology and more particularly of railway construction. A bridge plays a role in this story. The bridge collapsed. This was without doubt a catastrophe for the two hundred people who lost their lives, for their relatives, and for many others. Nevertheless, I wish to portray this disaster as no more than a minor episode in a great struggle from which human beings have emerged victorious and shall remain victorious unless they themselves destroy the work of their own hands once more.

As I was thinking about what to say to you today, I went back to one of my favorite books. It is a thick book, with illustrations, dating from around 1840, and is actually full of jokes and fanciful stories.[1] But we can acquire all sorts of curious knowledge from reading about what people in olden times found amusing and entertaining. For example, this book tells the adventures of a fantastic little imp who is trying to find his way about in the cosmos. When he arrives at the planets, he comes across a cast-iron bridge that links the countless heavenly bodies to one another. "A bridge whose two ends could not be glimpsed at the same time and whose piers rested on the various planets led, on a marvelously smooth asphalt surface, from one heavenly body to the next. The 333,000th pillar rested on Saturn. Then our imp noticed that the famous ring around this planet was nothing other than a balcony running entirely around the planet and on which the inhabitants of Saturn strolled in the evening to get a breath of fresh air." Do you see what I mean when I said that, at the time, people did not really know how they should react to technological advances? The latter were not without a comic side in their eyes. In particular, they thought it very funny that when iron buildings were constructed, only questions of form and matters of calculation should be taken into account. It was fitting, therefore, that there should have been a playful dimension in the first buildings of this kind to be built. Building in iron thus began with winter gardens and arcades—that is to say, with luxury buildings. But suitable technical applications were soon discovered, and this gave rise to buildings of a completely new type—constructions that had no precedent in the past. It was not just that they were founded on the new technology; they also satisfied quite new needs. It was at this time that the first exhibition palaces were built, the first covered markets, and above all the first train stations. They were still known then as "iron-railway stations" and they called up the strangest images in people's minds. Around the middle of the century a particularly audacious Belgian painter, Antoine Wiertz,[2] even put in an application to be allowed to paint the walls of these first stations with huge ceremonial pictures.

Before we take a look at the Firth of Tay—the vast, 3,000-meter-wide mouth of the River Tay in central Scotland—let's cast our minds back a little further into the past. In 1814 Stephenson built his first locomotive.[3] But it was not until 1820, when it became possible to manufacture the rails, that the first rail*way* became a possibility. You should not imagine, however, that all this was achieved systematically, step by step. On the contrary, a violent quarrel at once broke out on the subject of the rails. Under no circumstances, so it was claimed, would it ever be possible to provide enough iron for the English rail network—and at this time people thought in terms of a tiny network by today's standards. It would be necessary, according to many experts, to make the "steam carriages" run on granite tracks. Then, in 1825, the first railway line was opened, and even today

"Locomotive No. 1" can still be seen at one of the terminals—and if you were ever to go see it, you would undoubtedly be tempted to think it was a steamroller for smoothing pavement rather than a genuine locomotive. In Europe, on the Continent, they began with quite short stretches of line, over distances that could have been covered just as well by mail coach, or even on foot. You may have heard that the first two German towns to be linked by rail were Nuremberg and Fürth; they were followed by Berlin and Potsdam, and so on. But on balance these developments were regarded largely as a curiosity. When the Medical Faculty of Erlangen University was asked for an expert opinion about the proposed Nuremberg railway, they replied that it should not be permitted under any circumstances. The passengers' brains would be affected by the speed, and even the mere sight of these roaring trains might well cause people to faint. At the very least, it would be necessary to build fences three meters high on either side of the tracks. The second German railway, between Leipzig and Dresden, was the subject of legal proceedings brought by a miller who alleged it diverted the wind from his mill; and when it turned out that a tunnel would be required, physicians again protested on the grounds that elderly people might suffer a stroke as a result of the sudden change in air pressure. What people thought of the railroad in those days can best be seen from the comment of an English scholar, who in other respects was anything but a fool. He said that he could not regard going by rail as a form of travel; in reality, you were just being sent from one place to another, as if you were a package.

In addition to these arguments about the benefits or drawbacks of the railroad, there were also struggles associated with the building process itself. We find it difficult today to imagine the stamina required of these early engineers, or the huge timespans with which they were forced to reckon. In 1858, when they were constructing the twelve-kilometer-long tunnel through Mont Cenis, they calculated that the work would last seven years. It was similar with the bridge over the Tay. In the latter case, there was a further factor to be considered. They had to take into account not just the loads that the bridge had to bear, but also the terrible storms that rage around the Scottish coast, above all in autumn and spring. During the building of the bridge, which lasted from 1872 to 1878, there were whole months when the storms hardly ever ceased, and there were times when work could be done only five or six days in a month. In 1877, when the bridge was almost complete, a gale of unprecedented violence tore two iron girders, each forty-five meters in length, from their stone piers and at one fell swoop destroyed several years' worth of work. All the greater was the triumph, then, in May 1878, when the bridge was opened amid great celebration. Only one warning voice was to be heard, although that was the voice of J. Towler, one of the greatest of English bridge builders.[4] He expressed the view that it would be unable to withstand the storms for long and that people would soon be hearing of the Tay bridge once again.

A year and a half later, on December 28, 1879, at 4:00 in the afternoon, the regular passenger train left Edinburgh for Dundee, crowded with people. It was Sunday, and the six cars contained 200 passengers. Once again, it was one of those stormy Scottish days. The train was due to arrive in Dundee at 7:15 in the evening, but the time was already 7:14 when the signal box on the south side of the bridge announced its approach. I shall recount what happened next in the words of Theodor Fontane,[5] who describes the last that was heard of the train after that final signal. This is a passage from his poem "The Bridge over the Tay":

> It was the train. It chugs past
> the South Tower, the storm in its face,
> And Johnny says, "There's only the bridge!
> But it won't stop us—we'll win the race.
> A stout boiler, a great head of steam
> will carry the prize off in this fight.
> And though it may rage and batter and scream,
> We'll conquer the elements this very night.
>
> The bridge o'er the Tay is our pride and joy.
> It makes me laugh when I think of the past,
> with all of the trouble, the grief, and the woe
> the old ferryboat gave us right up to the last.
> Many and many a dear Christmas Eve
> Have I spent in the ferryman's cottage
> And gazed at our windows, lights burning so bright,
> And couldn't cross over there, wish though I might."
>
> On the northern shore, the bridge watchman's house,
> All the windows gaze out to the south,
> And the watchman's people full of alarm
> Anxiously gaze out through the storm.
> For the wind in furious play seemed to grow
> and down from the skies flames did glow,
> Bursting in glory as they descended
> to the water beneath . . . and all was ended.

There were no witnesses to the events of that night. Of those who were in the train, none was rescued. So to this very day no one knows what happened—perhaps the storm had blown away the middle of the bridge even before the train arrived, and the train simply plunged into the void. At all events, the storm is said to have raged so furiously that it drowned out all other sounds. But other engineers, especially those who actually built the bridge, maintained that the storm had blown the train off its tracks and hurled it against the parapet. It was this that caused a breach in the protective wall, and the bridge collapsed only much later.—So the first sign of the disaster was not the noise made by the falling train, but the flames that three fishermen noticed at the time, without suspecting that they came from the locomotive as it went hurtling down. These three men alerted the station on the south side, but when the latter tried to establish contact with the north station they received no response. The cables had been severed. They then contacted the stationmaster in Tay, who set out at once with a locomotive. He reached the spot a quarter of an hour later. Cautiously he inched the locomotive onto the bridge. He had barely reached the first central pier, about a kilometer out, when the driver applied the brakes so fiercely that the train almost leaped from the track. The moonlight had enabled him to see a gaping hole in the line. The central section of the bridge was gone.

If you look up the *Funkstunde* [Radio Times], you will find a picture of the damaged bridge that appeared at the time in the *Leipziger Illustrierte*. Even though the iron construction is evident at a glance, this bridge still had much in common with wooden bridges. Building in iron was in its infancy, and had not yet become fully confident of its own strengths. Of course, you are all familiar—from pictures, if from nowhere else—with the building in which iron first displayed itself with pride and utter self-confidence, a building which was also a monument to engineering calculation. I am referring to the tower that Eiffel completed for the World's Fair in Paris just ten years after the collapse of the Tay bridge. When the Eiffel Tower was built, it served no practical purpose of any kind; it was simply a landmark—a wonder of the world, as people say. But it was followed by the invention of radio telegraphy, and, at a stroke, the huge construction suddenly acquired a meaning. Today the Eiffel Tower is a Paris radio transmitter. Eiffel and his engineers had built the tower in seventeen months. Every rivet-hole had been precisely positioned in the workshops to within a tenth of a millimeter. Each of the twelve thousand metal fittings, each of the two and a half million rivets, had been machined to the millimeter. There was no sound of chisels on the work site; in the open air as much as in the builders' workshops, thought reigned over sheer muscle power, which it was able to transmit via cranes and secure scaffolding.[6]

Radio talk broadcast by Berliner Rundfunk, February 1932. *Gesammelte Schriften*, VII, 232–237. Translated by Rodney Livingstone.

Notes

1. The book in question is *Un Autre Monde* (Another World), first published in 1844, with satirical-oneiric drawings by the great illustrator Jean Ignace Isidore Gérard, known as Grandville (1803–1847).
2. Antoine Wiertz (1806–1865), a Belgian painter of colossal historical scenes, was lampooned by Baudelaire. See also Benjamin's comments in his *Passagen-Werk* (Arcades Project).
3. George Stephenson (1781–1848), English inventor and railroad pioneer, built and successfully demonstrated the first locomotive, at Killingworth, in 1814. He went on to invent a number of other locomotives and cofounded the locomotive works at Newcastle in 1823.
4. Benjamin surely means Sir John *Fowler* (1817–1898), English civil engineer, who designed the Pimlico Railway Bridge (1860) and, with Sir Benjamin Baker, the Forth Railway Bridge (1882–1890). He was also consulting engineer to Ismail Pasha, Khedive of Egypt.
5. Theodor Fontane (1819–1898), novelist, poet, and essayist, was Germany's greatest realist writer. He wrote his first novel when he was fifty-six. He is best-known in the English-language world for *Effi Briest* (1895).
6. The last two sentences are quoted without attribution from Alfred Gotthold Meyer, *Eisenbauten: Ihre Geschichte und Aesthetik* [Iron Constructions: Their History and Aesthetics] (Esslingen, 1907), p. 93. See Benjamin's *Passagen-Werk* (Arcades Project), F4a,2.

Privileged Thinking

On Theodor Haecker's *Virgil*

Virgil: Father of the West[1] is the title of a book in which Theodor Haecker presents us with the truths, teachings, and warnings from the works of Virgil that seem most relevant to him after the passing of two thousand years. The author, although a Catholic, is a disciple of Kierkegaard, not merely as a theologian but also as a polemicist. And his book must be considered in the light of its polemical intent. Haecker has two chief concerns: the overthrow of the traditional evaluation, which places Virgil in the shadow of Homer; and the demolition of every untheological—or, more exactly, un-Catholic—interpretation of the poet. This dual focus makes the book quite distinctive among the mass of commemorative writing, but it shares with other important works the goal of ascertaining Virgil's proper place beyond Homer, beyond Greek culture in general, and even beyond the realm of pure poetry. The radical nature of the change, undoubtedly the first for several hundred years, can be seen from a glance at any of the literary histories published around the turn of the century. "Virgil," we are told there quite baldly, "was no great poet." In contrast, the various writings that have appeared for the bimillennial celebration bespeak a very positive assessment of the poet, and also emphasize that his greatness is rooted in the religious. Vyacheslav Ivanov writes, for example,

> So what we have in Virgil's narrative of the wanderings and wartime toils of his *pater Aeneas* is not an old-style heroic saga, with tales of fame and suffering that amount to a mythological corroboration of the cult of the hero concerned, but a kind of hagiography reminiscent of Bible stories, inaugurating an endless series of deeds accomplished not by himself but by his successors, and serving as the launching pad for a vast destiny in the light of which the hero sees himself not so much as the enactor of those deeds but as the forerunner of the promised

> salvation and as the instrument of God . . . In consequence of this, Virgil's view
> of history falls historically between the Bible and Saint Augustine's masterwork,
> *The City of God*.[2]

It so happens that these words provide a very useful paraphrase of Haecker's
own basic conception. But the further development of this conception is
linked to a very curious methodology. The majority of the chapters in
Haecker's book bear epigraphs consisting of a Virgilian hemistich. These are
then subjected to a process of interpretation. This means that the analysis
largely becomes an exegesis of specific turns of phrase, or even single
words—which of course can come as no surprise, in view of Haecker's
language-mysticism. No interpretation—let alone a theological interpretation—can proceed without some violence. In order to penetrate to deeper
reserves of substance, it may blast apart the poetic framework, at the same
time allowing the most fruitful unfolding of the text from out of the core
of the word; it can be theological without sacrificing philology. Haecker's
interpretive practice, however, does violence to the text. It blasts apart the
Roman context rather than the poetic one; it violates the philological sphere
so that the words can unfold *ad majorem Dei gloriam*.[3] (If this were the
place to explore Haecker's entire doctrinal system, his ahistorical, idealist
language-mysticism would be a principal focus of attention. Even the present
account cannot afford, in what follows, to ignore it entirely.) Haecker's
mystical approach to interpretation gives his work the character of a tract,
and this accords well with both the elevated language and the authoritarian
assertiveness with which Christian dogmas and dicta are linked to every line
or hemistich. In one instance, the last line of the *Aeneid* is given a Pascalian
twist; in another, the famous "Sunt lacrimae rerum"[4] is made to invoke the
idea of justification. Elsewhere the "richness of Virgil's humanity" is interpreted as the readiness to "venerate the mystery—in other words, to believe
in a divine fate without any abatement of free will and human responsibility." Haecker even goes on to define it further as a double mystery, one that
is fulfilled "by Christianity through the gracious pleasure of the trinitarian
God who is Spirit and life, through the gracious pleasure of the God who
is inscrutable, inaccessible, like the Fates of old, who is obscure not by virtue
of the night but by virtue of the light, who brings suffering not through
whim but from wisdom, and who brings not merely perfect justice but also
the Passion and the flames of love." After further theological reflections, he
reverts to aesthetic considerations: "God is true and good and beautiful; no
sooner does the poet touch the hem of God's beauty, thereby touching also
the hem of the true and the good, than his work instantly acquires something
absolute and immortal." The book undoubtedly contains profounder and
more rigorous statements about Virgil than these. But this does not alter the
fact that Haecker's resolute neglect of any secular—in other words, authen-

tic—philological study of Virgil prevents him from recognizing such theological arguments for what they are: clichés inherited from the aesthetics of Late Romanticism.

We may frequently applaud the invective that Haecker unleashes against the translations of Virgil by Rudolf Alexander Schröder—but there can be no doubt that the latter's "Marginal Notes by a Reader of Virgil," which appeared at roughly the same time as Haecker's book, have chosen a superior approach.[5] Schröder, too, recognizes the importance of *pietas* for Virgil. But he can place it in its rich historical context, and in so doing he develops a novel and fertile concept of syncretism. In addition to everything he has to say about Virgil's importance for posterity, he is able to say something about Virgil's own view of history—unlike Haecker, who quite significantly, but also quite irritatingly, never transcends the sphere of the poet's individual soul, the *anima naturaliter christiana*,[6] and never attains a view of Roman *religio*. Thus, according to Schröder,

> There can be no doubt that a religious view of the world, in which every terrestrial manifestation, all earthly activities, seem to be reduplicated at a scarcely higher level of spirituality, can easily degenerate into crude animism in the vulgar mind, or into a jumble of more or less absurd observances in minds incapable of faith. But behind this we also find an overarching concept of such profundity as can move and inspire whole worlds—namely, the idea that something sacred which commands respect inhabits even the most profane aspects of the phenomenal world . . . The divine service that dedicated wreaths and offerings not just to the *lares* and *penates*[7] but also to boundary stones, the labor of ploughing and sowing, the *genius* of opening and shutting doors, and to many other objectifications of fleeting moments of time . . . may not inspire every person on every occasion with the image of a fully spiritualized or divine universe. Despite this, the world view represented here was an immanent entelechy that was articulated in each and every one of its component parts.

See how dessicated and pallid Haecker is in comparison: "We no longer have any vital interest in the outward practices of the Roman state religion—this is of concern to scholarship alone—nor can we warm to the entire Roman pantheon, which for the most part (aside from the rustic gods) has no more than a poetic importance, a purely external symbolic significance, even in Virgil." And describing the distinction between state religion and piety in the same context, he says: "In the pure spirit there is no possible antagonism between external piety, which is no piety at all, and internal piety, which despises the external one or maligns it; for in the pure spirit everything is *within*, both form and content. In mankind, however, this antithesis is real." The unassuming concept of the "pure spirit," as manifest here, is worthy of note. For it is precisely this concept which is the holder of those curious privileges characteristic of the kind of thinking practiced by Haecker. We have already seen that this thinking is authoritarian. Now, authority is a strange thing. It must be strong and immovable—no doubt. Yet it must also be inviting and captivating. It must be visible from far off—a fortress, if you like, but with a thousand gates. Knowing better is also a mighty fortress, but the knower has the privilege of inhabiting it alone.

In Germany, there have always been many people—nowadays they are particularly numerous—who believe that *what* they know, and the fact that *they* know it, are the key to the situation and that from now on everything will have to change. But they have only the vaguest notion about how to give this knowledge any direction and how to bring it to the people. They imagine you just have to express it, stress it. They are miles away from the idea that knowledge which contains no indication of how it should be propagated is of little use, and that in truth it is no knowledge at all. And if you tell them that every true knowledge always begins by testing its truth historically, that it tries itself out on new people unfamiliar with it, this will simply unnerve them. Nothing is so characteristic of their helplessness, their lack of realism, as the spurious immediacy with which the "pure spirit" inside them addresses itself to "mankind." In their heads "spirit" and "man" have concluded a spectral alliance; and so united, they join together here too. The introduction to Haecker's book contains a perhaps superfluous defense of "mankind" or "the human"—terms that anyway enjoy all the privileges of fashionable phrases. He writes: "There is scarcely anyone who, observing the countless different species of plants and animals and paying particular attention to the differences between them, nevertheless overlooks, or wishes to deny, the fact that there is such a thing as *the* plant or *the* animal, with eternally immutable qualities. Whereas there are people today who appear to believe that there have been radical changes in the nature of mankind in the course of time." For someone schooled in the tradition of scholasticism, as Haecker obviously is, a statement of this kind requires an uncommon freedom from intellectual scruple. For the question whether such species-beings exist—whether they exist *ante rem,* as the Schoolmen put it—was nowhere fought out so bitterly as in the dispute over universals, which nominalists carried on against realists. The fact that the author has chosen to come down so firmly on one side, particularly in this context, will perhaps raise some eyebrows. But only until it is realized what this partisanship achieves on behalf of the above-mentioned privileges. And this brings us back to "mankind" as beheld by the "spirit." "We have to say," Haecker writes further on, "that for the last 2,000 years Western man has had the ascendancy over all other nations and races. What this ultimately means is that it is *in principle* possible for him (regardless of the fact that he has often failed to make use of it in reality) to *understand* all other human beings, and this entails both his actual and possible political domination over them. And what has given him this possibility and this reality is his 'faith'." It is not our fault if the author makes the political implications of his "idea of humanity" so painfully clear—namely, that radically privileged understanding of non-Western man which is characterized by a combination of exploitation and the missionary spirit. The fact is that this is how contraband looks when wrapped in the fine muslin of the pure spirit which travelers take with them to cloud-cuckoo-land.

Theology should be the last place to be such a cloud-cuckoo-land. In fact, there have been theological thinkers, even in our generation, who have declared war against all idolatry of the spirit: Franz Rosenzweig, a Jew, who has done so from a linguistic point of view, and Florens Christian Rang, a Christian, who has done so from the perspective of politics.[8] Now, Haecker of course regards himself as both a politician and a philosopher of language, even if he might prefer not to be known as such. But he must be denied a place in the ranks of authentic theological thinkers in view of the fact that, on the basis of spirit alone, he imagines he can be master of both the philosophy of language and of politics without becoming conversant either with philology or with economics. Of course—and here we see the matter in its proper light—Rosenzweig, and even more clearly Rang, were essentially heretics in their attitudes; they saw no difficulty in advancing tradition by carrying it on their backs, instead of simply administering it in a sedentary way. It is Haecker's very moderation that cheats him of the fruits of his endeavors. For however radical his rereading of the sources, however great the art with which he interprets the texts, what is the use of all that if his mind clings to convention—a convention that is revealed to us here by his amateurish questions about Virgil's meaning for us today. This corresponds precisely to the false immediacy with which spirit addresses itself to mankind. (The great political significance of the doctrine of original sin is that it does away with immediacy and inwardness of this type.)

If Haecker had only managed to arrive at the genuine, mediated form of the problem—namely, what we can learn from the history of Virgil's poem and research on it, at a time when both threaten to come to an untimely end—he would have been able to provide us with proof of his brilliant gifts as a writer, without directing our gaze to his very modest talent as a thinker. There is no lack of models for such a project. If we think of the scholarly austerity with which Bezold has researched the afterlife of the ancient gods in medieval humanism,[9] we shall better understand how much more meaningful it would have been to embed not just Virgil but also Scholasticism in the context of medieval writing, whereas Haecker's formulas basically only repeat those that had once been used to conjure up the image of "Virgil the Sorcerer."

"A humanism emptied of theology will not stand the test of time," the author claims. But to recommend Thomism as a cure for an age whose humanism is intellectually and actually compromised is to take the joke too far. Haecker lives in an ivory tower and spends his time gazing out of the topmost window, belittling things. And the worst of it is that the ground on which this tower has been built is giving way. How otherwise could anyone use the phrase "adventistic paganism" as if it were in common use, while not noticing that the future approaching him and all of us is perfectly "adventistic," even when it is on the march? How could he describe "a merely philological and aesthetic interpretation of Virgil" as "a false approach, an undermining of civilization, carried out by minds themselves undermined," yet find no words for the barbaric conditions to which humanism of every kind is tied nowadays? It is the arrogance and lack of integrity on the part of intellectuals that is to blame for this inconsistency—the same features that allow them to speak of "the spiritual" without blushing and for no other reason than that they are unable to give an account of their own place in the production process. For if they were, an essayist of Haecker's gifts could not avoid the problem of every truly contemporary interpretation of Virgil: the possibility of humanism in our age. And the sight of the privileges which still enable a man to remain a humanist would liberate him from their most calcified accretion: privileged knowledge of the true path—a knowledge that turns out to be the most lethal metamorphosis of cultural privilege.

Published in *Die literarische Welt*, February 1932. *Gesammelte Schriften*, III, 314–322. Translated by Rodney Livingstone.

Notes

1. Theodor Haecker, *Vergil: Vater des Abendlandes* (Leipzig: Jacob Hegner, 1931), 148 pages. [Benjamin's note]
2. Vyacheslav Ivanov, "Vergils Historiosophie," *Corona*, May 1, 1931, p. 769.
3. *Ad majorem Dei gloriam:* "to the greater glory of God."
4. "Sunt lacrimae rerum et mentem mortalia tagunt": *Aeneid*, Book 1, line 461. "Here [in Tyre] as well, there are tears for misfortune, and mortal sorrows touch the heart."
5. R. A. Schröder, "Marginalien eines Vergil-Lesers," *Corona*, May 1, 1931, p. 752.
6. *Anima naturaliter christiana:* "the natural Christian soul."
7. *Lares* and *penates:* tutelary deities in Roman religion. *Lares,* originally gods of the fields, eventually came to be worshiped in the household in association with the *penates,* the gods of the storeroom.
8. Franz Rosenzweig (1886–1929) was a German religious thinker whose magnum opus, *Der Stern der Erlösung* (The Star of Redemption; 1921), made him one of the most influential modern Jewish theologians. After 1922, he was afflicted by progressive paralysis, but pushed ahead with a number of projects, including a new German translation of the Hebrew Bible in collaboration with Martin Buber. Benjamin's friend Florens Christian Rang, a conservative intellectual, had published a book entitled *Deutsche Bauhütte: Ein Wort an uns Deutsche über mögliche Gerechtigkeit gegen Belgien und Frankreich und zur Philosophie der*

Politik [German Masons' Guilds: A Word to Us Germans on the Possibility of Justice toward Belgium and France and on the Philosophy of Politics] (Leipzig: Sannerz, 1924), which included "replies" from a number of well-known figures, including Martin Buber, Alfons Paquet, and Benjamin.

9. Friedrich Bezold, *Das Fortleben der antiken Götter in mittelalterlichen Humanismus* [The Afterlife of the Ancient Gods in Medieval Humanism] (Bonn: Schroeder, 1922).

Excavation and Memory

Language has unmistakably made plain that memory is not an instrument for exploring the past, but rather a medium. It is the medium of that which is experienced, just as the earth is the medium in which ancient cities lie buried. He who seeks to approach his own buried past must conduct himself like a man digging. Above all, he must not be afraid to return again and again to the same matter; to scatter it as one scatters earth, to turn it over as one turns over soil. For the "matter itself" is no more than the strata which yield their long-sought secrets only to the most meticulous investigation. That is to say, they yield those images that, severed from all earlier associations, reside as treasures in the sober rooms of our later insights—like torsos in a collector's gallery. It is undoubtedly useful to plan excavations methodically. Yet no less indispensable is the cautious probing of the spade in the dark loam. And the man who merely makes an inventory of his findings, while failing to establish the exact location of where in today's ground the ancient treasures have been stored up, cheats himself of his richest prize. In this sense, for authentic memories, it is far less important that the investigator report on them than that he mark, quite precisely, the site where he gained possession of them. Epic and rhapsodic in the strictest sense, genuine memory must therefore yield an image of the person who remembers, in the same way a good archaeological report not only informs us about the strata from which its findings originate, but also gives an account of the strata which first had to be broken through.

Written ca. 1932; unpublished in Benjamin's lifetime. *Gesammelte Schriften*, IV, 400–401. Translated by Rodney Livingstone, on the basis of a prior version by Edmund Jephcott.

Oedipus, or Rational Myth

It must have been shortly after the war that we heard about the English stage experiment *Hamlet in Tails.* At the time, this was highly controversial. Here it perhaps suffices to note the paradox that the play is too modern to be modernized. Of course, there have always been periods when similar things could be done without a conscious purpose in mind. It is well known that in the mystery plays of the Middle Ages, the characters appeared wearing the clothing of their time, just as they did in contemporary pictures.[1] But we can be sure that in modern times such an approach must be the product of very precise artistic reflection if it is to be anything more than a snobbish joke. And in fact it has been possible to observe how, in recent years, major—or at least thinking—artists have undertaken such "modernizations," in music and painting as well as in literature. The trend represented by Picasso's pictures around 1927, Stravinsky's *Oedipus Rex,* and Cocteau's *Orphée* has been given the name "Neoclassicism." Now, we have mentioned this name here not in order to link Gide with this trend (he would undoubtedly object to any such procedure, and rightly so), but to indicate how artists of very different kinds came to divest Greek characters of their traditional clothing, or rather to disguise them by clothing them in modern dress. In the first place, they could derive an advantage from harnessing figures for their experiments who were at once familiar to their audience and also remote from contemporary concerns. For all these cases are instances of outspoken constructivist experiments—studio works, so to speak. In the second place, nothing could suit the agenda of constructivism so well as to set up in competition with the works of the Greeks, whose canonical authority as embodiments of the natural and organic had endured for hundreds of years. And in the third place, there is also a covert or open intention involved: namely, the desire to make a genuine test—one grounded in the philosophy of history—of the eternal character of Greek art, which is to say, its constantly self-renewing relevance. With this third consideration the observer finds himself at the very heart of André Gide's latest work.[2] In any event, he will soon realize that the milieu of this Oedipus has its own story to tell. For we hear about Sunday, repression, Lorrainers, decadents, and vestal virgins. The author makes it impossible for his spectators to fasten on any details of locale or situation; he deprives them of the illusion, and with his very first words he calls the stage by its name. In short, whoever wishes to follow him must allow himself to float freely, to take in stride the peaks and troughs of the sea of saga, which has ebbed and flowed for over two thousand years. Only then will he realize what this Greek culture can mean for him, or he for it. And what is it? This is to be found in Oedipus himself—and of all the profound or playful transformations that the saga undergoes at his hands, this is the most curious of all: "But I understand, I alone have understood, that the only watchword that could protect a person from the claws of the Sphinx is 'man.' No doubt a certain courage was required to utter this word, but I already had it in reserve even before I heard the riddle, and my strength was that I wanted no truck with any other answer, whatever the question might be."[3]

Oedipus had known beforehand the word that would break the power of the Sphinx. Gide, too, had known in advance the word that would dispel the horror of the Sophoclean tragedy. More than twelve years earlier, he had published his "Reflections on Greek Mythology," in which he wrote: "'How was it possible to believe such things?' cries Voltaire. Yet it is reason above all—and reason alone—to which every myth turns; no myth has been understood unless it has been accepted by reason. The Greek myths are fundamentally rational, and for this very reason a man may say, without its making him a bad Christian, that they are much easier to grasp than the teachings of Paul."[4] Now it is important not to misunderstand this. Gide does not claim that reason produced Greek myths, nor even that for the Greeks the meaning of myth lay in its rationality. What is important, rather, is how the modern meaning gains a distance from the old, and how that distance from the old interpretation is just a new closeness to the myth itself, from which the modern meaning inexhaustibly offers itself up for renewed discovery. This is why Greek myths are like Philemon's pitcher, "which no thirst can empty while you drink in Jupiter's presence."[5] The right moment is also a Jupiter, and therefore Neoclassicism is able today to discover meanings in the myths that have never been found in them before: construction, logic, and reason.

We must pause here to counter an objection: that explanation has been replaced at this point by a truly vertiginous paradox. Can it be true that on

the very site where the palace of Oedipus stood—the house that was surrounded by unparalleled darkness, horror, incest, parricide, doom, and
guilt—we are asked to watch the temple of the Goddess of Reason be erected
today? How can this be? What, then, has happened to Oedipus in twenty-
three centuries—from the time Sophocles first put him on the Greek stage
to the present day, when Gide has put him on the French stage? Very little.
And what has this little achieved? Much. *Oedipus has learned to speak.*
Sophocles' Oedipus is silent, or nearly so. A bloodhound after his own
blood, screaming with the pain inflicted by his own hands—he utters
speeches in which there can be no room for thought, for reflection. It is true
that he is insatiable in his need to keep repeating the horrific events:

> Incestuous sin! Breeding where I was bred!
> Father, brother, and son; bride, wife, and mother;
> Confounded in one monstrous matrimony!
> All human filthiness in one crime compounded![6]

But it is this very speech that makes him fall silent inwardly; and in the same
vein, he wishes to become like the night:

> Could I want sight to face this people's stare?
> No! Hearing neither! Had I any way
> To dam that channel too, I would not rest
> Till I had prisoned up this body of shame
> That I might be blind and deaf.[7]

And how could he not fall silent? How could thinking ever free him from
the entanglement that makes it impossible to decide what is destroying
him—the crime itself, Apollo's oracle, or the curse that he himself lays on
the murderer of Laius? Moreover, this silence characterizes not just Oedipus
alone, but the hero of Greek tragedy in general. This is why modern scholars
tend to dwell on it. "The tragic hero has but one language that is wholly
appropriate to him: silence."[8] Another writer claims that tragic heroes "tend
to speak more superficially than they act."[9] And a third writes: "In tragedy,
pagan man becomes aware that he is better than his gods, but the realization
robs him of speech, remains unspoken. Without declaring itself, it seeks
secretly to gather its forces . . . There is no question of the 'moral world
order' being restored; instead, the moral hero, still dumb, not yet of age—as
such he is called a hero—wishes to raise himself by shaking that tormented
world. The paradox that genius is born in moral speechlessness, moral
infantility, is the sublimity of tragedy."[10]

It is only from this vantage point that we can appreciate the boldness of
Gide's attempt to endow the hero of tragedy with speech. Now we understand the magnificent words about "fate" that the author wrote in the
above-mentioned essay long before he redeemed them in *Oedipe:* "With this

repellent word, we concede much to chance—more than is merited. The dreadful workings of fate are in evidence wherever we dispense with explanations. I now maintain, however, that the deeper we drive fate back into the myths, the more instructive they are."[11] At the close of Act 2 in Sophocles (the tragedy has five acts in all), the role of Tiresias is at an end. Oedipus has needed two thousand years to reply to him in their great debate, in which he says what he did not even venture to think in Sophocles: "God imposed this crime on me. He held it hidden on my path. The trap into which I was to fall had been set even before my birth, for either your oracle lied or I could not save myself. I was surrounded."[12]

Thanks to this unsought superiority on the part of the hero, we now find that in Gide the satyr-play takes up residence in the precincts of the ancient horror, as it shimmers through from time to time in Creon's words or in those of the Chorus. And never more authoritatively than in the warning that Oedipus gives the children whose conversation he had overheard. A habitué of La Rotonde could not have replied more uninhibitedly.[13] It is as if there lay before him in the inextricable relationships of his household all the domestic miseries of the petty bourgeoisie (magnified on a monstrous scale). Oedipus turns his back on them to follow the trail of the emancipated people who have gone before—that is to say, the younger brother from *Le retour de l'enfant prodigue* [The Return of the Prodigal Son] and the Wanderer from *Les nourritures terrestres* [Fruits of the Earth]. Oedipus is the eldest of the great escapers who take their cue from the man who wrote, "Il faut toujours sortir n'importe d'où."[14]

Published in *Blätter des hessischen Landtheaters*, April 1932. *Gesammelte Schriften*, II, 391–395. Translated by Rodney Livingstone.

Notes

1. Mystery plays were one of the kinds of vernacular drama common to the European Middle Ages (along with the miracle play and the morality play). The plays were usually based on biblical material, such as the Creation, the Last Judgment, or the murder of Cain.
2. André Gide, *Oedipe* (Paris: Pléiade, 1931). Benjamin refers to the German translation by Ernst Robert Curtius, *Oedipus, oder Der vernünftige Mythos*, which appeared in the same year.
3. Gide, *Oedipus, oder Der vernünftige Mythos*, p. 62.
4. André Gide, *Incidences* (Paris: Nouvelle Revue Française, 1924), p. 62.
5. See the story of Philemon and Baucis in Ovid, *Metamorphoses*, Book 8, lines 620–725.
6. Sophocles, *King Oedipus*, in *The Theban Plays*, trans. E. F. Watling (Harmondsworth: Penguin, 1949), p. 64.

7. Sophocles, *King Oedipus*, p. 64.
8. Franz Rosenzweig, *Der Stern der Erlösung* [The Star of Redemption] (Frankfurt: J. Kauffmann, 1921), p. 98.
9. Friedrich Nietzsche, *Werke in drei Bänden*, ed. Karl Schlechta, vol. 1 (Munich: Hanser, 1954), p. 94.
10. Benjamin is quoting himself here. See "Fate and Character," in Volume 1 of this edition.
11. Gide, *Incidences*, p. 81.
12. Gide, *Oedipus, oder Der vernünftige Mythos*, p. 81.
13. La Rotonde was one of the cafés in the Montparnasse district in Paris that was frequented by artists and intellectuals in the 1920s and 1930s.
14. "One must always make a departure, no matter from where." This seems to be a free quote from the preface to André Gide, *Les nourritures terrestres*.

On Proverbs

Let us lay, at the foundation, the image of the women who carry full, heavy vessels on their heads without the aid of their hands.

The rhythm with which they do this is what the proverb teaches.

From the proverb speaks a *noli me tangere* of experience.

With this, it proclaims its ability to transform experience into tradition.

Proverbs cannot be applied to situations. Instead, they have a kind of magical character: they transform the situation. It is scarcely within the powers of the individual to purify the lessons of his life completely by purging them of his particular experience. But the proverb can do this by taking possession of them.

It turns the lesson that has been experienced into a wave in the living chain of innumerable lessons that flow down from eternity.

Jean Paulhan: *Expérience du proverbe.*

Fragment written April–May 1932 or later; unpublished in Benjamin's lifetime. *Gesammelte Schriften*, VI, 206–207. Translated by Rodney Livingstone.

Theater and Radio

The Mutual Control of Their Educational Program

Theater and radio: for the unprejudiced reader, the contemplation of these two institutions will not perhaps evoke an impression of harmony. It is true that the competition between them is not as acute as between radio and the concert hall. Nevertheless, we know too much about the ever-expanding activities of radio, on the one hand, and the ever-increasing problems of the theater, on the other, to find it easy to envisage a collaboration between the two. For all that, collaboration does exist. And has existed, moreover, for a considerable time. They could only work together in the realm of education—so much must be admitted from the outset. But this collaboration has just been initiated with particular energy by Südwestfunk [Southwest Radio]. Ernst Schoen,[1] the artistic director, has been one of the first to take note of the works that Bert Brecht and his literary and musical colleagues have been introducing to public discussion over the last few years. It is no accident that these works—*Der Lindberghflug, Das Badener Lehrstück, Der Jasager, Der Neinsager,*[2] among others—were unambiguously geared toward education. On the other hand, they also represent a highly original combination of theater and radio. These foundations would soon prove viable. Radio plays of a similar kind could be broadcast—*Ford,* by Elisabeth Hauptmann, is one such.[3] In addition, problems of everyday life—school and education, the techniques of success, marriage difficulties—could be debated in the form of example and counterexample. So-called radio-models [*Hörmodelle*]—written by Walter Benjamin and Wolf Zucker—were also promulgated by the Frankfurt-based radio station (in collaboration with Berlin). Such extensive activity provides a welcome occasion for a closer look at work of this kind, and simultaneously helps prevent misunderstandings about it.

But taking a closer look of this sort means being unable to ignore the most obvious aspect of radio—namely, its technological dimension. Here we would be well advised to put all touchiness aside and simply to affirm that, in comparison to the theater, radio represents not only a more advanced technical stage, but also one in which technology is more evident. Unlike the theater, it does not have a classical age behind it. The masses it grips are much larger; above all, the material elements on which its apparatus is based and the intellectual foundations on which its programming is based are closely intertwined in the interests of its audience. Confronted with this, what can the theater offer? The use of live people—and apart from this, nothing. The theater's future development out of this crisis may very well take its lead above all from this fact. What is the significance of the use of live people? There are two very distinct possible answers to this: one reactionary and one progressive.

The first sees absolutely no reason to take note of the crisis at all. According to this view, universal harmony remains intact, and man is its representative. Man is conceived to be at the height of his powers, the Lord of Creation, a personality (even if he is the meanest wage laborer). His stage is modern culture, and he holds sway over it in the name of "humanity." This proud, self-confident, big-city theater is as indifferent to its own crisis as to that of the world outside it (even though its best-known magnate recently abandoned it). And whether it presents dramas of the poor in the modern style or libretti by Offenbach, it will always produce itself as "symbol," as "totality," as *Gesamtkunstwerk* [total artwork].

What we have described here is a theater of education and of entertainment [*Zerstreuung*].[4] Both functions, however opposed to each other they may seem, are merely complementary phenomena in the realm of a saturated stratum which turns everything it touches into stimuli. But it is in vain that this theater attempts to use complex machinery and a vast horde of extras in order to compete with the attractions of the mass-market film; in vain that its repertoire is expanded to include all times and places, when, with a much smaller apparatus, radio and the cinema can create space in their studios for anything ranging from ancient Chinese drama to the latest Surrealist experiments. It is hopeless to try to compete with the technological resources available to radio and cinema.

But not hopeless to debate with them. This is the only thing that can be expected from the progressive stage. Brecht, the first to have developed its theory, calls it "epic." This Epic Theater is utterly matter-of-fact, not least in its attitude toward technology. This is not the place to expound on the theory of Epic Theater, let alone to show how its discovery and construction of *gestus* is nothing but a retranslation of the methods of montage—so crucial in radio and film—from a technological process to a human one. It is enough to point out that the principle of Epic Theater, like that of montage, is based on interruption. The only difference is that here interruption has a pedagogic function and not just the character of a stimulus. It brings the action to a halt, and hence compels the listener to take up an attitude toward the events on the stage and forces the actor to adopt a critical view of his role.

The Epic Theater brings the dramatic *Gesamtkunstwerk* into confrontation with the dramatic laboratory. It returns with a fresh approach to the grand old opportunity of theater—namely, to the focus on the people who are present. In the center of its experiments stands the human being in our crisis. It is the human being who has been eliminated from radio and film—the human being (to put it a little extremely) as the fifth wheel on the carriage of its technology. And this reduced, debarred human being is subjected to various trials and judged. What emerges from this approach is that events are alterable not at their climactic points, not through virtue and decisionmaking, but solely in their normal, routine processes, through reason and practice. What Epic Theater means is the attempt to take the smallest possible units of human behavior and use them to construct what was known as "action" in the Aristotelian theory of drama.

Thus, Epic Theater challenges the theater of convention. It replaces culture with training, distraction with group formation. As to this last, everyone who has followed the development of radio will be aware of the efforts made recently to bring together into coherent groups listeners who are similar to one another in terms of their social stratification, interests, and environment generally. In like fashion, Epic Theater attempts to attract a body of interested people who, independently of criticism and advertising, wish to see realized on the stage their most pressing concerns, including their political concerns, in a series of "actions" (in the above-mentioned sense). Remarkably enough, what this has meant in practice is that older plays— such as *Eduard II* [Edward II][5] and *Dreigroschenoper* [Threepenny Opera]—have been radically transformed, while more recent ones—such as *Der Jasager* and *Der Neinsager*—have been treated as if they were parts of ongoing controversies. This may shed light on what it means to say that culture (the culture of knowledge) has been replaced by training (the training of critical judgment). Radio, which has a particular duty to take up older cultural products, will best do this by means of adaptations that not only do justice to modern technology, but also satisfy the expectations of an audience that is contemporary with this technology. Only in this way will the apparatus be freed from the nimbus of a "gigantic machine for mass education" (as Schoen has described it) and reduced to a format that is worthy of human beings.

Published in *Blätter des hessischen Landestheaters*, May 1932. *Gesammelte Schriften*, II, 773–776. Translated by Rodney Livingstone.

Notes

1. Ernst Schoen (1894–1960), German musician, poet, and translator, was the artistic director of a major radio station in Frankfurt. Just as Benjamin's relationship with Jula Cohn was allegorized in the essay "Goethe's Elective Affinities," so too was Dora Benjamin's with Ernst Schoen. Schoen provided Benjamin with opportunities to present his work on the radio during the 1920s and early 1930s.
2. Works by Brecht. *Der Lindberghflug* is a cantata (with text by Brecht and music by Kurt Weill) based on Brecht's radio play *Der Flug der Lindberghs* (The Lindberghs' Flight), which was later renamed *Der Ozeanflug* (The Flight over the Ocean). *Das Badener Lehrstück* (The Baden-Baden Didactic Play of Acquiescence), *Der Jasager* (He Who Said Yes), and *Der Neinsager* (He Who Said No) are all didactic plays intended for performance by amateur, politically engaged troupes.
3. Elisabeth Hauptmann (1897–1973), dramatist and important collaborator of Brecht's, emigrated in 1933, first to France, and then to the United States.
4. *Zerstreuung* means not only "entertainment" but also "distraction," a sense to which Benjamin turns later in this essay.
5. Benjamin is referring to Brecht's play *Leben Eduards des Zweiten von England* (Life of Edward the Second of England; 1924).

Ibizan Sequence

Ibiza, April–May 1932

Politeness

It is well known that the recognized imperatives of ethics—honesty, humility, brotherly love, compassion, and many others—come off second-best in the daily clash of interests. It is all the more surprising, then, that people have so seldom reflected on the mediating factor that human beings have sought and found for thousands of years. The true mediator, the product of the conflict between morality and the struggle for existence, is politeness. Politeness is neither the one nor the other—neither moral imperative nor a weapon in the struggle—yet it is nevertheless both. In other words, it is nothing and everything, depending on the way it is regarded. It is nothing in its capacity as beautiful appearance [*Schein*], as form, as an agreeable way of enabling us to overlook the cruelty of the conflict raging between the opposing parties. And just as it is anything but a rigorous moral prescription (but merely the representation of a morality that has been annulled), so too its value in the struggle for existence is a fiction (the representation of the fact that this struggle is unresolved). Alternatively, the very same politeness is everything—namely, when it frees itself, and thus the events concerned, from convention. If a negotiating room is entirely surrounded by the barriers of convention, like the lists of a jousting tournament, then true politeness comes into its own, since it tears down these barriers; in other words, it widens the conflict past all bounds, while at the same time granting entry—as helpers, mediators, and conciliators—to all those forces and authorities that it had excluded. Anyone who allows himself to be dominated by the abstract picture of the relationship in which he finds himself with his opponent will never be able to make anything but violent attempts to gain the upper hand in this conflict. He has every opportunity to remain impolite. Whereas an alert openness to the extreme, the comic, the private, and the surprising aspects in a situation is the advanced school of politeness. Anyone who practices this will be able to seize the reins in a negotiation, and ultimately also gain control of the interests at stake. Finally, he will be able to astonish his opponent by manipulating the conflicting elements of the situation as if they were cards in a game of patience [solitaire]. Patience is in any case at the heart of politeness and, of all the virtues, is perhaps the only one that politeness adopts without modification. As to the others, which a godforsaken conventionality imagines could receive their due only in a "conflict of duties," politeness as the muse of the middle way has long since given them this due—that is to say, a real chance for the underdog.

Do Not Seek to Dissuade

Anyone who is asked for his advice would do well to begin by finding out the asker's own opinion and then endorsing it.[1] No one is easily persuaded of another's greater cleverness, and few people ask for advice with the intention of following someone else's. The fact is that they have already made up their minds and now wish to hear it from the outside, to accept it as the "advice" of another. This confirmation is what they seek, and they are right to do so. For it is very risky to set out to implement one's own decisions without passing them through the give-and-take of conversation, as if through a filter. This is why the person who seeks advice is already halfway to a decision; and if what he is planning to do is a mistake, it is better to lend it skeptical support than to contradict it with conviction.

Space for Precious Objects

In the little villages in southern Spain, through open doors whose bead curtains have been gathered to one side, you can obtain glimpses into interiors from whose shadows the dazzling white of the walls stands out.[2] These walls are whitewashed many times a year. And in front of the wall, to the rear, there are usually three or four chairs in a strict symmetrical arrangement. On their central axis, however, rests an invisible pair of scales in which Welcome and Rejection are equally balanced. Much can be gleaned from these chairs as they sit there, unpretentious in form but with strikingly beautiful wickerwork. No collector could hang rugs from Isphahan[3] or pictures by Van Dyck on his vestibule walls with greater pride than the farmer who puts out such chairs in the otherwise bare hallway. Moreover, they are not just chairs. They change their function instantly when a sombrero is hung on the back of one of them. And in this new arrangement the straw hat appears no less precious than the simple chair. In this way fishermen's nets and copper kettles, rudders and clay jars, come together and are ready, as the need arises, to change places and form new combinations a hundred times a day. They are all more or less precious. And the secret of their value is the sobriety, the austerity, of the living space they inhabit. It means that they do not simply occupy, visibly, the spot they belong in, but have enough space to take possession of whatever new positions they are called upon to fill. In the house, which has no bed, there is the rug with which the occupant covers himself at night; in the cart, where there is no upholstery, the cushion you set on its hard planking is precious. In our well-appointed houses, however, there is no space for precious objects, because there is no scope for their services.

First Dream

I was going somewhere with Jula—it was halfway between an ordinary walk and a mountain hike—and now we were getting close to the summit.[4] For some strange reason I imagined I could recognize the top by a very tall pole sticking straight up into the sky and standing out against the overhanging rock wall. When we reached the top, it turned out to be not a peak but a plateau, with a broad street stretching along it and lined with rather tall, old-fashioned houses on both sides. Suddenly we were no longer on foot but instead sitting in a car, next to each other in the back seat (or so it seemed to me), driving along this road. But it may be that the car changed direction while we were sitting in it. I leaned over to give Jula a kiss. She offered me her cheek instead of her mouth. And as I kissed her I noticed that her cheek was made of ivory, furrowed from one end to the other by black, skillfully scooped-out grooves, whose beauty moved me deeply.

The Compass of Success

It is a deeply rooted prejudice that willpower is the key to success. This would be true enough if success concerned only the individual—if it were not also an expression of the fact that an individual's life intervenes in the structure of the world as a whole. An expression admittedly full of reservations. Yet are reservations any the less valid vis-à-vis individual existence and the structure of the world? So we may say that success, which some people so readily dismiss as the blind activity of chance, is the deepest expression of the contingencies of this world. Success is a caprice in the workings of the universe. To this extent, it has very little to do with the willpower that pursues it. And in general what reveals the true nature of success is not the reasons that account for it, but the human figures it affects. These are its favorites, and it makes itself known in them. Its spoiled children—and its stepchildren. This caprice of the universe corresponds to idiosyncrasy in the individual. To account for this has always been the prerogative of comedy, whose justice is the work not of heaven but of countless mistakes that end up producing an exact result, thanks to one last little error. But where can we locate the idiosyncrasy of the subject? In conviction. The sober man who has no idiosyncrasies lives without convictions; life and thought have long since ground them into wisdom, as millstones grind corn to meal. The comic figure, however, is never wise; he is a rogue, a simpleton, a fool, a poor devil. But whatever he is, the world fits him like a glove. In his eyes success is no lucky star, failure no unlucky star. He is quite unconcerned about destiny, myth, or doom. The key to his nature is a mathematical figure that is constructed around the axes of success and conviction. The compass of success:

Success at the cost of abandoning every conviction. Normal success: Chlestakoff, or the confidence trickster.[5]—The confidence man lets himself be guided by the situation, like a medium. *Mundus vult decipi.*[6] He even chooses his name to please the world.

Success in testing every conviction. Genius of success. Schweik, or the lucky devil.—The lucky devil is an honest fellow who wants to please everyone. Lucky Hans changes places with anyone who asks him to.[7]

Lack of success in testing every conviction. Normal failure: Bouvard and Pécuchet, or the philistine.[8]—The philistine is the martyr of convictions of every kind, from Lao-tze to Rudolf Steiner.[9] But for each conviction "only a quarter of an hour."

Lack of success at the cost of abandoning every conviction. Genius of failure: Chaplin or Schlemihl.[10] The schlemihl takes offense at nothing; he just stumbles over his own feet. He is the only angel of peace who is suited to this world.

This, then, is the compass by which to determine all the winds, favorable and unfavorable, that play their games with human existence. Nothing remains but to define their heart, the point of intersection of the axes, the site of the complete identity of success and failure. At this center we find Don Quixote, *the man with a single conviction,* whose story teaches us that in this, the best or worst of all conceivable worlds (except that his world is inconceivable), the conviction that stories of chivalry are true can make a whipped fool happy, if it is his only conviction.

Practice

The fact that in the morning the pupil knows by heart the contents of the book he has put under his pillow the night before, that the Lord inspires His own in their sleep, and that a pause is creative—to make space for such things to happen is the alpha and omega of all mastery, its hallmark.[11] This, then, is the reward before which the gods have placed sweat. For work which achieves only modest success is child's play, compared to the success conjured up by luck. This is why Rastelli's[12] stretched-out little finger attracts the ball, which hops onto it like a bird. The decades' worth of practice that came before does not mean that either his body or the ball is "in his power," but it enables the two to reach an understanding behind his back. To weary the master to the point of exhaustion through diligence and hard work, so that at long last his body and each of his limbs can act in accordance with their own rationality: this is what is called "practice." It is successful because the will abdicates its power once and for all inside the body, abdicates in favor of the organs—the hand, for instance. This is why you can look for something for days, until you finally forget it; then, one day, when you are looking for something else, you suddenly find the first object. Your hand has, so to speak, taken the matter in hand and has joined forces with the object.

Do Not Forget the Best

A man of my acquaintance was at his most well-organized at the unhappiest period in his life. He forgot nothing. He registered his current activities down to the last detail, and if he had an appointment—and he never forgot them—he was punctuality itself. His life's way seemed to have been smoothly paved, and there was not even the smallest crack for time to run out of control. And so matters rested for a while. Then circumstances brought about a change in his life. It began with his getting rid of his watch. He practiced arriving late, and if the person he was going to meet had already left, he sat down to wait. If he had to do something with an object close at hand, he managed to mislay it, and if he was supposed to clear something up somewhere, the confusion elsewhere increased. When he sat down at his desk, it looked as if someone had been living in it. But it was he himself who was building his nest in the ruins. Whatever he did, he made a little house for himself out of it, as children do when they play. Similarly, just as children keep coming across things they have hidden away and then forgotten—in their pockets, in the sand, in a drawer—so it was with his mind, with his entire life. Friends visited him when he least expected them but needed them most, and the gifts he sent, which were not sumptuous, arrived as punctually as if he had the paths of heaven in his hands. Around this time, he liked to recall the tale of the shepherd who one Sunday was given permission to enter the mountain with his treasures, but who also received the mysterious instruction, "Do not forget the best." At this period in his life, he felt quite well. He settled few things and thought of nothing as settled.

Habit and Attentiveness

Foremost among the human capacities, according to Goethe, is attention. But it shares this primacy with habit, which from the outset vies with it for preeminence. All attentiveness has to flow into habit, if it is not to blow human beings apart, and all habit must be disrupted by attentiveness if it is not to paralyze the human being. To note something and to accustom oneself to it, to take offense and to put up with a thing—these are the peaks and troughs of the waves on the sea of the soul. But this sea has moments of calm. There can be no doubt that a person who is wholly concentrated on a thought that torments him, on a pain and its sudden twinges, can suddenly be disconcerted by a barely perceptible noise, an insect humming or flying, that might well have escaped the notice of a more attentive and sharper ear. It might be presumed that the soul can be more easily distracted, the more concentrated it is. Yet isn't this concentrated listening not just the furthest development of attention, but also its end—the moment when it gives birth to habit? That humming or fluttering is the threshold, and imperceptibly the soul has crossed it. It is as if it no longer wished to return to the accustomed world—as if it now inhabited a new world, one in which pain is the quartermaster. Attentiveness and pain are complementary. But even habit has its complement, and we cross its threshold in sleep. For what comes to us when we dream is a new and unprecedented attentiveness that struggles to emerge from the womb of habit. Everyday experiences, hackneyed expressions, the vestiges that remain in a glance, the pulsating of one's own blood—all this, hitherto unnoticed and in a distorted and overly sharp form, makes up the stuff of dreams. In dreams there is no astonishment and in pain there is no forgetting, because both bear their opposites within them, just as in a calm the peaks and troughs of the waves lie merged in one another.

Downhill

The word "shattered" [erschüttert] has been used ad nauseam. So perhaps something may be said in its defense. It will not distance itself from the sensual for an instant and will above all else cling to one fact: that shock leads to collapse. Do those who assure us after every theater premiere or every new book that they were "shattered" really wish to tell us that something inside them has collapsed? Unfortunately, the phrase that stood firm beforehand will also stand firm afterward. How could they allow themselves the pause which is the precondition of collapse? No one has ever felt this more clearly than Marcel Proust did when he learned of the death of his grandmother—an event which he found shattering but unreal, until the evening he burst into tears while taking off his shoes.[13] Why? Because he bent down. In this way, the body is what rouses a profound pain; and it can serve no less to arouse profound thought. Both require solitude. Anyone who has climbed a mountain on his own and arrived at the top exhausted, and then turns to walk down again with steps that shatter his entire body— for such a person, time hangs loose, the partition walls inside him collapse, and he pushes on through the rubble of the moment as if in a dream. Sometimes he tries to stop, but cannot. Who knows whether it is his thoughts that shatter him, or the roughness of the way? His body has become a kaleidoscope that at each step presents him with ever-changing figures of the truth.

Published in the *Frankfurter Zeitung*, June 1932. *Gesammelte Schriften*, IV, 402–409. Translated by Rodney Livingstone.

Notes

1. For a variant of this text, see "Spain, 1932," in this volume.
2. For a variant of this text, see "Spain, 1932," in this volume.
3. Isphahan (Isfahan) rugs, made in Iran, are brightly colored and opulent. Their patterns recall European Renaissance and Baroque decorative motifs.
4. For a variant of this text, see "Spain, 1932," in this volume. "Jula" is Benjamin's friend, Jula Radt, *neé* Cohn, a sculptor and the sister of Benjamin's schoolfriend Alfred Cohn. Benjamin's relationship with her precipitated the crisis in his marriage. The essay "Goethe's Elective Affinities" (see Volume 1 of this edition) allegorizes this relationship.
5. Chlestakoff is the protagonist of *The Inspector General*, by Nikolai Gogol, first published in 1836.
6. "The world wishes to be deceived." The statement is attributed to Pope Paul IV (d. 1559). He added, "So let it be deceived."
7. Schweik is the protagonist of the satirical novel *The Good Soldier Schweik* (1920–1923), by the Czech writer Jaroslav Hašek. In the fairy tale "Hans im Glück," sometimes translated as "Hans in Luck," Hans is persuaded to exchange a piece of silver "as big as his head"—a treasure that cost him seven years' work—for a horse, the horse for a cow, the cow for a pig, the pig for a goose, and, finally, the goose for an ordinary rough stone that is allegedly a grindstone.
8. Bouvard and Pécuchet are the heroes of Gustave Flaubert's unfinished satirical novel *Bouvard et Pécuchet* (published posthumously in 1881), which satirizes the propensity of the bourgeoisie to accumulate knowledge in encyclopedias and museums.
9. Lao-tze, the reputed founder of Taoism. Rudolf Steiner (1861–1925), Austrian-born scientist and editor, was the founder of anthroposophy, a movement based on the notion that there is a spiritual world accessible only to the highest faculties of mental knowledge.
10. See Adelbert von Chamisso, *Peter Schlemihls wundersame Geschichte* (The

Strange Tale of Peter Schlemihl; 1814), the story of a man who sells his shadow in the hope of gaining social acceptability, but who succeeds only in making himself an outcast.

11. For a variant of this text, see "Spain, 1932," in this volume.

12. Enrico Rastelli (1896–1931) was a famous juggler. See also Benjamin's essay "Rastelli erzählt" (Rastelli's Story).

13. The incident is described in Part 2, Chapter 1, of Proust's *Sodome et Gomorrhe* (translated as *Cities of the Plain*).

Berlin Chronicle

For my dear Stefan

Now let me call back those who introduced me to the city. For although the child, in his solitary games, grows up in closest proximity to the city, he needs and seeks guides to its wider expanses, and the first of these—for a son of wealthy middle-class parents like me—are sure to have been nursemaids. With them I went to the Zoo—although I recall it only from much later, with blaring military bands and "Scandal Avenue" (as the adherents of Jugendstil [Art Nouveau] dubbed this promenade)—or, if not to the Zoo, to the Tiergarten.[1] I believe the first "street" I thus discovered that no longer had anything habitable or hospitable about it, emanating forlornness between the shopfronts and even danger at the crossings, was Schillstrasse; I like to imagine that it has altered less than others in the West End and that it could even now accommodate a scene rising irresistibly from the mist: the saving of the life of "little brother." The way to the Tiergarten led over Herkules Bridge, whose gently sloping embankment must have been the first hillside the child encountered—accentuated by the fine stone flanks of the lion rising above. At the end of Bendlerstrasse, however, began the labyrinth, not without its Ariadne: the maze surrounding Frederick William III and Queen Louise, who, rising sheer from the flower beds on their illustrated, Empire-style plinths, seemed as if petrified by the runes that a little rivulet inscribed in the sand. Rather than the figures, my eyes sought the plinths, since the events taking place on them, if less clear in their ramifications, were closer in space. But that a particular significance attaches to this Hohenzollern labyrinth I find confirmed even now by the utterly unconcerned, banal appearance of the forecourt on Tiergartenstrasse, where nothing suggests that you stand but a few yards from the strangest place in the city. At that time, it is true, it must have corresponded more than closely to what was waiting behind it, for here, or not far away, were the haunts of that Ariadne in whose proximity I learned for the first time (and was never entirely to forget) something that was to make instantly comprehensible a word that, since I was scarcely three, I cannot have known: love. Here the nursemaid supervenes, a cold shadow driving away what I loved. It is likely that no one ever masters anything in which he has not known impotence; and if you agree, you will also see that this impotence comes not at the beginning of or before the struggle with the subject, but in the heart of it. Which brings me to the middle period of my life in Berlin, extending from the whole of my later childhood to my entrance to the university: a period of impotence before the city. This had two sources. The first was a very poor sense of direction; but if it was thirty years before the distinction between left and right had become visceral to me, and before I had acquired the art of reading a street map, I was far from appreciating the extent of my ineptitude; and if anything was capable of increasing my disinclination to perceive this fact, it was the insistence with which my mother thrust it under my nose. On her I lay the blame for my inability even today to make a cup of coffee; to her propensity for turning the most insignificant items of conduct into tests of my aptitude for practical life I owe the dreamy recalcitrance with which I accompanied her as we walked through the streets, rarely frequented by me, of the city center. But to this resistance, in turn, is due who knows how much that underlies my present intercourse with the city's streets. Above all, a gaze that appears to see not a third of what it takes in. I remember, too, how nothing was more intolerable to my mother than the pedantic care with which, on these walks, I always kept half a step behind her. My habit of seeming slower, more maladroit, more stupid than I am had its origin in such walks, and has the great attendant danger of making me think myself quicker, more dexterous, and shrewder than I am.

I have long, indeed for years, played with the idea of setting out the sphere of life—*bios*—graphically on a map. First I envisaged an ordinary map, but now I would incline to a general staff's map of a city center, if such a thing existed. Doubtless it does not, because of ignorance of the theater of future wars. I have evolved a system of signs, and on the gray background of such maps they would make a colorful show if I clearly marked the houses of my friends and girlfriends, the assembly halls of various collectives, from the "debating chambers" of the Youth Movement to the gathering places of Communist youth,[2] the hotel and brothel rooms that I knew for one night, the decisive benches in the Tiergarten, the ways to different schools and the graves that I saw filled, the sites of prestigious cafés whose long-forgotten names daily crossed our lips, the tennis courts where empty apartment blocks stand today, and the halls emblazoned with gold and stucco that the terrors of dancing classes made almost the equal of gymnasiums. And even without this map, I still have the encouragement provided by an illustrious precursor, the Frenchman Léon Daudet, exemplary at least in the title of one of his works, which exactly encompasses the best that I might achieve here: *Paris vécu*.[3] "Lived Berlin" doesn't sound as good, but is as real. And it is not just this title that concerns me here; Paris itself is the fourth in the series of voluntary or involuntary guides that began with my nursemaids. If I had to sum up in one word what I owe to Paris for these reflections, it would be "caution." I would scarcely be able to abandon myself to the shifting currents of these memories of my earliest city life, had not Paris set before me, strictly circumscribed, the two forms in which alone this can legitimately—that is, with a guarantee of permanence—be done; and had I not forsworn the attempt to equal the first as firmly as I hope one day to realize the second. The first form was created in the work of Marcel Proust, and the renunciation of any dalliance with related possibilities could scarcely be more bindingly embodied than in the translation of it that I have produced. Related possibilities—do they really exist? They would certainly permit no dalliance. What Proust began so playfully became awesomely serious. He who has once begun to open the fan of memory never comes to the end of its segments. No image satisfies him, for he has seen that it can be unfolded, and only in its folds does the truth reside—that image, that taste, that touch for whose sake all this has been unfurled and dissected; and now remembrance progresses from small to smallest details, from the smallest to the infinitesimal, while that which it encounters in these microcosms grows ever mightier. Such is the deadly game that Proust began so dilettantishly, in which he will hardly find more successors than he needed companions.

The most remarkable of all the street images from my early childhood, however—more so even than the arrival of the bears, which I witnessed by the side of a nursemaid, or it may have been my French governess, and more remarkable than the racecourse that passed Schillstrasse or ended there— was (this must have been about 1900) a completely deserted stretch of road upon which ponderous torrents of water continuously thundered down. I had been caught up in a local flood disaster, but in other ways, too, the idea of extraordinary events is inseparable from that day; possibly we had been sent home from school. In any case, this situation left behind an alarm signal; my strength must have been failing, and in the midst of the asphalt streets of the city I felt exposed to the powers of nature. In a primeval forest, among the giant trees, I would not have been more abandoned than here on Kurfürstenstrasse, between the columns of water. How I reached the mouths of the bronze lions on our front door, with their rings that were now lifebelts, I cannot remember.

Rides to the station in the rattling taxi, skirting the Landwehr Canal at night, while, among the dirty cushions, the weekly evening gathering in the drawing room or the living room of my parents' apartment, which had just neared its end (for a week at least), was revived with stricken violence. And so it was not what impended that weighed so terrifyingly upon me, or even the parting from what had been, but that which still continued, persisted, asserting itself even in this first stage of the journey. The destination of such rides would usually have been Anhalt Station—where you took the train to Suderode or Hahnenklee, to Bad Salzschlirf or—in later years—to Freudenstadt. But now and again it was Arendsee, too, or Heiligendamm, and then you left from Stettin Station. I believe it is since that time that the dunes of the Baltic landscape have appeared to me like a *fata morgana* here on Chausseestrasse, supported only by the yellow, sandy colors of the station building and the boundless horizon opening in my imagination behind its walls.

The fourth guide. Not to find one's way in a city may well be uninteresting and banal. It requires ignorance—nothing more. But to lose oneself in a city—as one loses oneself in a forest—this calls for quite a different schooling. Then, signboards and street names, passers-by, roofs, kiosks, and bars must speak to the wanderer like a twig snapping under his feet in the forest, like the startling call of a bittern in the distance, like the sudden stillness of a clearing with a lily standing erect at its center. Paris taught me this art of straying; it fulfilled a dream that had shown its first traces in the labyrinths on the blotting pages of my school exercise books. Nor is it to be denied that I penetrated to its innermost place, the Minotaur's chamber—the only difference being that *this* mythological monster had three heads: those of the occupants of the small brothel on the rue de la Harpe, in which, summoning my last reserves of strength (and not entirely without an Ariadne's thread), I set my foot. But if Paris thus answered my most uneasy expectations, from another side it surpassed my graphic fantasies. The city, as it disclosed itself to me in the footsteps of a hermetic tradition that I can trace back at least as far as Rilke and whose guardian at that time was Franz Hessel, was a maze not only of paths but also of tunnels. I cannot think of the underworld of the Métro and the North-South line opening their hundreds of shafts all over the city, without recalling my endless *flâneries*.

And then my fifth guide: Franz Hessel.[4] I do not mean his book *Spazieren in Berlin* [On Foot in Berlin], which was written later, but his *Nachfeier*

[Celebration]—the celebration that our walks together in Paris received in our native city, as if we were returning to harbor, the jetty still rising and falling as on waves under the feet of strolling seamen. The centerpiece of this celebration, however, was the "Green Meadow"—a bed that still stands high above the couches spreading all around, on which we composed a small, complaisant, orientally pallid epilogue to those great, sleeping feasts with which, a few years earlier in Paris, the Surrealists had unwittingly inaugurated their reactionary career, thus fulfilling the text that the Lord giveth unto his own in sleep. On this meadow we spread out such women as still amused us at home, but they were few. From beneath lowered lids, our gaze often encountered—better than on drafty stairways—the palms, caryatids, windows, and niches from which the "Tiergarten mythology" was evolving as the first chapter of a science of this city. It prospered, for we had been astute enough to gather to us girls from the most latinate quarter and, in general, to observe the Parisian custom of residing in the *quartier.* True, the *quartier* in Berlin is unfortunately an affair of the well-to-do, and neither Wedding nor Reinickendorf nor Tegel[5] bears comparison on this account with Ménilmontant, Auteuil, or Reuilly. All the more gratifying, therefore, were marauding Sunday-afternoon excursions on which we discovered an arcade in the Moabit neighborhood, the Stettin tunnel, or liberty in front of the Wallner Theater. A young woman, a photographer, was with us.[6] And it seems to me, as I think of Berlin, that only the side of the city that we explored at that time is truly receptive to photography. For the closer we come to its present-day, fluid, functional existence, the narrower draws the circle of what can be photographed. It has been rightly observed that photography records practically nothing of the essence of, for example, a modern factory. Such pictures can perhaps be compared to railway stations, which, in this age when railways are beginning to be out of date, are no longer, generally speaking, the true "gateways" through which the city unrolls its outskirts as it does along the approach roads for motorists. A station gives the order, as it were, for a surprise attack, but it is an outdated maneuver that confronts us with the archaic, and the same is true of photography, even the snapshot. Only the cinema commands optical approaches to the essence of the city, such as conducting the motorist into the new center.

But this vista would indeed be delusive if it did not make visible the medium in which alone such images take form, assuming a transparency in which, however mistily, the contours of what is to come are delineated like mountain peaks. The present in which the writer lives is this medium. And, dwelling in it, he now cuts another section through the sequence of his experiences. He detects in them a new and disturbing articulation. First, his early childhood, enclosing him in the district where he lived—the old or the new West End, where the class that had pronounced him one of its number resided in a posture compounded of self-satisfaction and resentment that turned the district into something like a ghetto held on lease. In any case, he was confined to this affluent neighborhood without knowing of any other. The poor? For rich children of his generation, they lived at the back of beyond. And if at this early age he could picture the poor, it was, without his knowing either name or origin, in the image of the tramp who is actually a rich man, though without money, since he stands—far removed from the process of production and the exploitation not yet abstracted from it—in the same contemplative relation to his destitution as the rich man to his wealth. The child's first excursion into the exotic world of abject poverty characteristically took written form (only by chance, perhaps, one of his first such excursions): the depiction of a leafleter and his humiliation at the hands of the public, who did not trouble even to take the pamphlets he held out to them, so that the wretched man—thus the story ended—secretly jettisoned his entire consignment. Certainly a wholly unfruitful solution to the problem, already announcing the flight into sabotage and anarchism that later makes it so difficult for the intellectual to see things clearly. Perhaps the same sabotage of real social existence is to be found even later, in my manner (already described) of walking in the city, in the stubborn refusal under any circumstances to form a united front, be it even with my own mother. There is no doubt, at any rate, that the feeling of crossing for the first time the threshold of one's class had a part in the almost unequaled fascination of publicly accosting a whore on the street. At the beginning, however, this was a crossing of frontiers not only social but topographic, in the sense that whole networks of streets were opened up under the auspices of prostitution. But was it really a crossing? Is it not, rather, an obstinate and voluptuous hovering on the brink, a hesitation that has its most cogent motive in the fact that beyond this frontier lies nothingness? But in great cities, there are countless places where one stands on the edge of the void; and the whores in the doorways of tenement blocks and on the less sonorous asphalt of railway platforms are like the household goddesses of this cult of nothingness. So on these erring paths the stations became my special habitat, each with its outskirts like a city: the Silesian, Stettin, Görlitz stations, and Friedrichstrasse.

Just as there are, for children, fairy tales in which a witch or even a fairy holds a whole forest in thrall, as a child I knew a street that was ruled and occupied entirely by a woman, even though she was always enthroned in her bay window, one minute's walk from the house in which I was born: Aunt Lehmann. She was the ruler of Steglitzer Strasse. The stairs rose steeply to her room from just behind the hall door; it was dark on the staircase, until the door opened and the brittle voice bid us a thin "Good morning" and directed us to place before us on the table the glass rhombus containing the mineworks, in which little men pushed wheelbarrows, labored with pickaxes, and shone lanterns into the shafts in which buckets were winched perpetually up and down. On account of this aunt and her mineworks, Steglitzer Strasse could henceforth, for me, never be named after the district of Steglitz. A goldfinch [*Stieglitz*] in its cage bore greater resemblance to this street harboring the aunt at her window than that Berlin suburb, which meant nothing to me. Where it joins Genthiner Strasse, it is one of the streets least touched by the changes of the past thirty years. In its back rooms and attics, as guardians of the past, numerous prostitutes have established themselves, who, during the inflation period, brought the district the reputation of being a theater of the most squalid diversions. Needless to say, no one could ever determine on which floors the impoverished opened their drawing rooms, and their daughters their skirts, to rich Americans.

Climbing the stairs in this fashion, with nothing before me but boots and calves, and the scraping of hundreds of feet in my ears, I was often seized—I seem to remember—by revulsion at being hemmed in by this multitude; and again, as on those walks in the city with my mother, solitude appeared to me as the only fit state of man. Very understandably—for such a mob of schoolchildren is among the most formless and ignoble of all masses, and betrays its bourgeois origin in representing, like every assembly of that class in our day, the most rudimentary organizational form that its individual members can give their reciprocal relationships. The corridors, and the classrooms that finally came into view, are among the horrors that have embedded themselves most ineradicably in me—that is to say, in my dreams; and these have taken revenge on the monotony, the cold torpor, that overcame me at each crossing of the classroom thresholds, by turning themselves into the arena of the most extravagant events. The backdrop was often the fear of having to take the *Abitur* again (under more unfavorable conditions),[7] a situation in which I had been placed by my own recklessness and folly. Undoubtedly, these rooms lend themselves to dreamlike representation; there is something nightmarish even in the sober recollection of the damp odor of sweat emitted by the stone steps that I had to hasten up five times or more each day. The school, outwardly in good repair, was, in its architecture and setting, among the most desolate. It matched its emblem, a plaster statue of the Emperor Frederick, which had been deposited in a remote corner of the playground (admittedly one favored by hordes engaged in martial games), puny and pitiful against a firewall. According to school legend, it was—if I am not mistaken—a donation. This monument, unlike the classrooms, was never washed, and had acquired over the years an admirable coat of dirt and soot. It still stands today in its appointed place. But soot descends upon it daily from the passing municipal railway. It is far from impossible that my uncommon aversion to this railway dates from that time, since all the people sitting at their windows seemed enviable to me. They could afford to ignore the school clock that held sway above our heads, and quite unawares they cut through the invisible bars of our timetable cage. They could be seen only now and then, during the breaks, for the lower panes of the classroom windows were of frosted glass. "Vagabond clouds, sailors of the skies,"[8] had for us the same absolute precision that this line of verse holds for prisoners. Moreover, little about the actual classrooms has remained in my memory except these perfect emblems of imprisonment: the frosted windows and the infamous carved wooden battlements over the doors. It would not surprise me to hear that the cupboards, too, were crowned with such adornments, not to mention the pictures of the kaiser on the walls. Heraldic and chivalric obtuseness shone forth wherever possible. In the great hall, however, it was most ceremoniously united with Jugendstil. A crude, extravagant ornament stretched with stiff gray-green limbs across the paneling of the walls. References to objects were no more to be found in it than references to history; nowhere did it offer the eye the slightest refuge, while the ear was helplessly abandoned to the din of idiotic harangues. All the same, one of these occasions is perhaps noteworthy for the effect it continued to have on me for years afterward. It was the leavetaking ceremony for those who had graduated. Here, as in several other places, I find in my memory rigidly fixed words, expressions, verses that, like a malleable mass which has later cooled and hardened, preserve in me the imprint of the collision between a larger collective and myself. Just as, when you awake, a certain kind of significant dream survives in the form of words though all the rest of the dream-content has vanished, here isolated words have remained in place as marks of catastrophic encounters. Among them is one in which for me the whole atmosphere of the school is condensed; I heard it when, having previously received only private tutoring, I was sent for my first morning, on a trial basis, to what was later to become the Kaiser Friedrich School but at that time was still situated on Passauerstrasse. This word, which still adheres in my mind to a phlegmatic, fat, unbecoming figure of a boy, is "ringleader." Nothing else is left of this earliest school experience. It was reenacted in similar form, however, some six years later, when I spent my first day in alien and threatening circumstances in Haubinda[9] and was asked by a tall, hostile-seeming lout who played a prominent part in the class whether my "old man" had already left. This common piece of schoolboy parlance was entirely unfamiliar to me. An abyss opened before me, which I sought to bridge with a laconic protest. Here in the great hall, it was the verses with which the school choir began the farewell song to the leavers—"Brother, now may we / your companions be / in the world so wide"—followed by something containing the words "loyally by your side"; at any rate, these were the verses that enabled me year by year to take the measure of my own weakness. For no matter how palpably the abominable goings-on at school were before my eyes every day, the melody of this song seemed to surround the departure from this hell with infinite melancholy. But by the time it was addressed to me and my class, it must have made little impression, for I remember nothing of it. More remarkable are some other verses that I heard once in the gymnasium dressing room after the lesson, and never forgot. Why? Perhaps because "Schulze"—as the impudent boy who knew the lines was called—was rather pretty, perhaps because I thought them true, but most probably because the situation in which they were spoken, one of frenetic, military hyperactivity, was so utterly appropriate. "Loitering at the rear / you never need fear / neurasthenia."

First of all, let no one think we were talking of a *Markt-Halle* [covered market]. No: it was pronounced *"Mark-Talle"*; and just as these words were eroded by the habit of speech until none retained its original "sense," so by the habit of this walk all the images it offered were worn away, to the point that none of them conforms to the original concept of buying and selling.

If I write better German than most writers of my generation, it is thanks largely to twenty years' observance of one little rule: never use the word "I" except in letters. The exceptions to this precept that I have permitted myself could be quickly counted. Now, this has had a curious consequence that is intimately connected to these notes. For when one day it was suggested that I should write, from day to day in a loosely subjective form, for a newspaper, a series of glosses on everything that seemed noteworthy in Berlin—and when I agreed—it became suddenly clear that this subject, accustomed for years to waiting in the wings, would not so easily be summoned to the limelight. But far from protesting, it relied on ruse—so successfully that I believed a retrospective glance at what Berlin had become for me over the years would be an appropriate "preface" to such glosses. If the preface has now far exceeded the space originally allotted to the glosses, this is not only the mysterious work of remembrance—which is really the capacity for endless interpolations into what has been—but also, at the same time, the precaution of the subject represented by the "I," which is entitled not to be sold cheap. Now, there is one district of Berlin with which this subject is more closely connected than any other that it has consciously experienced. To be sure, there are parts of the city in which it was destined to have equally deep and harrowing experiences, but in none of them was the place itself so much a part of the event. The part I am speaking of is the Tiergarten district. There, in a back wing of one of the houses standing nearest the municipal railway viaduct, was the "Meeting House." It was a small apartment that I had rented jointly with the student Ernst Joël. How we had agreed on this I no longer remember; it can hardly have been simple, for the student "Group for Social Work" led by Joël was, during the term in which I was president of the Berlin Free Students' Union, a chief target of my attacks, and it was precisely as leader of this group that Joël had signed the lease, while my contribution secured the rights of the "debating chamber" to the Meeting House. The allocation of the rooms between the two groups—in terms of both space and time—was very sharply defined, and in any case, for me at that time only the debating group mattered.

My cosignatory, Ernst Joël, and I were on less than cordial terms, and I had no inkling of the magical aspect of the city that this same Joël, fifteen years later, was to reveal to me.[10] So his image appears in me at this stage only as an answer to the question whether forty is not too young an age at which to evoke the most important memories of one's life. For this image is already now that of a dead man; and who knows how he might have been able to help me cross this threshold, with memories of even the most external and superficial things? To the other threshold he had no access, and of all those who once had it, I alone remain. I should never have thought that I would seek him by this topographic route. But if I call to mind the first trial run I made in this direction, more than ten years ago now, the earlier and more modest essay comes off better in the comparison. It was in Heidelberg, during work that I had undoubtedly undertaken so as to forget myself, that I tried to summon up, in a meditation on the nature of the lyric, the figure of my friend Fritz Heinle, around whom all the happenings in the Meeting House arrange themselves and with whom they vanish. Fritz Heinle was a poet, and the only one of them all whom I met not "in real life" but in his work. He died at nineteen, and could be known in no other way.[11] All the same, this first attempt to evoke the sphere of his life through that of poetry was unsuccessful, and the immediacy of the experience that gave rise to my lecture asserted itself irresistibly in the incomprehension and snobbery of the audience, who came to hear it at the house of Marianne Weber.[12] No matter how much memory has subsequently faded, or how indistinctly I can now give an account of the rooms in the Meeting House, it nevertheless seems to me today more legitimate to attempt to delineate the outward space the dead man inhabited, indeed the room where he was "announced," than the inner space in which he created. But perhaps that is only because, in this last and most crucial year of his life, he traversed the space in which I was born. Heinle's Berlin was the Berlin of the Meeting House. He lived at this period in closest proximity to it, in a fourth-floor room on Klopstockstrasse. I once visited him there. It was after a long separation resulting from a serious disagreement between us. But even today I remember the smile that lifted the whole weight of those weeks of separation, that turned a probably insignificant phrase into a magic formula which healed the wound. Later, after the morning when an express letter

woke me with the words, "You will find us lying in the Meeting House"—
when Heinle and his girlfriend were dead—this district remained for a
period the central meeting place of the living. Today, however, when I recall
its old-fashioned apartment houses, its many trees dust-covered in summer,
the cumbersome iron-and-stone constructions of the municipal railway cutting through it, the sparse streetcars spaced at great intervals, the sluggish
water of the Landwehr Canal that marked the district off from the proletarian neighborhood of Moabit, the splendid but wholly unfrequented clus-
ter of trees in the Schlosspark Bellevue, and the unspeakably crude hunting
groups flanking its approach at the star-shaped intersection of roads—today
this point in space where we happened to open our Meeting House is for
me the consummate pictorial expression of the point in history occupied by
this last true elite of bourgeois Berlin. It was as close to the abyss of the
Great War as the Meeting House was to the steep slope down to the
Landwehr Canal; it was as sharply divided from proletarian youth as the
houses of this *rentiers'* district were from those of Moabit; and the houses
were the last of their line, just as the occupants of those apartments were
the last who could appease the clamorous shades of the dispossessed with
philanthropic ceremonies. In spite—or perhaps because—of this, there is no
doubt that the city of Berlin was never again to impinge so forcefully on
my existence as it did in that epoch when we believed we could leave it
untouched, only improving its schools, only breaking the inhumanity of
their inmates' parents, only making a place in it for the words of Hölderlin
or George. It was a final, heroic attempt to change the attitudes of people
without changing their circumstances. We did not know that it was bound
to fail, but there was hardly one of us whose resolve such knowledge could
have altered. And today, as clearly as at that time, even if on the basis of
entirely different reasoning, I understand that the "language of youth" had
to stand at the center of our associations. Nor do I know today of any truer
expression of our impotence than the struggle that seemed the pinnacle of
our strength and our exuberance, even if the shadow of downfall, cast by
the incomprehension of the audience, was seldom more palpable than on
that evening. I think here of an altercation between Heinle and myself on
an evening at *Die Aktion.*[13] Originally only a speech by me entitled "Youth"
had been on the agenda. I took it for granted that its text should be known
to our closest circle before it was delivered. Scarcely had this happened,
however, when Heinle raised objections. Whether he wanted to speak himself, or to impose alterations on me that I refused, the upshot was an ugly
quarrel into which, as always happens on such occasions, the whole existence of each participant was drawn—Heinle's side being taken by the
youngest of the three sisters[14] around whom the most important events used
to gravitate, as if the fact that a Jewish widow was living with her three
daughters represented, for a group seriously intent upon the abolition of the

family, an appropriate base from which to launch an attack. In short, the young woman reinforced her friend's demands. But I was not prepared to yield, either. So it happened that on that evening at *Die Aktion,* before an astonished but less-than-captivated audience, two speeches with the same title and almost exactly identical texts were delivered; and in truth the latitude within which the Youth Movement had to maneuver was no larger than the area bounded by the nuances of those speeches. Thinking about the two speeches today, I like to compare them to the clashing islands in the legend of the Argonauts, the Symplegades, between which no ship can pass in safety and where, at that time, a sea of love and hatred roiled.—Assemblies of bourgeois intellectuals were then far commoner than nowadays, since they had not yet recognized their limits. We may say, however, that we felt those limits, even if much time was to pass before the realization matured that no one can improve his school or his parental home without first smashing the state that needs bad ones. We felt these limits when we held our discussions, at which the younger among us spoke of the brutalities they had to endure at home, in drawing rooms kindly made available by parents who at bottom thought no differently from those we wished to oppose. We felt them when we older members held our literary evenings in rooms at beerhouses that were never for a moment safe from the waiters; we felt them when we were obliged to receive our lady friends in furnished rooms with doors we were not at liberty to lock; we felt them in our dealings with owners of public rooms and with porters, with relations and guardians. And when, finally, after August 8, 1914, the days came when those among us who were closest to the dead couple did not want to part from one another until they were buried, we felt the limits in the shame of being able to find refuge only in a seedy railway hotel on Stuttgart Square. Even the graveyard demonstrated the boundaries set by the city to all that filled our hearts: it was impossible to procure for the pair who had died together graves in one and the same cemetery. But those were days that ripened a realization that was to come later, and that planted in me the conviction that the city of Berlin would also not be spared the scars of the struggle for a better order.—If I chance today to pass through the streets of the neighborhood, I set foot in them with the same uneasiness that one feels when entering an attic unvisited for years. Valuable things may be lying around, but nobody remembers where. And in truth this dead district with its tall apartment houses is today the junkroom of the West End bourgeoisie.

That was the time when the Berlin cafés played a part in our lives. I still remember the first that I took in consciously. This was much earlier, immediately after my graduation. The Viktoria Café, where our first communal jaunt ended at three in the morning, no longer exists. Its place—on the corner of Friedrichstrasse and Unter den Linden—has been taken by one of the noisiest luxury cafés of new Berlin, against which the earlier one, however luxurious it may have been in its day, stands out with all the magic of the age of chandeliers, mirrored walls, and plush comfort. This old Viktoria Café was on that occasion our last port of call, and we doubtless reached it a depleted group. It must have been more than half empty—at any rate I can discern, through the veils that mask the image today, no one apart from a few whores, who seemed to have the spacious café to themselves. We did not stay long, and I do not know whether I paid the Viktoria Café, which must have disappeared soon after, a second visit. The time had not yet arrived when the frequenting of cafés was a daily need, and it can hardly have been Berlin that fostered this vice in me, however well the vice later adapted itself to the establishments of that city, which leads far too strenuous and deliberate a life of pleasure to know real coffeehouses. Our first café, accordingly, was more a strategic base than a place of siesta. And I have thus unmistakably revealed its name: as is well known, the headquarters of bohemians until the onset of the war was the old West End Café. It was in this café that we sat together in those very first August days, choosing among the barracks that were being stormed by the rush of volunteers. We decided on the cavalry on Belle-Alliance Strasse, where I duly appeared on one of the following days, no spark of martial fervor in my breast. Yet however reserved I may have been in my thoughts, which were concerned only with securing a place among friends in the inevitable conscription, one of the bodies jammed in front of the barracks gates was mine. Admittedly only for two days: on August 8 came the event that was to banish for long afterward both the city and the war from my mind. I often saw Heinle in the West End Café. We usually met there late, about twelve. I cannot say that we had close relations with the literary Bohemia whose days, or nights, were spent there; we were a self-contained group, the world of our "movement" was different from that of the emancipated people around us, and contacts with them were only fleeting. A mediator between the two sides for a period was Franz Pfemfert, editor of *Die Aktion;* our relations with him were purely Machiavellian. Else Lasker-Schüler once drew me to her table; Wieland Herzfelde, then a young student, was to be seen there, as well as Simon Guttmann, to whom I shall return;[15] but the list here reaches the boundaries of our narrower world. I believe we were alien to the café; the feverish concentration induced by concern with so many rival actions, the organization of the Free Students' Union and the development of the debating chambers, the elaboration of our speeches in large assemblies of students, help for comrades in need, care for those imperiled by entanglements either of friendship or of love—all this set us apart from the sated, self-assured bohemians around us. Heinle was more closely acquainted with one or another of them, such as the painter Meidner,[16] who sketched him; but this connection remained unfruitful for us. Then, one day in Switzerland,

I read that the West End Café had been closed. I had never been much at home in it. At that time I did not yet possess that passion for waiting without which one cannot thoroughly appreciate the charm of a café. And if I see myself waiting one night amid tobacco smoke on the sofa that encircled one of the central columns, it was no doubt in feverish expectation of the outcome of some negotiation at the debating chamber, or of one of the mediators who were brought into play when tensions had once again reached an unbearable pitch. I came to be on much more intimate terms with the neighboring café, which had its beginning during the period I now refer to. This was the Princess Café. In an attempt to develop a "Physiology of Coffeehouses," one's first and most superficial classification would be into professional and recreational establishments. If, however, one leaves aside the most brazen entertainment places run along industrial lines, it becomes very noticeable that in the development of most hostelries the two functions coincide. A particularly telling example is the history of the Romanische Café from exactly the moment when the proprietor of the West End Café evicted his clientele. Very soon the Romanische Café accommodated the bohemians, who, in the years immediately after the war, were able to feel themselves masters of the house. The legendary, now-departed waiter Richard, distributor of newspapers—a hunchback who on account of his bad reputation enjoyed high esteem in these circles—was the symbol of their dominance. When the German economy began to recover, the bohemian contingent visibly lost the threatening nimbus that had surrounded them in the era of the Expressionist revolutionary manifestos. The bourgeois revised his relationship to the inmates of the Café Megalomania (as the Romanische Café soon came to be called), and found that everything was back to normal. At this moment the physiognomy of the Romanische Café began to change. The "artists" withdrew into the background, to become more and more a part of the furniture, while the bourgeois, represented by stock-exchange speculators, managers, film and theater agents, literary-minded clerks, began to occupy the place—as a site of relaxation. For one of the most elementary and indispensable diversions of the citizen of a great metropolis, wedged, day in, day out, in the structure of his office and family amid an infinitely variegated social environment, is to plunge into another world, the more exotic the better. Hence the bars haunted by artists and criminals. The distinction between the two, from this point of view, is slight. The history of the Berlin coffeehouses is largely that of different strata of the public, those who first conquered the floor being obliged to make way for others gradually pressing forward, and thus to ascend the stage.

Such a stage, for Heinle and me, was the Princess Café, which we were in the habit of patronizing as occupants of "private boxes." The latter phrase should be taken almost literally, for this café, designed by Lucian Bernhard, an interior decorator and poster artist much in demand at that time, offered its visitors an abundance of snug recesses, standing historically midway between the *chambres séparées* and the coffee parlors. The profession primarily served by this establishment is therefore clear. And when we visited it, indeed made it for a time our regular meeting place, it was certainly on account of the *cocottes*. Heinle wrote "Princess Café" at that time. "Doors draw coolness over through the song." We had no intention of making acquaintances in this café. On the contrary—what attracted us here was being enclosed in an environment that isolated us. Every distinction between us and the literary coteries of the city was welcome to us. This one, to be sure, more so than all others. And that certainly had to do with the *cocottes*. But this leads into a subterranean stratum of the Youth Movement, reached by way of an artist's studio in Halensee, to which we shall return. It is quite possible that Simon Guttmann, its occupant, met us here, too, from time to time. I have no recollection of it, just as in general, here more than elsewhere, the human figures recede before the place itself. None of them is as vividly present to me as a forlorn, approximately circular chamber in the upper story, hung with violet drapery and illuminated with a violet glow, in which many seats were always empty, while on others couples took up as little space as possible. I called this amphitheater the "anatomy school." Later, when this epoch was long since closed, I sat long evenings there, close to a jazz band, discreetly consulting sheets and slips of paper, writing my *Ursprung des deutschen Trauerspiels* [Origin of the German Trauerspiel]. When one day a new "renovation" set in, turning the Princess Café into Café Stenwyk, I gave up. Today it has sunk to the level of a beerhouse.

Never again has music possessed so dehumanized and shameless a quality as that of the two brass bands that tempered the flood of people surging torpidly along "Scandal Avenue" between the café restaurants of the Zoo. Today I perceive what gave this flow its elemental force. For the city dweller there was no higher school of flirtation than this, surrounded by the sandy precincts of gnus and zebras, the bare trees and clefts where vultures and condors nested, the stinking enclosures of wolves, and the hatcheries of pelicans and herons. The calls and screeches of these animals mingled with the noise of drums and percussion. This was the air in which the glance of a boy fell for the first time on a passing girl, while he talked all the more zealously to his friend. And such were his efforts to betray himself neither by his eyes nor his voice that he saw nothing of her.

At that time the Zoological Garden still had an entrance by the Lichtenstein Bridge. Of the three gates it was the least frequented, and gave access to the park's most deserted area: an avenue that, with the milk-white orbs of its candelabras, resembled some deserted promenade at Wiesbaden or Pyrmont.

And before the economic crisis had so depopulated these resorts that they seemed more ancient than Roman spas, this dead corner of the Zoological Garden was an image of what was to come, a prophesying place. It must be considered certain that there are such places; indeed, just as there are plants that primitive peoples claim confer the power of clairvoyance, so there are places endowed with such power: they may be deserted promenades, or treetops, particularly in towns, seen against walls, railway crossings, and above all the thresholds that mysteriously divide the districts of a town. The Lichtenstein gate was really such a threshold, between the two West End parks. It was as if in both, at the point where they were nearest, life paused. And this daily desertion was the more keenly felt by one who remembered the dazzling approach to be seen on festal nights for a number of years from a doorway of the Adler ballrooms, which has fallen now into just such disuse as has this long-closed gate.

How totally unlike this (the music at the Zoo) was some other park music that had begun to reach my ears at an earlier time. It came from Rousseau Island and drove the skaters looping and whirling on New Lake. I was among them long before I had any conception of the source of the island's name, not to mention the difficulty of Rousseau's style. Through its position this skating rink was comparable to no other, and still more by virtue of its life through the seasons. For what did summer make of the rest? Tennis courts. But here, under the overhanging branches of the trees along the bank, stretched a lake connected to labyrinthine waterways, and now one skated under the little arched bridges where in summer one had leaned on balustrades, or on chains held by lions' mouths, watching the boats gliding on the dark water. There were serpentine paths near the lake and, above all, the tender retreats of lonely old men, benches for "adults only" at the edge of the sand pit with its ditches, where toddlers dig or stand absorbed in thought until bumped by a playmate or roused by the voice of a nursemaid from the bench of command. There she sits, stern and studious, reading her novel and keeping the child in check while hardly raising an eyelid, until, her labor done, she changes places with the nurse at the other end of the bench, who is holding the baby between her knees and knitting. Old, solitary men found their way here, paying due honor—amid these scatterbrained womenfolk, among the shrieking children—to the serious side of life: the newspaper. Even if the girl I loved, after long tarrying on the paths of this garden, had left at last, there was nowhere I liked better to think of her than while sitting on a backless bench in one of those playgrounds, and I never swept the sand from where I was going to sit down. All these images I have preserved. But none would bring back New Lake and a few hours of my childhood so vividly as to hear once more the bars of music to which my feet, heavy with their skates after a lone excursion across the bustling ice, touched the familiar planks and stumbled past the chocolate-dispensing machines, and past the more splendid one with a hen laying candy-filled eggs, through the doorway behind which glowed the anthracite stove, to the bench where you now savored for a while the weight of the metal blades strapped to your feet, which did not yet reach the ground, before resolving to unbuckle them. If you then slowly rested one calf on the other knee and unfastened the skate, it was as if in its place you had suddenly grown wings, and you went out with steps that nodded to the frozen ground.

Language has unmistakably made plain that memory is not an instrument for exploring the past but its theater.[17] It is the medium of past experience, just as the earth is the medium in which dead cities lie buried. He who seeks to approach his own buried past must conduct himself like a man digging. This determines the tone and bearing of genuine reminiscences. They must not be afraid to return again and again to the same matter; to scatter it as one scatters earth, to turn it over as one turns over soil. For the matter itself is merely a deposit, a stratum, which yields only to the most meticulous examination what constitutes the real treasure hidden within the earth: the images, severed from all earlier associations, that stand—like precious fragments or torsos in a collector's gallery—in the sober rooms of our later insights. True, for successful excavations a plan is needed. Yet no less indispensable is the cautious probing of the spade in the dark loam, and it is to cheat oneself of the richest prize to preserve as a record merely the inventory of one's discoveries, and not this dark joy of the place of the finding, as well. Fruitless searching is as much a part of this as succeeding, and consequently remembrance must not proceed in the manner of a narrative or still less that of a report, but must, in the strictest epic and rhapsodic manner, assay its spade in ever-new places, and in the old ones delve to ever-deeper layers.

It is true that countless façades of the city stand exactly as they stood in my childhood. Yet I do not encounter my childhood in their contemplation. My gaze has brushed them too often since; too often they have been the decor and theater of my walks and concerns. And the few exceptions to this rule—above all, St. Matthew's Church on St. Matthew's Square—are perhaps only apparently so. For did I as a child really frequent the remote corner where it stands? Did I even know it? I cannot tell. What it says to me today it owes solely to the edifice itself: the church with the two pointed, gabled roofs over its two side aisles, and the yellow-and-ocher brick of which it is built. It is an old-fashioned church, of which the same is true of many an old-fashioned building: although they were not young with us and perhaps did not even know us when we were children, they have much knowledge of our childhood, and for this we love them. But I should confront myself at that age in quite a different way had I the courage to enter a certain front door that I have passed thousands upon thousands of times. A front door in the old West End. True, my eyes no longer see it, or the façade of the house. My soles would doubtless be the first to send me word, once I had closed the door behind me, that they had discovered in me myself the distance and the number of steps I had to cross on the stairs, that on this worn staircase they trod in ancient tracks, and if I no longer cross the threshold of that house it is for fear of an encounter with this stairway interior, which has conserved in seclusion the power to recognize me that the façade lost long ago. For with its colored windows it has stayed the same, even if within the living quarters all is changed. Bleak verses filled the intervals between our heartbeats, when we paused exhausted on the landing between floors. They glimmered or shone from a pane in which, like a Raphael Madonna, a woman with nut-brown eyebrows floated aloft with a goblet from a niche, and while the straps of my satchel cut into my shoulders I was forced to read, "Industry adorns the burgher; blessedness is toil's reward." Outside, it may have been raining. One of the colored windows was open, and to the drumming of the rain the upward march resumed.

Epigraph: O brown-baked column of victory
        With children's sugar from the winter days.

I never slept on the street in Berlin. I saw sunset and dawn, but between the two I found myself a shelter. Only those for whom poverty or vice turns the city into a landscape in which they stray from dark till sunrise know it in a way denied to me. I always found quarters, even though sometimes tardy and also unknown ones that I did not revisit and where I was not alone. If I paused thus late in a doorway, my legs had become entangled in the ribbons of the streets, and it was not the cleanest of hands that freed me.

Reminiscences, even extensive ones, do not always amount to an autobiography. And these quite certainly do not, even for the Berlin years that I am exclusively concerned with here. For autobiography has to do with time, with sequence and what makes up the continuous flow of life. Here, I am talking of a space, of moments and discontinuities. For even if months and years appear here, it is in the form they have at the moment of commemoration. This strange form—it may be called fleeting or eternal—is in neither case the stuff that life is made of. And this is shown not so much by the role that my own life plays here, as by that of the people closest to me in Berlin—whoever and whenever they may have been. The atmosphere of the city that is here evoked allots them only a brief, shadowy existence. They steal along its walls like beggars, appear wraithlike at windows, to vanish again, sniff at thresholds like a *genius loci,* and even if they fill whole neighborhoods with their names, it is as a dead man's name fills his gravestone. Noisy, matter-of-fact Berlin, the city of work and the metropolis of business, nevertheless has more—not less—than some other cities of those places and moments when it bears witness to the dead, shows itself full of dead; and the obscure awareness of these moments, these places, perhaps more than anything else, confers on childhood memories a quality that makes them at once as evanescent and as alluringly tormenting as half-forgotten dreams. For childhood, knowing no preconceived opinions, has none about life. It is as dearly attached (though with just as strong reservations) to the realm of the dead—where it juts into that of the living—as to life itself. How far a child has access to the past is difficult to tell, and depends on many things—time, environment, the child's nature and education. The limitation of my own feeling for the Berlin that is not circumscribed by a few facts about the Stratau Fair and King Frederick in 1848—that is, for the topographic tradition representing the connection with the dead of this ground—results entirely from the fact that neither of my parents' families was native to Berlin. This sets a limit to the child's memory—and it is this limit, rather than childhood experience itself, that is manifest in what follows. Wherever this boundary may have been drawn, however, the second half of the nineteenth century certainly lies within it, and to it belong the following images, not in the manner of general representations, but of images that, according to the teachings of Epicurus, constantly detach themselves from things and determine our perception of them.[18]

Behind us lay the forecourt, with its dangerous, heavy swinging-doors on their whiplash springs. We were now walking on the flagstones, which were slippery with fish water or swill and where you could so easily lose your footing on carrots or lettuce leaves. Behind wire partitions, each bearing a number, were ensconced the ponderous ladies, priestesses of Venal Ceres, purveyors of all the fruits of field and tree and of all edible birds, fishes, and mammals, procuresses, untouchable wool-clad colossi exchanging vibrant signs from booth to booth with a flash of their large mother-of-pearl buttons or a slap on their booming black aprons or their money-filled pouches. Didn't the earth bubble and seethe below the hems of their skirts, and wasn't this truly fertile ground? Didn't a god of the market himself cast the goods into their laps? Berries, crustaceans, mushrooms, chunks of meat and cabbage, invisibly cohabiting with the people who abandoned themselves as they languidly and mutely eyed the unsteady procession of housewives who, laden with baskets and bags, laboriously drove their brood before them along these slippery alleyways of ill repute. But when, in winter, the gas lamps went on in the early evening, you at once had a feeling of sinking, becoming aware, in this gentle gliding, of the ocean depths that heaved opaque and sluggish below the glassy surface of the waters.

The more frequently I return to these memories, the less fortuitous it seems to me how slight a role is played in them by people: I think of an afternoon in Paris to which I owe insights into my life that came in a flash, with the force of an illumination. It was on this very afternoon that my biographical relationships to people, my friendships and comradeships, my passions and love affairs, were revealed to me in their most vivid and hidden intertwinings. I tell myself it had to be in Paris, where the walls and quays, the asphalt surfaces, the collections and the rubbish, the railings and the squares, the arcades and the kiosks, teach a language so singular that our relations to people attain, in the solitude encompassing us in our immersion in that world of things, the depths of a sleep in which the dream image waits to show the people their true faces. I wish to write of this afternoon because it made so apparent what kind of regimen cities keep over imagination, and why the city—where people make the most ruthless demands on one another, where appointments and telephone calls, sessions and visits, flirtations and the struggle for existence grant the individual not a single moment of contemplation—indemnifies itself in memory, and why the veil it has covertly woven out of our lives shows images of people less often than those of the sites of our encounters with others or ourselves. Now, on the afternoon in question I was sitting inside the Café des Deux Magots in Saint-Germain-des-Prés, where I was waiting—I forget for whom. Suddenly, and with compelling force, I was struck by the idea of drawing a diagram of my life, and knew at the same moment exactly how it was to be done. With a very simple question I interrogated my past life, and the answers were inscribed, as if of their own accord, on a sheet of paper that I had with me. A year or two later, when I lost this sheet, I was inconsolable. I have never since been able to restore it as it arose before me then, resembling a series of family trees. Now, however, reconstructing its outline in thought without directly reproducing it, I would instead speak of a labyrinth. I am concerned here not with what is installed in the chamber at its enigmatic center, ego or fate, but all the more with the many entrances leading into the interior. These entrances I call "primal acquaintances"; each of them is a graphic symbol of my acquaintance with a person whom I met not through other people but through neighborhood, family relationships, school comradeship, mistaken identity, companionship on travels, or other such—hardly numerous—situations. So many primal relationships, so many entrances to the maze. But since most of them—at least those that remain in our memory—for their part open up new acquaintances, relations to new people, after a time they branch off these corridors (the male may be drawn to the right, the female to the left). Whether cross-connections are finally established between these systems also depends on the intertwinements of our path through life. More important, however, are the astonishing insights that a study of this plan provides into the differences among individual lives. What part is played in the primal acquaintanceships of different people's lives by profession and school, family and travel? And above all: Is the formation of the many offshoots governed in individual existence by hidden laws? Which ones start early in life, and which ones start late? Which are continued to the end of life, and which peter out? "If a man has character," says Nietzsche, "he will have the same experience over and over again."[19] Whether or not this is true on a large scale, on a small one there are perhaps paths that lead us again and again to people who have one and the same function for us: passageways that always, in the most diverse periods of life, guide us to the friend, the betrayer, the beloved, the pupil, or the master. This is what the sketch of my life revealed to me as it took shape before me on that Paris afternoon. Against the background of the city, the people who had surrounded me drew close together to form a figure. It was many years earlier, I believe at the beginning of the war, that in Berlin, against the background of the people then closest to me, the world of things contracted to a symbol similarly profound. It was an emblem of four rings. This takes me to one of the old Berlin houses on Kupfergraben. With their plain, genteel façades and their wide hallways, they may have stemmed from the Schinkel period.[20] In one of them lived at that time a prominent antique dealer. He had no display window. You had to go into his apartment to admire, in a number of showcases, a selection of prehistoric brooches and clasps, Lombard earrings, Late Roman neck chains, medieval coins, and many similar valuables. How my friend A.C. had tracked him down I do not know.[21] But I remember distinctly the engrossment with which, under the impression of Alois Riegl's *Die spätrömische Kunst-Industrie*,[22] which I had recently studied, I contemplated the sheet-gold breastplates and garnet-studded bracelets. There were, if I am not mistaken, three of us: my friend, his fiancée at that time or Frau Dorothea J., and me. C. asked to see rings—Greek and Renaissance cameos, rings from the imperial period, work usually carved in semiprecious stone. Each of the four that he finally purchased is imprinted unforgettably on my mind. Except for one that I have lost sight of, they are still today with those for whom they were intended that morning. One, a bright-yellow smoky topaz, was chosen by Dorothea J. The workmanship was Grecian and depicted in a tiny space Leda receiving the swan between her parted thighs. It was most graceful. I was less able to admire the amethyst that the donor, Ernst S.,[23] selected for our mutual friend: a fifteenth- or sixteenth-century Italian had carved a profile in it which Lederer[24] claimed was that of Pompey. I was quite differently affected, however, by the last two rings. One was intended for me, but only as a very temporary owner; it was really destined to reach, through me, my then fiancée, Grete R.[25] It was the most fascinating ring I have ever seen. Cut in a dark, solid garnet, it portrayed Medusa's head. It was a work from the Roman imperial period. The proustite mounting was not the original. Worn on the finger, the ring seemed merely the most perfect of signet rings. You entered its secret only by taking it off and contemplating the head against the light. As the different strata of the garnet were unequally translucent, and the thinnest so transparent that it glowed with rose hues, the somber bodies of the snakes seemed to rise above the two deep, glowing eyes, which looked out from a face that, in the purple-black portions of the cheeks, receded once more into the night. Later I tried more than once to stamp a seal with this stone, but it proved easy to crack and in need of the utmost care. Shortly after giving it away, I broke off my relationship with its new owner. My heart had already gone with the last of the four rings, which the giver had reserved for his sister. And certainly this girl was the true center of the circle's fate, though years were to elapse before we realized it. For apart from her beauty—itself not dazzling, but inconspicuous and without luster—she had nothing that seemed to destine her for center stage. And in fact she was the center never of people but, in the strictest sense, of fates, as if her plantlike passivity and inertia had arranged the latter—which, of all human things, seem the most subject to vegetal laws—concentrically about her. Many years were needed before what at that time was in part beginning to unfold in its seed, and in part still dormant, emerged in its ramifications to the light of day: the fate by virtue of which she, who had a relationship with her brother that by its tenderness filled to the very edge the capacities of sisterly love, was to form a liaison with her brother's two closest friends—with the recipient of the ring depicting the head of Pompey and with me—and ultimately find her husband in the brother of the woman who married her own brother as her second husband.[26] She it was, on the day I am speaking of, who received from me the ring with the Medusa's head. It cannot have been many days later that I sent—after the lapis lazuli with the lute wreathed in foliage engraved in it, after the fourth ring and to its wearer—this sonnet: "To your finger constantly encircled [text breaks off]

The treasure-dispensing giant in the green pine forest[27] or the fairy who grants one wish—they appear to each of us at least once in a lifetime. But only Sunday's children remember the wish they made, and so it is only a few who recognize its fulfillment in their own lives. I know of such a wish that was fulfilled for me, and would not claim it to be any wiser than those of children in fairy tales. It goes back to my early childhood, and arose in me in connection with the lamp that on dark winter mornings at half past six was carried through my doorway and cast the shadow of our nursemaid on the ceiling. The fire was lit in the stove, and soon, amid reddish reflections, the grating was marked out on the bare floor. When the temperature—the night warmth from my bed and the morning warmth from the fire—had made me doubly drowsy, it was time to get up. Then I had no other wish than to finish my sleep. This wish accompanied me throughout the whole of my schooldays. Its inseparable attendant, however, was fear of being late. I can still feel today, when I pass the Savignyplatz, the dread with which, stepping into Carmerstrasse, where I lived, I read my judgment in the spellbound space between the ten and the twelve on the repulsive clock-face. The wish that animated me on such winter days, and even later, when, in an extremity of fatigue, I rose from the couch in the afternoon because of a gymnastics class, had been fulfilled. Only I did not always recognize this fulfillment when yet another of my attempts to find a professional "place," in the bourgeois sense of the word, had come to grief.

There is one other sound that, thanks to the decades in which it neither passed my lips nor reached my ears, has preserved the unfathomable mystery that certain words from the language of adults possess for children. It was not long ago that I rediscovered it, and indeed a number of indivisible finds of this nature have played a large part in my decision to write down these memories. My parents being wealthy, we moved every year, before I went to school and perhaps later, too, notwithstanding other occasional summer trips, to summer residences not far from home. First it was Potsdam, later Neubabelsberg. Whereas the latter period still survives in a number of images, of which I may perhaps have more to tell—the night of the great burglary when my parents locked themselves in my room, the hours I stood fishing beside my father on the bank of Lake Griebnitz, the visit to Peacock Island that brought the first great disappointment of my life, because I could not find peacock feathers in the grass as I had been promised—by contrast, the summer months in Potsdam have wholly vanished, unless I may situate the asparagus cutting (my first and only agricultural passion) as far back as the garden on the Brauhausberg. And I have thus divulged the word in which, like countless rose petals in a drop of Rose Malmaison, hundreds of summer days, forfeiting their form, their color, and their multiplicity, are preserved in their scent. The word is "Brauhausberg." To approach what it enfolds is almost impossible. These words that exist on the frontier between two linguistic regions, that of children and that of adults, are comparable to the words of Mallarmé's poems, which the conflict between the poetic and the profane word has, as it were, consumed and made evanescent, airy. Likewise, the word "Brauhausberg" has lost all heaviness, no longer contains any trace of a brewery [Brauhaus], and is at most a hill swathed in blue that rose up each summer to give lodging to me and my parents.

The economic basis on which the finances of my parents rested was surrounded, long past my childhood and adolescence, by deepest secrecy. Probably not only for me, the eldest child, but also for my mother. And it is certain that such a state of affairs was the rule in Jewish families, and no doubt in a great many Christian ones as well. More curious is the fact that consumption, too, was wrapped in some of the mystery that so deeply shrouded income and fortune. I remember, at any rate, that the mention of certain suppliers—"sources," as they were called—always took place with the solemnity befitting an initiation. There are, it is true, distinctions to be drawn. The purveyors who met the daily household needs no more belonged to that secret circle than did the Berlin firms of long-standing repute that my mother visited when she took me and the younger children "downtown." On such occasions it was as certain that our suits would be bought at Arnold Müller's, our shoes at Stiller's, and our suitcases at Mädler's, as that at the end of these commissions our hot chocolate with whipped cream would be ordered at Hillbrich's. These shopping places were strictly preordained by tradition—quite unlike the connections with traders, which were my father's responsibility. My father possessed at bottom, along with a number of inhibitions stemming not only from his decency but also from a certain civic worthiness, the entrepreneurial nature of a big-business man. Unfavorable influences brought about his very premature retirement from an enterprise that was probably by no means ill-suited to his capacities, the Lepke art-auction house, which at that time was still located on Kochstrasse and in which he was a partner. After he had relinquished his share in the firm, he concerned himself increasingly with speculative investments of his capital, and it would not surprise me if the interest he took in household transactions was far keener from this time on. What is certain is that a good many of the suppliers he henceforth searched out were indirectly connected with his investments. If, therefore, from my mother's shopping excursions, a traditional and as it were official image of the Berlin commercial world emerged, the hints and instructions of my father gave rise to an unknown and slightly sinister one, whose prestige derived as much from the authoritarian resonance that these names carried at the family table as from the fact that these firms, unlike the others, were never seen by me. At their head, so to speak, was the Lepke auction room itself, with which my father not only had connections but from which, from time to time, he also brought home a purchase. I doubt that this commerce was an altogether happy one, with the exception perhaps of his carpet buying. Shortly before his death, he told me that he could distinguish the quality of a carpet's pile with the ball of his foot, if his soles were suitably thin. In my childhood, however, what impressed me most was to imagine the gavel blows with which my father accompanied the auction. Later, when he had withdrawn from Lepke's, this gavel always lay on his desk. Even if I never heard the rap of this gavel, there is another sound that became indissoluble from the image of my father's power and grandeur—or, rather, from those of a man in his profession. It is (implausible as this may seem) the noise made by the knife that my mother used to butter the rolls that my father took to work in the morning, when it was scraped for the last time, to remove the butter still adhering to it, against the crisp surface of the cut roll. This signal preluding the labor of my father's day was no less exciting to me than, in later years, the sound of the bell that announced the start of a performance at the theater. Apart from this, the real token of my father's profession in our apartment was a Moor, almost life-size, who stood on a gondola reduced to one-thirtieth of its size, holding with one hand an oar that could be taken out, and lifting on the other a golden bowl. This work of art was made of wood, the Moor black, the gondola and oar glowing in many colors beneath the varnish. The whole, however, was so urgently oriented toward its companion piece that I cannot tell today whether a second Moor, whom I imagine with it, really stood there originally or is a figment of my imagination. So much for Lepke's auction house. There was, besides, a further purveyor of artwork—at least as far as bronzes were concerned; this was the firm of Gladenbeck. Whether the choice was affected here, too, by more intimate commercial ties, I do not know. Such was certainly the case, however, with our supply of mouthwash, hydrogen peroxide obtained in huge bottles from the "Medicinal Stores," of which my father was a director. Less transparent, on the other hand, was the state of affairs regarding the Stabernack firm, which for years held an uncontested monopoly on installations in our apartment. Here the intermediate party was perhaps a certain company of building contractors, one of whose directors, Herr Altgelt, filled the role of partner in countless telephone conversations with my father, and whose name has stayed in my memory because his son was a member, and one of the most inglorious, of my class. Leaving aside mealtime conversations, it was only the telephone that intimated to us the occult world of business and traders. My father telephoned a great deal. He, whose outward manner seems to have been almost always courteous and pliable, possessed perhaps only on the telephone the bearing and decisiveness corresponding to his sometimes great wealth. In conversations with mediating agencies, this energy not infrequently grew vociferous; and the "serious side of life," which was embodied tangibly in my father's activity, found in the altercations with telephone operators its true symbol. The telephone first came into use during my childhood. I have therefore known it nailed in some corner of the corridor, whence, shrilling from the darkness, it augmented the terrors of that Berlin apartment with the endless passage leading from the half-lit dining room to the back bedrooms. It became a truly infernal machine when my school friends phoned in the prohibited period between two and four. But not all my father's mysterious transactions were carried out by telephone. From earliest times he had had—like many husbands who do not always find life easy in marriage—a tendency to address himself independently to certain branches of the domestic economy. Thus, he had connections in the provinces, principally in the vicinity of Hamburg, which frequently called him away on business. Our house was regularly plied from this source with Holstein butter, and in autumn with duck. Wine, on the other hand, was furnished by a Berlin firm, whose share certificates were also in my father's possession: this was the Central Wine Distributors, who were trying out new methods of calculation in the wine business. Finally these names became entwined, in parental discussions, with others in which the traditions of the middle-class Berlin of that time converged from both sides: for notarial attestation, Oberneck was consulted; surgical operations were performed by Rinne; dancing instruction was entrusted to Quaritsch; the family doctor was Renvers, at least as long as he lived in the same building;[28] Joseph Goldschmidt was our banker. But as for me, I was most lastingly affected by a reckless attempt that my father embarked upon one evening to bring even the family's amusements into the harmony with his business enterprises that he had been able to establish for all its other needs. For when, about 1910, on Lutherstrasse in the West End, a consortium erected a building (the one that now houses the Scala) as an "Ice Palace," my father, with a sizable stake, was among their number. Now, one evening—I don't know whether it was the opening date or later—my father conceived the idea of taking me there. The Ice Palace, however, was not only the first skating rink in Berlin, but also a thriving nightclub. So it happened that my attention was held far less by the convolutions in the arena than by the apparitions at the bar, which I was able to survey at my ease from a box in the circle. Among these was a prostitute in a very tight-fitting white sailor's suit, who, though I was unable to exchange a word with her, determined my erotic fantasies for years to come.

In those early years I got to know "downtown" only as the theater of purchases, on which occasions it first became apparent how my father's money could cut a path for us between the shop counters and assistants and mirrors, and the appraising eyes of our mother, whose muff lay on the counter. In the ignominy of a "new suit" we stood there, our hands peeping from the sleeves like dirty price tags, and it was only in the confectioner's that our spirits rose with the feeling of having escaped the false worship that humiliated our mother before idols bearing the names of Mannheimer, Herzog and Israel, Gerson, Adam, Esders and Mädler, Emma Bette, Bud and Lachmann. An impenetrable chain of mountains—no, caverns—of commodities: this was "downtown."

There are people who think they find the key to their destinies in heredity, others in horoscopes, others again in education. For my part, I believe that I would gain numerous insights into my later life from my collection of picture postcards, if I were able to leaf through it again today. The main contributor to this collection was my maternal grandmother, a decidedly enterprising lady, from whom I believe I have inherited two things: my delight in giving presents and my love of travel. If it is unclear what the Christmas holidays—which cannot be thought of without the Berlin of my childhood—meant for the first of these passions, it is certain that none of my boys' adventure books kindled my love of travel as did the postcards with which she supplied me in abundance from her far-flung travels. And because the longing we feel for a place determines it as much as does its outward image, I shall say something about these postcards. And yet—was what they awakened in me longing? Didn't they have far too magnetic an attraction to leave room for a wish to travel to the places they showed? For I was there—in Tabarz, Brindisi, Madonna di Campiglio, Westerland— when I gazed, unable to tear myself away, at the wooded slopes of Tabarz covered with glowing red berries, the yellow-and-white-daubed quays at Brindisi, the cupolas of Madonna di Campiglio printed bluish on blue, and the bows of the "Westerland" slicing high through the waves. Visiting the old lady in her carpeted window alcove, ornamented with a little balustrade and looking out onto the Blumeshof, it was hard to imagine how she had undertaken long sea voyages or even camel rides with the guidance of Stangel's Travel Bureau. She was a widow; three of her daughters were already married when I was small. I can tell nothing about the fourth, but a good deal about the room that she occupied in her mother's apartment. Yet perhaps I should first say something about the apartment as a whole. With what words am I to describe the almost immemorial feeling of bourgeois security that emanated from these rooms? Paradoxical as it may sound, the idea of that particular protectedness seems to relate most directly to their shortcomings. The inventory that filled these many rooms—twelve or fourteen—could today be accommodated without incongruity in the shabbiest of secondhand furniture shops. And if these ephemeral forms were so much more solid than those of the Jugendstil that superseded them—what made you feel at home, at ease, comfortable, and comforted in them was the nonchalance with which they attached themselves to the sauntering passage of years and days, entrusting their future to the durability of their material alone, and nowhere to rational calculation. Here reigned a species of things that was, no matter how compliantly it bowed to the minor whims of fashion, in the main so wholly convinced of itself and its permanence that it took no account of wear, inheritance, or moves, remaining forever equally near to and far from its ending, which seemed the ending of all things. Poverty could have no place in these rooms where even death had none. They had no space for dying—which is why their owners died in a sanatorium, while the furniture went straight to the secondhand dealer. Death was not provided for in them—that is why they were so cozy by day, and by night the theater of our most oppressive dreams. It is for this reason that, when I think of this house (it was number 10 or 12 Blumeshof)—in which were spent so many of my childhood's happiest hours, such as when I was allowed, to the sound of piano études, to browse in *Herzblättchens Zeitvertreib* in an armchair—I am met on its threshold by a nightmare. My waking existence has preserved no image of the staircase. But in my memory it remains today the scene of a haunting dream that I once had in just those happy years. In this dream the stairway seemed under the power of a ghost that awaited me as I mounted, though without barring my way, making its presence felt when I had only a few more stairs to climb. On these last stairs it held me spellbound.—The rooms in this apartment on the Blumeshof were not only numerous but also in some cases very large. To reach my grandmother at her window, I had to cross the huge dining room and attain the farthest end of the living room. Only feast days, and above all Christmas Day, could give an idea of the capaciousness of these rooms. But if, when this day came, it seemed as though it had been awaited all year long in the front rooms, there were other occasions that brought other parts of the apartment to life: a visit by a married daughter unlocked a long-disused wardrobe; another back room opened to us children when the grownups wished to take their afternoon nap at the front of the house; and another part again was animated by the piano lessons received by the last daughter remaining at home. The most important of these remote, less-frequented rooms, however, was the loggia. Perhaps this was because, being the least furnished, it was least suited to the sojourn of adults, or because muted street noises drifted in, or finally because it opened onto back courtyards with children, domestic servants, hurdy-gurdy men, and porters. But of these it was more often the voices than the forms that were to be described from the loggia. Moreover, the courtyards of a residential neighborhood as genteel as this never really bustled with activity; something of the composure of the rich people whose work was being done there seemed to have permeated this work itself, and everything seemed to await the Sleeping Beauty slumber that descended here on Sundays. For this reason Sunday was properly the day of the loggia—Sunday, which none of the other rooms could ever quite contain, as if they were damaged. Sunday seeped out of them. Only our loggia, looking out onto the yard (with its racks where the carpets were beaten), and the other loggias (with their bare walls of Pompeian red) could hold it. And not a chime of its cargo of bell-peals, with which the churches—the Twelve Apostles, St. Matthew's, and the Kaiser Wilhelm Memorial Church—slowly loaded it throughout the afternoon, slipped over its balustrade; all remained piled high till evening. As I have already indicated, this grandmother did not die in the Blumeshof; nor did the other one, who lived opposite her in the same street and was older and more severe—my father's mother. So the Blumeshof has become for me an Elysium, a vague realm of the shades of deceased but immortal grandmothers. And just as imagination, having once cast its veil over a district, is apt to adorn its edges with incomprehensible, capricious frills, so, in the course of decades and to this day, it turned a long-established grocery store situated near this house but on Magdeburgerstrasse (to someone driving past without ever having set foot inside) into a monument to an early-departed grandfather, solely because the first name of its owner, like his, was Georg.

But isn't this, too, the city—the strip of light under the bedroom door on evenings when we were "entertaining"? Didn't Berlin itself find its way into the expectant childhood night, as later the world of William Tell or Julius Caesar invaded the night of an audience? The dream ship that came to fetch us on those evenings must have rocked at our bedside on the waves of conversation, or under the spray of clattering plates; and in the early morning it set us down on the ebb of the carpet beating that came in at the window with the moist air on rainy days, and engraved itself more indelibly in the child's memory than the voice of the beloved in that of the man—this carpet beating that was the language of the nether world, of servant girls, the real grownups, a language that sometimes took its time, languid and muted under the gray sky, breaking at other times into an inexplicable gallop, as if the servants were pursued by phantoms. The courtyard was one of the places where the city opened itself to the child; others, admitting him or letting him go, were railway stations. On departure, their openings were a panorama, the frame of a *fata morgana*. No distance was more remote than the place where the rails converged in the mist. On the return home, however, all was different. For within us still burned the melancholy lamps that had shone in isolation from courtyard windows often without curtains, from staircases bristling with filth, from cellar windows hung with rags. These were the backyards that the city showed me as I returned from Hahnenklee or Sylt, only to close upon them once more, never to let me see or enter them. But those five last fearful minutes of the journey before everyone got out of the train have been converted into the gaze of my eyes, and there are those perhaps who look into them as into courtyard windows in damaged walls, in which at early evening a lamp stands.

Among the postcards in my album, there are a number whose written side has lasted better in my memory than their picture. All bear the handsome, legible signature "Helene Pufahl." She was my first teacher. Long before I knew of classes at school, I was brought by her into close relationship to the children of my "class," in the sense of the word that I would not become acquainted with until two decades later. And that it was high on the social scale I can infer from the names of the two girls from the little circle that remain in my memory: Ilse Ullstein and Luise von Landau. What order of nobility these Landaus belonged to I do not know. But their name had an immense attraction for me and—I have grounds to suppose—for my parents. Yet this is hardly the reason their name has remained undimmed in my mind until today; rather, it happens that this was the first name on which I consciously heard fall the accent of death. This occurred, as far as I know, not long after I had grown out of the little private circle. Later, each time I passed the Lützow quay, my eyes sought her house; and when, toward the end of my schooldays, I wrote my first philosophical essay, entitled "Reflections on the Nobility," the alluring name of my first schoolmate—beside that of Pindar, with which I had begun—stood unuttered. Fraülein Pufahl was succeeded by Herr Knoche, whom I had to confront quite alone. He was the preschool teacher from the school for which my parents later intended me. His instruction does not appear to have entirely agreed with me. At any rate, I performed on occasion magical rites directed against his person, and I still remember the feeling of omnipotence that came over me one day on Herkules Bridge on receiving the news that Herr Knoche had canceled the next day's class. At that time I knew to what I might attribute this, but today, sadly, I have forgotten the magic formula. More than in his private appearances, Herr Knoche impressed me in the classroom lessons I had with him later, when I had started school. They were enlivened by frequent intermezzi for thrashing. Herr Knoche was a zealous exponent of the cane. He was also entrusted with our singing instruction. And it was in a singing lesson that he showed me one of the shut gates that we all know from our childhood, behind which, we were assured, the way to later, real life lay open. We were practicing the cuirassier's song from *Wallensteins Lager*.[29]

> To horse, trusty friends, to horse and away
> to the field of freedom and valiance,
> where a man's worth more than dust and clay
> and the heart's still weighed in the balance.

Herr Knoche wanted the class to tell him what these last words actually meant. No one, of course, could give an answer. It was one of those artful questions that make children obtuse. Our discomfiture seemed most agreeable to Herr Knoche, who said pointedly, "You'll understand this when you are grown up." Now I am grown up; I am today inside the gate that Herr Knoche showed me; but it is still firmly shut. I was not to make my entrance through that portal.

Just as lights on a foggy night are surrounded by gigantic rings, my earliest theatrical impressions emerge from the mist of my childhood with great aureoles. At the very beginning is a "monkey theater" that performed perhaps on Unter den Linden and at which I appeared, as I remember, heavily escorted, since neither parents nor grandmother was prepared to forgo witnessing the effect on me of my first theatrical performance. True, the source of the light, the actual happening on the stage, I can no longer discern in so much luminous haze. A pinkish-gray cloud of seats, lights, and faces has obliterated the pranks of the poor little monkeys on the stage. And while I can recount the sequence of theatrical events in the following six or seven years, I can say nothing more of them—neither of the *Veilchenfresser* I saw at the Spa Theater at Suderode; nor of the *Wilhelm Tell* that, as is customary, initiated me to the Berlin stage; nor of the *Fiesko,* with Matkowsky, that I saw at the Schauspielhaus; nor of the *Carmen,* with Destinn, at the Opera.[30] The latter two performances my grandmother had assumed responsibility for; hence not only the dazzling program but also the imposing dress-circle seats. And yet, more fondly than to them, my mind goes back to the *Wilhelm Tell,* because of the event that preceded it, the highly hermetic nature of which is still undimmed, while nothing remains in my memory of the same evening's performance. It must have been in the afternoon that a difference of opinion arose between myself and my mother. Something was to be done that I did not like. Finally, my mother had recourse to coercion. She threatened that unless I did her bidding I would be left at home in the evening. I obeyed. But the feeling with which I did so, or rather, with which, the threat hardly uttered, I measured the two opposed forces and instantly perceived how enormous was the preponderance of the other side, and thus my silent indignation at so crude and brutal a procedure, which put at stake something totally disproportionate to the end—for the end was momentary, whereas the stake, the gratitude for the evening that my mother was about to give me, as I know today and anticipated then, was deep and permanent—this feeling of misused and violated trust has outlived in me all that succeeded it that day. Many years afterward it was proved a second time how much more significant and enduring the anticipation of an event can be than what actually ensues. As a boy, I longed for nothing more than to see Kainz.[31] But his guest performances in Berlin were during school time. Since the advance bookings in the morning offered the only possibility of procuring seats at prices commensurate with my pocket money, my wish was denied for years. My parents, at any rate, did nothing to advance its fulfillment. One day—whether because the advance bookings were on a Sunday or for another reason—I was able after all to be one of the first at the ticket office, which was already that of the theater on Nollendorfplatz. I see myself standing at the box office and—as if memory wanted to prelude the approaching main theme—waiting there, sure enough, but not buying my ticket. At this point memory pauses, and picks up its thread again only when I am mounting the stairs to the dress-circle in the evening, before the performance of

Richard II. What is it that imposes once again on memory, at the door of the auditorium, a "so far and no further"? True, I see before me a scene from the drama, but entirely cut off, without my knowing whether it is really from this performance or from another, any more than I know whether I saw Kainz or not—whether his appearance was canceled or whether the disappointment of finding him less great than I had believed him annulled, with the image of his acting, the whole evening. So I confront uncertainty wherever I follow my earliest theatrical memories, and in the end I can no longer even distinguish dream from reality. This is true of a dark winter evening when I went with my mother to a production of *Die lustigen Weiber von Windsor.*[32] I really saw this opera, in a kind of people's theater. It was a noisy, cheerful evening, but all the more silent was the journey there, through a snow-covered, unknown Berlin spreading about me in the gaslight. It stood in the same relation to the city I knew as that most jealously guarded of my postcards, the depiction of the Halle Gate in pale blue on a darker blue background. The Belle-Allianceplatz was to be seen, with the houses that frame it; the full moon was in the sky. From the moon and the windows in the façades, however, the top layer of card had been removed; their contrasting white disrupted the picture, and one had to hold it against a lamp or a candle to see, by the light of windows and a lunar surface parading in exactly the same illumination, the whole scene regain its composure. Perhaps that evening the opera we were approaching was the source of light that made the city suddenly gleam so differently, but perhaps it was only a dream that I had later of this walk, the memory of which has displaced what previously stood in for reality.

The architect of the Kaiser Friedrich School must have had something on the order of Brandenburg brick Gothic in mind. At any rate, it is constructed of red brick and displays a preference for motifs commonly found at Stendal or Tangermünde. The whole, however, gives a narrow-chested, high-shouldered impression. Rising close by the precincts of the municipal railway, the building exudes a sad, spinsterish primness. Even more than to the experiences I had within, it is probably to this exterior that I should attribute the fact that I have not retained a single cheerful memory of it. Nor, since leaving, have I ever had the idea of going back. Of the walk to school I have already spoken. But if the portal had been reached just in time, or there was no longer sufficient time (and the nightmarish things to come did not weigh too heavily) to allow me to buy at the adjoining stationer's another piece of plasticine, a protractor, or, at the very beginning, wafers and the little ribbons used to attach blotting sheets to exercise-book covers—if finally the wrought-iron door, which the janitor was allowed to open only ten minutes before school started, was still closed—how melancholy and oppressed must this wait at the door have been, under the arch of the municipal railway, which crossed Knesebeckstrasse at this point, if nothing of it comes back to me besides the compulsion incessantly to remove my cap, to pay attention to myself, when I saw passing before me one of the teachers, who were permitted to enter, of course, anytime they pleased.

Only today, it seems to me, am I able to appreciate how much hatefulness and humiliation lay in the obligation to raise my cap to teachers. The necessity of admitting them by this gesture into the sphere of my private existence seemed presumptuous. I would have had no objection to a less intimate and in some way military display of respect. But to greet a teacher as one would a relation or a friend seemed inordinately unfitting, as if they had wanted to hold classes in my home. From this alone it can be seen how little school was ever able to win me over. And if I experienced the antiquated forms of school discipline—caning, change of seats, or detention—only in the lower forms, nevertheless the terror and the pall they placed me under in those years never lifted from me. I find this not only in the importance attached to promotion to the next grade and to the four report cards brought home each year, but also in smaller but more telling details. Above all in the unfathomable shock or, rather, bewilderment into which I was plunged by interruptions in the continuity of teaching—such as excursions to the country, games, and especially the great annual competition between the schools of Greater Berlin to decide the best team at prisoner's base. Needless to say, I never belonged to the school team, which seldom met with success. But in the mobilization of the whole school that took place on such occasions, I, too, was involved. The matches were normally played in May or June, on some field or drill ground in the vicinity of the Lehrter station. As a rule, the weather was blazing hot. Nervously I would alight at the Lehrter station. Uncertainly I would set off in the direction I vaguely remembered, and would find myself at last, with mixed feelings of relief and repugnance, amid some alien troop of schoolboys. From now on, my bewilderment was uninterrupted—whether I had to look for my own school party, or sought a resting place in the shade, whether I had to reach a stall without crossing the field in order to buy fruit for breakfast, or congregate, while avoiding any appearance of indifference, around one of the gentlemen who made known the day's results, or finally, although I had not understood these results, exchange with my schoolfellows during the homeward journey observations on the course of the game. Yet what made these sporting occasions most hated and most repellent of all was not the multitudes they attracted but their site. The broad, unfrequented avenues leading to it were flanked by barracks; barracks bordered the playing field; the field was a parade ground. And on those days the feeling never left me that if I relaxed my vigilance for only a moment, permitted myself only the briefest well-being in the shade of a tree or before a sausage vendor's stand, I would fall in ten years' time irredeemably into the power of this place: I would have to become a soldier.—The Kaiser Friedrich School stands close by the municipal railway yard on Savignyplatz. At Savignyplatz station you can look down into its playground. And because, once liberated from it, I frequently took the opportunity to do this, it now stands before me quite uselessly, like one of those Mexican temples that were excavated much too early and inexpertly, their frescoes having been long effaced by rain by the time the excavation of the ceremonial implements and papyri, which might have thrown some light on these images, could at last seriously begin. So I have to make do with what is resurrected only today—isolated pieces of interior that have broken away yet contain the whole within them, while the whole, standing there before me, has lost its details without trace. The first fragment to reappear is what was certainly, throughout my whole time at school, the idlest of my perceptions: the molding, crowned with crenelations, above the classrooms. And perhaps this is not so difficult to explain. For everything else that came within my visual field sooner or later became of use to me, became associated with a thought or a notion that swept it along into the sea of oblivion. The exception was this narrow molding, cast out innumerable times by the healthy beat of everyday waves until it was left stranded like a shell on the shore of my daydreaming. And there I now come across it. I pick it up and question it like Hamlet addressing the skull. It is, as I have said, a molding representing a row of battlements. Thus, what is visible between them is not empty space but the same wood, only beveled and notched. The intention was certainly to remind the onlooker of a castle. What he was to do with the recollection was another question. In any event, this molding reinforced the idea of the dense mass divined in the morning behind the closed doors: the class at lessons. Over the doors leading to the arts-and-crafts rooms it became the emblem of a certain guildlike solidarity. On the classroom cupboard I encountered it again—but how much more emphasis it had on the identically shaped cupboards standing along the faculty-room wall! In the first, second, and third grades, in the vicinity of the many little coats and caps on their racks, its impact was lost; but in the upper classes it acquired an allusion to the *Abitur* that was soon to crown the labors of their members. Yet never more than a shadow of meaning and reason passed across it in such places, and it remained, with the unspeakable gray-green ornaments adorning the wall of the auditorium, and with the absurd bosses and scrolls of the cast-iron balustrades, the refuge of all my minutes of terror and my nightmares. Nothing, however, could compare with the molding, unless it was the bell that shrilly marked the beginning and end of lessons and breaks. The timbre and duration of this signal never varied. Yet how different it sounded at the beginning of the first and at the end of the last period! To describe this difference would be to lift the veil that seven years of school cast ever more tightly over each of the days that composed them. In winter the lamps were often still on when it rang, but the light they cast was bereft of coziness, offering as little shelter as the light the dentist shines into the mouth on which he is about to work. Between two peals of the bell lay the break, the second precipitating the shuffling, chattering uproar with which the mass of pupils, streaming through only two doors, surged up the narrow stairway from floor to floor. These staircases I have always hated: hated when I was forced to climb them amid the herd, a forest of calves and feet before me, defenselessly exposed to the bad odors emanating from all the bodies pressing so closely against mine; hated no less when, arriving late, passing deserted corridors, I hastened up them quite alone to the very top, arriving breathless in the classroom. If that happened before the teacher's hand was on the door handle, even though he might be quite near, you got in unseen. But woe if the door was already shut! However wide open those next to it might still be—and even if above or below some time passed before the bang of a shutting door announced the start of a lesson, and no matter how harmlessly the eye of a strange teacher approaching along the corridor brushed you—the judgment was ineluctable within, once you had plucked up the courage to open it.

"Cease your sewing, little mother, on that sarafan; useless will your labors be, so strain no more." "Earthward sink the evening shadows over wood and dale, and silent grows the world." "I am Doctor Eisenbart; hosanna, shout for joy! I serve the people faithfully; hosanna, shout for joy!" "Drink up the sparkling wine, dear friends; farewell, 'tis time to part." "As clouds go wand'ring o'er heaven's brow, so I shall cross the wide, wide world."— These and many other lieder from the songbook of Ludwig Erk,[33] which, in the form of two thick green-and-gold-bound volumes, rested on the music stand, my mother used to play for me. I did not join in the singing, but I listened with pleasure. These melodies belonged to the household, just like the jingling of the basket of keys when my mother searched impatiently through it for the purse or notebook that lay at the very bottom; like the dull pop with which, at dusk, the gas mantle of the chandelier that hung above the dining-room table responded to the match; like the creaking of the dumbwaiter that brought up food and tableware from the kitchen; like the stir made by my father's returning home at noon, as he unlocked the front door and let his stick fall into the umbrella stand.

Many years earlier, in one of the streets I passed along on my endless wanderings, I was surprised by the first stirring of my sexual urge, under the oddest circumstances. It was on the Jewish New Year's Day, and my parents had made arrangements for me to attend some religious celebration. Probably it was a service at the Reformed synagogue, which my mother, on grounds of family tradition, held in some sympathy, whereas my father's upbringing inclined him more to the Orthodox rite. But he had to give way. For this visit to the synagogue I had been entrusted to a relative, whom I had to fetch on my way. But whether because I had forgotten his address or because I was unfamiliar with the district, it grew later and later without my drawing nearer to my goal. To make my way independently to the synagogue was out of the question, since I had no idea where it was. This bewilderment, forgetfulness, and embarrassment were doubtless chiefly due to my dislike of the impending service, in its familial no less than its divine aspect. While I was wandering thus, I was suddenly and simultaneously overcome, on the one hand, by the thought, "Too late, time was up long ago, you'll never get there"—and, on the other, by a sense of the insignificance of all this, of the benefits of letting things take what course they would. And these two streams of consciousness converged irresistibly in an immense pleasure that filled me with blasphemous indifference toward the service, but exalted the street in which I stood, as if it had already intimated to me the services of procurement it was later to render to my awakened drive.

We had our "summer residences" first at Potsdam, then at Babelsberg. They were outside, from the point of view of the city; but from that of the summer, inside: we were ensconced within it, and I must disengage my memories of it—like moss that one plucks at random in the dark from the walls of a cave—from its sultry, humid glimmer. There are memories that are especially well preserved because, although not themselves affected, they are isolated by a shock from all that followed. They have not been worn away by contact with their successors and remain detached, self-sufficient. The first such memory appears when I speak of these summer days: it is an evening in my seventh or eighth year. One of our maidservants stands a long while at the wrought-iron gate, which opens onto I know not what tree-lined walk. The big garden, where I have been roaming in overgrown border regions, is already closed to me. It is time to go to bed. Perhaps I have sated myself with my favorite game: shooting with the rubber bolts of my "Eureka" pistol, somewhere in the bushes by the wire fence, at the wooden birds, which, struck by a bolt, fell backward out of the green-painted foliage, to which they were attached by strings. The whole day I had been keeping a secret to myself: the dream of the previous night. It had been an eerie one. A ghost had appeared to me. The site of its operations did not, in truth, really exist, but nevertheless bore a very strong resemblance to one that was known, tantalizing, and inaccessible to me—namely, the corner of my parents' bedroom which was separated from the rest of the chamber by an arch draped with a heavy, faded-violet curtain, and in which my mother's dressing gowns, house dresses, and shawls were hung. The darkness behind the curtain was impenetrable, and this corner was the sinister, nocturnal counterpart of that bright, beatific realm that opened occasionally with my mother's linen cupboard, in which, piled up on the shelves, edged with white trimming and bearing a blue-embroidered text from "Die Glocke,"[34] lay the sheets, tablecloths, napkins, and pillowcases. A sweet lavender scent came from the brightly colored silk sachets hanging on the inside of the cupboard doors. These were the hell and paradise into which the ancient magic of hearth and home, which had once been lodged in the spinning wheel, had been sundered. Now my dream had risen from the evil world: a ghost busying itself at a trestle draped with a profusion of silken fabrics, one covering another. These silks the ghost was stealing. It did not snatch them up or carry them away; it did nothing with or to them that was actually visible and distinguishable. Yet I knew it stole them, just as in legends people who discover a spirits' banquet know that these dead beings are feasting, without seeing them eat or drink. It was this dream that I had kept secret. And in the night that followed it I noticed, half asleep, my mother and father coming quietly into my room at an unusual hour. I did not see them lock themselves in. When I got up next morning, there was nothing for breakfast. The house had been stripped of everything. At midday my grandmother arrived from Berlin with the bare necessities. A large band of burglars had descended on the house in the night. Fortunately the noise they made gave an indication of their number, so that my mother had succeeded in restraining my father, who, armed only with a pocketknife, had wanted to confront them. The dangerous visit had lasted almost until morning. In vain my parents had stood at the window in the first light, signaling to the outside world: the band had departed at their leisure with the baskets. Much later they were caught, and it emerged that their organizer, a murderer and criminal with many previous convictions, was a deaf-mute. It made me proud that I was questioned about the events of the previous evening—for a complicity was suspected between the housebreakers and the maidservant who had stood at the gate. What made me even prouder, however, was the question why I had kept silent about my dream, which I now, of course, narrated at length as a prophecy.

What my first books were to me—to remember this I should first have to forget all other knowledge of books. It is certain that all I know of them today rests on the readiness with which I then opened myself to books; but whereas now content, theme, and subject matter are extraneous to the book, earlier they were solely and entirely in it, being no more external or independent of it than are today the number of its pages or its paper. The world that revealed itself in the book and the book itself were never, at any price, to be divided. So with each book its content, too, its world, was palpably there, at hand. But, equally, this content and world transfigured every part of the book. They burned within it, blazed from it; located not merely in its binding or its pictures, they were enshrined in chapter headings and opening letters, paragraphs and columns. You did not read books through; you dwelt, abided between their lines, and, reopening them after an interval, surprised yourself at the spot where you had halted. The rapture with which you received a new book, scarcely venturing a fleeting glance between its pages, was that of the guest invited for a few weeks to a mansion and hardly daring to dart a glance of admiration at the long suites of ceremonial rooms through which he must pass to reach his quarters. He is all the more impatient to be allowed to withdraw. And so, each year, scarcely had I found on the Christmas table the latest volume of the *Neuer deutscher Jugend-freund* [New Companion of German Youth] when I retreated completely behind the ramparts of its cover, which was adorned with coats of arms, and felt my way into the spy or hunting story in which I was to spend the first night. There was nothing finer than to sniff out, on this first tentative expedition into the labyrinth of stories, the various atmospheres, scents, brightnesses, and sounds that came from its different chambers and corridors. For in reality the longer stories, interrupted many times to reappear as continuations, extended through the whole like subterranean passages. And what did it matter if the aromas that rose from the tunnels high into the air, where we saw globes or waterwheels glisten, mingled with the smell of gingerbread, or if a Christmas carol wove its halo around the head of Stephenson[35] glimpsed between two pages like an ancestral portrait through a door crack, or if the smell of gingerbread joined with that of a Sicilian sulfur mine that suddenly burst upon us in a full-page illustration as in a fresco. But if I had sat for a while immersed in my book and then went back to the table bearing the presents, it no longer stood almost imperiously over me as it had when I first entered the Christmas room; rather, I seemed to be walking on a small platform that led down to it from my fairy castle.

With this joy that I remember, however, another is fused: that of possession in memory. Today I can no longer distinguish them: it is as if it were only a part of the gift of the moment I am now relating, that it, too, received the gift of never again being wholly lost to me—even if decades have passed between the seconds in which I think of it.

Anyone can observe that the length of time during which we are exposed to impressions has no bearing on their fate in memory. Nothing prevents our keeping rooms in which we have spent twenty-four hours more or less clearly in our memory, and forgetting others in which we passed months. It is not, therefore, due to insufficient exposure time if no image appears on the plate of remembrance. More frequent, perhaps, are the cases when the half-light of habit denies the plate the necessary light for years, until one day from an alien source it flashes as if from burning magnesium powder, and now a snapshot transfixes the room's image on the plate. It is we ourselves, however, who are always standing at the center of these rare images. Nor is this very mysterious, since such moments of sudden illumination are at the same time moments when we separated from ourselves, and while our waking, habitual, everyday self is involved actively or passively in what is happening, our deeper self rests in another place and is touched by the shock, as is the little heap of magnesium powder by the flame of the match. It is to this immolation of our deepest self in shock that our memory owes its most indelible images. So the room in which I slept at the age of six would have been forgotten, had not my father come in one night—I was already in bed—with the news of a death. It was not really the news itself that so affected me: the deceased with a distant cousin. But in the way in which my father told me, there lay [text breaks off]

The first great disappointment of my life reached me one afternoon on Peacock Island. I had been told, on the way there, that I would find peacock feathers in the grass. Scarcely had I heard this when, with the speed of a spark leaping between two charged systems, a close connection must have been formed in me between the name of these islands and the peacock feathers. It was not that the spark took a roundabout path by way of the image of the peacock. This had no part in the process. And so my reproachful dismay as I scoured the turf so vainly was directed not against the peacocks that I saw strutting up and down, but, rather, against the soil of the island itself, which was a peacock island yet bore no peacock earth. Had I found the feather I craved in the grass. I would have felt expected and welcome at this spot. Now the island seemed to have broken a promise. Certainly the peacocks could not console me. Weren't they there for everybody to see? But I was to have had something intended only for me, concealed from all others, to be found in the grass only by me. This disappointment would not have been so great had it not been Mother Earth herself who inflicted it on me. Similarly, the bliss at having, after much toil, at last learned to ride a bicycle would have been less sweet had not Mother Earth herself let me feel her praise. One learned to ride in those days—it was the heyday of bicycle racing—in large indoor arenas specially established for the purpose. These arenas did not, however, have the snobbish character of the later ice palaces or indoor tennis courts; rather, they resembled skating rinks or gymnasiums, and bespoke a mentality for which sport and open air were not inseparable, as they are today. It was the era of "sporting costumes" that, unlike our present sports attire, sought not to adapt the body to immediate needs but rather to define the particular sport as sharply as possible and isolate it from all others, just as those arenas cut it off from nature and other exercises. The sport, as it was practiced in those arenas, still had about it all the eccentricities of its beginnings. On the asphalt floor, moving under the supervision of trainers among the ordinary bicycles for gentlemen, ladies, and children, were constructions with front wheels ten times larger than their small rear wheels, their airy seats probably occupied by artistes rehearsing a number.

The orchard at Glienicke, the broad, ceremonious promenade of Schloss Babelsberg, the narrow, concealed pathways of our summer garden, the shady ways through the foliage leading down to Lake Griebnitz at the places where there were jetties—all this I annexed to my domain, completing in an instant in fantasy the work of countless walks, games, and outings, kneeling in my nuptials with the billowing ground as a dynast conquers endless territories by means of a single felicitous union.

I have talked of the courtyards. Even Christmas was fundamentally a festival of the courtyards. There it began with the barrel organs, which continued the week before the festival with chorales, and there it ended with the Christmas trees, which, bereft of feet, leaned in the snow or glistened in the rain. But Christmas came, and all at once, before the eyes of the bourgeois child, it divided his city into two mighty camps. These were not the genuine ones, in which the exploited and their rulers lie irreconcilably opposed. No, it was a camp posed and arranged almost as artificially as the crèches made of paper or the wooden figures, but also as old and as honorable: Christmas came and divided the rich from the poor. Christmas came and divided the children into those who shuffled past the booths on Potsdam Square with their parents and those who, alone, indoors, offered their dolls and lambkins for sale to children of their age. Christmas came and with it a whole, unknown world of wares, [text breaks off]

The *déjà vu* effect has often been described. But I wonder whether the term is actually well chosen, and whether the metaphor appropriate to the process would not be far better taken from the realm of acoustics. One ought to speak of events that reach us like an echo awakened by a call, a sound that seems to have been heard somewhere in the darkness of past life. Accordingly, if we are not mistaken, the shock with which moments enter consciousness as if already lived usually strikes us in the form of a sound. It is a word, a tapping, or a rustling that is endowed with the magic power to transport us into the cool tomb of long ago, from the vault of which the present seems to return only as an echo. But has the counterpart of this entranced removal ever been investigated—the shock with which we come across a gesture or a word the way we suddenly find in our house a forgotten glove or reticule? And just as they cause us to surmise that a stranger has been there, there are words or gestures from which we infer this invisible stranger, the future, who left them in our keeping. I was perhaps five years old. One evening—I was already in bed—my father appeared, probably to say good night. It was half against his will, I thought, that he told me the news of a relative's death. The deceased was a cousin, a grown man who scarcely concerned me. But my father gave the news with details, took the opportunity to explain, in answer to my question, what a heart attack was, and was communicative. I did not take in much of the explanation. But that evening I must have memorized my room and my bed, the way you observe with great precision a place where you feel dimly that you'll later have to search for something you've forgotten there. Many years afterward I discovered what it was. Here in this room, my father had "forgotten" part of the news about the deceased: the illness was called syphilis.

Diabolo / The desk at which I did my schoolwork / Neubabelsberg railroad station / Schloss Neubabelsberg.

Fragment written during the first half of 1932; unpublished in Benjamin's lifetime. *Gesammelte Schriften*, VI, 465–519. Translated by Edmund Jephcott.

Notes

1. The Tiergarten is a district of central Berlin that includes the 630-acre, labyrinthine Tiergarten Park, a deer preserve until the eighteenth century. The park was destroyed in World War II but afterward restored, along with the Berlin Zoo and the zoological gardens at its southwest corner.

2. Benjamin himself had been a prominent member of the German Youth Movement. "Youth Movement" refers collectively to a broad range of attempts to establish a new culture of youth in Germany. It had its origins in the 1890s with groups of young boys, known as the Wandervögel, who tramped through the open countryside around Berlin and indulged in a kind of primitive nature worship. In the early years of the twentieth century, the elements within the movement ran the gamut from bland pedagogical reforms through vaguely philosophical programs for cultural change to the virulent nationalism and anti-Semitism of the radical Right. The "debating chambers" mentioned in this passage were the meeting place of the Freie Studentenschaft (Berlin Free Students' Union), the Youth Movement's organ at the University of Berlin. Benjamin had been the president of this organization. It was also in these chambers that his friends Friedrich Heinle and Rika Seligson committed suicide in protest against the onset of war in 1914. See the Chronology in Volume 1 of this edition, and the references to the couple later in this essay.

3. Léon Daudet (1867–1942), writer and journalist, was a cofounder of the royalist journal *L'Action Française* (1907). *Paris vécu* had been published in 1930.

4. Franz Hessel (1880–1941), German writer and journalist, collaborated with

Benjamin in translating Proust; see also Benjamin's review of his book *Heim-liches Berlin* (Unknown Berlin; 1927), in this volume. Hessel and his wife inspired two of the three figures in Henri Roché's novel *Jules et Jim,* which formed the basis of François Truffaut's film of the same title.

5. Wedding, Reinickendorf, and Tegel are all working-class districts of Berlin.

6. Probably Germaine Krull.

7. The *Abitur* is the final comprehensive exam in German secondary school *(Gymnasium)*—the exam that qualifies students for university study.

8. From Act 3, scene 1 (line 2098) of Schiller's *Maria Stuart* (1800).

9. From 1905 to 1907, Benjamin attended the Landerziehungsheim Haubinda, a distinctly progressive country boarding school in Thuringia. One of the directors of the school at this time was Gustav Wyneken. Wyneken's program of school reform became the first major intellectual influence on Benjamin, and his ideas on the role of youth in national cultural affairs left a lifelong imprint on Benjamin's thinking. See the Chronology in Volume 1 of this edition.

10. Ernst Joël became a physician in Berlin. He supervised Benjamin's experiments with hashish.

11. Friedrich (Fritz) Heinle, German poet and friend of Benjamin's, committed suicide on August 8, 1914.

12. Marianne Weber (1870–1954), author and feminist activist, was from 1919 to 1923 the head of the Union of German Women's Organizations. She wrote extensively on the professional role and development of women, especially in the university. She was the wife of Max Weber.

13. *Die Aktion,* a political journal founded in 1911 by Franz Pfemfert, was dedicated to revolution in literature and the visual arts.

14. The reference is to Rika (1891–1914), Carla (1892–1956), and Traute (1895–1915) Seligson.

15. Franz Pfemfert (1879–1954) was the founder and editor of the journal *Die Aktion.* Else Lasker-Schüler (1869–1945), German poet, short-story writer, playwright, and novelist, was one of the most widely recognized Expressionists. Wieland Herzfelde (1896–1988), German writer and publisher, was associated with the Dada movement in Berlin; he founded Malik Verlag, the main organ of Berlin Dada. He was the brother of John Heartfield, a prominent Berlin Dadaist and graphic artist. Simon Guttmann was a German photographer. In 1928, in Berlin, he founded the Deutsche Photodienst (German Photo Service), known as "Dephot" for short.

16. Ludwig Meidner (1884–1966), Expressionist painter and writer, was best-known for his playfully apocalyptic canvases of the years immediately before World War I.

17. Compare "Excavation and Memory" (1932), in this volume.

18. Epicurus (341 B.C.–270 B.C.) was a Greek philosopher, whose ideas initiated the direction in philosophy known as Epicureanism. Its adherents view pleasure as the sole good and as the first goal of morality.

19. See Nietzsche, *Beyond Good and Evil,* Aphorism 70.

20. Karl Schinkel (1781–1841), German architect, is best-known for his adaptations of classical Greek forms to modern structures.

21. The reference is to Alfred Cohn (1892–1954), a friend from Benjamin's youth

and the brother of Jula Cohn. Benjamin's relationship with Jula Cohn precipitated the crisis in his marriage. The essay "Goethe's Elective Affinities" (see
Volume 1 of this edition) allegorizes their relationship.

22. Alois Riegl (1858–1905) was an Austrian art historian. His book *Die spätrömis-che Kunst-Industrie* (The Late Roman Art Industry) appeared in 1901. This
    work exerted an enormous influence on Benjamin; he counted it as one of the
    seminal works of the century. See "The Rigorous Study of Art," in this volume.
23. The reference is to Ernst Schoen (1894–1960), a German musician, poet, and
    translator, and the artistic director of a major radio station in Frankfurt. Just
    as Benjamin's relationship with Jula Cohn was allegorized in the essay "Goethe's
    Elective Affinities," so too was Dora Benjamin's with Ernst Schoen. Schoen
    continued to provide Benjamin with opportunities to present his work on the
    radio into the early 1930s.
24. Emil Lederer (1882–1939), German economist, emigrated to the United States
    in 1934. He was the first dean of the New School for Social Research, in New
    York.
25. The reference is to Grete Radt, Benjamin's first fiancée, who later married Alfred
    Cohn.
26. This cryptic passage refers to a complex series of relationships centering around
    Jula Cohn (see note 21 above). Jula married Fritz Radt (brother of Grete Radt,
    Benjamin's first fiancée, who married Alfred Cohn, Jula's brother).
27. A reference to the fairy tale "Das kalte Herz" (The Cold Heart), by Wilhelm
    Hauff (1802–1827).
28. According to Gershom Scholem, Professor R. Renvers lived at 24 Nettelbeck-
    strasse in Berlin.
29. *Wallensteins Lager* (Wallenstein's Camp) is a play by Schiller of 1799; see scene
    11.
30. *Der Veilchenfresser* (The Ladies' Man; 1874) is a comedy by Gustav Moser.
    Wilhelm Tell (William Tell; 1804) is a drama by Schiller. *Fiesko* (1783) is a
    tragedy by Schiller. *Carmen* (1875) is an opera by Bizet. Adalbert Matkowsky
    (1857–1909) was a German actor. Emmy Destinn (1878–1930) was a Czech
    operatic soprano.
31. Josef Kainz (1858–1910) was a German actor.
32. *Die lustigen Weiber von Windsor* (The Merry Wives of Windsor; 1849) is a
    comic opera by the German composer Otto Nicolai.
33. Ludwig Erk (1807–1883) was a German singing teacher and editor who col-
    lected and popularized German folk songs.
34. The reference is to Schiller's poem "Das Lied der Glocke" (The Song of the Bell;
    1800).
35. George Stephenson (1781–1848), English inventor and railroad pioneer, built
    and successfully demonstrated a series of locomotives.

Spain, 1932

The first images worth pondering in San Antonio: the interiors that can be glimpsed through open doors whose bead curtains have been gathered to one side. Defying the shadows, the gleaming white of the walls stands out. And in front of the wall, to the rear, there are usually two to four chairs in a strict symmetrical arrangement. Much can be gleaned from them as they sit there, unpretentious in form but with strikingly beautiful wickerwork, all highly presentable. No collector could hang expensive rugs or pictures on his hallway walls with greater pride than the farmer who puts out his chairs in the otherwise bare room. Moreover, they are not just chairs. They change their function instantly when a sombrero is hung on the back of one of them. And in this new arrangement the straw hat appears no less precious than the chair. And it will no doubt generally be the case that in our well-furnished rooms, equipped with every conceivable comfort, there will be no place for what is truly precious, because there is no room for utensils. Chairs and clothes, locks and rugs, swords and planes can all be precious. And the true secret of their value is the sobriety, the austerity, of the living space they inhabit. It means that they do not simply occupy, visibly, the space they belong in, but have the scope to perform a variety of unforeseen functions which enables them constantly to surprise us anew. This is what makes them precious and elevates them above the level of a common object.[1]

A dream from the first or second night of my stay in Ibiza. I went home late—it was not actually my house, but rather a splendid apartment house in which, in my dream, I had put up the Seligmanns. Suddenly, close to the building's entrance, a woman came out of a side street toward me, and as she passed she whispered, as quickly as she was walking, "I'm going to tea! I'm going to tea!" I did not yield to the temptation to follow her but instead went into the Seligmanns' apartment, where an unpleasant scene took place, in the course of which their son pulled me by the nose. Protesting vigorously, I slammed the door behind me. Scarcely was I outside again than the same woman darted up to me from the same side street, with the same words, and this time I followed her. To my disappointment, however, she ignored my approach and kept hurrying down a rather steep alleyway until she reached an iron grille, where she joined a whole group of prostitutes who were obviously standing around in front of their quarters. Not far away a policeman had taken up his post. In the midst of all these embarrassments, I awoke. It then occurred to me that the girl's exciting silk blouse with the unusual stripes had shone brightly in green and violet: the colors of Fromm's nude (see Notebook 1, illustration 22).[2]

Another dream (this time in Berlin, some time before setting off on my journey). I was going somewhere with Jula[3]—it was halfway between an ordinary walk and a mountain hike—and now we were getting close to the summit. For some strange reason I imagined I could recognize the top by a very tall pole sticking straight up into the sky and standing out against the overhanging rock wall. When we reached the top, it turned out to be not a peak but a plateau, with a broad street stretching along it and lined with rather tall, old-fashioned houses on both sides. Suddenly we were no longer on foot but instead sitting in a car, next to each other in the back seat (or so it seemed to me), driving along this road. But it may be that the car changed direction while we were sitting in it. I leaned over to give Jula a kiss. She offered me her cheek instead of her mouth. And as I kissed her I noticed that her cheek was made of ivory, furrowed from one end to the other by black, skillfully scooped-out grooves, whose beauty moved me deeply.[4]

The economy on the island is quite archaic. Fifty years ago bread was quite unknown; the staple food was maize. Even today there are no more than four to six cows, some say because of the absence of fodder, although Don Rossiglio, a fishery owner and deputy, blames it on the backwardness of the inhabitants. How long will this backwardness continue? The fields are still irrigated using old Arab methods: bucket wheels drawn by mules. The grain is still threshed by the hooves of horses driven around the threshing floor on long reins. But we can also see half-built hotels in San Antonio and Ibiza which, for tourists, hold out the promise of running water. The time remaining before their completion has become precious. The paths are still unfrequented; the rambler (who is startled by the lizards) and the lizards (who are startled by the ramblers) still have the countryside to themselves for the moment. Nevertheless, it is with these unpretentious lizards that the modern trend began. We can all recall the terraria that made their appearance some years ago in the cactus niche of ladies' boudoirs or in winter gardens. Lizards started to become an international fashion item. Among present-day pet shop owners, these islands, the Balearics, are just as famous for their lizards as they were among generals in Antiquity for their adepts at the slingshot. And so, at some point, a man settled here and decided to make a living with the aid of a small mail-order business in lizards. There are many methods for catching lizards, but all of them seem to be based on the great curiosity of these creatures. Who knows what biological instinct led to this curiosity? It can scarcely be hunger. For on the one hand they are able to survive three or even four weeks without eating (and this makes it easy to transport them), while on the other they never tire of gazing at even the most inedible objects, such as a hand, if they find it remarkable. People rely on this curiosity when setting traps. The simplest is a deep, open tin can containing strong-smelling bait—cheese, fish, sausage. The can is then buried up to its lip in the ground. After a few days you find that it contains a number of animals that are unable to clamber up its smooth walls. Other, less trusting lizards have to be caught using a fine snare, likewise smeared with some strong-smelling substance to attract them. The strangest method, though, is said to have been practiced in Antiquity. A large bubble of saliva was dropped into a snare, and this was then held out in front of the lizard like a mirror. The moment the animal put its head through the noose, the string was pulled tight. But it was not that first trapper who knew how to tell about such things. He appears to have revealed his professional secrets only in exchange for money. At any rate, this is what can be gleaned from the franchise history of the second trapper. For one day it turned out that the fashion for keeping lizards as household ornaments had been put to rest by the crisis on the Continent. At around the same time—this was in 1922—an unemployed sculptor in Stuttgart who had lost his money in the inflation sat down full of gloomy thoughts to listen to the rarely used radio. This sculptor was a restless spirit, one of those people who have escaped from their parents at an early age. By the time he was fifteen he was already living as the only white man in an Indian village in South America. The ship on which he had served as cabin boy had been wrecked and the rest of the crew had been taken back to Germany, but his family wanted to prevent him from ever going to sea again. Because this did not suit him, he stayed with the Indians, ignoring the warnings of the German consul in Pernambuco about the multitudes of fleas in the Indian villages. So, having started out young, he was now listening to the radio. The talk he heard was being given by a German who had once been interned in Spain, but who, thanks to the generosity of the Spaniards during the war, had come to know the country very well. He had also been to Ibiza, and was now speaking about this "forgotten island." This is what brought the sculptor J. to the island, initially just to reconnoiter. Having discovered that conditions were favorable, lizards in plentiful supply, and the natives friendly, he came a second time and prepared to settle down. He paid his predecessor one thousand marks for his client list and for agreeing not to engage in any further trade in animals on the island. In the meantime, however, the world crisis had taken its course and eliminated the lizards from winter gardens and boudoirs. Orders for lizards failed to materialize, except from traders whose prices were too low to make catching them profitable. For every trip to one of the isolated, uninhabited islands on which the rarer and to some extent still unknown species were to be found meant two or three days' work, as well as a risk for the boat, which could not find anywhere to drop anchor. J., however, once installed, saw his dream of earning a living on the island in a more civilized and even emancipated way dissolve. With its ancient traditions and its archaic way of life, the island had the last word. J. became a fisherman. And when today he lights up a cigarette, he uses a flintstone and a fuse, like everyone else. "In a boat," he says, "that is the best way. The wind blows matches out, but the harder it blows, the more the fuse glows."

It is raining, and the light that here so relentlessly lays claim to all things under heaven retreats and gives them back to the earth.—The white houses behind their cactus hedges are pressed hard by a throng of stormy green spirits.

On the honesty of the natives and its opposite. Two stories.[5] A stranger who had spent several months on the island, during which time he had gained the friendship and trust of the inhabitants, saw the last day of his stay arrive. It happened to be a very hot day, and, having finished his travel preparations, he decided to banish his worries about his possessions as quickly as possible so that he could spend a couple of hours enjoying the shade on the terrace of an Ibizan wine merchant. The people on the boat promised to look after his luggage as well as his jacket, and, noticeably lighter, he went off to the wine merchant's, who welcomed him heartily even though he was only in his shirtsleeves. He effortlessly knocked back the first few *copitas* [mugs] of the local white wine. But the more time passed and the more he drank, the harder he found it to take his leave, especially in such an unfestive manner. Questions occurred to him. He wanted to know about the beautiful porch of the cathedral in Ibiza; about the strange customs of abduction, about which no one knew anything precise; about the origins of those curious names that the fishermen used for the mountains—names quite different from those used by the farmers. Soon he recollected that he had once heard his host described as an authority on the island's history. He thought he would like to clear up a few matters at the last moment, and in this way could perhaps survive the loneliness of his last evening. He ordered a bottle of the best wine, and even as his host uncorked it before his eyes, they were already deep in conversation. Now, in the past weeks the stranger had had ample opportunity to become acquainted with the fanatical hospitality of the islanders. He knew that if he wished to have the honor of inviting them, this had to be properly prepared and made into a quasi-legal stipulation. Accordingly, his first task was to invite his host to be his guest. He insisted on this during the second bottle and the third, all the more since it meant he could take brief notes about this or that piece of information with a good conscience. And (to dwell a little on these notes) there are some that can compete in vividness with those of Stendhal's Italian tales.[6] What an image! The marriageable girl, surrounded by suitors on holiday, but whose father sets strict limits to the time the suitors can have to plead their cause: an hour, an hour and a half at most, even if there are thirty of them or more, so that each one must compress what he has to say into a few brief minutes.—During the conversation, the weather had turned cool; his host would not be denied and insisted on lending him one of his own jackets. The last bottle was opened. A good half of it still remained, when they were interrupted by a siren. It was the steamer lying out at the breakwater, ten minutes away, ready to depart and with the stranger's luggage on board. In the pale evening light, you could see its top light. Even his host could perceive that there wasn't much time left for compliments, so he handed his guest the bill without much resistance, in accord with their agreement. But the latter felt a sudden panic even before he had looked at it. His wallet, which he always kept in his back trouser pocket, was gone. He cast a swift glance at his host. The latter's honest face was filled with consternation. It was inconceivable that he could have the wallet. With the most courteous expressions of concern, the merchant asked the stranger not to take the matter to heart. He maintained that he had felt uncomfortable at being the stranger's guest in his own house. And as for the wallet, it would undoubt-edly turn out to have been in his jacket on board the boat. The stranger, however, was only partly consoled by this. The banknotes it contained were not small, and they were quite numerous. Once he was on board, his worst fears were confirmed. His jacket pockets were empty, and he now knew what to think of the celebrated honesty of the island's people. Faced with the choice of suspecting the ship's crew or the wine merchant, he spent a sleepless night before deciding on the crew. But he was wrong. It was the wine merchant who had his wallet. Scarcely had he arrived back in Germany than he received proof of this in the form of the following telegram: "Wallet found in jacket you borrowed from me. Payment on its way."

Never dissuade a person from a course of action.[7] Anyone who is asked for his advice would do well to begin by finding out the asker's own opinion and then endorsing it. No one is easily persuaded of another's greater cleverness, and few people ask for advice with the intention of following someone else's. The fact is that they have already made up their minds and now wish to hear it from the outside, to accept it as the "advice" of another. This confirmation is what they seek, and they are right to do so. For it is very risky to set out to implement one's own decisions without passing them through the filter of conversation. This is why the person who seeks advice is already halfway to a decision; and if what he is planning to do is a mistake, it is better to lend it skeptical support than to contradict it with conviction.

The fact that in the morning the pupil knows by heart the contents of the book he has put under his pillow the night before, that the Lord inspires His own in their sleep, and that a pause is creative—to make space for such things to happen is the alpha and omega of all mastery, its hallmark.[8] This, then, is the reward before which the gods have placed sweat. For work which achieves only modest success is child's play, compared to the success conjured up by luck. This is why Rastelli's[9] stretched-out little finger attracts the ball, which hops onto it like a bird. The decades' worth of practice that came before does not mean that either his body or the ball is "in his power," but it enables the two to reach an understanding behind his back. To weary the master to the point of exhaustion through diligence and hard work, so that at long last his body and each of his limbs can act in accordance with their own rationality: this is what is called "practice." It is a form of post-hypnotic suggestion that starts to work inside the body, as it were, at the moment the will abdicates its power once and for all in favor of the organs—the hand, for instance. This is why you can look for something for days, until you finally forget it; then, one day, when you are looking for something else, you suddenly find the first object. Your hand has, so to speak, taken the matter in hand and has joined forces with the object which had successfully resisted the dogged efforts of the will.

A strange obsession has made travel writers become fixated on the idea of "fulfillment"—the desire to preserve for every country the blue haze that distance surrounds it with, or for every station in life the glamor that the imagination of the idler endows it with. The leveling of the globe through industry and technology has made such great strides that, by rights, each description should take place against a black backdrop of disillusionment, from which the truly strange incommensurability of the near at hand—of human beings in communication with one another and with the land—could then stand out more sharply. It has to be admitted that reportage in Germany, insofar as it can be regarded as a sort of inverted travelogue, does give expression to this. It is nothing more than a matter of time and study to make even the most distant lands appear immediately familiar. And naturally discipline is also required, of a sort which prevents the author from directly exploiting his first impressions; for if instead he allows them to fall like seeds into the womb of habit, they can subsequently give rise to the marvelous tree whose fruits have the scent of the near at hand.

Brief notes about the island.—Occasionally, when out walking, you hear a hollow sound. Perhaps there are hollow places in the lava (if indeed the island really is volcanic); but some say that there are graves.

There is a special breed of dog here that is said not to occur elsewhere. Dogs of this type are called galybs.

Very pretty, Jokisch's story about the way Customs treated his furniture shipper. Since Jokisch had influence from somewhere, they took the furniture apart as far as was possible, and made him pay duty only on the boards. When I was with him, he also told me how he had discovered that ants eat lizards. For some time after he had set his lizard traps, there was an uninterrupted spell of stormy weather. When he went back to his traps, he found one can full of lizards that had been able to survive cheerfully without food for three or four weeks on end. But others had been invaded by ants, which had killed off all the animals. Sometimes the lizards bite each other, and even themselves. On another occasion he lost some good customers when the lizards that he had kept segregated in various compounds at home all got mixed up. Since then he has ceased to keep a stock of them.

A book on the Balearics by Archduke Johann Salvator.[10]

The history of solitude. "How much land does a man need to live?" asks Tolstoy in one of his stories. The anchorites provided an answer: their way of life, restricted to the smallest speck of land possible, spread throughout the globe. The names of all the angels and devils that thronged around their souls or their camps descended from Athos or Montserrat, and spread throughout the world that once receded before the threshold of their hermitage. Throughout the still-unexplored globe, they asserted the claims of their faith to still-undiscovered climes and untutored creatures. They were the magical forerunners of the missionaries. But solitude is not so timeless that it does not change over time, albeit slowly. Today it is no more than a waste product of community. Hermits no longer exist, and whoever cuts himself off discovers no new community, but only the old one. Thus, there was one man who could not come to terms with the world and had retreated to the heart of a remote island. Few people came to disturb him, but those few were amazed to discover how well informed he was about the events and intrigues of the inhabitants of the coastal region. It was as if isolation had sharpened his ear and as if the wind had brought him news of the latest scandals that townsfolk learn about on the telephone. When they took their leave of him they would ask themselves, "How much gossip does a man need to live?"

There is nothing new about the fact that confidence men often find it easy to carry off their swindles once they have assumed a name that, as it were, dulls the senses of the people they are targeting. Rarely does it happen, however, that this is not the name of some ruling family or former ruling family ("They have all ruled at one time or another," as Fontane remarks), but the name of a remote island. To be sure, this too is not unprecedented; it goes back to the time of Marco Polo or Athanasius Kircher,[11] when one could gain an astonishing reputation through one's extensive travels and knowledge of distant lands. But the fact that an impoverished Mediterranean island can become the center of operations for a confidence man—and "in the name of global commerce"—perhaps deserves a more detailed account. Of course, there may be other minds that succumb to the magic of the name "Ibiza" [illegible phrase omitted]. But they must have two things in common: imagination and a lack of patience—in short, a passionate desire to escape from the conditions in which they live. This was the case with two friends, a writer and a publisher, who had no professional relationship with each other. [text incomplete]

The *Ciudad de Valencia,* which maintains communications between Barcelona and Ibiza, departs every Monday at six o'clock in the evening from the mainland and sails during the night. It is a fine new steamship to which one would like to assign a greater destiny than that of providing a ferry service for this small island. And in fact the image of the boat seemed to shrink before my eyes when I saw it the next day at the breakwater in Ibiza, waiting for the return voyage, for I had imagined that it would go on from there to the Canaries. In any case, toward six o'clock in the evening I stood on the empty promenade deck next to the wheelhouse, piecing together all the parts of the incomparable picture that large towns present to an observer gazing down from the heights of a ship. The sun was setting over the city, which seemed to have fallen silent. All life had retreated to the imperceptible transitions between the foliage on the trees, the cement of the buildings, and the rocks of the distant mountains. I stood and thought of Horace's famous truism, "What exile fleeing from his native land would ever flee his own mind?"[12]—and how questionable it is. For isn't traveling a purification, the overcoming of settled passions that are attached to one's accustomed environment, and hence an opportunity to develop new ones—something that in fact amounts to a metamorphosis? At any rate, I had just become conscious of a new passion, and the ten days at sea that now lay behind me had been sufficient to ignite it. This time I wanted to explore the epic vein—collect whatever facts and stories I could find, and test out my journey to see what it might yield once it was purified of all vague impressions. This should not be thought of as a travel account; rather, it is a matter of travel technique, one with a respectable pedigree—a technique, incidentally, that was the rule before journalism took over. I was standing thinking these thoughts when far below me on the quay I saw, or rather recognized, a stocky man with the most massive head that ever wore a captain's cap. It was Captain V., from the cargo boat on which I had arrived in port here ten hours previously. Anyone who is accustomed to a lonely departure from foreign towns will know what it means to encounter a familiar face—even if it is not a face one especially wants to see—at a moment when imminent departure sweeps aside all the difficulties of a prolonged conversation, but at the same time provides you with a handkerchief, a hand, or a hat in which the unaccommodated gaze may find refuge before venturing out over the sea. Here, however, few sights could have been more welcome to me than that of this captain, on whose boat I had begun to feel at home and who had provided me with the first of my collection of stories. That there was something unusual about him, something not altogether pleasant, had become clear to me very soon after we had left Hamburg. He had the sort of relationship with Tom, a dog he had borrowed from a German in Genoa, that is normally encountered only among eccentrics. It was strange to imagine his daily routine: he ignored breakfast and dinner, so that his working day really went from one lunch to the next, for when the sea is rough a nighttime's rest is a precarious business for a sea captain. And on leaving Hamburg, we had had stormy weather for over four days. Apart from this, he was never unfriendly, for all his reserve; and once he had produced the obligatory sailor's jokes even before we were clear of the estuary of the Elbe (to a somewhat unsympathetic audience, it must be said, since of the three passengers only one was a first-time traveler), he was occasionally not above spending five minutes in a more serious chat. In this way I obtained hints enough to be able to reconstruct for myself, all the way back to the time of the slave trade, the history of the shipping company in whose boat we were traveling. I learned about its beginnings as a ship broker, its trade with the first steamers, not to forget the later migrant transports—those masses of wretched passengers who meant far more to German shipping than the guests on luxury boats like the *Bremen* or the *Europa*. But these were no more than isolated highlights. It was not in such conversations that I heard so much about the history of the boat, and about the forces and interests that governed its voyage through timeless waves, that when I disembarked in Barcelona there seemed to be a whole seething mass of facts and figures in my mind. These included the original cost of the boat, its tonnage, the officers' wages, the year it was built, the cargo rates, and loading and unloading fees, right down to the salary of the most insignificant ship's boy, who was paid off on the day the boat arrived home and not signed on again until the day of the next sailing. Just to mention the first and last of these figures: in 1922 this boat had cost the buyer (who was not the person who had commissioned it) just a bit more than 25,000 marks; and twenty-five marks was a month's wages for a ship's boy. But even the captain of such a ship hasn't got much to laugh about. Indeed, it had been a different story in the days when the cargo business was still handled by sailing ships and when the ships' captains themselves negotiated the cost of transport in the harbors. Nowadays, however, the captain's position is less important, in relation not just to the shipowner but even to the inspector. And concerning the opportunities of rising to what is still a desirable post, an American officer seems to have spoken for many of his German colleagues when he complained about a certain kind of writer who described life on the sea as exciting and painted it in the rosiest of colors. It is of course true that the sailors on our steamships have a greater degree of comfort and their lives are significantly more pleasant than on the old sailing ships. In those says, the old sailor's joke could often be heard: Give up sailing and join a steamship! "But to get down to brass tacks. What are the prospects in the sailing business today? I guess we can assume that in recent years every shipowner has simply been overrun by young men who want to go to sea. But what work do they actually do on board? Scrub the deck, wash the paintwork, and polish the brass! The only chance they get to do anything a little more unusual is when they have to fetch some object that has torn loose on deck or been washed from its moorings and fix it back where it belongs. Only a minute proportion of these youths can stay the course and perhaps get as far as receiving their officer's commissions— and then they discover that supply exceeds demand even at sea. In this world where machines are making people redundant, the sailor's profession is marked by the same competition, the same desperate struggle for existence, as there is on land." I made them tell me about the entire process—from the training in a sailing ship to the helmsman's examination, from ship's boy to ship's officer, in all their various stages. I have also seen the textbook you have to study to prepare for the examinations; it is probably the only book in all the sciences that can claim to be in constant use. The first edition goes back to 1854. Nor is it easy to fom a picture of the world of books that a steamer like this carries with it, from *Quo vadis?* to the logarithmic tables.[13] Above all, there are the practical navigation books—alongside the sea charts, whose tiny clusters of figures reveal the presence of steep underwater mountains. Then there are the handbooks for all the coasts that the boat will, or conceivably could, encounter on its voyage. These are the Baedekers of places which are seldom visited by those who use the books. For here every peak and every promontory, every tower and settlement, is above all a signal, a reference point by which to locate a ship, as well as one for the officers who often find nothing in the examination but a set of data for taking their bearings, for which they have to provide so and so many hundred examples in their exercise books by way of proof if they want to pass the helmsman's examination. When darkness comes these are replaced by navigational beacons, which are likewise listed in the manuals, together with their colors and the intervals at which they flash; alternatively, the ship simply sails by the stars along "roads" that are as well worn as tracks across fields. Then come the best hours, the long ones during which the only diversion is a change of posture while you stand leaning on the bridge railing, or the steps you take walking up and down in front of the helm, which is tended by an ordinary seaman who is relieved by a comrade every three hours. None has remained so firmly in my memory as the one who had been to Iceland and who had been watching me with some resentment for a few nights, which I had spent listening to everything the third mate could tell me about his voyages. While the mate was gazing into the distance over the railing, the seaman suddenly erupted and a small cataract of names and numbers burst out of him: the 2 percent share he'd been given because he was on the Iceland run, the millions he possessed at the time (this was 1922), the vexation that was involved in earning his money, and how they were all so tired sometimes that they fell asleep over their food. I passed him a cigarette, but that was as far as it went. It was usually toward ten when I emerged from the radio operator's cabin. The deck had been cleared; the stars were in the sky. The conversation progressed slowly, but, like a fuse, it always burned its way toward an adventure or a story. My partner and I had discovered the best way of making the time pass quickly, and I never went back to my cabin without enjoying his hospitality for a while in the chart room over a cup of coffee or Van Houten's cocoa. The discussion of freeport dues was succeeded by an account of adventures on the coast of Panama or Schleswig. My host had left home young. At seventeen he had finished his apprenticeship on one of the sailing ships that Leist sent to Chile to bring back saltpeter and that sailed around Tierra del Fuego and Cape Horn, with their storms. At eighteen he got engaged, because he wanted to make use of a ring he had bought onshore. This turned out to be a good investment: he lodged for two weeks with his future mother-in-law, and whether, when he disappeared, his bride had any cause for complaint, even according to strict bourgeois criteria, did not become clear to me that night. For it was not just on topics of this kind that too many questions were impermissible. In this instance, curiosity might have excused my tactlessness; but nothing could have excused my ignorance, had I omitted to have explained to me the ins and outs of nautical maneuvers, the sailors' language, the meaning of the different ranks, or the names of the people and implements I did not understand. But this was not the right time for questions. The nights that week were dark; we couldn't see one another clearly; and the contours of the stories were just as fuzzy, like those of ships that crossed the path of our boat by night. I'm unable to retell them—least of all the one about the voyage of the *Prival*, which would most reward the telling. But since sailors' yarns are on the agenda, perhaps we could take up one particular comic subject with which few others, even from recent history, can compare. It was in 1919, when a number of Hamburg shipowners decided to try and repatriate some sailing ships, saltpeter cargo boats, that had been surprised by the outbreak of hostilities somewhere in Chile some five years previously. The legal position was quite straightforward: the ships had remained German property, and the only problem now was to procure the necessary crews to take possession of them in Rio de Janeiro. There were plenty of seamen available in German ports waiting for employment. But there was one little problem. How were the crews to be transported to Rio? This much was clear: they could travel from Hamburg only as passengers and could be put into service only at the various destinations. It was just as clear that the crews consisted of people who could not readily be managed with the kind of authority that the law of the sea gives captains over his passengers. Moreover, the date must be borne in mind: in 1919 the revolutionary mood of the Kiel uprising still permeated the navy, and much else besides.[14] The shipowners themselves knew this perfectly well, and had filled the higher ranks of the *Prival* with their most able and determined officers. They had gone even further, and the actual course of the voyage proved that their caution had been justified. For barely twelve hours after leaving the North Sea, there were signs that an alliance was being forged among the new recruits that might easily take on a threatening aspect in a voyage lasting over three weeks. On deck, in the cabins, in the crews' quarters, the officers' mess, and on the stairways, there were meetings from early until late of the most varied kinds of circles and associations. Off Finisterre, there were three gambling clubs and two boxing rings, with matches in constant progress. In the officers' mess, whose walls had been decorated with primitive but graphic drawings, the gentlemen from the audience tap-danced to a gramophone; on the steps a ship's exchange had been set up, where, as a sign of the approaching inflation, a lively barter trade had developed in boxes of cigars, dollar notes, binoculars, nude photos, and knives. In short, the boat had been transformed into a floating Magic City, and it would be easy to believe that even without women it was possible to conjure up all the depravity of harbor life. The captain—one of those people who combine a minimum of education and book learning with a maximum of true culture—managed to keep cool in this situation. Nor did he lose his composure when one fine afternoon off Dover, Frieda, a well-built girl from St. Pauli with a poor reputation, was found strolling up and down the stern with a cigarette in her mouth. No doubt there were people on board who knew where she had been hiding till then, and these were the same people who had agreed what measures to take if those in command made the slightest attempt to put the extra passenger back on shore. From then on the nightlife on board became even livelier, and anyone who insisted on his night's rest amid the din created by the 150 "passengers" would have fumed in vain. But it would not have been 1919 if, in addition to everything else, a political element had not appeared. This was no laughing matter, since it would have been easy for the mood to spread contagiously from the "passengers" to the "crew." Voices could already be heard claiming that this expedition would be the start of a new life in a new world; they wanted nothing to do with any work in the port they were heading for, let alone with any talk of returning home. Others saw the longed-for moment approach when there would be a grand reckoning with the rulers. There was no mistaking the fact that a harsher wind was blowing. It soon became plain where it was coming from. There was a certain Richard Schwenke, a tall fellow of slack demeanor who wore his red hair parted; the only thing known about him was that he had served as steward on various shipping lines. On the very first night he could be seen everywhere. He entered the bar, where the dancing was going on, and drew various people into such a loud quarrel that as soon as the record had come to an end, everyone gathered around him. In the boxing ring he provocatively inquired into the political opinions of the fighters, and the Reddest was always his man. And so he went to work, laboring tirelessly at the politicization of the ship, while the masses went in search of their primitive pleasures. By the fourth day, he had succeeded in organizing a general assembly; by the following evening, election fever was raging. And there was no lack of things to elect: a catering committee, a special inspection team, a political tribunal, a ship's secretariat—in short, an entire revolutionary apparatus was created in a few days out of nothing, without any bloodshed and without any serious conflict with the ship's command. Unfortunately, intrigues among the revolutionary leadership were all the more frequent. And they were all the more irritating because the closer you looked, the more apparent it became that in fact everybody belonged to the leadership. Anyone who did not yet have a post could expect one from the approaching elections; in fact, not an evening passed without there being a vote to verify here or there, or a report on various new abuses. When finally the action committee was asked to produce a plan for a coup for discussion in the general assembly, the *Mascot* had already passed Callao.[15] And on the morning of the day for which the final preparations had been set, the pilot from Rio came up the gangway. The last bearings noted in the ship's logbook turned out to be false. Forty-eight hours before the arrival date that the committee had reckoned on, the three-master was berthed at the breakwater as if nothing had happened. With this, my friend's story came to an end. The first week passed. We went into the chart room, where the cocoa already awaited us in two deep stoneware mugs. I had fallen silent, and only after a short interval did I realize that my nocturnal companion had asked me a question. I looked at him. "Yes, as I was saying. Surely you've understood?"—and when I said nothing, since I did not know what to say, he added, "You're right. I myself understood it only later on. One day I happened to go to the ship owner's office in Hamburg, and there I met Schwenke at the door. He still held in his hand the big cigar he had started to smoke in the boss's office. It was only then that I properly understood the story of the *Mascot*." Many of those stories I could never retell; but as I went down the steps to exchange a few words with the captain before the ship's departure, there wasn't one which failed to evoke a name or an image in my mind's eye. I had not formed a completely clear image of the man until the previous few hours—more precisely, until the previous evening, when I had sat with him in the cabin in Alicante before our departure, sharing a bottle, and he had told me the story of his son, who had started out as a sailor and now owned a little cigar shop. What lay between those two livelihoods was the kind of moment that anyone can experience who has stood and watched how a boat that has unloaded its cargo makes ready to cast off. I do not know the name of the large iron crossbeams that are then replaced in the frame that encloses the upper edge of the hold. But I know that they are not more than twenty centimeters wide and that the sailors who balance on them over the thirty-meter-deep hold have to be able to do so without feeling dizzy. And so they are for the most part; but every now and then one does fall, and this is what had happened to his son. He now moves about his shop with the aid of an artificial limb.

Once you've gone a good two hours in the direction of San Antonio, you'll come to a low hill among the last remote *fincas* [farms] that the road passes, up above San Antonio, which you can see lying down below by the bay. There you will see a peaceful farmhouse which seems to have been built in a style quite different from that of the other *fincas*—although at first sight you'd be hard put to say what this difference was.

Written April–July 1932; unpublished in Benjamin's lifetime. *Gesammelte Schriften*, VI, 446–464. Translated by Rodney Livingstone.

Notes

1. See also "Ibizan Sequence" (section entitled "Space for Precious Objects"), in this volume.
2. This notebook has never been found.

3. "Jula" is Benjamin's friend the German sculptor Jula Radt, neé Cohn, sister of Benjamin's schoolfriend Alfred Cohn. Benjamin's relationship with her precipitated the crisis in his marriage. The essay "Goethe's Elective Affinities" (in Volume 1 of this edition) allegorizes this relationship.

4. See also "Ibizan Sequence" (section entitled "First Dream"), in this volume.

5. A later version of this story can be found in this volume under the title "The Eve of Departure." The second story referred to here was never written or has not survived.

6. Stendhal based his *Chroniques italiennes* on unpublished accounts of crimes of passion and grim executions set in the Renaissance—accounts that he discovered in Rome during his consulate in the nearby port of Civitavecchia.

7. See also "Ibizan Sequence" (section entitled "Do Not Seek to Dissuade"), in this volume.

8. See also "Ibizan Sequence" (section entitled "Practice"), in this volume.

9. Enrico Rastelli (1896–1931) was a famous juggler. See also Benjamin's essay "Rastelli Erzählt" (Rastelli's Story).

10. Better-known as Ludwig Salvator, Archduke of Austria. He wrote *Die balearen geschildert in Wort und Bild* [The Balearics Depicted in Words and Pictures] (Leipzig, 1896).

11. Athanasius Kircher (1602–1680) was a Jesuit priest and a polymath. His astounding knowledge embraced archaeology, languages, science, alchemy, Egyptian hieroglyphs, mathematics, and philosophy.

12. "Patriae quis exsul / quoque fugit?" Horace, *Carmina*, Book 2, 16.

13. *Quo vadis?* is the best-known work of the Polish novelist Henryk Sienkiewicz (1846–1916). It deals with Rome under Nero, and was published in 1896.

14. The sailors' mutiny at Kiel in October 1918 was the first in the series of revolutionary actions that brought down the German Empire and led directly to the founding of the Weimar Republic.

15. This unfinished story about the *Prival* contains passages from another story, "Das Taschentuch" (The Handkerchief; see below in this volume), but also represents an early version of yet another story, "Die Fahrt der *Mascotte*" (The Voyage of the *Mascot*). Here the ship is introduced as the *Prival*, but is transformed into the *Mascot* in the course of the narrative.

Light from Obscurantists

Hans Liebstoeckl, *Die Geheimwissenschaften im Lichte unserer Zeit* [The Occult Sciences in the Light of Our Age] (Zurich: Amalthea Verlag, 1932), 432 pages.

In the realm of the occult sciences, the progress of the daily press is relatively slow and tentative. Its grasp of change in this area is usually belated. Rather like the husband who is the last to learn of his wife's infidelity, it is still very inadequately informed about the nature of suprasensual knowledge, in complete contrast to its journalistic quickness and competence in general.
—Liebstoeckl, *Die Geheimwissenschaften,* p. 9

There has always existed a literature that, alongside the need for education, also satisfies the desire of broad sections of the people for happiness. It was to be found in the newspaper shops of small towns just as much as in those of densely populated cities. It inducted its readers into "The Secrets of the Art of Love," "The Seventh Book of Moses," "The Key to Success," or "The Egyptian Interpretation of Dreams." Over the last few decades it has found its way from anonymous obscurity into the brightly lit window displays of more expensive shops that have made a specialty of selling occult writings. This improvement in status brought some changes in its train. The little magazines that attracted us as boys were destined for the classes of people who were excluded from higher education and who therefore aspired to better themselves at a stroke through some sort of magical divination or by mastering the art of winning a prize in the lottery. But the new magazines are addressed to people who have lost their faith in education. The stupidity, low cunning, and coarseness that are common to both types of writing do not prevent them from making a very clear distinction between the kinds of promise they hold out to their two very different readerships. What they promise the ordinary person is his elevation to a higher social class, whereas those who are already there are assured of the exclusive reality of the spirit and the meaninglessness of economic struggle. Not everyone, it must be said, is bold enough to go into such detail on this score as the author of *Die Geheimwissenschaften im Lichte unserer Zeit*, who declares:

> Now that the revival of spiritualism has enabled mankind to rediscover the occult, it has become possible for a poor proletarian—bound to Bolshevism and the comrades' shared store of funds by his compulsory subscriptions—to hear once more the knock on the door in his wretched little room . . . And since that day, the knock on the wall of the poor man has not ceased to make itself heard. Even worse, and most uncannily, when you ask a question of the spirit that is knocking, it answers quite precisely with a yes or a no . . . In broad daylight it plucks at your sleeve, pulls you by the ear, or suddenly hurls objects that miss you by a hair; tables float in the air, despite all the scientific talk of the force of gravity; a book opens of its own accord; a light suddenly shines; the footsteps of an invisible person shuffle through the room; a door opens by itself; and there is a scrabbling at the door, as if a poodle were asking to be let in. If our comrade secretly consults a wise woman or a fortuneteller, . . . he will mainly be given an answer he does not understand . . . But the shop steward will burst into laughter; of course he will soon laugh on the other side of his face, since even the most enlightened shop steward, who has effortlessly passed all the courses in freethinking, will be forced to admit that the supernatural is at work, even though it is broad daylight and he is in complete control of his faculties. I have met workers—loyal socialists and party members—who secretly attended spiritualist meetings and who were not to be deterred from informing me when new phenomena and messages were observed. (pp. 351–352)

The boss will not have many illusions about the reliability of the spirits summoned to besiege the shop steward in his tenement block. Rather, he will be inclined to quietly mutter to himself Wolfskehl's melancholy question, "Shouldn't we say that the spiritualists are fishing in the next world?"[1] This is done with even greater dexterity by the followers of Rudolf Steiner, who regard the author of these remarkable lines as one of themselves.[2] They presuppose a higher level of education than do the straightforward spiritualists, and for this very reason have had far more success in recent years among those who are placing their hopes in the occult. For if the "magic" of the good old penny magazines was the last pitiful by-product of more significant cultural traditions, "anthroposophy," with its associated swindles, is more closely linked to the "general education" of recent times. It is, in fact, the product of its dissolution.

Anyone who undertakes to account for the crisis which has befallen general education in the past few decades will become aware that the process is inadequately described in terms of the alienation of Europe from the works and traditions of its heyday, the withering of the humanities, the collapse of knowledge of the classical languages. For general education is not simply vanishing without a trace. Looked at more closely, it is being undermined. At this point in time, it has reached the stage where one can identify the products which have resulted from its decline and with which it is saturating the spiritual climate. The magic of blood and glitter in its manifold variants is just one of the two elements, neither of which is comprehensible in the absence of the other, that have appeared amid the decline. The oleaginous gibberish of the false prophets (to dwell on them for a moment) can easily be understood as a residue of the great philosophy of humanism that had formerly constituted an integral part of general education, along with the hard sciences. Among these prophets the adherents of anthroposophy are by far the most ambitious. They are concerned not just with the world of spirits, like spiritualists, or with supernatural ways of seeing, like mystics, or even with the stars, like astrologers. They regard the whole gamut of the sciences as their own realm. And it is undeniable that they have made new discoveries all along the line. As anthropologists, for example: "If, under the old Saturn, man's physical body was a body of heat, under the old sun-time it became an air-body that, like a gas, represents a new stage of density" (p. 61). Or as historians: "It cannot be maintained that the displacement of migrant nations (in the barbarian migrations) and the search for a new space was without meaning, if only because they were linked with the distribution of aether throughout the globe" (p. 228). Or as physicists: "Einstein slammed the doors of physics to it [i.e., the aether], but the presence of molecules—which Einstein, Smoluchowski, and Svedberg[3] regard as proven—does little credit to those who expelled the aether from physics, at least insofar as their capacity for logical thought is concerned" (p. 297). Even though we find these skirmishes a recurring feature, as here with Einstein, or again with Eduard Meyer, and Dessoir,[4] the essential thing for Steiner, as with Krishnamurti or Bo Yin Ra,[5] is the great universal harmony in which all individual details are subsumed. If we wish to gain a purchase on these details in the bizarre forms to which they have been condemned by the decay of general education, we have to look at their opposite pole. That the latter has just as powerful a magnetic attraction for the masses as the various essays in magic can be deduced from the popular "Ask Me" columns or the items along the lines of "Did you know . . . ?" that have been a permanent feature of certain daily papers for years now. The chaotic scattering of pieces of factual information that characterizes such diversions is not as senseless as might appear at first sight. At any rate, there is one great branch of economic activity that makes use of them—namely, advertising. Look through the advertising section of the illustrated weeklies. On every page, you'll find pictures of famous men and landscapes, cultural, historical, and technical information, classical rules on how to live, statistical tables, and chemical and physiological data. Commodities thus drape themselves in the world of knowledge and the human spirit, in order to stand out more alluringly. No wonder it was a trade-minded America that took the first great step here, by hiring its radio stations out by the hour to individual large companies and concerns, who are happy to sponsor at their own expense the greatest virtuosi and the most popular comedians to enhance the reputation of their products. In Europe the producers of commodities make do, for the time being at least, with less costly endeavors: they enlist general education in their service so as to anchor their products in the intellectual life of their customers, as well as in their needs. So much for the subterranean interplay between the newer techniques of advertising and the occult sciences, both of which have profited from the collapse of general education. If one of them has mastered the art of transforming the commodity into an arcanum, the other is able to sell the arcanum as a commodity. Just as a cigarette can be regarded as the best healer of the soul, so Steiner's "Goetheanum"[6] can be thought of as a solid business venture, and the occult science it purveys can be packaged as a brand-name product that does not hesitate to enlist the whole of world history as a marketing device.

All this may shed some light on what is at first glance the astonishing zeal with which the occult movement watches over its coverage in the press. We begin to understand why the master took time to reflect on "the press and its significance for the humanities," and on the extent to which "journalists were strong enough to liberate themselves from prejudices and their interest in ephemera" (p. 369). And now that, with this book, we see entering the stage a man who, as the publisher's blurb says, "enjoys a Europe-wide reputation as a music and theater critic," occult science should make the most of him. The reader, however, will think back with some nostalgia to the now-superseded brochures that offered for a few cents good luck at gambling or in love, and will confess how much purer they seemed than writings that summon up Ophir and Atlantis, Buddha and Christ, *The Book of the Dead* and the *Zohar,* merely to establish barbarism in the place occupied by culture a century ago.[7]

Published in the *Frankfurter Zeitung,* August 1932. *Gesammelte Schriften,* III, 356–360. Translated by Rodney Livingstone.

Notes

1. Karl Wolfskehl (1869–1948), a German-Jewish philosopher, was a friend of Stefan George and Ludwig Klages. He fled Germany in 1933.
2. Rudolf Steiner (1861–1925), Austrian-born scientist and editor, was the founder of anthroposophy, a movement based on the notion that there is a spiritual world

accessible only to the highest faculties of mental knowledge. His ideas exerted a broad influence on education in the early part of the twentieth century.

3. Maryan von Smoluchowski (1872–1917) was a Polish physicist. In 1906 he explained the movement of molecules suspended in fluid ("Brownian motion"). Theodor Svedberg (1884–1971) was a Swedish chemist who specialized in the study of colloids. He won the Nobel Prize for Chemistry in 1926.

4. Eduard Meyer (1855–1930) was a well-known classical historian. Max Dessoir (1867–1947) was a philosopher and psychologist. He coined the term "parapsychology."

5. Jiddu Krishnamurti (1895–1986), Indian mystic, enjoyed a prolonged career of writing and teaching. Beginning in the 1920s he spent much time in the United States and Europe, where his books have enjoyed considerable popularity. Bo Yin Ra (pseudonym of Joseph Anton Schneiderfranken; 1876–1943), German painter and writer, left behind thirty-two volumes of mystical writings. A self-described "medium of spiritual insights," his writings portray the world as a realm of spiritual powers inaccessible to the human senses, and the human task as the rediscovery of this divine realm.

6. The "Goetheanum" is the headquarters and the university of the anthroposophist movement. It was established near Basel in 1913.

7. Ophir was an area famous in Old Testament times for its fine gold; biblical texts offer contradictory information on its exact location. *The Book of the Dead* is an ancient Egyptian collection of funerary texts made up of spells and magic formulas, which were placed in tombs and were believed to protect and aid the deceased in the hereafter. The *Zohar*, or *Sefer ha-zohar* (Hebrew: "Book of Splendor"), dates from the thirteenth century; it is the central text of the esoteric system of interpretation known as the Kaballah.

The Handkerchief

Why is storytelling on the decline?—This is a question I often asked myself when I sat with other guests around a table for an entire evening feeling bored. One afternoon, however, when I was standing on the promenade deck of the *Bellver* next to the wheelhouse, surveying with the aid of my excellent binoculars every facet of the incomparable picture that Barcelona offers when viewed from the heights of a ship, I thought I had found the answer. The sun was setting over the city and seemed to be melting it. All life had retreated to the light-gray transitions between the foliage on the trees, the cement of the buildings, and the rocks of the distant mountains. The *Bellver* is a fine, spacious steamship that one would like to think deserved a greater destiny than providing a ferry service to the Balearics. And in fact the image before my eyes really did seem to shrink when, the following day, I saw her tied up at the breakwater in Ibiza, waiting for the return voyage, for I had imagined that it would go on from there to the Canaries. So I was standing there thinking of Captain O., from whom I had taken my leave a few hours before, the first and perhaps the last storyteller I ever met in my life. For, as I have said, the art of storytelling is coming to an end. And when I thought back to the many hours that Captain O. spent walking back and forth on the afterdeck, looking up idly from time to time and gazing into the distance, I realized that people who are not bored cannot tell stories. But there is no longer any place for boredom in our lives. The activities that were covertly and inwardly bound up with it are dying out. A second reason, then, for the decline in storytelling is that people have ceased to weave and spin, tinker and scrape, while listening to stories. In short, if stories are to thrive, there must be work, order, and subordination.

Storytelling is not just an art; it is a kind of dignity—if not, as in the East, an office. It culminates in wisdom, just as, for its part, wisdom often substantiates itself as story. For this reason the storyteller is always someone who knows what has to be done. And to receive such counsel, you yourself have to tell him something. But we know only how to moan and groan about our worries, not how to tell a story. And third, I called to mind the captain's pipe, a pipe that he knocked the ash out of when he started and again when he had finished; but in between, he would let it go out. It had an amber mouthpiece, while its bowl was made of horn with heavy silver mountings. It had come to him from his grandfather, and I think it was the storyteller's talisman. For another reason no proper stories can be heard today is that things no longer last the way they should. Anyone who wears a leather belt until it falls to pieces will always find that at some point in the course of time a story has attached itself to it. The captain's pipe must have known quite a number of them.

Thus I was dreaming, when far below me on the quay I caught sight of a stocky man with the most massive head that ever wore a captain's cap. It was Captain O., from the cargo boat on which I had arrived in port. Anyone who is accustomed to a lonely departure from foreign towns will know what it means to encounter a familiar face—even if it is not that of a close friend—at a moment when imminent departure sweeps aside all the difficulties of a prolonged conversation, but at the same time provides you with a hat, a hand, or a handkerchief in which the unaccommodated gaze may find refuge before venturing out over the sea. And here, then, was the captain, as if my thinking about him had made him appear. At fifteen he had left home, had spent three years on a training ship cruising around in the Pacific and the Atlantic, and had subsequently ended up on one of the steamers of the Lloyd Line on the America run. He had soon left this, however, although he did not say why. Nor could I discover more about him. There seemed to be a shadow lying over his life, but he did not wish to discuss it. And that, of course, means that he appeared to lack the most marvelous feature of a storyteller: the ability to narrate his own life, to allow that wick to be consumed in the gentle flame of the telling. Be that as it may, his life appeared poor compared with that of the ship, every one of whose ribs and spars he was able to bring to life. This was the ship I had before me when I went on board that morning. I was as well informed about the year it was built, the cargo rates, the size of its hold, and its tonnage as I was about the wages of the ship's boys and the worries of its officers. Indeed, those were the days when the cargo business was still handled by the sailing ships and when the ships' captains themselves negotiated the cost of transport in the harbors. In those days, the old sailor's joke could often be heard: "Give up sailing and join a steamship!" Now, however, . . . and there followed a string of sentences from which you could learn how radically things had been changed here too by the economic crisis.

On such occasions Captain O. sometimes let fall some remarks on politics.

But I never saw him with a newspaper. I have never forgotten his reply when one day I brought the matter up. "You can learn nothing from the papers," he said. "They always want to explain everything to you." And in fact isn't it half the art of journalism to keep the news free of explanations? And didn't the ancients set an example for us by presenting events, as it were, dry, draining them entirely of psychological explanations and opinions of every sort? It must be admitted that his own stories kept quite free of superfluous explanations, without losing anything in consequence—or so it seemed to me. There were some strange tales among them, but none that confirms this characterization more than the story below, which was to be followed that very afternoon on the breakwater off Barcelona by a most surprising sequel.

"It was many years ago," the captain had begun as we sailed off Cádiz, "on one of my first voyages to America, during which I was serving as the most junior officer. We'd been sailing for seven days and were due to reach Bremerhaven the following noon. I was making my rounds on the promenade deck as usual, pausing now and then to exchange a few words with the passengers, when suddenly I was startled to see that the sixth deckchair in the row was empty. A feeling of oppression overcame me, yet I fancy that on the previous days I had gone past it feeling even more apprehensive when I had turned with a silent greeting to the young lady who sat in it, her hands folded behind her head, gazing motionlessly before her. She was very beautiful, but her reserve was as striking as her beauty. This went so far that one seldom had the opportunity of hearing her voice—the most marvelous voice I can recollect hearing: soft, husky, dark, metallic. Once, when I had picked up her handkerchief (I can still remember how struck I'd been by the mark embroidered on it: a tripartite coat-of-arms with three stars in each field), I'd heard her say 'Thank you' in a tone that suggested I'd just saved her life. On this occasion, I finished my tour of the deck and was just looking around to see if I could see the ship's doctor to inquire whether she had been taken ill, when I was suddenly enveloped in a whirl of white scraps of paper. I looked up and saw the missing woman leaning over the railing on the sundeck, absentmindedly watching a mass of papers being tossed about by the wind and waves. The next day at noon—I'd taken up my post on deck and was watching the landing maneuver—I again saw the unknown woman, out of the corner of my eye. The ship was about to dock, and the keel was slowly edging closer to the quay to which the stern was already made fast. You could clearly see the faces of the people who were waiting; she scrutinized them feverishly. I was distracted by the sight of the anchor cables being let out. Then, suddenly, I heard shouts and screams. I turned around and saw that the unknown woman had disappeared; you could tell from the commotion of the crowd that she had fallen overboard. Every effort to rescue her seemed futile. If only the engine could have stopped the boat dead—the stern was not more than three meters from the quay and it was unstoppable. Anyone who came between the ship and the quay was lost. Then the implausible actually happened. There was someone who was willing to make the superhuman effort. You could see him straining every muscle, his eyebrows drawn together as if he were taking aim; then he leaped over the rail. And while—to the horror of the onlookers—the whole length of the steamer moved to starboard and came to rest against the quay, the rescuer suddenly surfaced with the woman in his arms on the port side, which was so abandoned that at first no one noticed him. He had in fact taken aim with his entire weight and borne her down with him under the water and beneath the keel before coming back to the surface. 'As I held her,' he told me later, 'she whispered "Thank you," as if I'd just picked up her handkerchief.'"

I could still hear the tone of voice with which the storyteller had uttered these last words. If I wanted to shake hands with him one last time, there was no time to be lost. I was just about to hurry down the steps when I noticed how the granaries, sheds, and cranes had begun to recede. We were under way. With my binoculars raised to my eyes, I let Barcelona pass in review before me one last time. I then lowered them toward the quay. There stood the captain among the crowd; he must have seen me, too. He lifted his hand in greeting; I waved mine. By the time I'd raised the binoculars to my eyes again, he had unfolded a handkerchief and waved. I could clearly see the mark in its corner: a tripartite coat-of-arms with three stars in each field.

Published in the *Frankfurter Zeitung*, November 1932. *Gesammelte Schriften*, IV, 741–745. Translated by Rodney Livingstone.

In the Sun

There are, so it is said, seventeen kinds of figs on the island. One ought—the man told himself as he walked in the sun—to know their names. Indeed, not only ought one to have seen the grasses and the animals that give the island its face, its sound, and its scent; not only ought one to have seen the strata of the mountains and the different kinds of soil, which vary from a dusty yellow to a violet brown, from the cinnabar; above all, one ought to know their names. Isn't every region governed by a unique confluence of plants and animals, and isn't every local name a cipher behind which flora and fauna meet for the first and last time? The farmer, however, has the key to this code. He knows their names. Yet it is not in his power to say anything about his domain. Is it that the names have made him taciturn? Would this mean that the cornucopia of language falls only to the man who has the knowledge without the names; and the cornucopia of silence, to the man who has nothing *but* the names?

It was evident that the man walking along deep in thought was not from here; and if, when he was at home, thoughts came to him in the open air, it was always night. With astonishment he would recall that entire nations—Jews, Indians, Moors—had built their schools beneath a sun that seemed to make all thinking impossible for him. This sun was burning into his back. Resin and thyme impregnated the air in which he felt he was struggling for breath. A bumble bee brushed his ear. Hardly had he registered its presence than it was already sucked away into the vortex of silence. The message of many summers that he had heedlessly let slip by unnoticed (for the first time, his ears were receptive), and now it had ceased to transmit. The nearly obliterated path broadened; tracks led to a charcoal kiln. Behind it the mountains, to which the gaze of the climber was drawn, cowered in the haze.

He felt something cold on his cheek. Thinking it was a fly, he struck at it. But it was only the first droplet of sweat. Soon he felt thirsty. The thirst came not from his palate but from his stomach. From there it spread everywhere, instructing his body, large as it was, in its ability to absorb and drink up the slightest breath of air with all its pores. His shirt had long since slipped from his shoulders, and when he hitched it up to protect them from sunburn, it felt like a damp shawl. In a hollow, almond trees cast their shadows straight down to the base of their trunks. Almonds are the wealth of the country. No other fruit brings the farmer a better price. At this time of year it is the only one ripe, and it is a pleasure to reach out for it among the branches as one walks. The hand is reluctant to part with the shells once the kernel has been removed. It continues to hold them for a while, and then lets them float away in a brook, which carries it along as well. The kernels are ripe, but not entirely ripe; the juice in them is fresher than it is later, when their skin is brown and can no longer be easily removed. At present it was still ivory-colored, like goat's cheese and women's silk shifts. Their taste is ivory, too. Whoever has them between his teeth can tranquilly hear creeks murmuring through the foliage of the fig trees. But the figs were green and hard, and were nestling, barely visible, in the axils. The moment had come when only the trees seemed alive. Amid the pines, you could hear the shrill chirping of cicadas; the noise they made echoed back from the dusty fields. The fields had been stripped of their harvest and now lay bare, with the expression of people who have given away everything. Their last possession—their shadows—lay shrunken, gathered in, at the foot of the tall haystacks. For this was the hour for gathering.

The forests themselves lay around the hilltops, as if harvested by the rake of summer. Only willows stood singly in the stubble, and their foliage gleamed black with white streaks, like tula metal. None was more decked out with bunting, yet more brittle, richer in signs—which were barely noticed. Nevertheless, one of them attracted the attention of the passer-by. He recalled the day he had felt at one with a tree. On that occasion, it had required only the woman he loved—she had stood, quite unconcerned about him, on the lawn—and his sadness or tiredness. So he had leaned with his back against the trunk, and the tree had taken his feelings in hand. He had learned to breathe in when the tree began to sway, and to breathe out when the trunk sprang back. Of course, that had been merely the well-tended trunk of an ornamental tree; it was impossible to imagine the life of a man who could learn from this gnarled willow trunk, deeply split three ways, leaning toward an unexplored world that spread out over the terrain in three directions. No pathway opened them up. But as he paused, uncertain whether or not to proceed along one that threatened to betray him at any moment—seeming now to peter out into a field path, now to come to a stop in a thorny hedge—he found he had himself under control once again as a man: stone blocks rose up in steps to form terraces, and cart tracks made their appearance, pointing to a farmstead in the vicinity.

No sound gives a clue to the neighboring environment of such settlements. Around them the intensity of noonday stillness appears redoubled. But now the fields thinned out, opening up the district with a second and even a third pathway; and while the walls and barns lay hidden behind trees or a ridge, a crossroads suddenly became visible in the abandoned stretch of fields and established the midpoint. There were no highways or mail routes leading here, but neither were these just paths made by animals. Instead, here in the open countryside converged the pathways on which farmers and their wives and children and herds, through the centuries, had moved from field to field, from house to house, from pasture to pasture, rarely in such a way that they did not return to sleep under their own roof at night. The ground here sounded hollow; the sound with which it responded to every step brought comfort to anyone walking this way. With this sound, the solitude of the passer-by laid the land at his feet. If he came to places where he felt good, he knew that solitude had brought him to that point; it had given him this stone to sit on, this hollow as a nest for his limbs. But he was already too tired to pause. Losing control of his feet, which carried him forward much too quickly, he became aware that his imagination had made itself independent of him and, poised against the broad slope that paralleled his path in the distance, had begun to operate on him of its own accord. Does imagination shift rocks and hilltops? Or does it just touch them with its breath? Does it leave no stone unturned, or does it leave everything as it was?

The Hasidim have a saying about the world to come. Everything there will be arranged just as it is with us. The room we have now will be just the same in the world to come; where our child lies sleeping, it will sleep in the world to come. The clothes we are wearing we shall also wear in the next world. Everything will be the same as here—only a little bit different. Thus it is with imagination. It merely draws a veil over the distance. Everything remains just as it is, but the veil flutters and everything changes imperceptibly beneath it.

Things change, and trade places; nothing remains and nothing disappears. From all this activity, however, names suddenly emerge; wordlessly they enter the mind of the passer-by, and as his lips shape them, he recognizes them. They come to the surface. And what further need has he of this landscape? They drift past him on the nameless distant horizon, without leaving a trace. The names of islands that rose out of the sea like marble sculptures, of steep rocks whose craggy peaks broke up the sky, of stars that surprised him in the boat when they came on guard duty in the early darkness. The chirping of the cicadas has fallen silent; the man's thirst has vanished; the day is waning. A sound rises up from somewhere down below. Is it a barking dog, some falling rocks, or a person calling from afar? As he listens, trying to identify it, a peal of bells wells up within him, note by note. Then it ripens and expands in his blood. Lilies blossom at the corner of the cactus hedge. In the distance a cart trundles silently across the fields between the olive and almond trees; and when the wheels vanish behind the foliage, women, larger than life, their faces turned toward him, seem to float motionlessly through the motionless countryside.

Published in the *Kölnische Zeitung*, December 1932. *Gesammelte Schriften*, IV, 417–420. Translated by Rodney Livingstone.

The Rigorous Study of Art

On the First Volume of the *Kunstwissenschaftliche Forschungen*

In the foreword to his 1898 study *Die klassische Kunst* [Classic Art], Heinrich Wölfflin made a gesture that cast aside the history of art as it was then understood by Richard Muther.[1] "Contemporary public interest" he declared, "seems nowadays to want to turn toward more specifically artistic questions. One no longer expects an art-historical book to give mere biographical anecdotes or a description of the circumstances of the time; rather, one wants to learn something about those things which constitute the value and the essence of a work of art . . . The natural thing would be for every art-historical monograph to contain some aesthetics as well." A bit further on, one reads: "In order to be more certain of attaining this goal, the first, historical, section has been furnished with a second, systematic, section as a counterpart."[2] This arrangement is all the more indicative because it reveals not only the aims but also the limits of an endeavor which was so epoch-making in its time. And, in fact, Wölfflin did not succeed in his attempt to use formal analysis (which he placed at the center of his method) to remedy the bleak condition in which his discipline found itself at the end of the nineteenth century. He identified a dualism—a flat, universalizing history of the art of "all cultures and times," on the one hand, and an academic aesthetic, on the other—without, however, being able to overcome it entirely.

Only from the perspective of the current situation does it become evident to what extent the understanding of art history as universal history—under whose aegis eclecticism had free play—fettered authentic research. And this is true not only for the study of art. In a programmatic explanation, the literary historian Walter Muschg writes: "It is fair to say that the most essential work being done at present is almost exclusively oriented toward the monograph. To a great extent, today's generation no longer believes in the significance of an all-encompassing presentation. Instead it is grappling with figures and problems which it sees marked primarily by gaps during that era of universal histories."[3] Indeed, the "turn away from an uncritical realism in the contemplation of history and the shriveling up of macroscopic constructions"[4] are the most important hallmarks of the new research. Sedlmayr's programmatic article "Toward a Rigorous Study of Art," the opening piece in the recently published yearbook *Kunstwissenschaftliche Forschungen* [Research Essays in the Study of Art], is entirely in accord with this position:

> The currently evolving phase in the study of art will have to emphasize, in a heretofore unknown manner, the *investigation of individual works*. Nothing is more important at the present stage than an improved knowledge of the individual artwork, and it is in just this task, above all, that the extant study of art manifests its incompetence . . . Once the individual artwork is perceived as a still unmastered task specific to the study of art, it appears powerfully new and close. Formerly a mere means to knowledge, a trace of something else which was to be disclosed through it, the artwork now appears as a self-contained *small world* of its own, particular sort.[5]

In accordance with these introductory remarks, the three essays which follow are thus rigorously monographic studies. G. A. Andreades presents the Hagia Sophia as a synthesis between Orient and Occident; Otto Pächt develops the historical task posed by Michael Pacher; and Carl Linfert explores the foundations of the architectural drawing.[6] What these studies share is a convincing love for—and a no less convincing mastery of—their subject. The three authors have nothing in common with the type of art historian "who, really convinced that artworks were meant not to be studied (but only 'experienced'), studied them nevertheless—only badly."[7] Furthermore, these authors know that headway can be made only if one considers contemplation of one's own activity—a new awareness—not as a constraint but as an impetus to rigorous study. This is particularly so because such study is not concerned with objects of pleasure, with formal problems, with giving form to experience, or any other clichés inherited from a belletristic consideration of art. Rather, this sort of studious work considers the formal incorporation of the given world by the artist

> not as a selection but rather always as an advance into a field of knowledge which did not yet "exist" prior to the moment of this formal conquest . . . This approach becomes possible only through a frame of mind that recognizes that the realm of perception itself changes over time and in accordance with shifts in cultural and intellectual [*geistig*] direction. Such a frame of mind, however, in no way presumes objects that are always present in an unvarying manner such that their formal makeup is merely determined by a changing "stylistic drive" within perceptual surroundings that remain constant.

For "we should never be interested in 'problems of form' as such, as if a form ever arose out of formal problems alone or, to put it in other words, as if a form ever came into existence for the sake of the stimulus it would produce."

Also characteristic of this manner of approaching art is the "esteem for the insignificant" (which the Brothers Grimm practiced in their incomparable expression of the spirit of true philology).[8] But what animates this esteem, if not the willingness to push research forward to the point where even the "insignificant"—no, *precisely* the insignificant—becomes significant? The bedrock that these researchers come up against is the concrete bedrock of past historical existence [*geschichtliches Gewesenseins*]. The "insignificance" with which they are concerned is neither the nuance of new stimuli nor the characteristic trait, which was formerly employed to identify column forms much the way Linné taxonomized plants.[9] Instead it is the inconspicuous aspect—or this *and* the offensive aspect (the two together are not a contradiction)—which survives in true works and which constitutes the point where the content reaches the breaking point for an authentic researcher. One need only read a study such as the one on the Sistine Madonna published years ago by Hubert Grimme (who does not belong to this group) in order to observe how much such an inquiry, based on the most inconspicuous data of an object, can wrest from even the most worn-out things. And thus, because of the focus on materiality in such work, the precursor of this new type of art scholar is not Wölfflin but Riegl. Pächt's investigation of Pacher "is a new attempt at that grand form of presentation exemplified in Riegl's masterly command of the transition from the individual object to its cultural and intellectual [*geistig*] function, as can be seen especially in his study 'Das holländische Gruppenportrait.'"[10] One could just as well refer to Riegl's book *Die spätrömische Kunst-Industrie* [The Late Roman Art Industry], particularly since this work demonstrates in exemplary fashion the fact that sober and simultaneously undaunted research never misses the vital concerns of its time.[11] The reader who reads Riegl's major work today, recalling that it was written at almost the same time as the work by Wölfflin cited in the opening paragraph, will recognize retrospectively how forces that are already stirring subterraneously in *Die spätrömische Kunst-Industrie* will surface a decade later in expressionism. Thus, one can assume that sooner or later contemporaneity will catch up with the studies by Pächt and Linfert as well.

There are some methodological reservations, however, regarding the advisability of the move that Sedlmayr attempts in his introductory essay, juxtaposing the rigorous study of art as a "secondary" field of study against a primary (that is, positivist) study of art. The kind of research undertaken in this volume is so dependent upon auxiliary fields of study—painting technique and painting media, the history of motifs, iconography—that it can be confusing to constitute these as a somehow separate "primary study of art." Sedlmayr's essay also demonstrates how difficult it is for a particular course of research (such as the one represented here) to establish purely methodological definitions without reference to any concrete examples whatsoever. This is difficult; but is it necessary? Is it appropriate to place this new aspiration [*Wollen*] so assiduously under the patronage of phenomenology and *Gestalt* theory? It could easily be that, in the process, one loses nearly as much as one gains. Admittedly, the references to "levels of meaning" in the works, to their "physiognomic character," to their "sense of orientation," can be useful in the polemic against positivist art chatter and even in the polemic against formalist analysis. But they are of little help to the self-definition of the new type of research. This type of study stands to gain from the insight that the more crucial the works are, the more inconspicuously and intimately their meaning-content [*Bedeutungsgehalt*] is bound up with their material content [*Sachgehalt*]. It is concerned with the correlation that gives rise to reciprocal illumination between, on the one hand, the historical process and radical change and, on the other hand, the accidental, external, and even strange aspects of the artwork. For if the most meaningful works prove to be precisely those whose life is most deeply embedded in their material contents—one thinks of Giehlow's interpretation of Dürer's *Melancolia*[12]—then over the course of their historical duration these material contents present themselves to the researcher all the more clearly the more they have disappeared from the world.

It would be difficult to find a better clarification of the implications of this train of thought than Linfert's study located at the end of the volume. As the text explains, its very subject matter, the architectural drawing, "is a marginal case."[13] But it is precisely in the investigation of the marginal case that material contents reveal their key position most decisively. If one examines the abundant plates accompanying Linfert's study, one discovers names in the captions that are unfamiliar to the layman and, to some extent, to the professional as well. As regards the images themselves, one cannot say that they *re*-produce architecture. They *produce* it in the first place, a production which less often benefits the reality of architectural planning than it does dreams. One sees, to take a few examples, Babel's heraldic, ostentatious portals, the fairy-tale castles which Delajoue has conjured into a shell, Meissonier's knickknack architecture, Boullée's conception of a library that looks like a train station, and Juvara's ideal views ["Prospettiva ideale"] that look like glances into the warehouse of a building dealer:[14] a completely new and untouched world of images, which Baudelaire would have ranked higher than all painting. In Linfert's work, however, the images are submitted to a descriptive technique that succeeds in establishing the most revealing facts in this unexplored marginal realm. There is, as is commonly known, a manner of representing buildings using purely painterly means. The architectural drawing is sharply distinguished from images of this sort and is found to have the closest affinity to nonrepresentational [*unbildmässige*] work—that is, the supposedly authentically architectonic presentations of buildings in topographic designs, prospects, and vedutas. Since in these, too, certain "errors" have survived up through the late eighteenth century despite all the progress in naturalism, Linfert takes this to be a peculiar imaginary world [*Vorstellungswelt*] of architecture, which is markedly different from that of the painters. There are various indications that confirm the existence of this world, the most important one being that such architecture is not primarily "seen," but rather is imagined as an objective entity [*Bestand*] and is sensed by those who approach or even enter it as a surrounding space [*Umraum*] *sui generis*—that is, without the distancing effect of the edge of the image space [*Bildraum*]. Thus, what is crucial in the consideration of architecture is not seeing but the apprehension [*durchspüren*] of structures. The objective effect of the buildings on the imaginative being [*vorstellungsmässige Sein*] of the viewer is more important than their "being seen." In short, the most essential characteristic of the architectural drawing is that "it does not take a pictorial detour."

So much for the formal aspects. In Linfert's analyses, however, formal questions are very closely tied to historical circumstances. His investigation deals with "a period during which the architectural drawing began to lose its principal and decisive expression."[15] But how transparent this "process of decay" becomes here! How the architectural prospects open up in order to take into their core allegories, stage designs, and monuments! And each of these forms in turn points to unrecognized aspects which appear to the researcher Linfert in their full concreteness: Renaissance hieroglyphics; Piranesi's visionary fantasies of ruins; the temples of the Illuminati, such as we know them from *Die Zauberflöte*.[16] Here it becomes evident that the hallmark of the new type of researcher is not the eye for the "all-encompassing whole" or the eye for the "comprehensive context" (which mediocrity has claimed for itself), but rather the capacity to be at home in marginal domains. The men whose work is contained in this yearbook represent the most rigorous of this new type of researcher. They are the hope of their field of study.

Written July–December 1932; abridged version published in the *Literaturblatt der Frankfurter Zeitung*, July 1933 (under the pseudonym Detlef Holz). *Gesammelte Schriften*, III, 363–369. Translated by Thomas Y. Levin.

Notes

1. Richard Muther (1860–1909) was an art historian and critic who is often cited as paradigmatic of the "old school" of nineteenth-century art history. His work was a mixture of religiosity, sentimentality, and eroticism.
2. Heinrich Wölfflin, *Die klassische Kunst: Eine Einführung in die italienische Renaissance* (Munich: F. Bruckmann, 1899), pp. vii–viii; translated by Linda Murray and Peter Murray as *Classic Art: An Introduction to the Italian Renaissance* (London: Phaidon, 1952), pp. xi–xii.
3. Walter Muschg, "Das Dichterporträt in der Literaturgeschichte" [The Writer's Portrait in Literary History], in Emil Ermatinger, ed. *Philosophie der Literaturwissenschaft* (Berlin: Junker und Dünnhaupt, 1930), p. 311. Compare also Benjamin's citation of the same passage in his essay "Literaturgeschichte und Literaturwissenschaft" (Literary History and the Study of Literature), *Gesammelte Schriften*, vol. 3, pp. 289–290. Walter Muschg (1898–1965) was a Swiss literary historian, poet, and dramatist.
4. Muschg, "Das Dichterportrait," p. 314.
5. Hans Sedlmayr, "Zu einer strengen Kunstwissenschaft" (Toward a Rigorous Study of Art), in Otto Pächt, ed., *Kunstwissenschaftliche Forschungen*, vol. 1 (Berlin: Frankfurter Verlags-Anstalt, 1931), pp. 19–20. Hans Sedlmayr (1896–1984) was a German art historian. Otto Pächt (1902–1988), Austrian art historian, was a leading figure in the "second Viennese school" of art history (the first school having formed around Alois Riegl at the turn of the century).
6. G. A. Andreades, "Die Sophienkathedrale von Konstantinopel" (The Hagia Sophia in Constantinople), in Pächt, ed., *Kunstwissenschaftliche Forschungen*, pp. 33–94; Otto Pächt, "Die historische Aufgabe Michael Pachers" (The Historical Task of Michael Pacher), ibid., pp. 95–132; Carl Linfert, "Die Grundlagen der Architektur-zeichnung" (Fundamentals of Architectural Drawing), ibid., pp. 133–246.
7. Pächt, ed., *Kunstwissenschaftliche Forschungen*, p. 31.
8. The phrase comes not from the Brothers Grimm but from Sulpiz Boisserée, who used it, in a letter to Goethe, to describe August Wilhelm Schlegel's review of the Grimms' book *Altdeutsche Wälder* (Old-German Woods).
9. Carl von Linné, also known as Carolus Linnaeus (1707–1778), was a Swedish naturalist credited with the founding of modern systematic botany. He based his classification of each genus and its species on the system of binomial scientific nomenclature, which he developed.
10. Alois Riegl (1858–1905) was an Austrian art historian. His book *Die spätrömische Kunst-Industrie* (The Late Roman Art Industry; 1901) effected a revolution in the study of artistic epochs previously held to be degenerate. Benjamin counted this text as one of the four most important books of the young century. Alois Riegl, "Das holländische Gruppenportrait" [The Dutch Group Portrait], *Jahrbuch der Kunsthistorischen Sammlungen des Allerhöchsten Kaiserhauses*, vol. 23, parts 3–4 (Vienna: F. Tempsky, 1902), pp. 71–278.
11. Alois Riegl, *Die spätrömische Kunst-Industrie nach den Funden in Oesterreich-Ungarn*, Part 1 (Vienna: K.K. Hof- und Staatsdruckerei, 1901); translated by

Rolf Winks as *Late Roman Art Industry* (Rome: Giorgio Bretschneider Editore, 1985).

12. Karl Giehlow, "Dürers Stich *Melancolia I* und der maximilianische Humanistenkreis" [Dürer's Engraving *Melancholy I* and the Humanist Circle under Maximilian], in *Mitteilungen der Gesellschaft für vervielfältigende Kunst: Beilage der "Graphischen Künste"* (Vienna, 1903). Giehlow (1863–1913) was a German art historian and a leading Dürer scholar.

13. Linfert, "Architektur-zeichnung," p. 153.

14. Paul Emile Babel (1720–1770), French designer and engraver, worked in a rococo style. Jacques Delajoue (1686–1761; also spelled "de Lajoue") did elegant drawings and paintings of rococo architecture, often in fanciful pastoral settings. Juste-Aurèle Meissonnier (1675–1750) was a French painter, sculptor, and architect whose work was characterized by fantasy and arabesque. Etienne-Louis Boullée (1728–1799) was a French visionary architect, theorist, and teacher. Filippo Juvara (1678–1736) was an Italian architect and stage designer.

15. Linfert, "Architektur-zeichnung," p. 231.

16. Benjamin is probably referring to the epoch-making stage sets for Mozart's opera *Die Zauberflöte* (The Magic Flute), produced in 1816 by the eminent architect Karl Friedrich Schinkel (1781–1841), whose neoclassical exoticism became a model for many subsequent stagings. Benjamin might even have seen a performance of *Die Zauberflöte* with these Schinkel sets, since they were still being used by the Berlin State Opera as late as 1937.

Hashish in Marseilles

Preliminary remark: One of the first signs that hashish is beginning to take effect is

a dull feeling of foreboding; something strange, ineluctable, is approaching . . . Images and chains of images, long-submerged memories appear; whole scenes and situations are experienced. At first they arouse interest, now and then enjoyment, and finally, when there is no turning away from them, weariness and torment. By everything that happens, and by what he says and does, the subject is surprised and overwhelmed. His laughter, all his utterances, happen to him like external events. He also attains experiences that approach inspiration, illumination . . . Space can expand, the ground tilt steeply, atmospheric sensations occur: vapor, an opaque heaviness of the air. Colors grow brighter, more luminous; objects more beautiful, or else lumpy and threatening. . . . All this does not occur in a continuous development; rather, it is typified by a continual alternation of dreaming and waking states, a constant and finally exhausting oscillation between totally different worlds of consciousness. In the middle of a sentence these transitions can take place . . . All this the subject reports in a form that usually diverges very widely from the norm. Connections become difficult to perceive, owing to the frequently sudden rupture of all memory of past events; thought is not formed into words; the situation can become so compulsively hilarious that the hashish eater for minutes on end is capable of nothing except laughing . . . The memory of the intoxication is surprisingly clear.

"It is curious that hashish poisoning has not yet been experimentally studied. The most admirable description of the hashish trance is by Baudelaire *(Les paradis artificiels).*" From Joël and Fränkel, "Der Haschisch-Rausch," *Klinische Wochenschrift,* 5 (1926), p. 37.

Marseilles, July 29. At seven o'clock in the evening, after long hesitation, I took hashish. During the day, I had been in Aix. With the absolute certainty (in this city of hundreds of thousands where no one knows me) of not being disturbed, I lie on the bed. Yet I am disturbed, by a little child crying. I think three-quarters of an hour have already passed. But it is only twenty minutes . . . So I lie on the bed, reading and smoking. Opposite me always this view of the belly of Marseilles. The street I have so often seen is like a knife cut.

At last I left the hotel, the effects seeming nonexistent or so weak that the precaution of staying at home was unnecessary. My first port of call was the café on the corner of the Cannebière and the Cours Belsunce. Seen from the harbor, the one on the right; therefore not my usual café. What now? Only a certain benevolence, the expectation of being received kindly by people. The feeling of loneliness is very quickly lost. My walking stick begins to give me a special pleasure. One becomes so tender, fears that a shadow falling on the paper might hurt it. The nausea disappears. One reads the notices on the urinals. It would not surprise me if this or that person came up to me. But when no one does I am not disappointed, either. But it's too noisy for me here.

Now the hashish eater's demands on time and space come into force. As is known, these are absolutely regal. Versailles, for one who has taken hashish, is not too large, or eternity too long. Against the background of these immense dimensions of inner experience, of absolute duration and immeasurable space, a wonderful, beatific humor dwells all the more fondly on the contingencies of the world of space and time. I feel this humor infinitely when I am told at the Restaurant Basso that the kitchen has just been closed, while I have just sat down to feast into eternity. Afterward, despite this, the feeling that all this is indeed bright, frequented, animated, and will remain so. I must note how I found my seat. What mattered to me was the view of the old port that one got from the upper floors. Walking past below, I had spied an empty table on the balcony of the second story. Yet in the end, I reached only the first. Most of the window tables were occupied, so I went up to a very large one that had just been vacated. As I was sitting down, however, the disproportion of seating myself at so large a table caused me such shame that I walked across the entire floor to the opposite end to sit at a smaller table that became visible to me only as I reached it.

But the meal came later. First, the little bar on the harbor. I was again just on the point of retreating in confusion, for a concert—indeed, a brass band—seemed to be playing there. I only just managed to explain to myself that it was nothing more than the blaring of car horns. On the way to the

Vieux Port, I already had this wonderful lightness and sureness of step that transformed the stony, unarticulated earth of the great square that I was crossing into the surface of a country road along which I strode at night like an energetic hiker. For at this time I was still avoiding the Cannebière, not yet quite sure of my regulatory functions. In that little harbor bar, the hashish then began to exert its canonical magic with a primitive sharpness that I had scarcely felt until then. For it made me into a physiognomist, or at least a contemplator of physiognomies, and I underwent something unique in my experience: I positively fixed my gaze on the faces that I had around me, some of which were of remarkable coarseness or ugliness. Faces that I would normally have avoided for a twofold reason: I would neither have wished to attract their gaze nor have endured their brutality. It was a very advanced post, this harbor tavern. (I believe it was the farthest accessible to me without danger—a circumstance I had gauged, in the trance, with the same accuracy with which, when utterly weary, one is able to fill a glass exactly to the brim without spilling a drop, something one can never do with sharp senses.) It was still sufficiently far from the rue Bouterie, yet no bourgeois sat there; at the most, besides the true port proletariat, a few petty-bourgeois families from the neighborhood. I now suddenly understood how, to a painter (hadn't it happened to Rembrandt and many others?), ugliness could appear as the true reservoir of beauty—or better, as its treasure chest: a jagged mountain with all the inner gold of beauty gleaming from the wrinkles, glances, features. I especially remember an infinitely bestial, vulgar male face in which the "line of renunciation" struck me with sudden violence. It was, above all, men's faces that had begun to interest me. Now began the game, which I played for quite a while, of recognizing someone I knew in every face. Often I knew the name, often not. The deception vanished as deceptions vanish in dreams: not in shame, not compromised, but peacefully and amiably, like a being who has performed his service. Under these circumstances, there was no question of loneliness. Was I my own company? Surely not so undisguisedly. I doubt whether that would have made me so happy. More likely this: I became my own most skillful, fond, shameless procurer, gratifying myself with the ambiguous assurance of one who knows from profound study the wishes of his employer.—Then it began to take half an eternity until the waiter reappeared. Or, rather, I could not wait for him to appear. I went into the barroom and paid at the counter. Whether tips are usual in such taverns I do not know. But under other circumstances, I should have given something in any case. Under the influence of hashish yesterday, however, I was on the stingy side; for fear of attracting attention by extravagance, I succeeded in making myself really conspicuous.

Similarly at Basso's. First I ordered a dozen oysters. The man wanted me to order the next course at the same time. I named some local dish. He came back with the news that none was left. I then pointed to a place on the menu in the vicinity of this dish, and was on the point of ordering each item, one after another, but then the name of the one above it caught my attention, and so on, until I finally reached the top of the list. This was not just from greed, however, but from an extreme politeness toward the dishes, which I did not wish to offend by a refusal. In short, I came to a stop at a *pâté de Lyon.* "Lion paste," I thought with a witty smile, when it lay clean on a plate before me; and then, contemptuously: "This tender rabbit or chicken meat—whatever it may be." To my lionish hunger, it would not have seemed inappropriate to satisfy itself on a lion. Moreover, I had tacitly decided that as soon as I had finished at Basso's (it was about half past ten) I would go elsewhere and dine a second time.

But first, back to the walk to Basso's. I strolled along the quay and read, one after another, the names of the boats tied up there. As I did so, an incomprehensible gaiety came over me, and I smiled in turn at all the Christian names of France. The love promised to these boats by their names seemed wonderfully beautiful and touching to me. Only one of them, *Aero II,* which reminded me of aerial warfare, I passed by without cordiality, exactly as, in the bar that I had just left, my gaze had been obliged to pass over certain excessively deformed countenances.

Upstairs at Basso's, when I looked down, the old games began again. The square in front of the harbor was my palette, on which my imagination mixed the qualities of the place, trying them out now this way, now that, without concern for the result, like a painter daydreaming on his palette. I hesitated before ordering wine. It was a half bottle of Cassis. A piece of ice was floating in the glass. Yet it went excellently with my drug. I had chosen my seat on account of the open window, through which I could look down on the dark square. And when I did so from time to time, I noticed that it had a tendency to change with everyone who stepped onto it, as if it formed a figure about him that, clearly, had nothing to do with the square as he saw it but, rather, had to do with the view that the great portrait painters of the seventeenth century—in accordance with the character of the dignitary whom they placed before a colonnade or a window—threw into relief with this colonnade, this window. Later I noted as I looked down, "From century to century, things grow more estranged."

Here I must observe in general: the solitude of such trances has its dark side. To speak only of the physical aspect, there was a moment in the harbor tavern when a violent pressure in my diaphragm sought relief through humming. And there is no doubt that truly beautiful, illuminating visions were not awakened. On the other hand, solitude works in these states as a filter. What one writes down the following day is more than an enumeration of impressions. In the night, the trance cuts itself off from everyday reality with fine, prismatic edges. It forms a kind of figure, and is more easily memorable. I would say: it shrinks and takes on the form of a flower.

To begin to solve the riddle of the ecstasy of trance, one ought to meditate on Ariadne's thread. What joy in the mere act of unrolling a ball of thread! And this joy is very deeply related to the joy of intoxication, just as it is to the joy of creation. We go forward; but in so doing, we not only discover the twists and turns of the cave, but also enjoy this pleasure of discovery against the background of the other, rhythmic bliss of unwinding the thread. The certainty of unrolling an artfully wound skein—isn't that the joy of all productivity, at least in prose? And under the influence of hashish, we are enraptured prose-beings raised to the highest power.

A deeply submerged feeling of happiness that came over me afterward, on a square off the Cannebière where the rue Paradis opens onto a park, is more difficult to recall than everything that went before. Fortunately I find in my newspaper the sentence, "One should scoop sameness from reality with a spoon." Several weeks earlier I had noted another, by Johannes V. Jensen,[1] which appeared to say something similar: "Richard was a young man with understanding for everything in the world that was of the same kind." This sentence had pleased me very much. It enabled me now to bring the political, rational sense it had had for me earlier into juxtaposition with the individual, magical meaning of my experience the day before. Whereas Jensen's sentence amounted (as I had understood it) to saying that things are, as we know them to be, thoroughly mechanized and rationalized, since the particular is confined today solely to nuances, my new insight was entirely different. For I saw only nuances, yet these were the same. I immersed myself in contemplation of the sidewalk before me, which, through a kind of unguent with which I glided over it, could have been—precisely like these very stones—also the sidewalk of Paris. One often speaks of stones instead of bread. These stones were the bread of my imagination, which was suddenly seized by a ravenous hunger to taste what is the same in all places and countries. Yet I thought with immense pride of sitting here in Marseilles in a hashish trance; of who else might be sharing my intoxication this evening, and of how few actually were. Of how I was incapable of fearing future misfortune, future solitude, for hashish would always remain. The music from a nearby nightclub that I had been following played a part in this stage. G. rode past me in a cab. It happened suddenly, exactly as, earlier, from the shadows of the boat, U. had suddenly detached himself in the form of a harbor loafer and pimp. But there were not only known faces. Here, while I was in the state of deepest trance, two figures (citizens, vagrants, what do I know?) passed me as "Dante and Petrarch." "All men are brothers." So began a train of thought that I am no longer able to pursue. But its last link was certainly much less banal than its first, and led on perhaps to images of animals.

"Barnabe," read the sign on a streetcar that stopped briefly at the square where I was sitting. And the sad confused story of Barnabas seemed to me no bad destination for a streetcar going into the outskirts of Marseilles.[2]

Something very beautiful was going on around the door of the dance hall. Now and then a Chinese man in blue silk trousers and a glowing pink silk jacket stepped outside. He was the doorman. Girls displayed themselves in the doorway. My mood was free of all desire. It was amusing to see a young man with a girl in a white dress coming toward me, and to be immediately obliged to think: "She got away from him in there in her shift, and now he is fetching her back. Well, well." I felt flattered by the thought of sitting here in a center of dissipation, and by "here" I meant not the town but the little, not-very-eventful spot where I found myself. But events took place in such a way that the appearance of things touched me with a magic wand, and I sank into a dream of them. At such hours, people and things behave like those little stage sets and figurines made of elder pith in the glazed tin-foil box, which, when the glass is rubbed, become electrically charged and fall at every movement into the most unusual relationships.

The music, which meanwhile kept rising and falling, I called the "rush switches of jazz." I have forgotten on what grounds I permitted myself to mark the beat with my foot. This is against my education, and it did not happen without inner disputation. There were times when the intensity of acoustic impressions blotted out all others. In the little bar, above all, everything was suddenly submerged in the noise of voices, not of streets. What was most peculiar about this din of voices was that it sounded entirely like dialect. The people of Marseilles suddenly did not speak good enough French for me. They were stuck at the level of dialect. The phenomenon of alienation that may be involved in this—which Kraus has formulated in the fine dictum, "The more closely you look at a word, the more distantly it looks back"—appears to extend to the optical.[3] At any rate, I find among my notes the surprised comment: "How things withstand the gaze!"

The trance abated when I crossed the Cannebière and at last turned the corner to have a final ice cream at the little Café des Cours Belsunce. It was not far from the first café of the evening, in which, suddenly, the amorous joy dispensed by the contemplation of some fringes blown by the wind had convinced me that the hashish had begun its work. And when I recall this state, I would like to believe that hashish persuades nature to permit us—for less egoistic purposes—that squandering of our own existence that we know in love. For if, when we love, our existence runs through Nature's fingers like golden coins that she cannot hold and lets fall so that they can thus purchase new birth, she now throws us, without hoping or expecting anything, in ample handfuls toward existence.

Published in the *Frankfurter Zeitung,* December 1932. *Gesammelte Schriften,* IV, 409–416. Translated by Edmund Jephcott.

Notes

1. Johannes Vilhelm Jensen (1873–1950) was a Danish novelist, poet, and essayist. He received the Nobel Prize for Literature in 1944.
2. The story of Barnabas is told in the New Testament (Acts 15).
3. Karl Kraus (1874–1936) was an Austrian journalist, critic, playwright, and poet. See the essays on Kraus in this volume.

The Eve of Departure

The economy on the island is archaic.[1] They do not mow, but cut the grain with sickles. In some places the women pull it up with their hands, so there is no stubble left. When it is harvested, the corn is brought to the threshing floor, where a horse, urged on by a farmer who stands in the middle of the floor holding the reins, separates with trudging hooves the grain from the ears. Sixty years ago bread was unknown here; the staple food was maize. And even today the fields are irrigated using an old-fashioned method: bucket wheels drawn by mules. There are only a few cows on the island. Some say because of the absence of fodder; but Don Rosello, the deputy and wine merchant, who represents progress here, blames it on the backwardness of the inhabitants. Not so long ago, a new arrival in Ibiza could learn from the first inhabitant he met: "Now we have so-and-so-many foreigners on the island." From that time dates the following story, which was told at Don Rosello's table:

"A stranger who had spent several months on the island, during which time he had gained the friendship and trust of the inhabitants, saw the last day of his stay arrive. It happened to be a very hot day, and, having finished his travel preparations, he decided to banish his worries about his possessions as quickly as possible so that he could spend a couple of hours enjoying the shade on the terrace of an Ibizan wine merchant. The people on the boat promised to look after his luggage as well as his jacket, and, noticeably lighter, he went off to the *tienda* [store] belonging to the wine merchant, who welcomed him heartily even though he was only in his shirtsleeves. He effortlessly knocked back the first few *copitas* [mugs] of the local white wine. But the more time passed and the more he drank, the harder he found it to take his leave, especially in such an unfestive manner. Questions occurred to him. He wanted to know about the history of the beautiful Galgos, the descendants of the dogs of the Pharaohs that roam the island without a master; about the old customs of courtship and abduction, about which he could never obtain any precise information; about the origins of those curious names that the fishermen used for the mountains—names quite different from those used by the farmers. Soon he recollected that he had once heard the owner of this little *tienda* described as an authority on the island's history. He thought he would like to clear up a few matters at the last moment, and in this way could perhaps get over the loneliness of his last evening. He ordered a bottle of the best wine, and even as his host uncorked it before his eyes, they were already deep in conversation. Now, in the past weeks the stranger had had ample opportunity to become acquainted with the fanatical hospitality of the islanders. He knew that if he wished to have the honor of inviting them, this had to be properly prepared and made into a quasi-legal stipulation. Accordingly, his first task was to invite his host to be his guest. He insisted on this during the second bottle and the third, all the more since it meant he could take brief notes about this or that piece of information with a good conscience. And as he leafed through his notebook by the light of the candle, he came across sketches (he was something of a draftsman) that he had made in the first few days after his arrival. There was the blind man with the red leg of goat or mutton who always walked around the streets led by a boy; on another page were the living profiles of the walls that had been built without any reference to standard measurements; then came the tiled steps with the mysterious numbers that he had seen at the very beginning when he was looking for a place to live. His host looked on with interest over his shoulder. Of course, he knew the story of the leg of mutton; he had himself been responsible for helping the blind man obtain permission to run a meagre little lottery and give out tickets whose only prize was this same leg of mutton. And he had himself seen the mysteriously numbered tiles on a street in which they had served as the house numbers. Even more, he knew the meaning of the white crosses that stood at the foot of a number of houses and that were so puzzling to outsiders. They were a kind of altar of rest. Each marked one of the places where the processions suddenly paused in their progress through the streets. And now the visitor suddenly remembered vaguely that he had come across something similar in Westphalian villages. During the conversation, the weather had turned cool; his host would not be denied and insisted on lending him one of his own jackets. The last bottle was opened.—But to return to those notes by the stranger: Where can you find in Stendhal's Italian tales a motif that could compete with this one from Ibiza?[2] The marriageable girl, surrounded by suitors on holiday, while her father sets strict limits to the time the suitors can have to plead their cause:

an hour, an hour and a half at most, even if there are thirty of them or more, so that each one must compress what he has to say into a few brief minutes.—A good half of the bottle still awaited them, when they were interrupted by a siren. It was the *Ciudad de Mahon* lying out at the breakwater, ten minutes away, ready to depart and with the stranger's luggage on board. Above the roofs you could see its top light piercing the darkness. Even his host could perceive that there wasn't much time left for compliments, so he handed his guest the bill without much resistance, in accord with their agreement. The visitor, however, felt a sudden panic even before glancing down at the bill. His money was gone. He cast a swift glance at his host. The latter's honest face was filled with consternation. It was inconceivable that he could have the envelope with the banknotes. With the most courteous expressions of concern, he asked the stranger not to take the matter to heart. He maintained that he had felt uncomfortable at being the stranger's guest in his own house. And as for the money, it would undoubtedly turn out to have been in his jacket on board the boat. The stranger, however, was only partly consoled by this. The banknotes he was missing were not small, and they were quite numerous. Once he was on board, his worst fears were confirmed. His jacket pockets were empty, and he now knew what to think of the celebrated honesty of the island's people. Faced with the choice of suspecting the steward or the wine merchant, he spent a sleepless night in his cabin before deciding on the steward. But he was wrong. It was the wine merchant who had his money. Scarcely had he arrived back home than he received proof of this in the form of the following telegram: 'Money found in jacket you borrowed from me. Payment on its way.'"

"As for the telegram," Don Rosello said, having listened with an obliging smile, "it must have been the first he'd ever sent."—"And what difference does that make?"—"I know what point you want to make," he replied. "You want to make me believe in the innocence of the inhabitants. In the Golden Age. Rousseauesque platitudes. Seven years ago the prison in an old Moorish castle was opened up, and has in fact not been needed since. But do you know why? I'll tell you in the words of the old warder, whom we had to dismiss at the time: 'Our people—they've all seen so much of the world nowadays. They've learned to distinguish between good and evil.' World travel promotes morality. That's the entire secret."

Written ca. 1932; unpublished in Benjamin's lifetime. *Gesammelte Schriften*, IV, 745–748. Translated by Rodney Livingstone.

Notes

1. An earlier version of this story appears in the autobiographical essay "Spain, 1932," in this volume.
2. Stendhal based his *Chroniques italiennes* on unpublished accounts of crimes of passion and grim executions set in the Renaissance—accounts that he discovered in Rome during his consulate in the nearby port of Civitavecchia.

On Astrology

An attempt to procure a view of astrology from which the doctrine of magical "influences," of "radiant energies," and so on has been excluded. Such an attempt may be provisional, if you like. It is very important because it would purify the aura surrounding these investigations. And we necessarily come across such research if we inquire into the historical origins of the concepts of a scientific humanism. Nowhere more pervasively, perhaps, than in astrology. I have shown the intensity it conferred on the concept of melancholy. Something along these lines could be adduced for many other concepts.

The approach looks like this: We start with "similarity." We then try to obtain clarity about the fact that the resemblances we can perceive, for example, in people's faces, in buildings and plant forms, in certain cloud formations and skin diseases, are nothing more than tiny prospects from a cosmos of similarity. We can go beyond this and attempt to clarify for ourselves the fact that not only are these resemblances imported into things by virtue of chance comparisons on our part, but that all of them—like the resemblances between parents and children—are the effects of an active, mimetic force working expressly inside things. Furthermore, not only are the objects of this mimetic force innumerable, but the same thing may be said of subjects, of the mimetic centers that may be numerous within every being. On top of all this, it must be remembered that neither the mimetic centers nor their objects, the mimetic objects, can have remained unchanged through time, and that in the course of the centuries both the mimetic force and the mimetic mode of vision may have vanished from certain spheres, perhaps only to surface in others. For example, there can be no doubt that people in Antiquity had a much sharper mimetic sense for physiognomic resemblances than does modern man, who really only recognizes facial similarities, and no longer has much ability to recognize bodily similarities. We may further reflect that in Antiquity, physiognomy was based on animal resemblances.

If these considerations bring us close to astrology, the decisive factor is still lacking. As students of ancient traditions, we have to reckon with the possibility that manifest configurations, mimetic resemblances, may once have existed where today we are no longer in a position even to guess at them. For example, in the constellations of the stars. The horoscope must above all be understood as an originary totality that astrological interpretation merely subjects to analysis. The panorama of the heavenly bodies presents a characteristic unity, and the characters of the individual planets, for example, are recognized only through their function within the constellation. (The word "character" is provisional here. We should really say "essence.") We must reckon with the fact that, in principle, events in the heavens could be imitated by people in former ages, whether as individuals or groups. Indeed, this imitation may be seen as the only authority that gave to astrology the character of experience. Modern man can be touched by a pale shadow of this on southern moonlit nights in which he feels, alive within himself, mimetic forces that he had thought long since dead, while nature, which possesses them all, transforms itself to resemble the moon. Nevertheless, these rare moments furnish no conception of the nascent promises that lay in constellations of the stars.

But if mimetic genius really was a life-determining force in Antiquity, then it is more or less unavoidable that the full possession of this gift, the most consummate expression of cosmic meaning, should be given to the newborn infant, who even today in the early years of his life will evidence the utmost mimetic genius by learning language.

This, then, is the complete prolegomenon of every rational astrology.

Fragment written probably in 1932; unpublished in Benjamin's lifetime. *Gesammelte Schriften*, VI, 192–193. Translated by Rodney Livingstone.

"Try to Ensure That Everything in Life Has a Consequence"

"Try to ensure that everything in life has a consequence."—This is without doubt one of the most detestable of maxims, one that you would not expect to run across in Goethe.[1] It is the imperative of progress in its most dubious form. It is not the case that the consequence leads to what is fruitful in right action, and even less that the consequence is its fruit. On the contrary, bearing fruit is the mark of evil acts. The acts of good people have no "consequence" that could be ascribed (or ascribed exclusively) to them. The fruits of an act are, as is right and proper, internal to it. To enter into the interior of a mode of action is the way to test its fruitfulness. But how to do this?

Fragment written probably in 1932; unpublished in Benjamin's lifetime. *Gesammelte Schriften*, VI, 205–206. Translated by Rodney Livingstone.

Notes

1. The precise source of this quotation is unknown, but there are similar formulations in Goethe. For example: "From this we can see that a man's life is worth something only insofar as it has a consequence." *Sankt-Rochus-Fest zu Bingen,* in J. W. von Goethe, *Gedenkausgabe der Werke, Briefe und Gespräche,* ed. Ernst Beutler (Zurich: Artemis Verlag, 1961–1966), vol. 12, p. 482.

Notes (IV)

I ought to investigate the way in which my concept of origin, as it is developed in the work on *Trauerspiel* and in the Kraus essay, relates to Rosenzweig's concept of revelation.[1]

To have presence of mind means to let oneself go at the moment of danger.

Feeble creativity: he created [*schuf*], but only in that he ousted [*schaffte fort*].

The great majority of intellectuals—particularly in the arts—are in a desperate plight.[2] The problem, however, is not one of character, pride, or inaccessibility. The journalists, novelists, and literati are for the most part ready for every compromise. It is just that they do not realize it. And this is the explanation of their failures. Because they do not know, or want to know, that they are venal, they do not understand that they should separate out those parts of their opinions, experiences, modes of behavior that might be of interest to the market. Instead they make it a point of honor to be wholly themselves on every issue. Because they want to be sold, so to speak, only "in one piece," they are as unsalable as a calf that the butcher will sell to the housewife only as an undivided whole.

The market will accept even the worst goods. But from each provider it will accept only his best.

Two mottos on Brecht:

"Methinks that was your good angel who inspired you to treat the drama in more epic fashion." Hölderlin, *Sämtliche Werke* [Complete Works], edited by Norbert von Hellingrath et al., volume 5 (Munich and Leipzig, 1913), p. 316, Letter to Böhlendorff, December 4, 1801.

"When thinking stops, the pointed heads have won, just as surely as they have when crooked thinking starts." Oskar Planer and Camillo Reissmann, *Johann Gottfried Seume* (Leipzig, 1898), p. 538. From the preface to *Mein Sommer 1805* [My Summer of 1805].[3]

As long as there is a single beggar, there will still be myth.

Fragment written 1931–1932 or later; unpublished in Benjamin's lifetime. *Gesammelte Schriften*, VI, 207–208. Translated by Rodney Livingstone.

Notes

1. See Franz Rosenzweig, *Der Stern der Erlösung* [The Star of Redemption] (Frankfurt: J. Kauffmann, 1921).
2. See also "Venal but Unusable" (1934), in this volume.
3. Benjamin is alluding to Brecht's play *Rundköpfe und Spitzköpfe* (Roundheads and Squareheads).

Thought Figures, 1933

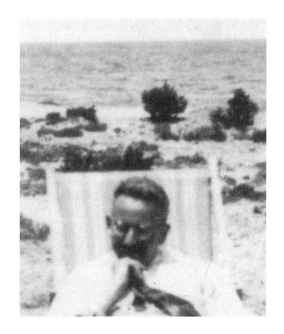

Walter Benjamin at the home of Jean Selz, Ibiza, 1933. Photographer unknown. Collection of the Werkbundarchiv Museum der Dinge, Berlin.

The Lamp

"In this way the marks on the bottom of a pewter plate tell the story of all
the meals it has been used for. In the same way, the form of every piece of
land—the shape of its sand dunes and rocks—contains in natural script the
history of the earth; every rounded pebble that the ocean casts on the shore
could tell that story to a soul that is chained to it, as our soul is chained
to our brain." Said to be found in Lichtenberg, *Schriften* [Writings], volume 1, p. 223.[1]

What is certain is that childhood chains us to things in this way; indeed,
it may be that in childhood we wander through the world of things like the
stations of a journey of whose extent we can form no conception. Couldn't
it be the case that childhood makes a start with the most remote things? At
first, at the moment of birth, it makes itself similar to the most distant things
in the deepest, most unconscious stratum of its own existence, so as subsequently to enable the objects of the world around to accrete, layer by layer.
Hence, what education and human influence do is only one factor in a field
of many active forces—forces the child responds to with that gift of mimesis
which was the natural heritage of mankind in its early stages and which
continues to function nowadays only in children. The gift we possess for
seeing similarity is nothing but a feeble vestige of the formerly powerful
compulsion to be similar and to behave mimetically. And the now-vanished
ability to become similar reached far beyond the narrow world of perception
in which we are still able to perceive similarity. Millennia ago, the effect of
the stars on a man's life at the moment of his birth was woven into his life,
on the basis of the similarity by virtue of which the spirits and forces of life
were shaped in accordance with a model that was inscribed in the cosmos.

It is possible, or even probable, that the formative powers familiar to recent generations are no longer able to extend their influence so far. And am I mistaken when I maintain that they have formed in me the image of chairs, stairwells, cupboards, net curtains, and even a lamp—objects that surrounded me in my childhood?

Thus, we must reckon with the fact that, basically, even events in the sky could be imitated by people in former times. Modern man can be touched by a pale shadow of this when he looks through a mask, or when, on southern moonlit nights, he feels mimetic forces alive in himself that he had thought long since dead, while nature, which possesses them all, transforms itself to resemble the moon. But he is transported into this very force field by his memories of childhood.

Here the lamp is fixed in position. Yet it was portable. And unlike our lighting systems, with their cables, cords, and electrical contacts, you could carry it through the entire apartment, accompanied always by the clatter of the tube in its casing and the glass globe on its metal ring—a clinking that is part of the dark music of the surf which slumbers in the laborious toil of the century. When I bring the lamp close to my ear, I do not hear the noise of field artillery, or the sounds of Offenbach's gala music, or factory sirens.[2]

Now the nineteenth century is empty. It lies there like a large, dead, cold seashell. I pick it up and hold it up to my ear. What do I hear? I do not hear the noise of field artillery or of Offenbach's gala music; nor do I hear the howling of factory sirens or the cry that goes up at midday on the stock exchange—not even the din of soldiers on parade or the long-drawn-out whistle of a train. I can of course imagine all these things. But what I hear when I put the shell up to my ear is something else: it is the rattling noise of the anthracite that is emptied from the coal scuttle into the furnace; it is the dull pop with which the flame lights up the gas mantle; it is the jangling of my mother's keys in her basket, the clatter of the tube in its casing, the clink of the glass globe on its metal ring when the lamp is carried from one room to another.

Has this lamp ever been lit? The little cap I see on top of the tube leads me to believe it has. For it was intended as a safety device that would protect the room from soot when it smoked. I undoubtedly had greater pleasure painting it than anything else. For I had intended it as a present for my grandmother on Christmas or on her birthday—long before it occurred to me to use it as a model. I had sown some brightly colored wool onto the upper section, and had then glued it onto cardboard. But just because it was a present it may have been put in a place of honor instead of having to suffer the indignity of being used. Thus, the picture reveals as little about the place the lamp stood as about the use to which it was put or which it was spared. And undoubtedly the light that was able to penetrate the globe of molded glass, with its blazing ornaments, must have been feeble and dim at best.

The hunting scenes depicted on this lamp, and on cake tins; birds on branches, with the golden orb of the sun—bisque, cloisonné, marquetry.

The gift we possess for seeing similarity is nothing but a feeble vestige of the formerly powerful compulsion to become similar and to behave mimetically. Even our parents still practiced it on us. Nowhere more painfully than at the photographer's. There we would stand, wearing a loden jacket, in front of a screen depicting an Alpine scene; and our right hand, which holding a little hat made of chamois leather, cast a shadow on the clouds and the snowfields depicted on the backdrop. Of this, nothing has remained. For the forced smile with which the little alpinist gazes out at us no longer concerns us. Unlike the other gaze—the one that falls on us from the earnest face in the shadow of the potted palm. I stand there bareheaded; in my hand, a large straw hat that I am holding nonchalantly, with carefully rehearsed gracefulness. My elbow leans anxiously on the edge of the little mahogany table. Behind me, but at a great distance, next to the heavy curtain covering the door, stands my mother, her narrow waist in a tight-fitting dress that matches my jacket, which is embroidered with naval emblems.

For this was the torture: we had to display ourselves, even though nothing lay further from our wishes. Thus, we made ourselves more like the embroidered cushion that someone had pushed toward us, or the ball we had been given to hold, than like a moment from our real lives.

Fragment written in early 1933; unpublished in Benjamin's lifetime. *Gesammelte Schriften,* VII, 792–794. Translated by Rodney Livingstone.

Notes

1. This text represents a transitional formulation of Benjamin's late mimetic theory of language; it was sketched during the final stages of the writing of "Berliner Kindheit um Neunzehnhundert" (Berlin Childhood around 1900; to appear in Volume 3 of this edition) and stands as a preliminary version of many of the ideas set down in "Doctrine of the Similar" (included in this volume). Georg Christoph Lichtenberg (1742–1799), German author and experimental psychologist, was a feared satirist in his time. Yet he is best-remembered today as the first great German aphorist. More than 1,500 pages of his notes were published posthumously; alongside jokes, linguistic paradoxes, puns, metaphors, and excerpts from other writers, they contain thousands of memorable aphorisms.
2. Jacques Offenbach (1819–1880), French composer, created the light comic opera we know as the operetta.

Doctrine of the Similar

Insight into the realms of the "similar" is of fundamental significance for the illumination of major sectors of occult knowledge. Such insight, however, is gained less by demonstrating found similarities than by replicating the processes which generate such similarities. Nature produces similarities—one need only think of mimicry. The very greatest capacity for the generation of similarities, however, belongs to human beings. Indeed, there may be no single one of their higher functions that is not codetermined by the mimetic faculty. This faculty has a history, however, in both the phylogenetic and the ontogenetic sense. As regards the latter, play is to a great extent its school. Children's play is everywhere permeated by mimetic modes of behavior, and its realm is by no means limited to what one person can imitate in another. The child plays at being not only a shopkeeper or teacher but also a windmill and a train. The question on which this turns, however, is the following: What advantage does this schooling in mimetic conduct bring to a human being?

The answer presupposes pointed thinking about the phylogenetic significance of mimetic conduct. To determine this, it is not enough to think, for example, of what we understand today by the concept of similarity. As is known, the sphere of life that formerly seemed to be governed by the law of similarity was much larger. This sphere was the microcosm and the macrocosm, to name only one version of many that the experience of similarity found over the course of history. It can still be claimed of our contemporaries that the cases in which they consciously perceive similarities in everyday life make up a tiny proportion of those numberless cases unconsciously determined by similarity. The similarities perceived consciously—for instance, in faces—are, compared to the countless similarities perceived unconsciously or not at all, like the enormous underwater mass of an iceberg in comparison to the small tip one sees rising out of the water.

These natural correspondences assume decisive importance, however, only in light of the consideration that they are all, fundamentally, stimulants and awakeners of the mimetic faculty which answers them in man. It must be borne in mind that neither mimetic powers nor mimetic objects have remained unchanged over time; and that, in the course of centuries, the mimetic power, and with it the gift of mimetic perception, have disappeared from certain fields—perhaps in order to flow into others. The supposition may not be too bold that, on the whole, a unified direction is perceptible in the historical development of this mimetic faculty.

This direction could, at first sight, lie solely in the increasing fragility of this mimetic faculty. For clearly the perceptual world [*Merkwelt*] of modern human beings seems to contain far fewer of those magical correspondences than did that of the ancients or even that of primitive peoples. The question is simply: Are we dealing with a dying out of the mimetic faculty, or rather perhaps with a transformation that has taken place within it? Of the direction in which the latter might lie, some indications could be derived, even if indirectly, from astrology. As researchers into old traditions, we must take account of the possibility that sensuous shape-giving took place—meaning that objects had a mimetic character—where we are today no longer capable even of suspecting it. For example, in the constellations of the stars.

In order to grasp this, we must above all understand the horoscope as an originary totality which astronomical interpretation merely analyzes. (The state of the stars represents a characteristic unity, and the character of the individual planets can be recognized only by the way they function in relation to this state of the stars.) We must assume in principle that processes in the sky were imitable, both collectively and individually, by people who lived in earlier times; indeed, that this imitability contained instructions for mastering an already present similarity. In this imitability by humans, or, as the case may be, in this mimetic faculty that humans have, we must discern what is for the time being the basis for astrology's experiential character. If, however, mimetic genius was really a life-determining force for the ancients, then we have little choice but to attribute full possession of this gift, and in particular its perfect adaptation to the form of cosmic being, to the newborn.

The moment of birth, which is decisive here, is but an instant. This directs our attention to another peculiarity in the realm of similarity. The perception of similarity is in every case bound to a flashing up. It flits past, can possibly be won again, but cannot really be held fast as can other perceptions. It offers itself to the eye as fleetingly and transitorily as a constellation of stars. The perception of similarities thus seems to be bound to a moment in time. It is like the addition of a third element—the astrologer—to the conjunction of two stars; it must be grasped in an instant. Otherwise the astrologer is cheated of his reward, despite the sharpness of his observational tools.

The reference to astrology may already suffice to make comprehensible the concept of a nonsensuous similarity. This concept is, obviously enough, a relative one: it indicates that we no longer possess in our perception whatever once made it possible to speak of a similarity which might exist between a constellation of stars and a human. Yet we, too, possess a canon, on whose basis we can attain more clarity regarding the obscurity which clings to the concept of nonsensuous similarity. And that canon is language.

From time immemorial, the mimetic faculty has been conceded some influence on language. But this was done without foundation—without serious consideration of a further meaning, still less a history, of the mimetic faculty. Above all, such considerations remained closely tied to the commonplace (sensuous) realm of similarity. All the same, imitative behavior in language formation was acknowledged as an onomatopoetic element. Now, if language, as is evident, is not an agreed-upon system of signs, we will be constantly obliged to have recourse to the kind of thoughts that appear in their rawest, most primitive form as the onomatopoetic mode of explanation. The question is whether this can be developed and accommodated to an improved understanding.

In other words, the question is whether one can establish an underlying meaning for Rudolf Leonhard's assertion in his instructive work, *Das Wort* [The Word]: "Every word—indeed, the whole language—is onomatopoetic." The key which finally makes this thesis fully transparent lies concealed in the concept of a nonsensuous similarity. For if words meaning the same thing in different languages are arranged about that signified as their center, we have to inquire how they all—while often possessing not the slightest similarity to one another—are similar to the signified at their center. Such an understanding is of course related in the most intimate way to mystical or theological theories of language, without, however, being alien to empirical philology. Yet it is well known that mystical language teachings do not content themselves with drawing the spoken word into the space of their considerations. They certainly also deal likewise with script. And here it is worth noting that script, perhaps even more than certain combinations of sound in language, clarifies—in the relationship of the written form [*Schriftbild*] of words or letters to the signified, or, as the case may be, to the one who gives the name—the nature of nonsensuous similarity. Thus, for instance, the letter *beth* [in Hebrew] is the root for the word meaning "house." It is thus nonsensuous similarity that establishes the ties not only between what is said and what is meant, but also between what is written and what is meant, and equally between the spoken and the written. And every time, it does so in a completely new, original, and underivable way.

The most important of these ties may, however, be the one mentioned last—that between what is written and what is said. For the similarity which reigns here is comparatively the most nonsensuous. It is also the one which takes the longest to be reached. And the attempt to represent the actual essence of this similarity can hardly be undertaken without a glance into the history of its birth, however impenetrable the darkness that is still spread over it today. The most recent graphology has taught us to recognize, in handwriting, images—or, more precisely, picture puzzles—that the unconscious of the writer conceals in his writing. It may be supposed that the mimetic process which expresses itself in this way in the activity of the writer was, in the very distant times in which script originated, of utmost importance for writing. Script has thus become, like language, an archive of nonsensuous similarities, of nonsensuous correspondences.

But this, if you will, magical aspect of language, as well as of script, does not develop in isolation from its other, semiotic aspect. Rather, everything mimetic in language is an intention which can appear at all only in connection with something alien as its basis: precisely the semiotic or communicative element of language. Thus, the literal text of the script is the sole basis on which the picture puzzle can form itself. Thus, the nexus of meaning which resides in the sounds of the sentence is the basis from which something similar can become apparent out of a sound, flashing up in an instant. Since this nonsensuous similarity, however, exerts its effects in all reading, at this deep level access opens to a peculiar ambiguity of the word "reading," in both its profane and magical senses. The schoolboy reads his ABC book, and the astrologer reads the future in the stars. In the first clause, reading is not separated out into its two components. Quite the opposite in the second, though, which clarifies the process at both its levels: the astrologer reads the constellation from the stars in the sky; simultaneously, he reads the future or fate from it.

If, at the dawn of humanity, this reading from stars, entrails, and coincidences was reading per se, and if it provided mediating links to a newer kind of reading, as represented by runes, then one might well assume that this mimetic gift, which was earlier the basis for clairvoyance, very gradually found its way into language and writing in the course of a development over thousands of years, thus creating for itself in language and writing the most perfect archive of nonsensuous similarity. In this way, language is the highest application of the mimetic faculty—a medium into which the earlier perceptual capacity for recognizing the similar had, without residue, entered to such an extent that language now represents the medium in which objects encounter and come into relation with one another. No longer directly, as they once did in the mind of the augur or priest, but in their essences, in their most transient and delicate substances, even in their aromas. In other words: it is to script and language that clairvoyance has, over the course of history, yielded its old powers.

So tempo, that swiftness in reading or writing which can scarcely be separated from this process, would then become, as it were, the effort, or gift, or mind to participate in that measure of time in which similarities flash up fleetingly out of the stream of things only in order to sink down once more. Thus, even profane reading, if it is not to forsake understanding altogether, shares this with magical reading: that it is subject to a necessary tempo, or rather a critical moment, which the reader must not forget at any cost lest he go away empty-handed.

Addendum

Our gift for seeing similarity is nothing but a weak rudiment of the once powerful compulsion to become similar and also to behave mimetically. And the lost faculty of becoming similar extended far beyond the narrow perceptual world in which we are still capable of seeing similarities. What the state of the stars—millennia ago, at the moment of their birth—wrought with one human existence was woven there on the basis of similarity.

Written January–February 1933; unpublished in Benjamin's lifetime. *Gesammelte Schriften,* II, 204–210. Translated by Michael Jennings, on the basis of prior versions by Knut Tarnowski and Edmund Jephcott.

Short Shadows (II)

Secret Signs. A word of Schuler's has been preserved for us.[1] Every piece of knowledge, he said, contains a dash of nonsense, just as in ancient carpet patterns or ornamental friezes it was always possible to find somewhere or other a minute deviation from the regular pattern. In other words, what is decisive is not the progression from one piece of knowledge to the next, but the leap implicit in any one piece of knowledge. This is the inconspicuous mark of authenticity which distinguishes it from every kind of standard product that has been mass produced.

A Saying of Casanova's. "She knew," Casanova says of a procuress, "that I would not have the strength to leave without giving her something." A strange statement. What strength was needed to cheat the procuress of her reward? Or, more precisely, what is the weakness on which she can always rely? It is shame. The procuress is venal—in contrast to the customer employing her services, who is ashamed. Filled with shame, he seeks a hiding place and finds one in the most hidden place of all: in money. Insolence throws the first coin down on the table. Shame follows it up with a hundred, in order to cloak it.

The Tree and Language. I climbed up an embankment and lay down under a tree. The tree was a poplar or an alder. Why have I not remembered which? Because while I was gazing up into the foliage, following its movements with my eyes, I suddenly found that, within me, language was so gripped by it that momentarily the age-old marriage with the tree was suddenly reenacted once again in my presence. The branches and the treetop swayed to and fro reflectively, or leaned over in rejection; the twigs bent down toward me or leaped upward; the foliage braced itself against a sharp gust of wind, shuddered, or met it halfway; the trunk was firmly planted in the solid ground; and one leaf cast its shadow over another. A gentle breeze signaled the start of a wedding and soon carried throughout the world the children who had quickly sprung from this bed, like an image speech.

Gambling. Gambling, like every other passion, can be recognized by the way in which the spark leaps within the body from one point to the next, imparting movement now to this organ, now to that one, concentrating the whole of existence and delimiting it. It is condensed to the time allowed to the right hand before the ball has fallen into the slot. The hand sweeps over the rows like a plane, spreading the seeds—the chips—into their furrows. The announcing of this time limit is a moment reserved exclusively for the ear, when the ball is poised to go into a whirl and the gambler listens for Lady Luck to tune her bass viols. Gambling addresses itself to all the senses, not excluding the atavistic sense of clairvoyance; hence, the eye has its turn as well. All the numbers wink at it. But because it has utterly forgotten the language of winking, it mainly leads astray those who still rely on it. On the other hand, these are the very people who are most deeply devoted to gambling. For a few moments, the stake that they have now forfeited remains on the table, before their eyes. It is kept there by the rules. Just as a lover is momentarily held by the displeasure of the person he adores. He sees her hand near his; but he will make no move to take it. Gambling has passionate devotees, who love it for its own sake and not for what it brings them. Indeed, if it strips them of everything, they tend to blame themselves: they say, "I played badly." And this love contains its own reward, to the point where they even love their losses because this enables them to demonstrate their capacity for self-sacrifice. The prince de Ligne was just such an irreproachable Knight of Fortune in the years following Napoleon's defeat, when he frequented the Paris clubs and was celebrated for the *sang froid* he displayed in the face of huge losses.[2] Day in, day out, he behaved in the same way. His right hand, which constantly wagered vast stakes on the tables, hung slackly. His left hand, however, was immobile, held horizontally across his right breast beneath his jacket. Later it became known, through his valet, that there were three scars on his chest—the precise imprint of the nails of the three fingers that had lain there so motionlessly.

Distance and Images. I wonder whether enjoyment of the world of images isn't fed by a sullen defiance of knowledge. I gaze out over the landscape. Before me lies the sea, smooth as a mirror in the bay; forests extend up to the hilltop—an immobile, silent mass; to one side, ruined castle walls lie there as they have for centuries; the sky is cloudless, a heavenly blue. This is what the dreamer wants to see. The fact that the ocean rises and falls in thousands and thousands of waves every moment; that the forests tremble anew at every instant, from their roots to the very last leaf; that in the stones of the castle ruins there is a constant crumbling and crashing; that, in the sky, gases surge invisibly to and fro in conflict with each other, and then condense into clouds—all this he must forget, so he can surrender to the images. These will give him peace, eternity. Every bird's wing that brushes past, every gust of wind that makes him shiver, everything he sees from up close gives the lie to his dreams. But every view from a distance rebuilds them again. They spring to life at every bank of clouds, at every lighted window. And the dream appears at its most perfect when he succeeds in removing the sting from movement itself—in translating the gust of wind into a rustling, and the flitting and darting of the birds above his head into a migratory flock. To command nature herself to stand still in this way in the name of faded images is the dreamer's delight. But to utter a call that will freeze it anew is the gift of poets.

To Live without Leaving Traces.[3] If you enter a bourgeois room of the 1880s, for all the coziness it radiates, the strongest impression you receive may well be, "You've got no business here." And in fact you have no business in that room, for there is no spot on which the owner has not left his mark—the ornaments on the mantlepiece, the monogrammed antimacassars on the armchairs, the transparencies in the windows, the screen in front of the fire. A neat phrase by Brecht helps us out here: "Erase the traces!" is the refrain in the first poem of his *Lesebuch für Städtebewohner* [Reader for City-Dwellers].[4] Here in the bourgeois room, the opposite behavior became the norm. And conversely, the *intérieur* forces the inhabitant to adopt the greatest possible number of habits. They are assembled in the image of the "furnished gentleman" as imagined by landladies. Living in these plush compartments was nothing more than leaving traces made by habits. Even the rage expressed when the least little thing broke was perhaps merely the reaction of a person who felt that someone had obliterated "the traces of his days on earth."[5] The traces that he had left in cushions and armchairs, that his relatives had left in photos, and that his possessions had left in linings and étuis and that sometimes made these rooms look as overcrowded as halls full of funerary urns. This is what has now been achieved by the new architects, with their glass and steel: they have created rooms in which it is hard to leave traces. "It follows from the foregoing," Scheerbart declared a good twenty years ago, "that we can surely talk about a 'culture of glass.' The new glass-milieu will transform humanity utterly.

And now it remains only to be wished that the new glass-culture will not encounter too many enemies."

Short Shadows. Toward noon, shadows are no more than the sharp, black edges at the feet of things, preparing to retreat silently, unnoticed, into their burrow, into their secret. Then, in its compressed, cowering fullness, comes the hour of Zarathustra—the thinker in "the noon of life," in "the summer garden." For it is knowledge that gives objects their sharpest outline, like the sun at its zenith.

Published in the *Kölnische Zeitung,* February 1933. *Gesammelte Schriften,* IV, 425–428. Translated by Rodney Livingstone.

Notes

1. Alfred Schuler (1865–1923) was a member of the George circle. He was a believer in ritual magical cults, through which he sought to establish communion with the dead. George broke with him in 1903 because of the "muddiness" and eccentricity of his thinking.
2. Charles-Joseph, prince de Ligne (1735–1814), Belgian military officer, diplomat, and man of letters, was a favorite at many European courts. His memoirs and his correspondence with figures such as Rousseau and Voltaire established him as an important literary voice in Belgium.
3. See also "Experience and Poverty" (1933), in this volume.
4. Brecht's text was published in Berlin in 1926–1927.
5. J. W. von Goethe, *Faust, Part II,* line 11,583: "The trace of my days on earth cannot perish in eons."

Kierkegaard

The End of Philosophical Idealism

The last attempt to take over or develop Kierkegaard's intellectual world in toto was that of Karl Barth's "dialectical theology."[1] At their outer limits the waves of this theological movement make contact with the concentric circles set in motion by Heidegger's existentialist philosophy. The present work—Theodor Wiesengrund Adorno's *Kierkegaard*[2]—approaches the subject from quite a different angle. Here Kierkegaard is taken not forward but back—back into the inner core of philosophical idealism, within whose enchanted circle the ultimately theological nature of his thought remained doomed to impotence.

Wiesengrund's approach can be called historical. But in its execution he shows how his cautious method actually springs from highly topical interests. It leads to a critique of German idealism, which he decodes from the point of view of its later developments. For Kierkegaard is a latecomer. Wiesengrund gives an illuminating description of the hybrid nature of his writings, and shows that his works are frequently the bastard offspring of poetry and knowledge. In so doing, he sheds light on the hidden elements of idealism that are still at work in them. For in the aesthetic idealism of Romanticism, the mythic elements of absolute idealism make their appearance. And the logical and historical description of these elements forms the centerpiece of Wiesengrund's account.

The author demonstrates the presence of myth not just in Kierkegaard's existential philosophy, but in "every idealism of Absolute Spirit." Yet nowhere, not even in the later Schelling or Baader,[3] is it given such an original, illuminating formulation, so completely true to its age, as in Kierkegaard. The extremely precise and exhaustive analysis and description of these formulations gives many pages of this study the character of a phantasmagoria. But Wiesengrund's insight and power of expression are never achieved at the cost of critical accuracy—as is so often the case in cultural history. And no cultural history of the nineteenth century will be able to compete with the vividness with which, from the very center of his thinking, Kierkegaard is here linked now with Hegel, now with Wagner, now with Poe, now with Baudelaire. The panorama of the century which Wiesengrund spreads out before us is as broad as his perspective on the past is deep. Pascal and the allegorical Hell of the Baroque are presented here as the vestibule to that cell in which Kierkegaard abandons himself to melancholy and which he shares with Irony, his false mistress.

This world of images whose labyrinths and halls of mirrors contain Kierkegaard's innermost experiences is something he himself considered insignificant, arbitrary, and idiosyncratic. All the arrogant pretensions of his existentialist philosophy rest on his conviction that he had found the realm of "inwardness," of "pure spirituality," which had enabled him to overcome appearance through "decision," through existential resolve—in short, through a religious stance. It is at this juncture that Wiesengrund's penetrating analysis of the concept of existence turns him into an incorruptible critic of Kierkegaard. He unmasks the "fraudulent theology of an existence based on paradox." In his view, "Kierkegaard's profundity (if we wish to retain this much abused concept) does not consist in his ability to reinstate an absolute, religious primal meaning disguised as idealist forms of thought." Instead, "in the historical decline of idealism" Kierkegaard discerned an underlying mythic content, which he declared "its primal meaning and at the same time its historical truth."

In this way, Kierkegaard's inward spirituality is assigned a specific place in history and society. Its model is the bourgeois interior, in which historical and mythical elements merge. Wiesengrund, with a sure hand, draws a whole series of fascinating descriptions of such interior spaces from Kierkegaard's writings. In these interiors, Kierkegaard's inwardness proves itself "the historical prison of a primordial humanity." And it is not, as Kierkegaard believed, the "leap" that will liberate mankind from this incarceration with the magical power of "paradox." Nowhere does Wiesengrund's insight go deeper than where he ignores the stereotypes of Kierkegaardian philosophy and where he looks instead for the key to Kierkegaard's thought in its apparently insignificant relics, in its images, similes, and allegories. He discerns the ultimate statement of this philosophy in the image of (a painter's) vanishing in a picture (painted by himself)—an image borrowed from the tradition of Chinese folktales. The self is "something vanishing that is rescued by a process of reduction." This entry into and dissolution in [Eingehen in] the image is not redemption but consolation—the consolation whose source is the imagination, "which is the organ by means of which the seamless transition from the mythic-historical into reconciliation can be effected."

This book contains much in a small space. The author's subsequent writings may someday emerge from it. It is, in any case, one of those rare first books in which inspiration manifests itself in the guise of criticism.

Published in the *Vossische Zeitung*, April 1933. *Gesammelte Schriften*, III, 380–383. Translated by Rodney Livingstone.

Notes

1. Karl Barth (1886–1968), Swiss theologian, was perhaps the most influential theologian of the twentieth century. The turn in Protestant thought that followed from his assertion that God is "wholly other" can still be felt today. His *Letters to the Romans* and monumental *Church Dogmatics* stand out among his many works.
2. Theodor Wiesengrund Adorno, *Kierkegaard: Konstruktion des Ästhetischen* [Kierkegaard: The Construction of the Aesthetic] (Tübingen: J. C. B. Mohr, 1933).
3. Friedrich Wilhelm Joseph von Schelling (1775–1854), German philosopher and educator, lent major impulses to the post-Kantian development of German idealism. His work incorporates mystical and pantheistic elements. Franz Xaver von Baader (1765–1841) was a Roman Catholic layman who became an influential mystical theologian and ecumenicist. Benjamin himself read Baader early in his career.

Stefan George in Retrospect

On a New Study of the Poet

Willi Koch, *Stefan George: Weltbild, Naturbild, Menschenbild* [Stefan George: His Image of the World, Nature, and Man] (Halle/Saale: Max Niemeyer Verlag, 1933), 114 pages.

Stefan George has been silent for years. With the passage of time, we have acquired a new ear for his voice. We recognize it as the voice of a prophet. This does not mean that George foresaw historical developments, and even less that he understood their causes—an ability which distinguishes the politician, not the prophet. Prophecy is a process in the moral world. What the prophet foresees is the wrath of God. This is what George has predicted for the race of "hurriers and gapers" in whose midst he has found himself. The night of the world, whose approach has darkened his days, arrived for him in 1914. And the fact that, in his view, its end has not yet come is indicated in his last collection of poems, in a title that speaks volumes: "Einem jungen Führer im ersten Weltkrieg" [To a Young Leader in the First World War]. New lights and shadows have migrated into his deeply furrowed features. But we do not yet know the aureole with which history will illuminate those features on the day they receive their expression for eternity.

Within this poet, however, there also lives an opponent of the prophet. The more audible the latter's voice becomes, the more the other voice—the reformer's voice—sinks into impotence. George, whose foreknowledge of the catastrophe springs from his strict discipline and innate sense of the powers of darkness, was, as leader and teacher, able to prescribe only feeble rules or courses of action, remote from the realities of life. In his eyes, art was that "Seventh Ring"[1] with which an order that was collapsing on all fronts was to be bound together one more time. This art has indisputably shown itself to be rigorous and valid, the ring well-fitting and precious. But what it binds together was the same order that was concerned to maintain the old powers that be—with far less noble methods than his. This is why George failed to extricate his poetry from the enchanted circle of symbols that—unlike those of Hölderlin—did not come to the surface like springs emerging from the rich soil of a great tradition. In his case, the symbolic work is the most fragile part of his oeuvre. At its core, it is not really different from the array of symbolic ideas and images derived from the church and the nation that were being proclaimed in France by Barrès at the same time that the "circle" was being formed around the Master. George's own array of symbols is defensive in character, often with a note of desperation. This is why the treasure of secret signs in his poetry already has the appearance of being the impoverished, anxiously preserved property of "style."

In his great review of *Der siebente Ring* [The Seventh Ring] in the *Hesperus* annual, Rudolf Borchardt was the first to attempt a general assessment of George's achievement as a poet.[2] And without ascribing to this question more importance than it deserves in the larger context of his work, he did focus attention on a significant number of feeble and failed stanzas. In the twenty-five years that have passed since the publication of the volume, such lapses strike us even more painfully. But basically we are saying the same thing if we note that in George's poems something like the "style" forces itself upon our attention in a way that overwhelms and eclipses the meaning. Poems in which his energy fails him are mainly those in which the style is triumphant. The style is that of Jugendstil—in other words, the style in which the old bourgeoisie disguises the premonition of its own impotence by indulging in poetic flights of fancy on a cosmic scale and abusing the word "youth" as a magic incantation with which to conjure up intoxicated visions of the future. Here, for the first time, and initially only as a program, we find regression migrating from the social sphere into the natural and biological world—a process which has since been increasingly confirmed as a symptom of the crisis. In the mind of the George circle, the biological and cosmic idols merge. This subsequently gives birth to the idea of the mythic ideal, Maximin.[3] Concerning the tortured ornamentation that was typical of the furniture and façades of the day, it has been said that they represented the attempt to translate forms which first made their appearance in modern technology back into the language of the arts and crafts. Jugendstil does in fact involve a great and quite conscious act of regression. What is expressed in its formal idiom is the will to evade imminent developments and the presentiments that rise up to confront it. The same may be said of that "spiritual movement" that aspired to the renewal of human existence without paying heed to politics. It, too, amounted to a retrospective transformation of societal contradictions into those hopeless, tragic tensions and convulsions that are so typical of the life of small conventicles.

Only historical reflection which goes far beyond the framework of literary history can lead to insights into George's figure and work that summoned the "spiritual movement" into life forty years ago. It is indisputable that Koch's study, too, stands well outside that framework. He is nowhere indebted to those dire stereotypes that are so often encountered in literary histories, particularly in their treatment of George. Nevertheless, a historical point of view is quite foreign to this book. It approaches George's work gingerly, fully accepting the "eternal" validity of the meanings that condition it. Yet this is done with such circumspection and methodological conscientiousness as to earn it a place of honor from which it will not easily be ousted.

The method underlying this study is "the analysis of a poetic work that aspires only to explicate the mode of expression, because it believes that it has understood the deeper meaning." And its achievement is an illuminating periodization of George's works, based on the phases—which are of course closely intertwined—in which George's view of the world has developed. The foundation of Koch's discussion is the terrible pervasiveness of chaos in George's deeper experience of nature. Chaos appears as the basic force of history:

> Unlovely, not wholly shapened forces;
> All-hearing time that entered in the book
> every feeble hubbub and every blast of dust,
> But heard not your subterranean stirrings.[4]

Yet this poet heard them from early on. The essence of Koch's account is to trace George's efforts to break the hostile spell—vainly at first with the aid of Christian symbolism, but then with the appearance of Maximin, when he feels that the spell has been lifted and reconciliation has been offered to him as a gift. Following the theological trend of rewriting the objects of religion, Koch classifies George's experience of nature under the concept of "the other." It is not difficult for him to provide some convincing evidence of the gloomy, chthonic elements that originally seemed to the poet to be dominant forces. At the same time, this starting point provides him with a link to problems that call on the latest developments in scholarly knowledge. He takes as his reference point the fact that, particularly since the later Romantic movement, the gaze of many poets has been fixed on opening up the world from its chthonic aspect. "The poetic treatment of this problem is still one for which the groundwork is lacking. The cause lies in the fact that, up to now, literary scholarship has been mainly concerned with formal aesthetics, focusing either on the *Gestalt* as an individual, sociological, or ideological factor, or else on the 'artistic' as an application of language. The factual 'ground' of a literary work, and with it the discipline for scrutinizing it, must always be sought in the religious sphere, which is the source of a writer's ideas, motifs, form, and language." A formulation in which a writer's language appears as the "product" of the religious—whereas in reality it is its medium—sets limits to even the most conscientious research. And the abrupt way in which Koch's study breaks off underlines the fact that the larger their object, the narrower these limits will prove to be. But this cannot detract from the very valuable insights he obtains in the process.

These involve constant variations on the theme of George's struggle with his experience of nature. "George's view that nature is a demonic being," Koch writes, "is rooted in his peasant feeling for the natural world." With these words, the author touches on the factors that might have given him insight into the historical workshop in which George's poetry was created. George is the son of a peasant who regards nature as a superior power "that he can never conquer, from whom he can at most copy a few habits, with which he lives in constant struggle and against which he must defend himself." And even though he is a writer and an inhabitant of big cities, nature is constantly present in his mind, with all its power and terrors. The hand that has ceased to grip the plow is still clenched in rage against nature. In this gesture of irreconcilability, the forces of his origins and those of his later life, far from his roots, meet and mingle. Nature appears to him "depraved—it has arrived at the point of being completely 'de-spiritualized' [*Entgottung*]. For this reason we are living in the 'night of the world,' in which formative forces are 'rigid and exhausted' and can be only feebly perceived." The author is quite right to see a chief source of George's poetic energies in the two famous stanzas from *Der siebente Ring*:

And when the great seamstress in rage
Stands to one side, leans at the lower bourn
In a world-night, rigid and tired, knocks:
So can only one man who always fought

And vanquished her, and never according to her rules,
Press her hand, seize her braid;
So that she compliantly continues her work:
Deifies the body and embodies the god.

But the possibility that this braid of *natura naturans* can be grasped only via the ordering and reordering of human conditions—certainly not through the cult of Maximin—is the insight needed to liberate the critical faculties of the investigator.

For knowledge of every kind, and not just criticism, contains the salt of negation—as Hegel insisted. It is possible to act from a stance of unreserved affirmation, but not to think. Hence, the "approach to his work" that

Eduard Lachmann has just published, under the title *Die ersten Bücher Stefan Georges* [Stefan George's First Books], does not get very far.[5] One cannot compare this book with Koch's valuable study. To a degree remarkable even for writings on George, the book lacks detachment and the ability to evaluate the poet's works as anything but perfect, or even to approach them with any other assumption in mind. The empty ceremonies once performed in verse by a Lothar Treuge, at the altar of the George circle, now turn up in prose at the end of the movement.[6] But this unstinting praise forms a barrier even for the reflective observer. In Koch's study the critical debate about the poetic figure of Maximin, who serves as the guardian angel at the threshold of George's late work, fails to take place. Instead, the author does not hesitate to comment on the Maximin experience as the "kernel of George's *religiosity*": "The history of ideas and the psychological approach must be complemented by a phenomenology of religious consciousness; indeed, everything must be based on this. *For the religious sense of responsibility is the impulse underlying the Maximin myth and is not explicable in psychological and historical terms.*"

Thus, we see once again that during the period dominated by George his great work has drawn to a close without attracting the genuine critic he merits. It approaches the judgment seat of history, almost unrecognizable amid a swarm of disciples, yet without an advocate. But not without witnesses. What manner of people are they? They are found among the young people who lived in those poems. Not among those who have ascended university chairs in the name of their master, nor among those who have used his teachings to strengthen their own positions in the power struggles between political parties, but rather among those who—the best of whom, at any rate—can serve as witnesses before the judgment seat of history because they are dead. The verses that hovered on their lips were not from *Der Stern des Bundes,*[7] and rarely from *Der siebente Ring.* In the priestly science of poetry, as this had been formulated in *Blätter für die Kunst,* they discovered no echo of the voice that had spoken "Das Lied des Zwergen" [The Song of the Dwarf], or the "Die Entführung" [The Abduction]. For these young people, George's poems were a song of consolation. Consolation in distress for which today he is unlikely to have a heart, a song of a kind for which today he is unlikely to have an ear.

"By making a hero of himself and of those who truly understand his work, George has rid the world of the purely aesthetic stance"—or so Koch asserts, ambiguously enough. For at the same time as he eliminated the aesthetic stance, he also eliminated life. The great regression of Jugendstil means that even youth shrinks to the size of a mummy, and its features are those of Eilert Lövborg as much as of Maximin. Both die in beauty.[8] The generation for whom George's most beautiful and perfect poems provided something of a refuge was doomed. The darkness that with the war had gathered above its head only what had long since been brewing in its heart seemed to that generation, as to the poet whose verses fulfilled it, to be the epitome of all the forces of nature. George was by no means the "prophet" [*Künder*] of "instructions," but a minstrel who moved the young as the wind moves the "flowers of the childhood home" that smilingly issue an invitation to the long summer. George was the great poet in the eyes of that generation, and he was so as the perfecter of the decadence whose playfulness he rejected in order to create for death the space it was to claim for itself at this crucial turning point. He stands at the end of an intellectual line that began with Baudelaire. It may well be that this statement once belonged to the history of literature. In the meantime, it has become part of history proper, and comes to claim its due.

Published in the *Frankfurter Zeitung*, July 1933. *Gesammelte Schriften*, III, 392–399. Translated by Rodney Livingstone.

Notes

1. *Der siebente Ring* (The Seventh Ring; 1907) was the title of one of George's collections of poems.
2. *Hesperus: Ein Jahrbuch*, ed. Rudolf Borchardt, Hugo von Hofmannsthal, and Rudolf Alexander Schröder (Leipzig: Insel, 1909). Rudolf Borchardt (1877–1945), a conservative author and essayist, promoted the literary models of classical Antiquity and the Middle Ages.
3. Maximin (pseudonym of Maximilian Kronberger; 1888–1904) was a youth of fifteen whom George regarded as an incarnation of the divine. In *Der siebente Ring*, inspired by Maximin, George celebrated the new youthful elite that would lead to the renewal of civilization.
4. Stefan George, *Der Stern des Bundes* (The Star of the Covenant), in *Werke* (Munich: H. Kupper, 1958), vol. 1, p. 366.
5. Eduard Lachmann, *Die ersten Bücher Stefan Georges: Eine Annäherung an das Werk* (Berlin: G. Bondi, 1933). [Benjamin's note]
6. Lothar Treuge (1877–1920), German poet, was a minor member of the circle around George. His poetry appeared frequently in George's journal, *Blätter für die Kunst*, which appeared from 1892 to 1919.
7. *Der Stern des Bundes* (The Star of the Covenant) was George's volume of poetry published in 1914.
8. Eilert Lövborg was the failed Dionysian poet in Henrik Ibsen's *Hedda Gabler* (1890). He is supposed to die beautifully, "with vine leaves in his hair" (though, in the event, his death by his own hand is rather messier).

Agesilaus Santander (First Version)

When I was born, it occurred to my parents that I might perhaps become a writer.[1] If that happened, it would be a good idea if people did not immediately notice I was a Jew. This is why they gave me two very unusual names, in addition to my first name. I do not wish to reveal them. It is enough to say that forty years ago it would have been very difficult for parents to be more prescient. What they regarded as a remote possibility has come to pass. But the precautions that were supposed to combat fate were nullified by the very person they concerned most. Instead of making the two prophylactic names public with his works, he kept them to himself. He watched over them as the Jews used to watch over the secret name that they gave to each of their children. These children did not learn of it until the day of their maturity. But because this day can come more than once in a lifetime, and perhaps because not every secret name can remain the same and untransformed, its transformation may well become manifest with a new maturity. Thus, it remains the name which gathers all the forces of life unto itself, and by which these forces can be conjured up and protected against outsiders.

But this name is by no means an enrichment of the person who bears it. It deprives him of many things—above all, of the gift of appearing entirely as the person he was before. In the room I was last living in, even before that person had emerged fully armored and accoutered from the old name, he had displayed his image: New Angel.[2] The Kaballah relates that, at every moment, God creates a whole host of new angels, whose only task before they return to the void is to appear before His throne for a moment and sing His praises. Mine had been interrupted in the process; his features had nothing human about them. Aside from that, he has made me pay for having disturbed him at his work. By turning to his advantage the fact that I was born under the sign of Saturn—the planet of slow revolution, the star of hesitation and delay—he sent his feminine aspect after the masculine one reproduced in the picture, and did so by the most circuitous, most fatal detour, even though the two had been such close neighbors.

He may have been unaware that in doing this he brought out the strength of the man against whom he was proceeding. For nothing can overcome my patience. Its pinions resemble those of the angel: they need but a few movements to hold it stationary in the face of the woman whom it is determined to await. But my patience has claws like the angel and razor-sharp pinions, and makes no attempt to pounce on her whom it has sighted. It learns from the angel and sees how he embraces his partner with a glance, but then retreats in a series of spasms, inexorably. He draws the angel after him on that flight into a future from which he has emerged. He hopes for nothing new from that future, other than the gaze of the person to whom he keeps his face turned.

And so, scarcely had I seen you the first time than I returned with you to where I had come from.

Ibiza, August 12, 1933

Written August 1933; unpublished in Benjamin's lifetime. *Gesammelte Schriften,* VI, 520–521. Translated by Rodney Livingstone.

Notes

1. The two autobiographical texts entitled "Agesilaus Santander" have provoked much speculation. There is now general agreement that the title does not refer to the Spartan king Agesilaos II (444–360 B.C.), who is mentioned by Xenophon, Cornelius Nepos, and Plutarch: no parallel between Benjamin and Agesilaos has been discovered. Nor is it now thought to refer to the name of the ferry linking Barcelona and Ibiza. Gershom Scholem has speculated that, if we set aside the extra *i* as an ornamental flourish, the name is an anagram of *Der Engel Satanas,* "Satan's angel."

2. Sometime in the spring of 1921, Benjamin bought a small ink wash drawing by Paul Klee entitled *Angelus Novus,* which was to become his best-known possession (see *Selected Writings,* vol. 1, p. 215). The image plays a role here and, in the last years of his life, was the inspiration for his meditation on the angel of history in "Über den Begriff der Geschichte" (On the Concept of History; 1940).

Agesilaus Santander (Second Version)

When I was born, it occurred to my parents that I might perhaps become a writer.[1] If that happened, it would be a good idea if people did not immediately notice I was a Jew. This is why they gave me two names in addition to my first name—eccentric names which showed neither that a Jew bore them, nor even that they were his first names. Forty years ago, it was impossible for parents to be more prescient. What they regarded as a remote possibility has come to pass. But the precautions that were supposed to combat fate were nullified by the very person they concerned most. Instead of making the names public with his works, he followed the Jewish custom of keeping them secret. Jews tell their children about a secret name only when the children reach maturity. Because this day can come more than once in a lifetime, and perhaps because even the secret name can remain the same and untransformed only for the pious, the man who is not pious may experience its transformation at a stroke with this new manhood. This was my situation. Thus, it remains the name that binds together all the forces of life and that is to be protected against outsiders.

But this name is by no means an enrichment of the person it designates. On the contrary, much of his image falls away when the name is heard. He loses, above all, the gift of appearing human. In the room I occupied in Berlin, even before that person had emerged fully armored and accoutered from my name, he had fixed his image to the wall: New Angel.[2] The Kaballah relates that, at every moment, God creates a whole host of angels, whose only task before they return to the void is to appear before His throne for a moment and sing His praises. The new angel presented himself as such before naming himself. I only fear that I had kept him excessively long from his hymn. Aside from that, he has paid me back. By turning to his advantage the fact that I was born under the sign of Saturn—the planet of the slowest revolution, the star of hesitation and delay—he sent his feminine aspect after the masculine one reproduced in the picture, and did so by the most circuitous, most fatal detour, even though the two had once (while remaining unknown to each other) been such close neighbors.

He may have been unaware that in doing this he brought out the strength of the man against whom he was proceeding—namely, his ability to wait. Whenever this man encountered a woman who held him in thrall, he at once determined to lie in wait for her on her journey through life and to wait until she fell into his hands, ill, aged, and in ragged clothes. In short, nothing could overcome the man's patience. And its pinions resembled those of the angels: they needed but a few movements to hold him stationary in the face of the woman whom he was determined not to abandon.

But the angel resembles everything from which I have had to part: the people, and especially the things. He dwells in the things I no longer possess. He makes them transparent, and behind each of them appears the figure of the person for whom they are intended. This is why no one can surpass me when it comes to giving presents. Indeed, the angel may have been attracted by a person who gives but who goes away empty-handed himself. For he, too, has claws and pointed, razor-sharp pinions, and makes no attempt to fall upon whomever he has his eye on. He looks him steadily in the eye, for a long time, and then retreats—in a series of spasms, but inexorably. Why? To draw him after himself on that road to the future along which he came, and which he knows so well that he can traverse it without turning round and letting him whom he has chosen out of his sight. He wants happiness— that is to say, the conflict in which the rapture of the unique, the new, the yet unborn is combined with that bliss of experiencing something once more, of possessing once again, of having lived. This is why he has nothing new to hope for on any road other than the road home, when he takes a new person with him. Just like myself; for scarcely had I seen you the first time than I returned with you to where I had come from.

Ibiza, August 13, 1933

Written August 1933; unpublished in Benjamin's lifetime. *Gesammelte Schriften*, VI, 521–523. Translated by Rodney Livingstone.

Notes

1. The two autobiographical texts entitled "Agesilaus Santander" have provoked much speculation. There is now general agreement that the title does not refer to the Spartan king Agesilaos II (444–360 B.C., who is mentioned by Xenophon,

Cornelius Nepos, and Plutarch: no parallel between Benjamin and Agesilaos has been discovered. Nor is it now thought to refer to the name of the ferry linking Barcelona and Ibiza. Gershom Scholem has speculated that, if we set aside the extra *i* as an ornamental flourish, the name is an anagram of *Der Engel Satanas,* "Satan's angel."

2. Sometime in the spring of 1921, Benjamin bought a small ink drawing by Paul Klee entitled *Angelus Novus,* which was to become his best-known possession (see *Selected Writings,* vol. 1, p. 215). The image plays a role here and, in the last years of his life, was the inspiration for his meditation on the angel of history in "Über den Begriff der Geschichte" (On the Concept of History; 1940).

Antitheses Concerning Word and Name

Word in the supreme sense[1]

The creative word of God.
Its likeness: the human proper name.
Its residue: mute nature.
Man is not created from the word.
"The more existent and real the mind,
the more it is expressible and ex-
pressed." [Vol. 1, pp. 66–67]

*Name, or the Adamite spirit of
language*

"All human language is only the
reflection of the word in name. The
name is no closer to the word than
knowledge is to creation." [Vol. 1,
p. 68]
The name is the translation of the
mute into sound and of the nameless
into the name.
The foundation of the name:
communication of matter in its
magic community.
"God made things knowable in their
names. Man, however, names them
according to knowledge." [Vol. 1,
p. 68]

The human word

"The name no longer lives in [the
human word] intact.
It has stepped out of . . . its own
immanent magic, in order to become
expressly, as it were externally,
magic. [Vol. 1, p. 71]

Similarity

"The communication of matter in its
magical community takes place
through similarity."
Are "to measure" [*ahmen*] and
"to have a presentiment" [*ahnen*]
related?[2]

The atonement for damaging the name lies in the word of judgment, which is also the root of abstraction.

The character of the name is damaged by that of the sign.

The magic of nature

In the things from which it shines back silently and in the mute magic of nature, God's word has become the communication of matter in magical community.

"Moreover, the communication of things is certainly communal in a way that grasps the world as such as an undivided whole." [Vol. 1, p. 73]

The fleeting appearance of a similarity in sound corresponds to the fleeting appearance of a similarity in the object.

Historically, the fleeting appearance of similarity has the character of an anamnesis, which takes possession of a lost similarity that was free from the tendency to become dissipated. This lost similarity, which exists in time, prevails in the Adamite spirit of language. Song holds fast to the image of such a past.

The determinate empirical (albeit nonsensuous) similarity always appears fleetingly in a heterogeneous substratum—namely, in the sign character of the word.

Selection [*herauslesen*]—on the basis of similarity—as the primal form of reading [*lesen*].[3] Runes as a transitional form between treetops, clouds, entrails, on the one hand, and letters, on the other. The magical function of the alphabet: to provide the nonsensuous similarity with the enduring semiotic ground on which it can appear.

The symbol is definable as a sign by means of which no similarity can appear.

Fragment written summer 1933; unpublished in Benjamin's lifetime. *Gesammelte Schriften*, VII, 795–796. Translated by Rodney Livingstone.

Notes

1. This fragment, a preliminary study for the essay "On the Mimetic Faculty," contains Benjamin's comparison of the theory of language he had recently set down in the essay "Doctrine of the Similar" and that formulated in the 1916 essay "On Language as Such and on the Language of Man." References in brackets are to Volume 1 of this edition.

2. *Ahmen*, a rare word meaning "to measure" or "to mark" (as in "to measure a ship's draught") is also the root of the common verb *nachahmen*, "to initiate"

or "to copy." It is etymologically distinct from *ahnen,* "to suspect," "to have a presentiment or foreboding," although the two words are close phonetically.

3. In Latin, reading was a "picking out" or selecting of letters. In contrast to English, German retains this Latin root in the words *lesen* ("to read") and *herauslesen* ("to gather," "to pick out," "to read into").

On the Mimetic Faculty

Nature produces similarities; one need only think of mimicry. The highest capacity for producing similarities, however, is man's. His gift for seeing similarity is nothing but a rudiment of the once powerful compulsion to become similar and to behave mimetically. There is perhaps not a single one of his higher functions in which his mimetic faculty does not play a decisive role.

This faculty has a history, however, in both the phylogenetic and the ontogenetic sense. As regards the latter, play is to a great extent its school. Children's play is everywhere permeated by mimetic modes of behavior, and its realm is by no means limited to what one person can imitate in another. The child plays at being not only a shopkeeper or teacher, but also a windmill and a train. Of what use to him is this schooling of his mimetic faculty?

The answer presupposes an understanding of the phylogenetic significance of the mimetic faculty. Here it is not enough to think of what we understand today by the concept of similarity. As is known, the sphere of life that formerly seemed to be governed by the law of similarity was comprehensive; it ruled both microcosm and macrocosm. But these natural correspondences are given their true importance only if we see that they, one and all, are stimulants and awakeners of the mimetic faculty which answers them in man. It must be borne in mind that neither mimetic powers nor mimetic objects remain the same in the course of thousands of years. Rather, we must suppose that the gift for producing similarities (for example, in dances, whose oldest function this is), and therefore also the gift of recognizing them, have changed in the course of history.

The direction of this change seems determined by the increasing fragility of the mimetic faculty. For clearly the perceptual world [*Merkwelt*] of modern man contains only minimal residues of the magical correspondences and analogies that were familiar to ancient peoples. The question is whether we are concerned with the decay of this faculty or with its transformation. Of the direction in which the latter might lie, some indications may be derived, even if indirectly, from astrology.

We must assume in principle that in the remote past the processes considered imitable included those in the sky. In dance, on other cultic occasions, such imitation could be produced, such similarity dealt with. But if the mimetic genius was really a life-determining force for the ancients, it is not difficult to imagine that the newborn child was thought to be in full possession of this gift, and in particular to be perfectly adapted to the form of cosmic being.

Allusion to the astrological sphere may supply a first reference point for an understanding of the concept of nonsensuous similarity. True, our existence no longer includes what once made it possible to speak of this kind of similarity: above all, the ability to produce it. Nevertheless we, too, possess a canon according to which the meaning of nonsensuous similarity can be at least partly clarified. And this canon is language.

From time immemorial, the mimetic faculty has been conceded some influence on language. Yet this was done without foundation—without consideration of a further meaning, still less a history, of the mimetic faculty. But above all, such considerations remained closely tied to the commonplace, sensuous realm of similarity. All the same, imitative behavior in language formation was acknowledged under the name of onomatopoeia. Now if language, as is evident to the insightful, is not an agreed-upon system of signs, we will, in attempting to approach language, be constantly obliged to have recourse to the kind of thoughts that appear in their most primitive form as the onomatopoeic mode of explanation. The question is whether this can be developed and adapted to improved understanding.

"Every word—and the whole of language," it has been asserted, "is onomatopoeic." It is difficult to conceive in any detail the program that might be implied by this proposition. But the concept of nonsensuous similarity is of some relevance. For if words meaning the same thing in different languages are arranged about that signified as their center, we have to inquire how they all—while often possessing not the slightest similarity to one another—are similar to the signified at their center. Yet this kind of similarity cannot be explained only by the relationships between words meaning the same thing in different languages, just as, in general, our reflections cannot be restricted to the spoken word. They are equally concerned with the written word. And here it is noteworthy that the latter—in some cases perhaps more vividly than the spoken word—illuminates, by the relation of its written form [*Schriftbild*] to the signified, the nature of nonsensuous similarity. In brief, it is nonsensuous similarity that establishes the ties not only between what is said and what is meant but also between what is written and what is meant, and equally between the spoken and the written.

Graphology has taught us to recognize in handwriting images that the unconscious of the writer conceals in it. It may be supposed that the mimetic process which expresses itself in this way in the activity of the writer was, in the very distant times in which script originated, of utmost importance for writing. Script has thus become, like language, an archive of nonsensuous similarities, of nonsensuous correspondences.

But this aspect of language, as well as of script, does not develop in isolation from its other, semiotic aspect. Rather, the mimetic element in language can, like a flame, manifest itself only through a kind of bearer. This bearer is the semiotic element. Thus, the nexus of meaning of words or sentences is the bearer through which, like a flash, similarity appears. For its production by man—like its perception by him—is in many cases, and particularly the most important, tied to its flashing up. It flits past. It is not improbable that the rapidity of writing and reading heightens the fusion of the semiotic and the mimetic in the sphere of language.

"To read what was never written." Such reading is the most ancient: reading prior to all languages, from entrails, the stars, or dances. Later the mediating link of a new kind of reading, of runes and hieroglyphs, came into use. It seems fair to suppose that these were the stages by which the mimetic gift, formerly the foundation of occult practices, gained admittance to writing and language. In this way, language may be seen as the highest level of mimetic behavior and the most complete archive of nonsensuous similarity: a medium into which the earlier powers of mimetic production and comprehension have passed without residue, to the point where they have liquidated those of magic.

Written April–September 1933; unpublished in Benjamin's lifetime. *Gesammelte Schriften*, II, 210–213. Translated by Edmund Jephcott.

Thought Figures

Death of an Old Man

The loss that a much younger person may feel directs his gaze, perhaps for the first time, to the laws that govern the relationship between people who are separated by a great distance in terms of age, but who may nevertheless be linked by bonds of affection. The dead man was a partner with whom the majority of things that concerned you, and the most important ones, could not possibly be discussed. Yet conversation with him had a freshness and a peaceful quality that could never be achieved with someone of the same age. This had two causes. First, any confirmation, however faint or uneffusive, that was forthcoming and that succeeded in bridging the gulf between the generations was far more convincing than confirmation between equals. Second, the younger partner found something that quite disappears later on, when the old have left him and until he himself grows old—namely, a dialogue that is free of calculation of every kind and the need to spare anyone's feelings, because neither has any expectations of the other and neither comes up against any feelings, except one that is rarely encountered: benevolence without admixture of any kind.

The Good Writer

The good writer says no more than he thinks.[1] And much depends on that. For speech is not simply the expression but also the making real of thought. In the same way that running is not just the expression of the desire to reach a goal, but also the realization of that goal. But the kind of realization—

whether it is precisely adapted to the goal, or whether it loosely and wantonly wastes itself on the desire—depends on the training of the person who is running. The more he has himself in hand and avoids superfluous, exaggerated, and uncoordinated movements, the more self-sufficient his position will be and the more economical his use of his body. The bad writer has many ideas which he lets run riot, just like the bad, untrained runner with his slack, overenthusiastic body action. And for that very reason, he can never say soberly just what he thinks. The talent of the good writer is to make use of his style to supply his thought with a spectacle of the kind provided by a well-trained body. He never says more than he has thought. Hence, his writing redounds not to his own benefit, but solely to the benefit of what he wants to say.

Dream

The O——s showed me their house in the Dutch East Indies. The room I found myself in was paneled in dark wood and gave the impression of affluence. But that was nothing, said my guides. What I must admire was the view from the upper story. I thought it must overlook the expanse of sea that was nearby, and so I climbed the stairs. At the top I stood at a window. I looked down. There before my eyes was the very same warm, paneled cozy-looking room I had just left.

Storytelling and Healing

The child is sick. His mother puts him to bed and sits down beside him. And then she begins to tell him stories. How are we to understand this? The answer dawned on me when N. told me about the strange healing powers of his wife's hands. What he said about her hands was this. "Their movements are highly expressive. But it is not possible to describe their expression . . . It is as if they were telling a story." We have learned about the healing powers of storytelling from the Merseburg magic spells.[2] It is not simply that they repeat Wotan's formula;[3] in addition, they explain the situation which led him to use it in the first place. We know, too, that the story a sick man tells the doctor at the start of his treatment can become the first stage in the healing process. And this provokes the question of whether storytelling may not provide the right climate and the most favorable precondition for many a healing—indeed, of whether every illness might be cured if it could only float along the river of narrative—until it reached the mouth. If we reflect that pain is a dam that offers resistance to the current of narrative, it is evident that the dam will be pierced when the gradient is steep enough for everything that crosses its path to be swept into an ocean of blissful oblivion. Stroking marks out a bed for this torrent.

Dream

Berlin. I sat in a coach in the company of two highly dubious girls. Suddenly the sky darkened. "Sodom," said a woman of a certain age in a bonnet who was suddenly in the coach too. In this way, we arrived at a railroad station where the tracks emerged from beyond the station roof. Here a court was in session, the two opposing parties sitting opposite each other on two street corners. I pointed to the outsize bleached moon low down in the sky, as a symbol of justice. Then I was part of a small expedition that was moving down a ramp of the sort you find in freight stations (and I was, and remained, in the precincts of the station). We stopped in front of a narrow rivulet. The rivulet flowed between two rows of porcelain slabs that seemed to be not fixed but floating, and that gave way like buoys under your feet. Whether the second row was really porcelain, I'm not certain. More like glass. At any rate, they were all filled with flowers—like onions in glass jars, only round and brightly colored ones, which gently bumped up against each other in the water, once again like buoys. I stepped into the flowerbed of the furthermost row for a moment. At the same time I could hear the explanations of a little junior official who was showing us the way. In this channel, he was saying, the suicides kill themselves, the poor devils who own nothing more than the flower they hold between their teeth. A light now fell on the flowers. An Acheron,[4] you might think; but in the dream nothing was said about that. As I stepped backward, someone told me where to put my foot on the first slabs. The porcelain at this point was white and full of grooves. Deep in conversation, we made our way out of the depths of the freight station. I drew attention to the strange pattern on the tiles that we were still walking on, and to their usefulness in a film. But no one wanted such projects to be spoken about so openly. Suddenly a boy all in rags came toward us. The others seemed to let him pass without comment, but I searched feverishly in all my pockets. I was looking for a five-mark piece. I could not find it. As he crossed my path—for he did not break his stride—I thrust a smaller coin at him, and awoke.

The "New Community"

I read *Das Friedensfest* [The Peace Festival] and *Einsame Menschen* [Lonely People].[5] People really were uncivilized in that Friedrichshagen milieu.[6] But the fact is that the members of Bruno Wille's and Wilhelm Bölsche's "New Community," which was so much talked about in Gerhart Hauptmann's youth, do indeed seem to have behaved childishly.[7] The modern reader cannot but ask himself whether he belongs to a new race of Spartans—so disciplined is he in comparison. That Johannes Vockerat, whom Hauptmann depicts with such evident sympathy, is certainly a nasty piece of work: bad manners and lack of discretion seem to be the prerequisites of heroism in these plays. In reality, however, the true prerequisite is nothing other than sickness.[8] Here, as in Ibsen, the various illnesses seem to be a cover for the sickness of the turn of the century, the *mal du siècle*. In those half-failed bohemians like Braun and Dr. Scholz, the yearning for freedom is at its most powerful; but on the other hand, it often seems as if it is the intense preoccupation with art, with social questions, and the like that is making them ill. In other words, illness here resembles a social emblem, much like madness among the ancients. Sick people have a special insight into the state of society; their private casting off of inhibitions is converted into an inspired sensitivity to the atmosphere their "contemporaries" breathe. But the form taken by this conversion is "nerves." The nerves are inspired threads; they resemble those fiber-like lines that trailed around furniture and house façades, redolent of unsatisfied rejuvenations and curves full of yearning. Jugendstil [Art Nouveau] liked to dwell on the figure of the Bohemian in the shape of a Daphne pursued by reality and changing into a bundle of nerves, laid bare, plantlike, trembling in the fresh air of the now [*Jetztzeit*].

Pretzel, Feather, Pause, Lament, Clowning

Such unconnected words are the starting point of a game that was very popular during the Biedermeier period.[9] What you had to do was link them up meaningfully, without changing their order. The shorter the sentence and the fewer the intervening clauses, the more the solution was admired. This game produced the most wonderful discoveries, especially among children. To children, words are still like caverns, with the strangest corridors connecting them. Now, however, imagine this game being turned back to front: think of a sentence as if it had been constructed according to these rules. This would, at a stroke, give it a strange, exciting meaning for us. In reality, something of this perspective is contained in every act of reading. It is not just ordinary people who read novels in this way—that is to say, for the names or formulas that leap out of the text at the reader. The educated person, too, is constantly on the lookout for turns of phrase or striking expressions, and the meaning is merely the background on which rests the shadow that they cast, like figures in relief. This is particularly apparent with texts that are regarded as sacred. The commentaries designed to serve such texts fix on particular words, as if they had been chosen according to the rules of the game and assigned to the reader as a task. And in fact the sentences that a child will compose from a group of words during a game really do have more in common with those in sacred texts than with the everyday language of grownups. Here is an example that shows how a child of twelve joined up some prescribed words: "Time sweeps through nature like a pretzel. The feather paints the landscape, and if a pause ensues, it is filled with rain. No lament is heard, for there is no clowning around."

Published in *Die literarische Welt*, November 1933, under the pseudonym Detlef Holz. *Gesammelte Schriften,* IV, 428–433. Translated by Rodney Livingstone.

Notes

1. See also "Little Tricks of the Trade" and "May–June 1931," in this volume.
2. The two Merseburg magic spells *(Zaubersprüche)* date back to the tenth century and are clearly of pre-Christian origin. They consist of a magical imperative formula, preceded by a narrative in which a similar past occurrence is described. The second spell describes the healing of a lame horse.
3. Wotan, the sovereign god of Germanic myth, was regarded as the divine founder of the Germanic dynasties in England and in Scandinavia. In the Merseburger Zaubersprüche, Wotan figures as the master of the most powerful spells.
4. The Acheron is a river in Epirus, Greece, that was thought in ancient times to go to Hades because it flowed through dark gorges and went underground in several places; an oracle of the dead was located on its banks. In Greek mythology it is a river in Hades, and the name sometimes refers to the Underworld generally.
5. These are plays by Gerhart Hauptmann (1862–1946), German playwright, poet, and novelist who was one of the founders of German Naturalism in Berlin in the 1890s; in 1912 he was awarded the Nobel Prize for Literature. *Das Friedensfest* (The Peace Festival; 1890) is an analysis of the troubled relations within a neurotic family. *Einsame Menschen* (Lonely People; 1891) describes the tragic end of an unhappy intellectual torn between his wife and a young woman with whom he can share his thoughts. For a slightly different version of this passage, see "Diary from August 7, 1931, to the Day of My Death," in this volume.
6. Friedrichshagen lies on the outskirts of Berlin.
7. Bruno Wille (1860–1928), German author, editor, and impresario, founded one of Berlin's most important theaters, the Freie Volksbühne Berlin, in 1901. He also established, with Wilhelm Bölsche (1861–1939), an alternative school called the Freie Hochschule. Bölsche, poet and novelist, was a founder of Berlin Naturalism in the 1890s.
8. Johannes Vockerat is a character in Hauptmann's *Einsame Menschen*. Vockerat is a hypersensitive scholar who suffers under the conservative and Christian ideas of his wife and parents.
9. "Biedermeier" refers to the German provincial style in interior decoration, furniture, and architecture of the first half of the nineteenth century. Originally a pejorative term stressing parochialism and apoliticism, Biedermeier came in the twentieth century to be esteemed for its sober, modest, and dignified qualities.

Little Tricks of the Trade

Good Writing

The good writer says no more than he thinks.[1] And much depends on that. For speech is not simply the expression but also the making real of thought. In the same way that running is not just the expression of the desire to reach a goal, but also the realization of that goal. But the kind of realization, whether it is precisely adapted to the goal, or whether it loosely and wantonly wastes itself on the desire—depends on the training of the person who is running. The more he has himself in hand and avoids superfluous, exaggerated, and uncoordinated movements, the more self-sufficient his position will be and the more economical his use of his body. The bad writer has many ideas which he lets run riot, just like the bad, untrained runner with his slack, overenthusiastic body action. And for that very reason, he can never say soberly just what he thinks. The talent of the good writer is to make use of his style to supply his thought with a spectacle of the kind provided by a well-trained body. He never says more than he has thought. Hence, his writing redounds not to his own benefit, but solely to the benefit of what he wants to say.

Reading Novels

Not all books are to be read in the same way. Novels, for example, are there to be devoured. To read them is a pleasure of consumption [*Einverleibung*]. This is not empathy. The reader does not put himself in the place of the hero; he absorbs what befalls the hero into himself. The vivid report on those events, however, is the enticing form in which a nourishing meal is presented at the table. Now, there is of course a raw, healthy form of experience, just as there is raw, healthy food for the stomach—namely, experiencing something for oneself. But the art of the novel, like the art of cooking, begins where the raw products end. There are many nourishing foodstuffs that are inedible when raw. Just as there are any number of experiences that are better read about than personally undergone. They affect many people so strongly that individuals would not survive them if they were to experience them in the flesh. In short, if there is a Muse of the novel—it would be the tenth—it must bear the features of a kitchen fairy. She raises the world from its raw state in order to produce something edible, something tasty. Read a newspaper while eating, if you must. But never a novel. For that involves two sets of conflicting obligations.

The Art of Storytelling

Every morning brings us news from all over the world.[2] Yet we are poor in remarkable stories. Why is that? It is because no events reach us without being permeated by explanations. In other words, hardly anything redounds to the advantage of the story; nearly everything, to that of information. In fact, half the art of storytelling is that of keeping it free of all explanations during the telling. In this respect the ancients, Herodotus above all, were masters. In Chapter 14 of Book III of his *Histories,* he tells the story of Psammenitus. The Egyptian king Psammenitus had been defeated and taken prisoner by the Persian king Cambyses; Cambyses was bent on humbling his captive. He gave orders to place Psammenitus on the road on which the Persian triumphal procession was to pass. And he further arranged that the prisoner should see his daughter as a serving girl, taking her pitcher to the well. While all the Egyptians stood lamenting and bewailing this spectacle, Psammenitus alone stood silent and motionless, his eyes fixed on the ground. And when soon after he saw his son in the procession, being led to execution, he likewise remained unmoved. But when he saw one of his old servants, an old man, reduced to beggary, in the ranks of the prisoners, he beat his head with his fists and gave every sign of the profoundest grief.— From this story we can see the nature of true storytelling. The value of information does not survive the moment when it was new. It lives only at that moment. It has to surrender to it completely and explain itself to the moment without loss of time. A story is different; it does not expend itself. It preserves its strength concentrated within itself and is capable of releasing it even after a long time. Thus, Montaigne referred to the story of this Egyptian king, and asked himself why the king mourned only when he caught sight of his servant and not before. Montaigne answers: "Since he was already overwhelmed by grief, it took only the smallest addition for the dam to burst." The story can be understood in this way. But there is room for other explanations, too. Anyone can find out what these reasons are by asking Montaigne's question in a circle of friends. For example, one of mine said, "The king is unmoved by the fate of those of royal blood, for it is his own." And another: "We are moved by much on the stage that does not move us in real life. To the king, this servant is only an actor." And a third: "Great suffering builds up and only breaks forth with relaxation. The sight of his servant was the relaxation."—"If this story had taken place today," said a fourth, "all the papers would claim that Psammenitus loved his servant more than his children." What is certain is that every reporter would find an explanation at the drop of a hat. Herodotus offers no explanations. His report is the driest. That is why this story from ancient Egypt is still capable of arousing astonishment and thought even after thousands of years. It resembles the seeds of grain that have lain hermetically sealed in the chambers of the Pyramids for thousands of years, and have retained their power to germinate to this very day.

After Completion

The origin of great works has often been conceptualized in terms of the image of birth. This image is dialectical; it embraces the process from two sides. One is concerned with creative conception and affects the feminine side of genius. This feminine aspect comes to an end with the completion of the work. It sets the work in motion and then it dies. What dies in the master with the finished creation is that part of him in which it was conceived. Now, however—and this is the other side of the coin—the completion of the work is no dead thing. It is not achievable from outside; filing and tinkering does not bring it about. It is perfected in the interior of the work itself. And here, too, we may speak of giving birth. In the act of completion, the created thing gives birth once more to its creator. Not in its feminine aspect, in which it was conceived, but on its masculine side. Ecstatic, the creator overtakes nature, for he will now be indebted to a brighter source for the existence that he received for the first time from the dark depths of the maternal womb. His home is not where he was born; rather, he comes into the world where his home is. He is the masculine firstborn of the work that he had once conceived.

Written 1928–1933; unpublished in Benjamin's lifetime. *Gesammelte Schriften,* IV, 435–438. Translated by Rodney Livingstone.

Notes

1. See also the essay "Thought Figures" (section entitled "The Good Writer") in this volume.
2. See also sections VI and VII of Benjamin's essay "Der Erzähler" (The Storyteller).

Experience and Poverty

Our childhood anthologies used to contain the fable of the old man who, on his deathbed, fooled his sons into believing that there was treasure buried in the vineyard. They would only have to dig. They dug, but found no treasure. When autumn came, however, the vineyard bore fruit like no other in the whole land. They then perceived that their father had passed on a valuable piece of experience: the blessing lies in hard work and not in gold. Such lessons in experience were passed on to us, either as threats or as kindly pieces of advice, all the while we were growing up: "Still wet behind the ears, and he wants to tell us what's what!" "You'll find out [*erfahren*] soon enough!" Moreover, everyone knew precisely what experience was: older people had always passed it on to younger ones. It was handed down in short form to sons and grandsons, with the authority of age, in proverbs; with an often long-winded eloquence, as tales; sometimes as stories from foreign lands, at the fireside.—Where has it all gone? Who still meets people who really know how to tell a story? Where do you still hear words from the dying that last, and that pass from one generation to the next like a precious ring? Who can still call on a proverb when he needs one? And who will even attempt to deal with young people by giving them the benefit of their experience?

No, this much is clear: experience has fallen in value, amid a generation which from 1914 to 1918 had to experience some of the most monstrous events in the history of the world. Perhaps this is less remarkable than it appears. Wasn't it noticed at the time how many people returned from the front in silence? Not richer but poorer in communicable experience? And what poured out from the flood of war books ten years later was anything but the experience that passes from mouth to ear. No, there was nothing remarkable about that. For never has experience been contradicted more thoroughly: strategic experience has been contravened by positional warfare; economic experience, by the inflation; physical experience, by hunger; moral experiences, by the ruling powers. A generation that had gone to school in horse-drawn streetcars now stood in the open air, amid a landscape in which nothing was the same except the clouds and, at its center, in a force field of destructive torrents and explosions, the tiny, fragile human body.

With this tremendous development of technology, a completely new poverty has descended on mankind. And the reverse side of this poverty is the oppressive wealth of ideas that has been spread among people, or rather has swamped them entirely—ideas that have come with the revival of astrology and the wisdom of yoga, Christian Science and chiromancy, vegetarianism and gnosis, scholasticism and spiritualism. For this is not a genuine revival but a galvanization. We need to remind ourselves of Ensor's magnificent paintings,[1] in which the streets of great cities are filled with ghosts; philistines in carnival disguises roll endlessly down the streets, wearing distorted masks covered in flour and cardboard crowns on their heads. These paintings are perhaps nothing so much as the reflection of the ghastly and chaotic renaissance in which so many people have placed their hopes. But here we can see quite clearly that our poverty of experience is just a part of that larger poverty that has once again acquired a face—a face of the same sharpness and precision as that of a beggar in the Middle Ages. For what is the value of all our culture if it is divorced from experience? Where it all leads when that experience is simulated or obtained by underhanded means is something that has become clear to us from the horrific mishmash of styles and ideologies produced during the last century—too clear for us not to think it a matter of honesty to declare our bankruptcy. Indeed (let's admit it), our poverty of experience is not merely poverty on the personal level, but poverty of human experience in general. Hence, a new kind of barbarism.

Barbarism? Yes, indeed. We say this in order to introduce a new, positive concept of barbarism. For what does poverty of experience do for the barbarian? It forces him to start from scratch; to make a new start; to make a little go a long way; to begin with a little and build up further, looking neither left nor right. Among the great creative spirits, there have always been the inexorable ones who begin by clearing a tabula rasa. They need a drawing table; they were constructors. Such a constructor was Descartes, who required nothing more to launch his entire philosophy than the single certitude, "I think, therefore I am." And he went on from there. Einstein, too, was such a constructor; he was not interested in anything in the whole wide world of physics except a minute discrepancy between Newton's equations and the observations of astronomy. And this same insistence on starting from the very beginning also marks artists when they followed the example of mathematicians and built the world from stereometric forms, like the Cubists, or modeled themselves on engineers, like Klee.[2] For just like any good car, whose every part, even the bodywork, obeys the needs above all of the engine, Klee's figures too seem to have been designed on the drawing board, and even in their general expression they obey the laws of their interior. Their interior, rather than their inwardness; and this is what makes them barbaric.

Here and there, the best minds have long since started to think in these terms. A total absence of illusion about the age and at the same time an unlimited commitment to it—this is its hallmark. It makes no difference whether the poet Bert Brecht declares that Communism is the just distribution of poverty, not of wealth, or whether Adolf Loos, the forerunner of modern architecture,[3] states, "I write only for people who possess a modern sensibility . . . I do not write for people consumed by nostalgia for the Renaissance or the Rococo." A complex artist like the painter Paul Klee and a programmatic one like Loos—both reject the traditional, solemn, noble image of man, festooned with all the sacrificial offerings of the past. They turn instead to the naked man of the contemporary world who lies screaming like a newborn babe in the dirty diapers of the present. No one has greeted this present with greater joy and hilarity than Paul Scheerbart.[4] There are novels by him that from a distance look like works by Jules Verne.[5] But quite unlike Verne, who always has ordinary French or English gentlemen of leisure traveling around the cosmos in the most amazing vehicles, Scheerbart is interested in inquiring how our telescopes, our airplanes, our rockets can transform human beings as they have been up to now into completely new, lovable, and interesting creatures. Moreover, these creatures talk in a completely new language. And what is crucial about this language is its arbitrary, constructed nature, in contrast to organic language. This is the distinctive feature of the language of Scheerbart's human beings, or rather "people"; for humanlikeness—a principle of humanism—is something they reject. Even in their proper names: Peka, Labu, Sofanti, and the like are the names of the characters in the book *Lesabéndio*, titled after its hero. The Russians, too, like to give their children "dehumanized" names: they call them "October," after the month of the Revolution; "Pyatiletka," after the Five-Year Plan; or "Aviakhim," after an airline. No technical renovation of language, but its mobilization in the service of struggle or work—at any rate, of changing reality instead of describing it.

To return to Scheerbart: he placed the greatest value on housing his "people"—and, following this model, his fellow citizens—in buildings befitting their station, in adjustable, movable glass-covered dwellings of the kind since built by Loos and Le Corbusier.[6] It is no coincidence that glass is such a hard, smooth material to which nothing can be fixed. A cold and sober material into the bargain. Objects made of glass have no "aura." Glass is, in general, the enemy of secrets. It is also the enemy of possession. The great writer André Gide once said, "Everything I wish to own becomes opaque to me." Do people like Scheerbart dream of glass buildings because they are the spokesmen of a new poverty? But a comparison will perhaps reveal more than theory.[7] If you enter a bourgeois room of the 1880s, for all the coziness it radiates, the strongest impression you receive may well be, "You've got no business here." And in fact you have no business in that room, for there is no spot on which the owner has not left his mark—the ornaments on the mantlepiece, the antimacassars on the armchairs, the transparencies in the windows, the screen in front of the fire. A neat phrase by Brecht helps us out here: "Erase the traces!" is the refrain in the first poem of his *Lesebuch für Städtebewohner* [Reader for City-Dwellers]. Here in the bourgeois room, the opposite behavior became the norm. And conversely, the *intérieur* forces the inhabitant to adopt the greatest possible number of habits—habits that do more justice to the interior he is living in than to himself. This is understood by everyone who is familiar with the absurd attitude of the inhabitants of such plush apartments when something broke. Even their way of showing their annoyance—and this affect, which is gradually starting to die out, was one that they could produce with great virtuosity—was above all the reaction of a person who felt that someone had obliterated "the traces of his days on earth."[8] This has now been achieved by Scheerbart, with his glass, and by the Bauhaus, with its steel. They have created rooms in which it is hard to leave traces. "It follows from the foregoing," Scheerbart declared a good twenty years ago, "that we can surely talk about a 'culture of glass.' The new glass-milieu will transform humanity utterly. And now it remains only to be wished that the new glass-culture will not encounter too many enemies."

Poverty of experience. This should not be understood to mean that people are yearning for new experience. No, they long to free themselves from experience; they long for a world in which they can make such pure and decided use of their poverty—their outer poverty, and ultimately also their inner poverty—that it will lead to something respectable. Nor are they ignorant or inexperienced. Often we could say the very opposite. They have "devoured" everything, both "culture and people," and they have had such a surfeit that it has exhausted them. No one feels more caught out than they by Scheerbart's words: "You are all so tired, just because you have failed to concentrate your thoughts on a simple but ambitious plan." Tiredness is followed by sleep, and then it is not uncommon for a dream to make up for the sadness and discouragement of the day—a dream that shows us in its realized form the simple but magnificent existence for which the energy is lacking in reality. The existence of Mickey Mouse is such a dream for contemporary man.[9] His life is full of miracles—miracles that not only surpass the wonders of technology, but make fun of them. For the most extraordinary thing about them is that they all appear, quite without any machinery, to have been improvised out of the body of Mickey Mouse, out of his supporters and persecutors, and out of the most ordinary pieces of furniture, as well as from trees, clouds, and the sea. Nature and technology, primitiveness and comfort, have completely merged. And to people who have grown weary of the endless complications of everyday living and to whom the purpose of existence seems to have been reduced to the most distant vanishing point on an endless horizon, it must come as a tremendous relief to find a way of life in which everything is solved in the simplest and most comfortable way, in which a car is no heavier than a straw hat and the fruit on the tree becomes round as quickly as a hot-air balloon. And now we need to step back and keep our distance.

We have become impoverished. We have given up one portion of the human heritage after another, and have often left it at the pawnbroker's for a hundredth of its true value, in exchange for the small change of "the contemporary." The economic crisis is at the door, and behind it is the shadow of the approaching war. Holding on to things has become the monopoly of a few powerful people, who, God knows, are no more human than the many; for the most part, they are more barbaric, but not in the good way. Everyone else has to adapt—beginning anew and with few resources. They rely on the men who have adopted the cause of the absolutely new and have founded it on insight and renunciation. In its buildings, pictures, and stories, mankind is preparing to outlive culture, if need be. And the main thing is that it does so with a laugh. This laughter may occasionally sound barbaric. Well and good. Let us hope that from time to time the individual will give a little humanity to the masses, who one day will repay him with compound interest.

Published in *Die Welt im Wort* (Prague), December 1933. *Gesammelte Schriften*, II, 213–219. Translated by Rodney Livingstone.

Notes

1. James Sydney Ensor (1860–1949) was a Belgian painter and printmaker whose works are known for their troubling fantasy, explosive colors, and subtle social commentary.
2. Paul Klee (1879–1940), Swiss painter, was associated in the teens with the group Der Blaue Reiter, which formed around Wassily Kandinsky. Klee was an instructor in the painting workshop at the Bauhaus between 1921 and 1931.
3. Adolf Loos (1870–1933), Austrian architect, was an important precursor of the

International Style. An influential essayist and social commentator, his attack on ornament drew broad attention in Europe before World War I.

4. Paul Scheerbart (1863–1915), German author, produced poetry and prose oriented toward a gently fantastic science fiction. In 1919, Benjamin wrote an unpublished review of his novel *Lesabéndio* (1913). Scheerbart's book *Glasarchitektur* (Glass Architecture), produced in collaboration with the architect Bruno Taut, was one of the inspirations for the present essay.

5. Jules Verne (1828–1905), French author, wrote remarkably popular novels which laid much of the foundation for modern science fiction.

6. Le Corbusier (pseudonym of Charles-Edouard Jeanneret; 1887–1965) was a Swiss architect and city planner whose designs combine the functionalism of the modernist movement with a bold, sculptural expressionism.

7. Compare the following passage with "Short Shadows (II)," in this volume.

8. J. W. von Goethe, *Faust, Part II,* lines 11,583–84: "The trace of my days on earth cannot perish in eons."

9. Compare the fragment "Mickey Mouse" (1931), in this volume.

The Author as Producer, 1934

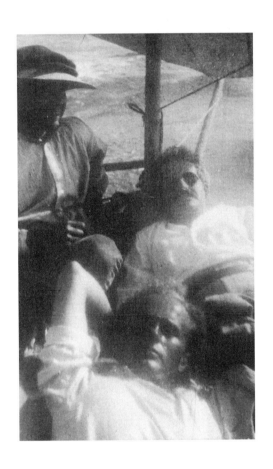

Walter Benjamin (center), with lobster-fisherman and (in foreground) Paul Gauguin, off Ibiza, May 1933. Photographer unknown. Collection of Marga Noeggerath, Munich.

Once Is as Good as Never

While writing, you sometimes pause over a purple passage—one which is more successful than everything else and after which you suddenly do not know how to go on. Something has gone awry. It is as if there were such a thing as a bad or unfruitful success; and perhaps you have to have a concept of precisely such a thing in order to grasp what a good success might be. Basically, there are two opposed adages that apply here: "Once and for all," and "Once is as good as never" [*Einmal ist keinmal*]. Of course, there are cases where "Once and for all" is entirely apt—in games, for example, or in examinations, or in a duel. But never at work. With work, "Once is as good as never" comes into its own. Only not everyone is eager to uncover the innermost nature of the practices and arrangements by which this wisdom can put down roots. Trotsky did so in a few sentences in which he erects a monument to his father's labor in the cornfields. He writes: "Touched, I watch him. My father moves simply and economically. You wouldn't think he was at work. His steps are measured; they're practice steps, as if he were looking for a spot where he could really make a start. His sickle makes its way without any artificial show of naturalness. You might be tempted to think he was not very sure of it—yet it cuts sharply and close to the ground, and throws off to the left in regular ribbons what it has cut down."[1] Here we have the work habits of the experienced man who has learned every day and with every swing of the scythe to make a fresh start. He does not pause to look at what he has achieved; indeed, what he has done seems to evaporate under his hands and to leave no trace. Only hands like those will succeed in difficult things as if they were child's play, because they are cautious when dealing with easy ones. "Never profit from an acquired élan," says Gide.[2] He is one of the writers in whose works "purple passages" are extremely rare.

Written ca. 1932; published in *Der öffentliche Dienst* (Zürich), February 1934. *Gesammelte Schriften*, IV, 433–434. Translated by Rodney Livingstone.

Notes

1. This citation differs from the corresponding passage in the German translation of Trotsky's autobiography, *Mein Leben* (Berlin: S. Fischer, 1930), p. 80. Benjamin may have translated the passage himself from the French edition: *Ma Vie* (Paris, 1930).
2. André Gide, *Journal des "Faux-monnayeurs"* (Paris: Gallimard, 1929), p. 89.

The Newspaper

In our writing, opposites that in happier ages fertilized one another have become insoluble antinomies.[1] Thus, science and belles lettres, criticism and literary production, culture and politics, fall apart in disorder and lose all connection with one another. The scene of this literary confusion is the newspaper; its content, "subject matter" that denies itself any other form of organization than that imposed on it by the reader's impatience. For impatience is the state of mind of the newspaper reader. And this impatience is not just that of the politician expecting information, or of the speculator looking for a stock tip; behind it smolders the impatience of people who are excluded and who think they have the right to see their own interests expressed. The fact that nothing binds the reader more tightly to his paper than this all-consuming impatience, his longing for daily nourishment, has long been exploited by publishers, who are constantly inaugurating new columns to address the reader's questions, opinions, and protests. Hand in hand, therefore, with the indiscriminate assimilation of facts goes the equally indiscriminate assimilation of readers, who are instantly elevated to collaborators. Here, however, a dialectical moment lies concealed: the decline of writing in this press turns out to be the formula for its restoration in a different one. For since writing gains in breadth what it loses in depth, the conventional distinction between author and public that the press has maintained (although it is tending to loosen it through routine) is disappearing in a socially desirable way. The reader is at all times ready to become a writer—that is, a describer or even a prescriber. As an expert—not perhaps in a discipline, but perhaps in a post that he holds—he gains access to authorship. Work itself has its turn to speak. And its representation in words becomes a part of the ability that is needed for its exercise. Literary competence is no longer founded on specialized training but is now based on polytechnical education, and thus becomes public property. It is, in a word, the literarization of the conditions of living that masters the otherwise insoluble antinomies. And it is at the scene of the limitless debasement of the word—the newspaper, in short—that its salvation is being prepared.

Published in *Der öffentliche Dienst* (Zürich), March 1934. *Gesammelte Schriften,* II, 628–629. Translated by Rodney Livingstone, on the basis of a prior version by Edmund Jephcott.

Notes

1. The following passage is a modification of similar ideas expressed in "Diary from August 7, 1931, to the Day of My Death," in this volume. Benjamin also cites from this essay in "The Author as Producer," also in this volume.

Venal but Unusable

The great majority of intellectuals—particularly in the arts—are in a desperate plight.[1] The fault lies, however, not with their character, pride, or inaccessibility. Journalists, novelists, and literati are for the most part ready for every compromise. It's just that they do not realize it. And this is the reason for their failures. Because they do not know, or want to know, that they are venal, they do not understand that they should separate out those aspects of their opinions, experiences, modes of behavior that might be of interest to the market. Instead they make it a point of honor to be wholly themselves on every issue. Because they want to be sold, so to speak, only "in one piece," they are as unsalable as a calf that the butcher will sell to the housewife only as an undivided whole.

Published in *Der öffentliche Dienst* (Zürich), April 1934. *Gesammelte Schriften,* II, 630. Translated by Rodney Livingstone.

Notes

1. See also "Notes (IV)" (1932), in this volume.

The Present Social Situation of the French Writer

When war broke out in 1914, a book by Guillaume *Apollinaire—Le poète assassiné* [The Poet Assassinated]—was in press.[1] Apollinaire has been called the Bellachini of literature.[2] Both his way of life and his style of writing contain all the theories and slogans whose time was ripe. He drew them out of his own nature just as a magician pulls objects out of a hat: pancakes, goldfish, ball gowns, pocket watches. As long as this man lived—he died on Armistice Day—no radical or eccentric fashion appeared, whether in painting or literature, that he had not created or at least launched. Together with Marinetti, he was the first to proclaim the main keywords of Futurism; he followed this up by making propaganda for Dada; then came the latest wave of painting, from Picasso to Max Ernst; and last, there was Surrealism, which he gave its name.[3] In the title story of the volume *Le poète assassiné*, Apollinaire prints an apocryphal article that allegedly appeared "on January 26 of this year" in *The Voice*, a paper published in Adelaide, Australia. The article, supposedly written by a German chemist, includes these words:

> True glory has abandoned literature in favor of science, philosophy, acrobatics, philanthropy, sociology, and so on. Nowadays, the only task of poets is to draw on money that they no longer earn, because they scarcely do any work; and the vast majority of them (with a few exceptions, such as cabaret artists) have not the slightest talent and hence not the slightest excuse. As for those who are not wholly without ability, they are even more pernicious, because they neither receive anything nor turn their hand to anything, yet they make more noise than an entire regiment . . . All these people have forfeited their right to exist. The prizes that are conferred on them have been purloined from workers, inventors, scholars, philosophers, acrobats, philanthropists, sociologists, and

so on. Poets have to go. Lycurgus drove them out of the republic; they should be driven from the face of the earth.

In the evening edition, the author is said to have published a postscript in which he argued: "You have to choose, O world, between literature and your own life; unless serious steps are taken to deal with literature, it will mean the end of civilization. This is no time for procrastination. The new age begins tomorrow. There will no longer be any poetry . . . Writers will be exterminated."[4]

These words do not look as if they had been written twenty years ago. Not that they are unmarked by the passing of twenty years. But their effect has been to transform a whim, an exuberant improvisation, and to lay bare the truth it contained. The landscape that is illuminated by these words as if by a lightning flash, and that at the time could barely be discerned in the distance, is one we have since become familiar with. It is the social climate of imperialism, in which the position of intellectuals has become increasingly intractable. The process of selection that has since taken place at the hands of the ruling classes has assumed forms that are scarcely less inexorable than the process Apollinaire described. Subsequent attempts to define the function of the intellectual in society are vivid testimony to the crisis in which he lives. Few people have had the wit or the resoluteness to perceive that this process of attrition, which has so undermined the intellectual's moral basis in society, if not his economic one, is predicated on the most radical changes in society itself. If this insight is unambiguously expressed by André Gide[5] and a number of other, younger writers, its value can be enhanced only by a scrutiny of the difficult conditions under which it was acquired.

The lightning shafts of Apollinaire's prophecies serve to discharge a stifling atmosphere. It is the atmosphere which gave birth to the work of Maurice *Barrès,* who had a decisive influence on the intelligentsia of the prewar years.[6] Barrès was a romantic nihilist. The disorientation of the intellectuals who succeeded him must have been great indeed if they could approve the utterances of a man who had said, "What do I care about the truth of ideas—it is the enthusiasm with which they are advanced that I respect." Barrès profoundly believed, and made a point of declaring, that "everything amounts to the same thing, with the exception of the excitement which we and people like us derive from certain ideas; for those who have managed to adopt the right point of view, there are no great events but only magnificent spectacles." The more thoroughly we become acquainted with his ideas, the more closely they seem to be related to the doctrines which the present age has everywhere brought forth. They consist of the same basic nihilistic outlook, the same set of idealistic gestures, and the same conformism that result from the synthesis of nihilism and idealism. La Rochefoucauld said that education can do nothing more than teach a man to peel a peach with decorum. In the same spirit, the entire romantic and ultimately political apparatus that Barrès sets in motion to propagate "the cult of the earth and the dead" ends up by subserving no higher purpose than "to transform chaotic feelings into more cultivated ones." These cultivated feelings never deny that they originate in an aestheticism which is merely the obverse side of nihilism. And just as modern Italian nationalism harks back to Imperial Rome and the Germans hark back to Teutonic paganism, Barrès believes that the time is ripe "for a reconciliation of the saints and the defeated gods." He wishes to salvage the pure springs and dense forests of France, as well as its cathedrals, on whose behalf he wrote a celebrated pamphlet in 1914. "And in order to preserve the spiritual vitality of the race, I call for an alliance between Catholic feeling and the spirit of the soil."

Barrès made his greatest impact with his novel *Les Déracinés* [Men without Roots], which follows the fortunes of seven Lorrainers who pursue their studies in Paris. The critic Thibaudet has made an illuminating comment on this novel: "As if by chance, four members of the group make something of their lives and become respectable people. They are the ones who have money. Of the two that receive scholarships, however, one becomes a blackmailer and the other a murderer. This is no accident. Barrès tells us that the great precondition of respectability is independence—in other words, wealth."[7]

Barrès' philosophy is the philosophy of inheritance. Significantly, one of the main figures in this weighty novel, in which he works out this philosophy, is a character study of one of his teachers, Jules *Lagneau*.[8] In real life, the two men failed to understand each other, and came from radically different parts of the social spectrum. Lagneau was genuinely without roots. He hailed from Metz; his family was ruined after they sided with France in 1871.[9] For the young Lagneau, France was the very opposite of a legacy. At the age of twenty, the philosopher had to assume the burden of supporting his family. At the same age, Barrès came into an inheritance that gave him the leisure to write *Le culte du moi*.[10]

Lagneau left few writings. But in the intellectual history of the last few decades, he is an important signpost. He produced two important students—two intellectuals whose work gives a more or less complete picture of the bourgeois ideology of France. What Barrès' work did for the ideologies of the Right, his other pupil, Emile Chartier,[11] did for the Left. Alain's political statement of faith, *Eléments d'une doctrine radicale* (the title refers to the doctrines of the Radical party),[12] are a kind of intellectual legacy of Jules Lagneau. The Radicals are, at least as far as their leaders are concerned, a party of professors and teachers. Lagneau was a very typical representative of this stratum. "We renounce," he writes, "every bid for popularity, every ambition to represent anything; we also deny ourselves the right to entertain or create any untruth, however slight, or any misguided opinions about what might be possible, whether in speech or in writing." He adds, "We will not store up any wealth: we renounce all claim to savings, to provision for ourselves and our families. This virtue, which shall be the death of us, needs no recommendation." The features of this intellectual—however real their basis in life—represent such a definite and deeply ingrained ideal of the bourgeois elites in the "republic of professors" that we would do well to shed as much light on them as possible. This can perhaps be achieved with the aid of a paragraph by Jacques *Chardonne,* in which this type of bourgeois intellectual is seen as the epitome of the petty bourgeois himself.[13] The fact that this depiction is stereotyped and exaggerated makes it all the more useful for our purposes:

> The bourgeois—and it is the petty bourgeois we have specifically in mind—is an artist. He is an educated character, but sufficiently independent of books to have his own ideas. Whether from experience or from close proximity, he has known enough wealth to enable him not to have to think about it constantly; he is fundamentally indifferent to indifferent matters, and was made for poverty like no one else. He is without prejudices, even exalted ones; without illusions and without hope. He is the first person to demand justice for others, and the first to suffer it, if need be. On earth, where he has received everything but his just deserts, he expects nothing more, nor does he expect to fare better in the world to come. Yet he takes pleasure in his unpretentious life, and is able to enjoy what it offers without maligning it. The world that has brought forth such people has not failed in its task. The path that leads to such wisdom is not an evil one. This is why there is still hope for the disinherited. This is why we must not dispute in advance a person's right to whatever society can offer.

As a political party, the Radicals have taken Barrès literally. He and they pose the problems in the same way, only his answers are diametrically opposed to theirs. To the inherited rights of the traditionalists he opposes the rights of the child; to the privileges of birth and wealth, the personal merits of the individual and success in state examinations. "And why not?" concludes Thibaudet. "Chinese civilization maintained itself for thousands of years as an examinocracy." Strange though the comparison with China may seem, it provides some insight. It has long since formed part of essayists' stock in trade. Paul *Morand* has used it to point out the striking similarities between the Chinese and the French petty bourgeois.[14] Both display the same "fanatical thrift, the art of constantly repairing things to prolong their usefulness . . . , distrust, a centuries-old politeness, a deep-rooted but passive hatred of foreigners, a conservatism punctuated by social squalls, an absence of public spirit, and the toughness of old people who have outlived their illnesses. One is tempted to think that all old civilizations resemble one another." The social subsoil on which the largest party in France has grown—for this is what the Radical party is—is far from being identical with the structure of the country as a whole. But the clubs and organizations (the so-called cadres) that this party possesses throughout the land undoubtedly constitute the climate in which the most important ideologies of the intelligentsia have been shaped, and from which only the most progressive have fully developed. The book that André Siegfried wrote three years ago under the title *Tableau des partis en France* [Portrait of the Parties in France] is a valuable tool for the study of these cadres.[15] Alain is by no means their leader, but he is the shrewdest interpreter of these groups. He defines their activities as "a constant battle of the small against the great." And in fact it has been asserted that the entire economic program of Radicalism consists in creating an aureole around the little word "small" and in defending the interests of the small farmer, the small businessman, the small property owner, the small depositor. So much for Alain. He is an interpreter more than a fighter. It is in the nature of the social substructure on which the activities of bourgeois intellectuals take place that any more determined course of action at once threatens to slip into Romantic sectarianism. The ideologies of Benda and Péguy are proof of this.[16]

In the intellectual situation fostered by Barrès and Maurras[17] and sanctioned by postwar developments, the appearance of Julien *Benda*'s book *La trahison des clercs* [The Treason of the Intellectuals] five years ago was like a bombshell. Here, Benda is concerned with the way in which intellectuals have begun to respond to politics over the past few decades. According to him, ever since intellectuals came into being, their world-historical task has been to teach the universal, abstract values of mankind: freedom, justice, and humanity. But now, with Maurras and Barrès, d'Annunzio and Marinetti, Kipling and Conan Doyle, Rudolf Borchardt and Spengler, they have begun to betray these values, whose guardians they have been for centuries. This new turn of events is marked by two signs. First, the unprecedented immediate relevance that politics has acquired for the writer. Wherever you look, you see political novelists, political poets, political historians, political reviewers.—But it is not just political passions that he finds incredible and unprecedented. Even more disconcerting and damaging is the direction this political activity is taking: he is shocked by the slogans of an intelligentsia that defends the cause of nations against that of mankind, of parties against justice, and of power against the mind. The bitter necessities of reality, the maxims of *Realpolitik,* were defended by the *clercs* in earlier times, but not even Machiavelli tried to embellish them with the pathos of ethical precepts.

Benda's general stance is prescribed by Catholicism. The thesis which underlies his book formally asserts a dual morality: that of force for states and peoples, and that of Christian humanism for intellectuals. His complaint is less that the norms of Christian humanism have no decisive effect on the world events than that they must forgo their claims to do so, because the intellectuals who defended them in the past have now gone over to the party of power. We cannot but admire the virtuosity Benda displays in confining his attention to the foreground of the problem. The decline of the independent intelligentsia is determined crucially, if not exclusively, by economic factors. The author understands as little of the economic basis of their crisis as he does of the crisis in the sciences—the undermining of the dogma of an objective research free from preconceptions. And he seems not to understand that the attachment of intellectuals to the political prejudices of classes and nations is for the most part no more than a disastrous, short-sighted attempt to break free of idealistic abstractions and come closer, closer than ever before, to reality. Admittedly, this entire movement was, in the end, violent and desperate. But instead of seeking an appropriate form for it, reversing it, and attempting to return intellectuals to the seclusion of their utopian idealism, he reveals—and no appeal to the ideals of democracy can disguise the fact—a thoroughly Romantic outlook. Benda recently proclaimed this openly in his *Discours à la nation européenne,* in which he gives an enticing description of a unified world whose economic forms have survived unaltered:

> This Europe will be scientific rather than literary, intellectual rather than artistic, philosophical rather than picturesque. And to more than a few of us it will come as a bitter lesson. For aren't poets more attractive than scholars? Aren't artists more captivating than thinkers? Here, however, we have to be more modest: either Europe will be serious, or it will not come into being. It will be far less entertaining than the various nations, which had been far less entertaining in their turn than the provinces. So we must choose: either we shall create Europe, or we shall remain eternal children. The nations have been lovable Clorindas; they will rejoice in the knowledge that they have been sensuous, passionately adored creatures. But Europe will come to resemble those youthful scholars of the thirteenth century who taught mathematics at the University of Bologna and who appeared before their audience veiled, so as not to confuse them with their beauty.[18]

It is not hard to discern in this very utopian Europe a disguised and, as it were, oversize monk's cell, to which intellectuals—"the spiritual"—retreat in order to weave the text of a sermon, undaunted by the thought that it will be delivered to rows of empty seats, if indeed it is delivered at all. This is why Berl is unanswerable when he says, "Revolt of the spirit? When Benda uses the word 'spirit,' isn't he thinking really of priests who minister to souls and see to earthly goods? . . . Doesn't his voice echo with nostalgia for the monastery, the Benedictines . . . a nostalgia that has become so powerful in the modern world? Must we continue to lament their loss?"[19]

The "spirit" to which Benda appeals so beseechingly, in an effort to counter the crisis, shows itself quickly enough in its true colors. It is nothing more than the manifestation of a figure from the past: the medieval cleric in his cell. But there has been no lack of attempts to breathe life into this notion of the "spirit," and no one has striven more fervently to give it flesh and bones than Charles *Péguy*, who appealed to the forces of the soil and of faith to assign intellectuals a place in the life of the nation and of history, although—unlike Barrès—he does not renounce the libertarian and anarchic elements they drew from the traditions of the French Revolution. Péguy fell early in the war. His life's work is still important today, thanks to the lucidity and energy with which he sought to define the role of the intellectual. Péguy might well be thought to fit the picture that Benda sketched of the *clerc trahissant,* the intellectual as traitor. But a closer inspection reveals that this is not the case. "You can say of Péguy what you will, but not that he is a traitor. And why? Because a particular attitude becomes treachery only when it is dictated by fear or indolence. The treason of intellectuals lies in their willingness to submit to prevailing moods and prejudices. Péguy does nothing of the sort. He was a nationalist, yet a supporter of Dreyfus. He was a Catholic, but was banned from taking Communion."[20] And when Berl, alluding to the title of a book by Barrès, sums up a certain type of writer with the words, "Enemy of the laws, indeed, but friend of the powers that be," this applies least of all to Péguy. He came from Orléans. There, according to the Tharauds, who describe their friend's origins, "he grew up surrounded by an ancient civilization, whose original complexion was determined by local traditions and a centuries-old history with no (or barely any) foreign element, in the womb of a population that was close to the earth and belonged to a peasant type . . . In short, he was surrounded by an ancient world that was closer to the France of the ancien régime than to the present."[21]

Péguy's great reform efforts bore in all respects the stamp of his origins. Even before he had established the *Cahiers de la Quinzaine* (acting as his own publisher and his own printer so as to create a vehicle for his own ideas), he had already consciously tried to maintain the traditions of his home, while he was still at the Ecole Normale. For the first time since the Renaissance, the generation he belonged to gave France great writers of peasant stock, with accompanying rustic language and way of thinking: Claudel, Jammes, Ramuz.[22] "Péguy was the first to provide the repellent spectacle of a student who had attended the Ecole Normale but who failed to exhibit the slightest evidence of a cultivated, classical, traditional style." On the contrary, Péguy's style comes from the soil; the long, coarse sentences that characterize it have been compared with long, coarse furrows intended for seed.

Thus, the forces to which Péguy appeals in order to form the type of the revolutionary intellectual are of prerevolutionary origin. According to André Siegfried, "the peasant and the French craftsman have come down to us from the Middle Ages; and if we gaze deeply into ourselves, we will have to confess that for good or ill, everything important in us was shaped before the Revolution. We are not a youthful nation."[23] This must be borne in mind if we are to understand that Péguy directed his appeal not to the young (as would be customary nowadays) but to those in their forties. The revolutionary task he set them was not of the defensive sort whose spirit was succinctly formulated by Alain when he said, "The attitude of the Left is that of a controlling authority." On the contrary, he urged his supporters to go on the attack, and his onslaught was directed not just at the rulers, but also at the cohorts of academics and intellectuals who had betrayed the people from whom they sprang. "I shall found the great party of forty-year-olds. Someone recently included me in that category, impulsively putting me in the class of forty-year-olds. I shall make use of this for my own purposes. An old politician makes use of everything. I will found the party of forty-year-olds."[24] That was in 1914. But those to whom Péguy was making his appeal were twenty in 1894; and that was the year in which Dreyfus was courtmartialed and demoted. So the controversy about Dreyfus had the same importance for Péguy's contemporaries as the Great War had for the generation that followed. With regard to the Dreyfus Affair, however, Péguy sought to distinguish between two aspects that point to the way in which he and his friends were to be cheated of the fruits of their victory. He speaks of "two Dreyfus Affairs, one good and one bad. The first is pure; the second, reprehensible. The first is religious; the second, political." And Péguy decisively repudiated the political struggle over Dreyfus. He opposed his allies on the left, accusing them of "Combes-like demagogy," and changed camps the moment the victors turned against the religious orders.[25] So before the bar of history it is Zola, not Péguy, who delivered the judgment of the intellectuals on the Dreyfus case.

And in this and other respects, it is *Zola* who provides the standard by which we must judge the historical outcome. The same may be said of great tracts of his fiction. It is well known that Zola's work is not based on a directly political theory. But it is a theory in the full sense of the word to the extent that Naturalism not only determined the subject of Zola's novels, and their form, but also supplied some of the basic ideas—such as the project of representing the heredity and social development of a single family. In contrast to this, what characterizes the social novel to which more than a few left-wing writers today have been devoting their energies is the absence of a theoretical foundation of any kind. As has been remarked by a sympathetic critic, the sheer impersonality and simplistic nature of the characters of the so-called *roman populiste* make them resemble characters in the popular fairy plays of times past, and their expressive power is so limited that it recalls the childish babble of those forgotten puppet-like figures.[26] It is the fatal, old confusion—we find it first, perhaps, in Rousseau—according to which the interior life of the disinherited and the oppressed is distinguished by a simplicity all its own, one to which authors often like to add an element of moral edification. It is obvious that such books have a very meagre yield. In fact, the *roman populiste* represents not so much an advance for the proletarian novel as a retreat on the part of bourgeois aesthetics. What is more, this corresponds to its origins. The fashion—if not the term—goes back to Thérive, the current critic for *Le Temps*.[27] But despite the enthusiasm with which he has sought to promote the new trend, its products—not least his own—show that what we are dealing with is just the old philanthropic impulses in a new form. The genre's only chance lies in choosing subjects that halfway conceal the author's lack of insight and education. It is no accident that the genre's first great success—*Voyage au bout de la nuit* [Journey to the End of Night], by *Céline*—is concerned with the *Lumpenproletariat*.[28] Like the *Lumpenproletariat*, which has no class consciousness that might enable it to fight for a life worthy of human beings, Céline, in his description of it, is quite unable to make visible this defect in his subject. Hence, the monotony in which the plot is veiled is fundamentally ambiguous. He succeeds in vividly portraying the sadness and sterility of a life in which the distinctions between workday and holiday, sex and love, war and peace, town and country have been obliterated. But he is quite incapable of showing us the forces that have shaped the lives of these outcasts. Even less is he able to convey how these people might begin to react against such forces. This is why nothing can be more treacherous than the judgment on Céline's book delivered by Dabit, who is himself a respected representative of the genre:[29] "We are confronted here with a work in which revolt does not proceed from aesthetic or symbolic discussions, and in which what is at issue is not art, culture, or God, but a cry of rage against the conditions of life that human beings can impose on a majority of other human beings." Bardamu—this is the name of the hero of the novel—"is made of the same stuff as the masses. He is made from their cowardice, their panic-stricken horror, their desires, and their outbursts of violence." So far so good. Were it not for the fact that the essence of revolutionary training and experience is to recognize the class structure of the masses and to exploit it.

If Zola was able to portray the France of the 1860s, this was because he rejected it. He rejected Haussmann's urban planning, La Païva's palace,[30] and Rouher's eloquence.[31] And if modern French novelists are unable to portray the France of our own day, this is because they are inclined to accept it at its face value. "Imagine," says Berl, "a reader in the year 2200 who tries to picture to himself the France of our day on the basis of our best novels. He would not even learn about the housing shortage. The financial crises of these years would be barely discernible. And there is no immediate prospect that our writers will begin to concern themselves with money matters."[32] This conformism turns a blind eye to the world in which it lives.

And it is the product of fear. Writers know that for the bourgeoisie the function of the intelligentsia is no longer that of defending its most human interests over the long term. For the second time in the bourgeois age, its intellectuals have entered a militant phase. But whereas between 1789 and 1848 they occupied a leading position as part of the bourgeois offensive, now their role is defensive. The less rewarding such a stance frequently is, the more urgent is the demand that intellectuals demonstrate their class reliability.

The novel is such an outstanding test of this reliability that the different attitudes displayed by authors in the process of adapting to society bring something resembling an ordered point of view into the chaos of producing literature. This does not mean, of course, that such literary production will automatically lend ideological support to the bourgeoisie. On the contrary, a large number of writers are much more likely to stand aloof from the middle class, at least in appearance. The position of a humanistic anarchism that seemed to hold sway for half a century or so—and in a real sense actually did so—has been irrevocably lost. Hence, the fata morgana of a new emancipation beckons, of a freedom between the classes—that is to say, the freedom of the *Lumpenproletariat*. The intellectual mimics the external appearance of proletarian existence without being even remotely connected to the working class. He thereby seeks the illusory state of standing outside the class system. While a Francis Carco could become the sensitive portrayer, the Richardson, of this new independence, a MacOrlan could become its ironic moralist, its Sterne.[33]

But conformism has even more elusive hiding places. And since even the greatest writer cannot be truly understood without defining the role of his works in society, and since, on the other hand, it is often those with the greatest talent who display a tendency to escape the consciousness of this role, even if they have to retreat to Hell to do so, this is the proper place to speak of Julien *Green*.[34] Green is undoubtedly one of the most important of the younger generation of writers, and he really has made the descent into Hell. His works are night-paintings of the passions. They burst the confines of the psychological novel in every respect. The antecedents of this writer take us back to the great Catholic and ultimately even the heathen depicters and interpreters of *passio*—to Calderón and even Seneca. But however deeply Green buries his characters in the provinces, and however subterranean the forces that move them, he does not always succeed in insulating them so completely from our own world that we should not expect them to make some sort of statement about it. Yet it is precisely at this point that we encounter the silence which is the expression of his conformism. I may perhaps be permitted to explore the traces of this attitude in his latest work, *Epaves* [Flotsam], if only because its conception makes it one of his greatest achievements.[35]

At the opening of the story, we encounter the hero taking a solitary evening walk along the banks of the Seine in the capital. In a remote corner of Passy, down by the waterside, he becomes the involuntary witness of a street fight between an old woman and a drunkard. It is a quite ordinary family scene, "but the man had been drinking and the woman was obviously afraid that he would throw her into the Seine." And further, "The man held her by the arm and shook her, loudly abusing her all the while. But she didn't take her eyes off Philippe"—this is the hero's name—"and shouted to him, 'Mister!' Her voice was coarse, but at the same time so subdued that he was transfixed with terror. He remained motionless." After this, he steps back. Then he goes home. "He arrived back home almost at the same time as usual."—That is all. Green's book now shows how this encounter begins to ferment inside his hero. It leads him, in the author's eyes, to a process of self-knowledge; it compels him to confront his cowardice, and it eventually undermines his entire life, over which the Seine increasingly gains a mysterious power. But he does not take his own life in the river.—Because this novel was written by a man of Green's qualities, it offers a pitiless example of the destruction of a great idea by conformism. No one will deny that the incident Green describes at the opening of his book is typical of life in our big cities. For this very reason, it clearly tells us nothing about the psychology of the man who refused to heed the cry for help. But it helps us understand his social character. For the involuntary witness who turns a blind eye is a bourgeois. An open quarrel between two bourgeois would scarcely take such a form in the street, in full view of the public. So what paralyzes Green's hero is the abyss that opens up in front of the bourgeois, while beyond it two members of the class of outcasts conduct their quarrel. It is not really the critic's task to make suggestions about how the author might have depicted this hidden meaning of the scene—the meaning that is actually its authentic one. The crass circumstance that unceremoniously opens the eyes of the bourgeois to the abyss that surrounds his class existence—the same crass circumstance might equally cause him to slip over the edge into madness, which could turn the abandonment and loneliness of his class into the abandonment and loneliness of his individual existence. The uncertainty about the fate of the woman who had appealed to him for help and of whom he hears nothing further seems to contain the seeds of such a development in Green.

Green's problem is old-fashioned, and no less old-fashioned is the standpoint of most of these novelists on questions of technique: "Most of these writers have an unshakable faith in their characters' statements, or pretend they do—even though, since Freud, this faith must be seen as misplaced. They refuse to see that a report which someone gives about his own past reveals more about his present state than about the past that is the report's ostensible subject. They insist on seeing the life of a character in a novel as an isolated process that has been fixed in advance within the framework of an empty time. They refuse to take cognizance of behaviorism, or even of psychoanalysis."[36] Thus writes Berl. In a word, it is characteristic of the present state of French literature that we are beginning to see a separation between leading intellectuals and novelists. The exceptions—Proust and Gide above all—confirm the rule. For both have made more or less crucial modifications to the technique of the novel. But neither Alain nor Péguy, neither Valéry nor Aragon, have published novels;[37] and those that we have from Barrès and Benda are really illustrations of theses. For the mass of writers today, however, we may venture this generalization: the more mediocre an author is, the greater his desire to use his activity as a novelist as an excuse to evade his responsibilities as a writer.

For this reason, it makes sense to inquire what the novel of the last decade has achieved for freedom. It is difficult to conceive of any answer, other than to note the defense of homosexuality that *Proust* has been the first to undertake. However, even though such a comment does justice to the meager revolutionary fruits of literature, it by no means exhausts the meaning of homosexuality in *A la recherche du temps perdu*. On the contrary, homosexuality appears in his work because both the most remote and the most primitive memories of the productive forces of nature are banished from the world he is concerned with. The world Proust depicts excludes everything that is involved in production. The attitude of the snob that predominates throughout is nothing other than the consistent, organized, and hardened observation of existence from the standpoint of the pure consumer. His work conceals a merciless and penetrating critique of contemporary society, and up to now criticism has scarcely done more than scratch the surface of his analysis. Still, this much is clear. Starting with the work's structure, which combines poetry, memoir, and commentary, down to the syntax of the overflowing sentences (the Nile of language pouring out over the plains of truth, fertilizing them in the process), the writer is everywhere present, adopting a point of view, giving an account of himself, and constantly placing himself at the disposition of the reader. In no instance can an author have any claim to making an impact on the public, unless he begins by asserting his claim to be regarded as a writer. France is fortunate that the highly suspect confrontation between "poetry" and writing has never really gained much currency there. Today, more than ever, what is decisive is the idea a writer forms of his work. And it is even more decisive if it is a true poet who attempts to make this concept a reality.

These remarks pertain to Paul *Valéry*. He has a symptomatic importance for the function of the writer in society. And this symptomatic importance is intimately connected with the unquestionable high quality of his work.

Among contemporary French writers, Valéry possesses the greatest technical expertise. He has reflected on the nature of technique in writing like no one else. And the unique position he occupies can perhaps best be summed up in the statement that, in his eyes, writing is primarily a matter of technique.

But it is equally important to note that writing, in his sense, includes poetry. He has appeared before the public, in a decisive capacity, both as essayist and lyric poet, and in neither case has he failed to provide repeated explanations of his technique. Valéry sets out to explore the writer's and especially the poet's intelligence like an inquisitor; he calls for a break with the widely held view that it is self-evident that writers are intelligent, as well as with the even more widely held idea that intellect is irrelevant to the poet. He himself possesses great intelligence, of a kind that is anything but self-evident. Nothing can be more disconcerting than its embodiment, Monsieur Teste. In his appearance, Monsieur Teste is a philistine; in his way of life, he is a man with a private income. He sits at home; he does not really mix with people; he is looked after by his wife. Monsieur Teste—in English, "Mr. Head"—is a personification of the intellect that reminds us very strongly of God as conceived by the negative theology of Nicholas of Cusa.[38] Everything we learn about Teste ends up in negation. "Every sense of excitement, every feeling is the sign of a failure of construction and adaptation." However human Monsieur Teste feels himself to be, he has taken to heart Valéry's aperçu that the most important ideas are those that contradict our feelings. He represents therefore the negation of the "human." "Behold, the twilight of the approximate is setting in; and before the door stands the reign of the dehumanized, which will emerge from the precision, rigor, and purity in human affairs."[39] No expansive, pathos-filled gestures, nothing "human," comes into the ambit of this Valéryesque eccentric, in whose image the pure writer is to be formed. Thought is the only substance from which the perfect can be created. "A classical writer," Valéry says, "is a writer who conceals or absorbs his associations of ideas."

But within the framework of the French bourgeoisie, Monsieur Teste represents nothing but the experience that Valéry attempted to trace on a human scale in a number of great artists. It was with this aim that he wrote one of his earliest works, *Introduction à la méthode de Léonard de Vinci*. Leonardo appears there as the artist who never in his work renounces his claim to give the most precise account possible of his activity and his methods. Valéry has said that he would prefer a mediocre page in which he was able to give an exact account of every word that flowed from his pen to a perfect work for which he was indebted to the power of chance and inspiration. Similarly, at another point, he writes: "The realms of chance, the powers of the gods, and Fate are nothing but the symptoms of our own mental deficiency. If we had an answer to everything—a precise answer, that is—these powers would not exist . . . We feel this ourselves, and this is why we end up turning against our own questions. But that should be just the beginning. We ought to be able to formulate a question within ourselves that precedes all others and tests them in turn to see what they are worth."[40]

The strict return of such ideas to their context in the heroic period of the European bourgeoisie allows us to master our surprise at encountering once more the idea of progress at such an advanced stage of the old European humanism. It is, furthermore, the valid and genuine idea of a progress transferable at the level of methodology, a term that corresponds to Valéry's concept of "construction" as neatly as it conflicts with the *idée fixe* of inspiration. As one of his interpreters has claimed, "The work of art is not a creation, but a construction in which analysis, calculation, and planning play the principal roles." The ultimate merit of the systematic process of leading the investigator to go beyond himself has proved its worth in Valéry. For who is Monsieur Teste if not the human subject who is ready to cross the historical threshold marking the dividing line between the harmoniously educated, self-sufficient individual and the technician and specialist who is ready to assume a place within a much larger plan? Valéry failed to extend the idea of planning from the realm of art to the sphere of the human community. That threshold he did not cross. The intellectual remains a private person, and this is the melancholy secret of Monsieur Teste. Two or three decades earlier, Lautréamont had said: "Poetry must be made by all. Not by a single person."[41] These words have not reached Monsieur Teste.

The threshold that constituted such a barrier for Valéry has recently been crossed by *Gide*. He has joined the Communists. This is a matter of significance for the development of the problems in the advanced intelligentsia in France that we are attempting to portray. It may be said that Gide has not missed any of its vital phases of the past forty years. The first stage could be seen in his critique of Barrès' *Déracinés*. It contained more than a sharp repudiation of his hymn to roots. It contained a reinterpretation. Of the four main characters in the novel who are made to exemplify Barrès' thesis about the nation, Gide can interest himself only in the one who has sunk furthest in the social scale and has become a murderer. "If Racadot had never left Lorraine, he would never have become a murderer. In that case, he would have been of absolutely no interest to me."[42] Being "deprived of his roots" forces Racadot into originality. In Gide's view, this is the true subject of the book. It was in the name of originality that Gide undertook to explore the entire range of possibilities that disposition and development had opened up for him. And the more astonishing these possibilities were, the more ruthlessly he fought to make room for them in his life—in the full glare of the public gaze, moreover. Self-contradictions were the last consideration that might have deterred him. "In every direction I started out in, I went right to the very end, so that I might turn round and pursue the opposite course with just as much determination." This fundamental rejection of the golden mean, this commitment to extremes, is dialectics—not as an intellectual method, but as life's blood and passion. Even at its extremes, the world is still whole, still healthy, still nature. And what drives him toward these extremes is not curiosity or apologetic zeal, but dialectical passion.

It has been said that Gide's nature is not rich. This is a judgment that is not just valid but decisive. And Gide's own attitude suggests he is not unaware of this himself. In his book on Dostoevsky, he writes: "At the origins of every great ethical reform we always encounter a small, physiological secret, a failing of the flesh, a restlessness, an anomaly . . . The discomfort from which the reformer suffers stems from the absence of inner equilibrium. The moral givens, positions, and values are in contradiction with one another, and he is laboring to bring them all under one roof; what he wants is a new equilibrium. His work is nothing but an attempt, with the aid of logic and reason, to sort out the confusion he feels within himself and to replace it with a new order . . . An action in which I do not recognize all the contradictions inside me betrays me."[43] The attitude that is expressed in these and similar statements has been questioned countless times. The critic Massis calls Gide "demonic."[44] But rather more illuminating is the fact that Gide has never claimed for himself that other kind of demonism which the bourgeoisie is always happy to concede to the artist—namely, the freedom of the genius. Just as Valéry succeeded in integrating his entire production into his intellectual life, Gide integrated his into his moral life. It is to this that he owes his pedagogical influence. After Barrès, he is the greatest leader the French intelligentsia has found. As Malraux writes: "It is perhaps incorrect to regard André Gide as a philosopher. I think he is something quite different: an advisor on matters of conscience. That is a highly important and unusual profession . . . For a long time, Maurice Barrès dedicated himself to the same cause. Gide likewise. It is certainly no small matter to influence the mindset of an entire epoch. But while Barrès could only give advice, Gide has drawn attention to the gulf between our desires and our dignity, between our aspirations and our wish to master or exploit them . . . He has awakened the intellectual conscience of half the people we call 'the young generation.'"

The effect described here can be closely linked to a particular character in Les caves du Vatican [The Vatican Cellars]. The novel appeared just before the outbreak of the Great War, when, for the first time in the younger generation, intellectual currents began to appear that would later flow, via Expressionism and Dadaism, into Surrealism. Gide had every reason to reprint in his selected writings, Pages choisis, which he has dedicated to the youth of France, the page from Les caves du Vatican in which Lafcadio's decision to commit murder is described. Traveling in a train, Gide's young hero is irritated by the ugliness of an old man who is sharing a compartment alone with him. It occurs to Lafcadio to do away with him. "Who would see?" he muses. "There within reach of my hand is this double lock that I can easily undo. The door would suddenly give way and he would topple over; the least push would do it; he would fall out like a stone; you wouldn't even hear a scream . . . It is not so much the events I am curious about, as about myself. Some people imagine themselves capable of anything, but when it comes to acting, they hold back . . . What a gulf between intention and deed. And you have no more right to take it all back than in chess. No matter; if you knew all the risks in advance, the game would lose all its interest."[45] And slowly, cold-bloodedly, Lafcadio counts to ten and then pushes his traveling companion out, for no reason—purely from curiosity about himself. In the Surrealists Lafcadio has found his most eager pupils. Like him they began with a series of *actes gratuits*—groundless or almost idle scandals. But the path taken by subsequent developments is well designed to shed a retrospective light on Lafcadio. For the Surrealists showed themselves increasingly intent on bringing scenes that had originally been initiated in a playful spirit or out of curiosity into harmony with the slogans of the Communist International. And if there could still be any doubt about the meaning of that extreme individualism under whose banner Gide's work was launched, it has lost all validity in the face of his recent statements. For these make clear how, once this extreme individualism had tested itself on the world around it, it inevitably became transformed into Communism.

"All things considered, what strikes one most immediately about the spirit of democracy is that it is asocial." This was written not by Gide, but by Alain.[46] Gide came late to this insight into the spirit of democracy. It was only at a late date that he prepared himself intellectually to recognize it. After his various travels into the interior of Africa, his descriptions of the living conditions of the indigenous populations under colonial rule created some unease among the political public. A few years earlier, when he had put himself forward as the advocate of homosexuals, he had caused offense, but now, as the champion of black people, he threatened to create an uproar.[47] For him, as for those who followed him, the factors that provided the occasion for his intervention were exclusively political. The war in Morocco has a special importance in this context, particularly for the younger generation.

Surrealism would have been spared many enemies (from which, incidentally, it derived enormous benefit) had it originated unambiguously in politics. But this was far from the case. Surrealism came to maturity in the confined space of the literary circle around Apollinaire. Aragon showed, in his *Vague de rêves* [Wave of Dreams] of 1924, in what an unprepossessing, homegrown substance the dialectical nucleus of Surrealism was originally found. At that time, the movement broke over its founders in an inspirational dream wave. Life appeared worth living only where the threshold between sleeping and waking had been eroded, as if by the footsteps of images ebbing and flowing by the thousand. Language was itself only where, with automatic exactitude, sound and image, image and sound, had merged with each other so utterly that there was no space left for "meaning," not even the smallest fissure. To enlist "the forces of intoxication for the revolution"—that was the real program. The dialectical development of the movement, however, was such that the image space which it had so boldly opened up for itself proved more and more to be identical with the image space of political praxis. It was within this space, at any rate, that the members of the group located the home of a classless society. It may well be that the promise of such a society owed less to the dialectical materialism of a Plekhanov or a Bukharin[48] than to an anthropological materialism derived from their own experiences, and from the earlier experiences of Lautréamont and Rimbaud.[49] However that may be, under the leadership of Breton and Aragon, this world of ideas established the rules that governed the actions and literary production of the group, until political developments permitted them to formulate their ideas in a simpler, more concrete way.

Since the end of the war the left-wing intellectuals, the revolutionary artists, have set the tone for a major segment of the public. It has now turned out, all too clearly, that this public esteem was not matched by any profounder impact on society. From this we may conclude, in Berl's words, that "an artist, however much he may have revolutionized the arts, is no more revolutionary than Poiret, who in his day revolutionized the world of fashion."[50] The most advanced and daring products of the avant-garde in all the arts have had only the haute bourgeoisie as their public—in France and Germany alike. This fact does not necessarily imply a judgment on their work, but it does point to the political uncertainty of the groups that stood behind these manifestations. Again and again we see the decisive influence of anarchism on the literary movements of the 1930s: the gradual displacement of anarchism characterizes the trajectory of Surrealism from its beginnings to the present. The crucial turning point came in the mid-1920s. In 1926 Blaise Cendrars' book *Moravagine* appeared.[51] In the type of revolutionary terrorist depicted in those pages, left-wing intellectuals could see the reflection of their former ideal, one they were in the process of discarding:

> What impulse did we obey when we undertook the assassination of the czar, and what was our frame of mind? I often asked myself this question when observing my comrades . . . Everything in them had withered and died. Feelings fell away from them like scales and became waste products. Their brittle senses had become fragile and were no longer capable of enjoyment; they disintegrated into dust at the merest attempt to enjoy anything. Inwardly we were all singed as if by a blazing fire, and our hearts were no more than a heap of ashes. Our souls had been laid waste. We had long since ceased to believe in anything, or

even in nothing. The nihilists of 1880 were a sect of mystics, dreamers, agents of a universal happiness. But we were the antithesis of these merry fellows and their opaque theories. We were men of action, technicians, specialists, the pioneers of a new generation who had dedicated our souls even unto death, the harbingers of world revolution . . . Angels or demons? No; in a word, we were automata . . . We dwelled not in the shadow of a guardian angel or in the folds of his robe, but rather at the feet of our own *Doppelgänger,* who gradually detached themselves from us to find a new shape of their own and to take on bodily form. As the alien projections of ourselves, these new beings absorbed us into them so that we imperceptibly slipped into their skin and became identical with them. And our final preparations were very similar to the final stages of production of those terrible, arrogant automata that are known to magic as Teraphim. Like them, we set about destroying a city, laying waste a whole country and crushing the imperial family between our fearsome jaws.[52]

The civil war in Russia is now part of history. In the meantime, civil wars have broken out elsewhere. And the fact that the climate and problems of Russia's civil war are of greater concern to the literary intelligentsia of the West than the evidence about the construction of society in Soviet Russia reflects not just the primitive nature of the political education in Western Europe, but also the situation there. *Malraux*'s work is symptomatic here.[53] The setting of his latest book—like that of his earlier novel *Les Conquérants* [The Conquerors]—is China during its civil war period. In *La condition humaine* [The Human Condition] Malraux forestalls neither the historian nor even the chronicler.[54] The episode of the revolutionary uprising in Shanghai that was successfully put down by Chiang Kai Shek is neither politically nor economically transparent. It serves as a backdrop for the depiction of a group of people who play an active role in these events. Different though their roles are, and different though these people are in character and background, and hostile to the ruling class as they may be, they have one thing in common: they all spring from it. They work either for that class or against it; they may have left it behind them or been expelled from it; they represent it or see through it. But whatever their situation, that ruling class is in their bones. This is equally true of the professional revolutionaries who are in the foreground in the book.

Malraux does not say this in so many words. Does he know it? He proves it, at any rate. For the work, which is laden with the dialectical tension from which the revolutionary activity of the intelligentsia is born, feeds on this secret homogeneity of his characters. The fact that these intellectuals have abandoned their own class in order to make common cause with the proletariat does not mean that the latter have accepted them into their ranks. Nor have they. Hence the dialectic in which Malraux's heroes move. They live for the proletariat; but they do not act as proletarians. At the very least, they act far less from their consciousness of class than from their consciousness of their own isolation. That is the torment that none of these people escapes. It is also the source of their dignity. "There is no dignity not based on suffering."[55] Suffering makes people lonely, and it feeds on the loneliness that it creates. To escape it is the fanatical desire of those who have the decisive say in this book. The pathos of the book owes much more to its nihilism than might be thought.

What human need is satisfied by revolutionary action? This question arises simply and solely from the special situation of the intellectual. His solitude is a major factor here. But when the intellectual elevates this to the essence of *la condition humaine,* the human condition, as Malraux does here, it prevents him from seeing quite different preconditions of revolutionary mass action—preconditions eminently worthy of study. The masses have quite different needs, and elicit quite different reactions—reactions that seem primitive only to primitive psychologists. Malraux's analysis is limited by its inability to explain the actions of the proletarian masses for whom revolutions are part of their experimental historical agenda. But (it will be objected) if his analysis is limited, his story is likewise. Without doubt. But we may legitimately ask how much freedom an author has when constructing a plot on this subject. Can he really afford not to anticipate the historian? Is there a genuine revolutionary literature without didacticism?

These questions highlight the crisis that besets literature, and their clarification remains the preserve of the Surrealists. The preconditions for a solution have been fulfilled, even if there is little to show for it at present. They lay in the emergence of the new nationalism that made manifest the true features of the "spiritual" which had been delineated by Barrès. They lay in the crisis of parliamentarianism that made the entry of young intellectuals into the ranks of those who adopted Alain's ideas increasingly precarious. They lay, furthermore, in the fact that internationalism, as a cultural concern, as Benda understands it, was about to undergo a series of very demanding trials. They lay in the speed with which the image of Péguy became the stuff of legend; in the impossibility of discovering in his writings any practical lessons for the situation in which intellectuals find themselves today. They lay in the insight that gradually imposed itself on the conscientious—namely, that they would have to learn to renounce a public which could not reconcile the satisfaction of its needs with its own better judgment. An indirect indication of these preconditions, however, can be found in an important writer like Valéry, who is a problematic figure only insofar as he lacked the strength to make clear to himself the contradiction between his technique and the society to which he was making it available. Last, these preconditions could be found in the example provided by André Gide.

What is crucial about all this is that the Surrealists approached the problem in a way that enabled them to exploit these preconditions to the full. Thus, they variously imitated Lafcadio's playful action before they tackled more serious ones. They lent a more pointed meaning to what appears as "pure poetry" in Valéry when they started to view literature as a key to the psychoses. In the same vein, they found a place for the intellectual as technologist by acknowledging the proletariat's right to make use of his technology, because only the proletariat depends on technology at its most advanced. In a word—and this is the decisive factor—they attained their achievements without compromise and as a result of constantly reexamining their own position. They reached their goal as intellectuals—that is to say, via the longest route possible. For the intellectual's path to the radical critique of the social order is the longest, just as that of the proletariat is the shortest. Hence their attack on Barbusse[56] and others who were concerned to shorten it by appealing to conviction. And this, too, is why they have no room for depictions of poverty and deprivation.

The petty bourgeois who means business with his libertarian and erotic aspirations ceases to provide the idyllic picture that Chardonne welcomes in him. The more uninhibitedly and resolutely he asserts his claims, the greater the certainty that he will find himself on the road to politics—albeit via the most circuitous route, the only one viable for him. At the same moment, he will cease to be the petty bourgeois he once was. "Revolutionary writers," Aragon maintains, "if they are of bourgeois stock, are essentially and crucially traitors to the class of their origins." They become militant politicians. As such, they are the only ones able to interpret that dark prophecy of Apollinaire's with which we began. They know from experience why literature—the only literature they still think worthy of the name—is dangerous.

Written April–June 1933 and January 1934; published in the *Zeitschrift für Sozialforschung*, spring 1934. *Gesammelte Schriften*, II, 776–803. Translated by Rodney Livingstone.

Notes

1. This collection of stories by Guillaume Apollinaire (1880–1918) was in fact first published in Paris in 1916, following his recovery from head wounds incurred in World War I.
2. Bellachini (1828–1885) was a well-known conjuror.
3. The first Futurist Manifesto, of which Filippo Tommas Marinetti (1876–1944) was the principal author, was published in *Le Figaro* on February 20, 1909. The first use of the term "surrealist" occurred in the subtitle of Apollinaire's play *Les mamelles de Tirésias: Drame surréaliste*.
4. These citations are from Barrès' *La grande pitié des églises de France* (Paris: Emile Paul Frères, 1914).

5. André Gide (1869–1951), French writer, humanist, and moralist, received the Nobel Prize for Literature in 1947. See "André Gide and Germany" and "Conversation with André Gide," in this volume.

6. Maurice Barrès (1862–1923) was a French writer and politician whose fervent individualism and nationalism made his ideas a rallying point for the Right.

7. Albert Thibaudet (1874–1936) was an eminent French literary historian. Benjamin here cites *La république des professeurs* (Paris: B. Grasset, 1927).

8. Jules Lagneau (1851–1894), French philosopher, is known for the idealist-spiritualist influence he exerted on a number of his students who later achieved prominence.

9. Metz, in the Lorraine, was lost to the Germans in October 1870. The defeat marked a turning point in the Franco-Prussian War.

10. While studying literature in Paris, Barrès embarked on a solitary project of self-analysis, through a rigorous method described in the trilogy of novels entitled *Le culte du moi* (The Cult of the Self). This work comprises *Sous l'oeil des barbares* (Under the Eye of the Barbarians; 1888), *Un homme libre* (A Free Man; 1889), and *Le jardin de Berénice* (The Garden of Bérénice; 1891).

11. Emile Chartier (1868–1951), French essayist, took his pseudonym, Alain, from a fifteenth-century poet. His collected essays, *Propos,* found a primarily youthful audience.

12. The Parti Radical (the name is an abbreviation of Parti Républicain Radical et Radical-Socialiste) was founded in 1901 as a coalition of various socialist and republican forces that had been brought together by their support for Dreyfus. Alain was a leading spokesman for the party. His *Eléments d'une doctrine radicale* appeared in Paris in 1925.

13. Jacques Chardonne (pseudonym of Jacques Boutelleau; 1884–1968), French novelist, detailed the tribulations of (mostly hopeless) marriages.

14. Paul Morand (1883–1976), French diplomat, novelist, and biographer, served as the Vichy government's ambassador to Romania and Switzerland.

15. André Siegfried (1875–1976) was a distinguished French sociologist and historian.

16. Julien Benda (1867–1956) and Charles Péguy (1873–1914) collaborated on the journal of politics and letters *Les Cahiers de la Quinzaine* (1900–1914). Both writers came to intellectual maturity during the Dreyfus Affair as champions of Dreyfus' innocence. After 1910, Benda emerged as an outspoken opponent of Henri Bergson and of what he saw as philosophical and political irrationalism in general; his most famous and influential work, *La trahison des clercs* (1927), condemns the European intelligentsia for their submission to the irrationalist temptation. Péguy, in contrast, favored Bergson and campaigned against "scientific" socialism and positivism.

17. Charles Maurras (1868–1952) was a French writer and political theorist whose "integral nationalism" anticipated some of the ideas of fascism.

18. Julien Benda, *Discours à la nation européenne* (Paris: Gallimard, 1933), pp. 70–71. Clorinda is a virgin warrior-maiden in Tasso's *Gerusalemme liberata.*

19. Emmanuel Berl, *Mort de la pensée bourgeoise* (Paris: B. Grasset, 1929), p. 32.

20. Ibid., pp. 45, 49–50.

21. Jérome Tharaud and Jean Tharaud, *Notre cher Péguy,* vol. 1 (Paris: Plon-Nourrit, 1926), pp. 19–20.

22. Paul Claudel (1868–1955), poet and dramatist, spent his childhood in the village of Villeneuve-sur-Fère, in northeastern France. Francis Jammes (1868–1938), poet, spent much of his life in villages in the French Pyrenees. Charles Ferdinand Ramuz (1878–1947), poet, came from a village in Switzerland's Vaud canton.

23. André Siegfried, *Tableau des partis en France* (Paris: B. Grasset, 1930), p. 10.

24. Charles Péguy, "Victor-Marie, Comte Hugo," *Oeuvres en prose, 1910–1914* (Paris: Gallimard, 1957), p. 838.

25. A reference to Emile Combes (1835–1921), a radical politician and minister. His anticlerical views helped enact the law separating Church and State.

26. Fairy plays, a genre established in the eighteenth century by the Venetian playwright Carlo Gozzi (1720–1806), were dramatizations of fairy tales, fables, puppet plays, and oriental stories. They were deliberately naive in characterization and expression. Gozzi, a defender of traditional dramatic forms such as the *commedia dell'arte*, was opposed to the innovations of such realist playwrights as Carlo Goldoni. His dramas were quite successful for a time, and formed the basis of many subsequent theatrical and musical works—especially in Germany, where he was admired by Goethe, Schiller, Lessing, and the Schlegels.

27. André Thérive (pseudonym of Roger Puthoste; 1891–1967) was a novelist whose work exemplifies the populist genre under discussion here. *Le Temps* (founded 1861) was one of France's most distinguished newspapers until its demise in 1942, on the day of the occupation of Lyon.

28. A German translation has just been published by Julius Kittl in Mährisch-Ostrau. [Benjamin's note. Louis-Ferdinand Céline's famous first novel, whose bleak vision and linguistic brilliance powerfully affected a generation of writers, was published in Paris in 1922.—*Trans.*]

29. Eugène Dabit (1898–1936), novelist, was the author of the popular novel *Hôtel du Nord*, which depicts life in a proletarian hotel. It was made into a film by Marcel Carné in 1938.

30. Thérèse Lachmann, known as La Païva, was a celebrated courtesan married to the Marquis de Païva, the Portuguese ambassador in Paris. The palace in question—which was built with money provided by her later husband, Count Henckel de Donnersmarck, and which still stands on the Champs-Elysées—is famous for such features as its monumental entrance and an onyx staircase.

31. Eugène Rouher (1814–1884), conservative politician, was one of the leading figures in the Bonapartist party during the Third Republic.

32. Berl, *Mort de la pensée bourgeoise*, p. 107.

33. Francis Carco (1886–1953) was a writer of memoirs and novels known for their realistic descriptions of low-life milieux. Pierre MacOrlan was the nom de plume of Pierre Dumarchey (1882–1970), a novelist who worked in the group around Apollinaire and Max Jacob. His novels are notable for their mixture of fantasy and reality, and for their sensitive portrayals of the marginalized and vagabond.

34. Julien Hartridge Green (1900–1998), French-American novelist, wrote bleak stories that were influenced by the gothic novel of the southern United States. His characters are typically neurotic and compulsive small-town figures. Green was elected to the Académie Française in 1971.

35. Green's novel *Epaves* appeared in Paris in 1932. An English translation, under the title *The Strange River,* appeared the same year.

36. Berl, *Mort de la pensée bourgeoise,* pp. 89–90.

37. Paul Valéry (1871–1945) was a French poet, essayist, and theorist. Louis Aragon (1897–1982) was a French poet, novelist, and essayist associated with the circle of Surrealists around André Breton. Aragon's *Paysan de Paris* and *Vague des rêves* were important stimuli in Benjamin's initial work on *Das Passagen-Werk* (The Arcades Project).

38. Nicholas of Cusa (1401–1464) propounded the idea that God is the "coincidence of opposites." Because God is infinite, He embraces all things in perfect unity; He is at once the maximum and the minimum. As for man's knowledge of the infinite God, he must be content with conjecture or approximation to the truth. Absolute truth escapes man; his proper attitude is "learned ignorance."

39. Paul Valéry, *Rhumbs,* in Valéry, *Oeuvres,* ed. Jean Hytier (Paris: Pléiade, 1971), vol. 2, p. 621.

40. Ibid., p. 647.

41. Comte de Lautréamont, "Poésies II," in Lautréamont, *"Maldoror" and the Complete Works* (Cambridge, Mass.: Exact Change, 1994), p. 244. "Lautréamont" was the pseudonym of Isidore Ducasse (1846–1870), whose work is notable for the violence, and the violent juxtaposition, of its images. He was a major influence on the Surrealists.

42. André Gide, *Prétextes* (Paris: Mercure de France, 1903), p. 56.

43. André Gide, *Dostoïevsky: Articles et causeries* (Paris: Plon, 1930), pp. 265–266.

44. Henri Massis (1886–1970), author and critic, was aligned with Péguy's Catholic nationalism. He attacked Gide for representing an anarchy supposedly originating in the East (and thought to comprise communism).

45. André Gide, *The Vatican Cellars* (Harmondsworth: Penguin, 1982), p. 139.

46. Alain, *Eléments d'une doctrine radicale* (Paris: Gallimard, 1925), p. 139.

47. See André Gide, *Corydon* (Paris: Nouvelle Revue Française, 1924); and idem, *Le retour du Tchad* (Paris: Gallimard, 1928).

48. Georgy Valentinovich Plekhanov (1856–1918), Marxist theorist, was the founder and for many years the leading exponent of the Marxist movement in Russia. A Menshevik, he opposed the Bolshevik seizure of power in Russia in 1917 and died in exile. Nikolai Ivanovich Bukharin (1888–1938), Bolshevik and Marxist theoretician and economist, was a prominent leader of the Communist International (Comintern).

49. Arthur Rimbaud (1854–1891) was a French poet and adventurer whose Symbolist poetry had a profound influence on modern literature.

50. Paul Poiret (1879–1944), couturier and decorator, is best-known for helping to eliminate the corset from feminine fashion.

51. This novel by Blaise Cendrars (pseudonym of Frédéric Sauser; 1887–1961) is, like much of his work, marked by striking images and an intense focus on rendering immediate experience.

52. Blaise Cendrars, *Moravagine* (Paris: Le Club Français du Livre, 1926), pp. 122–124, 134.

53. André Malraux (1901–1976) was a novelist, art historian, and statesman. His major works include the novel *La condition humaine* (The Human Condition, translated as *Man's Fate;* 1933); *Les voix du silence* (The Voices of Silence; 1951), a history and philosophy of world art; and *Le musée imaginaire* (The Imaginary Museum, translated as *Museum without Walls;* 1952–1954). Mal-

raux became an active supporter of General Charles de Gaulle and, after de Gaulle was elected president in 1958, served for ten years as France's minister of cultural affairs.

54. André Malraux, *Les Conquérants* (Paris: B. Grasset, 1928); *La condition humaine* (Paris: Gallimard, 1933).
55. Malraux, *La condition humaine*, p. 399.
56. Henri Barbusse (1874–1935), French writer and journalist, published novels, poems, and essays infused with pacifist and socialist views. His novels include *L'Enfer* (1908), *Le Feu* (1916), and *Clarté* (1919).

The Author as Producer

Address at the Institute for the Study of Fascism,
Paris, April 27, 1934[1]

The task is to win over the intellectuals to the working class by making them
aware of the identity of their spiritual enterprises and of their conditions as
producers.

—Ramón Fernandez

You will remember how Plato deals with poets in his ideal state: he banishes
them from it in the public interest. He had a high conception of the power
of poetry, but he believed it harmful, superfluous—in a *perfect* community,
of course. The question of the poet's right to exist has not often, since then,
been posed with the same emphasis; but today it poses itself. Probably it is
only seldom posed in this *form*, but it is more or less familiar to you all as
the question of the autonomy of the poet, of his freedom to write whatever
he pleases. You are not disposed to grant him this autonomy. You believe
that the present social situation compels him to decide in whose service he
is to place his activity. The bourgeois writer of entertainment literature does
not acknowledge this choice. You must prove to him that, without admitting
it, he is working in the service of certain class interests. A more advanced
type of writer does recognize this choice. His decision, made on the basis
of class struggle, is to side with the proletariat. This puts an end to his
autonomy. His activity is now decided by what is useful to the proletariat
in the class struggle. Such writing is commonly called *tendentious.*

Here you have the catchword around which has long circled a debate
familiar to you. Its familiarity tells you how unfruitful it has been, for it has
not advanced beyond the monotonous reiteration of arguments for and
against: *on the one hand,* the correct political line is demanded of the poet;

on the other, one is justified in expecting his work to have quality. Such a formulation is of course unsatisfactory as long as the connection between the two factors, political line and quality, has not been *perceived.* Of course, the connection can be asserted dogmatically. You can declare: a work that shows the correct political tendency need show no other quality. You can also declare: a work that exhibits the correct tendency must of necessity have every other quality.

This second formulation is not uninteresting, and, moreover, it is correct. I adopt it as my own. But in doing so I abstain from asserting it dogmatically. It must be *proved.* And it is in order to attempt to prove it that I now claim your attention. This is, you will perhaps object, a very specialized, out-of-the-way theme. And do I intend to promote the study of fascism with such a proof? This is indeed my intention. For I hope to be able to show you that the concept of political tendency, in the summary form in which it usually occurs in the debate just mentioned, is a perfectly useless instrument of political literary criticism. I would like to show you that the tendency of a literary work can be politically correct only if it is also literarily correct. That is to say, the politically correct tendency includes a literary tendency. And I would add straightaway: this literary tendency, which is implicitly or explicitly contained in every *correct* political tendency of a work, alone constitutes the quality of that work. The correct political tendency of a work thus includes its literary quality *because* it includes its literary *tendency.*

This assertion—I hope I can promise you—will soon become clearer. For the moment, I would like to interject that I might have chosen a different starting point for my reflections. I started from the unfruitful debate on the relationship between tendency and quality in literature. I could have started from an even older and no less unfruitful debate: What is the relationship between form and content, particularly in political poetry? This kind of question has a bad name; rightly so. It is the textbook example of the attempt to explain literary connections undialectically, with clichés. Very well. But what, then, is the dialectical approach to the same question?

The dialectical approach to this question—and here I come to the heart of the matter—has absolutely no use for such rigid, isolated things as work, novel, book. It has to insert them into the living social contexts. You rightly declare that this has been done time and again among our friends. Certainly. Only they have often done it by launching at once into large, and therefore necessarily often vague, questions. Social conditions are, as we know, determined by conditions of production. And when a work was subjected to a materialist critique, it was customary to ask how this work stood vis-à-vis the social relations of production of its time. This is an important question, but also a very difficult one. Its answer is not always unambiguous. And I would like now to propose to you a more immediate question, a question that is somewhat more modest, somewhat less far-reaching, but that has, it seems to me, more chance of receiving an answer. Instead of asking, "What is the attitude of a work to the relations of production of its time? Does it accept them, is it reactionary? Or does it aim at overthrowing them, is it revolutionary?"—instead of this question, or at any rate before it, I would like to propose another. Rather than asking, "What is the attitude of a work *to* the relations of production of its time?" I would like to ask, "What is its position *in* them?" This question directly concerns the function the work has within the literary relations of production of its time. It is concerned, in other words, directly with the literary *technique* of works.

In bringing up technique, I have named the concept that makes literary products accessible to an immediately social, and therefore materialist, analysis. At the same time, the concept of technique provides the dialectical starting point from which the unfruitful antithesis of form and content can be surpassed. And furthermore, this concept of technique contains an indication of the correct determination of the relation between tendency and quality, the question raised at the outset. If, therefore, we stated earlier that the correct political tendency of a work includes its literary quality, because it includes its literary tendency, we can now formulate this more precisely by saying that this literary tendency can consist either in progress or in regression of literary technique.

You will certainly approve if I now pass, with only an appearance of arbitrariness, to very concrete literary conditions. Russian conditions. I would like to direct your attention to Sergei Tretiakov, and to the type (which he defines and embodies) of the "operating" writer.[2] This operating writer provides the most tangible example of the functional interdependence that always, and under all conditions, exists between the correct political tendency and progressive literary technique. I admit, he is only one example; I hold others in reserve. Tretiakov distinguishes the operating writer from the informing writer. His mission is not to report but to struggle; not to play the spectator but to intervene actively. He defines this mission in the account he gives of his own activity. When, in 1928, at the time of the total collectivization of agriculture, the slogan "Writers to the *kolkhoz!*" was proclaimed, Tretiakov went to the "Communist Lighthouse" commune and there, during two lengthy stays, set about the following tasks: calling mass meetings; collecting funds to pay for tractors; persuading independent peasants to enter the *kolkhoz* [collective farm]; inspecting the reading rooms; creating wall newspapers and editing the *kolkhoz* newspaper; reporting for Moscow newspapers; introducing radio and mobile movie houses; and so on. It is not surprising that the book *Commanders of the Field*, which Tretiakov wrote following these stays, is said to have had considerable influence on the further development of collective agriculture.

You may have a high regard for Tretiakov, yet still be of the opinion that his example does not prove a great deal in this context. The tasks he performed, you will perhaps object, are those of a journalist or a propagandist; all this has little to do with literature. But I cited the example of Tretiakov deliberately, in order to point out to you how comprehensive the horizon is within which we have to rethink our conceptions of literary forms or genres, in view of the technical factors affecting our present situation, if we are to identify the forms of expression that channel the literary energies of the present. There were not always novels in the past, and there will not always have to be; there have not always been tragedies or great epics. Not always were the forms of commentary, translation, indeed even so-called plagiarism playthings in the margins of literature; they had a place not only in the philosophical but also in the literary writings of Arabia and China. Rhetoric has not always been a minor form: in Antiquity, it put its stamp on large provinces of literature. All this is to accustom you to the thought that we are in the midst of a mighty recasting of literary forms, a melting down in which many of the opposites in which we have been used to think may lose their force. Let me give an example of the unfruitfulness of such opposites, and of the process of their dialectical transcendence. And we shall remain with Tretiakov. For this example is the newspaper.

One left-wing author has declared:[3]

In our writing, opposites that in happier ages fertilized one another have become insoluble antinomies. Thus, science and belles lettres, criticism and literary production, education and politics, fall apart in disorder and lose all connection with one another. The scene of this literary confusion is the newspaper; its content, "subject matter" that denies itself any other form of organization than that imposed on it by readers' impatience. And this impatience is not just that of the politician expecting information, or of the speculator looking for a stock tip; behind it smolders the impatience of people who are excluded and who think they have the right to see their own interests expressed. The fact that nothing binds the reader more tightly to his paper than this all-consuming impatience, his longing for daily nourishment has long been exploited by publishers, who are constantly inaugurating new columns to address the reader's questions, opinions, and protests. Hand in hand, therefore, with the indiscriminate assimilation of facts goes the equally indiscriminate assimilation of readers, who are instantly elevated to collaborators. Here, however, a dialectical moment lies concealed: the decline of writing in the bourgeois press proves to be the formula for its revival in the press of Soviet Russia. For as writing gains in breadth what it loses in depth, the conventional distinction between author and public, which is upheld by the bourgeois press, begins in the Soviet press to disappear. For there the reader is at all times ready to become a writer—that is, a describer, or even a prescriber. As an expert—not perhaps in a discipline but perhaps in a post that he holds—he gains access to authorship. Work itself has its turn to speak. And its representation in words becomes a part of the ability that is needed for its exercise. Literary competence is no longer founded on specialized training but is now based on polytechnical education, and thus becomes public property. It is, in a word, the literarization of the conditions of living that masters the otherwise insoluble antinomies. And it is at the scene of the limitless debasement of the word—the newspaper, in short—that its salvation is being prepared.

I hope I have shown, by means of this quotation, that the description of the author as producer must extend as far as the press. For through the press, at any rate through the Soviet Russian press, one realizes that the mighty process of recasting that I spoke of earlier not only affects the conventional distinction between genres, between writer and poet, between scholar and popularizer, but also revises even the distinction between author and reader. Of this process the press is the decisive example, and therefore any consideration of the author as producer must include it.

It cannot, however, stop at this point. For in Western Europe the newspaper does not constitute a serviceable instrument of production in the hands of the writer. It still belongs to capital. Since, on the one hand, the newspaper, technically speaking, represents the most important literary position, but, on the other, this position is controlled by the opposition, it is no wonder that the writer's understanding of his dependent social position, his technical possibilities, and his political task has to grapple with the most enormous difficulties. It has been one of the decisive processes of the last ten years in Germany that a considerable proportion of its productive minds, under the pressure of economic conditions, have passed through a revolutionary development in their attitudes, without being able simultaneously to rethink their own work, their relation to the means of production, or their technique in a really revolutionary way. I am speaking, as you see, of so-called left-wing intellectuals, and will limit myself to the bourgeois Left. In Germany the leading politico-literary movements of the last decade have emanated from this left-wing intelligentsia. I shall mention two of them. Activism and New Objectivity [*Neue Sachlichkeit*], using these examples to show that a political tendency, however revolutionary it may seem, has a counterrevolutionary function so long as the writer feels his solidarity with the proletariat only in his attitudes, not as a producer.[4]

The catchword in which the demands of Activism are summed up is "logocracy"; in plain language, "rule of the mind." This is apt to be translated as "rule of the intellectuals." In fact, the concept of the intellectual, with its attendant spiritual values, has established itself in the camp of the left-wing intelligentsia, and dominates its political manifestos from Heinrich Mann to Döblin.[5] It can readily be seen that this concept has been coined without any regard for the position of intellectuals in the process of production. Hiller, the theoretician of Activism, means intellectuals to be understood not as "members of certain professions" but as "representatives of a certain characterological type."[6] This characterological type naturally stands as such between the classes. It encompasses any number of private individuals without offering the slightest basis for organizing them. When Hiller formulates his denunciation of party leaders, he concedes them a good deal. They may be "better informed in important matters . . . , have more popular appeal . . . , fight more courageously" than he, but of one thing he is sure: they "think more defectively." Probably. But where does this lead him, since politically it is not private thinking but, as Brecht once expressed it, the art of thinking in other people's heads that is decisive? Activism attempted to replace materialistic dialectics by the notion of common sense—a notion that in class terms is unquantifiable.[7] Activism's intellectuals represent at best a social group. In other words, the very principle on which this collective is formed is reactionary. No wonder its effect could never be revolutionary.

Yet the pernicious principle of such collectivization continues to operate. This could be seen three years ago, when Döblin's *Wissen und Verändern* came out.[8] As is known, this pamphlet was written in reply to a young man—Döblin calls him Herr Hocke—who had put to the famous author the question, "What is to be done?" Döblin invites him to join the cause of socialism, but with reservations. Socialism, according to Döblin, is "freedom, a spontaneous union of people, the rejection of all compulsion, indignation at injustice and coercion, humanity, tolerance, a peaceful disposition." However that may be, on the basis of this socialism he sets his face against the theory and practice of the radical workers' movement. "Nothing," Döblin declares, "can come out of anything that was not already in it—and from a murderously exacerbated class war, justice can come but not socialism." Döblin formulates the recommendation that, for these and other reasons, he gives Herr Hocke: "You, my dear sir, cannot put into effect your agreement in principle with the struggle [of the proletariat] by joining the proletarian front. You must be content with an agitated and bitter approval of this struggle. But you also know that if you do more, an immensely important post will remain unmanned . . . : the original communistic position of human individual freedom, of the spontaneous solidarity and union of men . . . It is this position, my dear sir, that alone falls to you." Here it is quite palpable where the conception of the "intellectual"—as a type of person defined by his opinions, attitudes, or dispositions, but not by his position in the process of production—leads. He must, as Döblin puts it, find his place *beside* the proletariat. But what kind of place is this? That of a benefactor, of an ideological patron—an impossible place. And so we return to the thesis stated at the outset: the place of the intellectual in the class struggle can be identified—or, better, chosen—only on the basis of his position in the process of production.

To signify the transformation of the forms and instruments of production in the way desired by a progressive intelligentsia—that is, one interested in freeing the means of production and serving the class struggle—Brecht coined the term *Umfunktionierung* [functional transformation]. He was the first to make of intellectuals the far-reaching demand not to supply the apparatus of production without, to the utmost extent possible, changing it in accordance with socialism. "The publication of the *Versuche*," the author writes in his introduction to the series of writings bearing this title, "occurred at a time when certain works ought no longer to be individual experiences (have the character of works) but should, rather, concern the use (transformation) of certain institutes and institutions."[9] It is not spiritual renewal, as fascists proclaim, that is desirable: technical innovations are suggested. I shall come back to these innovations. Here I would like to content myself with a reference to the decisive difference between the mere supplying of a productive apparatus and its transformation. And I would like to preface my discussion of the "New Objectivity" with the proposition that to supply a productive apparatus without—to the utmost extent possible—changing it would still be a highly censurable course, even if the material with which it is supplied seemed to be of a revolutionary nature. For we are faced with the fact—of which the past decade in Germany has furnished an abundance of examples—that the bourgeois apparatus of production and publication can assimilate astonishing quantities of revolutionary themes—indeed, can propagate them without calling its own existence, and the existence of the class that owns it, seriously into question. This remains true at least as long as it is supplied by hack writers, even if they are revolutionary hacks. I define "hack writer" as a writer who abstains in principle from alienating the productive apparatus from the ruling class by improving it in ways serving the interests of socialism. And I further maintain that a considerable proportion of so-called left-wing literature possessed no other social function than to wring from the political situation a continuous stream of novel effects for the entertainment of the public. This brings me to the New Objectivity. Its stock in trade was reportage. Let us ask ourselves to whom this technique was useful.

For the sake of clarity I will place its photographic form in the foreground, but what is true of this can also be applied to its literary form. Both owe the extraordinary increase in their popularity to the technology of publication: radio and the illustrated press. Let us think back to Dadaism. The revolutionary strength of Dadaism consisted in testing art for its authenticity. A still life might have been put together from tickets, spools of cotton, and cigarette butts, all of which were combined with painted elements. The whole thing was put in a frame. And thereby the public was shown: Look, your picture frame ruptures time; the tiniest authentic fragment of daily life says more than painting. Just as the bloody fingerprint of a murderer on the page of a book says more than the text. Much of this revolutionary content has gone into photomontage. You need only think of the work of John

Heartfield, whose technique made the book cover into a political instrument.[10] But now follow the path of photography further. What do you see? It becomes ever more *nuancé*, ever more modern; and the result is that it can no longer record a tenement block or a refuse heap without transfiguring it. Needless to say, photography is unable to convey anything about a power station or a cable factory other than, "What a beautiful world!" *The World Is Beautiful*—this is the title of the well-known picture anthology by Renger-Patzsch, in which we see New Objective photography at its peak.[11] For it has succeeded in transforming even abject poverty—by apprehending it in a fashionably perfected manner—into an object of enjoyment. For if it is an economic function of photography to restore to mass consumption, by fashionable adaptation, subjects that had earlier withdrawn themselves from it (springtime, famous people, foreign countries), it is one of its political functions to renew from within—that is, fashionably—the world as it is.

Here we have a flagrant example of what it means to supply a productive apparatus without changing it. To change it would have meant overthrowing another of the barriers, transcending another of the antitheses, that fetter the production of intellectuals—in this case, the barrier between writing and image. What we require of the photographer is the ability to give his picture a caption that wrenches it from modish commerce and gives it a revolutionary use value. But we will make this demand most emphatically when we—the writers—take up photography. Here, too, therefore, technical progress is for the author as producer the foundation of his political progress. In other words, only by transcending the specialization in the process of intellectual production—a specialization that, in the bourgeois view, constitutes its order—can one make this production politically useful; and the barriers imposed by specialization must be breached jointly by the productive forces that they were set up to divide. The author as producer discovers—even as he discovers his solidarity with the proletariat—his solidarity with certain other producers who earlier seemed scarcely to concern him. I have spoken of the photographer; here I will very briefly insert a word of Eisler's on the musician:[12]

In the development of music, too, both in production and in reproduction, we must learn to recognize an ever-increasing process of rationalization . . . The phonograph record, the sound film, jukeboxes can purvey top-quality music . . . canned as a commodity. The consequence of this process of rationalization is that musical reproduction is consigned to ever-diminishing but also ever more highly qualified groups of specialists. The crisis of the commercial concert is the crisis of an antiquated form of production made obsolete by new technical inventions.

The task, therefore, consisted of an *Umfunktionierung* of the form of the concert that had to fulfill two conditions: it had to eliminate the antithesis, first, between performers and listeners and, second, between technique and content. On this, Eisler makes the following illuminating observation: "One must beware of overestimating orchestral music and considering it the only high art. Music without words attained its great importance and its full extent only under capitalism." This means that the task of changing the concert is impossible without the collaboration of the word. It alone can effect the transformation, as Eisler formulates it, of a concert into a political meeting. But that such a transformation does indeed represent a peak of musical and literary technique, Brecht and Eisler prove with their didactic play *Die Massnahme* [The Measures Taken].

If you look back from this vantage point on the recasting of literary forms that I spoke of earlier, you can see how photography and music, and whatever else occurs to you, are entering the growing, molten mass from which the new forms are cast. You will find this confirmed: only the literarization of all the conditions of life provides an accurate conception of the range of this melting-down process, just as the state of the class struggle determines the temperature at which—more or less perfectly—it is accomplished.

I spoke of the process of a certain modish photography whereby poverty is made an object of consumption. In turning to New Objectivity as a literary movement, I must take a step further and say that it has made the *struggle against poverty* an object of consumption. The political importance of the movement was indeed exhausted in many cases by the conversion of revolutionary impulses, insofar as they occurred among bourgeoisie, into objects of distraction, of amusement, which found their way without difficulty into the big-city cabaret business. The transformation of the political struggle from a call-to-decision into an object of contemplative enjoyment, from a means of production into a consumer article, is the defining characteristic of this literature. A perceptive critic has explained this, using the example of Erich Kästner, as follows:[13]

> With the workers' movement, this left-wing radical intelligentsia has nothing in common. It is, rather, a phenomenon of bourgeois decomposition, a counterpart of the feudalistic mimicry that the Second Empire admired in the reserve officer. The radical-left publicists of the stamp of Kästner, Mehring, or Tucholsky are the proletarian mimicry of decayed bourgeois strata.[14] Their function is to produce, from the political standpoint, not parties but cliques; from the literary standpoint, not schools but fashions; from the economic standpoint, not producers but agents—agents or hacks who make a great display of their poverty, and a banquet out of yawning emptiness. One could not be more cozily accommodated in an uncozy situation.

This school, I said, made a great display of its poverty. It thereby shirked the most urgent task of the present-day writer: to recognize how poor he is and how poor he has to be in order to begin again from the beginning. For this is what is involved. The Soviet state will not, it is true, banish the poet, as Plato did; but it will—and this is why I evoked Plato's republic at the outset—assign him tasks that do not permit him to display in new master-pieces the long-since-counterfeit wealth of creative personality. To expect a renewal in terms of such personalities and such works is a privilege of fascism, which gives rise to such asinine formulations as that with which Günther Gründel, in his *Mission of the Young Generation,* rounds off the section on literature: "We cannot better conclude this . . . survey and prog-nosis than with the observation that the *Wilhelm Meister* and the *Green Henry* of our generation have not yet been written."[15] Nothing will be further from the author who has reflected deeply on the conditions of present-day production than to expect, or desire, such works. His work will never be merely work on products but always, at the same time, work on the means of production. In other words, his products must have, over and above their character as works, an organizing function, and in no way must their organizational usefulness be confined to their value as propaganda. Their political tendency alone is not enough. The excellent Lichtenberg has said, "What matters is not a man's opinions, but the kind of man these opinions make of him."[16] Now, it is true that opinions matter greatly, but the best are of no use if they make nothing useful out of those who hold them. The best political tendency is wrong if it does not demonstrate the attitude with which it is to be followed. And this attitude the writer can demonstrate only in his particular activity—that is, in writing. A political tendency is a necessary but never sufficient condition for the organizing function of a work. This further requires a directing, instructing stance on the part of the writer. And today this must be demanded more than ever before. *An author who teaches writers nothing teaches no one.* What mat-ters, therefore, is the exemplary character of production, which is able, first, to induce other producers to produce, and, second, to put an improved apparatus at their disposal. And this apparatus is better, the more consumers it is able to turn into producers—that is, readers or spectators into collabo-rators. We already possess such an example, to which, however, I can only allude here. It is Brecht's Epic Theater.

Tragedies and operas are constantly being written that apparently have a well-tried theatrical apparatus at their disposal, but in reality do nothing but supply a derelict one. "The lack of clarity about their situation that prevails among musicians, writers, and critics," says Brecht, "has immense consequences that are far too little considered. For, thinking that they are in possession of an apparatus that in reality possesses them, they defend an apparatus over which they no longer have any control and that is no longer, as they still believe, a means for the producers, but has become a means against the producers."[17] This theater, with its complicated machinery, its gigantic supporting staff, its sophisticated effects, has become a "means against the producers" not least in seeking to enlist them in the hopeless competitive struggle in which film and radio have enmeshed it. This theater (whether in its educating or its entertaining role; the two are complementary)[18] is that of a sated class for which everything it touches becomes a stimulant. Its position is lost. Not so that of a theater that, instead of competing with newer instruments of publication, seeks to use and learn from them—in short, to enter into debate with them. This debate the Epic Theater has made its own affair. It is, measured by the present state of development of film and radio, the contemporary form.

In the interest of this debate, Brecht fell back on the most primitive elements of the theater. He contented himself, by and large, with a podium. He dispensed with wide-ranging plots. He thus succeeded in changing the functional connection between stage and public, text and performance, director and actor. Epic Theater, he declared, had to portray situations, rather than develop plots. It obtains such situations, as we shall see presently, by interrupting the plot. I remind you here of the songs, which have their chief function in interrupting the action. Here—according to the principle of interruption—Epic Theater, as you see, takes up a procedure that has become familiar to you in recent years from film and radio, literature and photography. I am speaking of the procedure of montage: the superimposed element disrupts the context in which it is inserted. But here this procedure has a special right, perhaps even a perfect right, as I will briefly show. The interruption of action, on account of which Brecht described his theater as "epic," constantly counteracts illusion on the part of the audience. For such illusion is a hindrance to a theater that proposes to make use of elements of reality in experimental rearrangements. But it is at the end, not the beginning, of the experiment that the situation appears—a situation that, in this or that form, is always ours. It is not brought home to the spectator but distanced from him. He recognizes it as the real situation—not with satisfaction, as in the theater of Naturalism, but with astonishment. Epic Theater, therefore, does not reproduce situations; rather, it discovers them. This discovery is accomplished by means of the interruption of sequences. Yet interruption here has the character not of a stimulant but of an organizing function. It arrests the action in its course, and thereby compels the listener to adopt an attitude vis-à-vis the process, the actor vis-à-vis his role. I would like to show you, through an example, how Brecht's discovery and use of the *gestus* is nothing but the restoration of the method of montage decisive in radio and film, from an often merely modish procedure to a human event. Imagine a family scene: the wife is just about to grab a bronze sculpture and throw it at her daughter; the father is opening the window to call for help. At this moment a stranger enters. The process is interrupted. What appears in its place is the situation on which the stranger's eyes now fall: agitated faces, open window, disordered furniture. There are eyes, however, before which the more usual scenes of present-day existence do not look very different: the eyes of the epic dramatist.

To the total dramatic artwork he opposes the dramatic laboratory. He makes use in a new way of the great, ancient opportunity of the theater: to expose what is present. At the center of his experiment stands the human being. Present-day man; a reduced man, therefore, chilled in a chilly environment. But since this is the only one we have, it is in our interest to know him. He is subjected to tests, examinations. What emerges is this: events are alterable not at their climaxes, not by virtue and resolution, but only in their strictly habitual course, by reason and practice. To construct from the smallest elements of behavior what in Aristotelian dramaturgy is called "action" is the purpose of Epic Theater. Its means are therefore more modest than those of traditional theater; likewise its aims. It is concerned less with filling the public with feelings, even seditious ones, than with alienating it in an enduring way, through thinking, from the conditions in which it lives. It may be noted, incidentally, that there is no better trigger for thinking than laughter. In particular, convulsion of the diaphragm usually provides better opportunities for thought than convulsion of the soul. Epic Theater is lavish only in occasions for laughter.

It has perhaps struck you that the train of thought which is about to be concluded presents the writer with only one demand: the demand *to think*, to reflect on his position in the process of production. We may depend on it: this reflection leads, sooner or later, for the writers who *matter* (that is, for the best technicians in their field), to observations that provide the most factual foundation for solidarity with the proletariat. Thus, I would like to conclude by adducing a topical illustration in the form of a small extract from a journal published here, *Commune*. *Commune* circulated a questionnaire asking, "For whom do you write?" I quote from the reply of René Maublanc and from the comment added by Aragon.[19] "Unquestionably," says Maublanc, "I write almost exclusively for a bourgeois public. First, because I am obliged to" (here Maublanc is alluding to his professional duties as a grammar-school teacher), "second, because I have bourgeois origins and a bourgeois education and come from a bourgeois milieu, and so am naturally inclined to address myself to the class to which I belong, which I know and understand best. This does not mean, however, that I write in order to please or support it. I am convinced, on the one hand, that the proletarian revolution is necessary and desirable and, on the other, that it will be the more rapid, easy, and successful, and the less bloody, the weaker the opposition of the bourgeoisie . . . The proletariat today needs allies from the camp of the bourgeoisie, exactly as in the eighteenth century the bourgeoisie needed allies from the feudal camp. I wish to be among those allies."

On this Aragon comments:

Our comrade here touches on a state of affairs that affects a large number of present-day writers. Not all have the courage to look it in the face . . . Those who see their own situation as clearly as René Maublanc are few. But precisely from them more must be required . . . It is not enough to weaken the bourgeoisie from within; it is necessary to fight them *with* the proletariat . . . René Maublanc, and many of our friends among the writers who are still hesitating, are faced with the example of the Soviet Russian writers who came from the Russian bourgeoisie and nevertheless became pioneers in the building of socialism.

Thus Aragon. But how did they become pioneers? Certainly not without very bitter struggles, extremely difficult debates. The considerations I have put before you are an attempt to draw some conclusions from these struggles. They are based on the concept to which the debate on the attitude of Russian intellectuals owes its decisive clarification: the concept of the specialist. The solidarity of the specialist with the proletariat—herein lies the beginning of this clarification—can only be a mediated one. Proponents of Activism and of the New Objectivity could gesticulate as they pleased, but they could not do away with the fact that even the proletarianization of an intellectual hardly ever makes a proletarian. Why? Because the bourgeois class gave him, in the form of education, a means of production that, owing to educational privilege, makes him feel solidarity with it, and still more it with him. Aragon was thereby entirely correct when, in another connection, he declared, "The revolutionary intellectual appears first and foremost as the betrayer of his class of origin." In the case of the writer, this betrayal consists in conduct that transforms him from a supplier of the productive apparatus into an engineer who sees it as his task to adapt this apparatus to the purposes of the proletarian revolution. This is a mediating activity, yet it frees the intellectual from that purely destructive task to which Maublanc and many of his comrades believe it necessary to confine him. Does he succeed in promoting the socialization of the intellectual means of production? Does he see how he himself can organize intellectual workers in the production process? Does he have proposals for the *Umfunktionierung* of the novel, the drama, the poem? The more completely he can orient his activity toward this task, the more correct the political tendency of his work will be, and necessarily also the higher its technical quality. And at the same time, the more exactly he is thus informed about his position in the process of production, the less it will occur to him to lay claim to "spiritual" qualities. The spirit that holds forth in the name of fascism *must* disappear. The spirit that, in opposing it, trusts in its own miraculous powers *will* disappear. For the revolutionary struggle is not between capitalism and spirit; it is between capitalism and the proletariat.

Written spring 1934; unpublished in Benjamin's lifetime. *Gesammelte Schriften*, II, 683–701. Translated by Edmund Jephcott.

Notes

1. That the date given in the subtitle is erroneous can be gathered from a letter that Benjamin wrote to Adorno the following day (April 28, 1934), in which he mentions that the address has not yet been presented (*Gesammelte Schriften*, vol. 2, pp. 1460–1461). Gershom Scholem claims that the twenty-seventh was the date of Benjamin's *completion* of the text, which was *never* presented; see *The Correspondence of Walter Benjamin and Gershom Scholem, 1932–1940* (New York: Schocken, 1989), p. 111n. The Institute for the Study of Fascism was a Communist front organization.
2. Sergei Tretiakov (1892–1939) was a Russian writer whose work, based on a "literature of facts," was agitational and propagandistic. His book *Commanders of the Field* (1931) comprised two volumes of diaries and sketchbooks.
3. The "left-wing author" is Benjamin himself. See "The Newspaper" (1934), in this volume.
4. Centered around the yearbook *Das Ziel* (The Goal), "Activism" was a political stance that fused Nietzschean ideals with a pacifist socialism; it stood opposed to German Expressionism. Prominent figures associated with the movement included the German author and editor Kurt Hiller (1885–1972), who edited the yearbook; the theater critic Alfred Kerr; and the novelist Heinrich Mann. The young Benjamin had been a vocal opponent of Hiller's ideas. "New Objectivity" (Neue Sachlichkeit) was the term coined by the museum curator G. F. Hartlaub for a new tendency toward figuration in postwar German painting. It gradually came to designate the Weimar "period style" in art, architecture, design, literature, and film: cool, objective, analytical.
5. Heinrich Mann (1871–1950), German novelist and essayist, was the brother of Thomas Mann. Many of the disputes between the brothers over the years stemmed from Heinrich's left-liberal activism. Alfred Döblin (1878–1957), German novelist, is best-known for the novel *Berlin Alexanderplatz* (1929). He, too, was a prominent left-liberal voice in Weimar.
6. Kurt Hiller, *Der Sprung ins Helle* (Leipzig: Lindner, 1932), p. 314.
7. In place of this sentence, the original manuscript contained a different one, which was deleted: "Or, in Trotsky's words, 'If enlightened pacifists attempt to abolish war by means of rational argument, they simply make fools of themselves, but if the armed masses begin to use the arguments of reason against war, this means the end of war.'"
8. *Wissen und Verändern* (Know and Change; 1931) was Döblin's apology for his humane, party-independent, and frankly mystical socialism.
9. Bertolt Brecht, *Versuche 1–3* (Berlin: Kiepenheuer, 1930).
10. John Heartfield (pseudonym of Helmut Herzfelde; 1891–1968), German graphic artist, photographer, and designer, was one of the founders of Berlin Dada. He went on to reinvent photomontage as a political weapon.

11. Albert Renger-Patzsch, *Die Welt ist schön: Einhundert photographische Aufnahmen* (Munich: K. Wolff, 1928). Renger-Patzsch (1897–1966) was a German photographer who espoused a straight photographic realism, rejecting both the romanticism of photographers who tried to imitate painting and the photography that tried to gain its effects through startling techniques. His book *Die Welt ist schön* (The World Is Beautiful; 1928) established him as one of the leading European photographers.

12. Hanns Eisler (1898–1962) was a German composer best-known for his collaborations with Brecht. He became the leading composer in the German Democratic Republic, for which he wrote the national anthem.

13. The "perceptive critic" is Benjamin himself, in his essay "Left-Wing Melancholy," in this volume. Erich Kästner (1899–1974) was a German satirist, poet, and novelist who is especially known for his children's books. He was the most durable practitioner of the style of witty, laconic writing associated with the highbrow cabaret, the Berlin weekly *Die Weltbühne* (The World Stage), and the Neue Sachlichkeit (New Objectivity) movement of the mid-1920s.

14. Franz Mehring (1846–1919), German socialist historian and pamphleteer, is best-known for his biography of Karl Marx. Kurt Tucholsky (1890–1935) was a German satirist and journalist whose work is emblematic of the wit and savage irony of the Berlin cabaret.

15. E. Günther Gründel, *Die Sendung der jungen Generation: Versuch einer umfassenden revolutionären Sinndeutung der Krise* (Munich: Beck, 1932), p. 116. Gründel is referring to novels by Goethe and Gottfried Keller, respectively.

16. Georg Christoph Lichtenberg (1742–1799) was a German satirist and experimental psychologist. Although he was a feared satirist in his time, he is remembered today as the first great German aphorist.

17. Brecht, *Versuche 4–7* (Berlin: Kiepenheuer, 1930), p. 107.

18. See "Theater and Radio," in this volume.

19. René Maublanc (1891–1960) was a French Marxist historian whose books include *Fourier* (1937) and *Le Marxisme et la liberté* (1945). Louis Aragon (pseudonym of Louis Andrieux; 1897–1982) was a French poet, novelist, and essayist who, as a prominent Surrealist, was a political activist and spokesman for Communism. Benjamin's earliest work on *Das Passagen-Werk* (The Arcades Project) was inspired by Aragon's books *Vague de rêves* and *Paysan de Paris*.

Notes from Svendborg, Summer 1934

July 4. Long conversation in Brecht's sickroom in Svendborg yesterday.[1] It centered on my essay "The Author as Producer," in which I develop the theory that a decisive criterion of a revolutionary function of literature lies in the extent to which technical advances lead to a transformation of artistic forms and hence of intellectual means of production. Brecht was willing to concede the validity of this thesis only for a single type—namely, the upper-middle-class writer, a type he thought included himself. "Such a writer," he said, "experiences solidarity with the interests of the proletariat at a single point: the issue of the development of his means of production. But if solidarity exists at this single point, he is, as producer, totally proletarianized. This total proletarianization at a single point leads to a solidarity all along the line." Brecht thought my criticism of proletarian writers of the Becher type too abstract.[2] He tried to improve it with an analysis of a poem by Becher entitled "I Say Quite Openly . . . ," a poem that had appeared recently in one of the official proletarian literary reviews. Brecht compared it, on the one hand, with his didactic poem on acting, written for Carola Neher, and, on the other hand, with "Le bateau ivre."[3] "I have taught Carola Neher a variety of things," he explained. "She has not only learned to act, but, for example, she has learned how to wash herself. Up to then, she had washed so as not to be dirty. That was completely beside the point. I taught her how to wash her face. She acquired such skill in this that I wanted to make a film of her doing it. But nothing came of it because I was not making a picture at the time, and she did not want to be filmed by anyone else. That didactic poem was a model. Every learner was expected to take the place of his 'self.' When Becher says 'I,' he regards himself (since he's president of the Union of the Proletarian Revolutionary Writers of Germany) as exemplary. The only thing is that no one wants to emulate him. They simply conclude that he's pleased with himself." Brecht added that he had intended for a long time to write a number of model poems for various professions, such as engineering and writing.—On the other hand, Brecht compared Becher's poem with Rimbaud's. In the latter, he maintained that Marx and Lenin—if they had read it—would have detected the great historical movement of which it is an expression. They would have realized very clearly that it describes not just the eccentric stroll of an individual but the flight, the vagabondage, of a human being who can no longer bear to be confined within the limits of a class which—with the Crimean War and the Mexican adventure—has started to open up exotic parts of the globe to its own commercial interests. It was completely impossible to import into the model of the proletarian fighter the gesture of the footloose vagabond who leaves his own concerns to chance and turns his back on society.

July 6. Brecht said, in the course of yesterday's conversation, "I often imagine being interrogated by a tribunal: 'Tell us the truth. Are you in earnest?' I would have to confess that I am not completely in earnest. I think too much about artistic matters, about what might work on the stage, for me to be completely serious. But having uttered this disclaimer, I would go on to add an even more important claim—namely, that my behavior is *legitimate.*" Of course, this is a statement that came somewhat later in the course of the conversation. Brecht had begun by doubting not the legitimacy of his methods but their efficacy. In particular, with the statement provoked by some comments I had made about Gerhart Hauptmann: "I occasionally wonder whether they aren't the only writers who really achieve something— the *substance writers,* I mean." By this, Brecht means writers who are completely serious. And to explain this idea, he begins by imagining that Confucius had written a tragedy, or Lenin a novel. We would regard that as improper, he claims, and as an act unworthy of them. "Let's assume that you read an excellent political novel and discover subsequently that it was by Lenin. You'd change your opinion about both Lenin and the novel; they'd both go down in your estimation. Nor could Confucius have written a tragedy like those of Euripides; it would have seemed unworthy of him. But the same thing couldn't be said about his parables." In short, all this amounts to a distinction between two types of writers: the visionary, who is in earnest, and the reflective writer, who is not quite serious. And this leads me to raise the question of Kafka. Which group does he belong to? I realize that the question cannot be answered. And the very fact that it cannot be decided is, in Brecht's eyes, proof that Kafka (whom he regards as a great writer) is a failure, like Kleist and Grabbe, or Büchner.[4] His starting point is really the parable, the allegory, which is answerable to reason and hence cannot be entirely in earnest on the literal plane. But Kafka then develops the parable. It grows up into a novel. And a closer look reveals that it has contained the seed of the novel from the outset. It was never completely transparent. Furthermore, Brecht is convinced that Kafka would never have discovered his own proper form without Dostoevsky's Grand Inquisitor and that other parabolic passage in *The Brothers Karamazov,* where the corpse of the holy Staretz begins to stink. In Kafka, then, parable is in conflict with the visionary. But Brecht adds that, as a visionary, Kafka saw what was to come, without seeing what exists now. Brecht emphasizes the prophetic element in Kafka's works, as he did earlier, in Le Lavandou, and even more explicitly to me. Kafka had only one problem, that of organization. What gripped his imagination was his fear of a society of ants: the way in which people become alienated from each other by the forms of their life together. And he foresaw certain forms of this alienation, such as the methods of the Russian Secret Police. But he did not find any solution and has never awoken from his nightmare. Brecht added that Kafka's precision was the precision of an imprecise man, a dreamer.

July 12. Yesterday, after a game of chess, Brecht said: "When Karl Korsch comes, we ought to work out a new game with him.[5] A game in which the positions do not always remain constant, in which the functions of the pieces change after they have stood in the same place for a certain length of time. They would then become either stronger or weaker. At present, there is no development; things stay as they are for too long."

July 23. Yesterday, a visit from Karin Michaelis, who has just returned from a trip to Russia and is full of enthusiasm.[6] Brecht remembers being shown around by Sergei Tretiakov, who gave him a tour of Moscow and was proud of everything his visitor saw, no matter what. "That's not a bad thing," Brecht said. "It shows that what he showed me belongs to him. No one is proud of what belongs to someone else." After a while, he added: "But in the end, I did become a bit tired of it all. I couldn't admire everything, nor did I want to. After all, they are his soldiers and his trucks. Unfortunately, they are not mine."

July 24. On a horizontal beam supporting the roof of Brecht's study, there is a painted inscription: "The truth is concrete." On a window ledge stands a little wooden donkey that can nod its head. Brecht has hung a little notice round its neck with the words: "I, too, must understand it."

August 5. Three weeks ago I gave Brecht my essay on Kafka to read. He doubtless read it, but did not allude to it of his own accord; and on the two occasions when I brought the subject up, he responded evasively. Finally, I took the manuscript back without comment. Yesterday, he suddenly referred to the essay. With a somewhat abrupt and forced transition in the conversation, he remarked that I, too, could not entirely escape the charge of writing in diary form, in the style of Nietzsche. My Kafka essay, for example. It was interested in Kafka only as a phenomenon; looked at the work as if it—and likewise the author—were a product of nature and isolated it from every possible context, even the author's life. I was always interested exclusively in the question of *essence*. But how should such matters be addressed? The questions to be raised about Kafka are: What is he doing? How does he behave? And you should start with the general rather than the particular. What then emerges is that he lived, in Prague, in an unfortunate milieu of journalists and self-important literati. In that milieu, literature was the principal reality, if not the only one. And this view of things was inseparable from Kafka's own strengths and weaknesses—his artistic value, but also his uselessness in many respects. He was a Jewboy (you could also coin the term "Aryan-boy")—a feeble, unattractive figure, a bubble on the iridescent surface of the swamp of Prague's cultural life, and nothing more. But then, in this perspective, there were certain definite and highly interesting aspects. They could be made visible. One can imagine a conversation between Lao-tze[7] and his disciple Kafka: "'Very well then, Disciple Kafka, is it true that the organizations, the legal and economic institutions, around you have begun to give you the creeps?' 'Yes.' 'You cannot find your way around them any more?' 'No.' 'A stock certificate terrifies you?' 'Yes.' 'And now you are longing for a leader you can rely on, Disciple Kafka.'" "Of course, that is reprehensible," Brecht comments. "I reject Kafka." And he goes on to relate the parable told by a Chinese philosopher, concerning "the sufferings of usefulness." "In the forest, there are trees of different sorts. The thickest trunks are used for the beams of ships; the less massive but still quite serviceable trunks are used to make crates and coffins; the much thinner ones are used to make canes. But the twisted ones are not used for anything at all—they escape the sufferings of usefulness. You have to look around in Kafka's writings as if it were such a forest. You will find a number of very useful things. The images are good. The rest is just mystery-mongering. It is nonsense. You must ignore it. You cannot make progress with depth. Depth is simply a dimension; it is just depth—in which nothing can be seen." I end up telling Brecht that descending into the depths is my way of journeying to the antipodes. In my essay on Kraus, I had in fact managed to arrive there. I knew that the Kafka piece was less successful. I could not refute the criticism that it was a diary-like set of notes. In fact, I felt at home in the marginal space marked out by Kraus and, in a different way, by Kafka. Ultimately I had not yet fully managed to explore this space in the case of Kafka. I was well aware that his writings contained a lot of debris and rubbish—a lot of real mystery-mongering. But other things were crucial, and my study had touched on some of them. Brecht's judgment would have to be tested on particular works. I suggested "Das nächste Dorf" [The Next Village]. I saw right away the conflict that this suggestion produced in Brecht. He flatly rejected Hanns Eisler's assertion that this story was "worthless."[8] On the other hand, he was quite unable to define its value. "It has to be studied closely," he said. The discussion broke off at this point. It was ten o'clock—time for the news from Vienna on the radio.

August 31. The day before yesterday, a long, heated debate about my Kafka. Its foundation: the accusation that the essay promoted Jewish fascism. It increased and spread confusion about him, instead of dissipating it. Whereas the real task was to shed light on Kafka, and that meant formulating the practical proposals that could be distilled from his stories. One must assume that proposals can be distilled from them, if only because of the sovereign calm that characterizes the stance of the narrator. These proposals must be sought in the vicinity of the great evils that beset mankind today. Brecht attempted to point to their imprint on Kafka's writing. He concentrated mainly on *Der Prozess* (The Trial). What you find there above all, he said, is fear of the inexorable and never-ending growth of big cities. From his own intimate experience, he knows of the nightmare force with which this idea weighs on mankind. The incalculable mediations, dependencies, and complications that human beings find themselves in, thanks to modern forms of life, find expression in these cities. On the other hand, they also find expression in the longing for a "leader," for that *Führer* who—especially in the eyes of the petty bourgeois—can be held to account for all the latter's misfortunes in a world where everyone points the finger at someone else and everyone denies responsibility. Brecht calls *Der Prozess* a prophetic book. "You can see from the Gestapo what could become of the Cheka."[9] Kafka's perspective: that of a man who has fallen under the wheels. Symptomatic of this is Odradek: Brecht interprets "Die Sorge des Hausvaters" [The Cares of a Family Man] as those of the homeowner. The petty bourgeois necessarily gets it in the neck. His situation is Kafka's. But whereas the type of the petty bourgeois familiar today—the fascist, in other words— resolves to combat this situation by means of his invincible iron will, Kafka offers scarcely any resistance; he is wise. Where the fascist brings heroism into play, Kafka asks questions. He asks for guarantees of his situation. But his situation is such that the guarantees would have to exceed the bounds of reason. It is a Kafkaesque irony that the man was an insurance agent who appeared to be convinced of nothing more surely than the invalidity of all guarantees. Incidentally, his boundless pessimism is free from every tragic sense of fate. For not only is his expectation of disaster based entirely on empirical realities (although there it is total), but, in addition, the criteria of ultimate success are attached with incorrigible naïveté to the most trivial and commonplace activities, such as the visit of a commercial traveler or an inquiry addressed to a governmental department.—The discussion kept coming back to "Das nächste Dorf." Brecht said it was a companion piece to the story of Achilles and the tortoise. A rider can never reach the next village if he divides the journey up into its smallest components—even aside from any incidents en route. Because life is too short for such a journey. But the error lies in the concept of "a rider." For you have to divide up the traveler, as well as the journey. And since in doing this you abolish the unity of life, you likewise do away with its brevity. However short it may be. This doesn't matter, because the man who started out on his journey is different from the man who arrives.—For my part, I proposed the following interpretation: the true measure of life is memory. Looking back, it runs through life like lightning. The speed with which you can turn back a few pages is the same as the speed with which memory flies from the next village back to the place from which the rider decided to leave. Whoever, like the Ancients, has seen his life transformed into writing, let him read this writing backward. Only in this way will he encounter himself, and only in this way—in full flight from the present—will he be able to understand it.

September 27; Dragør. During an evening conversation a few days ago, Brecht displayed the strange indecisiveness that prevents him from making definite plans at the moment. The underlying cause of this indecisiveness is—as he himself emphasizes—the advantages that distinguish his personal situation from that of the majority of émigrés. Because in general he scarcely acknowledges the emigration as the foundation of plans and enterprises, it seems a fortiori to have no relevance for him. His plans operate on a larger scale. This presents him with alternatives. On one side, there are prose projects awaiting him. The smaller one about Ui—a satire on Hitler in the style of Renaissance historiography[10]—and the larger project of *Der Tui-Roman* [The Tui Novel]. *Der Tui-Roman* is intended to provide an encyclopedic survey of the follies of the Tellectuall-Ins (the intellectuals); it is set, partly at least, in China. A brief first draft of this work is finished. Alongside these prose plans, he is also preoccupied with projects that go back to very old studies and ideas. Whereas the reflections that arose in the context of the Epic Theater could be defined at a pinch in the notes and introductions to the *Versuche* [Experiments], ideas that originated in the same interests outgrew this narrow framework once they had been joined by the study of Leninism, on the one hand, and scientific empiricism, on the other. They have been concentrated for years now under one label or another, so that, in turn, non-Aristotelian logic, behavior theory, the new encyclopedia, and the critique of ideas became the focal point of his preoccupations. These different concerns are converging at present in the idea of a philosophical didactic poem. Brecht's misgivings revolve around the question whether he will have enough credit with the public for such a work—in the light of his entire past production, especially its satirical parts and above all *Der Dreigroschenroman* [The Threepenny Novel]. Such doubts are the meeting point of two different lines of thought. On the one hand, there are misgivings that concern his satirical and especially his ironic stance as such—the more so, the closer Brecht's involvement with the problems and methods of proletarian class struggle becomes. Such misgivings—which are essentially practical in nature—might be comprehensible, but not if they are identified with other, deeper-lying doubts. These deeper-lying reservations concern the artistic and playful aspect of art—above all, those impulses that from time to time make art resistant to reason. Brecht's sustained efforts to legitimate art vis-à-vis rationality have driven him again and again to the parable, a form in which artistic mastery is demonstrated by the fact that, in the end, the artistic elements cancel one another out. And these efforts to make use of the parable are at present emerging in a more radical form in the ideas connected with the didactic poem. In the course of this discussion, I tried to persuade Brecht that a didactic poem did not have to win over a bourgeois audience so much as a proletarian one, and that a proletarian audience was less likely to take its standards from Brecht's earlier, partly bourgeois-oriented works than from the dogmatic and theoretical content of the didactic poem itself. "If this didactic poem succeeds in mobilizing the authority of Marxism in its own cause," I told him, "the facts about your previous work are unlikely to undermine it."

October 4, 1934. Yesterday Brecht left for London.—Whether he sometimes feels especially challenged by me, or whether such behavior comes more easily to him now than it used to, what he himself thinks of as the inflammatory side of his thought comes to the fore in discussion much more often now than it did formerly. Indeed, I have been struck by a special vocabulary that turns up in his speech, in conjunction with this attitude. The concept of the *Würstchen* [little sausage] is a particular favorite of his in this respect. In Dragør I was reading Dostoevsky's *Crime and Punishment*. Brecht began by claiming that reading this novel was the main cause of my illness. And by way of proof he told me how, when he was young, a chronic illness whose germ had been latent in him for a long time broke out one afternoon when a schoolfriend played Chopin on the piano, at a time when Brecht was already too enfeebled to protest. He ascribes to Chopin and Dostoevsky particularly dire effects on health. Furthermore, on every possible occasion he took exception to the books I was reading, and since he was himself reading *The Good Soldier Schweik* he did not pass up the opportunity to compare the merits of the two writers. It turned out that Dostoevsky was no match for Hašek, and was relegated to the *Würstchen* without more ado. It would not have required much for Brecht to extend to Dostoevsky's writings the epithet that lately he has been ready to apply to any works that lack an enlightened tendency, or whose enlightened tendency he denies. He calls them a *Klump* [junk].

Written July–October 1934; unpublished in Benjamin's lifetime. *Gesammelte Schriften*, VI, 523–532. Translated by Rodney Livingstone.

Notes

1. Southern Funen Island, Denmark, on Svendborg Sound, Brecht's home in exile until 1939.
2. Johannes R. Becher (1891–1958) was a leading Expressionist poet who subsequently became a major force in Marxist literary circles, both as an émigré in Russia and, after 1945, in the German Democratic Republic, where he became minister of culture and president of the East German Academy of Arts.
3. Carola Neher (1905–ca. 1940) was one of Weimar's most gifted actresses. She played, among many other roles, Lulu in Frank Wedekind's *Büchse der Pandora* (Pandora's Box) and Eliza Doolittle in G. B. Shaw's *Pygmalion*. After she had played the role of Polly in the second cast of Brecht's *Dreigroschenoper* (Threepenny Opera), he wrote the play *Heilige Johanna der Schlachthofe* (Saint Joan of the Slaughterhouse) for her. She emigrated to the Soviet Union in 1933, was arrested in 1939, and died in a Soviet prison sometime thereafter. "Le bateau ivre" (The Drunken Boat; 1871) is perhaps the finest work by the French poet Arthur Rimbaud (1854–1891). He produced most of his writings before 1875, when, following an intense and violent relationship with Paul Verlaine, he began to wander through Europe and Africa.
4. Heinrich von Kleist (1777–1811), the first of the great German dramatists and short-story writers of the nineteenth century, wrote three plays that, although they received little acclaim in their time, have proven to be enduring classics: *Penthesilea* (1808), *Der zerbrochene Krug* (The Broken Pitcher; 1808), and *Prinz Friedrich von Homburg* (published posthumously in 1821 by Ludwig Tieck). His dramas combine remarkable intensity, psychological acuity, and a unique poetic voice. Christian Dietrich Grabbe (1801–1836), German dramatist, produced a number of plays that exceeded the capacities of the contemporary stage. Both *Napoleon, oder Die Hundert Tage* (Napoleon, or The Hundred Days; 1831) and *Don Juan und Faust* (1829) avoid continuous action in their use of rapidly changing, highly vivid scenes. Georg Büchner (1813–1837), German dramatist, produced two landmarks of the European theater, *Dantons Tod* (Danton's Death; 1835) and *Woyzeck* (1836). They combine harsh psychological realism with a fragmentary but highly suggestive dramatic technique.
5. Karl Korsch (1886–1961), German legal and Marxist theorist, had been one of Brecht's teachers. He was an outspoken opponent of Stalinist Russia, and settled in the United States after the Nazis rose to power. Benjamin used his work extensively in *Das Passagen-Werk* (The Arcades Project).

6. Karin Michaelis (1872–1950) was a celebrated Danish writer. In works such as *The Dangerous Age*, she addressed women's sexual needs.

7. Lao-tze (fl. sixth century B.C.) was the first philosopher of Chinese Taoism and the alleged author of the Tao-te Ching. Modern scholars discount the possibility that the text was written by one person but acknowledge the influence of Taoism on the development of Buddhism.

8. Hanns Eisler (1898–1962) was a German composer best-known for his collaborations with Brecht. He became the leading composer in the German Democratic Republic, for which he composed the national anthem.

9. The Cheka—also called the Vecheka—was an early Soviet secret-police agency and a forerunner of the KGB.

10. The "smaller one about Ui" is not the play about Arturo Ui, but *Die Geschichte des Giacomo Ui* (The History of Giacomo Ui).

Hitler's Diminished Masculinity

Hitler's diminished masculinity—
  to be compared with the feminine cast of the little tramp portrayed by Chaplin
So much luster surrounding so much shabbiness
Hitler's following
  to be compared with Chaplin's public
Chaplin—the plowshare that cuts through the masses; laughter loosens up the mass
  the ground of the Third Reich is stamped down hard and firm, and no more grass grows there
Ban on puppets in Italy, on Chaplin's films in the Third Reich—
  every puppet can put on Mussolini's chin, and every inch of Chaplin can become the Führer
The poor devil wants to be taken seriously, and instantly must call upon all hell
Chaplin's docility is apparent to all eyes; Hitler's, only to those of his bosses
Chaplin shows up the comedy of Hitler's gravity; when he acts the well-bred man, then we know how things stand with the Führer
Chaplin has become the greatest comic because he has incorporated into himself the deepest fears of his contemporaries
The fashion keynote for Hitler is not the image of the military man, but that of the gentleman in easy circumstances. The feudal emblems of authority are out of date; there remained only men's fashions. Chaplin, too, looks to men's fashions. He does this in order to take the master caste at its word. His cane is the rod around which the parasite creeps (the

vagabond is no less a parasite than the gent), and his bowler hat, which no longer sits so securely on his head, betrays the fact that the rule of the bourgeoisie is tottering.

It would be wrong to interpret the figure of Chaplin in a purely psychological light. Rarely do such popular figures fail to carry with them sundry properties or emblems that, from without, set the proper tone for them. In Chaplin's case, this role is played by his accoutrements—the cane and bowler hat.

"That happens only once, and never comes again." Hitler did not accept the title of president of the Reich;[1] his aim was to impress upon the people the singularity of his appearance. This singularity works in favor of his magically transposed prestige.

Fragment written ca. August 1934; unpublished in Benjamin's lifetime. *Gesammelte Schriften*, VI, 103–104. Translated by Howard Eiland, on the basis of a prior version by Lieven De Cauter.

Notes

1. After the death of Paul von Hindenburg on August 2, 1934, Hitler took over the office of Reichspräsident though officially renouncing the title. Chaplin's film parodying Hitler, *The Great Dictator,* was not released until 1940.

Franz Kafka

On the Tenth Anniversary of His Death

Potemkin

It is said that Potemkin suffered from states of depression which recurred more or less regularly.[1] At such times no one was allowed to go near him, and access to his room was strictly forbidden. This malady was never mentioned at court, and in particular it was known that any allusion to it would incur the disfavor of Empress Catherine. One of the chancellor's depressions lasted for an extraordinary length of time and caused serious difficulties; in the offices documents piled up that required Potemkin's signature, and the empress pressed for their completion. The high officials were at their wits' end. One day, an unimportant little clerk named Shuvalkin happened to enter the anteroom of the chancellor's palace and found the councillors of state assembled there, moaning and groaning as usual. "What is the matter, Your Excellencies?" asked the obliging Shuvalkin. They explained things to him and regretted that they could not use his services. "If that's all it is," said Shuvalkin, "I beg you gentlemen to let me have those papers." Having nothing to lose, the councillors of state let themselves be persuaded to do so, and with the sheaf of documents under his arm, Shuvalkin set out, through galleries and corridors, for Potemkin's bedroom. Without knocking or even stopping, he turned the door handle; the room was not locked. In semidarkness Potemkin was sitting on his bed, in a threadbare nightshirt, biting his nails. Shuvalkin stepped up to the writing desk, dipped a pen in ink, and without saying a word pressed it into Potemkin's hand while putting one of the documents on his knees. Potemkin gave the intruder a vacant stare; then, as though in his sleep, he started to sign—first one paper, then a second, finally all of them. When the last signature had been affixed, Shuvalkin took the papers under his arm and left the room without further ado, just as he had entered it. Waving the papers triumphantly, he stepped into the anteroom. The councillors of state rushed toward him and tore the documents out of his hands. Breathlessly they bent over them. No one spoke a word; the whole group seemed paralyzed. Again Shuvalkin came closer and solicitously asked why the gentlemen seemed so upset. At that point he noticed the signatures. One document after another was signed Shuvalkin . . . Shuvalkin . . . Shuvalkin . . .

This story is like a herald of Kafka's work, storming two hundred years ahead of it. The enigma which beclouds this story is Kafka's enigma. The world of offices and registries, of musty, shabby, dark rooms, is Kafka's world. The obliging Shuvalkin, who takes everything so lightly and is finally left empty-handed, is Kafka's K. Potemkin, on the other hand, who vegetates, somnolent and unkempt, in a remote, inaccessible room, is an ancestor of those holders of power in Kafka's works who live in the attics as judges or in the castle as secretaries. No matter how highly placed they may be, they are always fallen or falling men, although even the lowest and seediest of them, the doorkeepers and the decrepit officials, may abruptly and strikingly appear in the fullness of their power. Why do they vegetate? Could they be the descendants of those figures of Atlas that support globes with their shoulders? Perhaps this is why each has his head "so deep on his chest that one can hardly see anything of his eyes," like the Castellan in his portrait, or Klamm when he is alone. But it is not the globe they are carrying; it is just that even the most everyday things have their weight. "His fatigue is that of the gladiator after a fight; his job was to whitewash a corner of the office of an official!"[2]—Georg Lukács once said that in order to make a decent table nowadays, a man must have the architectural genius of a Michelangelo.[3] If Lukács thinks in terms of historical ages, Kafka thinks in terms of cosmic epochs. The man who whitewashes has epochs to move, even in his most insignificant gesture. On many occasions, and often for strange reasons, Kafka's figures clap their hands. Once, the casual remark is made that these hands are "really steam hammers" ["Auf der Galerie"].

We meet these holders of power in constant, slow movement, rising or falling. But they are at their most terrible when they rise from the deepest decay—from the fathers. The son in "Das Urteil" [The Judgment] calms his spiritless, senile father whom he has just gently put to bed:

"Don't worry, you are well covered up."
"No," cried his father, cutting short the answer. He threw the blanket off with such strength that it unfolded fully as it flew, and he stood up in bed. Only one hand lightly touched the ceiling to steady him.

"You wanted to cover me up, I know, my little scamp, but I'm not all covered up yet. And even if this is all the strength I have left, it's enough for you—too much for you . . . But thank goodness a father does not need to be taught how to see through his son" . . . And he stood up quite unsupported and kicked his legs out. He beamed with insight . . .

"So now you know what else there was in the world besides yourself; until now, you have known only about yourself! It is true, you were an innocent child, but it is even more true that you have been a devilish person!"

As the father throws off the burden of the blanket, he also throws off a cosmic burden. He has to set cosmic ages in motion in order to turn the age-old father-son relationship into a living and consequential thing. But what consequences! He sentences his son to death by drowning. The father is the one who punishes; he is drawn to guilt, just as the court officials are. There is much to indicate that the world of officials and the world of fathers are the same to Kafka. The similarity does not redound to this world's credit; it consists of dullness, decay, and filth. The father's uniform is stained all over; his underwear is dirty. Filth is the element of officials. "She could not understand why there were office hours for the public in the first place. 'To get some dirt on the front staircase'—this is how her question was once answered by an official, who was probably annoyed, but it made a lot of sense to her" [Das Schloß]. Uncleanness is so much the attribute of officials that one could almost regard them as enormous parasites. This, of course, refers not to the economic context, but to the forces of reason and humanity from which this clan makes a living. In the same way, the fathers in Kafka's strange families batten on their sons, lying on top of them like giant parasites. They not only prey upon their strength, but gnaw away at the sons' right to exist. Fathers punish, but they are at the same time accusers. The sin of which they accuse their sons seems to be a kind of original sin. The definition of it which Kafka has given applies to the sons more than to anyone else: "Original sin, the old injustice committed by man, consists in the complaint unceasingly made by man that he has been the victim of an injustice, the victim of original sin" ["Er"]. But who is accused of this inherited sin—the sin of having produced an heir—if not the father by the son? Accordingly, the son would be the sinner. But one must not conclude from Kafka's definition that the accusation is sinful because it is false. Nowhere does Kafka say that it is made wrongfully. A never-ending process is at work here, and no cause can appear in a worse light than the one for which the father enlists the aid of these officials and court offices. A boundless corruptibility is not their worst feature, for their essence is such that their venality is the only hope held out to the human spirit facing them. The courts, to be sure, have lawbooks at their disposal, but people are not allowed to see them. "It is characteristic of this legal system," conjectures K. in Der Prozeß [The Trial], "that one is sentenced not only in innocence but also in ignorance." Laws and definite norms remain unwritten in the prehistoric world. A man can transgress them without suspecting it and then must strive for atonement. But no matter how hard it may hit the unsuspecting, the transgression in the sense of the law is not accidental but fated, a destiny which appears here in all its ambiguity. In a side-glance at the idea of fate in Antiquity, Hermann Cohen came to a "conclusion that becomes inescapable": "The very rules of fate seem to be what causes and brings about the breaking away from them, the defection."[4] It is the same way with the legal authorities whose proceedings are directed against K. It takes us back, far beyond the time of the giving of the Law on twelve tablets, to a prehistoric world, written law being one of the first victories scored over this world. In Kafka the written law is contained in lawbooks, but these are secret; by basing itself on them, the prehistoric world exerts its rule all the more ruthlessly.

In Kafka's works, the conditions in offices and in families have multifarious points of contact. In the village at the foot of Castle Hill, people quote an illuminating saying. "'We have a saying here that you may be familiar with: Official decisions are as shy as young girls.' 'That's a sound observation,' said K., 'a sound observation. Decisions may have even other characteristics in common with girls.'" The most remarkable of these qualities is the willingness to lend oneself to anything, like the shy girls whom K. meets in *Das Schloß* [The Castle] and *Der Prozeß*—girls who indulge in unchaste behavior in the bosom of their family as they would in a bed. He encounters them at every turn; the rest give him as little trouble as the conquest of the barmaid.

> They embraced each other; her little body burned in K.'s hands. In a state of unconsciousness which K. tried to master constantly but fruitlessly, they rolled a little way, hit Klamm's door with a thud, and then lay in the little puddles of beer and the other refuse that littered the floor. Hours passed . . . in which K. constantly had the feeling that he was losing his way or that he had wandered farther than anyone had ever wandered before, to a place where even the air had nothing in common with his native air, where all this strangeness might choke one, yet a place so insanely enchanting that one could not help going on and losing oneself even further [*Das Schloß*].

We shall have more to say about this strange place. The remarkable thing is that these whorelike women never seem to be beautiful. Rather, beauty appears in Kafka's world only in the most obscure places—among accused persons, for example. "This, to be sure, is a strange phenomenon, a natural law, as it were . . . It cannot be guilt that makes them attractive . . . nor can it be the just punishment which makes them attractive in anticipation . . . So it must be the mere charges brought against them that somehow show on them."

From *Der Prozeß*, it may be seen that these proceedings are usually hopeless for those accused—hopeless even when they have hopes of being acquitted. It may be this hopelessness that brings out the beauty in them—the only creatures in Kafka thus favored. At least, this would be very much in keeping with the fragment of a conversation which Max Brod has related.

> I remember a conversation with Kafka which began with present-day Europe and the decline of the human race.
> "We are nihilistic thoughts, suicidal thoughts, that come into God's head," Kafka said. This reminded me at first of the Gnostic view of life: God as the evil demiurge, the world as his Fall.
> "Oh no," said Kafka, "our world is only a bad mood of God, a bad day of his."
> "Then there is hope outside this manifestation of the world that we know."
> He smiled. "Oh, plenty of hope, an infinite amount of hope—but not for us."[5]

These words provide a bridge to those extremely strange figures in Kafka, the only ones who have escaped from the family circle and for whom there may be hope. These are not the animals, not even those hybrids or imaginary creatures like the Cat Lamb or Odradek; they all still live under the spell of the family. It is no accident that Gregor Samsa wakes up as a bug in his parental home and not somewhere else, and that the peculiar animal which is half-kitten, half-lamb, is inherited from the father; Odradek likewise is the concern of the father of the family. The "assistants," however, are outside this circle.[6]

These assistants belong to a group of figures which recurs through Kafka's entire work. Their tribe includes the confidence man who is unmasked in *Betrachtung* [Meditation]; the student who appears on the balcony at night as Karl Rossmann's neighbor [in *Amerika*]; and the fools who live in that town in the south and never get tired [in "Kinder auf der Landstrasse"]. The twilight in which they exist is reminiscent of the uncertain light that surrounds the figures in the short prose pieces of Robert Walser—the author of *Der Gehülfe* [The Assistant], a contemporary novel of which Kafka was very fond.[7] In Indian mythology there are the *gandharvas,* mist-bound creatures, beings in an unfinished state. Kafka's assistants are of that kind: neither members of, nor strangers to, any of the other groups of figures, but, rather, messengers busy moving between them. Kafka tells us that they resemble Barnabas, who is a messenger. They have not yet been completely released from the womb of nature, and that is why they have "settled down on two old skirts on the floor in a corner. It was . . . their ambition . . . to use up as little space as possible. To that end they kept making various experiments, folding their arms and legs, huddling close together; in the darkness, all one could see in their corner was one big ball" [*Das Schloß*].

It is for them and their kind, the unfinished and the hapless, that there is hope.

What may be discerned, more tenderly subdued, in the activities of these messengers is the Law that reigns, in an oppressive and gloomy way, over this whole group of creatures. None has a firm place in the world, or firm, inalienable outlines. There is not one that is not either rising or falling, none that is not trading qualities with its enemy or neighbor, none that has not completed its period of time and yet is unripe, none that is not deeply exhausted and yet is only at the beginning of a long existence. To speak of any order or hierarchy is impossible here. Even the world of myth, which comes to mind in this context, is incomparably younger than Kafka's world, which has been promised redemption by myth. But if we can be sure of one thing, it is this: Kafka did not succumb to its temptation. A latter-day Ulysses, he let the Sirens pass before "his gaze, which was fixed on the distance; the Sirens disappeared, as it were, before his determination, and at the very moment when he was closest to them he was no longer aware of them." Among Kafka's ancestors in the ancient world, the Jews and the Chinese (whom we shall encounter later), this Greek one should not be forgotten. Ulysses, after all, stands at the dividing line between myth and fairy tale. Reason and cunning have inserted tricks into myths; their forces cease to be invincible. Fairy tales are the traditional stories about victory over these forces, and fairy tales for dialecticians are what Kafka wrote when he went to work on legends. He inserted little tricks into them; then he used them as proof "that inadequate, even childish measures may also serve as a means of rescue." With these words, he begins his story "Das Schweigen der Sirenen" [The Silence of the Sirens]. For Kafka's Sirens are silent; they have "an even more terrible weapon than their song . . . their silence." This they used on Ulysses. But he, so Kafka tells us, "was so full of guile, was such a fox, that not even the goddess of fate could pierce his armor. Perhaps he had really noticed (although here human understanding is out of its depth) that the Sirens were silent, and he opposed the aforementioned pretense to them and the gods merely as a sort of shield."

Kafka's Sirens are silent. Perhaps because for Kafka music and singing are an expression or at least a token of escape, a token of hope which comes to us from that intermediate world—at once unfinished and everyday, comforting and silly—in which assistants are at home. Kafka is like the lad who set out to learn what fear was. He has got into Potemkin's palace and finally, in the depths of its cellar, has encountered Josephine, the singing mouse, whose tune he describes: "Something of our poor, brief childhood is in it, something of lost happiness which can never be found again, but also something of active present-day life, of its small gaieties, unaccountable and yet real and unquenchable" ["Josefine, die Sängerin; oder, Das Volk der Mäuse"].

A Childhood Photograph

There is a childhood photograph of Kafka, a supremely touching portrayal of his "poor, brief childhood." It was probably made in one of those nineteenth-century studios whose draperies and palm trees, tapestries and easels, placed them somewhere between a torture chamber and a throne room. At the age of about six the boy is presented in a sort of greenhouse setting, wearing a tight, heavily lace-trimmed, almost embarrassing child's suit. Palm branches loom in the background. And as if to make these upholstered tropics still more sultry and sticky, the subject holds in his left hand an oversized, wide-brimmed hat of the type worn by Spaniards. Immensely sad eyes dominate the landscape arranged for them, and the auricle of a large ear seems to be listening for its sounds.

The ardent "wish to be a Red Indian" may have consumed this great sadness at some point. "If one were only an Indian, instantly alert, and on a galloping horse, leaning into the wind, kept on quivering briefly over the quivering ground, until one shed one's spurs, for there were no spurs, threw away the reins, for there were no reins, and barely saw the land before one as a smoothly mown plain, with the horse's neck and head already gone." A great deal is contained in this wish. Its fulfillment, which he finds in America, yields up its secret. That *Amerika* is a very special case is indicated by the name of its hero. While in the earlier novels the author never addressed himself otherwise than with a mumbled initial, here, on a new continent, he undergoes a rebirth and acquires a full name. He has this experience in the Nature Theater of Oklahoma.

> On a street corner, Karl saw a poster with the following announcement: "Today, from 6 A.M. until midnight, at Clayton Racetrack, the Oklahoma Theater will be hiring members for its company. The great Theater of Oklahoma calls you! The one and only call is today! If you miss your chance now, you miss it forever! If you think of your future, you belong with us! Everyone is welcome! If you want to be an artist, come forward! Our theater can use everyone and find the right place for everyone! If you decide to join us, we congratulate you here and now! But hurry, so that you get in before midnight! At twelve o'clock the doors will be shut and never opened again! A curse on those who do not believe in us! Set out for Clayton!"

The reader of this announcement is Karl Rossmann, the third and happiest incarnation of K., the hero of Kafka's novels. Happiness awaits him at the Nature Theater of Oklahoma, which is really a racetrack, just as "unhappiness" had once beset him on the narrow rug in his room on which he ran about "as on a racetrack." Ever since Kafka had written his "Nachdenken für Herrenreiter" [Reflections for Gentleman Jockeys]; ever since he had made the "new advocate" mount the courthouse steps, lifting his legs high, with a tread that made the marble ring; ever since he had made his "children on a country road" amble through the countryside with large steps and folded arms—this figure had been familiar to him. Even Karl Rossmann, "distracted by his sleepiness," may often make "leaps that are too high, too time-consuming, and useless." Thus, it can only be a racetrack on which he attains the object of his desire.

This racetrack is at the same time a theater, and this poses a puzzle. But the mysterious place and the entirely unmysterious, transparent, pure figure of Karl Rossmann are congruous. For Karl Rossmann is transparent, pure, without character, as it were, in the same sense in which Franz Rosenzweig says in his *Stern der Erlösung* [Star of Redemption] that in China people are—so far as their spiritual aspects are concerned—"devoid of individual character, as it were. The idea of the wise man, of which Confucius is the classic incarnation, blurs any individuality of character; he is the truly characterless man—namely, the average man . . . What distinguishes a Chinese is something quite different from character: a very elemental purity of feeling."[8] No matter how one conveys it intellectually, this purity of feeling may be a particularly sensitive gauge of gestural behavior. In any case, the Nature Theater of Oklahoma harks back to Chinese theater, which is a theater of gesture. One of the most significant functions of this theater is to dissolve events into their gestural components. One can go even further and say that a good number of Kafka's shorter studies and stories are seen in their full light only when they are, so to speak, put on as acts in the "Nature Theater of Oklahoma." Only then will one come to the certain realization that Kafka's entire work constitutes a code of gestures which surely had no definite symbolic meaning for the author from the outset; rather, the author tried to derive such a meaning from them in ever-changing contexts and experimental groupings. The theater is the logical place for such groupings. In an unpublished commentary on the story "Ein Brudermord" [A Fratricide], Werner Kraft perceptively identified the events in this little story as scenic events. "The play is ready to begin, and it is actually announced by a bell. This comes about in a very natural way. Wese leaves the building in which his office is located. But this doorbell (we are expressly told) is 'too loud for a doorbell; it rings out over the town and up to heaven.'"[9] Just as this bell, which is too loud for a doorbell, rings out toward heaven, the gestures of Kafka's figures are too powerful for our accustomed surroundings and break out into wider areas. The greater Kafka's mastery became, the more frequently he avoided adapting these gestures to common situations or explaining them. "It is strange behavior," we read in "Die Verwandlung" [The Metamorphosis], "to sit on the desk and talk down at the employee, who, furthermore, must come quite close because his boss is hard of hearing." *Der Prozeß* has already left such motivations far behind. In the penultimate chapter, K. stops at the first rows in the cathedral, "but the priest seemed to consider the distance still too great; he stretched out an arm and pointed with his sharply bent forefinger to a spot right in front of the pulpit. K. followed this direction, too; in that spot, he had to bend his head far back to see the priest at all."

Max Brod has said: "The world of those realities that were important for him was unfathomable." What Kafka could fathom least of all was the *gestus*. Each gesture is an event—one might even say a drama—in itself. The stage on which this drama takes place is the World Theater, which opens up toward heaven. On the other hand, this heaven is only background; to explore it according to its own laws would be like framing the painted backdrop of a stage and hanging it in a picture gallery. Like El Greco, Kafka tears open the sky behind every gesture; but as with El Greco—who was the patron saint of the Expressionists—the gesture remains the decisive thing, the center of the event. In "Der Schlag ans Hoftor" [The Knock at the Gate], the people who hear the knock double up with fright. This is how a Chinese actor would portray terror, but no one would give a start. Elsewhere, K. himself does a bit of acting. Without being fully conscious of it, "slowly, . . . with his eyes not looking down but cautiously raised upward, he took one of the papers from the desk, put it on the palm of his hand, and gradually raised it up to the gentlemen while getting up himself. He had nothing definite in mind, but acted only with the feeling that this was what he would have to do once he had completed the big petition which was to exonerate him completely" [*Der Prozeß*]. This animal gesture combines the utmost mysteriousness with the utmost simplicity. You can read Kafka's animal stories for quite a while without realizing that they are not about human beings at all. When you finally come upon the name of the creature—monkey, dog, mole—you look up in fright and realize that you are already far away from the continent of man. But it is always Kafka; he divests human gesture of its traditional supports, and then has a subject for reflection without end.

Strangely enough, these reflections are endless even when their point of departure is one of Kafka's philosophical tales. Take, for example, the parable "Vor dem Gesetz" [Before the Law]. The reader who read it in *Ein Landarzt* [A Country Doctor] may have been struck by the cloudy spot at its interior. But would it have led him to the never-ending series of reflections traceable to this parable at the spot where Kafka undertakes to interpret it? This is done by the priest in *Der Prozeß*, and at such a significant moment that it looks as if the novel were nothing but the unfolding of the parable. The word "unfolding" has a double meaning. A bud unfolds into a blossom, but the boat which one teaches children to make by folding paper unfolds into a flat sheet of paper. This second kind of "unfolding" is really appropriate to parable; the reader takes pleasure in smoothing it out so that he has the meaning on the palm of his hand. Kafka's parables, however, unfold in the first sense, the way a bud turns into a blossom. That is why their effect is literary. This does not mean that his prose pieces belong entirely in the tradition of Western prose forms; they have, rather, a relationship to religious teachings similar to the one Haggadah has to Halachah. They are not parables, yet they do not want to be taken at their face value; they lend themselves to quotation and can be recounted for purposes of clarification. But do we have the teachings which Kafka's parables accompany and which K.'s postures and the gestures of his animals clarify? It does not exist; all we can say is that here and there we have an allusion to it. Kafka might have said that these are relics transmitting the teachings, although we could just as well regard them as precursors preparing the teachings. In every case, it is a question of how life and work are organized in human society. This question increasingly occupied Kafka, even as it became impenetrable to him. If Napoleon, in his famous conversation with Goethe at Erfurt, substituted politics for fate, Kafka, in a variation of this dictum, could have defined organization as destiny. He faces it not only in the extensive hierarchy of officialdom in *Der Prozeß* and *Das Schloß*, but even more concretely in the difficult and incalculable construction plans whose venerable model he dealt with in "Beim Bau der Chinesischen Mauer" [The Great Wall of China].

> The wall was to be a protection for centuries; accordingly, the most scrupulous care in the construction, the application of the architectural wisdom of all known ages and peoples, and a constant sense of personal responsibility on the part of the builders were indispensable prerequisites for the work. To be sure, for the menial tasks, ignorant day laborers from the populace—men, women, and children, whoever offered his services for good money—could be used. But for the supervision of every four day laborers, a man trained in the building trade was required . . . We—and here I speak in the name of many people—did not really know ourselves until we had carefully scrutinized the decrees of the high command; then we discovered that, without this leadership, neither our book learning nor our common sense would have sufficed for the humble tasks which we performed in the great whole.

This organization resembles fate. Metchnikoff, who has outlined this in his famous book *La civilisation et les grands fleuves historiques* [Civilization and the Great Historical Rivers], uses language that could be Kafka's:

> The canals of the Yangtze and the dams of the Yellow River are in all likelihood the result of the skillfully organized joint labor of . . . generations. The slightest carelessness in the digging of a ditch or the buttressing of a dam, the least bit of negligence or selfish behavior on the part of an individual or a group in the maintenance of the common hydraulic wealth becomes, under such unusual circumstances, the source of social evils and far-reaching social calamity. Consequently, a life-giving river requires on pain of death a close and permanent solidarity among groups of people that frequently are alien or even hostile to one another; it sentences everyone to labors whose common usefulness is

revealed only by time and whose design quite often remains utterly incomprehensible to an ordinary man.[10]

Kafka wished to be numbered among ordinary men. He was pushed to the limits of understanding at every turn, and he liked to push others to them as well. At times he seems to come close to saying, with Dostoevsky's Grand Inquisitor: "So we have before us a mystery which we cannot comprehend. And precisely because it is a mystery we have had the right to preach it, to teach the people that what matters is neither freedom nor love, but the riddle, the secret, the mystery to which they have to bow—without reflection and even against their conscience." Kafka did not always evade the temptations of a modish mysticism. There is a diary entry concerning his encounter with Rudolf Steiner;[11] in its published form, at least, it does not reflect Kafka's attitude toward him. Did Kafka avoid taking a stand? His way with his own writings certainly does not exclude this possibility. Kafka had a rare capacity for creating parables for himself. Yet his parables are never exhausted by what is explainable; on the contrary, he took all conceivable precautions against the interpretation of his writings. One has to find one's way in them circumspectly, cautiously, and warily. One must keep in mind Kafka's way of reading, as exemplified in his interpretation of the above-mentioned parable. The text of his will is another case in point. Given its background, the directive in which Kafka ordered the destruction of his literary remains is just as unfathomable, to be weighed just as carefully as the answers of the doorkeeper in "Vor dem Gesetz." Perhaps Kafka, whose every day on earth brought him up against insoluble modes of behavior and imprecise communications, in death wished to give his contemporaries a taste of their own medicine.

Kafka's world is a world theater. For him, man is on stage from the very beginning. The proof is the fact that everyone is hired by the Nature Theater of Oklahoma. What the standards for admission are cannot be determined. Dramatic talent, the most obvious criterion, seems to be of no importance. But this can be expressed in another way: all that is expected of the applicants is the ability to play themselves. It is no longer within the realm of possibility that they could, if necessary, be what they claim to be. With their roles, these people look for a position in the Nature Theater the way Pirandello's six characters seek an author. For all of them this place is the last refuge, which does not preclude it from being their salvation. Salvation is not a premium on existence, but the last way out for a man whose path, as Kafka puts it in "Er" [He], is "blocked . . . by his own frontal bone." The law of this theater is contained in a sentence tucked away in "Ein Bericht für eine Akademie" [A Report to an Academy]: "I imitated people because I was looking for a way out, and for no other reason." Before the end of his trial, K. seems to have an intimation of these things. He suddenly turns to the two gentlemen wearing top hats who have come for him and asks them: "'What theater are you playing at?' 'Theater?' asked one, the corners of his mouth twitching as he looked for advice to the other, who acted as if he were a mute struggling to overcome a stubborn disability." The men do not answer this question, but there is much to indicate that it has hit home.

At a long bench which has been covered with a white cloth, all those who will henceforth be with the Nature Theater are fed. "They were all happy and excited." By way of celebration, extras act as angels. They stand on high pedestals that are covered with flowing drapery and have stairs inside— the makings of a country church fair, or perhaps a children's festival, which may have eliminated the sadness from the eyes of the tightly laced, dressed-up boy we discussed above.—But for the fact that their wings are tied on, these angels might be real. They have forerunners in Kafka's works. One of them is the impresario who climbs up on the luggage rack next to the trapeze artist beset by his "first sorrow," caresses him, and presses his face against his, "so that he was bathed by the trapeze artist's tears" ["Erstes Leid"]. Another, a guardian angel or guardian of the law, takes care of Schmar the murderer following the "fratricide" and leads him away, stepping lightly, with Schmar's "mouth pressed against the policeman's shoulder" ["Ein Brudermord"].—Kafka's *Amerika* ends with the rustic ceremonies of Oklahoma. "In Kafka," said Soma Morgenstern, "there is the air of a village, as with all great founders of religions."[12] Lao-tze's presentation of piousness is all the more pertinent here because Kafka has supplied its most perfect description in "Das nächste Dorf" [The Next Village].[13] "Neighboring countries may be within sight, so that the sounds of roosters and dogs may be heard in the distance. Yet people are said to die at a ripe old age without having traveled far." Thus Lao-tze. Kafka was also a writer of parables, but he did not found a religion.

Let us consider the village at the foot of Castle Hill, whence K.'s alleged employment as a land surveyor is so mysteriously and unexpectedly confirmed. In his postscript to *Das Schloß*, Brod mentioned that in depicting this village at the foot of Castle Hill, Kafka had in mind a specific place: Zürau in the Erzgebirge.[14] We may, however, also recognize another village in it. It is the village in a Talmudic legend told by a rabbi in answer to the question why Jews prepare a festive evening meal on Fridays. The legend is about a princess languishing in exile, in a village whose language she does not understand, far from her compatriots. One day this princess receives a letter saying that her fiancé has not forgotten her and is on his way to her. —The fiancé, so says the rabbi, is the Messiah; the princess is the soul; the village in which she lives in exile is the body. She prepares a meal for him because this is the only way in which she can express her joy in a village whose language she does not know. —This village of the Talmud is right in

Kafka's world. For just as K. lives in the village on Castle Hill, modern man lives in his own body: the body slips away from him, is hostile toward him. It may happen that a man wakes up one day and finds himself transformed into vermin. Strangeness—his own strangeness—has gained control over him. The air of this village blows about Kafka, and that is why he was not tempted to found a religion. The pigsty which houses the country doctor's horses; the stuffy back room in which Klamm, a cigar in his mouth, sits over a glass of beer; the manor gate which brings ruin to anyone who knocks on it—all these are part of this village. The air in this village is permeated with all the abortive and overripe elements that form such a putrid mixture. This is the air that Kafka had to breathe throughout his life. He was neither mantic nor the founder of a religion. How was he able to survive in this air?

The Little Hunchback

Some time ago it became known that Knut Hamsun was in the habit of expressing his views in an occasional letter to the editor of the local paper in the small town near which he lived.[15] Years ago, that town was the scene of the jury trial of a young woman who had killed her infant child. She was sentenced to prison. Soon thereafter the local paper printed a letter from Hamsun in which he announced his intention of leaving a town which did not impose the supreme punishment on a mother who killed her newborn child—the gallows, or at least a life term of hard labor. A few years passed. *Growth of the Soil* appeared, and it contained the story of a young woman who committed the same crime, suffered the same punishment, and, as is made clear to the reader, surely deserved no more severe one.

Kafka's posthumous reflections, which are contained in *Beim Bau der Chinesischen Mauer*, recall this episode to mind. Hardly had this volume appeared when the reflections served as the basis for a body of Kafka criticism which concentrated on an interpretation of these reflections to the neglect of his actual works. There are two ways to miss the point of Kafka's works. One is to interpret them naturally; the other is to interpret them from a supernatural perspective. Both the psychoanalytic and the theological interpretations miss the essential points. The first kind is represented by Hellmuth Kaiser; the second, by numerous writers, such as H. J. Schoeps, Bernhard Rang, and Bernhard Groethuysen.[16] To these last also belongs Willy Haas, although he has made revealing comments on Kafka in other contexts which we shall discuss later; such insights have not prevented him from interpreting Kafka's work after a theological pattern. "The powers above, the realm of grace," Haas writes, "Kafka has depicted in his great novel *Das Schloß;* the powers below, the realm of the courts and of dam-

nation, he has dealt with in his equally great novel *Der Prozeß*. The earth
between the two, earthly fate and its arduous demands, he attempted to
present in strictly stylized form in a third novel, *Amerika*."[17] The first third
of this interpretation has, since Brod, become a commonplace of Kafka
criticism. Bernhard Rang writes in a similar vein: "To the extent that one
may regard the Castle as the seat of grace, precisely these vain efforts and
attempts mean, theologically speaking, that God's grace cannot be attained
or forced by man willfully and deliberately. Unrest and impatience only
impede and confound the exalted stillness of the divine."[18] This interpretation is a convenient one; but the further it is carried, the more we realize
that it is untenable. This is perhaps seen most clearly in a statement by Willy
Haas. "Kafka goes back . . . to Kierkegaard as well as to Pascal; one may
call him the only legitimate heir of these two. In all three, there is an
excruciatingly harsh basic religious theme: man is always in the wrong
before God . . . Kafka's upper world, his so-called Castle, with its immense,
complex staff of petty and rather lecherous officials, his strange heaven,
plays a horrible game with people . . . yet man is very much in the wrong
even before this god."[19] This theology, lagging far behind the doctrine of
justification formulated by Saint Anselm of Canterbury, falls into barbaric
speculations which do not even seem consistent with the text of Kafka's
works.[20] "Can an individual official forgive?" we read in *Das Schloß*. "This
could be a matter only for the supreme authorities, but even they can
probably not forgive but only judge." This road soon leads into a blind
alley. "All this," says Denis de Rougemont, "is not the wretched situation
of man without a god, but the wretched state of a man who is bound to a
god he does not know, because he does not know Christ."[21]

It is easier to draw speculative conclusions from Kafka's posthumous
collection of notes than to explore even one of the motifs that appear in his
stories and novels. Yet only these give some clue to the prehistoric forces
that dominated Kafka's creativeness—forces which, to be sure, may
justifiably be regarded as belonging to our world as well. Who can say under
what names they appeared to Kafka himself? Only this much is certain: he
did not know them and failed to get his bearings among them. In the mirror
which the prehistoric world held up to him in the form of guilt, he merely
saw the future emerging in the form of judgment. Kafka, however, did not
say what it was like. Wasn't it the Last Judgment? Doesn't it turn the judge
into the defendant? Isn't the trial the punishment? Kafka gave no answer.
Did he expect anything of this punishment? Or wasn't he, rather, concerned
to postpone it? In the stories which Kafka left us, narrative art regains the
significance it had in the mouth of Scheherazade: its ability to postpone the
future. In *Der Prozeß*, postponement is the hope of the accused man only
if the proceedings do not gradually turn into the judgment. The patriarch

Abraham himself could benefit by postponement, even though he may have to trade his place in tradition for it.

> I could conceive of another Abraham (to be sure, he would never get to be a patriarch or even an old-clothes dealer), an Abraham who would be prepared to satisfy the demand for a sacrifice immediately, with the promptness of a waiter, but would be unable to bring it off, because he cannot get away, being indispensable; the household needs him, there is always something or other to take care of, the house is never ready. But without having his house ready, without having something to fall back on, he cannot leave—this the Bible also realized, for it says: "He set his house in order."[22]

This Abraham appears "with the promptness of a waiter." Kafka could understand things only in the form of a *gestus,* and this *gestus* which he did not understand constitutes the cloudy part of the parables. Kafka's writings emanate from it. The way he withheld them is well known. His will orders their destruction. This document, which no one interested in Kafka can disregard, says that the writings did not satisfy their author, that he regarded his efforts as failures, that he counted himself among those who were bound to fail. He did fail in his grandiose attempt to convert poetry into teachings, to turn it into a parable and restore to it that stability and unpretentiousness which, in the face of reason, seemed to him the only appropriate thing for it. No other writer has obeyed the commandment "Thou shalt not make unto thee a graven image" so faithfully.

"It was as if the shame of it were to outlive him." With these words *Der Prozeß* ends. Shame—corresponding as it does to his "elemental purity of feeling"[23]—is Kafka's strongest gesture. It has a dual aspect, however. Shame is an intimate human reaction, but at the same time it has social claims. Shame is not only shame in the presence of others, but can also be shame one feels *for* others. Kafka's shame, then, is no more personal than the life and thought which govern it and which he has described thus: "He does not live for the sake of his own life; he does not think for the sake of his own thought. He feels as though he were living and thinking under the constraint of a family . . . Because of this unknown family, . . . he cannot be released" ["Er"]. We do not know the makeup of this unknown family, which is composed of human beings and animals. But this much is clear: it is this family that forces Kafka to move cosmic ages in his writings. Doing this family's bidding, he moves the mass of historical happenings the way Sisyphus rolled the stone. As he does so, its nether side comes to light; it is not a pleasant sight, but Kafka is capable of bearing it. "To believe in progress is not to believe that progress has already taken place. That would be no belief."[24] Kafka did not consider the age in which he lived as an advance over the beginnings of time. His novels are set in a swamp world. In his works, the creature appears at the stage which Bachofen has termed the hetaeric stage.[25] The fact that this stage is now forgotten does not mean that it does not extend into the present. On the contrary: it is present by virtue of this very oblivion. An experience deeper than that of the average person can make contact with it. "I have experience [*Erfahrung*]," we read in one of Kafka's earliest notes, "and I am not joking when I say that it is a seasickness on dry land."[26] It is no accident that the first "Meditation" ["Kinder auf der Landstrasse"] was conceived on a swing. And Kafka does not tire of expressing himself on the fluctuating nature of experiences. Each gives way and mingles with its opposite. "It was summer, a hot day": so begins "Der Schlag ans Hoftor." "Walking home with my sister, I was passing the gate of a great house. I don't remember whether she knocked on the gate out of mischief or in a fit of absentmindedness, or merely shook her fist at it and did not knock at all." The very possibility of the third alternative puts the other two, which at first seemed harmless, in a different light. It is from the swampy soil of such experiences that Kafka's female characters rise. They are swamp creatures—like Leni, "who stretches out the middle and ring fingers of her right hand, between which the connecting web of skin reached almost to the top joint, short as the fingers were" [*Der Prozeß*]. "Fine times," the ambiguous Frieda reminisces about her earlier life; "You never asked me about my past" [*Das Schloß*]. This past takes us back to the dark, deep womb, the scene of the mating "whose untrammeled voluptuousness," to quote Bachofen, "is hateful to the pure forces of heavenly light and which justifies the term used by Arnobius, *luteae voluptates* [dirty voluptuousness]."[27]

Only from this vantage point can the technique of Kafka the storyteller be comprehended. Whenever figures in the novels have anything to say to K., no matter how important or surprising it may be, they do so casually and with the implication that he must really have known it all along. It is as though nothing new were being imparted, as though the hero were just being subtly invited to recall to mind something he had forgotten. This is how Willy Haas has interpreted the course of events in *Der Prozeß*, and justifiably so: "The object of the trial—indeed, the real hero of this incredible book—is forgetting, whose main characteristic is the forgetting of itself . . . Here it has actually become a mute figure in the shape of the accused man, a figure of the most striking intensity." It probably cannot be denied that "this mysterious center . . . derives from the Jewish religion." "Memory plays a very mysterious role as piousness. It is not an ordinary quality but . . . the most profound quality of Jehovah that He remembers, that He retains, an infallible memory 'to the third and fourth, even to the hundredth, generation.' The most sacred . . . act of the . . . ritual is the erasing of sins from the book of memory."[28]

What has been forgotten—and with this insight we stand before another threshold of Kafka's work—is never something purely individual. Everything forgotten mingles with what has been forgotten of the prehistoric world, forms countless uncertain and changing compounds, yielding a constant flow of new, strange products. Oblivion is the container from which the inexhaustible intermediate world in Kafka's stories presses toward the light. "Here the very fullness of the world is considered the only reality. All spirit must be concrete, particularized, in order to have its place and *raison d'être*. The spiritual, if it plays a role at all, turns into spirits. These spirits become definite individuals, with names and a very special connection with the name of the worshiper . . . Unhesitatingly, the fullness of the world is filled to overflowing with their fullness . . . Unconcernedly, the crowd of spirits is swelled . . . New ones are constantly added to the old ones, and each is distinguished from the others by its own name." All this refers not to Kafka, but to—China. This is how Franz Rosenzweig describes the Chinese ancestor cult in his book *Der Stern der Erlösung*.[29] To Kafka, the world of his ancestors was as unfathomable as the world of realities was important, and we may be sure that, like the totem poles of primitive peoples, the world of ancestors took him down to the animals. Incidentally, Kafka is not the only writer for whom animals are the receptacles of the forgotten. In Tieck's profound story *Der blonde Eckbert* [Fair Eckbert],[30] the forgotten name of a little dog, Strohmi, stands for a mysterious guilt. One can understand, then, why Kafka never tired of hearing about the forgotten from animals. They are not the goal, to be sure, but one cannot do without them. A case in point is the hunger artist, who, "strictly speaking, was only an impediment on the way to the menagerie" ["Ein Hungerkünstler"]. Can't one see the animal in *Der Bau* [The Burrow] or the giant mole ["Der Riesenmaulwurf"] ponder as they dig in? Yet this thinking is extremely flighty. Irresolutely, it flits from one worry to the next; it nibbles at every anxiety with the fickleness of despair. Thus, there are butterflies in Kafka, too. The guilt-ridden hunter Gracchus, who refuses to acknowledge his guilt, "has turned into a butterfly" ["Der Jäger Gracchus"]. "Don't laugh," says the hunter Gracchus. This much is certain: of all of Kafka's creatures, the animals have the greatest opportunity for reflection. What corruption is in the law, anxiety is in their thinking. It messes a situation up, yet it is the only hopeful thing about it. But because the most forgotten source of strangeness is our body—one's own body—one can understand why Kafka called the cough that erupted from within him "the animal." It was the vanguard of the great herd.

In Kafka's work, the most singular bastard which the prehistoric world has begotten with guilt is Odradek ["Die Sorge des Hausvaters"]. "At first sight it looks like a flat, star-shaped spool for thread, and it really seems to have thread wound around it; to be sure, this is probably just old, broken-off bits of thread that are knotted and tangled together, of all sorts and colors. But the object is not just a spool, for a small wooden crossbar sticks out of the middle of the star, and another small rod is joined to it at right angles. With the aid of this latter rod on one side and one of the extensions of the star on the other, the whole thing can stand upright as if on two legs." Odradek "stays alternately in the attic, on the staircase, in the corridors, and in the hall." So it prefers the same places as the court of law which investigates guilt. Attics are the places of discarded, forgotten objects. Perhaps having to appear before a court of justice gives rise to a feeling similar to that with which one approaches trunks in the attic which have been locked up for years. One would like to put off this chore till the end of time, just as K. regards his written defense as suitable "for occupying one's senile mind someday during retirement."

Odradek is the form which things assume in oblivion. They are distorted. The "cares of a family man," which no one can identify, are distorted; the bug, which we know all too well represents Gregor Samsa, is distorted; the big animal, half-lamb, half-kitten, for which "the butcher's knife" might be "a release," is distorted. These Kafka figures are connected by a long series of figures with the prototype of distortion: a hunched back. Among the images in Kafka's stories, none is more frequent than that of the man who bows his head far down on his chest: the fatigue of the court officials, the noise affecting the doormen in the hotel, the low ceiling facing the visitors in the gallery. In the penal colony, those in power use an archaic apparatus which engraves letters with curlicues on the back of every guilty man, multiplying the stabs and piling up the ornaments to the point where the back of the guilty man becomes clairvoyant and is able to decipher the script from which he must derive the nature of his unknown guilt. It is the back on which this is incumbent. It was always this way with Kafka. Compare this early diary entry: "In order to make myself as heavy as possible, which I believe is an aid to falling asleep, I had crossed my arms and put my hands on my shoulders, so that I lay there like a soldier with his pack."[31] Quite palpably, being loaded down is here equated with forgetting—the forgetting of a sleeping man. The same symbol occurs in the folksong "The Little Hunchback." This little man is at home in distorted life; he will disappear with the coming of the Messiah, who (a great rabbi once said) will not wish to change the world by force but will merely make a slight adjustment in it.

When I come into my room,
My little bed to make,
A little hunchback is in there,
With laughter he does shake.

This is the laughter of Odradek, which is described as sounding "something like the rustling of falling leaves."

When I kneel upon my stool
And I want to pray,
A hunchbacked man is in the room
And he starts to say:
My dear child, I beg of you,
Pray for the little hunchback too.[32]

So ends the folksong. In his depths, Kafka touches ground which neither "mythical divination" nor "existential theology" supplied him with. It is the ground of folk tradition, German as well as Jewish. Even if Kafka did not pray—and this we do not know—he still possessed in the highest degree what Malebranche called "the natural prayer of the soul": attentiveness.[33] And in this attentiveness he included all creatures, as saints include them in their prayers.

Sancho Panza

In a Hasidic village, so the story goes, Jews were sitting together in a shabby inn one Sabbath evening. They were all local people, with the exception of one person no one knew, a very poor, ragged man who was squatting in a dark corner at the back of the room. All sorts of things were discussed, and then it was suggested that everyone should tell what wish he would make if one were granted him. One man wanted money; another wished for a son-in-law; a third dreamed of a new carpenter's bench; and so each spoke in turn. After they had finished, only the beggar in his dark corner was left. Reluctantly and hesitantly he answered the question. "I wish I were a powerful king reigning over a big country. Then, some night while I was asleep in my palace, an enemy would invade my country, and by dawn his horsemen would penetrate to my castle and meet with no resistance. Roused from my sleep, I wouldn't have time even to dress and I would have to flee in my shirt. Rushing over hill and dale and through forests day and night, I would finally arrive safely right here at the bench in this corner. This is my wish." The others exchanged uncomprehending glances. "And what good would this wish have done you?" someone asked. "I'd have a shirt," was the answer.[34]

This story takes us deep into the household that is Kafka's world. No one says that the distortions which it will be the Messiah's mission to set right someday affect only our space; surely they are distortions of our time as well. Kafka must certainly have thought this. And in this certainty he made the grandfather in "Das nächste Dorf" say: "Life is astonishingly short. As I look back over it, life seems so foreshortened to me that I can hardly understand, for instance, how a young man can decide to ride over to the next village without being afraid that, quite apart from accidents, even the span of a normal life that passes happily may be totally insufficient for such a ride." This old man's brother is the above-mentioned beggar, whose "normal" life that "passes happily" does not even leave him time for a wish, but who is exempted from this wish in an abnormal, unhappy life (that is, the flight which he attempts in his story) and who exchanges the wish for its fulfillment.

Among Kafka's creations, there is a clan which reckons with the brevity of life in a peculiar way. It comes from the "city in the south . . . of which it was said: 'People live there who—imagine!—don't sleep!' 'And why not?' 'Because they don't get tired.' 'Why don't they?' 'Because they are fools.' 'Don't fools get tired?' 'How could fools get tired?'" ["Kinder auf der Landstrasse"]. One can see that the fools are akin to the indefatigable assistants. But there is more to this clan. It is casually remarked of the assistants' faces that they seem to be those of "grown-ups, perhaps even students" [*Das Schloß*]. Actually, the students who appear in the strangest places in Kafka's works are the spokesmen for and leaders of this clan. "'But when do you sleep?' asked Karl, looking at the student in surprise. 'Oh, sleep!' said the student. 'I'll get some sleep when I'm finished with my studies.'" This reminds one of the reluctance with which children go to bed; after all, while they are asleep, something might happen that concerns them. "Don't forget the best!" We are familiar with this remark "from a nebulous bunch of old stories, although it may not occur in any of them."[35] But forgetting always involves the best, for it involves the possibility of redemption. "The idea of helping me is an illness and requires bed rest for a cure," ironically says the restlessly wandering ghost of the hunter Gracchus.— While they study, the students are awake, and perhaps their being kept awake is the best thing about their studies. The hunger artist fasts, the doorkeeper is silent, and the students are awake. This is the veiled way in which the great rules of asceticism operate in Kafka.

The crowning achievement of asceticism is study. Reverently Kafka unearths it from long-lost boyhood. "In a way not very different from this—a long time ago—Karl had sat at home at his parents' table doing his homework, while his father read the newspaper or did bookkeeping and correspondence for some organization and his mother was busy sewing, drawing the thread high out of the fabric in her hand. To avoid disturbing his father, Karl would put only his exercise book and his writing materials on the table, while he arranged the books he needed on chairs to the right and left of him. How quiet it had been there! How seldom strangers had entered that room!" [*Amerika*]. Perhaps these studies had amounted to nothing. But they are very close to that nothing which alone makes it possible for a something to be useful—that is, they are very close to the Tao. This is what Kafka was after with his desire "to hammer a table together with painstaking craftsmanship and, at the same time, to do nothing—not in such a way that someone could say 'Hammering is nothing to him,' but 'To him, hammering is real hammering and at the same time nothing,' which would have made the hammering even bolder, more determined, more real, and, if you like, more insane" ["Er"]. This is the resolute, fanatical mien which students have when they study; it is the strangest mien imaginable. The scribes, the students, are out of breath; they fairly race along. "Often the official dictates in such a low voice that the scribe cannot even hear it sitting down; he has to jump up, catch the dictated words, quickly sit again and write them down, then jump up again, and so forth. How strange that is! It is almost incomprehensible!" [Das Schloß]. It may be easier to understand this if one thinks of the actors in the Nature Theater. Actors have to catch their cues in a flash, and they resemble those assiduous students in other ways as well. Truly, for them "hammering is real hammering and at the same time nothing"—provided that this is part of their role. They study this role, and only a bad actor would forget a word or a gesture from it. For the members of the Oklahoma troupe, however, the role is their earlier life; hence the "nature" in this Nature Theater. Its actors have been redeemed. But this is not true of the student whom Karl watches silently at night on the balcony as the student reads his book, "turning the pages, occasionally looking something up in another book which he always snatched up quick as a flash, and frequently making notes in a notebook, which he always did with his face surprisingly close to the paper."

Kafka does not grow tired of making the *gestus* present in this fashion, but he invariably does so with astonishment. K. has rightly been compared with the Good Soldier Schweik: the one is astonished at everything; the other, at nothing.[36] The invention of motion pictures and the phonograph came in an age of maximum alienation of men from one another, of unpredictably intervening relationships which have become their only ones. Experiments have proved that a man does not recognize his own gait on film or his own voice on the phonograph. The situation of the subject in such experiments is Kafka's situation; this is what leads him to study, where he may encounter fragments of his own existence—fragments that are still within the context of the role. He might catch hold of the lost *gestus* the way Peter Schlemihl caught hold of the shadow he had sold.[37] He might understand himself, but what an enormous effort would be required! It is a tempest that blows from forgetting, and study is a cavalry attack against it. Thus, the beggar on the corner bench rides toward his past in order to catch hold of himself in the figure of the fleeing king. This ride, which is long enough for a life, corresponds to life, which is too short for a ride— "until one shed one's spurs (for there were no spurs), threw away the reins (for there were no reins), and barely saw the land before one as a smoothly mown plain, with the horse's neck and head already gone." This is the fulfillment of the fantasy about the blessed horseman who rushes toward the past on an untrammeled, happy journey, no longer a burden on his galloping horse. But accursed is the rider who is chained to his nag because he has set himself a future goal, even though it is as close as the coal cellar—accursed is his animal, accursed are both of them: bucket and rider. "Seated on the bucket, my hands up on the handle, with the simplest kind of bridle, I propel myself with difficulty down the stairs. But once I am down below, my bucket ascends, superbly, superbly; camels lying flat on the ground do not rise any more handsomely as they shake themselves under the sticks of their drivers" ["Der Kübelreiter"]. There is no more hopeless vista than that of "the regions of ice mountains" in which the bucket rider drops out of sight forever. From the "nethermost regions of death" blows the wind that is favorable to him—the same wind which so often blows from the prehistoric world in Kafka's works, and which also propels the boat of the hunter Gracchus. "At mysteries and sacrifices, among Greeks as well as barbarians," writes Plutarch, "it is taught that there must be two primary essences and two opposing forces, one of which points to the right and straight ahead, whereas the other turns around and drives back."[38] Reversal is the direction of study which transforms existence into script. Its teacher is Bucephalus, "the new advocate," who takes the road back without the powerful Alexander—which means, rid of the onrushing conqueror. "His flanks free and unhampered by the thighs of a rider, under a quiet lamp far from the din of Alexander's battles, he reads and turns the pages of our old books."—Werner Kraft once wrote an interpretation of this story. After giving careful attention to every detail of the text, Kraft notes: "No-where else in literature is there such a powerful and penetrating criticism of myth in its full scope."[39] According to Kraft, Kafka does not use the word "justice," yet it is justice which serves as the point of departure for his critique of myth.—But once we have reached this point, we are in danger of missing Kafka by stopping here. Is it really the law which could thus be invoked against myth in the name of justice? No, as a legal scholar Bucephalus remains true to his origins, except that he does not seem to be practicing law—and this is probably something new, in Kafka's sense, for both Bucephalus and the bar. The law which is studied but no longer practiced is the gate to justice.

The gate to justice is study. Yet Kafka doesn't dare attach to this study the promises which tradition has attached to the study of the Torah. His assistants are sextons who have lost their house of prayer; his students are pupils who have lost the Holy Writ [Schrift]. Now there is nothing to support them on their "untrammeled, happy journey."[40] Kafka, however, has found the law of his journey: on at least one occasion, he succeeded in bringing its breathtaking speed in line with the slow narrative pace that he presumably sought all his life. He expressed this in a little prose piece which is his most perfect creation—and not only because it is an interpretation.

Without ever boasting of it, Sancho Panza succeeded over the years, by sup-plying a lot of romances of chivalry and adventure for the evening and night hours, in so diverting from him his demon, whom he later called Don Quixote, that his demon thereupon freely performed the maddest exploits—which, however, lacking a preordained object, which Sancho Panza himself was supposed to have been, did no one any harm. A free man, Sancho Panza philosophically followed Don Quixote on his crusades, perhaps out of a sense of responsibility, and thus enjoyed great and profitable entertainment to the end of his days." ["Die Wahrheit über Sancho Pansa"]

Sancho Panza, a sedate fool and a clumsy assistant, sent his rider on ahead; Bucephalus outlived his. Whether it is a man or a horse is no longer so important, if only the burden is taken off the back.

Published in *Jüdische Rundschau*, December 1934. *Gesammelte Schriften*, II, 409–438. Translated by Harry Zohn.

Notes

1. Grigori Potemkin (1739–1791) was a Russian soldier and statesman who became the chief favorite of Catherine II. The immediate source of Benjamin's story is Aleksandr Pushkin, *Anecdotes and Tabletalk,* no. 24.
2. Kafka, *Beim Bau der Chinesischen Mauer* (Berlin: Kiepenheuer, 1931), p. 231: "Betrachtungen über Sünde, Leid, Hoffnung und den wahren Weg" (Observations on Sin, Suffering, Hope and the True Way), aphorism 34. See also Benjamin's essay "Franz Kafka: *Beim Bau der Chinesischen Mauer,* in this volume. The Castellan and Klamm are officials in the castle in Kafka's novel *Das Schloß* (The Castle).
3. Cited in Ernst Bloch, *Geist der Utopie* (Munich: Duncker und Humblot, 1918), p. 22.
4. Hermann Cohen, *Ethik des reinen Willens* (Berlin: Cassirer, 1907), p. 362. Cohen (1842–1918) did important work that combined philosophy (he was the cofounder of the Marburg school of neo-Kantianism and published books on ethics, epistemology, and aesthetics) and Jewish theology. His work figures prominently in Benjamin's essay "Goethe's Elective Affinities" (see Volume 1 of this edition).
5. Max Brod, "Der Dichter Franz Kafka," *Die neue Rundschau* 11 (1921): 1213. Brod (1884–1968) was a Czech-born, German-language novelist and essayist known primarily as Kafka's friend and as the editor of his major works, most of which were first published after Kafka's death. Brod had a major influence on the first wave of Kafka interpretations, many of which were religiously oriented.
6. For the Cat Lamb, Odradek, and Gregor Samsa, see the stories "Eine Kreuzung" (A Crossbreed), "Die Sorge des Hausvaters" (The Cares of a Family Man), and "Die Verwandlung" (The Metamorphosis), respectively.
7. Robert Walser (1878–1956), Swiss prose writer, was much cherished by Benjamin (as well as by Kafka and Robert Musil) for his literary miniatures, which mix keen observation of detail with wit, irony, and a sense of paradox.
8. Franz Rosenzweig, *Der Stern der Erlösung* (Frankfurt: J. Kauffmann, 1921), p. 96: Part 1, Book 3. Rosenzweig (1886–1929) was a German-Jewish religious

Existentialist who, through his fresh handling of traditional religious themes, became one of the most influential modern Jewish theologians. While on active service in World War I, he began his magnum opus, *Der Stern der Erlösung* (The Star of Redemption; 1921). From 1922 he was afflicted with progressive paralysis but continued work on numerous projects, including a new German translation of the Hebrew Bible in collaboration with Martin Buber.

9. Werner Kraft, *Franz Kafka: Durchdringung und Geheimnis* (Frankfurt: Suhrkamp, 1968), p. 24. Kraft (1896–1991), German essayist, poet, and novelist, was a friend of Benjamin's. He emigrated to Palestine in 1933.

10. Léon Metchnikoff, *La civilisation et les grands fleuves historiques* (Paris: Hachette, 1889), p. 189.

11. See Kafka, *Tagebücher, 1910–1923* (New York: Schocken, 1951), pp. 54–58: entry for March 26, 1911. Rudolf Steiner (1861–1925) was an Austrian-born scientist and editor, and the founder of anthroposophy, a movement based on the notion that there is a spiritual world comprehensible to pure thought but accessible only to the highest faculties of mental knowledge. Steiner's ideas exerted a remarkable influence on educational philosophy in the early years of the twentieth century.

12. Conversation with Benjamin (ms. 334 in the Benjamin archive).

13. Lao-tze (fl. sixth century B.C.) was the first philosopher of Chinese Taoism and the alleged author of the Tao-te Ching. Modern scholars discount the possibility that the text was written by one person but acknowledge the influence of Taoism on the development of Buddhism.

14. Brod's remark is not in the postscript to *Das Schloß*, but was recorded by Willy Haas in *Gestalten der Zeit* (Berlin: Kiepenheuer, 1930), pp. 183ff.

15. Knut Hamsun (pseudonym of Knut Pedersen; 1859–1952) was a Norwegian writer. *Growth of the Soil* appeared in 1917.

16. Hans Joachim Schoeps (1901–1980) was a German historian who published widely on Jewish religious history. Bernhard Groethuysen (1880–1946), German cultural historian, was a student of Wilhelm Dilthey and applied Dilthey's method of "intellectual history" to studies of the intellectual development of the European bourgoisie.

17. Haas, *Gestalten der Zeit*, p. 175. Willy Haas (1891–1973), German critic and essayist, founded (along with Ernst Rowohlt) the weekly journal *Die literarische Welt*, which he edited until 1933 and in which he published numerous pieces by his friend Benjamin.

18. Bernhard Rang, "Franz Kafka," *Die Schildgenossen* (Augsburg) 12, nos. 2–3 (1932).

19. Haas, *Gestalten der Zeit*, p. 176.

20. Saint Anselm of Canterbury (1033/34–1109) was the founder of Scholasticism, the school of thought that dominated the Middle Ages. Anselm first proposed the ontological argument for the existence of God. His satisfaction theory of redemption was based on the feudal notion of making satisfaction or recompense according to the status of the person against whom the offense had been committed. According to Anselm's notion, God was the offended party and man the offender.

21. Denis de Rougemont, "*Le Procès*, par Franz Kafka," *Nouvelle Revue Française* 22 (May 1934): 869.

22. Kafka, *Briefe, 1902–1924* (New York: Fischer, 1958), p. 333: letter of June 1921 to Robert Klopstock.

23. Rosenzweig, *Der Stern der Erlösung,* p. 96.

24. Kafka, *Beim Bau der Chinesischen Mauer,* p. 234: "Betrachtungen," aphorism 48.

25. Johann Jakob Bachofen (1815–1887) was a Swiss anthropologist and jurist, best-known as the author of *Das Mutterrecht* (1861) and *Urreligion und antike Symbole* (1861). See Benjamin's review of Bernoulli's book on Bachofen, in Volume 1 of this edition.

26. Kafka, in *Hyperion* 2, no. 1 (1909).

27. Bachofen, *Urreligion und antike Symbole* (Leipzig: Reclam, 1926), vol. 1, p. 386. Arnobius (fl. A.D. 300) was an early Christian apologist.

28. Haas, *Gestalten der Zeit,* pp. 195, 196–197.

29. Rosenzweig, *Der Stern der Erlösung,* pp. 76–77: Part 1, Book 2.

30. Ludwig Tieck (1773–1853) was a German Romantic writer, critic, and translator. His novella *Der blonde Eckbert* appeared in 1797.

31. Kafka, *Tagebücher, 1910–1923,* p. 76: entry for October 3, 1911.

32. *Des Knaben Wunderhorn: Alte deutsche Lieder* (1808; rpt. Meersburg, 1928), p. 297: "Das buckliche Männlein."

33. Nicolas de Malebranche (1638–1715) was a French metaphysician whose work sought a synthesis of Cartesianism, Neoplatonism, and the thought of Augustine.

34. This joke was current in books of Jewish humor around 1900.

35. Kafka, *Beim Bau der Chinesischen Mauer,* p. 248: "Betrachtungen," aphorism 108.

36. *The Good Soldier Schweik* (1920–1923) is an unfinished sequence of satirical novels by the Czech writer Jaroslav Hašek (1883–1923).

37. In the 1814 prose tale *Peter Schlemihl,* by the German Romantic writer Adalbert von Chamisso, a man sells his shadow to the Devil for an inexhaustible purse of gold, but then regrets the bargain.

38. Plutarch, *On Isis and Osiris;* cited in Bachofen, *Urreligion und antike Symbole,* vol. 1, p. 253.

39. Kraft, *Franz Kafka: Durchdringung und Geheimnis,* pp. 13–14.

40. Kafka, *Beim Bau der Chinesischen Mauer,* p. 233: "Betrachtungen," aphorism 45.

A Note on the Texts · Chronology, 1927–1934 · Index

The hardcover edition of this book was printed in one volume. For ease of use, the complete Chronology and Index for Parts 1 and 2 of Volume 2 are reprinted here.

A Note on the Texts

Most of the texts included in this second volume of Benjamin's selected writings were published during his lifetime. In the years 1927–1933, Benjamin established himself as a public intellectual in the Weimar Republic; this volume, with its mix of essays, critical glosses, travel writings, reviews, and radio talks, documents that emergence. The volume also offers a rich selection of the form Benjamin had pioneered in *One-Way Street* (reprinted in Volume 1): the "thought figure" [*Denkbild*], a prose form which combines aspects of the aphorism and the Romantic fragment with a decidedly materialist interest in things. Benjamin published dozens of these short texts in the period under scrutiny here. Alongside this array of texts that Benjamin succeeded in publishing, the volume also includes a representative selection of unpublished writings from the period. Some, like the "Introductory Remarks on a Series for *L'Humanité*," are simply parts of projects that were never completed. Others are fragments found in Benjamin's notebooks long after his death; many of these fragments, such as "Mickey Mouse" or "Notes on a Theory of Gambling," articulate important stages and aspects of his thought, and provide much of what we know about Benjamin's ideas on a wide range of topics. But the bulk of these posthumously published texts are autobiographical. They range from résumés through protocols of hashish experiments and on to extensive journals ("Diary of My Journey to the Loire") and intensive self-examination ("Agesilaus Santander").

The German edition of Benjamin's collected writings groups texts generically (volumes of essays, of reviews, of fragments, and so on). In the present volume, all texts are arranged chronologically by date of composition; if this differs markedly from the date of publication, both dates are given. Each text is accompanied by the following information: date of composition; place of publication, or a statement that the piece was unpublished during Benjamin's lifetime; and the word "Fragment" if the text is designated as such in the German edition. All endnotes other than Benjamin's were produced by the editors in collaboration with the translators.

The *Selected Writings* aims to present to English-language readers a very broad and representative selection from Benjamin's oeuvre. Every major text published during Benjamin's lifetime is included in this edition. We have attempted to supplement these major texts with examples of every *form* in which Benjamin worked: thought figures, radio plays, autobiographical writings, book reviews, letter collections, essays, fragments, cultural histories, travel accounts. Examples of each of the remarkable number of *fields* to which Benjamin contributed are likewise included: cultural theory; epistemology; art history; toys; the French avant-garde, especially Surrealism; the new Soviet Union; cinema; radical pedagogy; contemporary writers ranging from André Gide and Julien Green through Karl Kraus and Hugo von Hofmannsthal (to say nothing of Proust and Kafka, the subjects of two of Benjamin's most famous essays); graphology; political and social analysis; media theory; the theory of experience; marginalized popular forms such as novels by the mentally ill and penny romances; photography; and the theory of language. We hope that the English-language reader will for the first time be able to assess the remarkable breadth and intensity of Benjamin's achievement.

All translations are based on the text of the standard German edition: Walter Benjamin, *Gesammelte Schriften,* seven volumes (Frankfurt: Suhrkamp Verlag, 1972–1989), edited by Rolf Tiedemann and Hermann Schweppenhäuser. The editors of the present volume are indebted to Benjamin's German editors for the meticulous dating and preparation of his texts.

The editors would like to thank a number of friends, colleagues, and collaborators who provided information and assistance at crucial stages of the project. Above all, an immense debt of gratitude is due two research assistants, Joel Golb in Berlin and Daniel Magilow in Princeton, whose vigorous research formed the basis for a number of the notes to the text. Eduardo Cadava, Stanley Corngold, Michael Curschmann, James Eggleston, Barbara Hahn, Thomas Levin, Michael Wachtel, and Christian Wildberg answered our questions with patience and generosity. Hans Puttnies gave us his time and energy as we sought to procure images of Benjamin from the period in question. Very special thanks are due our colleagues at Harvard University Press. The idea for an expanded edition of Benjamin's writings came from Lindsay Waters, and without his now patient, now insistent godfathering, the edition would certainly never have been completed. And Maria Ascher, through her consistently insightful and meticulous editing—based on a brilliant ear for the sound of English prose—of the final manuscript, improved not just the texts themselves but the conception and the apparatus of this second volume of the edition.

Chronology, 1927–1934

1927

On New Year's Day Benjamin was in Moscow, where the long winter of the Stalinization of Soviet cultural policy was beginning. He had arrived some three weeks earlier, after learning that the Latvian-born Bolshevik actress and educator Asja Lacis—his "holiday love" from a vacation on Capri—had suffered a nervous breakdown. Benjamin had financed the trip by securing an advance from the journal *Die Kreatur* for an article on Moscow. He found the city in ferment, rundown yet extremely expensive—"an improvised metropolis," as he calls it in the extensive diary he kept during his two-month stay there.[1] A letter written at the end of December reflects his own excitement: "In the current state of affairs, the present— though fleeting—is of extraordinary value. Everything is being built or rebuilt, and almost every moment poses very critical questions. The tensions of public life— which, for the most part, are actually of a theological sort—are so great that they block off all private life to an unimaginable degree . . . It remains to be seen to what extent I'll be able to establish concrete relations with developments here" (*MD*, 127). In this matter of establishing contacts, Benjamin, who did not speak Russian, was almost entirely dependent on the good graces of his Moscow host, the German-born Bernhard Reich, a prominent theater critic then living in Moscow and a rather tolerant rival for the affections of Asja Lacis. (She and Reich would remain together through banishment and imprisonment during the Stalin era, and after the war would write about and produce the plays of Bertolt Brecht.) Benjamin's position as a freelance writer, "without party or profession," was a subject of conversation among his friends in Moscow, and to Reich he admitted that he "was in a critical situation" insofar as his "activity as an author was concerned" (*MD*, 60, 47).

Benjamin was weighing the advantages and disadvantages of becoming a professional fellow traveler. In his diary, at the beginning of January, he wrote about the choice that was facing him: either join the Communist party and gain a solid institutional framework and mandate, at the sacrifice of his private independence; or seek to consolidate a marginal position as "a left-wing outsider," and organize his existence on "this narrow base" (MD, 72–73). At issue, of course, was the continuation of his scholarly work, "with its formal and metaphysical grounding"—something that in itself might have a revolutionary function. He asked himself whether his "illegal incognito among bourgeois authors makes any sense," and whether, for the sake of his work, he should "avoid certain extremes of 'materialism'" (73). "As long as I continue to travel," he concluded, "joining the party is obviously something fairly inconceivable" (73).

Benjamin was intent on observing a wide variety of the daily affairs—as well as the cultural and political affairs—of Moscow, for, as he believed, "one knows a spot only after one has experienced it in as many dimensions as possible" (MD, 25). He visited shops (toy shops were his delight), restaurants, pubs, museums, offices, a factory manufacturing Christmas tree decorations, a children's clinic, a famous monastery. He took in life on the streets—beggars, children, street vendors, shop signs and posters, the relative absence of cars and church bells, the clothing and idiosyncrasies of the inhabitants. He went to plays, films, and ballets. He saw Sergei Eisenstein's film Potemkin, and the ballet Petrushka, set to Igor Stravinsky's music. He saw a shortened production (still more than four hours long) of Vsevolod Meyerhold's adaptation of Gogol's Inspector General, whose extravagant staging—involving a series of tableaux—he compared to the architecture of a Muscovite cake. And he was present at the Meyerhold Theater for a crowded public debate involving writers such as Vladimir Mayakovsky, Andrei Bely, Anatoly Lunacharsky, and Meyerhold himself. He was interviewed by a Moscow newspaper as an expert on literature and the plastic arts. Everywhere in the city he witnessed the "thoroughgoing politicization of life" (MD, 71). His observations on these particulars, and on more general features of Russian society as it pursued its grand experiment, were recorded in his Moscow diary, which he then mined, over the next four years, for articles and radio scripts. And throughout all the organized flânerie in the stunning cold, there was the lure of Asja Lacis, as mercurial and difficult of access as the city itself.

On his return, at the beginning of February, from Moscow to Berlin, where he was living with his wife and son in an apartment in his parents' villa, Benjamin found that the translation of Proust's Within a Budding Grove, which he had undertaken together with Franz Hessel, had just appeared and was getting generally respectful reviews. Hessel was editor-in-chief of the Rowohlt publishing house, which was due to bring out Benjamin's books One-Way Street and Origin of the German Trauerspiel (though their publication was on hold for the moment; they would not appear until 1928). Meanwhile, and amid "a great deal of idleness,"[2] Benjamin was busy on a number of fronts. Through Reich he had obtained a commission for a compendious article on Goethe for the Great Soviet Encyclopedia, although in February he heard from Reich that the editorial board was balking at his synopsis. (The article would eventually be written the following year and would appear, in 1929, drastically modified by the editors.) The article on Moscow for Die Kreatur was now claiming his attention. To Martin Buber, who ran the journal, he wrote of his intention to allow the "creatural" to speak for itself; in his picture of Moscow, he said (adapting Goethe), "everything factual is already theory" (Letters,

313). This statement seems prophetic for the direction of much of his future activity as an author, as does what he wrote to Siegfried Kracauer on the same day: his presentation of Moscow would take the form of "small, disparate notes, and for the most part the reader will be left to his own devices."[3] The critic Kracauer, with whom Benjamin had become friendly in 1923, was cultural affairs editor at the *Frankfurter Zeitung;* this newspaper, along with *Die literarische Welt* (published by Rowohlt under the editorship of Willy Haas), was to become a mainstay of Benjamin's work for the duration of the Weimar Republic.

It was at this point, in the second half of the Weimar Republic's brief life, that Walter Benjamin emerged as a public intellectual. In 1927 he not only brought out a number of articles stemming from his visit to Moscow—articles on the city itself, on Russian literature, and on Russian film—but he also published the first results of his intense involvement with French culture. And he made his debut at the microphone of a radio station on March 23, when he broadcast a talk entitled "Young Russian Writers." Regular work in this medium would begin for him two years later; between 1929 and 1932, he would be heard more than eighty times on Frankfurt and Berlin radio stations, usually presenting material he himself had written or was improvising. In an overview of the work he had undertaken in 1931, Benjamin could in fact write that he had succeeded in getting every word he had written published. This commercial activity—along with that of his wife, Dora, who in 1926 had become editor of a Berlin fashion magazine—helped to fund his few independent projects of these years, especially his work on the Paris arcades, begun in the summer of 1927.

In April, Benjamin traveled to Paris for what he expected would be a two- or three-month stay, to assess new developments in French literature. Much of the time he was reading Proust. At the end of the month, he met for a few days with his old friend Gershom Scholem, who had become a lecturer in Jewish mysticism at the newly founded Hebrew University in Jerusalem and was visiting libraries in England and France to research kabbalist texts. Benjamin remarked to Scholem that he wanted to settle permanently in Paris because he found the city's "atmosphere" suited him.[4] In mid-May he was joined by Dora and his son, Stefan; they went on to the Riviera and Monte Carlo, where Benjamin won enough money in the casinos to finance a week's vacation in Corsica on his own. He took a plane back from Corsica to Antibes, "and this brought me up to date on the latest means of human transportation" (Scholem, 132).

At the beginning of June, Benjamin sent a letter to the Austrian writer Hugo von Hofmannsthal, whose journal, *Neue deutsche Beiträge,* had published Benjamin's essay "Goethe's Elective Affinities" in 1924–1925 and would publish a chapter on melancholy from the forthcoming *Trauerspiel* book in August. The letter describes his current projects, including the essay on Moscow, in which he claims to have concentrated on "rhythmic experiences" more than on purely visual ones. At the moment, he says, his work is mainly devoted to consolidating his position in Paris, to gaining proximity "to the French spirit in its modern form," given that "it incessantly preoccupies me in its historical form" (Letters, 315). In Germany, he adds, he feels "completely isolated" among those of his generation (315). He mentions that he is writing a piece on the Swiss poet and novelist Gottfried Keller, covering matters that have long run through his mind. This work would continue into July, and the piece would appear in *Die literarische Welt* in August, inaugurating a series of major essays on important literary figures for the German newspapers. The Keller essay announces a characteristic set of motifs, ranging from the revaluation of the nineteenth century to the concepts of image space and mirror world, from the interfusion of humor and choler to the efflorescence of Antiquity within the smallest cell of the present day.

Another trip, in August, took him to Orléans, Blois, and Tours, where he visited some of the châteaus on the Loire. In a travel diary he noted the peace, the "immediate sense of presence," that comes with gazing at great works of architecture; he also felt gloom at being stood up by "a Parisian woman . . . with whom he had fallen in love—something he did rather easily and frequently in those years" (Scholem, 133). In mid-August, Scholem again came to Paris to examine manuscripts at the Bibliothèque Nationale and often met with Benjamin, mostly in cafés around the Boulevard Montparnasse. On one occasion, he visited Benjamin's "shabby, tiny, ill-kept room, which contained hardly more than an iron bedstead and a few other furnishings" (133). They went to the movies (Benjamin especially admired the American actor Adolphe Menjou) and took part in violent mass demonstrations in the boulevards against the execution of Sacco and Vanzetti on August 23. Benjamin spoke of his plans for an (unrealized) anthology of Wilhelm von Humboldt's writings on the philosophy of language, and he read to Scholem from the early drafts of *The Arcades Project,* which at that epoch wore the guise of an essay that would number "about fifty printed pages" (135). After parting in Paris, he and Scholem would see each other only one more time, in February 1938, when they met for a few days, again in Paris.

Benjamin's letters of the period point to his rapidly growing interest in photography. In October, Benjamin attended an International Exhibition of Photography in Paris but was disappointed in the selection of early photographs of that city. In a letter to his old schoolmates Grete and Alfred Cohn, he comments that photos of persons mean more than those of localities, because fashions in clothing provide such a reliable temporal index (*GB,* III, 291). He was reading Flaubert's *Sentimental Education* and, under the great impression which this novel was making on him, felt unable to focus on contemporary French literature (291–292). And "with fear and trembling" in his heart, he was giving himself up to "a new work that deals with Paris," on which he was spending every available hour in documentation at the Bibliothèque Nationale (292–293).

Benjamin returned from Paris to Berlin in November, and soon afterward came down with a case of jaundice. A letter of November 18, to Scholem, mentions that he was reading Kafka's novel *The Trial* in bed. It also comments on the cover for the upcoming Rowohlt edition of *One-Way Street,* with its collage by Sasha Stone; he calls it "one of the most effective covers ever" (*GB,* III, 203). At the end of this letter he adds a short allegorical spinoff of Kafka's novel—a piece entitled "The Idea of a Mystery," in which history itself is represented as a trial. While he was ailing, Benjamin received a visit from the poet and philosopher Karl Wolfskehl, a friend of Stefan George and Ludwig Klages: "It's a good thing I've hardly read a line of his; it enabled me to follow his wonderful conversation without any scruples" (312). An account of this visit would appear in *Die literarische Welt* in 1929. In November and December, Benjamin stepped up his efforts to gain entry into the circle sur-

rounding the German art historian Aby Warburg, but Warburg's Hamburg associate
Erwin Panofsky, to whom Hofmannsthal had written at Benjamin's request, was put
off by his work. On December 12, he wrote to Alfred and Grete Cohn that he had
finished *The Trial* in a state verging on agony, "so overwhelming is the unpretentious
abundance of this book" (312).

Soon after this, Benjamin made his first experiment with hashish, which he took
orally under the supervision of two doctors with whom he was friendly. Baudelaire's
writings on hashish and opium, as well as the influence of Surrealism, played a part
in this experiment, which he repeated at various times over the next seven years or
so. It would seem that he owed his idea of the aura, at least in part, to his experience
with hashish. Benjamin was particularly interested in what he called the "colportage
phenomenon of space," a kind of spatiotemporal palimpsest effect afforded by the
drug. This played a role in the concept of the *flâneur*, which he was developing in
connection with *The Arcades Project*. Over the next few years his letters sometimes
refer to a book on hashish intoxication, but he never managed to write the work;
it was only in 1972, under the title *On Hashish*, that the protocols he kept for the
experiments, along with related texts, were first collected and published.

1928

The competing claims on Benjamin's attention continued to intensify during 1928.
His unflagging efforts as strategist in the literary wars were balanced by greater
immersion in his independent study of the Paris arcades, while his engagement with
Marxism, in part mediated through Asja Lacis (with whom he would live in Berlin
at the end of the year), and later through Brecht, was carried on in conjunction with
constantly revamped plans to emigrate to Palestine. In August of the previous year,
in Paris, Scholem had introduced Benjamin to the chancellor of the Hebrew University in Jerusalem, Rabbi Judah L. Magnes, who listened with emotion to Benjamin's
description of his career in the philosophy of language. Their two-hour conversation,
in which Benjamin maintained that he "had already done what he could as a critic
of significant texts" and "that his position had found virtually no response in
Germany," so that the interpretation of Hebrew literature remained his only viable
option (Scholem, 138), led to Magnes' request for letters of recommendation as a
first step in considering Benjamin for a teaching position in Jerusalem. Naturally,
such a position would require that he learn Hebrew. Benjamin therefore set about
collecting copies of his published work to send to Magnes and requesting academic
references (including one from Hofmannsthal) attesting to his scholarly qualifica-
tions; these reached Magnes in the spring and were pronounced excellent. His
immediate goal was to secure some sort of financial support from Jerusalem.

In January, at long last, *One-Way Street* and the *Trauerspiel* book were published
by Rowohlt Verlag. Among the reviews which appeared in Germany, France, Switzerland, Holland, and Hungary, the most important for Benjamin were those by
Kracauer, Willy Haas, Franz Hessel, Ernst Bloch, and Marcel Brion (a friend of
Hofmannsthal's who was associated with the *Cahiers du Sud*). He also found it
noteworthy that Hermann Hesse wrote very favorably to Rowohlt about *One-Way
Street*. He was bothered, however, by a rather catty review by Werner Milch (later
a specialist in Romanticism at Marburg) which appeared in a Berlin daily. Yet this

review, despite its unpleasant tone, nevertheless made the fundamental point that what unites these two texts, outwardly so different, is a formal predisposition, reminiscent of Friedrich Schlegel, for the collection of fragments.

One incident gives some indication of Benjamin's growing recognition. When André Gide came to Berlin in January, he took part in a two-hour interview with Benjamin, who was the only German journalist he agreed to see. This encounter, which Benjamin found "enormously interesting" and "delightful," resulted in two articles on Gide, published soon afterward in the *Deutsche allgemeine Zeitung* and *Die literarische Welt*.

At the end of January, Benjamin wrote to Scholem outlining his need for a subsidy of 300 marks a month if he was "now to jump off the cart that, although slow-moving, is traveling the career path of a German writer" (Letters, 322). He declared himself ready to take up the study of Hebrew just as soon as he completed his current project—"the highly remarkable and extremely precarious essay 'Paris Arcades: A Dialectical Fairy Scene' . . . [with which] one cycle of work, that of *One-Way Street*, will have come to a close for me in much the same way in which the *Trauerspiel* book concluded the German cycle. The profane motifs of *One-Way Street* will march past in this project, hellishly intensified" (322). At this point Benjamin could not have known that the project initially conceived as a newspaper article (to be written in collaboration with Hessel) would expand exponentially during the subsequent decade, coming eventually to fill two fat, posthumously published volumes.

Early 1928 was a period in which Benjamin cultivated a number of old and new intellectual relationships. In February, Theodor Wiesengrund Adorno spent some weeks in Berlin, and he and Benjamin were able to resume the discussions they had begun in Frankfurt in 1923. Benjamin reported to Kracauer in mid-February that he was "often and profitably together with Wiesengrund," who had just met Ernst Bloch (*GB*, III, 334). Adorno and Benjamin would see each other again in Königstein in early June and, a month after that, would begin their historic twelve-year correspondence. Earlier in the year, Benjamin had come to know Margarete (Gretel) Karplus, later Adorno's wife, another important correspondent of his in the Thirties and a provider of financial aid in 1933. Also that February, Benjamin became personally acquainted with the critic Ernst Robert Curtius, and he had his first meetings with Hofmannsthal, to whom he had sent his two books. The *Trauerspiel* book carried the dedication: "For Hugo von Hofmannsthal, / who cleared the way for this book, / with thanks, / February 1, 1928, WB" (333n), a sentence clarified by his remark to Marcel Brion that Hofmannsthal had been the first reader of the work (336). About *One-Way Street* he wrote to Hofmannsthal—echoing here the Baudelairean concept of *modernité*—that its object was "to grasp topicality [*Aktu-alität*] as the reverse of the eternal in history and to make an impression of this, the side of the medallion hidden from view" (Letters, 325). His conversation with Hofmannsthal touched on his own relation to his Jewishness and to Hebrew, as well as on his ideas about "Paris Arcades"—"an essay," he told Scholem, "that might turn out to be more extensive than I had thought" (327). To Scholem he described "an almost senile tendency" in Hofmannsthal, moments "when he sees himself completely misunderstood by everybody" (328).

Although Dora had been hard at work translating a detective novel by G. K. Chesterton, giving radio lectures on the education of children, and contributing book reviews to *Die literarische Welt* (including one that concerned Joyce's "Work in Progress"—*Finnegans Wake*), Benjamin told Scholem that their current situation was "gloomy" (*GB,* III, 348). He himself had just completed an essay, "Old Toys," which at the end of February he had sent to Kracauer, along with a routine request for a book to review. In his accompanying letter he observes that this essay (which would appear in the *Frankfurter Zeitung* in March) stands in close proximity to his study of the Paris arcades. About the latter he says that he knows one thing: what it's like, "for weeks on end, to be carrying around a subject in one's head and, for the present, enjoying its only success in the fact that I am totally incapable of occupying myself with anything else whatsoever" (359). The emerging intellectual centrality of his work on the arcades, which he liked to call the *Passagen-Werk,* is further indicated by the investigations he was now undertaking into the philosophical significance of fashion—"into the question of what this natural and wholly irrational temporal measure of historical process is all about" (Letters, 329)—and by his response to Karl Kraus's reading of Offenbach's *La vie parisienne* at the end of March, which set in motion, as he remarks to Alfred Cohn, "a whole mass of ideas" connected to the arcades project (*GB,* III, 358). His account of Kraus's performance was published the following month in *Die literarische Welt.*

In April, Benjamin moved into a new room located "in the deepest, most forgotten section of the Tiergarten," where "nothing but trees peer at me through two high windows" (Letters, 335). For the two months that he lived there, before subletting it to Ernst Bloch, he took advantage of the easy access it provided to the Prussian State Library, where he pursued his research on the arcades. He characterized the project in a pointed manner to Scholem: "The work on the Paris arcades is taking on an ever more mysterious and insistent mien, and howls into my nights like a small beast if I have failed to water it at the most distant springs during the day. God knows what it will do when . . . I set it free. But this will not happen for a long time, and though I may already be constantly staring into the abode in which it does what comes naturally, I let hardly anyone else have a look inside" (335). This beast of his was inhabiting "an old and somewhat rebellious quasi-apocryphal province of my thought," and what he had in mind with its subjugation was a testing of "the extent to which it is possible to be 'concrete' in the context of the philosophy of history" (333). An advance which he had received from Rowohlt for "a projected book on Kafka, Proust, and so on" (335–336) was helping to maintain the *Passagen-Werk.*

In his letter of May 24, he announced to Scholem: "I have firmly put an autumn visit to Palestine on my agenda for the coming year. I hope that, before then, Magnes and I will have reached an agreement about the financial terms of my apprenticeship" (Letters, 335). A few weeks later he met with Magnes in Berlin, and the latter "promised, on his own and without further ado," to provide him with a stipend to study Hebrew (338). Meanwhile, he interrupted his research on the arcades to resume work on his Goethe article for the *Soviet Encyclopedia;* this would occupy him until October. At the same time, he was working on a translation of part of Louis Aragon's *Paris Peasant* for *Die literarische Welt;* on an article eventually entitled "The Path to Success, in Thirteen Theses," which would appear in the *Frankfurter Zeitung* in September (and which bears a close relation to the theory of gambling elaborated in *The Arcades Project*); and on a short meditative piece called simply "Weimar," to be published in the *Neue schweizer Rundschau* in October. This last was a by-product of his encyclopedia article on Goethe, which in June had taken him to the Goethe house in Weimar to check his documentation. There, quite unexpectedly, he had suddenly found himself alone for twenty minutes in the great author's study, without even the shadow of a guard to disturb him. "And thus it happens," he wrote to Alfred and Grete Cohn, drawing the moral, "that the more cold-bloodedly one accosts things, the more tenderly they sometimes respond" (*GB*, III, 386).

Amid "all the deadlines" for articles long and short, including "some long articles about French literary currents" (Letters, 335), and amid drawn-out, ultimately fruitless negotiations in May regarding the transfer of rights for the Proust translation to Piper Verlag (a development that led to his and Hessel's abandonment of any further work on this project which had had such "an intense effect on my own writing"; 340), Benjamin characteristically began, that summer, to meditate an escape from Berlin: "I sit and brood—a penguin on the barren rocks of my thirty-seven [*sic*] years—on the possibility of a lonely Scandinavian cruise. But it is probably too late in the year" (*GB*, III, 399). In fact, this plan would have to wait two years for its realization. Meanwhile, he had received news of Asja Lacis' transfer to the Soviet Embassy in Berlin, where she was to work as a trade representative for Soviet films, and so he wrote to Scholem at the beginning of August that the trip to Palestine was "a settled matter" and that he would be staying in Jerusalem "for at least four months," but that his departure "may have to be delayed until mid-December. This will depend, first of all, on whether I can make up my mind to complete the arcades project before I leave Europe. Second, on whether I get together with a Russian woman friend in Berlin in the fall" (Letters, 339). He goes on to mention that Dora has no fixed income of any kind at the moment, while there is nothing presently in the works at Rowohlt for him; "therefore, please have Magnes send something on September 1" (339). In this matter, too, he would have to wait a little longer.

His alleged lack of funds did not stand in the way of a trip to Italy in September. From Lugano, whence he would travel to Marseilles at the end of the month, he wrote to Scholem that the encyclopedia article on Goethe was nearly finished and that he would be returning soon to the arcades project. "It would be splendid," he affirms, "if the ignominious writing I do for profit did not, for its part, need to be maintained at a certain level, so as not to become disgusting to me. I cannot say that I have lacked the opportunity to publish bad stuff; what I have always lacked, despite everything, is only the courage to compose it" (*GB*, III, 414). After this rueful boast, he put off his arrival in Palestine to January.

In October, Benjamin received a check from Magnes for 3,642 marks. The thank-you would come only eight months later, after he finally got around to arranging some Hebrew lessons. On October 22, he wrote to Alfred Cohn of the leisure he had been enjoying "for the past few weeks" since finishing the Goethe article (*GB*, III, 418). Soon, though, he was immersed in a new round of reviewing and feuilleton work. This included reviews of Kraus's reading and of a novel by Julien Green, for the Dutch journal *Internationale Revue;* a series of sketches of Marseilles, for the *Neue schweizer Rundschau;* reviews of a new edition of Goethe's book on color theory and of a startling volume of botanical photographs by Karl

Blossfeldt, for *Die literarische Welt;* and the essay "Hashish in Marseilles," for the *Frankfurter Zeitung.* But the most important of the journalistic projects undertaken at this time was the essay "Surrealism," which would appear in three installments in *Die literarische Welt* in February 1929. The preoccupation with Surrealism had a particular bearing on his ideas for the *Passagen-Werk.* He spoke of this in a letter to Scholem at the end of October: "An all too ostentatious proximity to the Surrealist movement might become fatal to the project, . . . well-founded though this proximity might be. In order to extricate the project from this situation, I have had to expand my ideas of it . . . , making it so universal within its most particular and minute framework that it will take possession of the inheritance of Surrealism . . . Enough of it exists now . . . for me to be able to accept the great risk entailed in slowing the pace of the work while expanding the subject matter" (Letters, 342–343). From this, of course, it followed that his trip to Palestine would have to be postponed again: "I now think I will be coming in the spring of next year" (343).

In November, Asja Lacis came to Berlin in the company of Bernhard Reich (who was there for a short visit only, while Brecht was finishing *The Threepenny Opera*). Before she returned to Moscow in 1930, she would try to arrange for Benjamin's emigration to the Soviet Union, in another of her vain attempts to find something for her friend there. According to Scholem, she advised Benjamin against moving to Palestine. Through her, he would get to meet Brecht in the course of the following year, along with a number of "revolutionary proletarian" authors. And for two months, from December 1928 through January 1929, he would live with her in an apartment at 42 Düsseldorfer Strasse.

1929

At the end of January, Benjamin moved back into his parents' villa on Delbrück-strasse in the Grunewald section of Berlin West—a wealthy haven from Berlin's poverty and misery—where Dora and Stefan were living with his mother. In the spring, after a series of turbulent scenes, he asked his wife for a divorce so that he could marry Asja Lacis and provide her with German citizenship. In August, Dora would insist that he leave his parents' house, which he described rather pathetically as his home of "ten or twenty years," and he would go to live for a while with the Hessels. The legal process that began on June 29 and ended on March 27, 1930, the date of their divorce, would prove financially draining (he would sign over his entire inheritance—including his cherished collection of children's books—to cover the 40,000 marks he owed her). It was because of this, and also to escape the nervous exhaustion of the entire process, that Benjamin flew to his writing desk. In 1929 he would produce more writings (including many newspaper reviews and radio scripts) than in any year before or after. "The year 1929 constituted a distinct turning point in his intellectual life," writes Scholem, "as well as a high point of intensive literary and philosophical activity. It was a visible turning point, which nevertheless did not exclude the continuity of his thought . . .—something that is more clearly discernible now than it was then" (Scholem, 159).

Benjamin was working on his Surrealism essay and also thinking about Proust. To Max Rychner, editor of the *Neue schweizer Rundschau,* which was practically the only German-language periodical to have published articles on Proust on a regular basis, he wrote: "German Proust scholarship is sure to have a different look to it, when compared to its French counterpart. There is so much to Proust that is greater and more important than the 'psychologist,' who, as far as I can tell, is almost the exclusive topic of conversation in France" (Letters, 344). His essay "Surrealism," which he described as "an opaque screen placed before the arcades" (347), began appearing in *Die literarische Welt* on February 1. It, too, announced a movement beyond psychology: "Language takes precedence. / Not only before meaning. Also before the self." The priority of language was, of course, a longstanding concern of Benjamin's—indeed, the hallmark of his thought. And reaching just as far back in his thinking was the emphasis on an expanded concept of experience, which, in Surrealism, takes the form of a "profane illumination" of the world of things, a recognition of mystery within the orders of the everyday. Occupying "its highly exposed position between an anarchistic *Fronde* and a revolutionary discipline," Surrealism, in Benjamin's presentation, discloses a crisis of the intellect, or, more specifically, of "the humanistic concept of freedom."

That the question of revolution was, for Benjamin, necessarily a question of tradition is nicely indicated by a letter of February 15 to the Swiss art historian Sigfried Giedion, whose 1928 study *Architecture in France* had had an "electrifying" effect on Benjamin and was to figure prominently in the pages of *The Arcades Project*. "As I read through your book (together with so many others claiming my attention at the moment), I am struck by the heart-quickening difference between a radical attitude and radical knowing. What you exemplify is the latter, and therefore you are capable of highlighting tradition—or rather, discovering it—within the present day itself" (*GB*, III, 144). The present day had become a kind of well from which tradition could be drawn, or a ground in which mystery was embedded. This was the logic of his work on the Paris arcades, which was aimed at excavating the everyday life of the nineteenth century in France. Benjamin touched on this conception in a letter to Scholem in March: "The issue here is . . . to attain the most extreme concreteness for an era, as it occasionally manifested itself in children's games, in a building, or in a particular situation. A perilous, breathtaking enterprise, repeatedly put off over the course of the winter—not without reason" (Letters, 348).

In the same letter, Benjamin informed Scholem of his latest projects and personal contacts. He had been seeing the political philosopher Leo Strauss, whom he found "sympathetic," and Martin Buber, to whom he detailed his plans for visiting Palestine, and he had received "a delightful, delighted, even enthusiastic letter from Wolfskehl" praising his Surrealism article, "as well as one or two friendly notices" (Letters, 349). He had recently completed a piece called "Marseilles," which would be coming out in April in the *Neue schweizer Rundschau* (of all his cityscapes, he found this one the most difficult to write), and he was working on a piece called "Short Shadows," which would form part of the sequence "Thought Figures" published in November in the same periodical. And he had begun an essay entitled "On the Image of Proust": "I have produced a pack of reviews for the next French issue of *Die literarische Welt*, and am currrently hatching some arabesques on Proust" (349). This "very provisional but cunning essay on Proust," he later tells Scholem, was "begun from a thousand and one different angles" (*GB*, III, 462)—in this respect it resembled *The Arcades Project*, which he had been working "toward, not nearly on" (459). He wanted to know which of all these things, or of his other things, Scholem considered part of the Benjaminian "experimental demonology" (Letters, 349). To borrow a moment from Thomas Mann: he was playing Leverkühn to Scholem's Zeitblom.

A quite different sort of relationship developed in May, when Asja Lacis introduced Benjamin to Brecht. Benjamin was nearly thirty-seven at the time; Brecht, thirty-one. Together with Lacis, they met for long discussions in Brecht's apartment near the zoo—discussions on the crucial importance of winning over the petty bourgeoisie to the side of the Left before Hitler appropriated it first; or on the instructive example afforded by Charlie Chaplin, whose film *The Circus* had opened in Berlin at the beginning of 1929 and had impressed Benjamin as "the first work of maturity in the art of film." Brecht encouraged Benjamin's efforts in radio and introduced him to fellow Marxists, such as the philosopher Karl Korsch, whom Benjamin would cite extensively in *The Arcades Project*. Scholem's portrait is just: "Brecht brought an entirely new element, an elemental force in the truest sense of the word, into his life . . . As early as June 6, he informed me of his rather close acquaintance with Brecht: 'There is a lot to say about him and about it' . . . Three weeks later he wrote: 'You will be interested to know that a very friendly relationship between Bert Brecht and me has recently developed, based less on what he has produced (I know only *The Threepenny Opera* and his ballads) than on the well-founded interest one must take in his present plans'" (Scholem, 159). During the years of exile, Benjamin would find at Brecht's house near Svendborg, Denmark, one of his oases, and with Brecht he would continue the sort of personal confrontation with German thinking that he had begun with Fritz Heinle and Florens Christian Rang. It was also around this time that his relationship with Adorno became closer.

From Scholem's point of view, Benjamin seemed to be Janus-faced: turned simultaneously toward Moscow and Jerusalem. On May 22, he had written to Scholem that his daily Hebrew lessons were beginning the next week, although "inwardly" he was preoccupied with the historical significance of the movement in art and literature known as Jugendstil, partly in the context of the *Passagen-Werk*, partly as a subject for the collection of essays he was planning with Rowohlt (but which never materialized). On June 6 he wrote to Magnes, apologizing for the long delay in thanking him for the stipend, and announcing that his study of Hebrew with the Orthodox rabbi Max Mayer of the *Jüdische Rundschau* had been going on "for a month." He reassured Magnes of his own earnestness, as witnessed in their Paris conversation of 1927, and he went on to express the hope that he would be in Palestine in the fall. To Scholem, the same day, he wrote that his "coming in the fall depends strictly on my material circumstances" (Letters, 350). He countered his friend's "reproaches" by admitting that he was up against "a truly pathological inclination to procrastinate in this matter," although he would "absolutely go on with Hebrew" (350). He even declared that he kept his Hebrew grammar book with him at all times. In fact, the Hebrew lessons were discontinued in July, when Benjamin went off on a trip to Italy with an old friend, and they never resumed.

Before this, he had taken a two-day trip with the same friend—the dramatist and novelist Wilhelm Speyer, with whom he had been a pupil at Haubinda twenty-three years earlier, and with whom he was now collaborating on a detective play. On June 24, from Bansin, France, he wrote to Scholem of his satisfaction with his current literary relations (a feature article on *One-Way Street* had just appeared in a Rotterdam newspaper), and of his dissatisfaction with his friend Ernst Bloch. Back in February, he had complained to Scholem of Bloch's shameless, if subtle, pilferings of his ideas and terminology; now he announced the appearance of "two new books by Bloch, *Traces* and *Essays,* in which a not insubstantial proportion of my immortal works, in part somewhat damaged, has been transmitted to posterity" (*GB,* III, 469). On his return to Berlin he wrote to Hofmannsthal, enclosing some of his recent publications, of which the essay on Proust then appearing in *Die literarische Welt* was to serve as the showpiece. Benjamin's "synthetic interpretation" of Proust underscores the novelist's "impassioned cult of similarity" and his unprecedented revelation of the world of things, arguing that the Proustian idea of happiness transforms existence into "a preserve of memory." As it happened, these were all key motifs of Benjamin's own writing at that period.

Hofmannsthal died on Benjamin's birthday, July 15, and a couple of weeks later Benjamin wrote to Scholem from Italy to express his sadness at the event. He was busy with a number of other articles in July and August, including a review entitled "The Return of the *Flâneur*" (concerning his friend Hessel's book about Berlin) and "a hostile essay" on the Swiss prose writer Robert Walser (Letters, 357). At the end of August, he published in *Die literarische Welt* a piece entitled "Conversation with Ernst Schoen," in which he and the composer Schoen—one of his oldest friends, who had just become director-general of the radio station Südwestdeutscher Rundfunk in Frankfurt—discussed the educational possibilities of radio and television. Benjamin renounced the use of these media for any specific propaganda purposes, although he was interested in combating "false consciousness" among the bourgeoisie. In the latter half of 1929, he began to do radio broadcasts (lectures and readings) more regularly.

In September, Benjamin sent a telegram to Scholem announcing his upcoming arrival in Palestine on November 4—this at a time when his financial situation had stabilized with his steady work for the newspapers, when his relationship with Brecht was blossoming, and when Asja Lacis (as he informed Scholem in a letter of September 18) had suddenly fallen ill again and he had put her on a train to Frankfurt to see a neurologist. He visited her often in Frankfurt during September and October. In the course of these visits, Benjamin also met with Adorno, Gretel Karplus, and Max Horkheimer for intensive discussions of the key theoretical elements of his work. Benjamin now read early drafts of his *Arcades Project,* including "the magnificently improvised theory of the gambler," as Adorno later described it. These "Königstein conversations" left a deep imprint on the thought and writings of all concerned; an important strand of the Frankfurt School's thinking on cultural theory had its beginnings here.

On November 1 Benjamin wrote to Scholem of the unexpectedly "cruel" dimensions that the divorce process was assuming, of Dora's "relentless bitterness," and of the help she was getting from "one of the most cunning and dangerous lawyers in Germany" (*GB,* III, 489). Dora—and the judges—saw the matter rather differently. She had already written, in 1915 (two years before their marriage), "If you love him, then you already know that his words are grand and divine, his thoughts and works significant, his feelings petty and cramped, and his actions of a sort to correspond to all of this."[5] Now, deeply embittered by Benjamin's initiation of divorce proceedings (which centered on accusations of her infidelity) and by his behavior toward her and his son, Stefan (Benjamin had by his own admission lived for years on Dora's earnings as a journalist; he now refused to repay her the 40,000 marks from her inheritance that he had borrowed, and in addition refused all requests to assist in the support of his son), Dora became even more explicit in a letter to Scholem: "The thing with Asja began as early as April 1924, on Capri. Since then he has always made his pacts: with Bolshevism, which he was unwilling to negate, so as not to lose his last excuse (for in the moment of denial he would have had to admit that it is not the sublime principles of this lady that bind him to her, but rather only sexual things); with Zionism, partly for your sake, partly (don't be angry, but these are his own words) 'because his home lies there, where someone can give him the possibility of spending money'; . . . with the literary life (not with literature), for he is naturally ashamed to admit his Zionist leanings in front of Hessel and in front of the little ladies that Hessel brings him during the breaks in his affair with Asja."[6] The judges, in granting a divorce, found that the fault in the marriage lay unequivocally on Benjamin's side. The text of their decision confirms that the accuser "had denied the accused marital intercourse since 1921 (aside from a brief period in 1923) and since then had had sexual relations with other women, in particular with a Frau Lacis. He has, furthermore, repeatedly conceded, orally and in writing, the same freedom to the accused that he, the accuser, has for years claimed for himself in the sexual realm."[7] Benjamin naturally spared Scholem such details, merely remarking that, aside from this all-consuming process (which had even brought on a ten-day nervous collapse), nothing was keeping him in Germany. Nevertheless, he could not for the moment think of leaving.

At the end of December, however, he did leave the country—not for Jerusalem, but for Paris. *Die literarische Welt* was covering his traveling expenses. In return, the periodical expected him to write a "Paris Diary," based on his interviews with literary celebrities.

1930

Benjamin's deepening friendship with Brecht was an important motivating factor in a good deal of his writing during the years 1930–1933; although his political convictions had gradually deepened, he had up to now produced little that could be called engaged writing. In 1930 and 1931, though, Benjamin overtly sought to claim for himself a role as "strategist in the literary struggle." He first issued a series of challenges to the political Right. On the cultural front, he published a long review of "the most astonishing publication to have come out of the George circle in the past few years": Max Kommerell's *The Poet as Leader in German Classicism*. Benjamin's review, "Against a Masterpiece," is his most detailed encounter with the conservative forces that dominated the German cultural scene. And the long review "Theories of German Fascism" offers a devastating critique of the war mysticism that characterized the writings of Ernst Jünger and his circle. If Benjamin was uncompromising in his critique of the Right, however, he was positively merciless in his attacks on left-liberal intellectuals. The review "Left-Wing Melancholy," with Erich Kästner's poems as its ostensible topic, accuses such moderate-left writers as Kästner, Kurt Tucholsky, and Walter Mehring of providing not ammunition in the class struggle but commodities for the entertainment industry. The tone of this review was sufficiently bitter to cause its rejection by the *Frankfurter Zeitung*; like many of Benjamin's political writings of the period, it finally appeared in the social-democratic periodical *Die Gesellschaft*.

In Paris, Benjamin met with acquaintances of Proust and with various Surrealists, including Louis Aragon and Robert Desnos. He was able to follow at first hand the quarrel that had just erupted in the Surrealist group after the publication of André Breton's second *Surrealist Manifesto* in December 1929 and its rejection by the dissidents gathered around Desnos. He interviewed Julien Green, Marcel Jouhandeau, Emmanuel Berl, and the bookseller Adrienne Monnier, who told him that all methods of mechanical reproduction were basically techniques of reduction. Benjamin's "Paris Diary," a kind of supplement to the essays on Proust and Surrealism which he extracted from the actual diary kept during his trip, would appear in *Die literarische Welt* in three installments from April to June.

From his hotel on the Boulevard Raspail, Benjamin wrote to Marcel Brion, at the beginning of January, that he had had "to abandon, at least provisionally," his plans for going to Palestine (*GB*, III, 498). His communication to Scholem was less bald. Ending a silence of nearly three months, during which Asja Lacis had returned to Moscow, he wrote, on January 20, an extraordinary letter in French, beginning "Cher Gerhard."[8]

"You will probably think me crazy," the letter begins, "but I find it immensely difficult to end my silence and write you about my projects. I find it so difficult that I may never manage it without resorting to this mode of alibi that French is for me.

"I cannot delude myself any longer that the question I have been putting off for so long threatens to turn into one of my life's most serious failures. Let me begin by saying that I will not be able to think about my trip to Palestine at all until my divorce becomes final. It does not look like this will happen very soon. You will understand that this subject is so painful to me that I do not want to speak about it" (Letters, 358–359). He added that he had to give up all hope of learning Hebrew as long as he remained in Germany.

On the one hand, requests for contributions were coming in "from all quarters"; on the other—and here he sounded a note that would become a constant refrain through the next decade—his economic situation was "too precarious" for him to think of ignoring such opportunities. Of course, it was not in itself the worsening economic situation of the country (the number of unemployed would reach three million by March) but rather the change in political climate that would spell the end of his career as a man of letters in Germany.

This career was the real subject of his letter to Scholem: "I have already carved out a reputation for myself in Germany, although of modest proportions . . . The goal is that I be considered the foremost critic of German literature. The problem is that literary criticism is no longer considered a serious genre in Germany, and has not been for more than fifty years . . . One must thus recreate criticism as a genre [*le créer comme genre*]. Others have made some progress in doing this, but myself especially" (Letters, 359). His expression of confidence in a positive reception of his work by his contemporaries, if it did not give the lie to his assertions to Magnes of two and a half years earlier, at least signaled his sense of accomplishment since his last stay in Paris. For not only was he the author of two respected, and highly original books of criticism, but he was now publishing regularly with the two most important literary journals of the day. Furthermore, there was the negotiation with Rowohlt for a collection of his essays, on which he laid particular emphasis to Scholem. In 1930 and 1931 Benjamin sought to further solidify this position by publishing a major statement on the theory of literary criticism. A rich variety of preliminary studies and partial drafts of this planned work are included in this volume under titles such as "Program for Literary Criticism" and "Criticism as the Fundamental Discipline of Literary History." The work would never appear, although central ideas that emerged from this process found their way into two little-noticed reviews, "The Rigorous Study of Art" and "Literary History and the Study of Literature."

But he was founding his hopes, above all, on his study of the Paris arcades. "This book," he told Scholem, "is the theater of all my struggles and all my ideas" (Letters, 359). His plan was to pursue the project on "a different plane," in comparison to what, under the influence of Surrealism, he had conceived in 1927 and 1928. Faced with the problem of "documentation" on one side, and of "metaphysics" on the other, he was looking to Hegel and Marx to provide "a solid scaffolding" for his work. An explicit discussion of the theory of historical knowledge would be necessary: "This is where I will find Heidegger on my path, and I expect sparks will fly from the shock of the confrontation between our two very different ways of looking at history" (359–360). In actual fact, though, Benjamin now put his arcades work on the back burner for the next four years. Other projects, in combination with the rapidly worsening political situation in Germany, began to intervene. Not until late 1934 would Benjamin again turn to the arcades and begin to follow the direction he was laying out here.

In February, Scholem wrote a tart letter to Benjamin seeking an end to all equivocation. He accused his friend of "indulging in false illusions" and of lacking candor. He demanded to know where Benjamin really stood vis-à-vis Palestine and Hebrew, and whether or not he was serious about a "true confrontation with Judaism . . . outside the medium of our friendship" (Letters, 363–364). He was also upset about Benjamin's securing a stipend from Magnes under what now appeared to be false pretenses. He would have to wait another two months for Benjamin's response, on April 25, in which he again vaguely suggested that he would be coming to Palestine "before the end of the year" (365). Benjamin offered a direct rejoinder to Scholem's challenge in the matter of Judaism ("I have come to know living Judaism in absolutely no form other than you"; 364), but otherwise sidestepped the issues Scholem had raised by alluding to "that procrastination . . . which is second nature to me in the most important situations of my life" (364), and by shifting attention to his recent divorce with Dora and the "makeshift existence" into which he had been forced as a result. Benjamin, of course, had long since spent the stipend granted him from Jerusalem, and he had no intention of paying it back. When Scholem's wife brought the matter up again in June, while Benjamin was visiting her in Berlin, he once more changed the subject.

That April, Benjamin signed a contract with Rowohlt for the collection of essays he had been meditating. In addition to already published articles—"The Task of the Translator" and "Surrealism," as well as essays on Keller, Hebel, Hessel, Walser, Green, Gide, and Proust—the book was to contain pieces entitled "The Task of the Critic," "Novelist and Storyteller," and "On Jugendstil."

Benjamin was also busy with his broadcasts for radio stations in Berlin and Frankfurt. In February and March, he had presented a series of talks for young listeners on the city of Berlin, and these were followed by lectures on E. T. A. Hoffmann and on Bertolt Brecht, among others. With the journalist Wolf Zucker, he was working on a series of "radio models" (*Hörmodelle*), which consisted of dialogues and short scenes on everyday situations, followed by spontaneous discussions. He was planning an article (unrealized) on the political aspects of radio for the *Frankfurter Zeitung;* it was to incorporate ideas of his colleague Ernst Schoen on the feasibility of transforming radio from a medium of entertainment to one with educational and political significance as well—one that would work against "the limitless spread of a consumer mentality" (as he put it in a sketch of 1930–1931, "Reflections on Radio") and would serve as a model for a new "people's art." On April 4, he wrote to Schoen, listing some thirteen points to be discussed in his proposed article. These include the trivialization of radio as a consequence, in part, of the failure of a liberal and demagogic press and, in part, of the failure of Wilhelminian ministers; the domination of radio by trade unionism; radio's indifference to things literary; and the corruption in the relations between radio and the press (*GB*, III, 515–517).

Among his publications that spring was a review of Kracauer's book *White-Collar Workers*, in *Die Gesellschaft*. Entitled "An Outsider Makes His Mark," it suggests something of Benjamin's own conception of himself as a left-wing outsider, alienated from the "morally rosy" adaptation of the white-collar workers to "the inhuman side of the contemporary social order," yet sufficiently aware—in pointed contrast to Brecht's position—that "the proletarianization of the intellectual hardly ever turns him into a proletarian." Rejecting both the depoliticized "sensation seeking of the snobs" and the depoliticized subordination of white- and blue-collar workers, the writer "rightly stands alone." At the conclusion of the piece, Benjamin compares the writer to a "ragpicker, at daybreak, picking up rags of speech and verbal scraps with his stick." If Benjamin here outlines a materialist criticism in terms of the unmasking of false consciousness among the bourgeoisie, his essay "Food," which appeared in the *Frankfurter Zeitung* at the end of May, is a small masterpiece of materialism in a very different vein, one more personal and, above all, bodily oriented. What he would call "anthropological materialism" was centered in the body as understood philosophically.

His divorce had left him, after he had finally found the "strength" to end his marriage, "at the threshold of my forties, without property or position, dwelling or resources," as he wrote, somewhat exaggerating, to Scholem in June (*GB*, III, 530). Applying himself diligently to labors that (in writing to Scholem) he often derided as "tomfoolery" or "stupidities," he felt overworked and exhausted. He was longing for some sort of "relaxation" (531). The idea of a trip to Scandinavia, first broached some two years earlier, now came to his rescue. At the end of July, he set sail on a voyage that took him over the Arctic Circle into northern Finland. On board ship, he translated a novel by Jouhandeau and read Ludwig Klages, whom he considered, despite Klages' "clumsy metaphysical dualism" and his suspect political tendencies, a great philosopher (Letters, 366). Benjamin's spirits, as he indicated in a letter to Gretel Karplus, were restored: "Once Berlin has been left behind, the world becomes spacious and beautiful, and it even has room on a 2,000-ton steamer, swarming with assorted tourists, for your quietly exhilarated servant" (GB, III, 534). An account of his trip would appear in the *Frankfurter Zeitung* in September.

In October, Benjamin moved into a quiet two-room studio apartment in the Wilmersdorf section of Berlin, opposite his cousin Egon Wissing. Sublet from the artist Eva Boy, it would remain his home until he emigrated from Germany in 1933. He had a large study, with space for his 2,000-volume library and for Paul Klee's drawing *Angelus Novus*. Someone had given him a gramophone and he was putting together a record collection, which he enjoyed with his son, Stefan. As Scholem remarks, "it was the last time he had all his possessions together in one place" (Scholem, 178). Pressured by money worries, he was busy, as usual, on several fronts. A major essay on Karl Kraus was nearing completion, and he was working on the review essay "Left-Wing Melancholy." He was preparing his sparkling radio script "Myslovice—Braunschweig—Marseilles" for publication in the humor periodical *Uhu*. He had been present at a conference of the National Socialists' Strasser group (a branch of the Sturmabteilung, or SA—the Storm Troopers) and had witnessed a "debate that was in part fascinating" (GB, III, 546–547). He was reading Karl Korsch's *Marxism and Philosophy*, and he would soon be quite absorbed in a German translation of Charles Dickens' *Old Curiosity Shop*.

With Brecht, who had now become the *enfant terrible* of the Berlin theater world, he was engaged in long conversations about a plan for a new journal to be published by Rowohlt, one oriented toward the recognition of a crisis in art and science. "Its formal stance," he told Scholem, "will be scholarly, even academic, rather than journalistic, and it will be called *Krisis und Kritik*. I have completely won Rowohlt over to the plan . . . Beyond this is the difficulty inherent in working with Brecht. I of course assume that I am the one who will be able to deal with that, if anyone can" (Letters, 368). The journal was to be edited by the theater critic and dramatist Herbert Ihering, with Benjamin and Brecht as coeditors. Potential contributors included Adorno, Kracauer, Korsch, Georg Lukács, Robert Musil, and Alfred Döblin. Benjamin's own first contribution was to be an essay on Thomas Mann.

Furthermore, Benjamin was planning, with Adorno and Horkheimer, to deliver a lecture at the end of 1930 entitled "The Philosophy of Literary Criticism" at Frankfurt's Institut für Sozialforschung, of which Horkheimer had become the director in October. On November 2, however, Benjamin's mother died after a long illness (his father had died in 1926), and he asked for a postponement of the lecture, which then was never rescheduled. At this time, he was helping to support himself by working as a publisher's reader for Rowohlt. His translation of Proust's *The Guermantes Way* appeared about a month later, from Piper Verlag.

In December, Benjamin wrote a brief letter accompanying the delivery of his *Trauerspiel* book to the conservative political philosopher Carl Schmitt, whose treatise *Political Theology* had been a principal source. "You will quickly notice how much this book, in its exposition of the doctrine of sovereignty in the seventeenth century, owes to you" (GB, III, 558). He referred to Schmitt's recent work in political philosophy as a confirmation of his own work in the philosophy of art. Schmitt would later make use of Benjamin's book in his *Hamlet or Hecuba* of 1956. A different sort of influence is indicated in a letter of mid-December to the literary historian Franz Glück, who had sent Benjamin a volume of the selected writings of the Viennese architect Adolf Loos. To Glück, Benjamin speaks of the importance of

Loos's work to his present studies in particular (559). Loos would be cited at pivotal moments in the essay on Kraus.

1931

Unusually for the peripatetic Benjamin, he spent much of 1931 in Berlin. The pleasure he derived from the security of his apartment in Berlin-Wilmersdorf is a recurrent theme in his letters: "The study is pleasant and livable. All of my books are here now and, even given these times, their number has increased gradually from 1,200—although I certainly have not kept all of them, by a long shot—to 2,000. The study . . . has a panoramic view of the old filled-in bog, or, as it is also called, Lake Schramm—almost *l'atelier qui chante et qui bavarde;* and now that the weather is cold, a view of the ice-skating rinks and a clock is in sight at all seasons. As time goes by, this clock, especially, becomes a luxury it is difficult to do without" (Letters, 387). The lovely essay "Unpacking My Library" is the result of this sentiment. Yet the apartment was not merely the kind of bourgeois refuge Benjamin depicted with such glee throughout his work; if his thought was, as he described it, a "contradictory and mobile whole," then this apartment certainly mirrored that configuration. Benjamin wrote to Scholem with self-mocking irony: "To my horror, I already have to answer for the fact that only saints' pictures are hanging on the walls of my communist cell" (Letters, 386).

The security and continuity of this Berlin existence had a marked effect on Benjamin's self-conception. He could write in October: "I feel like an adult for the first time in my life. Not just no longer young, but grown up, in that I have almost realized one of the many modes of existence inherent in me" (Letters, 385). This state of mind was highly productive. In 1931 he published two of his most important essays, "Karl Kraus" and "Little History of Photography," as well as a number of fine literary and political essays, some radio talks, and several autobiographical pieces. And this was only the completed work. In February, Benjamin mentioned to Scholem that he was at work on what he hoped would be his definitive statement on literary criticism, "The Task of the Critic" (which would stand as the preface to his collection of literary essays), as well as on a "major essay on Jugendstil" (Scholem, 167). A letter to Scholem from October 28 gives an indication of the "ridiculous variety of projects" on which he typically worked: "The series of letters is to be continued;[9] there is a somewhat more detailed physiognomic attempt to describe the connections between Kant's feeblemindedness (in old age) and his philosophy; additionally, a shattering review of Haecker's Virgil;[10] a position as a judge in an open competition for sound-film scripts, for which I am reading and judging approximately 120 drafts a week; a short study of Paul Valéry . . . and I do not know whether the list is complete" (Letters, 385). This diversity in his writing was complemented by the diversity in his reading at the time: Shmarya Levin's *Childhood in Exile,* a life of Johann Heinrich Pestalozzi, Brecht's *Versuche,* and works by Nikolai Bukharin.

From his base in Wilmersdorf, Benjamin made sorties into the social world of the Berlin intelligentsia. He continued to meet frequently with Ernst Bloch and Franz Hessel and discuss ideas; he formed a close friendship with the bank official Gustav Glück; and he continued to frequent the company of journalists such as Willy Haas and Albert Salomon. Max Rychner, editor of the *Neue schweizer Rundschau,* dined with Benjamin in November 1931 and left us a portrait of him in this period: "I observed the massive head of the man across from me and couldn't break free from this observation: of the eyes—hardly visible, well fortified behind the glasses—which now and then seemed to awaken; of the moustache, obliged to deny the youthful character of the face and functioning like two small flags of some country I couldn't quite identify."[11]

But of all of Benjamin's social and intellectual contacts at this time, it was the ones with Brecht that had the most obvious and immediate impact. The two writers debated the relative merits of Stalin and Trotsky, and Benjamin was keen to collaborate on a study of Heidegger's *Being and Time,* which had appeared in 1927. "We were planning to annihilate Heidegger here in the summer," he reported to Scholem, "in the context of a very close-knit circle of readers led by Brecht and me. Unfortunately, Brecht . . . will be leaving soon, and I will not do it on my own" (Letters, 365).

In early 1931, though, the plans for *Krisis und Kritik,* the journal they had hoped to coedit, foundered. It was not merely the foreseeable financial difficulties that brought the journal to a halt before it had begun; differences between Brecht's conception of the work and Benjamin's soon arose. Benjamin had placed enormous weight on the project, not only because of its potential for solidifying the increasingly important relationship with Brecht, but also because it would have embodied the strongest form of Benjamin's now overtly political criticism. Feeling that his intellectual independence would be compromised by further participation, though, Benjamin withdrew from the enterprise in February 1931. Notes on the discussions between Brecht and Benjamin have survived, as has a programmatic memorandum written by Benjamin in October or November.

But the contact with Brecht and his circle was by no means the only manifestation of Benjamin's political will. Just as characteristic is his great essay on Karl Kraus, which appeared in March 1931. Kraus himself, who may well have met Benjamin through a common acquaintance, the composer Ernst Krenek, judged the essay with his own very typical irony: "I can only express the hope that other readers have understood his writings better than I have. (Perhaps it is psychoanalysis.)"[12] The essay, which intertwines a radical politics and a no less radical theology, provoked a series of queries and attacks from friendly quarters and a series of highly revealing defenses and justifications from Benjamin. In a letter of March 7, 1931, to Max Rychner, Benjamin offered a direct apology for the mixture of political and theological elements in his work. He described himself as "a scholar to whom the stance of the materialist seems scientifically and humanely more productive in everything that moves us than does that of the idealist. If I might express it in brief: I have never been able to do research and think in any sense other than, if you will, a theological one—namely, in accord with the talmudic teaching about the forty-nine levels of meaning in every passage of Torah. That is: in my experience, the most trite Communist platitude possesses more hierarchies of meaning than does contemporary bourgeois profundity" (Letters, 372–373). Scholem, in a letter of March 30, delivered what can only be described as a frontal assault on the position Benjamin now occupied: he asserted that Benjamin was "engaging in an unusually intent kind of self-deception" based on a "disconcerting alienation and disjuncture between your *true* way of thinking and your *alleged* way of thinking." Scholem objected to what he saw as a tendency in the Kraus essay to conflate "the metaphysician's insights into the language of the bourgeois" with the insights "of the materialist into the economic dialectic of society" (Letters, 374–375). Benjamin's reply was a model of restraint—and of no little evasion: he finally, much later, sent Scholem a copy of the letter to Rychner, as a kind of belated answer. If he did not defend his politics, though, he did issue Scholem an apology for his continued failure to make good on his promise to learn Hebrew and come to Palestine. "Where is my productive base? It is—and I have not the slightest illusion about this—in Berlin W[ilmersdorf-West]. WW, if you will. The most advanced civilization and the most 'modern' culture not only are part of my private comforts but are, in part, simply the means of my production" (Letters, 378).

In late spring, Benjamin made an extended trip to the south of France, in the company of his friends the Speyers and his cousins the Wissings; they stayed in Juan-les-Pins, Saint-Paul de Vence, Sanary, Marseilles, and Le Lavandou, where they met Brecht, Carola Neher, Emil Hesse-Burri, Elisabeth Hauptmann, Marie Grossman, and Bernhard and Margot von Brentano. As always when he was together with Brecht, Benjamin engaged in a series of long and heated discussions on a wide range of problems and writers—from the Hegelian dialectic and Trotsky to Proust, Kafka, and Schiller.

During this trip, Benjamin's letters and diaries began to show signs that his new stability and self-confidence were being increasingly punctuated—and not for the first time in his life—by periods of deep depression and thoughts of suicide.

"I feel tired. Tired above all of the struggle, the struggle for money, of which I now have enough in reserve to enable me to stay here. But tired also of aspects of my personal life with which, strictly speaking—apart from my economic situation—I have no reason to be dissatisfied . . . This dissatisfaction involves a growing aversion to and also a lack of confidence in the methods I see chosen by people of my kind and my situation to assert control over the hopeless situation of cultural politics in Germany . . . And to take the full measure of the ideas and impulses that preside over the writing of this diary, I need only hint at my growing willingness to take my own life."[13]

This "growing willingness" is most evident in a diary Benjamin kept in August, 1931—a diary on whose first page he wrote "Diary from August 7, 1931, to the Day of My Death."

"This diary does not promise to become very long. Today there came the negative response from [Anton] Kippenberg, and this gives my plan the relevance that only futility can guarantee. I need to discover 'a method that is just as convenient, but somewhat less definitive,' I said to I[nge] today. The hope of any such discovery is fast disappearing. But if anything can strengthen still further the determination—indeed, the peace of mind—with which I think of my intention, it must be the shrewd, dignified use to which I put my last days or weeks. Those just past leave a lot to be desired in this respect. Incapable of action, I just lay on the sofa and read. Frequently, I fell into so deep a reverie at the end of each page that I forgot to turn the page. I was mainly preoccupied with my plan—with wondering whether or not it was unavoidable, whether it should best be implemented here in the studio or back at the hotel, and so on."

Suicide—whether thoughts of his own or that of people close to him—had played a remarkable role in his work starting as early as 1914, with the writing of "Two Poems by Friedrich Hölderlin" and its commemoration of the suicide of his friends Fritz Heinle and Rika Seligson. An attempted suicide emerges as the "secret" that organizes his reading of Goethe's *Elective Affinities*. And the problem of suicide informs one of Benjamin's most provocative short texts, "The Destructive Character" of 1931. Now, however, despite his deepening depression, Benjamin failed to carry through on his plan; but thoughts of taking his life would never be far from him in the years to come.

Benjamin returned to Berlin in July 1931 and remained there until April 1932. In August he published his "Little History of Photography." Benjamin here establishes himself as an early and significant theorist of photography; the essay contains, in addition, an important early formulation of his concept of the aura. His letters from these months are full of capsule descriptions of the political situation and, naturally, of foreboding. "The economic order of Germany has as firm a footing as the high seas, and emergency decrees collide with each other like the crests of waves. Unemployment is about to make revolutionary programs just as obsolete as economic and political programs already are. To all appearances, the National Socialists have actually been delegated to represent the unemployed masses here; the Communists have not as yet established the necessary contact with these masses and, consequently, the possibility of revolutionary action" (Letters, 382).

It was in late 1931 that Benjamin began to sense the end of his career as a public intellectual in Germany. "The constriction of the space in which I live and write (not to mention the space I have for thought) is becoming increasingly difficult to bear. Long-range plans are totally impossible" (Letters, 384). This is one of the first soundings of what will be the dominant theme of his letters in the years to come: the progressive elimination of all but a very few sites for the publication of his work, and with that elimination, his gradual reduction to abject poverty.

1932

Benjamin's long preoccupation with the bourgeois letter as a literary form bore fruit in early 1932. First in a radio talk called "On the Trail of Old Letters," delivered in January, and then in a series of letters called "From World Citizen to Haut Bourgeois," coedited with Willy Haas, Benjamin began to explore possibilities for grouping and commenting on a series of letters that he hoped would have revelatory and potentially revolutionary potential. This line of his thought would culminate in the pseudonymously published *Deutsche Menschen* of 1936, one of the keystones of Benjamin's work in the 1930s.

In January and February 1932, he also began to set down the first drafts of the recollections of his childhood and youth that Scholem would eventually publish as *Berlin Chronicle*. The short texts, for which he had received a contract from *Die literarische Welt* in the fall, took advantage of the form Benjamin had first developed in *One-Way Street*: often aphoristic but always dense and allusive meditations on things and places. He would continue to refine his drafts in the months to come. But no longer in Berlin.

Driven by the bleakness of his long-term economic prospects and the short-term presence of a bit of cash, Benjamin boarded a ship in Hamburg on April 7, bound for Barcelona. From there he took the mail boat to Ibiza, the Balearic island on which he would spend important parts of the coming years. While on the island, he shared lodgings with Felix Noeggerath (a friend from the days of the Youth Movement) and Noeggerath's family. His first remarks on Ibiza, contained in a letter to Scholem of April 22, reflect a subdued hope. He was prepared to do without "any kind of comfort" because of the "composure the landscape provides; the most untouched landscape I have ever come across" (Letters, 390). In a letter to Gretel Karplus written early in his stay, he elaborated on the particular forms of "deprivation" he had to endure. After rising early, swimming, and sunbathing, he faced "a long day of doing without countless things, less so because they shorten life than because none of them is available, or, when they are, they are in such bad condition that you are glad to do without them—electric light and butter, liquor and running water, flirting and reading the paper" (Letters, 393). Nothing, of course, could deter Benjamin from reading (Stendhal's *Charterhouse of Parma*—an already familiar text; Theodor Fontane's *Der Stechlin;* Trotsky's autobiography and his history of the February Revolution). Or, apparently, from flirting. While on Ibiza, he proposed marriage to a German-Russian woman named Olga Parem, who turned him down. In subsequent months, Benjamin saw a number of other women, including the divorced wife of a Berlin physician.

While on the island, he pushed forward with his autobiographical project. He brought *Berlin Chronicle* to a provisional conclusion, though he remained unsure of just what to do with it. The short form that he was developing there, which he now came to call a "thought figure," found other uses. "Ibizan Sequence," a series of these short texts, was published in June. Benjamin also used the time on Ibiza to produce an unusual number of novellas, travel reports, and landscape sketches. "Spain, 1932," "The Handkerchief," and "In the Sun" all date from this period. He complained, meanwhile, of the island's relative lack of detective novels, which were always a passion with him; and he commented on his reading of Thornton Wilder's novel *The Cabala* and Proust.

Although Benjamin had planned to extend his stay on Ibiza at least through August, on July 17 he boarded a ship for the French mainland. His departure was undoubtedly comical: "When we finally arrived at the quay, the gangplank had been taken away and the ship had already begun to move . . . After calmly shaking hands with my companions, I began to scale the hull of the moving vessel and, aided by curious Ibizans, managed to clamber over the rail successfully."[14] His reasons for leaving Ibiza were considerably less comical: he planned to take his life in a hotel in Nice. In a letter to Scholem of July 26, written in Nice, Benjamin spoke of his "profound fatigue" and of his horror and disgust at events in Germany. On July 20, 1932, Franz von Papen, who had been German chancellor for only a month, suspended the democratically elected Prussian government, naming himself "Imperial Commissar for Prussia" and preparing the way for Hitler's assumption of power. Benjamin was all too aware of the immediate and possibly future results of Germany's political demise. By the end of July he had already, as a Jew, received a letter from the building-safety authorities ordering him to abandon his apartment because of alleged code violations; his radio work had also been brought to a halt by the dismissal of the left-leaning directors of the Berlin and Frankfurt stations. The tone of the July 26 letter, in which he compiles a retrospective assessment of his accomplishments and failures, leaves little to the imagination. "The literary forms of expression that my thought has forged for itself over the last decade have been utterly conditioned by the preventive measures and antidotes with which I had to counter the disintegration constantly threatening my thought as a result of such contingencies. And though many—or a sizable number—of my works have been small-scale victories, they are offset by large-scale defeats." He goes on to name the "four books that mark off the real site of ruin or catastrophe" in his life: the unfinished work on the arcades of Paris, his collected essays on literature, the edited series of old letters, and a truly exceptional book about hashish (Letters, 396).[15]

Now, in the Hôtel du Petit Parc, he prepared to put an end to his life. He wrote out a will, leaving his manuscripts and those of his friends Fritz and Wolf Heinle to Scholem as executor, and he drafted farewell letters to Egon Wissing, Ernst Schoen, Franz Hessel, and Jula (Cohn) Radt. Whether it was a change of heart or a failure of will that led Benjamin to stop short of suicide itself will undoubtedly remain a mystery (Scholem, 185–188).

From Nice, Benjamin went to join the Speyers in Povoremo, Italy, in order to collaborate with Speyer on a detective play. "I live away from all the bustle, in a simple but quite satisfactory room, and I am rather content, insofar as conditions and prospects allow me to be" (Scholem Letters, 16). In Povoremo, Benjamin turned again to the series of short autobiographical texts he had completed on Ibiza three months before, and the project underwent a decisive conceptual change. In the early texts finished on Ibiza that Scholem would later publish as *Berlin Chronicle*, the autobiographical element of the project had been predominant. But in Italy, Benjamin began to turn the texts toward the poetical and philosophical form of the "thought figure"—an attempt to capture the essence of a place and a time. He soon began referring to this project as *A Berlin Childhood around 1900*. Benjamin worked hard on the project, and was able to send a provisionally completed text to Scholem from Berlin in December. That mailing inaugurated the long and troubled publication history of the *Childhood*. The version of December 1932 contains thirty sections; the version published in 1972, in the fourth volume of the Suhrkamp edition of Benjamin's writings, contains forty-one sections, in a different order; and the "definitive" version, published in Volume 7 of the Suhrkamp edition and based on a manuscript long believed lost, contains thirty again, but in a still different order.

The collaboration with Speyer at least held out some prospect of eventual remuneration; all other prospects seemed to be vanishing. Just as his radio contracts had disappeared during the summer, his two major publishing venues were rendered inaccessible. The *Frankfurter Zeitung* left his letters unanswered, and *Die literarische Welt* asked explicitly that he submit no more work. Even the few hopes that dangled from Berlin were to prove futile. Rowohlt again hinted at the publication of the volume of literary essays that he had hoped, in 1931, would make his career and that was now seen only as a source of a few marks; but this, too, led to nothing. Benjamin was now destitute, totally dependent upon Speyer's generosity. "I am now engulfed in [the economic crisis] like a fish in water, but I am hardly as well off as the fish" (Scholem Letters, 20). Scholem had been in Europe, working at a series of archives on kabbalistic texts, since early in the year; Benjamin had avoided a meeting for reasons he never articulated, but which undoubtedly were bound up with his commitments to Brecht and his politics. Now, in the fall, when Benjamin expressed an interest in seeing Scholem, he was unable to afford the return fare to Berlin, where Scholem stayed until mid-October. Benjamin returned only when Speyer—along with his automobile—was ready, in mid-November. While Benjamin wrote and worried, he read Arthur Rosenberg's *A History of Bolschevism* and Rudolf Leonhard's *The Word*.

Returning directly from Italy to Berlin, Benjamin had to turn down a gratifying invitation to visit, in Frankfurt, the first university seminar devoted to his work. The young *Privatdozent* Theodor Wiesengrund Adorno was offering a seminar to selected students on Benjamin's *Origin of the German Trauerspiel*. In turning down Adorno's invitation, Benjamin affirmed that he was "less than ever the master of my decisions . . . As such, the temptation to stay in Germany for any length of time is not very great" (Letters, 398).

In Berlin, Benjamin detailed to Scholem the way in which intellectuals were continuing to betray one another. He had been stung by a letter from his former collaborator Willy Haas, the editor of *Die literarische Welt,* one of his central organs of publication. "In order to know how someone fares who deals with such 'intellectuals,' in the form of editors or newspaper owners, you need only remember that the 'intellectuals' among our 'coreligionists' are the first to offer the oppressors hecatombs from their own circles, so as to remain spared themselves. True, I have been able to stem the boycott led against me simply by showing up. But whether the energy I invested over these first few weeks will avert the worst cannot yet be judged" (Scholem Letters, 23).

1933

In early 1933, Benjamin made the acquaintance of a woman who would figure prominently in his correspondence with Scholem in the coming years: Kitty Marx (who would soon become Kitty Marx-Steinschneider, after her marriage to Scholem's friend Karl Steinschneider). Unusually for Benjamin, a deep and lasting friendship sprang up between them almost immediately; their subsequent correspondence is filled with a courtly irony that borders on long-distance flirtation. This new friendship represented, though, only a temporary respite from concerns that were becoming more pressing every day.

Benjamin was experiencing first-hand the preparations for the "opening ceremonies of the Third Reich" that he had already prophesied in spring of 1932. The persecution of political opponents, the book burnings, the unleashing of the Brownshirts—all this was part of daily life in Germany's capital. "The little composure that people in my circles were able to muster in the face of the new regime was rapidly spent, and one realizes that the air is hardly fit to breath anymore—a condition which of course loses significance as one is being strangled anyway" (Scholem Letters, 27). After the night of February 27, 1933, when the Reichstag was burned, Benjamin's friends began to disappear: Ernst Schoen and Fritz Fränkel into hastily erected concentration camps; Brecht, Bloch, Kracauer, and Speyer into exile. Benjamin was prescient regarding the implications for his own work. "I don't know how I will be able to make it through [the coming months], either inside or outside Germany. There are places where I could earn a minimal income, and places where I could live on a minimal income, but not a single place where these two conditions coincide" (Letters, 402).

What is perhaps most remarkable about these months is Benjamin's ability to suppress the ugly clamor in the streets outside his window and push on with his work. While still in Berlin, he completed a radio play on the German aphorist Lichtenberg (long one of his heroes), began an essay on Kafka, and, above all, finished one of his most important "private" essays, intended only for his own use and the eyes of a few adepts. This essay, "Doctrine of the Similar," represented a "new theory of language," an important building on the foundations of his language essay of 1916, "On Language as Such and on the Language of Man." In a letter of this period to Scholem, he continued to press his friend to read two texts about which Scholem has a host of reservations: Adorno's *Kierkegaard* and Brecht's *Versuche*.

On about March 18, Benjamin left Berlin. From Paris, his first stop, he wrote to Scholem: "I can at least be certain that I did not act on impulse, out of panic: the German atmosphere in which you look first at people's lapels, and after that usually do not want to look them in the face anymore, is unbearable. Rather, it was pure reason which bid all possible haste" (Letters, 406). Another letter sounded a note that would become recurrent: Benjamin's concern for friends and family who, for various reasons, delayed their departure from Germany. He was anxious first and foremost about the safety of his son. "All of this . . . would be bearable, if only Stefan weren't where he still is. In my first letter from here, I urged Dora to send him to Palestine, where her brother owns a plantation" (Scholem Letters, 36). In Paris, where Benjamin stayed only a short time, he met acquaintances from his stay on Ibiza in 1932: Jean Selz and his wife. He left Paris for the island in their company on April 5, arriving ten days later after a stay of several days in Barcelona.

On Ibiza, Benjamin returned to his former, remarkably simple lifestyle. He lodged with acquaintances (including the Noeggeraths) or in rented accommodations; for a good part of his stay, he lived in an isolated house that was half finished and devoid of any conveniences. Ibiza represented for Benjamin a reduction of his living expenses to "the European minimum of about sixty or seventy reichsmarks a month." He was able to raise this sum through a combination of income from his writings, income from the slow selling-off of the most valuable contents of his library, and regular contributions from friends such as Gretel Adorno and Fritz and Jula Radt (Letters, 410). But even Ibiza had begun to change, with many new residents, many new buildings, and not a few Nazis. Without knowing how long he would—or could—remain there, Benjamin began to learn Spanish. His reports from the island contrast markedly with those from his stay in 1932, which had been so idyllic in tone; now he gave way to irritation with the "blastings and hammer blows, the gossip and debates that constitute the atmosphere of San Antonio" (Scholem Letters, 58). Only on occasional rambles in the interior of the island, some of them in the company of Paul Gauguin, a grandson of the famous painter, could he escape the tumult and recover some of the earlier sense of place. Benjamin's account of one such walk takes even this encounter with a more primitive side of the island and organizes it around a symbol of death: "A man came walking toward us, carrying a tiny white child's coffin under his arm" (Letters, 420).

News from Germany persistently added to his sense of despair. In early May, he learned that his brother Georg, who had been active in Germany's Communist party, had been arrested. First reports had him in the hands of the SA, tortured, and blinded in one eye. Benjamin soon learned that his brother was in fact in "preventive detention" in a regular prison, and relatively healthy; better news, but hardly the sort to allay his fears. Dora and Stefan remained in Berlin. And a new source of anxiety soon made itself felt: his passport would expire at the end of the summer, and he was doubtful that he would be allowed to reenter France without one.

Among his most pressing personal concerns was, naturally, the problem of finding new sources of income. He was surprised to learn that Germany was, at first, not as closed to him as he had feared. Both the *Vossische Zeitung* and the *Frankfurter Zeitung* continued to publish reviews and short prose (including individual sections of *A Berlin Childhood*). These and other efforts were published under a series of pseudonyms, "Detlev Holz" remaining his favorite. The first major statement from his time of exile to appear in Germany was his final reckoning with an author who had preoccupied him since his earliest encounters with literature: Stefan George. "Stefan George in Retrospect" is predictably cautious in its political assessment of George, the most important figure in the conservative literary world in the first half of the twentieth century. Benjamin's remarks on this aspect of George are more direct in a letter to Scholem: "If ever God has smitten a prophet by fulfilling his prophecies, then this is the case with George" (Scholem Letters, 59). Benjamin's published critique takes on George, instead, in the coded language he had developed in his own work: the terms "nature," "daemonic," and "hero" carry with them philosophical and theological associations first developed in the 1921 essay "Goethe's Elective Affinities." The George essay was followed by a commission to write a piece commemorating the two hundredth anniversary of the birth of Christoph Martin Wieland, one of the chief literary figures of the German Enlightenment.

Older journals now in exile represented further publishing outlets. One of the first such opportunities was a commission from the Institut für Sozialforschung, which had managed to transfer its endowment from Germany to Switzerland. Benjamin agreed to produce a very substantial review of the current state of French letters, although he repeatedly expressed reservations about his ability to carry out this task on Ibiza, with no scholarly library and few books; early in the process, he called the essay "sheer fakery" (Scholem Letters, 41). By late May, however, when he had finished "The Present Social Situation of the French Writer," he accorded himself grudging approval: "It wasn't possible to produce something definitive. Nonetheless, I believe that the reader will gain insight into connections that until now have not been brought out so clearly" (Scholem Letters, 54). And late in the year in Paris, with the Bibliothèque Nationale at his disposal, he began to work on two further commissions from the Institut: a major essay on the collector and historian Eduard Fuchs, and a collective review of recent publications on the philosophy and sociology of language.

But the paths to the exile journals were often tortuous. At Scholem's urging, Benjamin overcame a strong personal disinclination and submitted two pieces to Max Brod for publication in the *Prager Tageblatt*. Brod not only rejected the pieces, but gave them without the author's permission to Willy Haas, editor of the periodical *Die Welt im Wort*. Haas, now an object of Benjamin's scorn, agreed to publish both "Experience and Poverty" (Benjamin's important reflection on the thoroughly positive reduction of modern experience to a "new barbarism") and a small piece on Johann Peter Hebel. Before they appeared, and certainly before Benjamin had been paid, *Die Welt im Wort* failed—an event which Benjamin described as "gratifying" (Scholem Letters, 100). Brod eventually published both pieces in the *Tageblatt*.

Despite isolated successes, most of Benjamin's efforts to find new venues failed. A review of Brecht's *Threepenny Novel* had initially been accepted and indeed typeset by the journal *Die Sammlung,* edited by Klaus Mann; Benjamin was bold enough to ask for 250 francs rather than the offered 150, and Mann returned the piece without comment. And an attempt late in the year to find a home for some longer works with an émigré press planned in Jerusalem by Shoshanah Persitz came to nothing.

By late May, Benjamin's isolation and the poor nutrition that resulted from his lack of funds began to take effect. He reported to Scholem that his health was not good and that he saw no hope of relief. Unable to work on "what matters most to me"—the continuation of *A Berlin Childhood*—he began to work with Jean Selz on a French translation of his text. Selz knew no German, but Benjamin paraphrased in French, leading to results that Benjamin deemed excellent. And he continued to think about his new language theory; he asked Scholem to forward a copy of the 1916 essay, so that he could compare it with the new writings.

With the increasing desperation of exile and poverty, Benjamin again began to weigh a possibility he had discarded with seeming finality early in the decade: emigration to Palestine. Scholem had written him a few mildly discouraging sentences regarding possibilities for work for European professionals and intellectuals. Benjamin now responded with a long, circuitous account of his current state of mind.

"Thousands of intellectuals have made their way to you. One thing distinguishes them from me—and this seems to work in my favor at first glance. But thereafter—as you well know—the advantage becomes theirs. Precisely this: they represent blank pages. Nothing would have more fateful consequences than an attitude on my part that could be construed as though I were attempting to cover up a private calamity with a public one . . . I would be glad and fully prepared to come to Palestine if you, or others concerned, assume that I could do so without provoking such a situation . . . Is there more room for me—for what I know and what I can do—there than in Europe? If there is not more, then there is less . . . If I could improve upon my knowledge and my abilities there without abandoning what I have already accomplished, then I would not be the least bit indecisive in taking that step" (Scholem Letters, 59–60).

Translated into the plain language which Benjamin was incapable of using with Scholem on this topic, the letter indicates that Benjamin was at this point willing neither to give up his engagement with European ideas, nor to use Palestine as a mere base for that engagement. Scholem, long a shrewd reader of Benjaminian prose, understood immediately. He replied that he found it "questionable whether a person could possibly feel well in this country without directly participating in the life here, whether . . . this would not rapidly bring about a morally unbearable state of estrangement in which life cannot be sustained" (Scholem Letters, 66).

Late spring and early summer brought an intense fascination with the work of Arnold Bennett. Benjamin recommended the novel *Clayhanger* to each of his correspondents, wrote a review of the German translation of *Constance and Sophie,* and described Bennett as a kind of Benjaminian alter ego. He recognized in Bennett "a man whose stance is very much akin currently to my own and who serves to validate it—that is to say, a man for whom a far-reaching lack of illusion and a fundamental mistrust of where the world is going lead neither to moral fanaticism nor to embitterment but to an extremely cunning, clever, and subtle art of living. This leads him to wrest from his own misfortune the chances, and from his own wickedness the few respectable ways to conduct himself, that amount to a human life" (Letters, 422).

In mid-July the first of a series of illnesses overtook Benjamin. Upon his return from Majorca, where he had succeeded in obtaining a new passport, a leg wound became inflamed while he was visiting friends in the town of Ibiza, and the resultant fever combined with bouts of intense summer heat to keep Benjamin from returning to his room in San Antonio. Even so, he managed during his illness to write one of the most compelling sections of *A Berlin Childhood*, "Loggias," which he described as a "kind of self-portrait" (Letters, 427). And a glimmer of hope revealed itself to him when, through Wilhelm Speyer's intervention, he received an invitation to live, free of charge, in a house in Paris funded by the Baroness Goldschmidt-Rothschild for refugee Jewish intellectuals.

A relationship with a woman to whom Benjamin alluded only in the vaguest terms in his letters seems to have been a dominant element in his life during these months. By the end of the summer, he could pay her the highest of compliments—calling her the female counterpart to the *Angelus Novus*—while continuing to conceal her identity. Whether or not this relationship played a role, during the summer Benjamin produced two of his most important "private" writings of the period of exile: "On the Mimetic Faculty" (the later version of his new theory of language) and two pieces entitled "Agesilaus Santander" (versions of a highly esoteric meditation on naming and identity). Scholem speculates that the lovely last line of "Agesilaus Santander"—"And so, scarcely had I seen you the first time than I returned with you to where I had come from"—could well refer to the unnamed woman of the summer. During the summer Benjamin was also able to arrange for the transfer of part of his "archive" (his own writings and those of the Heinles) from Berlin; he continued to be anxious about the fate of his library, whose packing and shipping he simply could not afford.

By early September, Benjamin's condition had not improved; he continued to run a fever, and experienced prolonged periods of exhaustion during which he was bedridden in an isolated country house. He realized that his recovery was made difficult by his sparse diet and his emotional state. Ill as he was, Benjamin retained his sense of humor, at least when it came to reading. Commenting to Scholem on their shared interest in Christian theology (he had just finished a book on Luther), Benjamin claimed: "I have now grasped for the fifth or sixth time in my life what is meant by justification through faith. But I have the same trouble here as I have with infinitesimal calculus: as soon as I have mastered it for a few hours, it vanishes again for just as many years" (Scholem Letters, 77).

He planned to return to Paris when he had regained his health, but even Paris seemed to be less a superior haven for an exile than a marginally preferable place of suffering. "It hardly needs to be stated that I am facing my stay in Paris with the utmost reserve. The Parisians are saying, 'Les émigrés sont pires que les boches' [The émigrés are worse than the Krauts]" (Scholem Letters, 72). When he finally did make the trip to the French capital in early October, it was under "unimaginable conditions" (82): he was diagnosed on his arrival with malaria and treated with a course of quinine. Exactly when the lingering illness related to his leg wound gave way to this far more serious disease remains unclear.

Paris was all he had feared. The lodging in the house provided by the baroness proved to be "by no means free of charge" (83); it soon revealed itself as no option at all. And the possibility of earning a living from his writings in French was just as hopeless. "I am faced here with as many question marks as there are street corners in Paris. Only one thing is certain: that I have no intention of making a futile attempt to earn my living by writing for French journals" (82). He would eventually receive a commission from *Le Monde* for a piece on Baron Haussmann, but this was never completed; like so much of Benjamin's work, the research for the newspaper article found its way into *The Arcades Project*.

By the end of the year, Paris had begun to present difficulties to which Benjamin had no solution. "Life among the émigrés is unbearable, life alone is no more bearable, and a life among the French cannot be brought about" (Scholem Letters, 93). And although the city was far too expensive, he had no other place to go. Brecht had invited him to follow in his footsteps and emigrate to Denmark, luring him with attractive estimates of living costs. "But I am horrified by the winter, the travel costs, and the idea of being dependent on him and him alone" (Scholem Letters, 93). Dora and Stefan were still in Berlin; his brother Georg had been released from the Sonnenburg concentration camp, but refused to flee Germany. It was the beginning of a Parisian exile that would, with a few interruptions, extend to the end of Benjamin's life.

1934

Material hardship and intellectual isolation remained the key elements in Benjamin's existence in Paris. "I have hardly ever been as lonely as I am here," he wrote to Scholem in January. "If I were seeking opportunities to sit in a café with émigrés, they would be easy to find. But I avoid them" (Letters, 434). He wandered into Sylvia Beach's bookshop, and lingered over the portraits and autographs of British and American writers; he strolled the boulevards as a latter-day *flâneur;* and trapped by day, he dreamed at night. "In these times, when my imagination is preoccupied with the most unworthy problems between sunrise and sunset, I experience at night, more and more often, its emancipation in dreams, which nearly always have a political subject . . . They represent a pictorial atlas of the secret history of National Socialism" (Scholem Letters, 100).

Benjamin's first letters in the new year inaugurated what would be the dominant theme for the year as a whole: Franz Kafka. In a letter to Scholem, he expressed the hope that he would some day be able to lecture on Kafka and S. J. Agnon, the Jewish writer whose story "The Great Synagogue" would have figured prominently in the first issue of Benjamin's planned journal *Angelus Novus* in 1921. Discussions on Kafka also opened the way for Benjamin to take up new, albeit cautious, relations with his old friend Werner Kraft, with whom he had broken in 1921. Kraft had, until 1933, been a librarian in Hannover; he now shared Benjamin's exile and experienced the same dilemmas that confronted the émigré intellectual.

Rejections and disappointments continued to frustrate Benjamin's attempts to find venues for his work. He placed great hopes in some talks on the German avant-garde, to be delivered in French—a series of subscription lectures that he was to hold in a Parisian art salon; aside from the funds they would have brought, Benjamin hoped that they might establish a bridgehead on the French intellectual scene. The talks, which would have included an introduction on the German reading public and individual lectures on Kafka, Bloch, Brecht, and Kraus, were canceled when their sponsor, a prominent gynecologist, fell ill. Similarly, a commission from the *Nouvelle Revue Française* for an article on Johann Jakob Bachofen led to much research, a completed essay, and a rejection. And a major project intended for the *Zeitschrift für Sozialforschung* fell prey not to rejection but to Benjamin's failure to complete it. He devoted months to the preparation of this "retrospective recapitulation of the cultural politics of *Die neue Zeit*" (Scholem Letters, 139), the ideological organ of Germany's Social Democratic party; he hoped to "demonstrate for once how collective literary products are particularly suited to materialist treatment and analysis and, indeed, can be rationally evaluated only when treated in such a way" (Letters, 456). Though he mentioned the project in nearly every letter he wrote in the late summer and early fall, the project simply disappeared. One notable exception to this pattern of frustration and failure was the championing of *A Berlin Childhood* by Hermann Hesse, who approached two publishers, S. Fischer and Albert Langen, in an effort to find a home for the text. His efforts ultimately came to nothing, but Benjamin was gratified by the attention paid to his work by the prominent novelist.

In addition to the small gifts of money from friends, Benjamin was able to supplement his income through stipends paid by various organizations and by the ongoing sale of his books. In the spring, he began to receive 700 francs a month from the Israélite Alliance Universelle; at about the same time, the Institut für Sozialforschung initiated a stipend of 500 francs per month that would continue throughout the 1930s. And the institute, in the person of Friedrich Pollack, performed another important service: it funded the transfer of Benjamin's books—"about half the library, but the more important half"—from Berlin to Denmark, care of Brecht (Letters, 437). This transfer not only put the library at Benjamin's disposal for his writing, but allowed him to make important sales, foremost among them a tortuously negotiated sale of the complete works of Franz von Baader to the library of the Hebrew University in Jerusalem.

In March, his fortunes had so declined that he was forced to move from his cheap hotel in the sixth arrondissement. Fortunately, his sister Dora had recently moved to Paris. Benjamin's relations with his sister had long been troubled, but now, in Paris, they improved, and Benjamin moved into her small apartment on a temporary basis. Sometime that month, Benjamin also broke with one of his few remaining French acquaintances, Jean Selz, under circumstances that remain clouded. His family in Germany was still an object of intense concern. Dora and Stefan remained in Berlin, while Benjamin's brother Georg, freed from prison, returned to Berlin from a trip to Switzerland and Italy and immediately resumed his clandestine political work.

Despite these conditions, Benjamin continued to write. He finished the long review essay "Problems of the Sociology of Language" for the *Zeitschrift für Sozialforschung,* and a review of Max Kommerell's book on Jean Paul, which he published under the pseudonym K. A. Stempflinger in the *Frankfurter Zeitung.* In late spring, he finished a long piece on literary politics, "The Author as Producer." The text, as published twenty-six years after Benjamin's death, indicates that it was delivered as a lecture at the "Institute for the Study of Fascism" in Paris on April 27. This institute, with Arthur Koestler at its head, was a research group controlled by the Comintern but financed by French workers and intellectuals. The essay is one of Benjamin's most significant analyses of the relations between literary form and politics; whether it was ever delivered remains a mystery.

Once again, he sat in the Bibliothèque Nationale and took up his work on the Paris arcades. "The arcades project is the *tertius gaudens* these days between fate and me. I have not only been able to do much more research recently, but also—for the first time in a long while—to imagine ways in which that research might be put to use. That this image diverges greatly from the first, original one is quite understandable" (Scholem Letters, 100).

A letter from Scholem of April 19 opened the way for one of Benjamin's most significant essays, "Franz Kafka." Scholem had approached Robert Weltsch—editor of the *Jüdische Rundschau,* the largest-circulation Jewish publication still allowed in Germany—regarding the possibility of Benjamin's contributing an essay on Kafka. When Weltsch followed up Scholem's suggestion with an invitation, Benjamin on May 9 accepted enthusiastically, while warning Weltsch that his essay would not conform to the "straightforward theological explication of Kafka" (Letters, 442). And this was not the only activity on Benjamin's behalf that his friend had undertaken: he also asked Moritz Spitzer, editor of the Schocken Library (a series of small, somewhat popular volumes with a largely German-Jewish readership), to solicit "one or more small books" from Benjamin (Scholem Letters, 106). Despite Benjamin's willingness, this plan, too, foundered, as the German exchange office soon stopped all payments to Schocken authors living abroad.

Scholem's important letter also rekindled the old, uncomfortable debate between the friends regarding Benjamin's politics. After reading the relatively mild and straightforward essay "The Present Social Situation of the French Writer," Scholem claimed that he was unable to understand it and asked Benjamin if the essay was a "Communist credo" (107). Scholem wanted to know where Benjamin stood, and reminded him that he had been unwilling to give clear answers to this question in the past. Scholem's letter elicited an important and highly revealing response from Benjamin. A draft later found in East Berlin reads: "I have always written according to my convictions—with perhaps a few minor exceptions—but I have never made the attempt to express the contradictory and mobile whole that my convictions represent in their multiplicity" (109). In the letter he finally sent, he defined his communism as "absolutely nothing other than the expression of certain experiences I have undergone in my thinking and in my life. That it is a drastic, not infertile expression of the fact that the present intellectual industry finds it impossible to accommodate my life; that it represents the obvious, reasoned attempt on the part of a man who is completely or almost completely deprived of any means of production to proclaim his right to them, both in his thinking and in his life . . . Is it really necessary to say all this to you?" (110). Benjamin continued with a passage on Brecht that showed he was all too aware of the real stakes here: Scholem's objection to his incorporation of a Brechtian, engaged politics alongside both his theological inclinations and the carefully considered, though still markedly leftist social analyses that allied him with the Institut für Sozialforschung. In a letter written that summer, Benjamin again alluded to this controversy while also claiming that he could not send Scholem the much more provocative essay "The Author as Producer," because he had failed to have enough copies made; when Scholem asked for a copy in person in 1938, Benjamin said (as Scholem later recalled), "I think I had better not let you read it" (113).

In early summer 1934, Benjamin undertook the trip to Skovsbostrand (near Svendborg), where Brecht and Helene Weigel were living in an isolated farmhouse; it was to be the first of three such extended summer visits, the others coming in 1936 and 1938. Shortly before leaving Paris for Denmark, Benjamin had suggested to Brecht that a series of affinities exist between his plays and the game of Go, with its initially empty board and its strategy of placing, rather than moving, pieces. "You place each of your figures and formulations on the right spot, whence they fulfill their proper strategic function on their own and without having to act" (443). He now took a room in a neighboring house in the countryside, which limited his social relations to Brecht and Weigel. His entertainment consisted of his customary walks (solitary, because neither of his hosts was interested) and evenings in front of Brecht's radio. "Thus, I was able to listen to Hitler's Reichstag speech, and because it was the very first time I had ever heard him, you can imagine the effect" (Scholem Letters, 130).

Despite the manifest difference in their personalities, Brecht and Benjamin shared a remarkable friendship. As Ruth Berlau, a member of Brecht's circle, remembers: "Whenever Benjamin and Brecht were together in Denmark, an atmosphere of confidence and trust immediately arose between them. Brecht had an enormous liking for Benjamin; in fact, he loved him. I think they understood each other without saying a word. They played chess wordlessly, and when they stood up, they had had a conversation."[16] When they did speak, the conversations were extensive and memorable. In the summer of 1934, they discussed Rimbaud and Johannes R. Becher, Confucius and Euripides, Gerhart Hauptmann and Dostoevsky. But most of their conversations concerned Kafka and the essay Benjamin was writing (see "Notes from Svendborg," in this volume).

An odd, three-part conversation on this topic soon arose, with Scholem the silent partner in Palestine. His frequent letters challenged Benjamin to answer a series of explicitly theological questions. Benjamin's replies are noteworthy. In reflecting on the question as to how one is to conceive, "in Kafka's sense, the Last Judgment's projection into world history," Benjamin emphasized not the answers to such questions, but rather Kafka's failure. "I endeavoured to show how Kafka sought—on the nether side of that 'nothingness,' in its inside lining, so to speak—to feel his way toward redemption. This implies that any kind of victory over that nothingness . . . would have been an abomination for him" (Scholem Letters, 129). A few weeks later, Benjamin admitted a "small, nonsensical hope" intended for Kafka's creatures and helpers, so memorably portrayed in the essay. "That I do not deny the component of revelation in Kafka's work already follows from my appreciation—by declaring the work to be 'distorted'—of its messianic aspect. Kafka's messianic category is the 'reversal' or 'study'" (135). Just as the great essay on Karl Kraus had done, the essay on Kafka marked a point of crystallization in Benjamin's thought. In a letter of November 12 to Werner Kraft, he asserted that "the study brought me to a crossroads in my thoughts and reflections. Devoting additional thought to it promises to do for me precisely what using a compass would do to orient a person on uncharted terrain" (Letters, 462).

The world and its politics penetrated, if somewhat slowly, to Skovsbostrand. In September, Benjamin was dismayed by what he saw as Kraus's "capitulation to Austro-fascism, the glossing-over of the white terror instituted against the Viennese workers, the admiration of the rhetoric . . . of Starhemberg." He was led to ask, "Who can still give in?" (Letters, 458). By October, Benjamin was clearly desperate to leave Denmark, and this despite continuing productive and cordial relations with Brecht. He badly wished to return to his arcades work, an undertaking impossible on an isolated farm with no access to a library. This to some extent explains Benjamin's enthusiastic response to a proposal by Horkheimer that he follow the Institut für Sozialforschung, which was moving to New York. "I would most gratefully welcome the chance to work in America, regardless of whether it is to do research at your institute or at an institute associated with yours. Indeed, allow me to say that you have my prior consent to any arrangement that seems appropriate to you" (Letters, 460).

In late October, Benjamin left Denmark for Italy. After a layover of a few days in Paris, he continued on to San Remo, where Dora had bought and was running a pension, the Villa Verde. In the years since the divorce, her relations with her former husband had gradually improved. She had actively sought publication possibilities for him while she remained in Berlin, and she now offered him food and shelter in Italy, and not for the last time. As one can imagine, Benjamin was acutely aware of the ambiguous position in which his acceptance of Dora's hospitality placed him. In a moment of self-laceration, he said it was "pitiful and a disgrace to nest, as it were, in the ruins of my own past" (465). But in the relative peace and security of the Italian countryside, he returned to his habits of long walks, much reading, and a good deal of writing. Aside from the customary detective novels (Somerset Maugham and the ever-present Simenon), he read Julien Green's latest book, *Visionnaire* (which he found quite disappointing) and Karl Thieme's *The Old Truth: A Cultural History of the West*, a gift from the author. He also told each of his correspondents of his esteem for Robert Louis Stevenson's *Master of Ballantrae*, which he ranked "ahead of almost all great novels, and right behind *The Charterhouse of Parma*" (Letters, 464).

In December, his sense of isolation was relieved by a visit from Stefan, who intended to return to Berlin and his schooling at least until he could be registered in the Italian school system in the spring. Benjamin found his son composed, confident, and rather too serious. Even this visit was not enough, though, to lend Benjamin a sense of rootedness, and he continued to cast about for opportunities for movement. Scholem, having abandoned all hope of bringing Benjamin back onto the path of a fully committed Judaism, now proposed for the first time that Benjamin pay a short, three-to-four-week visit to Palestine. As the year came to an end, Benjamin responded to this idea with the same enthusiasm he had expressed at Horkheimer's theoretical invitation to visit America.

Notes

1. Walter Benjamin, *Moscow Diary,* ed. Gary Smith, trans. Richard Sieburth (Cambridge, Mass.: Harvard University Press, 1986), p. 31. Subsequent references to this work will appear in the text as *MD.*
2. *The Correspondence of Walter Benjamin,* trans. Manfred R. Jacobson and Evelyn M. Jacobson (Chicago: University of Chicago Press, 1994), p. 312. Subsequent references to this work will appear in the text as Letters.
3. Walter Benjamin, *Gesammelte Briefe,* vol. 3, 1925–1930, ed. Christoph Gödde and Henri Lonitz (Frankfurt: Suhrkamp, 1997), p. 233. Subsequent references to this work will appear in the text as *GB.*
4. Gershom Scholem, *Walter Benjamin: The Story of a Friendship,* trans. Harry Zohn (Philadelphia: Jewish Publication Society of America, 1981), p. 130. Subsequent references to this work will appear in the text as Scholem.
5. Dora Pollak to Herbert Blumenthal and Carla Seligson, June 29, 1915. Cited in Hans Puttnies and Gary Smith, *Benjaminiana* (Giessen: Anabas Verlag, 1991), p. 140.
6. Dora Benjamin to Gerhard Scholem, July 24, 1929. Cited in Puttnies and Smith, *Benjaminiana,* p. 150.
7. Divorce Decree, April 24, 1930. Cited in Puttnies and Smith, *Benjaminiana,* p. 159.
8. Benjamin always addressed Scholem as "Gerhard," using his original name. (Scholem took the name "Gershom" only after moving to Palestine.
9. See the essay "German Letters," in this volume.
10. See the essay "Privileged Thinking," in this volume.
11. Puttnies and Smith, *Benjaminiana,* p. 33.
12. Karl Kraus in *Die Fackel* 33, nos. 852–856 (1931): 27.
13. See "May–June 1931," in this volume.
14. Gershom Scholem, ed., *The Correspondence of Walter Benjamin and Gershom Scholem, 1932–1940,* trans. Gary Smith and André Lefevere (New York: Schocken, 1989), p. 13. Subsequent references to this work will appear in the text as Scholem Letters.
15. Benjamin refers here to (1) an early conception of *The Arcades Project;* (2) a book of his collected criticism on which he had pinned the greatest hopes; (3) a series of selected examples of bourgeois prose that would eventually be published pseudonymously in Switzerland as *Deutsche Menschen;* and (4) a book that would include his hashish protocols and commentary.
16. Ruth Berlau, *Brechts Lai-tu* (Darmstadt, 1985); cited in Momme Brodersen, *Spinne im eigenen Netz* (Bühl-Moos: Elster Verlag, 1990), p. 233.

Index